Jane Williams DEwins
1-410-643-6301
Gail Huff
410-721-1279
541-2868 2283
215 I Hum
Else Gilmore 410 7579182

Para empezar: Interacciones

PARA EMPEZAR:
INTERACCIONES

Dave McAlpine
University of Arkansas at Little Rock

Leon Book
Southeast Missouri State University

Karen Hardy Cárdenas
South Dakota State University

Instructor's Edition

. . . .

BEGINNING SPANISH

. . . .

A Companion to
Para empezar:
Exploraciones

. . . .

McGraw-Hill, Inc.

New York St. Louis San Francisco Auckland Bogotá
Caracas Lisbon London Madrid Mexico City Milan
Montreal New Delhi San Juan Singapore Sydney Tokyo
Toronto

This is an  book

Para empezar: Interacciones
Beginning Spanish

1 2 3 4 5 6 7 8 9   VNH   VNH   9 0 9 8 7 6 5 4

ISBN 0-07-044978-3 (Student Edition)
ISBN 0-07-044979-1 (Instructor's Edition)

This book was set in New Baskerville by CRWaldman Graphic Communications Inc.
The editors were Thalia Dorwick, Danielle Havens, and Phyllis Larimore.
The designer was Adriane Bosworth.
The production supervisor was Tanya Nigh.
The cover was designed by BB&K Design, Inc.
The photo researcher was Darcy Wilding.
Illustrations were done by Tim Jones and maps by Lori Heckelman.
Project supervision was done by Phyllis Larimore.
Von Hoffmann Press was printer and binder.

Cover painting by Silvia Ordóñez, *Amanecer en el pueblo,* oil on canvas, courtesy of Galería de Arte Mexicano.

Library of Congress Cataloging-in-Publication Data

McAlpine, Dave.
    Para empezar. Interacciones : beginning Spanish / Dave McAlpine,
  Leon Book. Karen Hardy Cárdenas.
        p.   cm.
    "A companion to Para empezar: Exploraciones."
    Includes index.
    ISBN 0-07-044978-3
    1. Spanish language—Textbooks for foreign speakers—English.
  I. Book, Leon.   II. Cárdenas, Karen Hardy.   III. Title.
  PC4129.E5M43   1995
  468.2'421—dc20   94-25158
                                                          CIP

Grateful acknowledgment is made for use of the following:
PHOTOGRAPHS   **Page iv–v:** Frerck/Odyssey/Chicago; **v:** (man at computer) Cameramann/The Image Works; (Tula) Frerck/Odyssey/Chicago; (older woman in traditional dress) Suzanne L. Murphy/D. Donne Bryant Stock Photography; **2–3:** Chip and Rosa Maria de la Cueva Peterson; **17:** (left) J.P. Courau/D. Donne Bryant Stock Photography; (right) Frerck/Odyssey/Chicago; **21:** Bob Daemmrich/The Image Works; **31:** (top) Frerck/Odyssey/Chicago; (middle) Matthew Nathons/Stock, Boston; **36:** Norman Prince; **36–37:** (Monterrey) Chip and Rosa Maria de la Cueva Peterson; **37:** (top) Frerck/Odyssey/Chicago; (bottom) Michael Herron/Woodfin Camp and Associates;
(Continued after the index)

Bienvenidos
a México, D.F.

Avila, España

Saludos
de Oaxaca

Tula, México

Contents

Capítulo 2: La identidad 38

DIÁLOGOS

VOCABULARIO

CONCEPTOS

FACETAS CULTURALES

EN ACCIÓN

México y los mexicanos

Capítulo 3: El horario 74

DIÁLOGOS

México y los mexicanos

Capítulo 4: Las viviendas   104

Capítulo 5: La vida urbana 134

Capítulo 6: Los pasatiempos   174

Otros mundos

México y los mexicanos

Capítulo 7: La comida   206

FACETAS CULTURALES

EN ACCIÓN

Otros mundos

México y los mexicanos

Capítulo 8: El mundo de los negocios   234

DIÁLOGOS

VOCABULARIO

CONCEPTOS

FACETAS CULTURALES

EN ACCIÓN

Otros mundos

México y los mexicanos

Capítulo 9: Los eventos de la vida   260

Otros mundos

México y los mexicanos

Capítulo 10: El medio ambiente   294

CONCEPTOS

Review and expansion of grammar learned in previous chapters

FACETAS CULTURALES

EN ACCIÓN

Otros mundos

México y los mexicanos

Capítulo 11: Las comunicaciones   324

DIÁLOGOS

VOCABULARIO

CONCEPTOS

Review and expansion of grammar learned in previous chapters

FACETAS CULTURALES

EN ACCIÓN

Otros mundos

México y los mexicanos

Capítulo 12: Los hispanos en los EE. UU.   350

DIÁLOGOS

CONCEPTOS

FACETAS CULTURALES

EN ACCIÓN

Otros mundos

Appendixes 370

To the Instructor

Welcome to *Para empezar,* a new introductory Spanish language program. We think that *Para empezar* is different from other beginning Spanish textbooks for a number of reasons, and we hope that these reasons will motivate you to take a close look at all the parts of the program: the student text, *Para empezar: Interacciones;* the student workbook/laboratory manual, *Para empezar: Exploraciones;* and the ancillary materials available to help you achieve your goals in beginning Spanish classes.

Para empezar is different from other programs in the following ways.

- It is truly a pair of textbooks—a hardcover and a softcover manual (with perforated pages)—that can accommodate a number of teaching and learning styles.
- It is a brief program of language instruction that you can complete in one year and that will sufficiently prepare your students to continue with second-year courses.
- Its cultural coverage is extensive and unique, paying particular attention to the cultures of Mexico and to the diverse cultures of the Hispanic world.

In the pages that follow, you will learn more about these unique features of the *Para empezar* program as well as about the organization of the text, the manual, and the ancillary package.

What Is Unique About *Para empezar?*

A Pair of Textbooks

Most Spanish language programs have a textbook and a workbook / laboratory manual. *Para empezar* takes this concept one step further to give you greater flexibility in the classroom and help you accommodate different learning styles.

Interacciones

The main textbook, *Para empezar: Interacciones,* which you are reading now, is the one you and your students will always use in the classroom. *Interacciones* provides opportunities for instructor–student and student–student interaction in Spanish. It offers lively yet focused activities with vocabulary presentations and basic grammar concepts, together with a wealth of cultural information and plentiful reading material.

As you work with your students in class, you will find ample opportunity for exposing them to spoken Spanish in the "teacher talk," or comprehensible input, that is so essential for language acquisition. And you will find activities to help students develop all four language skills (listening, speaking, reading, and writing). The authors of *Para empezar* believe that it is essential to expose students to Spanish in the receptive mode—via listening and reading—to help them become successful *producers* of language—in speaking and in writing.

Only the essential details of Spanish grammar are presented in *Interacciones,* just enough so that students can do the activities and be successful communicators in Spanish. By doing the carefully guided activities in *Interacciones,* many students will intuitively grasp, or induce, the grammar rules that they can confirm using the grammar charts and brief explanations that follow the activities. They will then practice these rules in a more focused way in *Exploraciones.*

Exploraciones

The softcover companion manual, *Para empezar: Exploraciones,* is not an optional ancillary. It is a truly integral part of the *Para empezar* approach. *Exploraciones* can be used in class if you desire and if time permits. Alternatively, its explanations, exercises, and activities can be assigned primarily as homework. *Exploraciones* supports the hardcover textbook, *Interacciones,* by offering detailed grammar explanations that are conveniently organized in charts; written grammar and vocabulary exercises; and speaking and listening comprehension practice (coordinated with the *Audiocassette Program*).

The exercises in *Exploraciones* "walk" students through the language-learning process, allowing them to verify their comprehension of grammar rules and vocabulary, and to feel comfortable with their understanding of certain vocabulary groups and grammatical forms of Spanish. Whereas *Interacciones* focuses on inductive learning, *Exploraciones* accommo-dates the needs of students who learn through a more deductive approach. In addition, ample opportunity for personalized use of Spanish is provided and is appropriate for grading.

Used together, *Interacciones* and *Exploraciones* provide you with an appropriate amount of material for teaching a beginning Spanish course that is compatible with your individual philosophy and approach. The activities in *Interacciones* provide an appropriate vehicle for teaching in a Natural Approach or Direct Method style. If you prefer, however, you can start with or emphasize the more cognitive exercises in *Exploraciones*. The companion volumes will also provide your students with a well-rounded approach to the acquisition of the Spanish vocabulary, grammar, language skills, and cultural content stressed in contemporary Spanish courses.

A Text You Can Truly Finish in One Year

Para empezar: Interacciones is indeed a brief beginning Spanish text. The word "brief," of course, can mean many things. *Interacciones* is brief in a number of ways.

First, *Interacciones* has fewer pages than most texts currently available for beginning Spanish courses. However, the brevity of *Interacciones* has not been achieved at the expense of practice materials and activities. Instead, *Para empezar* offers a reduced grammar syllabus, to benefit both students and instructors.

With *Interacciones,* you can easily complete the text in one year, and students will have the time to learn to use—not simply cover—the most important first-year grammar structures: the four basic verb tenses (present indicative, preterite, imperfect, and present subjunctive), and the essential details of the noun, adjective, and pronoun systems of Spanish. By covering fewer grammar topics, students will spend more time practicing the essentials and will have a stronger foundation for intermediate and upper division courses. Of course, most of the other grammar commonly covered in beginning Spanish texts is contained in the readings in *Interacciones* and may be explained in greater detail in **A propósito** boxes, so that students are exposed to the whole language system.

To strengthen students' knowledge of the essentials, the last three of the twelve chapters in *Interacciones* present no new grammar topics. In these chapters, students are given the chance to consolidate what they have learned throughout the course. In this way students will have a sense of satisfaction at the end of the year, and you won't feel that you have four more tenses to cover in the last two weeks.

Unique Cultural Coverage

Para empezar: Interacciones integrates coverage of Hispanic cultures throughout the text, in English language cultural features as well as in abundant reading materials in Spanish, including the reading sections called **Otros mundos**. If these enrichment materials are made an integral part of the course, students will come to understand the importance of Spanish as a world language and achieve an appreciation for the diversity of Hispanic cultures world-wide.

But *Interacciones* also goes one step further. It focuses, in addition, on the culture of one country in particular, Mexico, via the on-going story of two students. *Interacciones* follows David, a U.S. college student of Hispanic descent, and Elena, his Mexican cousin, as they spend a summer traveling through Mexico. This feature provides context and continuity to the text's dialogues and activities. In addition, optional reading sections called **México y los mexicanos** offer students additional information about this Spanish-speaking country that is the closest to the United States and the one students are most likely to visit.

Finally, *Para empezar: Interacciones* is accompanied by a video, filmed exclusively for McGraw-Hill and coordinated with the main chapters of the text. The video is designed to be used with the end-of-chapter **En acción** section. It features native speakers of Spanish using simple, yet authentic, language to perform the functions of everyday life—greetings, ordering in a restaurant, talking about the past, and so on.

Organization of the Student Text, *Para empezar: Interacciones*

Interacciones is divided into twelve chapters, making it convenient to use in semester- or quarter-length courses. The unique chapter organization, a description of which follows, divides the chapters into smaller units that provide convenient places at which to quiz students on the material covered up to that point. (See the opening pages of each chapter in the annotated *Instructor's Edition* for a description of appropriate quiz points for each chapter.)

All chapters of the text contain the following types of sections. Most of them occur as needed throughout the chapter. The **México y los mexicanos** and **Otros mundos** sections occur between chapters.

- **México y los mexicanos**   optional reading
- *Chapter-opening spread*   visual display
- **Diálogo**   authentic discourse
- **Vocabulario**   thematic vocabulary presentation
- **Concepto**   grammar section
- **Faceta cultural**   culture note
- **En acción**   four-skill chapter review
- **Vocabulario**   active chapter vocabulary
- **Otros mundos**   optional reading

The following discussion of each repeating section of the chapters highlights the function of each as well as some additional features of the text.

- MÉXICO Y LOS MEXICANOS   Each chapter of the text is preceded by one of these sections, which offers two types of optional readings. The first, **De viaje**, provides detailed information about the Mexican cities and sites visited by U.S. student David and his Mexican cousin Elena on their trip through Mexico. The second, **Perspectivas de México**, provides more in-depth information about a specific aspect of the Mexican people and their culture. The **Perspectivas** sections will help students and instructors be more aware of what many Mexican people think and how they feel about a number of topics. (Optional activities, comprehension questions, and additional information about the topics covered in each of these sections are found in the *Instructor's Manual.*)

- *CHAPTER-OPENING SPREAD*   Chapters open with a visual display that serves as an advance organizer for the chapter theme. The display provides a focus for conversation about the chapter theme and provides you with a base of comprehensible input using the chapter's vocabulary and structures. (Suggestions for maximizing use of these pages are found in the *Instructor's Manual.*) In addition, the chapter-opening spread provides students with a list of grammar goals and language functions for the chapter.

- DIÁLOGO   Interspersed throughout each chapter are short dialogues that move the story line forward. Other dialogues follow events in the lives of international students and faculty at David's campus, the University of Wisconsin–Eau Claire. Because the students are from many different parts of the Spanish-speaking world, additional information about Hispanic cultures is provided to complement the cultural information revealed on the trip through Mexico.

As well as adding a narrative flavor and context to the text and providing cultural information, the dialogues also "seed" new vocabulary, grammar, and functional language that are targeted for acquisition by students. Each dialogue is followed by two sets of activities. The first type, **De inmediato**, helps students check their comprehension of the dialogue. Then, **A ti te toca** sections guide students toward personalized use of the key concepts presented in the dialogue. Thus, the dialogues are not intended for memorization; rather, they serve as springboards for student production of simple Spanish.

- VOCABULARIO   Each **Vocabulario** section begins with a visual representation of the section's vocabulary. In this way, theme vocabulary targeted for student mastery is clearly indicated, and the display itself serves as the point of departure for conversation and input about the chapter theme.

Vocabulary displays are followed by **Actividades** that create opportunities for students to use the new vocabulary. Activity formats range from discrete items to more creative and complex activities such as partner/pair interaction, role plays, interviews, and surveys.

- CONCEPTO   Each new grammar topic is presented in a section called **Concepto**. As happens with new vocabulary, grammar concepts are introduced with a visual display that can serve as the basis for teacher talk with the new grammar. Each **Concepto** section is also followed by a series of **Actividades** that involve instructor–student and student–student interaction.

Each **Concepto** section ends with a succinct grammar chart and a very brief grammar discussion. Here students find the essential information for the section and can confirm what they may already have induced from working with the concept in the **Actividades** and from hearing your use of the concept in the classroom.

- FACETA CULTURAL   Occurring throughout the chapter as needed, these sections provide students with cultural information about Hispanic peoples and places. When appropriate, **Faceta cultural** sections also contain subsections called **En México**, which point out how the topic relates specifically to Mexico.

- A PROPÓSITO   These sections, occurring as needed throughout the chapters of *Interacciones*, introduce grammar that will not be taught for active use in the text but that has been used in a preceding **Diálogo**. No practice activities are offered for these grammar topics in the hardcover text, but the concepts do appear, for passive recognition, in readings and Diálogo sections throughout the text. Grammar topics presented in **A propósito** sections include the perfect tenses, the past subjunctive, and so on. (A complete listing of these topics is provided in the Contents listing. Note also that brief practice is provided for **A propósito** material in the student manual, *Exploraciones.*)

- **EN ACCIÓN** As its name implies, this section allows students to practice the vocabulary and grammar of the entire chapter in integrative, four-skills activities that focus on listening, speaking, reading, and writing skills. For your convenience, the listening comprehension sections of **En acción** have been designed to be read by the instructor. This eliminates the need to reserve cassette players and carry them to each classroom. (The scripts for the listening comprehension passages are bound into the back of the *Instructor's Edition.* The sections are also available in the *Audiocassette Program.*)

  The **En acción** sections in the last three chapters offer students the chance to practice material from the entire text. In addition, they provide ample practice of all skills in drawing-based sections called **Episodios** and **Actividad comprensiva**. In this way, review and recycling, hallmarks of the *Para empezar* approach, are built into the structure of the materials.

- **VOCABULARIO** This end-of-chapter vocabulary section is a complete list of all new vocabulary considered active in the chapter, whether formally presented in **Vocabulario** sections or less formally presented in dialogues and readings. (The annotated *Instructor's Edition* notes each place that new vocabulary is presented for active use.)

- **OTROS MUNDOS** Beginning at the end of **Capítulo 4** and continuing with each chapter to the end of the text, **Otros mundos** sections present glimpses of the Hispanic world, beyond Mexico, seen through the eyes of the international students from the University of Wisconsin–Eau Claire who are characters in the book. Intended to spark students' interest in the diversity of language usage and customs throughout the Spanish-speaking world, **Otros mundos** also provides facts about each country with a **¿Sabías que... ?** section and demographic information about each with **En breve.**

Organization of the Student Manual, *Para empezar: Exploraciones*

Exploraciones was written by the authors of *Interacciones*, with the collaboration of Paul Hoff (University of Wisconsin–Eau Claire). Each chapter of *Exploraciones* corresponds to a chapter of *Interacciones*, and the material

is presented in the same order. All chapters of the manual contain the following sections.

- **Conceptos**   grammar charts and expanded explanations
- **Ejercicios escritos**   written exercises with vocabulary and grammar
- **Ejercicios de laboratorio**   listening and speaking activities to accompany the audiocassette program

Features of the manual include the following.

- Grammar explanations (**Conceptos**) that expand and build on those in *Interacciones*. In this manual, students who learn deductively can benefit from the rules and models presented.
- Written activities corresponding to the **Diálogos, Vocabulario,** and **Conceptos** sections of *Interacciones*
- Additional **Faceta cultural, A propósito,** and **Diálogo** sections
- Corresponding listening comprehension and speaking activities, tied to the *Audiocassette Program*, as well as pronunciation practice with the Spanish sounds that are challenging for non-native speakers
- End-of-chapter review sections

Answers to mechanical exercises in both the workbook and the laboratory manual sections are included in the *Instructor's Manual.*

Supplementary Materials

A variety of additional components have been developed to support *Para empezar*. Many are free to adopting institutions. Please contact your local McGraw-Hill representative for details on policies, prices, and availability.

- The *Audiocassette Program*, coordinated with *Para empezar: Exploraciones*, is free to adopting institutions and is also available for student purchase upon request. The audio program also includes, on a separate tape, presentations of the **Para escuchar** listening comprehension passages (from the **En acción** sections), for in-class use. A *Tapescript* is also available.
- The annotated *Instructor's Edition* of the student text contains on-the-page suggestions, many supplementary exercises for developing listening and speaking skills, and abundant variations and follow-ups on student text material. In addition, listening scripts for all

listening comprehension sections are bound into the back of the *Instructor's Edition.*

- The *Instructor's Manual / Testbank* offers an introduction to teaching techniques appropriate for use with *Para empezar*, general guidelines for instructors, suggestions for lesson planning and for semester/quarter schedules, tests for each chapter, and suggestions for using the **México y los mexicanos, Otros mundos**, and chapter-opening-spread visual displays. Instructors will find the supplementary materials on Mexico to be especially useful, in particular the detailed timeline that shows significant events in the history of Mexico in relation to United States history.

- The *Video Program to Accompany* **Para empezar** was filmed entirely in Mexico and is coordinated with activities in the **En acción** sections. Additional suggestions for using the video are included in the *Instructor's Manual.*

- Additional video materials that can be used with *Para empezar* include the **Destinos** *Video Modules* (vocabulary, functional language, situational language, and culture, taken from the popular *Destinos* television series as well as original footage shot on location) and the *McGraw-Hill Video Library of Authentic Spanish Materials.*

- The *McGraw-Hill Electronic Language Tutor* (MHELT 2.0) offers many of the more controlled exercises from the student text and manual. The MHELT program is available in both IBM and Macintosh formats.

- Also available is a new software program for purchase by students—*Spanish Partner*. Developed at Vanderbilt University by Monica Morley and Karl Fisher, *Spanish Partner* is a user-friendly program that helps students master vocabulary and grammar topics that all beginning Spanish students need to know. *Spanish Tutor* offers clear, student-oriented feedback that helps students learn from their mistakes.

- A set of *overhead transparencies* offers all new visuals in full color that you can use for vocabulary or grammar presentations.

- A set of *slides* from various parts of the Spanish-speaking world, with activities for classroom use, is also available.

- A *training/orientation manual* for use with teaching assistants, by James F. Lee (University of Illinois, Urbana-Champaign), offers practical advice for beginning language instructors and language coordinators.

- *A Practical Guide to Language Learning*, by H. Douglas Brown (San Francisco State University), provides beginning foreign language students with a general introduction to the language learning process. This guide is free to adopting instructors, and it can also be made available for student purchase.

Acknowledgments

We would like to thank our colleagues and students at the University of Arkansas at Little Rock, Southeast Missouri State University, and South Dakota State University for their considerable support for this project. We are also indebted to Dr. Stella Clark (California State University, San Marcos), who served as our Mexican language and cultural consultant. Stella led us to many of the source materials on which the **México y los mexicanos** sections are based, and provided a constant reminder of the need to help students and instructors alike go past the surface to understand Mexico and the Mexican people in their wonderful complexity.

The authors would also like to thank the members of our profession whose valuable comments on an earlier draft of this project helped us shape the final product. The appearance of their names in this list does not necessarily constitute their endorsement of the text or of its methodology.

Julian L. Bueno
Southern Illinois University at Edwardsville

Susan de Carvalho
University of Kentucky

Walter Chatfield
Iowa State University

Cecilia Colombi
University of California, Davis

Donna J. Gustafson
San Jose State University

Mary Jane Kelley
The University of Kansas

Jeffrey A. Kirsch
Tulane University

José L. Mas
California State University, Chico

Nadine F. Olson
Oklahoma State University

Gerald W. Petersen
University of Nevada, Reno

Alfredo Torrejón
Auburn University

Robert Valero
George Washington University

Gwen Yount
University of California, Riverside

Many individuals deserve recognition for their contributions to this project. Thalia Dorwick served as our editor and publisher and gave us the opportunity to try something different, the encouragement to persevere, and the guidance and direction to improve. For her patience with this team of authors and for her care and support, we are gratefully indebted. We also wish to thank Thalia for making it possible for us to work with our development editor, Danielle Havens, who played a crucial role in determining the content and appearance of these volumes. Danielle's insightful treatment of many aspects of each chapter as well as her constant attention to the details of how a textbook works in the hands of instructors and students is much appreciated. Thanks are also due to Dr. Robert DiDonato (Miami University) for his perceptive comments on an early draft of these materials and to Laura Chastain, whose tireless efforts helped shape the language and content of all drafts.

Special thanks are also due to the many people at McGraw-Hill who worked on aspects of the program's production. Phyllis Larimore, Charlotte Jackson, Francis Owens, Adriane Bosworth, Tim Jones, Lori Heckelman, and Tanya Nigh are among those who have made the debut of *Para empezar* possible. We would be remiss if we did not recognize the support of our families, notably Marva, Patrick and Elizabeth McAlpine, Patricia Book, and Joseph Cárdenas. They provided love and affection as well as encouragement and support. We hope this work justifies your patience and your faith in us.

Finally, we thank each other. Throughout this project we have remained friends and friendly, even on those days when we wondered whether it was worth the effort, when frustration and fatigue overtook cooperation and humor. We managed to laugh among and at ourselves, to enjoy each other's company, and (we hope) to do some good work in the process.

Capítulo preliminar: Para empezar

¿Están ustedes listos *para empezar?* Are you ready *to begin?* The subtitle of this preliminary chapter, which is also the main title of this book, invites you to start using Spanish. To accomplish this goal, you will listen to and speak Spanish, as well as read and write the language, and learn about the great variety of Hispanic cultures.

Several people will help you get started learning Spanish. Throughout the text, you will follow David Nelson, a student at the University of Wisconsin–Eau Claire, and his Mexican cousin, Elena Muñoz, as they travel through Mexico. The cousins meet at the United States–Mexico border, then travel south to visit family and friends and to make new friends in Mexico.

A second group of people will also help you: university students and professors at David's home campus, the University of Wisconsin–Eau Claire. These characters will enable you to relate your growing knowledge of Spanish to everyday life and learn about the Spanish-speaking countries they come from.

Two important tools will help you achieve your goals: *Para empezar: Interacciones* (this textbook) and *Para empezar: Exploraciones* (the companion workbook/ laboratory manual). *Interacciones* will help you interact

David   Elena

with your classmates in Spanish, using vocabulary and grammar concepts immediately to communicate with them. *Exploraciones* offers you more in-depth information on how the Spanish language system works, and it provides opportunities for writing and listening practice. You may want to work with both texts simultaneously, as they are intended to support each other and provide you with a complete approach to learning Spanish.

¿Están ustedes listos para empezar? ¿Sí? Entonces, ¡vámonos!

Jorge   Joaquin   Tomás   Felipe   Luis   Marisol   Luisa   Profesora Martínez   María   Profesor Ramos   Alfonsina   Profesor Brewer

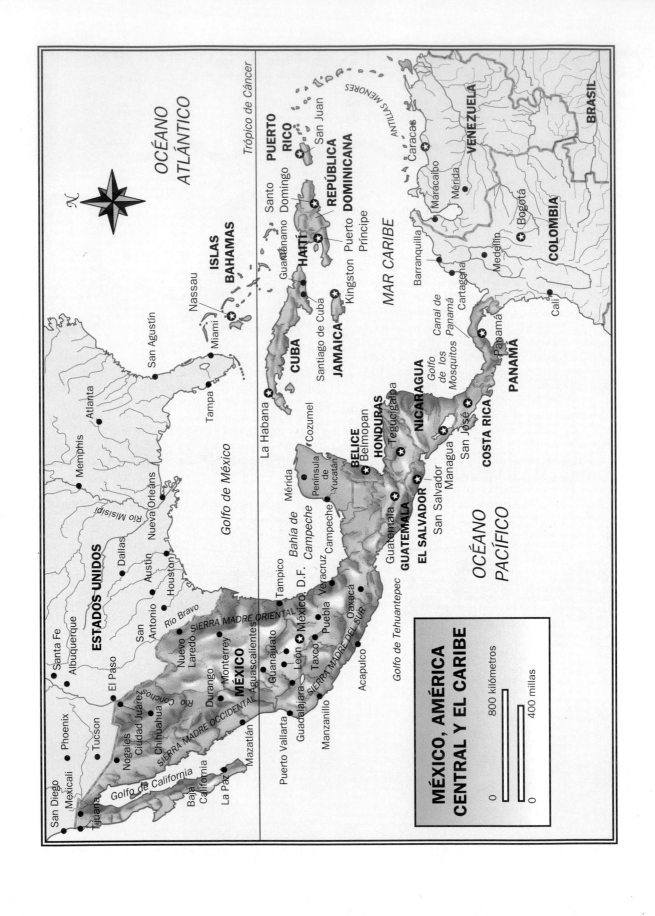

MÉXICO, AMÉRICA CENTRAL Y EL CARIBE

OCÉANO ATLÁNTICO

Trópico de Cáncer

OCÉANO PACÍFICO

MAR CARIBE

Golfo de México

Golfo de California

Bahía de Campeche

Golfo de Tehuantepec

Golfo de los Mosquitos

Canal de Panamá

ESTADOS UNIDOS

MÉXICO

BELICE
GUATEMALA
EL SALVADOR
HONDURAS
NICARAGUA
COSTA RICA
PANAMÁ

ISLAS BAHAMAS
CUBA
JAMAICA
HAITÍ
REPÚBLICA DOMINICANA
PUERTO RICO
ANTILLAS MENORES

VENEZUELA
COLOMBIA
BRASIL

SIERRA MADRE ORIENTAL
SIERRA MADRE OCCIDENTAL
SIERRA MADRE DEL SUR

Península de Yucatán
Baja California

San Diego
Mexicali
Tijuana
Phoenix
Tucson
Nogales
Ciudad Juárez
Chihuahua
Durango
Mazatlán
La Paz
Santa Fe
Albuquerque
El Paso
Nuevo Laredo
Monterrey
Aguascalientes
Guanajuato
León
Guadalajara
Manzanillo
Puerto Vallarta
Taxco
Acapulco
Oaxaca
Puebla
México, D.F.
Veracruz
Tampico
Mérida
Cozumel
Dallas
Austin
San Antonio
Houston
Nueva Orleans
Memphis
Atlanta
San Agustín
Miami
Tampa
Nassau
La Habana
Santiago de Cuba
Kingston
Guantánamo
Puerto Príncipe
Santo Domingo
San Juan
Caracas
Maracaibo
Mérida
Barranquilla
Cartagena
Medellín
Bogotá
Cali
Panamá
San José
Managua
Tegucigalpa
San Salvador
Guatemala
Belmopan

Río Misisipi
Río Bravo
Río Conchos

N

OCÉANO ATLÁNTICO

0   800 kilómetros
0   400 millas

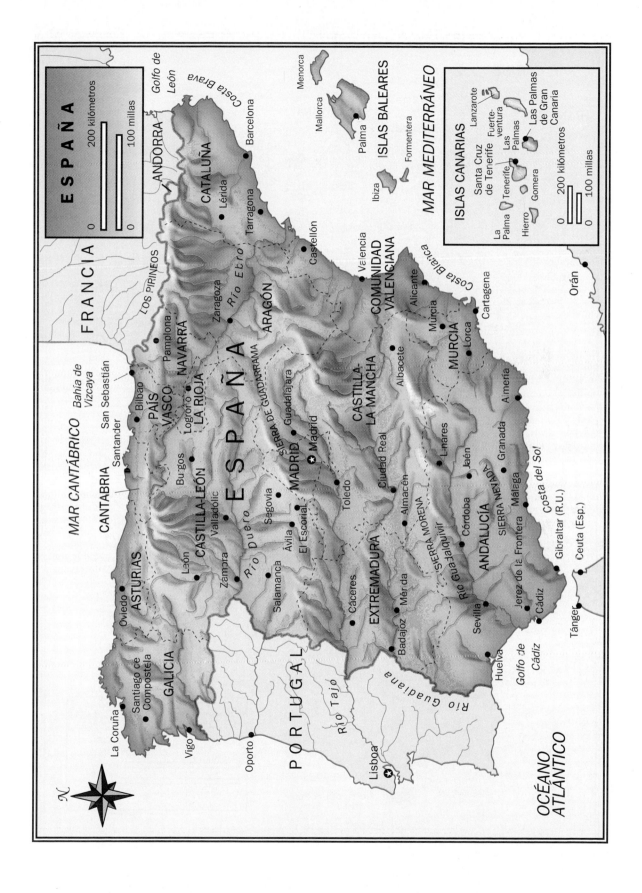

MAR CARIBE

OCÉANO
ATLÁNTICO

Maracaibo

Barranquilla

PANAMÁ

Caracas

VENEZUELA

GUYANA

Medellín

Panamá

Georgetown

Paramaribo

Río Orinoco

Cayena

Cali

Bogotá

SURINAM

GUYANA FRANCESA

COLOMBIA

Quito

Ecuador

ECUADOR

Río Amazonas

Belém

Guayaquil

Manaus

PERÚ

BRASIL

CORDILLERA DE LOS ANDES

Recife

Cuzco

Lima

La Paz

Brasília

Arequipa

BOLIVIA

Sucre

Antofagasta

PARAGUAY

Río de Janeiro

Trópico de Capricornio

CHILE

San Miguel
de Tucumán

Asunción

São Paulo

OCÉANO
PACÍFICO

La Serena

Córdoba

Rosario

OCÉANO
ATLÁNTICO

URUGUAY

Valparaíso

Santiago

ARGENTINA

Buenos Aires

Montevideo

N

Concepción

Río de la Plata

Bahía Blanca

Puerto Montt

Bariloche

Chiloé

AMÉRICA DEL SUR

Islas Malvinas

0   1500 kilómetros

Estrecho de Magallanes

Punta Arenas

Tierra del Fuego

0   1000 millas

Cabo de Hornos

PARA EMPEZAR:
INTERACCIONES

México y los mexicanos

NOTE: Detailed suggestions for teaching the **De viaje** and **Perspectivas** sections of **México y los mexicanos** cannot be accommodated in the margins of the *Instructor's Edition*. For this reason, the notes for these sections are in the *Instructor's Manual*.
NEW VOCABULARY: es, está, hay, tiene; la aduana, la ciudad, las cosas, el estado, los Estados Unidos, la frontera, los norteamericanos, el país, el río, las tiendas, el valle, el viaje; México; estadounidense, mexicanos, muchas, otro/a; más; de, del, en; o, y

De viaje: Laredo y Nuevo Laredo

David Nelson's trip to Mexico with his cousin, Elena Muñoz, will start in two border cities. The reading about the first city is in English; the second one is in Spanish. Read the descriptions of both cities. Your instructor will help you with the Spanish passage. However, you will be able to guess the meaning of many of the Spanish words, and the meanings of numerous others are provided.

named the city Villa de San Augustín de Laredo to honor a town in the Spanish province of Santander. Throughout its long and sometimes tumultuous history, Laredo has been known for its role in transportation. In the early days, mule teams and steamboats used the city as a base of operation. Today, the city serves as a vital commercial link between the United States and Mexico.

Nuevo Laredo

Al otro lado[1] de la frontera de la ciudad estadounidense de Laredo está la ciudad mexicana de Nuevo Laredo. Nuevo Laredo, una ciudad del estado mexicano de Tamaulipas, está en el valle del Río Bravo[2]—o Río Grande,[3] como lo llaman[4] los norteamericanos. Nuevo Laredo tiene la aduana más importante de la República y es la entrada principal del turismo en el país. En Nuevo Laredo hay muchas diversiones, como carreras de caballos y galgos,[5] además de[6] otras cosas interesantes, como[7] tiendas de artesanías[8] muy variadas.

[1]Al... *On the other side* [2]*Wild, Ferocious* [3]*Big* [4]como... *as it is called by* [5]carreras... *horse and greyhound races* [6]además... *in addition to* [7]*such as* [8]*handicrafts*

Laredo

The Texas city of Laredo is older but smaller than its Mexican neighbor, Nuevo Laredo. The city was founded by Spaniards in 1755, even before the Declaration of Independence was written. The Spaniards

Miles de vehículos cruzan cada día la frontera entre México y los Estados Unidos. Ésta es la aduana en Laredo, Texas.

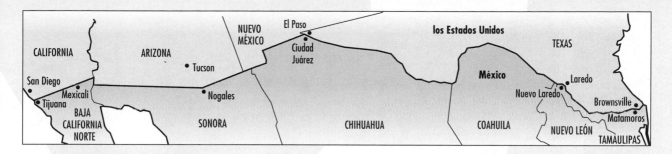

Perspectivas de México:
La identidad mexicana

As David and Elena begin their trip into Mexico, they will discover that the country's inhabitants have a strong awareness of and deep pride in their history. The identity of the Mexican people is formed by the heroes and anti-heroes of Mexico's long, colorful past. In this very short segment of a famous bilingual poem by the Chicano author Rodolfo Gonzales, you may be able to get a sense of this pride.

I Am Joaquín

I am Cuauhtémoc,
proud and noble,
    leader of men,
king of an empire
civilized beyond the dreams
    of the gachupín[1] Cortés
who also is the blood,
    the image of myself.
I am the Maya prince.
I am Netzahualcóyotl,
great leader of the Chichimecas.
I am the sword and flame of Cortés
        the despot.
          And
I am the eagle and serpent of
      the Aztec civilization.

Yo soy Joaquín

Yo soy Cuauhtémoc
majestuoso y noble,
    guía de hombres,
rey de un imperio civilizado
incomparablemente a los sueños
    del gachupín Cortés,
quien igualmente es la sangre,
    la imagen de mí mismo.
Yo soy el príncipe de los mayas.
Yo soy Netzahualcóyotl
líder famoso de los chichimecas.
Yo soy la espada y llama de Cortés
        el déspota.
          Y
yo soy el águila y la serpiente
      de la civilización azteca.

[1] *pejorative term for a Spaniard who relocated to Mexico without adopting Mexican ways*

3

Encuentros[1]

David

David Nelson Muñoz
134 North Willow Street
Eau Claire, WI 54701

Dear David,
    It was so good to get your letter telling us that you will be coming to Mexico this summer to help the family celebrate Grandmother's 80th birthday. Everyone is looking forward to seeing you again, especially Grandmother (or Abuelita, as we prefer to call her).
    In fact, Abuelita has come up with a wonderful idea! She has suggested, since you are already coming for her birthday, that you and I take time to see a little of Mexico. We could meet in Laredo, Texas, in June, spend the summer traveling through Mexico, and you can be back at the University of Wisconsin in time for the fall term. ¿Qué opinas?[a]
    I hope to hear from you soon.

    Tu prima,

    Elena

[a]¿Qué... ? *What do you think?*

Elena

NEW VOCABULARY: la abuelita, la prima

NOTE: See the *Instructor's Manual* for suggestions on using the chapter-opening pages.

[1]*Encounters*

CASA de las
ARTESANIAS
de NUEVO LEON

Una aventura
a tu alcance en el...
**Estado de
Nuevo
León**

Balnearios y
manantiales.
Grutas.
Cascadas.
Centros recreativos.
Monumentos
coloniales.
Museos.
Caza y pesca.
Dónde comer y
hospedarse.

**Todo esto y más
en 23 destinos y 10
recorridos turísticos.**

M E T A S

FUNCIONES

- to introduce people to each other, and to greet and say good-bye to people in familiar and formal situations

- to describe your classroom, to give your age and telephone number, and to tell time, using numbers from 0 to 99

- to express courtesy in a variety of situations

- to talk about the geographical features of an area

- to describe a person's physical and emotional state

GRAMÁTICA

- Spanish subject pronouns (the equivalents of *I, you, . . .*)

- the verb **estar**

- Spanish articles (the equivalents of *the, a, an, some*)

- the concept of agreement

APPROPRIATE TESTING POINTS:
Diálogo (2), Los saludos y las despedidas, Los números del 0 al 99, Los pronombres personales, **Quiz 1**
Diálogo (2), El verbo *estar*, Diálogo (2), Expresiones de cortesía, La geografía, **Quiz 2**
Diálogo (2), Los artículos, Estados físicos y emocionales, Los adjetivos, ¿Qué hora es?, **Quiz 3**
Diálogo (2), En acción
Chapter test

En la estación de autobuses

David and Elena greet each other at the bus station in Laredo, Texas.

DAVID: Hola, Elena. ¿Qué tal?* ¿Cómo estás?
ELENA: Muy bien, David. ¡Qué gusto de verte![1]
DAVID: ¿Y la familia? ¿Cómo están todos[2]?
ELENA: Bien, gracias.

[1]¡Qué... *How nice to see you!*   [2]*everybody*

PREPARATION: Ask students to look at the drawing that precedes the dialogue. Ask who these people are and what they are doing? Ask students to focus on the title of the dialogue and on the dialogue introduction. Where are David and Elena (city and place)? Ask students to react to the way David and Elena greet each other. Does the fact that they are hugging indicate that they are very close?

NEW VOCABULARY: la estación (de autobuses), la familia; ¿Cómo están?, ¿Cómo estás?, Hola, (Muy) bien., ¿Qué tal?, gracias

De inmediato

SUGGESTION: Before beginning the dialogue, explain to students that glossed words and expressions are useful to know, but they are not part of the vocabulary that students are expected to master.

1. What phrases does David use to ask Elena how she is?
2. How does Elena feel?
3. How is Elena's family doing?

EXTENSION: 4. How does David say "Hi?" 5. How does David ask about Elena's family? 6. How does he indicate that he wants to know about everyone in the family?

A ti te toca

Practice the preceding dialogue with a classmate, substituting your names for those of David and Elena.

OPTIONAL: Ask students to turn to the people around them and ask how they are. Their classmates should respond appropriately.

En la universidad

NEW VOCABULARY: la fiesta (de despedida), el profesor, la universidad; Buenas noches, ¿Cómo está usted?, Nada (de particular), Oye, ¿Qué hay de nuevo?, ¿qué pasa?, ¿Y contigo?, ¿Y tú?

A week earlier in Eau Claire, David's friends from the University of Wisconsin's **Club Hispánico** gave him a farewell party, **una fiesta de despedida**. Here are two conversations from the first moments of that party.

JORGE: Buenas noches, profesor Ramos. ¿Cómo está usted?
EL PROFESOR RAMOS: Bien, gracias, Jorge. ¿Y tú?
JORGE: Muy bien, gracias.

TOMÁS: Oye, Joaquín, ¿qué pasa?
JOAQUÍN: Nada. ¿Y contigo? ¿Qué hay de nuevo?
TOMÁS: Nada de particular.

SUGGESTION: Mention that in responding to the question *How are you?* it is considered polite to return the inquiry. The full sentence **¿Y cómo estás tú?** is not necessary.

PREPARATION: Call attention to the drawing. Ask students what is happening? What do people say when they arrive at a party? When they leave?

*Note the use of inverted question marks and exclamation points.

The following conversations take place at the end of the evening.

MARISOL: Bueno,[1] David, nos vemos. Que te vaya bien.
DAVID: Gracias, Marisol. Hasta luego.

LUISA: Chao, Alfonsina. Hasta mañana.
ALFONSINA: Hasta el lunes,[2] Luisa.

[1]*Well*   [2]*Hasta... See you (on) Monday*

NEW VOCABULARY: Chao, Hasta luego, Hasta mañana, nos vemos, Que te vaya bien.

SUGGESTION: Note that **chao** comes from the Italian *ciao*. The word may have gained acceptance in the Hispanic world because it is often used in Argentina where many citizens are of Italian heritage.

---

1. What phrase does Jorge use to ask Professor Ramos how he is?
2. What's new in the lives of Tomás and Joaquín?
3. How does Marisol convey her best wishes to David?
4. According to Luisa and Alfonsina's conversation, on what night of the week does the party take place?

De inmediato

EXTENSION: 5. How does Professor Ramos ask Jorge how he is? 6. How does Tomás ask Joaquín what's going on? 7. What are three ways of saying good-bye that begin with **hasta**?

Practice the preceding dialogues with a classmate, substituting your names for those of the characters.

OPTIONAL: Ask students to create two-line dialogues depicting the following situations. 1. Alfonsina and David

A ti te toca

as they meet at the party, 2. Jorge and Tomás as they say good-bye.

Los apellidos hispánicos

NEW VOCABULARY: los apellidos

Hispanics often use two last names (**apellidos**): the father's surname followed by the mother's surname. Children are typically known by their father's surname, despite the fact that the mother's name comes last. Therefore, Elena Muñoz López is called Elena Muñoz and David Nelson Muñoz is called David Nelson. You know that David and Elena are cousins. Which of their parents are siblings?

SUGGESTION: Ask students what their names would be if they used the Hispanic last-name system.

Faceta cultural

SUGGESTION: Draw students' attention to several names in the directory. Ask them to identify the father's and mother's last names for these individuals. You may wish to note the use of **de** in a married woman's name.

```
COELLO SOCORRO DOMINGUEZ DE-ARCOS PTE 301 ZP 23
  MFAM JUAREZ EDIF A-2 DEPTO 502 ZP 7 .........  676-4782
COELLO TOVILLA MA DE CARMEN
  CALLE 313 N° 10 ZP 14 .......................  584-2861
COELLO TREJO Y ASOCIADOS SA
  HOMERO 404-101 CP 05600 .....................  781-6718

COELLO UGALDE GUSTAVO A-HDA CONDESA 83 ZP 16..  545-3301
COELLO Y CORDOVA MERCEDES GPE ...............  545-3480
  ORIENTE 162 NO 261 ZP 9 .....................  382-7213
COELLO YOLANDA S DE-TEMOLUCO AND 8 GPO 5-1 ZP 14  571-6978
COELLO YOLANDA SANTOS DE-ALLENDE 212 CP 02080.  391-3557
COELLO Z FERNANDO A
  AV MORELOS 613 EDIF CH-4 ZP 8 ...............  396-5928
COELLO ZENTENO MARCELO A
  OYAMEYO 11 EDIF 28-11 ZP 8 ZP 08 ...........  552-7208
COEN ANITUA ARRIGO
  U LOMA HERMOSA EDIF 17 ENT A-204 ZP 10 .....  650-3281
COEN ARISTIDES-INSURG SUR 480-31 CP 06760....  650-2891
COEN AVILA ARNALDO JOSE-LOS JUAREZ 3 ZP 19...  557-0708
COEN MENACHE SAMUEL-BOSQUE MOLINO 32 CP 52750  574-0336
COEPFERT RAMOS ERNESTO-DR VERTIZ 908-4 ZP 12.  598-2686
COESA SA-VISTA HERMOSA 136-B CP 03300 .......  294-4767
COETO BUSTAMANTE ENRIQUE ...................  682-1694
  U CUITLAHUAC EDIF 78 ENT A-302 ZP 16 .......  688-8139
                                                355-8472
```

```
COHEN COHEN SAMY-EL SALVADOR 26-11 CP 06000..  512-5060
COHEN COHEN SIMON-FUENTE DE TREVI 190 ZP 10 .  589-2546
COHEN DABAH EDUARDO-BOSQUES 244 ZP 10 .......  294-3138
  F PETRARCA 223-102 CP 11560 .................  250-2324
COHEN DABBAH JOSE-FUENTE DE TIROL 21 ZP 10...  251-4857
  HOMERO 1303-101 ZP 5 ........................  520-5531
COHEN DABBAH RAUL-HOMERO 1405-302 ZP 05 .....  395-5352
COHEN DABBAH SALVADOR-FUENTE JUPITER 12 ZP 10  251-6026
COHEN DAVID-FUENTE AGUILAS 299-A ZP 10 ......  251-3816
COHEN DAYAN ABRAHAM-FUENTE DEL REY 86-A ZP 10  251-3959
  FUENTE REY 86-A CP 53950 ....................  251-3950
  HOMERO 1337 ZP 5 ............................  540-3958
COHEN DOLORES ASSE DE-LAMARTINE 144-301 ZP 5   531-0956
COHEN DUEK MOISES-HORACIO 1709-101 ZP 10 ....  540-1700
  LOPE DE VEGA 148 PISO 4 ZP 5 ................  531-0524
COHEN E ALBERTO-SANCHEZ AZCONA 403 PISO 3 ZP 12  543-8889
COHEN EDITH HATTEM DE-HOMERO 1837 EDIF A-901 ZP5  395-1952
COHEN ELIAS D-EDGAR A POE 349 ZP 5 ..........  545-8408
COHEN ELIE-GUADALAJARA 94-12 ZP 7 ...........  286-4861
COHEN ELISA JAFIF DE-BOSQUE SECRETO 9 ZP 12..  589-9097
COHEN ELVIRA LEVY DE-SN BORJA 302-4 ZP 12 ...  536-0142
COHEN EMILIA GALANTE DE-LAURELES 15 ZP EM ...  373-7232
COHEN EMILIA Y DE-BOSQUE MAGNOLIAS 127 ZP 10   596-3968
COHEN ENRIQUE-HORACIO 1210 ZP 5 .............  545-7789
COHEN ESTELA DESATNIK DE-AV MEXICO 13-4 ZP 11  528-6413
COHEN ESTHER CREDI DE-LUIS VIVES 210-601 ZP 10  540-5755
```

SUGGESTION: Explain that there are prefixes and suffixes in many languages that once meant *son of:* Johnson, McDonald, etc. The suffix **-ez** served this function in Spanish. **Ramírez** meant *son of Ramiro.* What did Fernández and López mean?

Los saludos y las despedidas

«Hola. ¿Qué tal?»
«Buenos días. ¿Cómo estás?»

«Adiós.»
«Hasta luego.»

Saludos

Buenos días.	*Good morning.*
Buenas tardes.	*Good afternoon.*
Buenas noches.	*Good evening. / Good night.*
Hola.	*Hello.*

FORMAL*

—¿Cómo está usted?	*How are you (form. sing.)?*
—¿Y usted?	*And you (form. sing.)?*
—¿Cómo están ustedes?	*How are you (pl.)?*
—¿Y ustedes?	*And you (pl.)?*

FAMILIAR*

—¿Cómo estás?	*How are you (fam. sing.)?*
—¿Y tú?	*And you (fam. sing.)?*

—(Muy) Bien.	*(Very) Well. / Fine.*
—(Muy) Mal.	*(Very) Ill. / Poorly.*
—Regular.	*Okay.*

¿Qué hay?	*What's going on?*
¿Qué hay de nuevo?	*What's new?*
¿Qué pasa?	*What's happening?*
¿Qué tal?	*What's up?*

—Nada (de particular).	*Nothing (much).*
—¿Y contigo?	*And with you (fam. sing.)?*

Despedidas

Adiós.	*Good-bye.*
Chao.	*'Bye.*
Hasta luego.	*See you later.*
Hasta mañana.	*See you tomorrow.*
Nos vemos.	*See ya.*
Que le vaya bien.	*Hope all goes well (form. sing.).*
Que te vaya bien.	*Hope all goes well (fam. sing.).*

*The concept of formality in address is introduced on page 12. In brief, familiar address is used with people you address on a first-name basis and formal address is used with all others.

Ⓐ **Al saludar.**[1] What greeting could Elena use with the following people? Consult the **Vocabulario** at the end of the chapter if necessary to be certain you understand who these individuals are.

NEW VOCABULARY: la amiga, el compañero de clase, el español, el papá; su, mejor

1. su papá
2. su mejor amiga
3. su profesor(a) de español
4. un compañero de clase

[1]Al... (*Upon*) *Greeting.*

Ⓑ **Al despedirse.**[1] Now imagine a farewell Elena could use with the following people. Consult the **Vocabulario** at the end of the chapter if necessary to be certain you understand who these individuals are.

NEW VOCABULARY: el chófer del autobús, el dentista, la mamá, el novio, el policía

1. su mamá
2. el chófer del autobús
3. su novio
4. un policía
5. su dentista

[1]Al... (*Upon*) *Saying good-bye.*

SUGGESTION: Use the picture as a way of introducing the new vocabulary, numbers and the verb **hay**. Read the description below the drawing and point to the items referred to either in the book or on an overhead transparency. Indicate that not all of some items (e.g., desks, students, books) can be seen in the drawing.

SUGGESTION: Pronounce the numbers and ask students to repeat them. This should be done quickly, just to ensure that students are comfortable with pronunciation. Mention that beyond fifteen, numbers in Spanish are simply combinations of the tens and digits the students already know. Give hints for remembering the numbers,

e.g., suggest that student learn 1–10 in pairs with their multiples of 10: **cinco-cincuenta, seis-sesenta**, etc.

Los números del 0 al 99

VOCABULARIO

En la sala de clase de Felipe hay dos puertas, seis ventanas, cincuenta pupitres y una mesa para el profesor. Hay sólo un profesor en la sala de clase, pero hay veintiocho alumnos. Hay dieciocho mochilas y cuarenta y seis libros en total.

Los números

0 cero	13 trece			
1 uno	14 catorce			
2 dos	15 quince			
3 tres	16 dieciséis			
4 cuatro	17 diecisiete			
5 cinco	18 dieciocho			
6 seis	19 diecinueve			
7 siete	20 veinte	26 veintiséis	40 cuarenta	70 setenta
8 ocho	21 veintiuno	27 veintisiete	44 cuarenta y cuatro	77 setenta y siete
9 nueve	22 veintidós	28 veintiocho	50 cincuenta	80 ochenta
10 diez	23 veintitrés	29 veintinueve	55 cincuenta y cinco	88 ochenta y ocho
11 once	24 veinticuatro	30 treinta	60 sesenta	90 noventa
12 doce	25 veinticinco	33 treinta y tres	66 sesenta y seis	99 noventa y nueve

Actividades

A **¿Es cierto o no es cierto?** According to what you've read about **La sala de clase de Felipe,** are the following statements true (**Es cierto**) or false (**No es cierto**)?

1. Hay 2 puertas en la sala de clase de Felipe.
2. Hay 8 ventanas.
3. Hay 50 pupitres.
4. Hay 1 profesora.
5. Hay 35 alumnos en total.
6. Hay 18 mochilas.
7. Hay 64 libros.

B **¿Cuántos años tienes?** Ask various classmates how old they are, using the model to the right.

C **Un viaje breve.**[1] Imagine that you are interested in spending two days and one night in Ciudad Juárez, so you decide to call ahead to make some arrangements. Following the model, inform a classmate of the phone numbers of the hotels and restaurants listed. HINT: To ask the question, simply raise your voice at the end of the phrase.

NEW VOCABULARY: el número de teléfono

EJEMPLO: ¿el Ballet Folklórico? / 14-01-23 →
El número de teléfono es el catorce, cero uno, veintitrés.

1. ¿el Hotel Calinda Juárez? / 16-34-21
2. ¿el Motel Colonial Las Fuentes? / 15-50-10
3. ¿el Hotel del Prado? / 11-88-12
4. ¿el Restaurante Florida? / 18-41-54
5. ¿el Restaurante Dega? / 13-98-35
6. ¿el Restaurante Casa del Sol? / 19-65-09

[1] *brief*

Los pronombres personales

yo

tú

nosotros

nosotras

él

ellos

vosotros

usted   usted

ustedes

ella

ellas

vosotras

A **¿Quién?** Which subject pronoun would you use to address each of the following individuals?

EJEMPLO: Felipe → tú

1. Profesor Brewer

2. Jorge y Joaquín

3. Alfonsina

SUGGESTION: If students seem to have difficulty with the distinction between formal and familiar, singular and plural, use photos from magazines or from a picture file to help them master the concept before moving on.

4. Carmen y Luisa

5. Profesora Martínez

6. Tomás

T **B** **¿Quién más?** Which subject pronoun would you use to talk *about* each of the following people?

PREPARATION: Point out that in this activity the students are not talking *to* people; they are talking *about* them.

EJEMPLO: a male instructor → él

1. yourself

2. yourself and a male companion

3. yourself and a female companion

4. a woman

5. two women

6. two men

7. one man

8. one man and one woman

Test

Remember, to express English *you*, use pronouns of familiar address (**tú** and **vosotros/as**) with people you address on a first-name basis and pronouns of formal address (**usted** and **ustedes**) with all others. NOTE: In writing, **usted** and **ustedes** are frequently abbreviated as **Ud.** and **Uds.**, respectively.

LOS PRONOMBRES PERSONALES

Singular		Plural	
yo	*I*	nosotros nosotras	*we*
tú usted (*abbrev.*: Ud.)	*you*	vosotros vosotras ustedes (*abbrev.*: Uds.)	*you*
él ella	*he* *she*	ellos ellas	*they*

Use **nosotros, vosotros,** and **ellos** for groups that consist of all males *or* males and females. Use **nosotras, vosotras,** and **ellas** for groups consisting of only females.

DIÁLOGO

Por teléfono

SUGGESTION: Explain the concept of first, second, and third person: I am always first; you are second only when I am talking to you; you become third (and last) when I am talking about you. Point out that English does not have the concept of familiar and formal forms of address. We use the same pronoun *you* for the President as for a cat.

PREPARATION: Ask students to look at the drawings. Who are the people and what are they doing? Ask students to look at the dialogue introduction and to brainstorm about the content of the conversation.

NEW VOCABULARY: estoy, estamos; contentos; ¿dónde?; ¡Qué bueno!

Before beginning his trip with Elena, David places a phone call to his family in Wisconsin.

ANA: Hello.
DAVID: ¡Mamá! ¿Qué tal?
ANA: ¡Hola, David! ¿Dónde estás?
DAVID: Estoy en la aduana de Laredo. Elena está conmigo.[1]
ANA: ¡Qué bueno! ¿Cómo están los dos[2]?
DAVID: ¡Estamos muy contentos! Ya empieza[3] el viaje.

[1] *with me* [2] los... *both (of you)* [3] Ya... *Is about to start*

De inmediato

1. Who is Ana?
2. What does Ana ask about as soon as the conversation begins?
3. From what city does David place the call?

4. How are David and Elena?

_____

1. ¿Dónde están David y Elena, en México o en Texas?
2. ¿Cómo están David y Elena, bien o mal?

With a classmate, practice placing a phone call to a friend or family member, using the dialogue as a model. Remember to substitute the city you are in and the name of the friend with whom you are traveling.

En la universidad

PREPARATION: Review the names of objects in the classroom by having students name the objects in the picture that they can identify. Ask whether students recognize any characters from previous dialogues. What are the characters doing?

DIÁLOGO

The faculty and students of the **Club Hispánico** go about their routine activities during the summer session on the University of Wisconsin–Eau Claire (UW-EC) campus.

JORGE: ¿Dónde está Marisol?
LUISA: Hoy no está aquí. Está enferma.

_____

EL PROFESOR RAMOS: Pero... ¿dónde están mis libros?
JOAQUÍN: Aquí están, profesor, en uno de los pupitres.

_____

ALFONSINA: La biblioteca está allí, María.
MARÍA: ¡Qué bueno! Está cerca.

NEW VOCABULARY: están; la biblioteca; enferma, mis; allí, aquí, cerca, hoy, no

---

Use information from the preceding dialogues to form as many true sentences as possible from the phrases in the columns.

Marisol	(no) está	en clase hoy
la biblioteca	(no) están	en el pupitre
los libros del profesor		cerca
Jorge y Luisa		mal hoy
Alfonsina y María		

OPTIONAL: Ask students to create minidialogues between instructor and students about objects in the classroom or their own classmates by following one of these models.
—¿Dónde está Fred/Tammy hoy? —Hoy no está aquí. Está enfermo/a.
—¿Dónde está la mochila? —Aquí/ Allí está.

Practice the preceding dialogues with three different classmates, substituting names and information as appropriate.

El verbo *estar*

¿Cómo **estás**, Elena?

Estoy muy contenta.

David y Elena **están** en la frontera.

Ana **está** en Wisconsin.

La abuelita **está** en Saltillo.

Actividades

A **Más saludos.** Use either **¿Cómo estás (tú)?** or **¿Cómo está Ud.?** to ask the following people how they are.

EJEMPLOS: tu mamá → ¿Cómo estás?

tu dentista → ¿Cómo está Ud.?

1. tu papá
2. tu mejor amigo/a
3. el rector (la rectora) de la universidad
4. tu profesor(a) de español
5. un compañero de clase
6. el chófer del autobús
7. tu novio/a
8. tu primo/a

B **¿Dónde están?** Indicate where the following items are located by combining elements from each column.

1. la torre Eiffel	estoy	en la sala de clase
2. yo	está	en la frontera
3. el puente Golden Gate	estamos	en Washington, D.C.
4. nosotros	están	en San Francisco
5. la Casa Blanca y el Capitolio		en París
6. El Paso y Ciudad Juárez		en ¿ ?

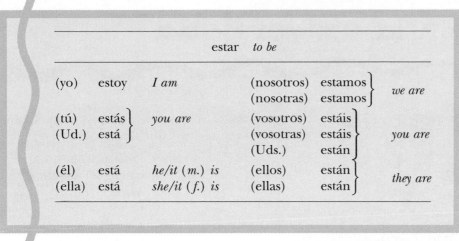

		estar	*to be*			
(yo)	estoy	*I am*		(nosotros)	estamos	
				(nosotras)	estamos	*we are*
(tú)	estás	*you are*		(vosotros)	estáis	
(Ud.)	está			(vosotras)	estáis	*you are*
				(Uds.)	están	
(él)	está	*he/it (m.) is*		(ellos)	están	
(ella)	está	*she/it (f.) is*		(ellas)	están	*they are*

The verb **estar** is used to discuss health, location, and current emotions and conditions.

PREPARATION: Call the students' attention to the drawing. Who are these people? What are they doing? Why? Ask students to look at the dialogue introduction for clues. What physical gestures (handshakes, hugs) do students normally use to greet the following people: close friends, members of their family, teachers, people they don't know?

Otro encuentro

DIÁLOGO

While waiting for the bus, Elena sees people she knows from Saltillo. After greeting them, Elena introduces David.

ELENA: David, quiero presentarte a Ricardo y Francisca Guzmán. Son mis padrinos[1] y amigos de la abuelita.[2]

DAVID: Mucho gusto.

RICARDO: Tanto gusto en conocerte,[3] David.

FRANCISCA: Encantada.

[1] *godparents* [2] *amigos... grandmother's friends* [3] Tanto... *So pleased to meet you*

NEW VOCABULARY: son; Encantada, Mucho gusto, quiero presentarte a, Tanto gusto en conocerte.

De inmediato

1. What are the names of the two people to whom David is introduced?
2. What is the relationship between Elena and Mr. and Mrs. Guzmán.
3. What phrase does Elena use to initiate the introduction of David?
4. What is one way to respond to an introduction?

A ti te toca

In groups of three, practice introducing yourself to your neighbors in the class, and respond when your neighbors introduce themselves to you. Use the dialogue as a model.

En la universidad

PREPARATION: Who are the three women in the drawing? Under what circumstances do women shake hands in the United States? Under what circumstances do students introduce classmates to professors?

NEW VOCABULARY: la librería; De nada, El gusto es mío, Perdón, quiero presentarle a, Tanto gusto en conocerla; cerca de, junto a, sí

On the UW-EC campus, the members of the **Club Hispánico** are also meeting new people.

LUISA: Profesora Martínez, quiero presentarle a María Gómez, de Colombia.

LA PROFESORA MARTÍNEZ: Tanto gusto en conocerla, María.

MARÍA: Gracias. El gusto es mío. Perdón, profesora. ¿Hay una librería cerca de aquí?

LA PROFESORA MARTÍNEZ: Sí, claro.[1] La librería está junto a la biblioteca.

MARÍA: Gracias.

LA PROFESORA MARTÍNEZ: De nada.

[1] *of course*

De inmediato

The following sentences all contain incorrect information. Correct them using information from the dialogue.

1. La profesora Martínez presenta a María.
2. María es de Venezuela.
3. No hay una librería en la universidad.
4. La librería está cerca de la carretera.

A ti te toca

In groups of three, practice introducing each other, using the dialogue as a model.

PREPARATION: Prepare students for this reading by asking them whether in their culture holding hands, hugging, and kissing are reserved for one special person. Can these gestures be used with family members? Close friends? Acquaintances? Total strangers? Point out that some cultures are more physically demonstrative than others. (See the *Instructor's Manual* for a discussion of comfort zones.) Ask students to comment on variations they have seen in their own experience. How do we react to such differences?

NEW VOCABULARY: el abrazo, el beso

Faceta cultural

Al saludar

In every culture, there are rules that govern how people interact. In the Hispanic world, manners are particularly important. Failure to follow certain social customs is considered rude. There are even correct and incorrect ways for people to greet each other. For example, in Hispanic countries, shaking hands is common in both business and social settings. Men shake hands with men and women. The **abrazo** (*hug* or *embrace*) is often used between friends, both males and females. The **beso** (*kiss*) is a greeting shared primarily between women who already know each other. How do we greet each other in this country?

el abrazo

el beso

Expresiones de cortesía

VOCABULARIO

Por favor.	*Please.*
(Muchas) Gracias.	*Thanks (a lot).*
	Thank you (very much).
De nada.	*You're welcome.*
No hay de qué.	*You're welcome.*
Con permiso.	*Excuse me.*
(Ay,) Lo siento.	*(Oh,) I'm sorry.*
Perdón.	*Forgive me.*
Quiero presentarte a...	*I'd like you (fam. sing.) to meet . . .*
Quiero presentarle a...	*I'd like you (form. sing.) to meet . . .*
Mucho gusto.	*Pleased to meet you.*
El gusto es mío.	*The pleasure is mine.*
Encantado/a.	*Delighted. / Pleased to meet you.*
Igualmente.	*Likewise. / Same to you. / Same here.*

Con permiso.

Perdón. Lo siento.

PREPARATION: Call attention to the drawing. What is happening in the two parts? What would we say, typically, in English in these situations? Mention that in the Hispanic world appearances and showing good manners are considered a sign of a proper upbringing.

A **Cortesía.** Use the expression of courtesy that fits each situation.

Actividades

1. You have received a gift from your parents.   *Gracias*
2. You are introducing your friend Paul to the dean of Liberal Arts, Dean Harris.   *Dean H, quiero presentarle a mi amigo, Paul*
3. You are introducing Dean Harris to your friend Paul.   *Paul, quiero presentarte a D.H.*

17

4. You have just met someone. *Mucho gusto*
5. You ask someone to do a favor for you. *Por favor*
6. You step on someone's toes. *Ay, lo siento, Perdon*
7. You are in the middle of a row at the movies and want to go get popcorn. *Con permiso, Excúsame*
8. You have forgotten to bring the money you owe your friend. *Lo siento Perdon.*

B **Situaciones.** Act out the following situations with two classmates.

1. You and an elderly relative meet one of your instructors in a shopping mall. Exchange greetings and introduce your relative to the instructor, addressing both of them formally. They exchange pleasantries. You all inquire about each other's health, then say good-bye.

2. You and a good friend run into one of your classmates. Greet the classmate and introduce him/her to your friend. You are all approximately the same age, so there is no need to be formal. Your classmate and friend exchange pleasantries. You all inquire about each other's health, then say good-bye.

VOCABULARIO

La geografía

Mirar en el diccionario

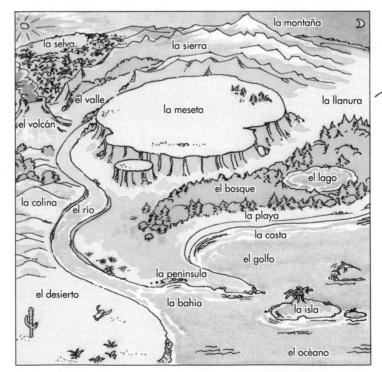

Otro vocabulario

el istmo　*isthmus*
el mar　*sea*

A ¿Qué es? What geographical feature do you associate with these places? Consult a map or an atlas if necessary.

EJEMPLO:　Tehuantepec → el istmo

1. Yucatán　Pen.
2. Cozumel　Isla
3. el Caribe　Mar
4. Hawai　Isla
5. el Pacífico　Oceano
6. el Amazonas　Río/Silva
7. Iberia　Pen.
8. Michigan　Lago
9. Cuba　Isla
10. los Alpes　Montaña Sierra
11. el Sáhara　Desierto
12. el Vesubio　Volcan.

B La geografía. Create as many sentences as you can by combining at least two of the features in the preceding drawing to describe the location of a geographical feature.

EJEMPLO:　La playa está en la costa.

En la Avenida Reforma en Nuevo Laredo

DIÁLOGO

Elena and David have to change buses in Nuevo Laredo. While they wait they explore the city.

DAVID:　¿Dónde estamos? Digo,[1] ¿en qué calle?
ELENA:　Estamos en la Avenida Reforma. Hay tiendas muy buenas aquí.
DAVID:　¡Sí! A propósito,[2] ¿qué hora es?
ELENA:　Son las dos. El autobús sale a las tres. Tenemos tiempo[3] todavía.[4]

[1] *I mean*　[2] *A... By the way*　[3] *time*　[4] *still, yet*

Complete the following sentences to form correct statements based on the dialogue.

De inmediato

1. David y Elena están en la ciudad de _____.
2. David y Elena están en la Avenida _____.

3. Las tiendas en la ciudad son muy _____.

4. Su autobús sale a las _____.

A ti te toca

Imagine that you and a classmate are in the downtown area of the city where your university is located. Using the preceding dialogue as a model, substitute real information for the street name and times. Use **Son las...** for all hours except one o'clock, which is expressed as **Es la una.**

DIÁLOGO

En la universidad

At the UW-EC cafeteria, David's friends and instructors are concerned about how others are doing.

MARÍA: ¿Qué le pasa a[1] Carmen? ¿Está enojada?

JOAQUÍN: No. Está preocupada por su familia en España.

EL PROFESOR RAMOS: ¿Qué les pasa a[1] Uds. hoy? ¿Están aburridos?

LUISA: No, profesor. Los lunes[2] siempre estamos cansados.

ALFONSINA: Hola, amigos. ¿Qué tal?

FELIPE: Estamos nerviosos. Son las ocho y media y tenemos un examen a las nueve.

NEW VOCABULARY: España, el examen; aburridos, cansados, enojada, nerviosos, preocupada por; siempre, y media
PREPARATION: Ask students to focus on the drawing. Do they recognize any of the characters? Ask them to make statements about the drawing or ask them questions that require simple answers.
SUGGESTION: Point out the adjectives and note their agreement with the nouns they describe: **Carmen → enojada, preocupada; ustedes → aburridos, cansados; (nosotros) → nerviosos.**

[1]¿Qué... *What's up/wrong with*   [2]Los... *On Mondays*

De inmediato

With which of the characters (**Carmen, Felipe y sus amigos, Luisa y los otros alumnos**) do you associate the following statements?

NEW VOCABULARY: tienen

1. Está preocupada. Carmen
2. Están nerviosos. Felipe + amigos
3. Están cansados. Luisa y los otros alumnos
4. Tiene una familia en España. Carmen
5. Tienen un examen a las nueve. Felipe + friends.

A ti te toca

Practice the preceding dialogues with a classmate, substituting names and information as appropriate.

Los artículos

U.S. Border Station
Laredo, Texas

INFORMATION

- All persons must report for inspection.
- Aliens must show identification.
- Smuggling narcotics, marijuana or dangerous drugs is a felony.

Estacion Fronteriza de los Estados Unidos
Laredo, Texas

INFORMACION

- Todas las personas deben de venir a inspeccion.
- Todos los extranjeros tienen que mostrar su identificacion.
- El contrabando de narcoticos, de marihuana o de drogas peligrosas es un delito.

PREPARATION: Ask what the English articles are. What is the difference between a definite article and an indefinite article? Is there a difference between *I want the book* and *I want a book*? When do we use *a*? when do we use *an*?

Nuevo Laredo está en **la** frontera. Laredo también está en **la** frontera. **Una** frontera es **una** división política; separa dos países.

Ⓐ **Identificación.** Indicate whether the following nouns that denote geographical features are masculine (**masculino**) or feminine (**femenina**).

1. bahía
2. península
3. río
4. valle
5. golfo
6. costa
7. montaña
8. lago
9. volcán

Ⓑ **¿Singular o plural?** Indicate whether the following nouns that denote geographical features are singular (**singular**) or plural (**plural**).

1. montañas
2. playas
3. colina
4. desiertos
5. islas
6. océano
7. istmo
8. selva
9. mares

¡OJO! Note that nouns ending in a vowel are made plural by adding **-s**. Nouns that end in a consonant are made plural by adding **-es**.

Ⓒ **El artículo definido.** Give the definite article (**el/la**) of the words in **Actividad A**.

Ⓓ **El artículo indefinido.** Give the indefinite article (**un/una, unos/unas**) of the words in **Actividad B**.

Actividades

PREPARATION: Ask how students can determine whether a noun is masculine or feminine. (They can look at the article or at an adjective modifying the noun.) Indicate that nouns ending in **-o** are usually masculine while nouns ending in **-a** are usually feminine. You might point out that nouns ending in the letters **-l, -o, -n, -e, -r** are usually masculine, and those ending in **-ión, -dad** are usually feminine. Students will have to learn the gender of nouns with other endings.
EXTENSION: Ask which of the following words are masculine and which are feminine: **aduana, autobús, biblioteca, calle, clase, estación, frontera, libro, pupitre, universidad**.

EXTENSION: Ask students to provide **un, una, unos** or **unas**: **valle, sierra, penínsulas, mesetas, bahía, ríos, costa, volcanes, lago, bosques**.

PREPARATION: Spanish, like English, uses the concept of singular versus plural. Unlike in English, in Spanish virtually everything is either masculine or feminine. Also, the articles that accompany each noun must agree with the noun.

LOS ARTÍCULOS

El artículo definido: el, la, los, las   = *the*
El artículo indefinido: un, una   = *a, an*
                    unos, unas   = *some, any, a few*

EJEMPLOS

Artículos masculinos

el río → los ríos   el país → los países
un río → unos ríos   un país → unos países

Artículos femeninos

la playa → las playas   la ciudad → las ciudades
una playa → unas playas   una ciudad → unas ciudades

NEW VOCABULARY: la ciudad

PREPARATION: Ask students to look at the drawings. What kinds of emotions or conditions are being portrayed?
SUGGESTION: Use pictures from magazines or from a picture file to ask students to identify emotion(s) a person is feeling.

VOCABULARIO

Estados físicos y emocionales

aburrido

cansado

contento

enfermo

enojado

entusiasmado

furioso

nervioso

ocupado

preocupado

triste

Actividad

¿Cómo se siente Jorge?[1] Jorge's day has had its ups and downs. Describe his emotional state in each of the following situations. (There may be more than one possible answer.)

EJEMPLO: He is waiting for a friend at the bus station. →
             Jorge (no) está aburrido.   *o*   Jorge (no) está contento.

1. He lost his wallet.   *enojado, furioso, pre*   **4.** He studied all night long. *cans, enf nrv*
2. He has an exam tomorrow. *nerv, oup*   **5.** He has a sore throat and a fever. *enf*
3. He got an A in history. *ent, cont.*   **6.** He won the lottery. *cont, enlus.*

SUGGESTION: If an item has a number of possible answers, after the first response, say: **Muy bien, y ¿otra cosa?**

[1]¿*Como... How does Jorge feel?*

Los adjetivos

Mercedes está enferm**a**.   Luisa está preocupad**a**.

PREPARATION: Call students' attention to the drawing. Read the captions. Point to a drawing of a healthy, smiling David (e.g., page 4). Say **David no está enfermo. David no está preocupado.** Repeat, emphasizing adjective endings. **Mercedes está enferma. David no está enfermo. Luisa está preocupada. David no está preocupado.** Ask **¿Está preocupada Luisa?**, etc.

🅐 **Armonía perfecta.** You can tell Elena and David have really hit it off because they always feel the same. Say how they feel in each of these situations.

EJEMPLOS: Cuando[1] Elena está contenta,... → David está contento.
             Cuando David está contento,... → Elena está contenta.

1. Cuando Elena está enferma,...
2. Cuando David está nervioso,...
3. Cuando David está enojado,...
4. Cuando Elena está preocupada,...
5. Cuando David está aburrido,...
6. Cuando Elena está cansada,...

[1]*When*

🅑 **Estados de ánimo.**[1] After a long, difficult week, Luisa recounts how all her friends and her daughter Mercedes are feeling. Working from the point of

[1]*mind*

Actividades

EXPANSION: Ask students to give four similar sentences to describe a couple they know or an imaginary one.

SUGGESTION: Before you begin the activity, use a photo or a rough sketch of four happy/sad/nervous people (two men and two women) to demonstrate adjective endings. Point to one man and say **Está contento.** Point to both men and say **Están contentos**, and so on.

view of Luisa (**yo**), match the people in the first column with the appropriate verb form in the second column and an adjective from the third column. You can identify the proper adjective by its ending. Some sentences may have more than one possible adjective.

Mercedes y yo	estoy	aburrida
Joaquín y Jorge	está	cansada
Alfonsina	estamos	enfermas
yo	están	enojado
Marisol y Carmen		furiosos
Tomás		nervioso
		ocupadas
		pesimistas
		tristes

Adjectives that end in **-o** or **-dor** have four forms. Most other adjectives have two.

Los adjetivos

-o/-a		-e		-ista	
furioso	furiosa	triste	triste	optimista	optimista
furiosos	furiosas	tristes	tristes	optimistas	optimistas

-dor(a)		ANY OTHER ENDING	
hablador	habladora	joven	joven
habladores	habladoras	jóvenes	jóvenes

Faceta cultural

La hora

Spanish speakers use the expressions **de la mañana, de la tarde,** and **de la noche** to indicate *A.M., in the morning,* and *P.M., in the afternoon* or *at night.* The exact definition of **la tarde** and **la noche** varies from country to country, but usually *afternoon* continues later than it does in the United States, until between 7:30 and 9:30 P.M.

Time schedules for transportation, invitations, programs, and business hours often use the twenty-four-hour clock system. Therefore, if a concert begins **a las 17 horas,** you would need to arrive **a las cinco de la tarde.**

En México

In Mexico, the exact definition of **la noche** varies from region to region, from city to city, even from family to family. Depending on the speaker, **la noche** may begin after supper, around 7:00, about 9:00, or simply when it gets dark. Visitors will have to inquire about and follow local customs.

¿Qué hora es?

VOCABULARIO

Es la una
(en punto).

Son las tres
(en punto).

Son las nueve
(en punto).

Son las dos y
cuarto de la tarde.

Son las siete y media de
la mañana.

Son las diez menos
cuarto de la noche.

Faltan cinco para la una.

Es mediodía.

Es medianoche.

A **Dime la hora.** *Paso 1.* Listen as your instructor announces a time to you, then give the number of the clock face to which it corresponds.

Actividades

1.

2.

3.

4.

5.

6.

7.

8.

9.

Paso 2. Now your instructor will say the number of one of the preceding clocks. State the time depicted on that clock.

B **El reloj internacional.** Mr. Larra, a businessman in Monterrey, is planning a sales trip to sites where his company has offices. It is 8.00 A.M. in Monterrey. What time is it in the other offices?

EJEMPLO: Si[1] son las once en Monterrey, ¿qué hora es en las otras ciudades? →
En Los Ángeles, son las nueve. En Denver, son...

LA HORA INTERNACIONAL

Los Ángeles   Denver

México, D.F.   Nueva York

Madrid

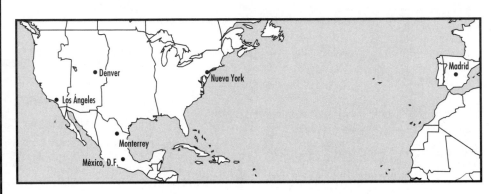

1. ¿Y si es mediodía?
2. ¿Y si son las tres y media en Monterrey?
3. ¿Y si son las once y cuarto de la noche?

SUGGESTION: Point out that the verticle lines in the map are international time zones.

[1]*If*

DIÁLOGO

En la universidad

PREPARATION: Ask questions about the art: **¿Qué pasa aquí? ¿Quiénes son las personas sentadas a la mesa? ¿Dónde están? ¿Qué hay en la biblioteca? ¿Qué tiene en la mano Felipe, una postal o un pupitre?**
NEW VOCABULARY: la postal; tonto; ¿Qué día es hoy?, Hoy es el día doce.

David's friend Felipe has just received a postcard (**una postal**) from him. Felipe shows it to his friends in the library.

FELIPE: Acabo de recibir[1] una postal de David.
ALFONSINA: ¿Sí? ¿Dónde está?
FELIPE: ¿Qué? ¿La postal?
ALFONSINA: No, tonto... David.
FELIPE: Está en Laredo. No... espera.[2] ¿Qué día es hoy?
MARISOL: Hoy es el día doce.
FELIPE: Pues,[3] David acaba de salir hoy para[4] Monterrey.

[1]*Acabo... I've just received*   [2]*wait*   [3]*Well*   [4]*acaba... has just left today for*

1. ¿Dónde están los amigos?
2. ¿Qué acaba de recibir Felipe?
3. ¿Qué día es hoy?
4. ¿David acaba de salir para Monterrey o para Laredo?

A ti te toca

Practice the preceding dialogue with two classmates. Then, using the dialogue as a model, imagine that you and your classmates have just received a postcard from a friend. Substitute the following information and today's date to form new dialogues.

YOUR FRIEND . . .	WAS IN . . .	BUT HAS JUST LEFT FOR . . .
1. Karen	Chicago	Springfield
2. Mark	Los Ángeles	San Francisco
3. ¿ ?	¿ ?	¿ ?

¡Vamos a Monterrey!

NEW VOCABULARY: mira; la carretera, la Carretera Panamericana, el mapa; ahora

DIÁLOGO

The bus from Nuevo Laredo to Monterrey has just left. David and Elena have begun their tour of Mexico.

ELENA: Mira, David. Son las tres de la tarde. Estamos ahora en Nuevo Laredo. A las siete estamos en Monterrey. ¿Estás cansado?

DAVID: No, estoy muy entusiasmado de estar en México. Oye, no veo[1] Monterrey en el mapa.

ELENA: Aquí está, y aquí, muy cerca, está la ciudad de Saltillo.

DAVID: O sea,[2] vamos a tomar[3] la carretera 85... la Carretera Panamericana.

[1]no... *I don't see* [2]O... *So (that means)* [3]*take*

De inmediato

1. ¿Qué hora es?
2. El viaje de Nuevo Laredo a Monterrey, ¿es de tres horas o de cuatro horas?
3. ¿Cómo está David?
4. ¿Qué ciudad está cerca de Monterrey?
5. ¿Qué número tiene la Carretera Panamericana, el ochenta y siete o el ochenta y cinco?

A ti te toca

Imagine that you and a classmate are looking at a map to plan the next leg of a journey you are making. Using the following exchange as a model, inform your classmate of the highway you are going to take to get from one city to another, and the approximate driving time. You may use information from any region with which you are familiar or you may use the map provided.

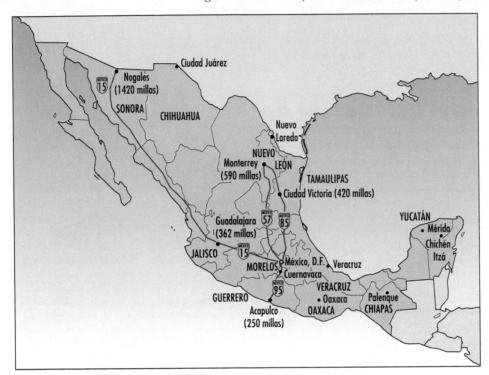

EJEMPLOS:
—Aquí estamos en Little Rock. Estoy muy entusiasmado/a de estar en Arkansas.
—Vamos a tomar la carretera 40. En dos horas estamos en Memphis.

o

—Aquí estamos en México, D.F. Estoy muy entusiasmado/a de estar en México.
—Vamos a tomar la carretera 57. En diez horas estamos en Monterrey.

NEW VOCABULARY: vamos

EN ACCIÓN

This section recombines material you studied previously. It provides additional opportunities for you to practice what you have learned in **Capítulo 1** while focusing on your speaking, reading, writing, and listening skills.

Antes de ver

In this part of the **En acción** section, you will see authentic video segments, shot in Mexico, that relate to the chapter's theme, vocabulary, and functions.

In this chapter, you will watch and listen as a series of people meet and greet each other as well as say good-bye. Try to determine whether their relationships are formal or informal, and be alert to any actions or gestures that may be different from those used by speakers of English.

Una llamada telefónica

Much to his surprise, David receives a telephone call from one of his friends shortly after his arrival in Saltillo.

Antes de escuchar

Have you ever made or thought about making a phone call to another country? What aspects of placing an international call might be confusing to a first-time caller? What differences do you think there might be between a long-distance conversation and a local call? Review the vocabulary for greeting someone and saying good-bye, since you would expect to hear some of these expressions in the conversation. Read the questions that pertain to each portion of the telephone call to alert yourself to the content of the conversation.

Now, listen carefully to each part of the conversation. You will hear only David's side of the conversation, and you will be asked to make some inferences and draw some conclusions based on what you hear. After listening, answer the questions that follow.

Después de escuchar

Paso 1

1. Where is David when he receives the call?
2. Is the caller male or female? Where is he/she from?
3. How is everyone (David, Elena, and David's grandmother) feeling?
4. At what time is the call made?
5. David reassures the caller. What concern does the caller seem to have?
6. Whose telephone number does David give the caller? What is the number?

Paso 2. List the geographic terms mentioned and explain why they come up in the conversation.

Dime más

With a classmate, take turns asking and answering questions about the location of the Mexican cities on page 30. Use the map of Mexico on page 28 to locate the cities. See how many answers you can give.

> EJEMPLO: ESTUDIANTE 1: ¿Dónde está (la ciudad de) Veracruz?
>   ESTUDIANTE 2: Está en la costa.
>   E1: Dime más.
>   E2: Está en el Golfo de México.
>   E1: Dime más.
>   E2: Está en el Estado de Veracruz.

1. Guadalajara	**4.** México, D.F.	**7.** Ciudad Juárez
2. Mérida	**5.** Acapulco	**8.** Cuernavaca
3. Monterrey	**6.** Nuevo Laredo	

Miniencuesta

How do you and your classmates feel when you are at the dentist's office (**en el consultorio del dentista**), at a party (**en una fiesta**), or washing the dishes (**al lavar los platos**)?

Paso 1. Which of the following adjectives describes you in these situations?
Paso 2. Working in small groups, determine how many in the group feel the same way in each situation. Be prepared to report to the class what you learned.

aburrido/a	enojado/a	ocupado/a
cansado/a	entusiasmado/a	preocupado/a
contento/a	furioso/a	triste
enfermo/a	nervioso/a	

1. En el consultorio del dentista estoy _____.
2. En una fiesta estoy _____.
3. Al lavar los platos estoy _____.

La guía turística

As David and Elena travel to Monterrey, David decides to read about some other areas along the Mexico–United States border.

NOTE: The readings in this activity are adapted from a guidebook for tourists who are native-speakers of Spanish. The goal is for students to learn to scan material written in Spanish to find the answers to questions that are asked in English.

Antes de leer

SUGGESTION: Read and discuss readings in class if possible. Review new words and expressions for each reading with the students. Note that many have not been glossed or included in the end-of-chapter vocabulary because they are cognates or are guessable in context.

Review the readings on Laredo and Nuevo Laredo in the **México y los mexicanos** section that precedes this chapter. These will help you anticipate the general kind of information that David might find in a guidebook about the northern Mexican states of Baja California Norte, Chihuahua, and Tamaulipas.

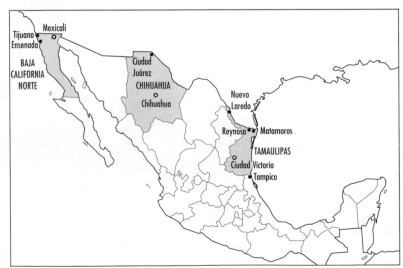

Next, study the map of Mexico that accompanies the following reading. Locate the three states that will be mentioned in the passages. On which U.S. states do they border? Based on what you might already know about the geography and climate of the regions, what differences would you expect in the climate and economic base of the three states?

Read the questions that follow the reading to prepare yourself for the content of each passage. Now read the paragraphs and answer the questions that follow.

Un viaje por tres estados mexicanos

Baja California Norte es uno de dos estados que están en la Península de Baja California. Sus tres ciudades principales son Tijuana, Mexicali y Ensenada, un puerto de gran importancia.

El clima de la península es muy caluroso;[1] a veces pasan 5 ó 6 años sin lluvia.[2] Sin embargo,[3] la economía se basa en la agricultura y también en el turismo.

Chihuahua es el estado más grande de los 32 estados mexicanos. Una de las ciudades más importantes de este estado es Ciudad Juárez, que limita con[4] la ciudad estadounidense de El Paso. Ciudad Juárez y Tijuana son las dos ciudades mexicanas fronterizas con más de un millón de habitantes.

El clima del estado de Chihuahua es desértico seco[5] extremo, con poca lluvia en todas las estaciones.[6] En el verano,[7] en junio, hay temperaturas de 38° C. (103° F.) pero en el invierno[8] hay mucha nieve[9] y hace mucho frío.[10]

Tamaulipas es uno de los estados mexicanos que limita con el Golfo de México. Hay petróleo en las costas de este estado y por esto[11] es uno de los estados más prósperos de la República.

Este estado tiene una economía muy industrializada. Sus ciudades más importantes son Matamoros, Reynosa, Tampico y, en un punto remoto de la parte noroeste del estado, Nuevo Laredo.

[1]hot [2]rain [3]Sin... *Nevertheless* [4]limita... *borders on* [5]dry [6]seasons [7]summer [8]winter [9]snow [10]hace... *it's very cold* [11]por... *for this reason*

El clima de Baja California Norte es ideal para el cultivo de una variedad de frutas como la naranja y la tuna, fruto del nopal.

NEW VOCABULARY: poca

La Barranca del Cobre en el estado de Chihuahua es más honda que el famoso Gran Cañón del Colorado en Arizona.

El Golfo de México todavía produce mucho petróleo, pero la industria petrolera ha declinado mucho.

Despues de leer

BAJA CALIFORNIA NORTE

1. How many Mexican states are on the California peninsula?
2. What is a very important port in the state of Baja California Norte?
3. How many years can go by without rain in this region?
4. What are the two economic bases of the peninsula?

CHIHUAHUA

1. Which Mexican state has the largest area?
2. Which two Mexican border cities have more than one million inhabitants? In which two states are they located?
3. Describe the climate of the region.

TAMAULIPAS
1. What body of water forms one of the borders of this state?
2. Why is this state one of the most prosperous in the country?
3. What one word can describe the economy of this region?
4. Why might one be surprised to find that Nuevo Laredo is part of this state?

Una conversación

Write a dialogue of eight to twelve sentences in which you exchange information with one of your instructors. First, exchange greetings, then inquire about each other's current health, feelings, and/or emotions. The instructor asks about a female friend who is a mutual acquaintance. Say that your friend is excited about a trip to Monterrey. Then take your leave.

CONSIDERACIONES
- Which greetings and farewells are appropriate for the social situation and time of day?
- Which pronouns for *you* are appropriate?
- Which courtesy expressions seem appropriate?
- Which forms of **estar** are needed?
- What punctuation marks do you need?

VOCABULARIO

Los verbos	Verbs
es	it is
estar	to be (*with locations, conditions*)
estoy	I am
estás	you (*fam. sing.*) are
está	you (*form. sing.*) are; he/she/it is
estamos	we are
estáis	you (*fam. pl.*) are
están	you (*pl.*) are; they are
hay	there is; there are
llega (a)	arrives (in, at)
mira	look
oye	hey; listen
sale	leaves
son	they are

tener	to have
tengo	I have
tienes	you (*fam. sing.*) have
tiene	he/she/it has
tenemos	we have
tienen	they have
va	goes
vamos	we are going

Los términos geográficos	Geographic terms
la bahía	bay
el bosque	woods, forest
la colina	hill
la costa	coast
la isla	island
el istmo	isthmus

el lago	lake
la llanura	plain
el mar	sea
la meseta	plateau
la montaña	mountain
la playa	beach
el río	river
la selva	jungle
la sierra	mountain range
el valle	valley

Palabras semejantes (*Cognates*): **el desierto, el golfo, el océano, la península, el volcán.**

Las personas — *People*

la abuelita	grandma
el alumno / la alumna	student, pupil (*m./f.*)
el amigo / la amiga	friend (*m./f.*)
el compañero / la compañera	companion (*m./f.*)
el compañero / la compañera de clase	classmate (*m./f.*)
el chófer del autobús	bus driver
el novio / la novia	boyfriend/girlfriend
el policía	police officer (*m.*)
la mujer policía	police officer (*f.*)
el primo / la prima	cousin (*m./f.*)
el rector / la rectora	university president (*m./f.*)

Palabras semejantes: el/la dentista, el/la estudiante, la mamá, el papá, el profesor / la profesora.

En la ciudad y la universidad — *In the city and at the university*

el autobús	bus
la avenida	avenue
la biblioteca	library
la calle	street
la carretera	highway
la Carretera Panamericana	Pan-American Highway
la ciudad	city
la clase (de español)	(Spanish) class
el club	club
el español	Spanish
el examen	exam, test
la fiesta	party
la fiesta de despedida	farewell party

la librería	bookstore
el libro	book
el mapa	map
la mesa (para el profesor / la profesora)	table (for the professor)
la mochila	backpack; bookbag
la puerta	door
el pupitre	student desk
la sala de clase	classroom
la tienda	store
la universidad	university
la ventana	window

Los lugares — *Places*

la aduana	customs office
España	Spain
la estación (de autobuses)	(bus) station
el estado	state
los Estados Unidos (EE. UU.)	United States (U.S., U.S.A.)
la frontera	border (*political*)
México	Mexico
el país	country (*political*)

Otros sustantivos — *Other nouns*

el abrazo	hug, embrace
el apellido	family name, surname, last name
el beso	kiss
la cosa	thing
la familia	family
la geografía	geography
el mapa	map
el número	number
el número de teléfono	telephone number
la postal	postcard
el viaje	trip

Los números (*Numbers*)

0	cero	5	cinco
1	uno	6	seis
2	dos	7	siete
3	tres	8	ocho
4	cuatro	9	nueve

10	diez	24	veinticuatro
11	once	25	veinticinco
12	doce	26	veintiséis
13	trece	27	veintisiete
14	catorce	28	veintiocho
15	quince	29	veintinueve
16	dieciséis	30	treinta
17	diecisiete	40	cuarenta
18	dieciocho	50	cincuenta
19	diecinueve	60	sesenta
20	veinte	70	setenta
21	veintiuno	80	ochenta
22	veintidós	90	noventa
23	veintitrés		

mi(s)	my
tu(s)	your (*fam. sing.*)
su(s)	his, her
¿cuántos/as?	how many?

Los estados físicos y emocionales

Physical and emotional states

estar...	to be (*with conditions*)
aburrido/a	bored
cansado/a	tired
contento/a	happy
enfermo/a	sick
enojado/a	angry
entusiasmado/a	enthused, excited
furioso/a	furious
nervioso/a	nervous
ocupado/a	busy
preocupado/a (por)	worried (about)
triste	sad

Los adverbios

Adverbs

ahora	now
hoy	today
siempre	always
allí	there
aquí	here
cerca	nearby; near
sí	yes
no	no, not
sólo	only
más	more
muy	very
¿dónde?	where?

Otros adjetivos

Other adjectives

ser...	to be (*with characteristics*)
bueno/a	good
estadounidense	U.S., American
hablador(a)	talkative; gossipy
hispanico/a	Hispanic
joven (*pl.:* jóvenes)	young
mexicano/a	Mexican
norteamericano/a	(North) American
optimista	optimistic
pesimista	pessimistic
tonto/a	silly, foolish
mejor	better; best
mucho/a	much; (*pl.*) many, a lot (of)
otro/a	other; another
poco/a	few; little

Las preposiciones

Prepositions

a	at; to
cerca de	near (to)
de	of; from
del	of; from the
en	in; on
junto a	next to
para	for; (in order) to

Las conjunciones

Conjunctions

o	or
pero	but
y	and

Los saludos

Greetings

Buenos días.	Good morning.
Buenas tardes.	Good afternoon.
Buenas noches.	Good evening; Good night.
Hola.	Hello, Hi.
¿Cómo estás?	How are you (*fam. sing.*)?
¿Cómo está usted?	How are you (*form. sing.*)?
¿Cómo están ustedes?	How are you (*pl.*)?
(Muy) Bien.	(Very) Well. / Fine.

(Muy) Mal.	(Very) Ill. / Poorly.
Regular.	Okay.
¿Y tú?	And you (*fam. sing.*)?
¿Y usted?	And you (*form. sing.*)?
¿Y ustedes?	And you (*pl.*)?
¿Qué hay?	What's going on?
¿Qué hay de nuevo?	What's new?
¿Qué pasa?	What's happening?
¿Qué tal?	What's up?
Nada (de particular).	Nothing (much).
¿Y contigo?	And with you (*fam. sing.*)?

Las despedidas — *Farewells*

Adiós.	Good-bye.
Chao.	'Bye.
Hasta luego.	See you later.
Hasta mañana.	See you tomorrow.
Nos vemos.	See ya.
Que le vaya bien.	Hope all goes well (for you [*form. sing.*]).
Que te vaya bien.	Hope all goes well (for you [*fam. sing.*]).

Las expresiones de cortesía — *Expressions of courtesy*

Quiero presentarle a...	I'd like you (*form. sing.*) to meet . . .
Quiero presentarte a...	I'd like you (*fam. sing.*) to meet . . .
Encantado/a.	Delighted. / Pleased to meet you.
Mucho gusto.	Pleased to meet you.
Tanto gusto en conocerlo/la.	So pleased to meet you. (*form. sing., m./f.*)
Tanto gusto en conocerte.	So pleased to meet you. (*fam. sing.*)
El gusto es mío.	The pleasure is mine.
Igualmente.	Likewise. / Same to you. / Same here.
(Ay,) Lo siento.	(Oh,) I'm sorry.

Con permiso.	Excuse me.
Perdón.	Forgive me.
Por favor.	Please.
(Muchas) Gracias.	Thanks (a lot). / Thank you (very much).
De nada.	You're welcome.
No hay de qué.	You're welcome.

La hora — *(Telling) Time*

¿Qué hora es?	What time is it?
Es la una.	It's one o'clock.
Son las dos (tres,...).	It's two (three, . . .) o'clock.
Es mediodía.	It's noon.
Es medianoche.	It's midnight.
Faltan cinco para la una.	It's five 'til one.
en punto	sharp, on the dot
menos cuarto	quarter 'til
y cuarto	quarter past
y media	half past
de la mañana	A.M., in the morning
de la tarde	P.M., in the afternoon
de la noche	P.M., at night
¿A qué hora... ?	(At) What time . . .
A las tres (cuatro,...).	At three (four, . . .) o'clock.

Palabras y expresiones útiles — *Useful words and expressions*

¿Cuántos años tienes?	How old are you?
Tengo... años.	I'm . . . years old.
¿No?	Right?
¿Qué... ?	What . . . ?
¡Qué bueno!	How nice!
¿Qué día es hoy?	What day is today?
Hoy es el día doce (trece,...).	Today is the twelfth (thirteenth, . . .).
¿Quién más?	Who else?
¿Verdad?	Right?

DOS

México y los mexicanos

NOTE: Suggestions for teaching the **De viaje** and **Perspectivas** sections of **México y los mexicanos** are very detailed and cannot be easily accommodated in the margins of the text. For this reason, the notes for these two sections are in the *Instructor's Manual*.

NEW VOCABULARY: con, también

De viaje: Monterrey y Saltillo

Monterrey es la capital del estado mexicano de Nuevo León. Está en una de las carreteras más populares entre los Estados Unidos y la capital de México, la Carretera Panamericana. Para muchas personas Monterrey es el Pittsburgh de México. Es una ciudad industrial que domina esta parte de México. El Instituto Tecnológico de Monterrey es una de las universidades más importantes[1] de México.

Saltillo es la capital del estado mexicano de Coahuila. Está en el Valle de Saltillo en la Sierra Madre Oriental. Es una ciudad con mucha actividad industrial, agrícola y comercial.

Saltillo y Monterrey son ciudades coloniales. Fueron fundadas[2] en el siglo[3] XVI. En la época colonial Saltillo era[4] la capital de los estados actuales[5] de Tamaulipas, Nuevo León, Texas y también de todos los territorios hasta llegar al Polo Norte.[6] ¡Sí! El territorio mexicano se extendía hasta[7] el Polo Norte en esa época.[8]

[1]más... *most important* [2]Fueron... *They were founded* [3]*century* [4]*was* [5]*present-day* [6]hasta... *to the North Pole* [7]se... *stretched to* [8]en... *in those days*

En Saltillo, como en casi todos los pueblos y ciudades de México, la catedral y la plaza central son el foco de la ciudad.

NEW VOCABULARY: el hombre, la mujer, los hijos; mucho

Perspectivas de México: La familia mexicana

La familia nuclear es formada generalmente por un hombre, una mujer y sus hijos. Constituye[1] una unidad social de gran cohesión y solidaridad. La familia es el centro y fundamento del sistema social. Cuando la familia cambia,[2] la sociedad cambia.

En los años[3] recientes la familia mexicana ha cambiado[4] mucho. La familia ha delegado[5] unas funciones tradicionales a la escuela,[6] a la iglesia[7] y al gobierno.[8] Ha adoptado[9] nuevos valores,[10] principalmente respecto al papel[11] y posición de la mujer en la familia y en la comunidad.

Los logros[12] de la mujer en la lucha[13] por obtener más dignidad y libertad en el trabajo y la política han tenido[14] un impacto en los hogares[15] mexicanos. Ahora existe menos sexismo y mayor igualdad[16] entre los cónyuges.[17]

México, D.F. Hay muchas oportunidades para ejecutivos competentes de ambos sexos.

[1]*It constitutes, makes up* [2]*changes* [3]*years* [4]*ha... has changed* [5]*ha... has delegated* [6]*school* [7]*church* [8]*government* [9]*Ha... It has adopted* [10]*values* [11]*role* [12]*achievements* [13]*struggle* [14]*han... have had* [15]*homes* [16]*equality* [17]*spouses*

El Instituto Tecnológico de Monterrey. Las universidades mexicanas son parte importante del desarrollo de los habitantes.

Para la familia mexicana, la hora de la comida es muy apreciada, como lo es para todas las familias ocupadas de hoy día.

CAPÍTULO

2

NOTE: See the *Instructor's Manual* for suggestions on using the chapter opening pages.

La identidad[1]

Esta orgullosa familia chicana es ejemplo de la familia extendida.

[1] *Identity*

Dora López de Muñoz, la madre de Elena

Harvey Nelson, el padre de David

Yolanda Inés García de Muñoz, la abuelita de David y Elena

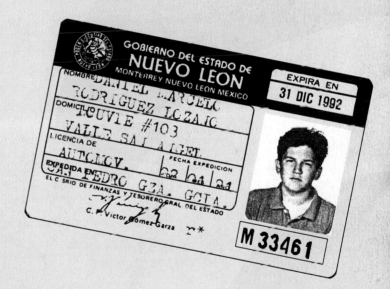

M E T A S

FUNCIONES

- to identify and describe yourself and others with vocabulary for talking about family, clothes, colors, physical characteristics, personality, and nationalities
- to ask for information
- to express ownership

GRAMÁTICA

- the verbs **ser, tener, ir**
- expression of possession with possessive adjectives
- expression of possession with **de**
- questions

APPROPRIATE TESTING POINTS:
Diálogo (2), La familia, El verbo *ser*, La posesión, El uso de *de* para expresar posesión, **Quiz 1**

Diálogo (2), La ropa, Los colores, El verbo *tener*, Diálogo (2), La descripción física, La personalidad, **Quiz 2**

Las preguntas con palabras interrogativas, Las preguntas con respuestas de *sí* o *no*, Diálogo (2), Los países y las nacionalidades, El verbo *ir*, **Quiz 3**
Diálogo (1), En acción
Chapter test

DIÁLOGO

En casa de la abuela

Alfonso Inés Bartolomé Yolanda
Raúl Fernando Dora Ana Harvey
Elena David

PREPARATION: Ask questions about the art: **¿Quiénes son estas personas? ¿Conoces al hombre? ¿Y a la mujer?** Aquí David y su abuelita miran un álbum de fotografías... un álbum de fotos. En el álbum hay fotos de la familia de la abuelita. Hay fotos de David, de tíos, tías, primos, primas... hay fotos de muchos de los parientes de David.

NEW VOCABULARY: la abuela, el esposo, el hermano, la hermana, el pariente, el tío

When David and Elena arrived in Monterrey, their cousin Amalia picked them up at the bus station and drove them to Saltillo to visit their grandmother, Yolanda. David and Yolanda stay up late looking at family photos.

DAVID: Abuelita, ¿es Raúl mi tío?

YOLANDA: No, Raúl es tu primo. Es el hijo de Inés, la hermana de tu mamá.

DAVID: ¿Y Alfonso? Él es mi tío, ¿no?

YOLANDA: Sí, Alfonso es el esposo de Inés.

DAVID: ¡Ay! Tengo muchos parientes mexicanos.

De inmediato

¿Sí o no?

1. ¿Es Raúl el tío de David?
2. ¿Es Raúl el hijo de Inés?
3. ¿Es Inés la abuela de David?
4. ¿Es Alfonso el esposo de Inés?

A ti te toca

Practice the preceding dialogue with a classmate. Then exchange roles, substituting the following names for those of the characters.

Raúl → Alberto
Inés → Cecilia
Alfonso → Fernando

En la universidad

At UW-EC, David's friends spend time looking at family photos also.

LUISA: Tu familia es grande, ¿verdad?
ALFONSINA: Sí, mi padre tiene ocho hermanos y mi madre tiene seis. Tengo treinta y ocho primos en total.

ALFONSINA: Entonces,[1] Emilio es el hermano de tu papá.
FELIPE: Sí, es mi tío, y su hijo Roberto es mi primo.

FELIPE: La niña en esta[2] foto, ¿es tu sobrina?
LUISA: No. Es mi hija Mercedes. Tiene ocho años. Ahora está en Miami, con mi esposo. Pero la semana que viene[3] va a estar aquí.

[1]*Then*   [2]*this*   [3]*que... next*

NEW VOCABULARY: va a + *inf.*; la madre, la niña, el padre, la semana, la sobrina; grande, en total
DIÁLOGO
PREPARATION: Ask whether students recognize any of the people in the drawing? What items in the picture can students identify in Spanish? What are the people in the drawing doing? What do you think they are talking about?
SUGGESTION: Remind students that glossed words and expressions are useful to know, but they are not part of the vocabulary that students are expected to master.

De inmediato

Complete the following statements using information from the dialogues.

ALFONSINA
1. Su familia es _____ (**adjetivo**).
2. Tiene treinta y ocho _____ en total.

FELIPE
3. Emilio es su _____.
4. Roberto es su _____.

MERCEDES
5. Es la _____ de Luisa.
6. Tiene _____ años.
7. Está ahora en _____ (**ciudad**).

OPTIONAL: Read the following sentences as students look at the dialogue in the text. Ask students to tell which character is being described, Alfonsina, Felipe, or Luisa. 1. **Su madre tiene seis hermanos.** 2. **Emilio es su tío.** 3. **Roberto es su primo.** 4. **Su hija es Mercedes.**

OPTIONAL: Using the information in the dialogue, have students indicate as many family relationships as possible. You may wish to put a model on the board or the overhead. (**Persona) es (relación a otra persona). → Raúl es primo de David. Raúl es hijo de Inés.**

A ti te toca

Practice the preceding dialogues with a classmate. Then try the following exchange with one or more classmates.

—Tu familia es grande, ¿verdad?
—Sí, tengo _____ (**número**) tíos/primos/hermanos/parientes en total.
o —No, tengo sólo _____ (**número**) tío(s)/primo(s)/hermano(s)/pariente(s) en total.

La familia

LA FAMILIA DE DAVID

Relationship with David.

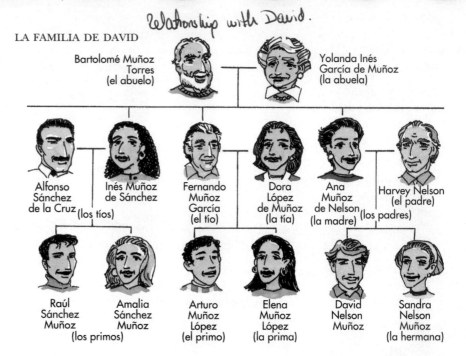

Bartolomé Muñoz Torres (el abuelo)

Yolanda Inés García de Muñoz (la abuela)

Alfonso Sánchez de la Cruz

Inés Muñoz de Sánchez
(los tíos)

Fernando Muñoz García (el tío)

Dora López de Muñoz (la tía)

Ana Muñoz de Nelson (la madre)

Harvey Nelson (el padre)
(los padres)

Raúl Sánchez Muñoz

Amalia Sánchez Muñoz
(los primos)

Arturo Muñoz López (el primo)

Elena Muñoz López (la prima)

David Nelson Muñoz

Sandra Nelson Muñoz (la hermana)

Otros miembros de la familia

el esposo	husband	el nieto	grandson	el suegro	father-in-law
la esposa	wife	la nieta	grandaughter	la suegra	mother-in-law
el hijo	son	el sobrino	nephew	el yerno	son-in-law
la hija	daughter	la sobrina	niece	la nuera	daughter-in-law

Actividades

A **Los parientes de David.** What is the relationship to David of each person in David's family?

EJEMPLO: Sandra → Sandra es la hermana de David.

1. Bartolomé *abuelo*
2. Ana *madre*
3. Elena *prima*
4. Arturo *primo*
5. Harvey *padre*
6. Yolanda *abuela*
7. Dora *tía*
8. Amalia *prima*

B **Parentescos.**[1] Using David's family tree for reference, work with a classmate to ask the identities of each of the people in David and Elena's families. Mention at least two relationships for each person named.

EJEMPLO: —¿Quién es Sandra?
—Es la hermana de David. Es la hija de Ana y Harvey.

[1] *Family relationships.*

La familia

Throughout the Hispanic world, bonds between family members have traditionally been very close. The term **familia** includes members of the extended family (aunts, uncles, cousins, and so on) whom many in the United States might designate as *relatives* (**parientes**). Social occasions tend to be family-centered, and family members are expected to support each other emotionally, and sometimes financially. However, as economic conditions produce an ever more mobile society, the family unit has become increasingly limited to the nuclear family (parents and children), but ties with the extended family remain strong.

Faceta cultural

PREPARATION: Ask whether students consider their families close. Whom do they include when describing their families? When they or their parents have a party, do they invite other family members? Whom? Do they live within 200 miles of most of the members of their nuclear family? And of their extended family? Do they think that ties with members of the extended family are important?

El verbo *ser*

David y Sandra **son** altos.
Los hermanos **son** jóvenes.

La abuelita **es** baja.
La abuelita **es** vieja.

NEW VOCABULARY: ser; altos, baja, jóvenes, vieja
PREPARATION: Direct the students' attention to the drawings of David, Sandra, and Yolanda. Expand on the model by using comparisons between students and the instructor. Point out that earlier we used the verb **estar** to express *to be*. What kinds of things did we talk about that use **estar**? (health/condition [**Está bien.**] and location [**Están en Laredo.**]) What kinds of things are we talking about that use **ser**? Note that Spanish speakers use at least two verbs to talk about being, but each is used in different ways.
SUGGESTION: Introduce **ser** to discuss general age and origin by using pictures from magazines or a picture file. Hold up a picture and ask one of the following questions with students responding ¿Sí or no? 1. ¿Es joven? 2. ¿Es viejo/a? 3. ¿Es de los EE. UU.? 4. ¿Es de México (Rusia, ...)?

A **¿Jóvenes o viejos?** Since David is in his early twenties, he may well consider anyone in his parents' generation "old," regardless of their age. Using David's family tree for reference, state whether David would consider the following individuals to be *young* (**joven/jóvenes**) or *old* (**viejo/vieja/viejos/viejas**).

EJEMPLOS:　la abuela → Es vieja.
　　　　　　Raúl y Amalia → Son jóvenes.

1. Harvey y Ana
2. Sandra
3. Dora y Fernando
4. Bartolomé y Yolanda

(*Continúa.*)

Actividades

OPTIONAL: Ask students to make as many sentences as possible to express *young* and *old*: **Mi abuela es vieja. Mi compañera de cuarto es joven.**
OPTIONAL: Ask students to describe the relative height of people they see in pictures with **alto/a, bajo/a,** and **de estatura mediana.**

5. Elena
6. Inés
7. Raúl y Amalia

EXTENSION: 5. Ana Muñoz de Nelson 6. Amalia y Raúl Muñoz Sánchez 7. Luisa, una amiga de David de Miami

B **¿De México o de los Estados Unidos?** Indicate whether the following people are from Mexico or from the United States.

EJEMPLOS: Yolanda Muñoz →
Es de México.

David y Sandra Nelson →
Son de los Estados Unidos.

1. Fernando y Dora Muñoz
2. Harvey Nelson
3. Elena Muñoz
4. Bartolomé y Yolanda Muñoz

OPTIONAL: Ask students to name current singers, sports figures, actors, or politicians. The other students will attempt to identify the occupation of each person named.

C **Identificaciones.** Use a form of **ser** to identify the following people.

¡OJO![1] This text uses symbols to represent persons whom you will choose to include in your responses. For example, in this and subsequent activities, the icon Ⓔ represents another student (**estudiante**) in the class, whereas the icon Ⓟ represents the instructor (**profesor[a]**) of the class. When you see one of these symbols, state the name of someone you know that fits the description of the symbol. For instance, when you see Ⓟ, say the name of your instructor.

EJEMPLO: Bill Clinton   político/a[2] → Bill Clinton es político.

1. Gloria Estefan actor (actriz)
2. Emilio Éstevez amigos (amigas)
3. los «Padres» de San Diego cantante[3]
4. yo estudiante(s) en la clase de español
5. David y Elena jugadores[4] profesionales de béisbol
6. Ⓔ y yo primos
7. Ⓟ, Ud. político/a
  profesor(a) de español

[1] *Careful! Note!* [2] *politician* [3] *singer* [4] *players*

The verb **ser** is used to identify as well as to describe the physical and personality traits and characteristics of people and things. It can also indicate where people and things originate (when used with **de**).

ser	to be		
(yo) soy	*I am*	(nosotros/as) somos	*we are*
(tú) eres (Ud.) es	*you are*	(vosotros/as) sois (Uds.) son	*you are*
(él/ella) es	*he/she is*	(ellos/as) son	*they are*

La posesión

David es **mi** primo y yo soy **su** prima.

Mi familia. Name the following members of your family. When appropriate, use **No tengo...**

Actividad

EJEMPLOS: padre → Ed Lewis es mi padre.
hermanos → Daniel y Martha son mis hermanos.
hijos → No tengo hijos.

1. padre
2. madre
3. hermanos
4. hijos
5. tío/a
6. primos
7. abuelo/a
8. esposo/a
9. suegro/a

Los adjetivos posesivos

mi(s) *my*	nuestro/a/os/as *our*
tu(s) *your* (*fam.*)	vuestro/a/os/as *your* (*fam.*)
su(s) *his, her, its, your* (*form.*)	su(s) *their, your*

mi padre	mi madre	nuestro primo	nuestra prima
mis hijos	mis hijas	nuestros primos	nuestras primas
tu amigo	tu amiga	vuestro profesor	vuestra profesora
tus amigos	tus amigas	vuestros profesores	vuestras profesoras
su abuelo	su abuela	su nieto	su nieta
sus abuelos	sus abuelas	sus nietos	sus nietas

As in other adjectives, the endings of possessive adjectives agree in number (singular/plural) with the nouns they modify. **Nuestro/a** and **vuestro/a** also match the gender of the nouns they modify. Possessive adjectives are placed before the noun.

El uso de *de* para expresar posesión

PREPARATION: 1. Draw students' attention to the drawing of David and Elena's respective houses. Repeat the captions several times as you point to the two houses. Use objects in the classroom to expand on the model: **Es el libro del profesor / de la profesora. Son los libros de Mary,** **etc.** 2. Expand the model in a different direction by using David's family tree to show the relationships between the characters: **David es el hermano de Sandra. David y Sandra son los hijos de Ana y Harvey.**

Es la casa **de** David.   Es la casa **de** Elena.

Actividades

SUGGESTION: Before beginning the activity, have students look at the family tree while you read statements about the relationships between the people in David's family. **¿Sí o no?** 1. **Elena es la hija de Fernando y Dora.** 2. **Alfonso es el hermano de Inés.** 3. **Raúl es el hermano de Amalia.** 4. **David es el primo de Sandra.** 5. **Dora es la esposa de Fernando.**

A **¿Cuál es la relación?** Using David's family tree on page 42 for reference, express the relationship between the following people.

EJEMPLOS: Elena / David → Elena es la prima de David.

David y Sandra / Elena →
David y Sandra son los primos de Elena.

1. Ana / David
2. Arturo / Dora
3. Yolanda / Elena
4. David / Sandra
5. Sandra y David / Harvey

6. Ana y Harvey / Elena
7. Elena y David / Bartolomé y Yolanda
8. Inés y Alfonso / David y Elena

OPTIONAL: Hold up books and backpacks belonging to students. As you take each item, ask the owner **¿Cómo te llamas?** After the student answers with **Me llamo ___,** ask **¿Es la mochila / el libro (Son las mochilas / los libros) de ___?** Repeat activity, asking **¿De quién es ___?** or **¿De quiénes son ___?**

B **¿De quién es?** Express the relationship between the objects and people indicated.

EJEMPLO: clase/Felipe → Es la clase de Felipe.

LA SALA DE CLASE

Para expresar posesión: *noun* + **de** + *noun*

Although English uses *'s* to show possession, Spanish uses **de** + noun. *David's book* is expressed by **el libro de David** in Spanish. Note that when **de** precedes the masculine definite article **el,** the two words contract to **del.**

la oficina **de la** profesora Martínez

but

la oficina **del** profesor Brewer

Un café en Monterrey

David, Elena, and Amalia return to Monterrey, where they spend the morning seeing the sights. They take a break to get a cold drink and sit for a while.

AMALIA: Me gusta ver[1] la ropa que la gente[2] lleva.

ELENA: Sí, a mí[3] también. Mira, esa[4] mujer lleva un traje muy bonito, ¿no?

AMALIA: Sí, el verde es un color atractivo en una mujer morena. Y su compañera tiene una blusa azul muy bonita.

DAVID: ¿Qué te parece[5] ese[6] hombre de la guayabera blanca?

AMALIA: Muy elegante.

NEW VOCABULARY: lleva; la blusa, el color, la guayabera, la ropa, el traje; atractivo, bonito, morena; azul, blanca, verde

[1]Me... *I like to see*   [2]que... *that people*   [3]a... *me*   [4]*that*   [5]¿Qué... *What do you think of*   [6]*that*

Create as many sentences as you can by combining items from both columns and using **lleva** to describe the people in the preceding dialogue and sketch.

EJEMPLO: Una mujer lleva un traje muy bonito.

una mujer
su compañera
un muchacho
un hombre
una niña

jeans
pantalones azules
pantalones blancos
un traje muy bonito
un traje verde
un vestido rosado
una blusa muy bonita
una camiseta blanca
una guayabera blanca
¿ ?

De inmediato

NEW VOCABULARY: el muchacho; la camiseta, los *jeans*, los pantalones, el vestido, los zapatos; rosado
OPTIONAL: To ensure that students know to whom you are referring in this exercise, point to each character in the drawing. **¿Es cierto o no es cierto?** 1. **El hombre elegante lleva jeans.** 2. **La mujer morena lleva un traje verde.** 3. **El muchacho lleva una guayabera.** 4. **La muchacha lleva un traje azul.** 5. **El hombre elegante lleva una guayabera.** 6. **La compañera de la mujer morena lleva una blusa azul.** 7. **La muchacha lleva un vestido verde.**

A ti te toca

Ask a classmate which of the characters depicted in the following drawings is wearing a particular item of clothing. Your classmate will respond with the name of the character.

EJEMPLO: —¿Quién lleva pantalones blancos?
—Alfonsina.

Felipe   la profesora Martínez   Alfonsina   el profesor Ramos

VOCABULARIO

La ropa

PREPARATION: Ask students to list in English as many articles of clothing as possible. Have them check the drawing and the list of additional vocabulary to find the Spanish equivalents. You may choose to provide translations for items of clothing on the students' list that are not given in the book.

una corbata
una camisa
los pantalones
un abrigo
los calcetines
los guantes
los zapatos

una blusa
un suéter
una falda
una chaqueta
los zapatos

Otro vocabulario

la camiseta	*T-shirt*
la gorra	*cap*
los *jeans*	*jeans*
los pantalones cortos	*shorts*
el paraguas	*umbrella*
el pijama	*pajamas*
la ropa interior	*underwear; undergarments*
las sandalias	*sandals*
el traje	*suit*
el traje de baño	*swimsuit*
el vestido	*dress*
los zapatos de tenis	*tennis shoes*

COMPREHENSION: Call out the name of various articles of clothing; have all students wearing each article stand. Students who are seated will be asked **¿Dónde está?**, and request that they point to the piece of clothing indicated.

COMPREHENSION: Ask students to say whether the following items are typically worn by men (**los hombres**), by women (**las mujeres**), or by both (**los dos**): **un traje** → **los dos** 1. **un vestido** 2. **una chaqueta** 3. **una corbata** 4. **los zapatos** 5. **los guantes**

Actividades

NEW VOCABULARY: lógico

Ⓐ **Asociaciones.** Indicate whether you typically associate the following articles of clothing with the situation or place given. Comment on each pair with **Es lógico** or **No es lógico**.

EXTENSION: Ask students to make up additional items using the same format. They may work in small groups sharing only a few of their favorites with the entire class, or this could be a whole-class activity.

EJEMPLOS: un abrigo / la playa → No es lógico.

los *jeans* / una clase → Es lógico.

1. los pantalones cortos / el tenis
2. unos guantes / el desierto
3. una chaqueta / las montañas
4. un traje de baño / la playa
5. un traje / una fiesta elegante
6. una corbata / la selva
7. un pijama / la biblioteca

B **Preguntas.** Interview a classmate about his or her clothing choices. Be prepared to report to the class what you discover.   **NEW VOCABULARY:** llevo; la pregunta; largas

1. ¿Qué ropa llevas a una fiesta elegante? (Llevo...)
2. ¿Qué ropa llevas a un partido[1] de fútbol americano? ¿a un club de tenis?
3. Generalmente, ¿qué ropa llevas a la playa? ¿a las montañas?
4. Generalmente, ¿prefieres las minifaldas o las faldas largas? ¿las sandalias o los zapatos de tenis? ¿los trajes o los *jeans*? ¿las camisas o las camisetas? (Prefiero...)

[1]*game*

SUGGESTION: You may need to help students with their reports to the class. Provide a model to show the difference between the first- and third-person forms. **Yo llevo un traje a una fiesta elegante; mi compañera de clase Joyce lleva un vestido.**

Los colores

COMPREHENSION: Ask students to stand. As you call out the name of a color they must find someone in the class who is wearing something of that color and touch or point to that person.

COMPREHENSION: Say the name of an article of clothing illustrated. The students will respond with its color: **gorra → anaranjado/a.** Accept any form of the adjective, but pattern correct agreement by saying, **Sí, la gorra es anaranjada.**

VOCABULARIO

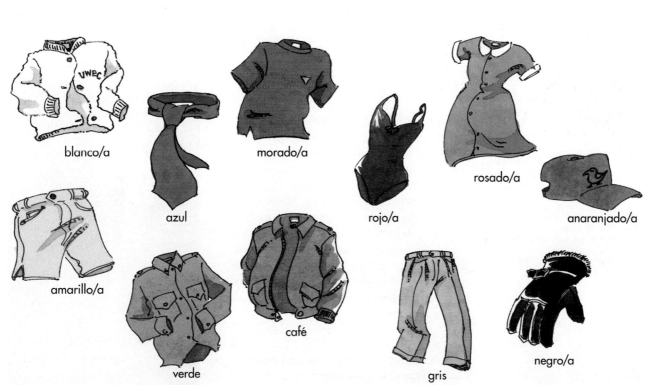

blanco/a
azul
morado/a
rojo/a
rosado/a
anaranjado/a
amarillo/a
verde
café
gris
negro/a

Actividades

A **¿De qué color es?** What color(s) do you associate with each item? There may be more than one possible answer.

EJEMPLO: la bandera[1] de México → Es roja, verde y blanca.

1. una planta
2. una banana
3. un elefante

4. un tomate
5. la noche
6. un pingüino

7. el cielo[2]
8. una calabaza[3]
9. una uva[4]

[1] *flag*　[2] *sky*　[3] *pumpkin*　[4] *grape*

B **Mis colores.** Complete the following statements to express the color of something you have with you or that you are wearing.

EJEMPLOS: Mi (*noun*) es (*color*). →
Mi mochila es verde.

Mis (*plural noun*) son (*color*). →
Mis zapatos de tenis son blancos y anaranjados.

C **Preguntas.** Interview a classmate about his or her favorite things. Be prepared to report to the class what you discover. To answer, you may refer to the models from **Actividad B** for help. When appropriate, use **No tengo... .**

1. ¿Cuál es tu color favorito?　NEW VOCABULARY: la casa; favorito; ¿De quién?
2. ¿De qué color es tu coche[1]? ¿tu mochila? ¿tu cuarto[2]?
3. ¿De qué color es tu casa favorita? ¿De quién es?
4. ¿De qué color es tu libro favorito? ¿Qué libro es?
5. ¿De qué color son tus calcetines favoritos?

[1] *car*　[2] *(bed) room*

OPTIONAL: Ask students to tell what color objects of clothing and personal belongings of other students are. Students may choose to say the wrong color. The class confirms or denies the statements by saying **Es cierto** or **No es cierto**.
E1: La camiseta de ___ es roja.
LA CLASE: Es cierto.
E2: El pelo del profesor (de la profesora) es verde.
LA CLASE: No es cierto.
OPTIONAL: Ask students to describe what someone in the room is wearing. The class will guess whom they are describing: —**Hoy lleva una camiseta roja y** *jeans* **negros. ¿Quién es?** —**Es** ___.

Faceta cultural

PREPARATION: 1. Ask students to define the word *stereotype*. What stereotypes do people have of college/university students? Of professors? Of people from certain states or countries? Why do people have stereotypes? 2. Explain that stereotypes are often based on knowledge of the past or on colorful and memorable individuals in a group. Stereotypes are not necessarily false; they are simply incomplete visions of reality.

La ropa

In the United States, most ideas about how people in the Hispanic world dress are based on stereotypes created by American movies. In fact, people in the Hispanic world today dress much like their counterparts in this country. Many large cities in Spain and Latin America, such as Madrid, Mexico City, and Buenos Aires, are centers of high fashion. When Spanish-speaking people wear traditional dress, it is either because it is appropriate for their lifestyle or because a special occasion requires it.

Carolina Herrera es una famosa modista hispanoamericana que diseña ropa para muchas personas importantes.

En México

Some of the most beautiful examples of traditional Mexican dress are worn by the performers of folkloric dances. Virtually all major cities and tourist centers sponsor at least one folkloric dance troupe, and showtimes are frequent. Many of the native dances call for the women to wear colorfully embroidered blouses and matching, flowing, pleated skirts while the men wear western-style pants and shirts, often with a colorful sash tied at the waist. Boots and sombreros complete the men's ensemble. This traditional wear, however, is seldom if ever seen on the street for everyday wear. Business and professional people dress conservatively, whereas jeans and T-shirts are major components of younger people's wardrobes.

Estos trajes típicos mexicanos se usan los días de fiesta, como el 16 de septiembre, el Día de la Independencia mexicana.

El verbo *tener*

PREPARATION: See the student manual, *Exploraciones,* for other ways to introduce this material.

CONCEPTO

PREPARATION: Remind students that they have already seen and used some forms of the verb **tener** in expressing age. The most common use of the verb **tener** is to show possession. Read the sentences that accompany the drawing.

You may wish to point out that the verb **tener** is irregular and to give the forms of the verb. Remind students that all verbs have six forms in the present indicative, each one corresponding to the subject nouns or pronouns that accompany them.
NEW VOCABULARY: ¿Cuántos?

Yo **tengo** nueve suéteres.

Tomás **tiene** tres suéteres.

¿Cuántos suéteres **tienes** tú?

🅐 **Un inventario.** Joaquín is taking stock of some items in the apartment that he and Jorge share. What does he say? With a classmate, play the role of Joaquín and express how many of the items indicated he and Jorge have individually, and how many they have total.

EJEMPLO: 2 diccionarios   3 diccionarios   ¿ ? →
—Yo tengo dos diccionarios. Jorge tiene tres.
—Jorge y yo tenemos cinco diccionarios en total.

	YO	JORGE	NOSOTROS
1.	20 fotos	50 fotos	¿ ?
2.	35 cassettes	28 cassettes	¿ ?
3.	26 discos compactos	60 discos compactos	¿ ?
4.	50 libros	40 libros	¿ ?
5.	11 discos	14 discos	¿ ?

Actividades

NEW VOCABULARY: los cassettes, los diccionarios, los discos (compactos), las fotos
SUGGESTION: Model the pronunciation of the borrowed word **cassettes**.
OPTIONAL: Ask students to work in groups of three to expand on this activity. Two students will take the roles of Jorge and Joaquín. Each states how many of a certain item he has. The third student provides the total: E1: **Tengo 50 cassettes.** E2: **Tengo 35 cassettes.** E3: **Ustedes tienen 85 cassettes.**
OPTIONAL: Remind students that the sum should not exceed 99.

B **¿Cuántos años tiene?** Say how old each of the following people is, based on the cues given. When appropriate, use **No tengo...**

EJEMPLOS: Jorge (20) → Jorge tiene veinte años.

hijo/a (¿ ?) → Mi hija tiene cinco años.

o No tengo hijos.

1. Elena (21)
2. la abuelita (80)
3. Sandra (16)
4. Harvey Nelson (49)

5. Carmen Campos (19)
6. mi hermano/a (¿ ?)
7. Ⓟ ¡OJO!
8. yo (¿ ?)

Tener is used to express possession and age. As you will see later in this chapter, it is also used for some physical descriptions and in some idiomatic expressions.

tener	*to have*		
(yo) tengo	*I have*	(nosotros/as) tenemos	*we have*
(tú) tienes (Ud.) tiene	*you have*	(vosotros/as) tenéis (Uds.) tienen	*you have*
(él/ella) tiene	*he/she has*	(ellos/as) tienen	*they have*

DIÁLOGO

En casa de Elena

The cousins are now at Elena's house in Monterrey, where David looks at more photographs with Elena's father, Fernando.

DAVID: ¿Son altos todos los hermanos de mi mamá?

FERNANDO: Tres sí, pero tu tío Alfonso es bajito.[1] Mira la foto de tus tíos.

DAVID: Es cierto. Mi hermana Sandra es alta también. Es una de las muchachas más altas de[2] la escuela.[3]

FERNANDO: ¿Es más alta que tu mamá?

DAVID: Sí, pero no es tan alta como[4] mi papá.

[1] *kind of short* [2] *más... tallest in* [3] *school* [4] *tan... as tall as*

1. ¿Es el tío Alfonso alto o bajo?
2. ¿Quién es una de las muchachas más altas de la escuela de Sandra?
3. ¿Quién es más alta, Sandra o su mamá?
4. ¿Es Sandra más alta que su papá?

Practice the preceding dialogue with a classmate. Then, exchange roles and repeat it. Next, substitute the following characters for those in the dialogue, being sure to make all necessary changes.

A ti te toca

hermanos	→	hermanas
Alfonso	→	Alfonsina
mi hermana Sandra	→	mi hermano Carlos

OPTIONAL: Ask students to use the last two lines of the dialogue to compare their siblings (cousins, friends) to other people in their families, creating as many sentences as possible: **Mi hermana no es tan alta como mi mamá. Mi primo es más alto que su padre.**

En la universidad

DIÁLOGO

NEW VOCABULARY: perezosa, trabajadora; ¿Por qué?, ¡Qué + *adj.*!

While David relaxes in Monterrey, some of his friends in Wisconsin meet in the library to study.

MARISOL: ¡Ay! ¡Soy tan perezosa!

MARÍA: No, Marisol, no eres trabajadora, pero tampoco[1] eres perezosa.

TOMÁS: Los hombres son más lógicos que las mujeres.

ALFONSINA: ¡Qué tonto eres, Tomás! ¡Es al revés[2]!

LUISA: ¿Por qué creen[3] que[4] van a sacar[5] «A» en el examen?

FELIPE: Somos *muy* optimistas.

[1] *neither*   [2] *al... the opposite*   [3] *do you believe, think*   [4] *that*   [5] *to get*

PREPARATION: Ask students to focus on the picture and on the dialogue introduction. **¿Dónde están las personas en este dibujo? ¿Quiénes son las personas? ¿Cómo se llaman? ¿Cómo están hoy las personas en el dibujo? ¿Están contentos/cansados? ¿Qué más? ¿Quién está aburrido/preocupado?**
  Note that in this dialogue, the people will be discussing their characteristics, not their conditions. Ask students whether they can see any difference in how these are expressed.

With which of the characters from the dialogues do you associate the following statements?

1. Es optimista.
2. Cree[1] que los hombres son más lógicos que las mujeres.
3. Cree que su amiga no es perezosa.
4. Cree que Tomás es tonto.
5. Cree que es perezosa.

[1] *He/She believes*

5. simpático/a, tonto/a, aburrido/a
6. desagradable, estudioso/a, interesante
7. antipático/a, divertido/a, estudioso/a
8. hablador(a), serio/a, perezoso/a

B **¿Cómo eres?** Describe yourself to a classmate using **ser** and any of the descriptive phrases from the lists of physical and personality characteristics. Remember to use **no** to make negative statements. Then check your partner as he or she describes you to the class.

EJEMPLO: Soy alto y rubio. Tengo pelo corto y rizado. Soy un poco tímido. No soy extrovertido. →

_____ es alto y rubio. Tiene pelo corto y rizado. Es un poco tímido. No es extrovertido.

Las preguntas con palabras interrogativas

¿**Qué** es esto?
¿**De dónde** es?
¿**Cómo** se usa?
¿**Quién** lo usa?
¿**Cuánto** cuesta?

Actividades

A **¿Cuál es la respuesta?** Match the questions in the first column with the most logical response from the second.

1. ¿Cómo estás?
2. ¿Dónde están los estudiantes?
3. ¿Quién es el profesor?
4. ¿Cuánto tiempo necesita el profesor?
5. ¿Cuál tienes, el libro rojo o el azul?
6. ¿Cuántos años tiene David?
7. ¿Adónde van David y Elena mañana[1]?
8. ¿Cuándo van David y Elena a Guadalajara?
9. ¿Qué tiene David en la mochila?
10. ¿Por qué no está en clase Joaquín?

a. Bien.
b. El doctor Brewer.
c. Un mapa.
d. 21
e. A Guadalajara.
f. Está enfermo.
g. En la clase.
h. El rojo.
i. Una hora.
j. Mañana.

[1] _tomorrow_

B **Preguntas.** Interview a classmate, and be prepared to report to the class what you discover. When appropriate, use **No tengo...** in your answer or **No tiene...** in your summary.

1. ¿Cómo estás hoy?
2. ¿Cuántos años tienes?
3. ¿De dónde eres?
4. ¿Cuál es tu color favorito?
5. ¿De qué color es tu suéter favorito?

6. ¿Cuándo tienes una clase de matemáticas?
7. ¿Qué tienes en tu mochila?
8. ¿Quién es tu persona especial? ¿Cómo es? ¿Dónde está ahora?

SUGGESTION: Ask students, working in groups of two or three, to write five questions using any of the interrogatives given.

Las palabras interrogativas

¿qué?	*what (definition or explanation)*
¿cuál? ¿cuáles?	*which, what (when choosing from two or more possibilities)*
¿dónde?	*where?*
¿adónde?	*(to) where? (indicates movement)*
¿de dónde?	*(from) where? (origin)*
¿a qué hora?	*when?, (at) what time?*
¿cuándo?	*when?*
¿cómo?	*how?*
¿por qué?	*why?*
¿quién? ¿quiénes?	*who?*
¿cuánto? ¿cuánta?	*how much?*
¿cuántos? ¿cuántas?	*how many?*

Use question words to ask for information. Remember to place an inverted question mark (¿) before a written question.

SUGGESTION: Point out that some interrogatives in Spanish (**¿cuál? ¿cuánto? ¿cuántos?**) vary in gender and/or number, although their English equivalents do not. Note also that the interrogative concept of *where* in Spanish has multiple forms: **¿Adónde? ¿De dónde? ¿Dónde?**

Las preguntas con respuestas de *sí* o *no*

¿**Tienes tú** el mapa?

No, no tengo el mapa.

Actividades

Ⓐ **Al revés.** Form questions from the following statements by changing the word order of the sentences.

EJEMPLO: Elena tiene hermanos. →
       ¿Tiene Elena hermanos?
   o ¿Tiene hermanos Elena?

1. Raúl es simpático.
2. La abuela está contenta.
3. Los primos están en México.

4. Sandra es alta.
5. Tu padre es doctor.
6. Las blusas son azules.

Ⓑ **¿Verdad?** With a classmate, practice reacting to each statement with an expression to indicate astonishment. Then repeat the statement as a question by using rising inflection. Some expressions that indicate surprise include the following.

   ¿Verdad? (¿De veras?) *Really?*
   ¡No me digas! *You're kidding!*
   ¡Imposible! *Impossible!*

EJEMPLO: Luisa tiene ocho hermanos. →
       ¿De veras? ¿Luisa tiene ocho hermanos?

1. El profesor Ramos tiene ocho hijas.
2. Elena tiene veinte primas.
3. Alfonsina tiene trece tías.
4. Los señores Guzmán tienen ocho hijos.

5. Joaquín tiene cincuenta sobrinos.
6. Felipe tiene tres abuelas.

There are several ways to form yes/ no questions in Spanish: by inverting the subject and verb (or the subject and the verb + complement/ adjective), by using rising intonation, or by using "tag" questions that are added to the end of a statement.

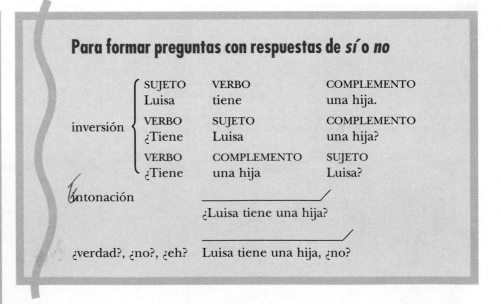

Para formar preguntas con respuestas de *sí* o *no*

	SUJETO	VERBO	COMPLEMENTO
	Luisa	tiene	una hija.
inversión	VERBO	SUJETO	COMPLEMENTO
	¿Tiene	Luisa	una hija?
	VERBO	COMPLEMENTO	SUJETO
	¿Tiene	una hija	Luisa?

intonación _____
       ¿Luisa tiene una hija?

         _____
¿verdad?, ¿no?, ¿eh? Luisa tiene una hija, ¿no?

En casa de Elena

NEW VOCABULARY: la nacionalidad, el señor, la señora, la señorita, el verano; alemana; ¿cuánto tiempo?, ¡Qué + *adv*.!

DIÁLOGO

While David and Elena are at her home in Monterrey, Mr. Oscar Kolb, a business associate of Elena's father, stops by for a visit.

EL SR.* KOLB: ¡Qué bien hablas[1] español! ¿Cuál es tu nacionalidad?

DAVID: Soy norteamericano... perdón, estadounidense. Mi mamá es mexicana. Nació[2] en Saltillo. ¿Y Ud., Sr. Kolb?

EL SR. KOLB: Mis padres son mexicanos. Mi padre es de ascendencia[3] alemana. ¿Cuánto tiempo vas a estar aquí en México?

DAVID: Voy a pasar[4] el verano aquí.

EL SR. KOLB: Bueno. Mi familia vive[5] en Guadalajara. ¿Por qué no nos visitas[6] allí?

DAVID: Con mucho gusto,[7] si[8] es posible. Gracias por la invitación.

[1] *you speak* [2] *She was born* [3] *heritage* [4] *to spend* [5] *lives* [6] *no... don't you visit us* [7] *Con... With pleasure,* [8] *if*

PREPARATION: Looking at the drawing, **¿Cuántas personas hay en el dibujo? ¿Quiénes son? ¿Es Kolb un típico apellido mexicano?** You may choose to discuss ethnic diversity in Mexico and the rest of the Hispanic world. Mexico has large populations of African and Asian descent and has areas where Germans, Lebanese, and Poles constitute a significant presence. Although we know nothing of Oscar Kolb's background, ask when in history his German ancestors might have come to Mexico?

De inmediato

1. ¿Qué dos palabras usa David para expresar su nacionalidad?
2. ¿Dónde nació la madre de David?
3. ¿Cuánto tiempo va a pasar David en México?
4. ¿Dónde vive la familia del Sr. Kolb?

A ti te toca

Use the following model to have a brief conversation with a classmate. If necessary, look at the next **Vocabulario** section, **Los países y las nacionalidades** on page 61, to find out how to describe your nationality.

EJEMPLO: E1: ¡Qué bien hablas el español!

E2: Muchas gracias. Eres muy amable.

E1: ¿Cuál es tu nacionalidad?

E2: Soy (*nationality*).

E1: Mi familia vive en (*city/state/country*). ¿Por qué no nos visitas allí?

E2: Con mucho gusto, si es posible. Gracias por la invitación.

OPTIONAL: Write the following model on the board. Ask students to construct as many logical sentences as possible using the model.

E1: ¿Cuánto tiempo vas a estar en (la universidad, la biblioteca, la librería, la clase de español, ¿ ?)? →

E2: (*number*) años/días/horas/minutos

---

*In writing, **señor** (*Mr.*), **señora** (*Mrs.*), and **señorita** (*Miss*) are frequently abbreviated as **Sr., Sra.,** and **Srta.,** respectively.

En la universidad

PREPARATION: Call students' attention to the drawing that precedes the dialogue and to the dialogue introduction. **¿Quiénes son las personas en el dibujo? ¿Cómo es Tomás, físicamente? ¿Cómo es Marisol?** (Encourage students to describe each of the characters depicted in at least two ways.) **¿Cómo están las personas en el dibujo? ¿aburridos? ¿cansados? ¿contentos?**

NEW VOCABULARY: el Brasil; holandés, japonés, ruso

Many of David's friends from the **Club Hispánico** are also members of the International Club. At the first meeting of the summer, there are many new faces.

TOMÁS: ¿Quién es la muchacha[1] alta que habla[2] con João?

MARISOL: Es Sandra, la hermana de David Nelson. Está aquí para practicar su portugués. Va a estudiar[3] en el Brasil y va a vivir[4] con la familia de João en Rio de Janeiro.

FELIPE: ¿Dónde vive[5] la familia de Misha?

JOAQUÍN: En Rusia. Leon, su compañero de cuarto, es holandés.

MARÍA: ¿Cuántos estudiantes japoneses hay en el Club Internacional?

ALFONSINA: No sé.[6] Conozco[7] a cuatro... no, a cinco. Pero hay muchos más.

[1]*girl*   [2]*que... who is talking*   [3]*to study*   [4]*to live*   [5]*lives*   [6]*No... I don't know.*   [7]*I know, am acquainted with*

De inmediato

OPTIONAL: Read the following statements and ask students to tell if they are true (**Es cierto**) or false (**No es cierto**). 1. **Sandra Nelson habla con João, un hombre brasileño.** 2. **João va a vivir con la familia de Sandra.** 3. **Misha es de Rusia.** 4. **Leon es de Rusia también.**

1. ¿Con quién habla Sandra Nelson?
2. ¿De qué ciudad es la familia de João?
3. ¿Cómo se llama el hombre ruso?
4. ¿Cómo se llama el compañero holandés?
5. ¿En qué club hay muchos estudiantes japoneses?

A ti te toca

Using Felipe and Joaquín's dialogue as a model, ask a classmate about others in the class and where their families live.

Los países y las nacionalidades

VOCABULARIO

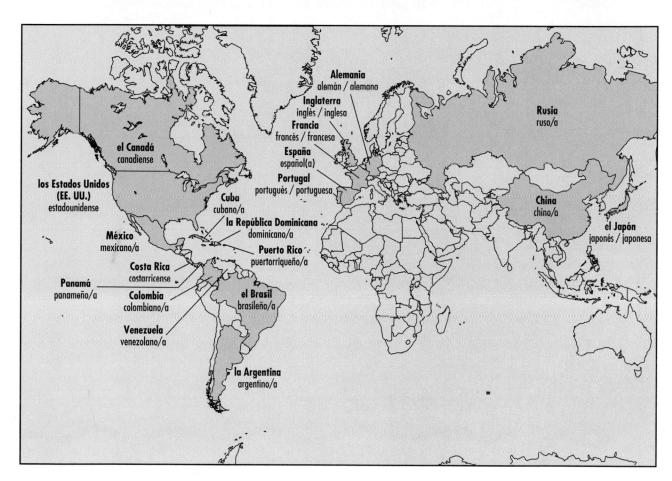

Alemania
alemán / alemana

Inglaterra
inglés / inglesa

Francia
francés / francesa

España
español(a)

Portugal
portugués / portuguesa

Rusia
ruso/a

China
chino/a

el Japón
japonés / japonesa

el Canadá
canadiense

**los Estados Unidos
(EE. UU.)**
estadounidense

Cuba
cubano/a

la República Dominicana
dominicano/a

Puerto Rico
puertorriqueño/a

México
mexicano/a

Costa Rica
costarricense

Panamá
panameño/a

Colombia
colombiano/a

el Brasil
brasileño/a

Venezuela
venezolano/a

la Argentina
argentino/a

Actividades

Ⓐ ¿Cuál es su nacionalidad? Say where these famous people are from and what their nationalities are.

EJEMPLOS: Bill Clinton →
Es de los Estados Unidos. Es estadounidense.

Los príncipes Carlos y Andrés →
Son de Inglaterra. Son ingleses.

1. el rey Juan Carlos
2. Catherine Deneuve
3. Boris Becker y Steffi Graf
4. Fidel Castro
5. Tom Cruise y Kevin Costner
6. Pelé y Emerson Fittipaldi
7. John Major y Margaret Thatcher
8. Fernando Valenzuela

61

B **Un dialoguito.** Use the following dialogue, which is based on David's conversation with Mr. Kolb, to discuss with a classmate the nationality of your own family members.

—¿Cuál es tu nacionalidad?
—Soy...
—¿Y tus padres?
—Mi papá es... Nació en... Mi mamá es... Nació en...

Whereas most other adjectives ending in a consonant have only two forms (singular and plural), adjectives of nationality that

end in a consonant have four forms.

Los adjetivos de nacionalidad

-o	-a		-e	
ruso	rusa		canadiense	canadiense
rusos	rusas		canadienses	canadienses

CONSONANT	CONSONANT + **a**
inglés	inglesa
ingleses	inglesas

CONCEPTO

El verbo *ir*

Mi hermano David **va** a Guadalajara, y yo **voy** a Río de Janeiro.

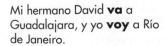

Actividades

A **¿Adónde vas?** Share with the class where you are going on the following days or at the following times. **Vocabulario útil: a la biblioteca, a mi residencia,[1] a la librería, a mi casa, al trabajo.[2]**

EJEMPLO: mañana → Mañana voy a mis clases.

1. después de[3] la clase de español
2. esta tarde
3. esta noche
4. este fin de semana[4]
5. durante las vacaciones de Navidad[5]
6. durante las vacaciones de verano

EXPANSION: Ask students to use the model to tell when they will be going to the homes of various family members (**a casa de mis abuelos / mis padres / mis primos / mi hermano/a / mis tíos / mis suegros**).

[1]*dormitory*   [2]*al... to work*   [3]*después... after*   [4]*fin... weekend*   [5]*Christmas*

B **Dos itinerarios.** Jorge and Joaquín have planned trips during the break after summer classes. Each has included stops in six cities. Imagine that you are Jorge. Compare your itinerary to that of Joaquín, following the model.

EJEMPLOS: Des Moines → Yo voy a Des Moines.
Iowa City → Tú vas a Iowa City.
Chicago → Los dos[1] vamos a Chicago.

1. Springfield
2. Minneápolis
3. Louisville
4. Milwaukee
5. St. Louis
6. Bloomington

[1]*Los... The two of us*

Itinerario de Jorge	Itinerario de Joaquín
Milwaukee	Chicago
Chicago	Bloomington
Springfield	Louisville
St. Louis	Springfield
Des Moines	St. Louis
Minneápolis	Iowa City

SUGGESTION: Students have seen **del** used with possession and **al** used with direction. You may wish to give a brief explanation of contractions in Spanish.

ir *to go*			
(yo) voy	*I go, am going*	(nosotros/as) vamos	*we go, are going*
(tú) vas / (Ud.) va	*you go, are going*	(vosotros/as) vais / (Uds.) van	*you go, are going*
(él/ella) va	*he/she goes, is going*	(ellos/as) van	*they go, are going*

Speakers indicate where they are going with the verb **ir.** Notice that **ir** is often followed by **a,** which contracts with the masculine definite article **el** to form **al.**

Voy **al** lago.
   a la playa.
   a los estados de Tamaulipas y Chihuahua.
   a las montañas.

¡Vamos a Guadalajara!

NEW VOCABULARY: pues

PREPARATION: Direct students' attention to the drawing. **David y Elena están en Monterrey, ¿verdad? En este dibujo están en una plaza de la ciudad. Están tomando refrescos y están hablando de su salida. ¿Cómo se sienten? (¿Cómo están?)** Ask students to make statements about what they see in the drawing.

Their stay in Monterrey is ending, and David and Elena discuss the next city they will visit.

ELENA: Bueno, David, mañana[1] vamos a salir[2] para Guadalajara.

DAVID: Estás triste, ¿no? No quieres dejar[3] a tus padres y a tu abuelita, ¿verdad?

ELENA: Es cierto. Pero también estoy entusiasmada con la idea del viaje.

DAVID: Yo también estoy muy entusiasmado porque vamos a conocer[4] a la familia del Sr. Kolb.

ELENA: Y Guadalajara es una ciudad muy bonita.

DAVID: Vamos a casa[5] pues. Tenemos que hacer las maletas,[6] ¿no?

[1] *tomorrow*   [2] *to leave*   [3] *No... You don't want to leave*   [4] *to meet*   [5] *a... home*   [6] *hacer... to pack*

De inmediato

Create as many sentences as you can by combining items from the three columns to summarize the preceding dialogue.

Elena	está	en Monterrey.
David	están	en Guadalajara.
La familia del Sr. Kolb		entusiasmado/a.
Los padres de Elena		un poco triste.
Las maletas		en un café.
David y Elena		en casa.

A ti te toca

Practice the preceding dialogue with a classmate. Then exchange roles, acting out the parts of Elena and David.

EN ACCIÓN

Antes de ver

In this chapter, you will watch and listen as a series of people talk about their families and describe other people. Listen carefully for the names of family members and the relationships they describe, and try to visualize the people who are described if you cannot see them in the video segment.

Un reportaje sobre el béisbol

While in Monterrey, David hears a radio program in which two commentators discuss the popularity of baseball in Japan and the success of Hispanics in Major League baseball.

NEW VOCABULARY: panameño, venezolano
OPTIONAL: When students have completed the **Despues de escuchar** activities, ask them to listen to the passage once more. This time ask them to write, in English, as many factual statements about the passage as they can.

Antes de escuchar

What do you know about baseball in Japan? Is it a popular sport? Do you know the names of any Japanese baseball players? Have you watched or heard of any movies about baseball in Japan? Read the questions that pertain to each section of the radio show to alert yourself to the content of the program.

Now, listen carefully to each part of the report. After listening, answer the questions that follow.

Después de escuchar

Paso 1

1. Which U.S. actor is mentioned in the report and why?
2. Who is Sidharita Oh, and what is said about him?

Paso 2. Which of the following Major League players are mentioned and what are their nationalities?

BEISBOLISTAS		NACIONALIDADES
René Arocha	Juan González	cubano
Carlos Baerga	Pedro Guerrero	dominicano
José Canseco	Iván Rodríguez	mexicano
Roberto Clemente	Rubén Sierra	panameño
David Concepción	Danny Tartabull	puertorriqueño
Andrés Galarraga	Fernando Valenzuela	venezolano

OPTIONAL: Ask students to work with a classmate and decide on a person to describe to the class, whether it is a fellow classmate or someone famous. They should take turns describing this person to the class in Spanish and include clothing, colors, and physical and personality characteristics in the description. Other students may guess only after they hear the third clue about the person.

La familia y los problemas

While Elena is on the bus to Guadalajara, she reads a magazine in which the following article catches her attention.

Antes de leer

This reading presents the results of a survey that asked, To whom do Mexicans turn when they have a serious problem? Before you read the article, review the vocabulary for family members. As you will discover, in times of trouble many people find comfort in their families. Who do you think would be more likely to turn to their mothers when they had a serious problem, men or women? Who do you think would turn to their fathers? Who would be more likely to ask a priest for help, an older or a younger man?

Because the results of surveys are often reported in percentages, review the numbers 0–99. To express a percentage in Spanish, say **el,** then the number, and follow with **por ciento.** Thus, 18% is read as **el dieciocho por ciento.**

Now look at the graphs that accompany the reading. Notice that the horizontal axis indicates the person to whom someone might turn (**acude**) when in need, whereas the vertical axis indicates the percentage of respondents that indicated they would turn to that individual. The first graph compares the responses of men and women, and the second compares the responses of three age groups.

Next, read the questions that pertain to each of the graphs to familiarize yourself with their content and with the article as a whole. Now, scan the article and the graphs to find the information requested.

NEW VOCABULARY: la encuesta; más

¿En quién confían[1] los mexicanos?

Cuando una persona tiene un problema, normalmente habla[2] con otra[3] persona que conoce y respeta. Una encuesta reciente indica que, cuando los mexicanos necesitan ayuda,[4] prefieren hablar[5] con su esposo o esposa,

[1] *confide* [2] *he/she speaks* [3] *another* [4] *help* [5] *to speak*

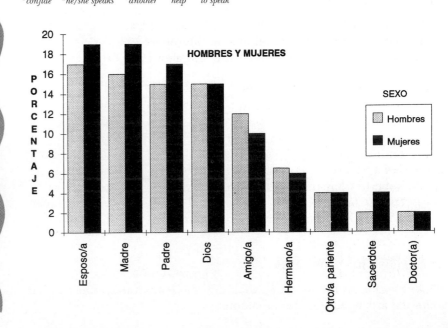

con sus padres o con Dios.[6] La encuesta también indica que estas tendencias generales varian según[7] muchos factores, entre otros,[8] el sexo y la edad[9] del individuo. Las gráficas indican los resultados de la encuesta.

[6]*God*   [7]*according to*   [8]*entre... among others*   [9]*age*

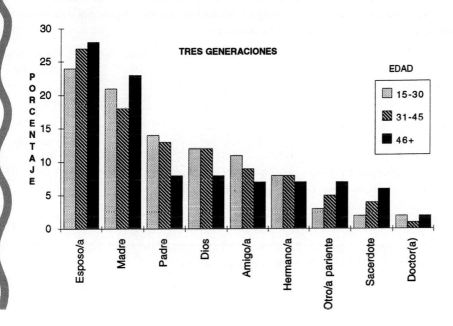

Después de leer

Hombres y mujeres. Indica que comprendes las estadísticas contestando **Sí** o **No,** o **No dice,** a estas frases.

1. Los hombres y las mujeres confían más que nada[1] en sus esposos.
2. Los hombres confían más en sus amigos que las mujeres.
3. Los hombres y las mujeres confían más en Dios que en el sacerdote o el doctor.
4. Las mujeres confían más en Dios que los hombres.
5. Las mujeres de menor ingreso[2] confían más en sus hermanos que las mujeres de mayor[3] ingreso.

[1]*más... more than anything*   [2]*menor... lower income*   [3]*higher*

Edad. Ramón tiene 18 años; su padre Carlos tiene 42 y su abuelo Efraín tiene 60. Si Ramón, su padre y su abuelo son mexicanos «típicos» ¿cuál de los tres es la persona que confía... ?

1. más en su esposa
2. menos en su madre
3. más en su padre
4. menos en un amigo pero más en un pariente
5. más en un sacerdote
6. menos en un doctor

Miniencuesta

Conduct a survey of your classmates to determine whether their habits and beliefs coincide with those represented in the previous reading. You may wish to ask only one question: **¿A quién acudes¹ en caso de tener un problema serio?** Or you may wish to ask a series of questions, such as **¿Confías² más en tu madre o en tu padre? ¿en tu amigo o en tu hermano? ¿en un pariente o en un sacerdote? ¿en un sacerdote o en un doctor?**

Keep track of the respondents' answers and be prepared to report them by age or gender.

¹*do you turn to*   ²*Do you confide*

Una conversación

Write a brief dialogue of eight to twelve sentences in which you exchange information with a classmate about a potential blind date.

Antes de escribir

Here are some things to think about before you write your dialogue. You can also check for them as you edit your first draft.

- Which greetings and farewells are appropriate for the social situation?
- Which pronoun for *you* is appropriate?
- What five adjectives best describe your friend's physical appearance? How would you describe his or her hair and eye color?
- What five adjectives best describe your friend's personality? How do these characteristics make your friend and classmate compatible?
- Will you need masculine or feminine adjectives to describe your friend?
- What transition or reaction words and phrases included in the dialogues in this chapter could help the flow of your conversation?
- Have you included the punctuation marks you need?

A escribir

First, exchange greetings and inquire about each other's health, feelings, and current emotions. Next, try to get your classmate interested in a blind date. Say that you have a friend, and tell your classmate your friend's name. Mention that your friend is perfect for your classmate (**Es perfecto/a para tio.**). Then give a thorough description of the friend's physical appearance, personality, and typical dress. Answer the questions that the classmate asks about your friend's age, where he or she is from, and who his or her parents are. The classmate then thanks you for the information (**por la información**) but explains that he or she has a boyfriend or girlfriend. Say your farewells.

Es perfecto/a para ti

Work with a partner to practice the conversations you wrote for the previous activity.

Los verbos — Verbs

ir	to go
ir a + *inf.*	to be going to (*do something*)
lleva	he/she wears, is wearing
llevo	I wear, am wearing
necesita	he/she needs
necesito	I need
scr	to be
tener (R)*	to have
tener... años	to be . . . years old
usa	he/she uses, is using; he/she wears, is wearing

La familia — Family

el abuelo / la abuela	grandfather/ grandmother
el abuelito / la abuelita (R)	grandma/grandpa
los abuelos	grandparents
el esposo / la esposa	husband/wife
los esposos	married couple, spouses
el hermano / la hermana	brother/sister
los hermanos	brothers and sisters, siblings; brothers
el hijo / la hija	son/daughter
los hijos	children; sons and daughters; sons
la madre	mother
el nieto / la nieta	grandson/ granddaughter
la nuera	daughter-in-law
el padre	father
los padres	parents; fathers
el/la pariente	relative
el primo / la prima (R)	cousin (*m./f.*)
el sobrino / la sobrina	nephew/niece
el suegro / la suegra	father-in-law/mother-in-law
los suegros	in-laws
el tío / la tía	uncle/aunt
los tíos	uncles and aunts; uncles
el yerno	son-in-law

La ropa — Clothes

el abrigo	overcoat
la blusa	blouse
el calcetín	sock
los calcetines	socks
la camisa	shirt
la camiseta	T-shirt
la corbata	tie
la chaqueta	jacket
la falda	skirt
la gorra	cap
el guante	glove
la guayabera	*loose-fitting man's shirt worn in tropical climates*
los *jeans*	jeans
las medias	stockings, pantyhose
los pantalones	pants
los pantalones cortos	shorts
el paraguas	umbrella
el pijama	pajamas
la ropa interior	underwear, undergarments
las sandalias	sandals
el suéter	sweater
el traje	suit
el traje de baño	swimsuit
el vestido	dress
el zapato	shoe
los zapatos de tenis	tennis shoes

Los países — Countries

Alemania	Germany
España (R)	Spain

*(R), meaning **Repaso** (*Review*), indicates that a vocabulary term has appeared previously.

69

los Estados Unidos (EE. UU.) (R)	United States (U.S.)
Inglaterra	England
el Japón	Japan
la República Dominicana	the Dominican Republic

Palabras semejantes: la Argentina, el Brasil, el Canadá, Colombia, Costa Rica, Cuba, China, Francia, México (R)**, Panamá, Portugal, Rusia, Venezuela.**

Otros sustantivos / *Other nouns*

el/la atleta	athlete
la casa	house
el cassette	cassette
el diccionario	dictionary
el disco	record
el disco compacto	compact disc
la encuesta	survey, poll
la foto(grafía)	photo(graph)
el hombre	man
el muchacho / la muchacha	boy/girl
la mujer	woman
el niño / la niña	boy/girl; child
la pregunta	question
la respuesta	answer
la semana	week
el señor (Sr.)	Mr.; sir; gentleman
los señores	gentlemen; Mr. and Mrs.
la señora (Sra.)	Mrs.; ma'am; lady
la señorita (Srta.)	Miss; young lady
el tiempo	time
el verano	summer

La descripción física / *Physical description*

Es...	He/She is . . .
alto/a	tall
atractivo/a	attractive
bajo/a	short
bonito/a	pretty
débil	weak
de estatura mediana	(of) average height
delgado	slender
de peso mediano	(of) average weight
feo/a	ugly
fuerte	strong
gordo/a	fat
grande	large, big
guapo/a	good-looking, handsome

joven (*pl.:* jóvenes) (R)	young
moreno/a	dark-haired, dark-skinned
pelirrojo/a	redheaded
pequeño/a	small, little
rubio/a	blond(e)
viejo/a	old
Tiene...	He/She has . . .
barba	a beard
bigote	a moustache
ojos azules	blue eyes
castaños	brown eyes
grises	hazel/gray eyes
negros	black/dark eyes
verdes	green eyes
pelo blanco	gray/white hair
castaño	brown hair
corto	short hair
lacio	straight hair
largo	long hair
negro	black hair
rizado	curly hair
rubio	blond hair

Las características / *(Personality) Characteristics*

aburrido/a	boring
agradable	pleasant
antipático/a	not likable, obnoxious
callado/a	quiet
desagradable	unpleasant
divertido/a	fun, funny
hablador(a) (R)	talkative, gossipy
perezoso/a	lazy
simpático/a	nice, friendly
tonto/a (R)	foolish, silly
trabajador(a)	hardworking

Palabras semejantes: estudioso/a, extrovertido/a, inteligente, interesante, lógico/a, optimista (R)**, pesimista** (R)**, serio/a, tímido/a.**

Los colores / *Colors*

amarillo/a	yellow
anaranjado/a	orange
azul	blue
blanco/a	white
(de color) café	brown
gris	gray
morado/a	purple

negro/a	black
rojo/a	red
rosado/a	pink
verde	green

Las nacionalidades / *Nationalities*

alemán/alemana	German
costarricense	Costa Rican
español(a)	Spanish
estadounidense (R)	U.S., American
francés/francesa	French
holandés/holandesa	Dutch
inglés/inglesa	English
japonés/japonesa	Japanese
norteamericano/a (R)	(North) American
puertorriqueño/a	Puerto Rican

Palabras semejantes: argentino/a, brasileño/a, canadiense, colombiano/a, cubano/a, chino/a, dominicano/a, mexicano/a (R)**, panameño/a portugués/portuguesa, ruso/a, venezolano/a.**

Otros adjetivos / *Other adjectives*

favorito/a	favorite
imposible	impossible
nuevo/a	new

Las palabras interrogativas / *Interrogative words*

¿adónde?	(to) where?
¿a qué hora? (R)	when?, (at) what time?
¿cómo?	how?
¿cuál(es)?	which, what?
¿cuándo?	when?
¿cuánto/a?	how much?
¿cuántos/as? (R)	how many?
¿de dónde?	(from) where?
¿de quién?	whose
¿dónde? (R)	where?
¿por qué?	why?
¿qué? (R)	what?
¿quién(es)?	who?

Palabras y expresiones útiles / *Useful words and expressions*

¿Cómo eres?	What are you like?
con	with
¿cuánto tiempo?	how long?
¿De veras?	Really?
durante	during
¿eh?	right?
en total	total
es cierto	that's true; it's true
esta noche	tonight
esta tarde	this afternoon
más	more
más (+ *adj.*) **que**	more (+ *adj.*) than, (*adj.*)-er than
más alto/a	taller
mucho	a lot
¿no? (R)	right?, isn't he/she/it?, aren't you/we/they?
¡No me digas!	You're kidding!
por ciento	percent
porque	because
pues	well; then
¡Qué + *adj./adv.*!	How + *adj./adv.*!
¡Qué bien hablas español!	How well you speak Spanish!
también	also, too
todavía	still
¿verdad? (R)	right?, isn't he/she/it?, aren't you/we/they?

México y los mexicanos

NEW VOCABULARY: la música, la palabra; todos

De viaje: Guadalajara

Guadalajara es la capital del estado de Jalisco. Es la segunda[1] ciudad más grande del país. Actualmente[2] hay más de tres millones de personas en esta ciudad encantadora conocida[3] por los mariachis, los charros[4] y los murales del famoso pintor José Clemente Orozco.

La música que tocan[5] los mariachis se originó[6] en el estado de Jalisco. La palabra *mariachi* procede de la palabra francesa *mariage* (*wedding*). ¿Por qué? Posiblemente porque los músicos mariachis solían tocar en las bodas.[7] En muchas fiestas mexicanas hoy en día hay un grupo de mariachis que toca canciones[8] para los invitados.[9] En Guadalajara hay una plaza, muy famosa y muy popular, que está dedicada a la música de los mariachis. Se llama, por supuesto,[10] la Plaza de los Mariachis.

Los charros, los *cowboys* mexicanos, representan la fascinación mexicana con el pasado[11] y la historia del país. Como los *cowboys*, los charros usan un traje especial. También celebran jaripeos[12] donde exhiben sus habilidades[13] ecuestres. Aunque[14] hay charros en todas partes[15] de México, algunos[16] creen que es en Guadalajara donde mejor observamos sus habilidades.

En Guadalajara, hay muchas obras[17] del muralista José Clemente Orozco, quien nació[18] en la ciudad en el año 1883.* Orozco es considerado[19] con frecuencia como el mejor de los muralistas mexicanos que pintaron[20] en su época. Era[21] un artista trágico y apasionado[22] que se inspiró[23] en la Revolución mexicana (1910–1920).† Fue[24] un idealista muy afectado por la sordidez[25] de la historia. Utilizó[26] el mural para transmitir sus sentimientos.[27] El mensaje[28] de su arte trasciende la situación nacional y puede ser comprendido por todos.

La idea del rodeo viene de las charreadas.

[1] *second* [2] *Currently* [3] *known* [4] *cowboys* [5] *que... that (they) play* [6] *se... originated* [7] *solían... tended to play at weddings* [8] *songs* [9] *guests* [10] *por... of course* [11] *past* [12] *rodeos* [13] *skills* [14] *Although* [15] *en... everywhere* [16] *some (people)* [17] *works* [18] *was born* [19] *es... is considered* [20] *painted* [21] *He was* [22] *passionate* [23] *se... was inspired* [24] *He was* [25] *sordidness* [26] *He used* [27] *feelings* [28] *message*

*1883: mil ochocientos ochenta y tres
†1910–1920: de mil novecientos diez a mil novecientos veinte

NOTE: The detailed suggestions for teaching the **De viaje** and **Perspectivas** sections of **México y los mexicanos** cannot be accommodated in the margins of this *Instructor's Edition.* For this reason, notes for these sections are in the *Instructor's Manual.*

Perspectivas de México: Las metas[1] profesionales

NEW VOCABULARY: trabajan; el amo / la ama de casa, el maestro, el/ la profesional, el trabajo; difícil

Para los mexicanos, la familia tiene mucha importancia. El trabajo también es importante. Este consenso[2] sobre los objetivos personales se demostró[3] en una encuesta nacional. Éstas eran las dos metas más importantes para los mexicanos.

1. proporcionar[4] mejores oportunidades a los hijos (o sea, a la familia)
2. realizarse[5] en el trabajo

En los hospitales en México, D.F., el servicio médico es bastante avanzado.

Esta encuesta también demuestra que las metas de los hombres se demuestran[6] a ser diferentes de las de[7] las mujeres. Para los hombres las principales metas profesionales son las siguientes.

1. ser profesionista*
2. ser deportista[8]
3. ser maestro

Para las mujeres las metas más comunes son las siguientes.

1. ser maestra
2. ser profesionista*
3. ser ama de casa

Es posible que la elección de ocupación, entre las mujeres y los hombres, refleje[9] los papeles[10] que, por tradición, la sociedad ha determinado.[11] Una persona, normalmente, imita[12] los modelos que ve.[13] En una cultura tradicional, como la mexicana, es difícil que una persona aspire[14] a una carrera[15] que nadie[16] en su mundo tiene. Pero la sociedad cambia.[17] Ahora, 23 por ciento de las mujeres entre los 12 y 65 años de edad[18] trabajan. Al entrar más mujeres[19] en la población[20] económicamente activa, se cambiarán[21] las aspiraciones de las mujeres y las de los hombres.

[1]*goals*   [2]*consensus*   [3]*se... was demonstrated*   [4]*to provide*   [5]*to fulfill oneself*   [6]*se... are found*   [7]*de... from those of*
[8]*athlete*   [9]*reflects*   [10]*roles*   [11]*ha... has determined*   [12]*imitates*   [13]*que... that he/she sees*   [14]*to aspire*   [15]*career*   [16]*no one*   [17]*changes*   [18]*age*   [19]*Al... As more women enter*   [20]*population*   [21]*se... will change*

Este minero trabaja en las minas de plata en Guanajuato, México. En el siglo XVIII unas de las minas de plata y oro más ricas del mundo se encontraron allí.

*The word **profesionista** is widely used in Mexico to mean *professional*, that is, not blue-collar or working class. The term **profesional** is the preferred term in the rest of the Spanish-speaking world.

NEW VOCABULARY: el horario

El horario

NOTE: See the *Instructor's Manual* for suggestions for using the chapter-opening pages.

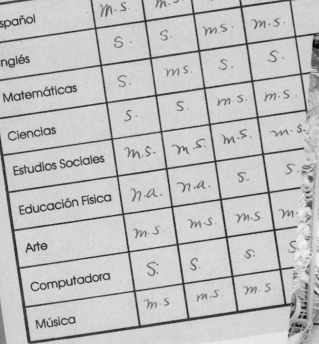

Clave

M.S.	Muy Satisfactorio
S.	Satisfactorio
N.A.	Necesita Ayuda

	1er. Semestre		2do. Semestre		Promedio
	Oct.	Dic.	Marzo	Mayo	
Español	m.s.	m.s.	m.s.	m.s.	
Inglés	s.	s.	m.s.	m.s.	
Matemáticas	s.	m.s.	s.	s.	
Ciencias	s.	s.	m.s.	m.s.	
Estudios Sociales	m.s.	m.s.	m.s.	m.	
Educación Física	n.a.	n.a.	s.	s.	
Arte	m.s.	m.s.	m.s.	m.	
Computadora	s.	s.	s.	s.	
Música	m.s.	m.s.	m.s.		

En el aeropuerto en la capital mexicana, esta dependiente arregla una variedad de regalos que compran los turistas.

Estos agrimensores miden la región alrededor de Monte Albán, la antigua capital zapoteca.

Esta aeromoza tiene que hablar varias lenguas.

Los mexicanos son fanáticos del fútbol.

FUNCIONES

- to talk about class schedules using school subjects and days of the week
- to identify people's professions and occupations
- to identify additional classroom items

GRAMÁTICA

- when to use **ser** and when to use **estar**
- use of **ir a** + an infinitive to talk about the future
- the present tense conjugations of regular verbs
- use of the personal **a**

En México hay muchas oportunidades para los profesionales, como estos ingenieros hidráulicos.

APPROPRIATE TESTING POINTS:
Diálogo (2), Las materias, **ser** y **estar**, **Quiz 1**
  Diálogo (2), Las profesiones y las ocupaciones, ir a + *inf.*, **Quiz 2**
  Diálogo (1), La sala de clase, El presente del indicativo, Diálogo (2), Los días de la semana, La *a* personal, **Quiz 3**
  Diálogo (1), En acción
  Chapter test

75

En casa del Sr. Kolb

NEW VOCABULARY: estudias, hablan, llegar, visitan; el cálculo, las ciencias políticas, la estadística, los estudios, la física, la ingeniería, las materias; segundo, universitario; en casa (de)

¡OJO! In these dialogues you will see some new present tense verb forms. You should be able to guess their meanings easily from the context.

Al llegar a Guadalajara, David y Elena visitan a Héctor y Matilde, los hijos del Sr. Kolb. Hablan de sus estudios universitarios.

PREPARATION: Direct students' attention to the drawing and to the dialogue introduction. Ask questions about the identity of the characters in the drawing, their locations, and their attire, e.g., **¿Quiénes son las personas en este dibujo? ¿Dónde están? ¿Están en Monterrey? ¿Están en Saltillo? ¿Qué ropa llevan?**

ELENA: Héctor, ¿qué tienes?[1] ¿Estás muy cansado?

HÉCTOR: Sí. Tengo mucho trabajo en mis clases.

ELENA: ¿Qué materias estudias?

HÉCTOR: Estoy en el segundo curso[2] de ingeniería. Tengo que estudiar cálculo, física, estadística...

MATILDE: ¿Qué estudias tú, David?

DAVID: Estudio ciencias políticas y también español.

[1] ¿qué... *what's with you?*   [2] segundo... *second level, year*

SUGGESTION: Remind students that glossed words and expressions are useful to know, but they are not part of the vocabulary that students are expected to master.

SUGGESTION: Point out the construction **tengo que** + *inf.* used here as *to have to* (*do something*). Ask what students have to do: **¿Tienes que ir a la librería/biblioteca/¿? ¿hoy? ¿Tienes que ir a México?** etc.

De inmediato

Which of these statements refer to David and which refer to Héctor?

1. Estudia español.
2. Está cansado.
3. Tiene mucho trabajo en sus clases.
4. Estudia ciencias políticas.
5. Está en el segundo curso de ingeniería.
6. Estudia cálculo.

A ti te toca

NEW VOCABULARY: escribir; la composición
SUGGESTION: Point out **tengo que**.
OPTIONAL: Have students work in groups of four to do a **miniencuesta**. Each student takes one of the subjects mentioned (**cálculo, física, estadística, ciencias políticas**) and asks all others in the group if they study the subject: **¿Estudias cálculo?** Students then report to the class the results from their group.

Practice the preceding dialogue with a classmate, substituting your names and personal information as appropriate. Then act out the first two lines, substituting the following information for **cansado** and **Tengo mucho trabajo en mis clases**.

preocupado/a → Tengo dos exámenes hoy.
contento/a → Tengo clases excelentes este semestre.
triste → Tengo que escribir una composición difícil.
ocupado/a → Tengo que estudiar mucho.

En la universidad

NEW VOCABULARY: compran; el inglés, la psicología, la sociología; nuestra, rápido

En la Universidad de Wisconsin–Eau Claire, los amigos de David también tienen mucho trabajo en sus clases. Ahora compran libros en la librería y hablan de sus estudios universitarios.

MARISOL: Tu clase de sociología es a la una, ¿no?

JORGE: Sí, y estoy preocupado. El profesor habla muy rápido.

LUISA: ¿No están Misha y Leon en nuestra clase de cálculo?

FELIPE: No, a las diez Leon está en su clase de inglés. Misha tiene una clase de psicología.

MARÍA: ¿Qué le pasa a la profesora Martínez hoy? Normalmente sus clases son muy interesantes. Pero hoy...

CARMEN: Hoy está muy cansada. Dicen que[1] uno de sus hijos está enfermo.

[1]Dicen... *They say that*

PREPARATION: Draw the students' attention to the drawing and the dialogue introduction. Ask questions, **¿Dónde están las personas en este dibujo? ¿Cómo están? ¿Conocen Uds. a estas personas? ¿Qué objetos ven en la sala de clase?**

---

1. ¿A qué hora tiene Jorge su clase de sociología?
2. ¿Por qué está Jorge preocupado?
3. ¿Qué clase tiene Misha a las diez? ¿Y León?
4. ¿Por qué está cansada la profesora Martínez?

De inmediato

Practice the preceding dialogues with a classmate. Then substitute the following information where Marisol and Jorge say **sociología** and **El profesor habla muy rápido**.

A ti te toca

NEW VOCABULARY: leer; el álgebra, la biología, los conceptos

inglés	→ Hay muchas composiciones.
historia	→ Tenemos que leer muchos libros.
álgebra	→ Hay muchos exámenes.
biología	→ El profesor no explica bien los conceptos.
psicología	→ La profesora está enferma.

La educación

NEW VOCABULARY: el colegio, el curso, la escuela secundaria, la Facultad (de Filosofía y Letras / de Ingeniería), la pensión

Faceta cultural

Hispanic students complete their general education when they finish secondary school (**la escuela secundaria** or **el colegio**) and receive their diploma (**el bachillerato**). Before they enter college, they may take an additional year or two of pre-university training in a special school called a **preparatoria**.

Unlike American universities, where students may spend two years or more studying a wide range of subjects before electing a major, at Hispanic universities students enroll immediately in a single school, called **una facultad**. This could be **la Facultad de Filosofía y Letras** (*humanities*), **la Facultad de Ingeniería** (where Héctor Kolb would be a student), and so on. Every year or level of study in the **facultad** is called **un curso**. The courses are predetermined by the professors of the school (**el profesorado**) or by the ministry of education. Few, if any, electives are allowed.

There are few extracurricular activities at the universities in Hispanic countries; students who want to participate in a sport generally do so by joining a private club. In addition, residence halls are not common at Hispanic universities. Students typically stay with relatives, reside in a boarding house (**una pensión**), or rent an apartment during their time at the university.

En México

At the Universidad Autónoma de Guadalajara, the various **facultades** are located not only in different buildings (as in this country), but often in completely different parts of town as well. Thus, whereas music and theater students might study downtown near the cathedral, business and law students might attend courses several miles away in another commercial district. This pattern is true of many urban universities in Mexico.

FOLLOW-UP: To help students understand the differences between educational experiences in the Hispanic world and the United States, ask students to interview a student from a Hispanic country regarding her or his educational preparation. The interview might include questions regarding the content and scheduling of classes, the importance of education, the amount of homework students were assigned each day, and extracurricular activities available.

VOCABULARIO

Las materias

NEW VOCABULARY: el cuaderno, el otoño

Joaquín, un amigo de David que estudia en la Universidad de Wisconsin–Eau Claire, siempre escribe su horario en su cuaderno. Aquí está su horario para el otoño.

	lunes	martes	miércoles	jueves	viernes
			mi horario		
8:00	historia		historia		historia
9:00	francés	francés	francés	francés	laboratorio de lenguas
10:00		inglés		inglés	
11:00					
12:00	almuerzo	almuerzo	almuerzo	almuerzo	almuerzo
1:00					
2:00	física	física	laboratorio	física	física
3:00		arte		arte	
4:00					
5:00					
6:00					

PREPARATION: Read the description of Joaquín's schedule aloud pausing to mime any passages that may not be clear, e.g., **escribe, cuaderno, otoño.** Ask students: **Miren ustedes el horario. Ahora bien, ¿es cierto o no es cierto?** 1. **Joaquín tiene la clase de historia/física/francés/inglés a las ___.** 2. **Tiene la clase de historia/francés los lunes, miércoles y viernes.** 3. **Tiene la clase de inglés/física antes del almuerzo.**

And then: **Ahora, unas preguntas más difíciles: Joaquín tiene la clase de historia a las ocho, ¿verdad? ¿A qué hora (Qué días) tiene Joaquín la clase de inglés / el almuerzo / el laboratorio de física?** etc.

Las materias

LAS BELLAS ARTES	FINE ARTS
la arquitectura	architecture
el arte	art
la música	music

LAS CIENCIAS SOCIALES	SOCIAL SCIENCES
las ciencias políticas	political science
la geografía	geography
la psicología	psychology
la sociología	sociology

LAS CIENCIAS Y LA INGENIERÍA	SCIENCE AND ENGINEERING
la biología	biology
el cálculo	calculus
las ciencias veterinarias	veterinary science
la computación	computer science
la enfermería	nursing
la física	physics
la geología	geology
las matemáticas	mathematics
la medicina	medicine
la química	chemistry

EL COMERCIO	BUSINESS
la contabilidad	accounting
la economía	economics

LA FILOSOFÍA Y LAS LETRAS	HUMANITIES
la composición	composition
las comunicaciones	mass communications
la filosofía	philosophy
la historia	history
las lenguas (los idiomas)	languages
el alemán	German
el chino	Chinese
el español	Spanish
el francés	French
el inglés	English
el italiano	Italian
el japonés	Japanese
el latín	Latin
el portugués	Portuguese
el ruso	Russian
la literatura	literature
la religión	religion

COMPREHENSION: Beginning with the academic subjects listed on Joaquín's schedule and continuing with the list of **materias**, ask: **¿Tenemos clases de ___ en esta universidad? ¿Estudias ___?**

SUGGESTION: If there are **facultades/departamentos** or **materias** offered at your institution that are not on the list but are critical for students to have for talking about their own schedules, add them.

Actividades

A **¿Qué materias cursa?** Match the activity in the first column with the course (listed in the second column) in which a student would most likely carry out the activity.

1. Lee *La República* de Platón.
2. Estudia el organismo animal.
3. Escribe composiciones.
4. Estudia mapas.
5. Trabaja con operaciones de aritmética.
6. Estudia la conducta humana.

a. inglés
b. contabilidad
c. filosofía
d. biología
e. psicología
f. geografía

NEW VOCABULARY: cursa
SUGGESTION: See whether students can guess the meaning of the new words used in the activity. Note that knowing the verbs is not as important in doing the activity as understanding the nouns that follow them.

B **¿Qué cursos tomas tú?** With a classmate, take turns asking and answering the following questions. Be prepared to report similarities and differences in schedules and in opinions about your classes.

1. ¿Qué clases tienes este semestre/trimestre?
2. ¿Cuál es tu clase favorita?
3. ¿Cuál es la clase que te gusta[1] menos?
4. ¿Qué clases vas a tomar el próximo semestre/trimestre?
5. ¿Cuál es tu clase más fácil?
6. ¿Cuál es tu clase más difícil?

jtus ask each other.

NEW VOCABULARY: tomar; el semestre, el trimestre; fácil, próximo; menos
VARIATION: Use questions 2, 3, 5, and 6 as a basis for a **miniencuesta**.

[1]te... *you like*

C **Nuestros horarios.** Using Joaquín's class schedule as a model, write out your own schedule. Next, follow the model provided to tell your partner what your schedule is. He or she will record what you say on a grid similar to the one you have made. Then reverse roles. When you have finished, check the schedules you have prepared for each other. Are they correct?

EJEMPLO:　Tengo la clase de francés a las nueve los lunes, martes, miércoles y jueves.

CONCEPTO

Ser y estar

Elena **es** la prima mexicana de David. **Es** delgada, de estatura mediana y tiene pelo negro. **Es** estudiante en el Instituto Tecnológico de Monterrey. Elena **está** en Guadalajara con David ahora. **Está** muy contenta con el viaje.

Actividades

Ⓐ **Mi nieto, David.** David's **abuelita** is telling her best friend about her American grandson, David. Indicate whether she should use **es** or **está** in each statement she makes about him.

1. David _____ mi nieto.
2. Él _____ alto y guapo.
3. La familia de David _____ en Eau Claire, Wisconsin.
4. David _____ estudiante en la Universidad de Wisconsin–Eau Claire.
5. Él _____ contento con sus estudios.
6. Él _____ popular en la universidad.
7. Ahora, David _____ en México.
8. David _____ el primo de Elena.
9. Hoy, David _____ en Guadalajara.
10. David _____ ocupado con los planes para el viaje a Guanajuato.

Ⓑ **¿Y tú?** Now adapt the preceding description of David to describe yourself. Remember that you can make the sentences negative.

EJEMPLO: Yo soy estudiante. Soy alto/a; no soy delgado/a. Mi familia está en Chicago. Soy estudiante en la Universidad de Chicago. Estoy contento/a con mis estudios. Soy popular en la universidad. Ahora estoy en la clase de español. Soy el primo (la prima) de Carla. Hoy estoy ocupado/a con muchos libros y muchos exámenes.

Usos de *ser* y *estar*

ser:	identificación	Felipe es estudiante.
	descripción	Es guapo y de estatura mediana.
estar:	condición / estado	Está enfermo hoy.
	localidad	Está en Eau Claire.

The verbs **ser** and **estar** are not interchangeable. They have even more uses than those shown in this chart. Allow yourself some time to get comfortable with all of their uses.

SUGGESTION: Emphasize that each of the verbs has particular uses. Misusing them may result in miscommunication.

En la Universidad de Guadalajara

D I Á L O G O

NEW VOCABULARY: enseñar, hacer, terminar; la administradora de empresas, el futuro, los planes

En la Universidad de Guadalajara, Elena y David hablan con unos estudiantes universitarios sobre sus planes para el futuro.

ELENA: Pedro, ¿qué vas a hacer después de terminar[1] tus estudios?
PEDRO: Voy a enseñar lenguas.
ELENA: La enseñanza[2] es muy importante. ¿Y tú, Beatriz?
BEATRIZ: Voy a ser administradora de empresas.

[1]después... *after finishing*   [2]*teaching*

PREPARATION: Focus students' attention on the drawing and the dialogue introduction. Ask students to describe the drawing in as much detail as possible.

De inmediato

1.   ¿Qué va a hacer Pedro después de terminar sus estudios?
2.   ¿Quién cree que la enseñanza es importante?   NEW VOCABULARY: cree
3.   ¿Qué va a ser Beatriz?

A ti te toca

In groups of three, practice the preceding dialogue. Then use the dialogue as a model to discuss your own plans for the future.

OPTIONAL: Ask students, ¿Qué vas a hacer después de terminar tus estudios? You might suggest that they look at the list of regular verbs and the list of professions at the end of the chapter. Give the models **Voy a** + *inf.* and **Voy a ser** + *profession.*

DIÁLOGO

En la universidad

NEW VOCABULARY: la abogada, el enfermero, la médica

SUGGESTION: Point out **tengo que** in the dialogue. Ask what it means.

Los estudiantes de UW-EC también hablan de sus planes para el futuro.

LUISA: ¿Vas a estudiar en la biblioteca esta noche?
JORGE: Sí, claro. Quiero hacerme[1] enfermero. Tengo que estudiar todas las noches.

FELIPE: ¿Vas a seguir[2] con tus estudios de historia?
MARÍA: Desgraciadamente,[3] no. Voy a hacerme médica y no tengo tiempo para la historia.

CARMEN: Luisa estudia para abogada, ¿verdad?
JOAQUÍN: Sí. Quiere poner un bufete[4] en Miami.

[1]*to become*   [2]*to continue*   [3]*Unfortunately*   [4]*Quiere... She wants to set up a law office*

PREPARATION: Discuss the drawing in Spanish. Then prepare students for the content of the dialogue by asking: Before reading the dialogues, can you guess what any of the characters might be studying?

De inmediato

OPTIONAL: Ask ¿Es cierto o no es cierto? 1. María va a hacerse médica. 2. Jorge va a estudiar en la biblioteca esta noche. 3. Luisa estudia para abogada.

What do the characters in the preceding dialogues say about their future plans? Create as many sentences as you can combining items from each of the following columns.

Jorge   (no) va a   estudiar   con sus estudios de historia
Luisa   hacerse   en la biblioteca esta noche
María   poner   enfermero/a
                      seguir   médico/a
                      tener   tiempo para la historia
                                  un bufete en Miami

A ti te toca

NEW VOCABULARY: el ingeniero, la veterinaria

Practice the preceding dialogues several times with a classmate. Then substitute the following information.

1. enfermero → ingeniero
2. médica → veterinaria
3. abogada → médica
   un bufete → una clínica

Términos correctos para las profesiones

The terms used in different Hispanic countries to refer to professional people vary. One issue in which there is a notable difference and even some controversy is that of titles for women who work in what have been historically all-male professions. In some areas, speakers use only the masculine form: **La doctora Campos es el médico de turno.** (*Dr. Campos is the physician on duty.*) In other places, the noun remains unchanged, but speakers change the article to indicate gender: **La doctora Campos es *la* médico de turno.** Still other speakers use a feminine form of the noun: **La doctora Campos es la *médica* de turno.**

En México

Despite the fact that most dictionaries list a feminine form for *physician* (**la médica**), most people in Mexico refer to a female physician as **la médico.** However, in urban areas such as Mexico City, where feminism is a significant force, many women prefer using a feminine form of nouns that denote profession when the professional is a woman. In such areas you will hear **la médica, la abogada,** and even **la miembra** (*member*). FOLLOW-UP: Ask students to interview a student or professor from a Hispanic country. The student should ask her or him whether the terms **la abogada, la médica,** and **la miembra** are accepted in her or his country.

Las profesiones y las ocupaciones

PREPARATION: Review the nouns that students have already learned for professions. You can do this by showing a photograph or drawing and asking, **¿Qué es esta persona? ¿Es profesor? ¿médico?** Point to the pictures in the book and continue the activity.

VOCABULARIO

un artista

una cocinera

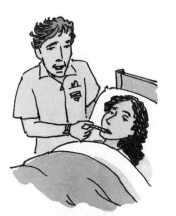

un enfermero

un ingeniero

un mecánico

una médica

una peluquera

una profesora

Otras profesiones y ocupaciones

el abogado / la abogada	*lawyer*	el/la dentista	*dentist*
el actor / la actriz	*actor/actress*	el/la dependiente	*clerk*
el administrador / la administradora de empresas	*administrator, businessperson*	el empleado / la empleada	*employee*
		el escritor / la escritora	*writer*
el/la agente	*agent (travel agent); traveling salesperson*	el/la gerente	*manager*
		el granjero / la granjera	*farmer*
		el hombre / la mujer de negocios	*businessman/ businesswoman*
el amo / el ama (*f.*) de casa	*homemaker*	el músico / la música	*musician*
		el obrero / la obrera	*worker*
el/la artista	*artist*	el/la periodista	*journalist*
el autor / la autora	*author*	el policía / la mujer policía	*police officer*
el cajero / la cajera	*cashier*	el reportero / la reportera	*reporter*
el consejero / la consejera	*counselor*	el secretario / la secretaria	*secretary*
		el veterinario / la veterinaria	*veterinarian*
el contador / la contadora	*accountant*		

COMPREHENSION: Bring pictures of various types of buildings (schools, hospitals, office buildings, service stations, barns, etc.). As you hold up each picture, ask **¿Quién trabaja aquí?** The pictures may be captioned in Spanish; the important thing is that students be able to recognize what they are.

Actividades

(A) **Preguntas profesionales.** Interview a classmate about career choices. Be prepared to report to the class the career choices of your classmate's family members and whether you and your classmate have family members with the same career. When appropriate, use **No tengo/tiene...** or **Nadie es...**

1. ¿Cuál es tu ocupación?
2. Después de graduarte en la universidad, ¿qué vas a ser? (Voy a...)
3. ¿Cuál es la ocupación de tu padre/madre/esposo/esposa?
4. ¿Qué ocupación tienen otros dos miembros de tu familia?
5. De tus amigos y parientes, ¿quién es mecánico o mecánica? ¿estudiante? ¿secretario o secretaria? ¿artista? ¿enfermero o enfermera? ¿policía?

(B) **¿Quién lo hace?** Match the job description in the first column with the most logical occupation from the second column.

1. limpia, cocina, lava,[1] cuida[2] a los niños[3]
2. aconseja[4] a los estudiantes
3. cocina en un restaurante
4. enseña en la universidad
5. planta y cosecha[5]
6. escribe libros
7. repara automóviles
8. cuida a los pacientes
9. recibe y da dinero
10. representa una compañía

  a. un enfermero
  b. una escritora
  c. un mecánico
  d. una profesora
  e. un cajero
  f. un ama de casa
  g. un agente
  h. una consejera
  i. un cocinero
  j. una granjera

[1]*washes* [2]*takes care of* [3]*children* [4]*advises* [5]*harvests*

NEW VOCABULARY: cocina, limpia
VARIATION: Ask students to act out the situations in the first column. The rest of the class will guess the profession depicted.

Ir a + infinitivo

CONCEPTO

PREPARATION: Focus students' attention on the caption that accompanies the drawing. **¿David y Elena van a visitar muchas o pocas ciudades mexicanas?** (Make large and small gestures with your hands.) **¿A quién va a conocer David en Oaxaca?** etc. Expand: **Ahora estoy en la clase de español. Pero, esta tarde voy a estar...**

«**Vamos a visitar** muchas ciudades mexicanas. En Oaxaca, **voy a conocer**[1] al tío de Elena.»

[1]*meet*

Ⓐ La semana que viene. Imagine that a friend asks you about the following activities. Indicate that they are not happening today, but on Friday.

EJEMPLO: ¿Tienes laboratorio de lenguas hoy? →
              No, voy a tener laboratorio de lenguas el viernes.

1. ¿Tienes cuatro clases hoy?
2. ¿Hablas con Ⓟ hoy?
3. ¿Estudias los verbos hoy?
4. ¿Vas a la biblioteca hoy?
5. ¿Estás en una reunión[1] hoy?
6. ¿Visitas a tu familia hoy?

[1]*meeting*

Actividades

VARIATION: Change the activity slightly to allow students to tell you what they plan to do tomorrow:—**¿Vas a tener laboratorio de lenguas mañana?** —**No, no voy a tener laboratorio de lenguas mañana.**

NEW VOCABULARY: confirmar, escuchar, invitar, preparar
VARIATION: Explain to the class that María has just found that nothing is working out. No one is going to do what she thought. They must change all the sentences to the negative: **Carmen no va a preparar los sándwiches para el viaje.**

B **Van a visitar Chicago.** The International Club at the university is planning a trip to Chicago. Taking María's point of view, mention what each person is going to do to prepare for the trip. If an activity does not seem appropriate or is not to your liking, make the sentence negative.

EJEMPLO: Carmen / preparar los sándwiches para el viaje →
Carmen va a preparar los sándwiches para el viaje.

1. Luisa / escribir un artículo que anuncia[1] el viaje para el periódico[2] estudiantil
2. yo / invitar a los otros estudiantes
3. Felipe / confirmar las reservaciones de los asientos[3] en el autobús
4. Luis y yo / hacer las reservaciones en un buen restaurante
5. Isabel y Joaquín / escuchar el pronóstico de tiempo[4] en la radio
6. tú / comprar las entradas[5] del concierto

[1]*announces* [2]*newspaper* [3]*seats* [4]*pronóstico... weather forecast* [5]*tickets*

NEW VOCABULARY: aprender, comer, llamar, mirar, practicar, viajar; el fin de semana, el sábado; por la noche
OPTIONAL: Use questions 1–3 as the basis for a **miniencuesta** and tabulate the results reported on the board or overhead.

C **¿Qué vas a hacer?** Using the following questions and possible answers as a guide, discuss your future plans with a classmate. Be prepared to report to the class the plans your classmate and his or her family and friends have, and whether they coincide with your own plans.

aprender el vocabulario nuevo	leer novelas
comer en casa / en un restaurante	llamar a... por teléfono
	practicar el fútbol
dar[1] una fiesta	trabajar
escribir cartas	ver televisión
estudiar	viajar a España/México
ir a la biblioteca	visitar a mi familia
	¿otra cosa?

1. ¿Qué vas a hacer esta noche?
2. ¿Qué van a hacer tú y tus amigos el sábado por la noche?
3. ¿Qué vas a hacer este verano?
4. ¿Qué va a hacer Ⓟ mañana?
5. ¿Qué van a hacer tus padres este fin de semana?
6. ¿Qué va a hacer tu hermano/a este verano?

[1]*to give*

NEW VOCABULARY: vivir; hasta

To indicate what you are going to do in the immediate future, use a form of the verb **ir** followed by **a** and an infinitive.

ir a + infinitivo

David	va a	estar en México hasta agosto.
María y Tomás	van a	vivir en las residencias.
Jorge,	¿vas a	ir a la biblioteca esta noche?

Antes de[1] clase

PREPARATION: Direct students' attention to the drawing and to the dialogue introduction. **¿Quién es el joven en este dibujo? ¿Cómo es? ¿Dónde está? ¿Está Matilde con él? ¿Adónde va Héctor ahora? ¿Tiene las cosas necesarias para ir a clase?**

DIÁLOGO

NEW VOCABULARY: conversan, llevas; el bolígrafo, el papel, la pizarra; sólo

David y Elena conversan con Héctor, que se prepara[2] para ir a su próxima clase.

ELENA: ¿Vas a una clase ahora?

HÉCTOR: Sí. Tengo la clase de estadística a las once.

DAVID: Pero no tienes ningún[3] libro. ¿No llevas tus libros a clase?

HÉCTOR: No. Leemos los libros en casa. En clase escuchamos al profesor. Llevo sólo papel y bolígrafo porque tengo que escribir.

DAVID: Las clases de estadística son muy difíciles, ¿no? ¿Entiendes[4] bien las explicaciones[5] del profesor?

HÉCTOR: Sí, es muy buen profesor. Explica los conceptos con cuidado[6] y siempre escribe los puntos importantes en la pizarra.

[1]Antes... *Before* [2]se... *is preparing* [3]no... *you have no* [4]*Do you understand* [5]*explanations* [6]con... *carefully*

Choose the word that most accurately completes the sentence, based on the preceding dialogue.

1. Ahora Héctor va a su clase de (estadística, física).
2. La clase es a (la una, las once).
3. Héctor (escribe, lee) sus libros en casa.
4. Héctor lleva papel y un bolígrafo porque tiene que (escribir, leer).
5. El profesor es muy (bueno, malo).
6. El profesor explica los (conceptos, libros) con cuidado y también escribe los puntos importantes en (la pizarra, la ventana).

De inmediato

OPTIONAL: Ask students to indicate whether the following sentences describe **Héctor, el profesor,** or both. In some cases, students may have to make an educated guess about **el profesor.** 1. **No lleva libros a clase.** 2. **Explica los conceptos con cuidado.** 3. **Lee el libro en casa.** 4. **Tiene la clase de estadística a las once.** 5. **Escribe los puntos importantes en la pizarra.** 6. **Escucha las explicaciones en clase.**

Practice the preceding dialogue with two classmates. Then exchange roles, substituting a class you are taking for Héctor's statistics class. Remember to use **la profesora** if the instructor of your class is a woman.

A ti te toca

PREPARATION: Ask what students expect from a good instructor. Is it more important that teachers be brilliant in their field, that they be good instructors, or that they be available to help the students learn? How are students evaluated in most courses at this institution? Do they have any courses in which the entire grade is based on one examination? How would they feel about such a method of evaluation?

Profesores y exámenes

Faceta cultural

The atmosphere in a Hispanic university tends to be somewhat different from that of a typical college in the United States. One of the most important differences is in the relationship between students and professors. Professors, particularly in technical fields, are seen more as specialists in their area than as instructors. For example, professors of law are frequently practicing lawyers who give lectures in their area of expertise at a nearby university. Thus, they are lawyers first and professors second; their function is to impart knowledge, not to help the student learn. Such professors usually have no office on campus and are not readily available to help students.

Professors usually do not give quizzes and rarely administer examinations during a course, although there may be final examinations covering material in individual courses. It is not uncommon for the university to require students to take one examination at the end of the year that tests all the subjects covered in that term. Students are expected to have mastered the material and to be able to write about it in an essay-format exam.

SUGGESTION: Point out that in many Hispanic countries, full-time teachers are not highly regarded. Often, they must teach heavy loads at several institutions in order to support a family. The professional who is invited to lecture at a university, however, is seen as having reached a position of respect in the profession.

FOLLOW-UP: Ask students to interview a student or faculty member from a Hispanic country. Students should ask specific questions on the content of the reading as it relates to the interviewee's country. How would the person compare the two educational systems? What are the advantages/disadvantages of each?

VOCABULARIO

La sala de clase

SUGGESTION: To present the new vocabulary, point to objects in the classroom as you say their names. Do this a couple of times with students' books closed, then ask students to look at the drawing as you point out each new item in the book, to reinforce the correct spelling.
COMPREHENSION: Ask, **¿Hay una pizarra (una pantalla, etc.) en esta sala de clase? ¿Dónde? ¿De qué color(es) es?**

Actividad

En la sala de clase. *Paso 1.* What classroom word(s) do you associate with the following?

EJEMPLO: cuadernos →
              bolígrafos, papeles

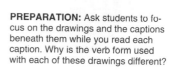

1. bolígrafos
2. pizarras
3. sillas
4. cuadernos
5. lápices
6. mochilas
7. mesas
8. profesores
9. libros
10. mapas
11. sacapuntas
12. pantalles

EXPANSION: Add the following items: **borradores, países, estudiantes, tiza, escritorios, pupitres.**

Paso 2. How many of the preceding items are in your classroom?

EJEMPLOS: ventanas → Hay seis (No hay) ventanas en mi sala de clase.

El presente del indicativo

PREPARATION: Ask students to focus on the drawings and the captions beneath them while you read each caption. Why is the verb form used with each of these drawings different?

JORGE: Yo **aprendo** inglés.

LUISA: Mercedes, tú **necesitas** estudiar más.

David **viaja** con Elena.

NEW VOCABULARY: necesitas; arreglar, buscar; beber, comprender, correr, deber, vender; abrir, decidir

SANDRA: Mi familia y yo **vivimos** en Wisconsin.

Vosotros **miráis** la profesora, ¿no?

Los estudiantes **leen** mucho.

SUGGESTION: Ask students to scan the lists of other verbs. What do they notice? What are the three different endings? Review the list, focusing on the meaning of each verb.

Otros verbos   15-8 . leer / entender vor.

verbos en -ar

arreglar (el cuarto)	to fix; to arrange, straighten (up) (the room)
buscar	to look for
cocinar	to cook
comprar	to buy
confirmar	to confirm
conversar	to converse, talk
enseñar	to teach; to show
escuchar	to listen (to)
estudiar	to study
hablar	to talk; to speak
invitar a	to invite
limpiar	to clean

llamar a	to call
llegar a	to arrive (in, at)
llevar	to wear; to carry; to take
practicar	to practice
preguntar	to ask
preparar	to prepare
pronunciar	to pronounce
regresar	to return
terminar	to finish
tomar	to take; to eat; to drink
trabajar	to work
visitar	to visit

verbos en -er

beber	to drink
comer	to eat
comprender	to understand
correr	to run
creer	to believe, think
deber	ought to, should
vender	to sell

verbos en -ir

abrir	to open
asistir (a)	to attend
decidir	to decide
escribir	to write

VIVIR

2. ¿Pierdes las clases con frecuencia?

   a. Sí, a las cuatro.
   b. No, quiero recibir buenas notas.
   c. A veces, especialmente las clases a las ocho de la mañana.

3. ¿Qué haces cuando pierdes una clase?

   a. Hablo con el profesor para saber qué pasó.
   b. Nada. Mis amigos siempre llaman por la noche para decirme[1] qué pasó.
   c. Trabajo a las ocho de la mañana.

[1] *tell me*

DIÁLOGO

En la universidad

NEW VOCABULARY: los domingos

En la Universidad de Wisconsin–Eau Claire, los amigos de David conversan sobre sus planes para la semana.

JORGE: ¿A quién llamas?
TOMÁS: Llamo a María. Tenemos un examen de química el martes y ¡necesito ayuda[1]!

CARMEN: ¿Tienes clase con Leon hoy?
JOAQUÍN: No, sólo los martes y jueves.

FELIPE: El lunes es un día pesado,[2] ¿no crees?
LUIS: Sí, los lunes son difíciles para todos. Yo prefiero los sábados y domingos.
FELIPE: ¡Como todo el mundo![3]

[1] *help* [2] *difficult, boring* [3] ¡Como... *Like everyone!*

De inmediato

1. ¿Por qué llama Tomás a María?
2. Joaquín tiene clase con Leon hoy, ¿no?
3. ¿Qué día es difícil para Felipe?
4. ¿Qué días prefieren Luis y Felipe?

A ti te toca

Practice the preceding dialogues with a classmate, substituting courses and days of the week to make the dialogues reflect your own academic activities.

PREPARATION: Ask questions about the drawing and the dialogue introduction, ask students to work in small groups to discuss the drawing, or allow students to study the drawing and then make statements or questions about it.

Los días de la semana

enero						
lunes	martes	miércoles	jueves	viernes	sábado	domingo
		1	2	3	4	5
6	7	8	9	10	11	12
13	14	15	16	17	18	19
20	21	22	23	24	25	26
27	28	29	30	31		

COMPREHENSION: Quickly check comprehension by asking **Si hoy es ____, ¿qué día es mañana?** and/or **Si hoy es ____, ¿qué día fue ayer?** Indicate the meaning of the questions using gestures.

Actividades

A **¿Qué día es hoy?** Use the preceding calendar to answer the following questions.

1. ¿Cuál es el primer día de la semana?
2. ¿Qué día es el 25 de enero? ¿el 6? ¿el 31? ¿el 15?
3. ¿Qué día es el Día del Año Nuevo?
4. Si hoy es el 23 de enero, ¿qué día es mañana?
5. ¿Cuántos viernes hay en el mes de enero?
6. ¿Cuántos domingos hay?

NEW VOCABULARY: el mes

B **El calendario.** Ask a classmate the following questions about the days of the week.

1. ¿Qué día de la semana es hoy?
2. ¿Qué día es mañana?
3. ¿Qué día es pasado mañana?
4. ¿Qué día es el último día del mes?
5. ¿Qué día tienes más clases?
6. ¿Qué día de la semana es el más difícil para ti este semestre? ¿Y el más fácil?

NEW VOCABULARY: el calendario; último; pasado mañana

SUGGESTION: Point out the difference between **voy a clase el martes** (*this Tuesday*) and **voy a clase los martes** (*on Tuesdays,* in general). If there is a holiday scheduled, point to the calendar and ask **¿Tenemos clase el lunes? Generalmente, ¿tenemos clase los lunes?**

LOS DÍAS DE LA SEMANA EN ORACIONES

singular: **el** + día → Voy a clase el martes.
I am going to class on Tuesday.

plural: **los** + día → No tengo clase los martes.
I don't have class on Tuesdays.

Use **el** or **los** to express *on* with days of the week. Note that the days are not capitalized in Spanish.

93

Faceta cultural

El calendario

Differences between cultures can be reflected in the calendar and in the way people view the passage of time. The Hispanic calendar is typically arranged differently from the one used in this country. Monday, **lunes,** is the first day of the week, whereas **domingo** is the seventh day. Days that are not linked to a universally recognized religious festival may be observed in one culture but not in another, or may be observed on different days. For example, Friday the thirteenth is not dreaded as an unlucky day in Spanish-speaking countries; however, Tuesday the thirteenth (**el martes trece**) is. In addition, certain periods of time are expressed in a somewhat different manner in the Hispanic world. A one-week trip is **un viaje de ocho días,** and events that will occur two weeks from today happen (**de hoy**) **en quince días.**

SUGGESTION: Ask students why some people might regard Sunday as the seventh day of the week and others might see it as the first day of the week.

CONCEPTO

La a personal

PREPARATION: Call attention to the drawing. Read the caption, emphasizing the personal **a** when it occurs. Now read, **Los alumnos miran la pizarra. Los alumnos miran al profesor (a la profesora). El profesor (La profesora) mira el libro. El profesor (La profesora) mira a la alumna.** Point out that, in Spanish, the untranslated particle **a** precedes a direct object when it is a person.

David busca el mapa. ¡Ah! Elena tiene el mapa. David debe buscar **a** Elena.

Actividad

¿A quién llamas cuando... ? ¿Qué buscas cuando... ? What or whom would you seek in each of these situations? You may choose from the suggestions or provide your own original responses.

EJEMPLOS: quieres ir a las montañas →
          Llamo a mis amigos.
          o Busco el mapa.

mis amigos/as	el mapa	el rector (la rectora) de la
el calendario	mis padres	universidad
el diccionario	el profesor	un pariente rico[1]
la enciclopedia	(la profesora)	¿ ?

1. tienes un problema   **2.** necesitas saber qué día es mañana

[1] *rich*

94

3. tienes un examen mañana

4. quieres quejarte[2] de una clase

5. necesitas información sobre la guerra[3] civil española

6. necesitas dinero

7. pierdes una clase

8. necesitas información sobre una palabra

NEW VOCABULARY: el dinero; sobre

[2]*to complain*   [3]*war*

SUGGESTION: You may wish to discuss this construction with students since it has no equivalent in English.

Usos de la *a* personal

Se usa cuando el complemento directo es...

una persona	Busco **a** la amiga de Amalia.
	Busco **al** tío Ramón.
un grupo de personas	Busco **a** mi familia.
EXCEPCIÓN	Tengo dos hermanos.

No se usa cuando el complemento directo es...

una cosa	Busco mi mochila.
un lugar	Busco el Restaurante Tres Estrellas.

This **a** is called the personal **a**; it precedes a direct object that is a specific person or group of people. The **a** contracts with the article **el** (**a** + **el** = **al**). Note that the personal **a** is not used after **tener**.

PREPARATION: Draw the students' attention first to the title of the dialogue. Ask where they have seen this term before. (David's classmates gave him a **fiesta de despedida** before he left Eau Claire for Mexico. Students have also learned **las despedidas** as *farewells/good-byes*.) Discuss the drawing by asking questions about it or by having students make short, simple statements about it.

La despedida

DIÁLOGO

NEW VOCABULARY: la visita; algún; allá

La familia Kolb invita a David y a Elena a cenar[1] en la Plaza de los Mariachis. Allí todos conversan y escuchan la música.

> DAVID: Nunca voy a olvidar[2] mi visita a la ciudad de Guadalajara. Uds. han sido[3] muy amables conmigo, digo[4], con nosotros.
>
> EL SR. KOLB: Gracias, David. Vamos a extrañar[5] mucho a nuestro nuevo amigo.
>
> HÉCTOR: Matilde y yo esperamos[6] ir a los EE. UU. algún día. Quizás podamos[7] ir a Wisconsin también.
>
> DAVID: Allá tienen su casa.

[1]*to have dinner*   [2]*to forget*   [3]*han... have been*   [4]*I mean*   [5]*to miss*   [6]*hope*   [7]*we can*

Summarize the dialogue by combining items from each of the two columns.

De inmediato

1. David nunca va a olvidar

2. la familia Kolb ha sido

3. el Sr. Kolb dice que van a

4. Matilde y Héctor esperan

5. David dice que allá

a. extrañar mucho a su nuevo amigo.

b. Héctor y Matilde tienen su casa.

c. ir a los EE. UU.

d. muy amable con David y Elena.

e. su visita a Guadalajara.

A ti te toca
Practice the preceding dialogue with two classmates. Then use the dialogue as a model to talk about the following.

1. to tell about a trip to a place you will never forget
2. to identify someone you are going to miss
3. to tell about a country you hope to visit

EN ACCIÓN

Antes de ver

In this chapter you will watch and listen to a series of people talk about their classes, their class schedules, and their instructors. Some of them will also discuss their career plans. Listen carefully for the names of their favorite and least favorite subjects and for the professions for which they are preparing.

El horario de Luisa

You will hear Felipe describe Luisa's class schedule. Before you listen, make a chart like the one shown to record the courses that Luisa is taking. Then, listen to Felipe's description, which will be read twice. During the first reading, fill in the schedule with Luisa's courses. Listen carefully to the description a second time to check your answers and fill in what you have missed.

	lunes	martes	miércoles	jueves	viernes
8:00					
9:00					
10:00					
11:00					
12:00					
1:00					
2:00					
3:00					
4:00					
5:00					

El hombre, la mujer y el trabajo

While David is waiting for Héctor to get out of class, he spots the following survey results on a bulletin board near an academic adviser's office.

Antes de leer

This reading presents the results of a survey that asked what professions Mexicans would choose, and analyzed the preferences by sex. Before you read the survey, review the vocabulary for professions and occupations, because you will find many of the professions listed here. Who do you think would more likely choose to be a teacher, a man or a woman? Who would more likely choose to be a businessperson? A professional athlete? A doctor? Would you expect the same differences based on sex in this country?

Next, look at the graph that presents the results of the survey. The professions are listed down the side of the graph and the order of preference for each profession is listed across the bottom. What are some of the obvious differences that you observe between the choices of Mexican men and women?

Scan the introductory paragraph and the graph to find the information requested.

PREPARATION: Before beginning this activity, use the list of professions on pages 83–84 to assess students' opinions regarding sex-related career choices. As you read each item, ask students to raise their right hands if it is a career more frequently chosen by men, their left hands if it is a career more frequently chosen by women, and both hands if an equal number of men and women would choose this career.
SUGGESTION: Read the list of occupations and ask students to raise their hands for each one that is a career they have considered. You may wish to count the responses and report the results to the class.

Preferencias profesionales

En México, según una encuesta reciente, hay una relación entre el sexo de la persona y el trabajo que escoge.[1] En la gráfica que sigue[2] se ve[3] cómo el sexo afecta el orden de preferencia de varias profesiones.

[1]*he or she chooses* [2]*follows* [3]*se... one sees*

Preferencias profesionales

Después de leer

Paso 1. ¿Es cierto o no es cierto? Si Héctor y Matilde son mexicanos típicos, ¿cuáles de estas declaraciones son ciertas?

1. Héctor prefiere ser comerciante a maestro.
2. Héctor prefiere ser doctor a enfermero.
3. Héctor prefiere ser amo de casa a mesero.

4. Matilde prefiere ser secretaria a maestra.
5. Matilde prefiere ser deportista a mesera.
6. Matilde prefiere ser doctora a enfermera.
7. Héctor va a decidir ser militar antes que[1] Matilde.
8. Matilde va a decidir ser doctora antes que Héctor.
9. Ninguno[2] quiere ser mesero.

[1]antes... *before* [2]*Neither*

Paso 2. David's interest in the effect of sex differences on career choices is piqued by the preceding survey results, and he decides to interview some of Héctor and Matilde's friends from the University of Guadalajara about their career choices. He discovers that their choices conform to those indicated by the study. David then writes a letter to the academic adviser outside whose office he read the article. He tells the adviser about his own survey results. Complete the following letter to indicate David's findings.

Muy estimada profesora Suárez:

NEW VOCABULARY: ayer, entre

Ayer visité[a] la Universidad de Guadalajara. Hablé[b] con un grupo de estudiantes universitarios acerca de[c] la elección de su profesión. Para su información, entre los hombres ____[1] tiene el primer lugar; las mujeres prefieren en primer lugar ser ____.[2] En segundo lugar los hombres prefieren ser ____.[3] También prefieren ser ____[4] a ser comerciantes. Por otra parte, en segundo lugar las mujeres prefieren ser ____[5] a ser doctora. Lo interesante[d] es que las mujeres elegirían[e] una profesión médica como ____[6] o ____[7] antes que los hombres.

[a]*I visited* [b]*I spoke* [c]acerca... *about* [d]Lo... *The interesting thing* [e]*would choose*

Miniencuesta

Paso 1. Work in groups of four or five to interview each other about your job preferences, using the following questions.

De las diez profesiones mencionadas en la lectura,[1] ¿cuál tienes en primer lugar? ¿en segundo lugar? ¿en tercer lugar?

NEW VOCABULARY: tercer

Paso 2. Working together, write a brief report on the professional preferences in your group, listing how many people select which professions as first, second, and third choices.

EJEMPLO: En nuestro grupo, ____ persona(s) tiene(n) ____ en primer/ segundo/tercer lugar...

Paso 3. Read the results of your survey to the class. Your instructor will chart the information on the board or the overhead projector. When you see the final results, comment on the career preferences of the entire class. You may also wish to discuss how the results of your class survey differ from those of the Mexican survey just studied.

EJEMPLO: En nuestra clase, ____ persona(s) tiene(n) ____ en primer/ segundo/tercer lugar...

[1]*reading*

Una conversación

With a classmate, write a dialogue of eight to twelve lines in length in which you and a friend exchange information about one of your friend's classes. Be prepared to act out your scene for the entire class.

First, exchange greetings. Next, inquire what class your friend is going to. After your friend responds, ask what the class is like—interesting, boring, difficult, and so on. Then inquire what your friend needs for that class. Your friend should have at least five things in his or her backpack that are appropriate for such a course. Ask what kinds of things the students do in the class. In response, your friend should list at least three activities. Find out at what time the class is held and on which days of the week. Then say good-bye.

CONSIDERACIONES
- Which greetings and farewells are appropriate for the social situation and for the time of day?
- What are the appropriate pronouns for *you*?
- Will you need masculine or feminine adjectives to describe the school subject?
- What transition or reaction words and phrases (such as those included in the dialogues in this and previous chapters) could help the flow of your conversation?
- What verb form is most appropriate for your friend to use to describe the activities of all the students in the class?
- Which forms of **estar, ser, ir,** and **tener** do you need?
- Have you included all necessary punctuation marks?

VOCABULARIO

Los verbos regulares	Regular verbs		
abrir	to open	confirmar	to confirm
aprender (a)	to learn (how to)	conversar	to converse, talk
arreglar (el cuarto)	to fix; to arrange, straighten (up) (the room)	correr	to run
		creer *creyó*	to believe in, think
		cursar	to study (*a subject*)
asistir (a)	to attend	deber	ought to, should
beber	to drink	decidir	to decide
buscar	to look for	enseñar	to teach; to show
cocinar	to cook	escribir	to write
comer	to eat	escuchar	to listen (to)
comprar	to buy	estudiar	to study
comprender	to understand	hablar	to talk; to speak
		invitar	to invite

leer *leyó*	to read
limpiar	to clean
llamar	to call
llegar	to arrive
llevar	to wear; to carry; to take
mirar	to look at
necesitar	to need
practicar	to practice
preguntar	to ask
preparar	to prepare
pronunciar	to pronounce
regresar	to return (*to a place*)
terminar	to finish
tomar	to take; to eat; to drink
trabajar	to work
vender	to sell
viajar	to travel
visitar	to visit
vivir	to live

Otros verbos / *Other verbs*

hacer	to do; to make
haces	you (*fam. sing.*) do, are doing
hacen	you (*pl.*) / they do, are doing
ver	to see, watch
veo	I see

Las profesiones, las ocupaciones y los oficios / *Professions, occupations, and trades*

el abogado / la abogada	lawyer
el administrador / la administradora de empresas	administrator, businessperson
el/la agente	agent, salesperson
el amo de casa / el ama (*f.*) de casa	homemaker
el cajero / la cajera	cashier
el cocinero / la cocinera	cook
el consejero / la consejera	counselor, adviser
el contador / la contadora	accountant
el/la dependiente	clerk
el empleado / la empleada	employee
el enfermero / la enfermera	nurse
el escritor / la escritora	writer

el/la gerente	manager
el granjero / la granjera	farmer
el hombre de negocios	businessman
el ingeniero / la ingeniera	engineer
el maestro / la maestra	teacher
el médico / la médica	doctor, physician
la mujer de negocios	businesswoman
el músico / la música	musician
el obrero / la obrera	worker, laborer
el peluquero / la peluquera	hair stylist; barber
el/la periodista	journalist
el/la profesional	professional person, white-collar worker

Palabras semejantes: el actor / la actriz, el/la artista, el autor / la autora, el/la dentista (R), el mecánico / la mecánica, el profesor / la profesora (R), el reportero / la reportera, el secretario / la secretaria, el veterinario / la veterinaria.

Las materias / *School subjects*

LAS BELLAS ARTES	*FINE ARTS*
la arquitectura	architecture
LAS CIENCIAS SOCIALES	*SOCIAL SCIENCES*
las ciencias políticas	political science
la psicología	psychology
LAS CIENCIAS Y LA INGENIERÍA	*SCIENCE AND ENGINEERING*
las ciencias veterinarias	veterinary science
la computación	computer science
la enfermería	nursing
la estadística	statistics (*science, course*)
la física	physics
la química	chemistry
EL COMERCIO	*BUSINESS*
la contabilidad	accounting
la economía	economics
LA FILOSOFÍA Y LAS LETRAS	*HUMANITIES, LIBERAL ARTS*
las comunicaciones	mass communications
la filosofía	philosophy
los idiomas (las lenguas)	languages
el alemán	German
el chino	Chinese
el español	Spanish

el francés	French
el inglés	English
el japonés	Japanese
el ruso	Russian

Palabras semejantes: el álgebra (*f.*), **el arte** (*f.*), **la biología, el cálculo, la composición, la geografía** (R), **la geología, la historia, el italiano, el latín, la literatura, las matemáticas, la medicina, la música, el portugués, la religión, la sociología.**

La sala de clase — *The classroom*

el bolígrafo	ballpoint pen
el borrador	chalkboard eraser
el cuaderno	notebook
el escritorio	(teacher's) desk
el lápiz (*pl.* lápices)	pencil
la pantalla	screen
el papel	paper
la pizarra	chalkboard
el sacapuntas	pencil sharpener
la silla	chair
la tiza	chalk

Los días de la semana — *Days of the week*

el lunes	Monday
el martes	Tuesday
el miércoles	Wednesday
el jueves	Thursday
el viernes	Friday
el sábado	Saturday
el domingo	Sunday

Otros sustantivos — *Other nouns*

el almuerzo	lunch
el calendario	calendar
la cena	dinner
el colegio	secondary/high school
el concepto	concept
el curso	course
el dinero	money
el enero	January
la escuela secundaria	secondary/high school
los estudios	studies, schooling
la facultad	school/college (*of a university*)
la Facultad de Filosofía y Letras	School/College of Humanities, Liberal Arts
la Facultad de Ingeniería	School/College of Engineering
el fin de semana	weekend
el futuro	future
el horario	schedule
el laboratorio (de lenguas/física/química)	(language/physics/chemistry) laboratory
el mes	month
el otoño	autumn, fall (*season*)
la palabra	word
la pensión	boarding house
el plan	plan
el reloj	clock; watch
la residencia	dorm(itory)
la tarea	homework
el trabajo	work
el trimestre	trimester, quarter

Los adjetivos — *Adjectives*

difícil	difficult, hard
fácil	easy
todo/a	all
todos/as	every, all
universitario/a	university
primer, primero/a	first
segundo/a	second
tercer, tercero/a	third
próximo/a	next, following
último/a	last, final

Expresiones adverbiales — *Adverbial expressions*

allá	there, over there
anoche	last night
a veces	sometimes, at times
ayer	yesterday
con frecuencia	often, frequently
en casa (de)	at (the) home (of)
menos	less, least, fewer
nunca	never, not ever
pasado mañana	the day after tomorrow
por la noche	at night

Las preposiciones — *Prepositions*

entre	between; among
hasta	until
sobre	about

México y los mexicanos

De viaje: La región entre Guadalajara y México, D.F.

Entre Guadalajara y la capital de México queda una de las regiones más encantadoras[1] del país: el Bajío, el valle más amplio[2] de México central. Aquí se encuentran depósitos de minerales, especialmente de plata,[3] que han tenido[4] tanta importancia en la historia del país. Algunas de las ciudades de esta región son: en el estado de Guanajuato, Guanajuato y San Miguel de Allende; en el estado de Querétaro, su

capital del mismo nombre; y en el estado de Hidalgo, Tula, famosa por sus ruinas.

Guanajuato, la capital del estado de Guanajuato, ha sido[5] declarada monumento histórico nacional por su arquitectura colonial. La ciudad mantiene un aspecto encantador con avenidas subterráneas o túneles, para acomodar el tránsito[6] tremendo que

sufre esta ciudad colonial. Hoy en día Guanajuato tiene menos de 100.000 habitantes, pero era más grande cuando sus famosas minas de plata estaban en plena explotación.[7]

San Miguel de Allende, otro monumento histórico nacional en el estado de Guanajuato, es una atracción turística por su encanto[8] colonial y por ser un centro artístico. La ciudad es bien conocida[9] por haber atraído[10] a muchos artistas y escritores[11] a México. Estudiantes de arte vienen de varios países, especialmente de los EE. UU., para estudiar en el famoso Instituto Allende. Pero el crecimiento[12] de la población trae consigo[13] problemas: un aumento[14] de tránsito y una amenaza[15] al abastecimiento[16] de agua de la región.

Querétaro, capital del estado de Querétaro, es una ciudad que atrae[17] a personas que tienen interés en el arte y la arquitectura colonial. Esta ciudad ha sido el escenario[18] de algunos de los episodios más importantes de la historia de México. Aquí en 1848 se firmó[19] el Tratado[20] de Guadalupe Hidalgo, en el que México cedió[21] más de la mitad[22] de su territorio a los EE. UU.

Tula, una zona arqueológica en el estado de Hidalgo que probablemente tenía unos 35.000 habitantes, atrae a muchos turistas. Aquí se estableció[23] en el año 856 la tribu de los chichimecas, que después llegó a ser[24] la de los toltecas. En Tula, en el Templo de los Guerreros,[25] hay figuras de tres metros de altura[26] que son uno de los ejemplos más destacados[27] de la escultura precolombina.

Cuatro sitios y cuatro aspectos[28] de México. ¿Cuál representa el México verdadero[29]? Pues, todos.

---

[1]*enchanting* [2]*large* [3]*silver* [4]*han... have had* [5]*ha... has been* [6]*traffic*
[7]*en... operating at full capacity* [8]*charm* [9]*known* [10]*haber... having attracted*
[11]*writers* [12]*growth* [13]*with it* [14]*increase* [15]*threat* [16]*supply* [17]*attracts*
[18]*setting* [19]*se... was signed* [20]*Treaty* [21]*ceded* [22]*half* [23]*se... settled*
[24]*llegó... became* [25]*Warriors* [26]*de... in height* [27]*outstanding* [28]*views, facets*
[29]*true*

NEW VOCABULARY: los cambios, el gobierno, las manos, el norte, los pobres, el pueblo, los siglos, el sur; importantes, muchos, ricos, todavía

Perspectivas de México: Los EE. UU. y México—algunos paralelos

La independencia

En los siglos XVIII y XIX ocurrieron muchos cambios en México y en los Estados Unidos. Las colonias norteamericanas declararon su independencia de Inglaterra en 1776*: Los colonos[1] no querían que Inglaterra controlara su política y su economía.

En México ocurrió algo parecido.[2] Los mexicanos declararon su independencia de España en 1810.*

Conflictos en las nuevas repúblicas

Muchos países europeos y latinoamericanos tomaron como[3] modelo la revolución y la constitución norteamericanas. Pero en los EE. UU. y en México, la independencia no resolvió todos sus problemas. En México surgieron[4] entre 1858* y 1861* las Guerras[5] de la Reforma. Y, en los EE. UU., entre 1861* y 1865,* tuvo lugar[6] la Guerra Civil entre los estados del norte y los del sur.

Estas dos guerras—la Guerra Civil en los EE. UU. y las Guerras de la Reforma en México—fueron[7] importantes porque señalaron[8] conflictos básicos en las dos repúblicas nuevas. En los EE. UU. el conflicto que llamamos la Guerra Civil tenía que ver[9] con la esclavitud.[10] Pero el derecho[11] de los estados de controlar su propio destino era de mayor importancia. En México, las Guerras de la Reforma fueron ocasionadas[12] por la lucha[13] entre dos ideologías. Una de las ideologías daba[14] el poder a los que siempre[15] lo habían tenido[16]—los ricos y la iglesia.[17] La otra daba el poder a los que[18] nunca habían tenido poder, es decir, al pueblo.

En Guanajuato se puede ver edificios de estilo colonial junto a los de estilo francés e italiano.

Hoy en día

Es importante notar que esas opiniones conflictivas todavía existen en estos países. En los EE. UU. hay muchos que creen que el poder debe estar en manos de los estados, no en las del gobierno nacional. En México la lucha sigue[19] entre los pocos, que tienen dinero y poder, y los pobres, que no tienen ninguno.

[1] *colonists*   [2] *algo... something similar*   [3] *as a*   [4] *arose*   [5] *Wars*   [6] *tuvo... took place*   [7] *were*   [8] *they pointed out*   [9] *tenía... had to do*   [10] *slavery*   [11] *right*   [12] *fueron... were caused*   [13] *struggle*   [14] *gave*   [15] *always*   [16] *lo... had had it*   [17] *church*   [18] *los... those who*   [19] *continues*

*1776: mil setecientos setenta y seis; 1810: mil ochocientos diez; 1858: mil ochocientos cincuenta y ocho; 1861: mil ochocientos sesenta y uno; 1865: mil ochocientos sesenta y cinco

Las viviendas[1]

NOTE: See the *Instructor's Manual* for suggestions on using the chapter opening pages.

NEW VOCABULARY: las viviendas

En México muchas fábricas construyen viviendas para sus empleados.

En México, D.F., por ser una de las ciudades más grandes del mundo, se necesita una gran cantidad de apartamentos.

[1]*Dwellings; Housing*

En México, dos características típicas de las casas en el campo son las tejas rojas y un patio con plantas y árboles.

En México hay muchas casas elegantes del período colonial, o sea, del siglo XVI.

APPROPRIATE TESTING POINTS:
Diálogo (2), Las viviendas, Algunos verbos irregulares, **Quiz 1**
Diálogo (2), Los cuartos y los muebles de la casa, Los verbos de cambio radical, **Quiz 2**
Diálogo (2), El cuerpo, Los verbos reflexivos, **Quiz 3**
Diálogo (1), En acción
Chapter test

METAS

Un dormitorio estudiantil. Muchos estudiantes mexicanos asisten a la universidad de su localidad, lo que les permite vivir con sus padres o parientes.

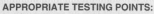

FUNCIONES

- to talk about where you live and what your home looks like

- to refer to the parts of the body and to tell someone where you hurt

- to describe your daily routine

GRAMÁTICA

- the present-tense conjugations of stem-changing verbs

- the present-tense conjugations of verbs that have some irregularities

- verbs that are used reflexively

105

DIÁLOGO

En las afueras de la ciudad

NEW VOCABULARY: dicen, muestra, ve; los apartamentos, el centro, los condominios, los edificios, el socio, el tipo, la urbanización, la zona; ese, típico; rápido

El Sr. Eugenio Cardoza, socio del Sr. Kolb, les muestra la ciudad de Guadalajara a David y a Elena. Ahora miran una urbanización nueva en las afueras de la ciudad.

ELENA: Hay mucha construcción en esta zona, ¿verdad?

EL SR. CARDOZA: Sí, dicen que en esta zona la población aumenta[1] muy rápido.

DAVID: Los edificios allí... ¿son condominios?

EL SR. CARDOZA: No, son edificios de apartamentos.

DAVID: ¿Es típico ese tipo de construcción?

ELENA: Sí, es típico en una urbanización moderna.

[1]la... *the population is growing*

De inmediato

NEW VOCABULARY: ve; el centro; despacio

¿Es cierto o no es cierto?

1. David, Elena y el Sr. Cardoza miran una urbanización en el centro de la ciudad.
2. Hay mucha construcción en esta zona.
3. La población en esta zona aumenta despacio.
4. Los edificios que David ve son condominios.
5. Este tipo de construcción es típico en una urbanización moderna.

A ti te toca

With a classmate, list as many words as you can that are related to housing.

DIÁLOGO

En la universidad

NEW VOCABULARY: celebrar; el cumpleaños

Los amigos de David en Eau Claire conversan en la cafetería.

LUIS: Vamos a hacer una fiesta esta noche para celebrar el cumpleaños de Tomás.

CARMEN: ¿Dónde? ¿En tu apartamento, Luis?

LUIS: No. Vamos a la casa de Jorge y Joaquín.

NEW VOCABULARY: pasar por, sales, traer, venir; la casa particular, la residencia; conmigo, contigo

MARISOL: ¿Alfonsina, a qué hora sales para la fiesta hoy?

ALFONSINA: Salgo de la residencia a las cuatro. Pero primero tengo que pasar por la biblioteca. ¿Quieres venir conmigo a la biblioteca?

MARISOL: Voy contigo a la fiesta, pero a la biblioteca, no. Quiero pasar por la oficina de mi profesora de filosofía porque le debo un trabajo escrito.[1]

———————————————————————

TOMÁS: Oye, Luisa. Tu esposo y tus padres viven en Miami, ¿no? ¿Tienes otros parientes que viven en los EE. UU.?

LUISA: Sí. Mis tíos viven en la Florida también.

TOMÁS: ¿Viven ellos en una casa particular?

LUISA: No. Viven en un condominio. Mañana voy a traerte las fotos que sacamos[2] el verano pasado.[3]

[1]trabajo... *paper, report*   [2]*we took*   [3]*last*

PREPARATION: Review the identity of the characters in the drawing and ask where they are. Ask students to identify objects and clothing in the drawing.

De inmediato

1. ¿Quién celebra hoy su cumpleaños?
2. ¿Dónde van a celebrar el cumpleaños?
3. ¿A qué hora sale Alfonsina de la residencia?
4. ¿Va a pasar Alfonsina por la librería o por la biblioteca?
5. ¿Dónde tienen un condominio los tíos de Luisa?
6. ¿Cuándo va a traer Luisa las fotos?

OPTIONAL: Make statements about characters in the dialogue. Ask students to tell you to whom they refer. **Viven en un condominio.** → **los tíos de Luisa.**

A ti te toca

¿Dónde o cómo celebras los siguientes eventos?

EJEMPLO: mi cumpleaños →   Celebro mi cumpleaños con una fiesta.
               o No celebro mi cumpleaños.

con mis amigos   en la sala de clase
con mis padres   en mi casa/condominio/
con un *picnic*   apartamento/residencia
con una fiesta   en un restaurante

NEW VOCABULARY: el fin, el *picnic*

1. mi cumpleaños
2. mi aniversario de bodas[1]
3. el fin de semestre/trimestre
4. la Navidad[2]

[1]aniversario... *wedding anniversary*   [2]*Christmas*

La vivienda

NEW VOCABULARY: el piso

Faceta cultural

In many areas of the Hispanic world, new houses vary in style from those typically found in the United States. But apartments (**apartamentos**), flats (**pisos**), and condominiums (**condominios**), the types of housing in which many people in the Hispanic world live, are similar in style and arrangement to those in many

areas of the United States. It is interesting that the condominium, which has only recently become popular in the United States, has been common in the Hispanic world for centuries. The existence of such "modern" housing developments is frequently an indication of economic growth, but unlike the residents in many cities of the United States, Hispanic city dwellers do not abandon older neighborhoods, especially in downtown areas. Instead, these neighborhoods are frequently coveted as prestigious housing areas.

Because of the prevalence of **apartamentos** or **pisos,** the private or single-family home is not as common in Hispanic cities as it is in the United States. People with middle to high incomes, however, often own a country home, or **casa de campo,** that they use on weekends or during vacations.

SUGGESTION: Comment that a society that prizes its private space places less importance on public space. Contrast the relative importance of parks and plazas in Hispanic countries with the relative importance of private homes in the United States.

FOLLOW-UP: Ask students to interview a student from another country or someone in the community who has lived abroad about how housing differs between the two countries.

PREPARATION: Ask students to list the kinds of dwellings referred to in previous dialogues.
COMPREHENSION: Use a transparency of the drawing without labels on the overhead and ask students to name the places you point to.

VOCABULARIO

Las viviendas

la colonia

el condominio

una casa particular

el vecino

la residencia

BROWN HALL

el apartamento

el coche

Actividad

VARIATION: Use questions 1, 2, 4, and 5 as the basis for a **mini-encuesta**.

NEW VOCABULARY: me/te gusta

¿Dónde vives? With a classmate, take turns asking and answering the following questions about your living situations.

1. ¿Prefieres vivir en una casa, en un apartamento o en una residencia?
2. ¿En qué tipo de vivienda vives tú?
3. ¿Dónde vive la mayoría[1] de los estudiantes de tu universidad?
4. ¿Te gusta la colonia donde vives?
5. ¿Hay tiendas cerca de tu casa?
6. ¿Viven muchas personas en apartamentos en esta ciudad?

[1] *majority*

7. ¿Dónde hay muchos condominios en esta ciudad? ¿en el centro o en las afueras? ¿al norte, al sur, al este o al oeste?

8. ¿Vive tu familia en una casa, un condominio o en un apartamento? ¿Cómo es la casa (el condominio / el apartamento) de tu familia?

NEW VOCABULARY: el este, el oeste

Algunos verbos irregulares

PREPARATION: Read the captions, emphasizing the pronunciation of irregular verb forms and pantomiming meaning if necessary. Read the captions again, noting the infinitive on the board. Ask what these verbs have in common with the verb **tener**.

Las actividades de Jorge

NEW VOCABULARY: hago, oigo, pongo la mesa; la verdad; siempre, temprano

«**Salgo** de casa temprano.»

«**Traigo** los libros a clase todos los días.»

«Siempre **hago** la tarea.»

«Siempre les* **digo** la verdad a mis amigos.»

«**Vengo** de la universidad a las cinco.»

«No **oigo** bien porque escucho música.»

«**Pongo** la mesa todas las noches.»

---

*The pronouns **le** and **les** are often used with **dar** and **decir** to indicate to whom something is given or said.

Actividades

SUGGESTION: Refer students to **Las actividades de Jorge** for the **yo** forms of these verbs.

Ⓐ **Comparaciones: Luisa y yo.** Compare yourself with Luisa.

EJEMPLO: Luisa tiene una hija. → Yo también tengo una hija.
o Yo no tengo una hija. Tengo un hijo.

1. Luisa sale para la universidad a las siete de la mañana.
2. Luisa viene a clase todos los días.
3. Luisa trae la mochila a clase.
4. Luisa hace la tarea todos los días.
5. Luisa les* dice la verdad a sus amigas.
6. Luisa oye bien.
7. Luisa pone la mesa antes de comer.

PREPARATION: Read the captions, emphasizing the pronunciation of irregular verb forms and pantomiming meaning if necessary. Read the captions again, noting the infinitive on the board.

Las actividades de Joaquín

«Les* **doy** regalos a mis primos.»

NEW VOCABULARY: doy, sé; los regalos, la televisión

«En clase, no **sé** todas las respuestas.»

«**Veo** televisión todas las noches.»

SUGGESTION: Refer students to **Las actividades de Joaquín** for the **yo** forms of these verbs.

Ⓑ **Más comparaciones entre Luisa y yo.** Now compare yourself to Luisa again.

1. Luisa ve la televisión todas las noches.
2. Luisa les* da regalos a sus profesores.
3. Luisa sabe todas las respuestas.

SUGGESTION: Have students work with a partner. Both students should give a response for each item.

Ⓒ **¿Qué hacemos en la clase?** Rank the activities from the most to the least necessary to do in order to succeed in school. Then indicate which ones you and your classmates do in class and which you do at home.

EJEMPLO: oír al instructor (a la instructora) →
Oímos al instructor (a la instructora) en la sala de clase.

NEW VOCABULARY: las mentiras, los pies; a tiempo

_____ hacer la tarea
_____ venir a tiempo
_____ saber las respuestas
_____ poner los libros en el pupitre
_____ darle dinero a la profesora
(al profesor) (Le...)

_____ decir mentiras
_____ oír música
_____ ver televisión

---

*Note again the pronouns **le** and **les** are often used with **dar** and **decir** to indicate to whom something is given or said.

SUGGESTION: Point out the verbs with only an irregular **yo** form and those with other irregularities. Have students give you the forms of each verb. Then, ask a series of personalized questions to help students remember the verbs. **(Siempre traigo mi libro de español a clase. ¿Y tú, ___? ¿Siempre traes tu libro de español a clase?)**

Las viviendas   ●   **111**

Some verbs with irregular *yo* forms

"only yo cambia"

dar *to give*	doy, das, da...
saber *to know*	sé, sabes, sabe...
ver *to see*	veo, ves, ve...
hacer *to do; to make*	hago, haces, hace...
poner *to put, place*	pongo, pones, pone...
salir *to leave*	salgo, sales, sale...
traer *to bring*	traigo, traes, trae...

otros forms

decir *to say, tell*   digo, dices, dice, decimos, decís, dicen
oír *to hear*   oigo, oyes, oye, oímos, oís, oyen
venir *to come*   vengo, vienes, viene, venimos, venís, vienen

Several verbs have irregular **yo** forms, although their other forms are regular. **Decir, venir,** and **oír** have irregular **yo** forms as well as other stem or spelling changes.

Se alquilan cuartos

PREPARATION: Ask students to focus on the drawing and the dialogue introduction. Ask questions about the drawing and the dialogue introduction. **(¿Quién es la Sra. Santos? ¿Cómo es su casa? ¿A quiénes alquila cuartos?)**

DIÁLOGO

David y Elena viajan con el Sr. Cardoza a Guanajuato para visitar a la Sra. Santos, la hermana del Sr. Cardoza. La Sra. Santos vive en una casa enorme y alquila[1] cuartos* a los estudiantes de la Universidad de Guanajuato.

ELENA: ¡Qué bonita es su casa, Sra. Santos!
LA SRA. SANTOS: Bueno, es vieja pero cómoda.
DAVID: Las alcobas son muy grandes.
LA SRA. SANTOS: Pues, los estudiantes que vienen aquí para estudiar quieren tener mucho espacio.[2]
ELENA: Sí, y también prefieren los armarios grandes, ¿no es verdad?

NEW VOCABULARY: profieren; las alcobas, los armarios, los cuartos; cómoda, enorme

[1]*rents*   [2]*space*

---

1. En la opinión de Elena, ¿cómo es la casa?
   a. grande   **b.** bonita   **c.** cómoda
2. Y en la opinión de la Sra. Santos, ¿cómo es?
   a. grande   **b.** bonita   **c.** cómoda
3. ¿Cómo son las alcobas?
   a. grandes   **b.** bonitas   **c.** cómodas

De inmediato

---

*There are many words for *bedroom* in Spanish. Depending on the country that one visits, it may be called **la alcoba, el cuarto, la habitación, la recámara,** or **el dormitorio.** (Remember that a college or university *dormitory* is **una residencia** in Spanish.)

4. ¿Quiénes prefieren tener mucho espacio?
    a. David y Elena **b.** los Santos **c.** los estudiantes

5. ¿Qué prefieren también?
    a. la cocina grande **b.** el patio grande **c.** los armarios grandes

NEW VOCABULARY: la cocina, el patio

A ti te toca

NEW VOCABULARY: las alfombras, la cama, las cortinas, la cómoda, la mesita, las paredes
OPTIONAL: Ask students to use Sra. Santos's second line to tell what students want in a room at a residence hall or apartment. (**Los estudiantes que vienen aquí para estudiar quieren armarios grandes.**)

Make several statements about the bedrooms in a house you like, using the words provided when appropriate.

las alcobas	la cama	la cómoda
las alfombras	las cortinas	la mesita
los armarios	los colores	las paredes

EJEMPLOS: La alfombra es bonita.
              Las alcobas son cómodas.

DIÁLOGO

En la universidad

NEW VOCABULARY: almuerzas, desayunar, piensas, se reúnen; el horno de microondas, la lavadora, el lavaplatos, la sala, la secadora, los sillones, los sofás, el sótano; las veces; hispanos
PREPARATION: Ask students, working in small groups, to prepare a list of questions about the drawing and the dialogue introduction. Let them call on other students to answer the questions.

Los amigos de David conversan en la biblioteca.

MARÍA: ¿Almuerzas en la cafetería hoy, Jorge?
JORGE: No, a veces como allí. Pero para desayunar y almorzar, prefiero comer en un restaurante en el centro.

ALFONSINA: Oye, Joaquín. Los hispanos del Club Internacional se reúnen el martes en casa del profesor Brewer.
JOAQUÍN: ¿De veras? Pero somos muchos.
ALFONSINA: No hay problema. La sala de su casa es enorme; tiene dos sofás grandes y no sé cuántos sillones.

TOMÁS: ¿En qué piensas, Luisa?
LUISA: Estoy pensando[1] en la casa que mi esposo y yo vamos a comprar algún día. Tendremos[2] en la cocina un horno de microondas y un lavaplatos. Y, en el sótano pondremos[3] la lavadora y la secadora.

[1]Estoy... *I am thinking*   [2]*We will have*   [3]*we will put*

De inmediato

NEW VOCABULARY: el grupo

1. Jorge come en... a veces.
2. Jorge prefiere desayunar y almorzar en...
3. El grupo hispano se reúne en... el...

4. La sala de la casa del profesor Brewer es...
5. La sala tiene...
6. Luisa y su esposo van a tener... en la cocina.
7. Van a poner la lavadora y la secadora en...

Ask several classmates where they generally eat lunch and where they will have lunch today, using the following model.

EJEMPLOS: E1: ¿Dónde almuerzas, generalmente?
E2: Casi siempre almuerzo en...
E1: ¿Y dónde vas a almorzar hoy?
E2: Hoy almuerzo en..., como siempre.
  o Hoy no voy a almorzar en... Voy a almorzar en...

NEW VOCABULARY: casi siempre, generalmente

A propósito: Las formas progresivas

"Estoy pensando en la casa que mi esposo y yo vamos a comprar." Luisa's words from the previous dialogue provide a good example of the present progressive construction. The progressive is easily recognizable and simple to use. It indicates that an action is going on at the moment in question. The form of **estar** indicates the relative time of the action (*present*) and the person doing it (in this case *I*, the speaker). The verb form ends in **-ando** (for **-ar** verbs) or **-iendo** (for **-er** and **-ir** verbs) and indicates the activity that is going on (in this example, *thinking*). Use the progressive construction when you want to talk about things that you are doing right now.

> **Estoy bebiendo** una Coca-Cola.
> **¿Estás estudiando** en este momento?
> Mauricio **está escuchando** a la profesora.
> **Estamos limpiando** el sótano ahora.
> **¿Están trabajando** Uds. ahora?

NEW VOCABULARY: en este momento

NOTE: The structures presented in **A propósito** are for recognition only.

The **A propósito** section will appear at various times in this text. It is intended to give you a quick introduction to a language structure used by Spanish speakers that is not formally taught in *Para empezar*. In most cases, the construction and its use are quite simple. You should have little trouble recognizing it and, with practice, should be able to use it with confidence.

3 DORMITORIOS
MAS CASA PARA
INVITADOS

Viva en la casa de enfrente y adquile la otra para ayudar con los pagos. Casa para invitados tiene su propia cocina, baño y 2 dormitorios. Para más información llame a Carlos Martinez o Juan Mora.

CASA NUEVA

3 dormitorios, 2 baños, chimenea, estacionamiento para vehículos de recreación, construida en 1985. Garaje doble gigantesco. Sólo $139,900. Pregunte por Carlos Martinez o Juan Mora.

SUGGESTION: Point out differences between the use of the simple present tense and the present progressive. Only when the speaker focuses on the ongoing nature of an action is the present progressive used. The sentence should make sense with **ahora** or **en este momento** for the present progressive to be appropriate.

Los cuartos y los muebles de la casa

COMPREHENSION: Name furnishings and ask students to list the room(s) where each might be found. Then name a room in the house and ask for one piece of furniture that they might find there.

el desván

el baño

la pared

el dormitorio, la alcoba

el jardín

la escalera

el suelo

el garaje

el comedor

la sala

el vestíbulo

el portal

la cocina

el patio

el sótano

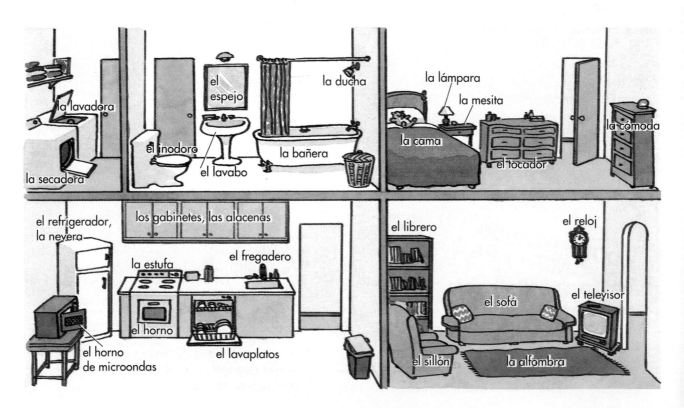

la lavadora

el espejo

la ducha

la lámpara

la mesita

la cómoda

el inodoro

la bañera

la cama

la secadora

el lavabo

el tocador

el refrigerador, la nevera

los gabinetes, las alacenas

el fregadero

el librero

el reloj

la estufa

el sofá

el televisor

el horno

el horno de microondas

el lavaplatos

el sillón

la alfombra

Ⓐ ¿En qué sitio? With which areas of the house do you associate these activities?

EJEMPLO: hacer la cama → el dormitorio (la alcoba)

1. preparar una pizza
2. ver tele
3. hablar por teléfono
4. comer
5. hacer una fiesta
6. hacer una barbacoa
7. poner el coche
8. lavarse las manos
9. lavar los platos
10. dormir

NEW VOCABULARY: dormir, hacer la cama, lavar, lavarse; la barbacoa, los platos, la tele, el teléfono
VARIATION: Ask students to make sentences to indicate where they perform the activities given. (**Hago la cama en el dormitorio.**)

Ⓑ Los muebles y los aparatos. With which home furnishings or appliances do you associate the following?

EJEMPLO: una siesta → la cama, el sofá, un sillón...

1. leer por la noche
2. lavar los platos
3. ver tele
4. preparar el almuerzo
5. decir la hora
6. la ropa
7. el arreglo personal[1]

NEW VOCABULARY: la ropa

[1]arreglo... *grooming, getting ready*

Ⓒ ¿Dónde vives? Interview a classmate about where he or she lives. Be prepared to report to the class what you discover.

1. ¿Cuántos cuartos hay en tu casa o apartamento? ¿Cuántos baños? ¿y cuántos dormitorios?
2. ¿Qué muebles hay en tu dormitorio? ¿en tu cocina? ¿y en tu sala?
3. ¿Qué aparatos eléctricos hay en tu casa o apartamento?
4. ¿Qué cuarto de tu casa o apartamento te gusta más? ¿Por qué?

NEW VOCABULARY: los aparatos eléctricos

Los verbos de cambio radical

CONCEPTO

DAVID Y SUS PADRES

NEW VOCABULARY: pido, quiero; el café, el refresco

«En Wisconsin almuerzo en la universidad.»
«Quiero ir a Guanajuato.»
«Siempre pido un refresco. No me gusta el café.»

«Nosotros almorzamos en casa.»
«Nosotros queremos ir a Madrid.»
«Nosotros pedimos café.»

Actividades

Ⓐ Una encuesta sociológica. In your sociology class, your instructor has asked you to conduct a survey among your classmates to determine their habits and attitudes. Use the following questions to interview three of your classmates. Then tabulate the responses and be prepared to report to the class what you discover.

EJEMPLO: ¿a qué hora / almorzar? →
E1: ¿A qué hora almuerzas?
E2: Almuerzo a las doce.
E1: Gracias.

NEW VOCABULARY: empezar, entender, jugar, poder, servir, soler, volver; la cerveza; por teléfono

1. ¿a qué hora / empezar / tu primera clase?
2. ¿a qué hora / almorzar?
3. ¿cuántas veces a la semana / almorzar / en tu casa?
4. ¿cuántas lenguas / poder / entender?
5. ¿qué materia / preferir / estudiar?
6. ¿cuándo / volver / a casa después de estudiar?
7. ¿cuántas horas / dormir / por la noche?
8. ¿cuántas veces a la semana / jugar / al tenis?
9. ¿soler / llamar / por teléfono o escribir cartas?
10. cerveza o Coca-Cola, ¿cuál / servir / en una fiesta?

Escuelas, Institutos y Universidades
¡Inscríbase yá!
Inglés En harmon hall
¡Sin Pretextos!
AV. INDEPENDENCIA No. 1108 CENTRO ESQ. XICOTENCATL C.P. 68000 OAXACA, OAX.
TELS. 4-21-78 4-20-41

Ⓑ Dame tu firma. Ask various classmates about the following activities. When a classmate answers affirmatively, ask him or her to sign on the blank line next to the item. Do not ask the same classmate two consecutive questions.

EJEMPLO: recordar el nombre de su primer maestro (primera maestra) →
E1: ¿Recuerdas el nombre de tu primer maestro o tu primera maestra?
E2: Sí, recuerdo el nombre de mi primera maestra. La Sra. Jackson.
E1: Bien. Dame tu firma aquí, por favor.

NEW VOCABULARY: la firma, el tenis

1. dormir hasta las once de la mañana los sábados _____
2. volver a casa todos los fines de semana _____
3. almorzar en la cafetería el domingo _____
4. jugar al tenis _____
5. entender francés _____
6. soler estudiar hasta la medianoche _____
7. querer vivir en Italia _____
8. pedirles dinero a sus padres/amigos (¿les pides... ?) _____
9. pensar estudiar japonés _____
10. recordar el nombre de su primer maestro (primera maestra) _____
11. preferir estudiar o ver televisión _____
12. poder hablar español bien _____

Los verbos de cambio radical

e → ie		o → ue	
pensar (ie) *to think*		**poder (ue)** *to be able, can*	
pienso	pensamos	puedo	podemos
piensas	pensáis	puedes	podéis
piensa	piensan	puede	pueden

e → i		u → ue	
servir (i) *to serve*		**jugar (ue)** *to play*	
sirvo	servimos	juego	jugamos
sirves	servís	juegas	jugáis
sirve	sirven	juega	juegan

Other infinitives that follow these patterns include the following.

e → ie	o → ue	e → i
empezar (ie)	almorzar (ue)	pedir (i)
entender (ie)	devolver (ue)	repetir (i)
preferir (ie)	dormir (ue)	
querer (ie)	mostrar (ue)	
	recordar (ue)	
	soler (ue)	
	volver (ue)	

To conjugate any verb, you must change the verb endings. To ~as in regular~ conjugate a stem-changing verb, you must also make changes in the stem of some of the forms. In vocabulary lists, the stem change will always be shown after the infinitive: **poder (ue)**.

NEW VOCABULARY: devolver, repetir

Note : la forme del Nosotros, NO cambia

Turistas de los EE. UU.

DIÁLOGO

Los primos visitan la ciudad de San Miguel de Allende, monumento histórico nacional. Allí conocen[1] a un estadounidense, Roger Austin, y a su familia. Roger es estudiante de arte en el Instituto Allende. Ahora conversan en la Biblioteca Pública.

[1] *they meet*

NEW VOCABULARY: se llama; la forma, el mundo, los ojos, el pelo; distintos, uniformes; de habla española, de vacaciones

ELENA: ¿Tu familia está aquí de vacaciones, Roger?

ROGER: Sí. Yo llevo un año aquí,[2] pero mis padres y mi hermana acaban de llegar.[3]

DAVID: ¿Cómo se llama tu hermana?

ROGER: Jennifer. ¿Por qué?

DAVID: Pues, por el color del pelo y de los ojos parece[4] mexicana.

ELENA: ¡David! Y tú, que eres de ascendencia[5] mexicana, con tus ojos azules y tu pelo rubio... ¿cómo puedes decir esto? En el mundo de habla española hay personas de distintos tipos. El color del pelo y de los ojos, la forma de las facciones,[6] no son uniformes.

[2]llevo... *I've been here a year* [3]acaban... *have just arrived* [4]*she looks* [5]*background, heritage* [6]*(facial) features*

De inmediato

1. ¿Cuánto tiempo lleva Roger Austin en México?
2. ¿Quiénes acaban de llegar a San Miguel de Allende para visitar a Roger?
3. ¿Cómo se llama la hermana de Roger?
4. ¿Por qué cree David que Jennifer parece mexicana?
5. ¿Es David de ascendencia española o mexicana?
6. ¿De qué color son los ojos de David? ¿y el pelo?

A ti te toca

OPTIONAL: Have students use David's first line to ask various class members the names of some of their family members.

Practice the preceding dialogue with two classmates. Then tell your classmates about yourself, using the following model. Be prepared to report to the class what you discover about each other.

EJEMPLOS: Soy de ascendencia... Tengo los ojos... y el pelo... →
(estudiante) es de ascendencia _____. Tiene los ojos _____ y el pelo _____.

En la universidad

En la UW-EC los amigos del Club Hispánico conversan y hacen planes.

NEW VOCABULARY: me acuesto, me afeito, me baño, divertirnos, irme, te levantas, te pones; la cabeza, las gafas de sol, las orejas; rígido, suficiente; antes de; mientras

JOAQUÍN: ¿A qué hora te levantas generalmente?

FELIPE: A las seis y media.

JOAQUÍN: ¿Por qué tan temprano?

FELIPE: Me gusta hacer la tarea en la mañana. Luego me baño y me afeito antes del desayuno, y veo tele mientras como.

CARMEN: ¿Por qué te pones blusa y pantalones para ir al lago, Marisol?

MARISOL: Porque hace mucho sol,[1] ¿no?

CARMEN: No hace tanto. Ponte[2] la gorra para protegerte[3] la cabeza y las orejas. Con gafas de sol para protegerte los ojos, y crema bronceadora,[4] tienes suficiente.

ALFONSINA: Vamos a divertirnos mucho en la fiesta esta noche, ¿verdad Luis?

LUIS: Sí, pero yo tengo que irme a las diez. Siempre me acuesto a las once.

ALFONSINA: ¡Qué horario más rígido tienes! ¡Qué aguafiestas[5] eres!

[1]*hace... it's very sunny*   [2]*Put on*   [3]*protect*   [4]*crema... suntan lotion*   [5]*party-pooper*

PREPARATION: Ask students to look at the drawing and be prepared to give details about it in Spanish (such as, the identity of the people, their location, and what they are wearing).

De inmediato

1. ¿A qué hora se levanta Felipe generalmente?
2. ¿A Felipe le gusta bañarse y afeitarse antes o después del desayuno?
3. ¿Qué se pone Marisol cuando cree que hace sol?
4. ¿Qué recomienda Carmen para protegerse la cabeza y las orejas? ¿y para protegerse los ojos?
5. ¿A qué hora tiene que irse Luis?
6. ¿A qué hora se acuesta siempre Luis?

NEW VOCABULARY: después del
OPTIONAL: Read the statements and ask students which character is being identified. 1. **Cree que hace mucho sol.** 2. **Se levanta a las seis y media.** 3. **Siempre se acuesta a las once.** 4. **Le gusta hacer la tarea en la mañana.**

A ti te toca

Tell a classmate when you usually get up and go to bed.

EJEMPLOS: Generalmente me levanto a las ____ y me acuesto a la(s) ____.

OPTIONAL: Have students use the first line of Felipe's second speech to tell one thing they like to do in the morning, in the afternoon, and at night. (**Me gusta estudiar en la mañana.**)

El tipo hispano

NEW VOCABULARY: hispano
SUGGESTION: Use pictures of Hispanic people from as many countries as possible. Some should fit common stereotypes; others should not. Ask which of the people in the pictures are from Hispanic countries.

Faceta cultural

Many people have a stereotypical notion of what people from different areas of the world look like. For them, a Hispanic person has dark eyes and hair and an olive complexion. And indeed, the appearance of many people from the Hispanic world would confirm their impression.

There are millions of Hispanic people, however, who do not fit this stereotype. People from northern Spain, for example, or from areas in Latin America where there is a strong European influence (such as Argentina), do not conform to the stereotype. Furthermore, there are many native Spanish speakers of African, Asian, or Middle Eastern descent. Their ancestors emigrated to Spanish-speaking countries for the same reasons that people of similar ancestry immigrated to the United States.

El cuerpo

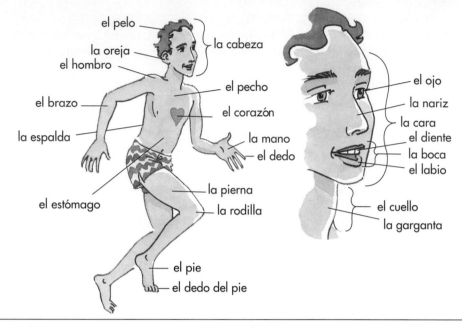

el pelo
la cabeza
la oreja
el hombro
el pecho
el brazo
el corazón
la espalda
la mano
el dedo
el estómago
la pierna
la rodilla
el pie
el dedo del pie

el ojo
la nariz
la cara
el diente
la boca
el labio
el cuello
la garganta

SUGGESTION: Ask students to listen as you pronounce the parts of the body while pointing to them either on the drawing or on a transparency of the drawing without labels on the overhead. Go over each part of the body until students can name them.

Actividades

A **¿Puedes asociar?** What parts of the body do you associate with the following items of clothing? There may be more than one possible answer.

EJEMPLO: las gafas → los ojos

1. los guantes
2. la gorra
3. las sandalias
4. las medias
5. el suéter
6. la corbata
7. el traje
8. las gafas de sol
9. los pantalones

B **¿Qué le duele(n) a Elena?** After walking all day sightseeing in San Miguel de Allende, and sampling many new foods, Elena has several aches and pains and doesn't feel very well. Tell where it hurts according to the drawing and the model.

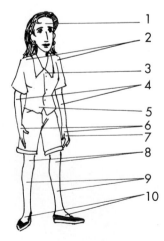

EJEMPLOS: A Elena le duele
la mano.
A Elena le duelen
las manos.

NEW VOCABULARY: le duele(n)
OPTIONAL: Have each student draw a monster and then describe it to a partner, who will also draw it. The monster may have as many/few eyes, arms, etc. as its creator wishes. Encourage students to use adjectives (**enorme, grotesco,** etc.) when giving their descriptions.

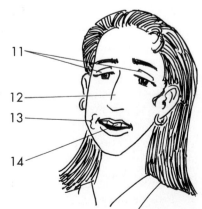

C **Preguntas.** Responde en español.

1. ¿Haces mucho o poco ejercicio?[1]
2. ¿Qué partes del cuerpo usas cuando nadas[2]? ¿Qué usas cuando corres? ¿y cuando levantas pesas[3]? ¿y cuando manejas un carro?
3. ¿Qué partes del cuerpo usa un jugador de tenis? ¿y un jugador[4] de básquetbol? ¿y un jugador de fútbol?
4. ¿Con qué ropa te cubres[5] las manos? (Me cubro...) ¿los pies? ¿la cabeza? ¿las piernas? ¿la espalda?

[1]*exercise*   [2]*you swim*   [3]*levantas... you lift weights*   [4]*player*   [5]*te... do you cover*

Los verbos reflexivos

CONCEPTO

	ALFONSINA	LUIS
7:00	**se despierta** y **se levanta**	duerme
7:30	**se ducha** y **se lava** el pelo	**se despierta**
8:00	**se seca** y **se cepilla** el pelo	**se levanta**
8:30	**se pone** la ropa	**se baña** y **se seca**
9:00	**se maquilla**	**se viste** y **se peina**
9:15	**se sienta** a la mesa y desayuna	**se afeita** y **se lava** los dientes
9:30	**se lava** los dientes y **se va** para la universidad	**se va** para la universidad

A **Alfonsina, Luis y yo.** Compare your routine with Alfonsina's and Luis's.

Actividades

EJEMPLO: Alfonsina se maquilla todos los días. →
             Yo me maquillo todos los días también.
             o Yo no me maquillo.

1. Alfonsina se ducha todos los días.
2. A veces Luis se despierta tarde.
3. Alfonsina siempre se seca después de ducharse.
4. Generalmente Luis se levanta a las 8:00.
5. Alfonsina se viste antes de desayunar.
6. Luis se pone *jeans* y camiseta los días de clase.
7. Luis se peina antes de salir para la universidad.
8. Luis se afeita todos los días.
9. Alfonsina se cepilla el pelo por la mañana y por la noche.

B **¿Qué hacen estas personas?** What are the following people doing?

EJEMPLO: Joaquín →
Joaquín se ducha.

1. Luisa

2. Alfonsina

3. el profesor Ramos

NOTE: Point out that **acostarse,** used in item 6, was introduced in the previous **En la universidad** dialogue.
OPTIONAL: Ask students to pantomime three of the new verbs. The class will guess what action is being depicted.
SUGGESTION: Point out the difference between verbs used reflexively and their nonreflexive counterparts: **levantar (Miguel levanta la mano.)** and **levantarse (Miguel se levanta.).** Ask which verbs students have seen in a nonreflexive form. Verbs used reflexively in Spanish will be listed in the vocabulary with the reflexive pronoun **se** attached to the infinitive.

4. Joaquín y Jorge

5. Tomás

6. la profesora Martínez

Los verbos reflexivos

bañarse *to take a bath*
(to bathe oneself)

(yo)	me	baño
(tú)	te	bañas
(Ud., él, ella)	se	baña
(nosotros/as)	nos	bañamos
(vosotros/as)	os	bañáis
(Uds., ellos, ellas)	se	bañan

Some Spanish verbs are used with a set of reflexive pronouns which indicate that the action of the verb is done to the subject: *I bathe* (*myself*), *I get* (*myself*) *up.* The reflexive pronoun precedes the conjugated form and may be attached to the infinitive. The verbs for many routine activities are used reflexively.

bañar+se

La fiesta de cumpleaños

NEW VOCABULARY: económico

Alfonsina y Luis llegan a la casa de Jorge y Joaquín. Son los primeros en llegar a la fiesta de cumpleaños de Tomás.

JORGE: Bienvenidos.[1] Vengan[2] a sentarse.

ALFONSINA: Tienes una casa muy bonita, Jorge. ¡Te envidio![3]

JORGE: Gracias. Y la casa es muy cómoda. Tenemos nuestro televisor y podemos preparar la comida[4] que nos gusta.[5]

JOAQUÍN: Somos seis, como sabes, Alfonsina. Es más económico alquilar[6] una casa que dos o tres apartamentos.

JORGE: También podemos hacer fiestas en el patio.

LUIS: Es fácil comprender por qué prefieren vivir en una casa.

ALFONSINA: ¡Oigan,[7] chicos! Sandra Nelson me dice[8] que David sale hoy para la Ciudad de México.

LUIS: David ya ha visto[9] las ciudades de Nuevo Laredo, Monterrey, Saltillo,... ¿y qué otras?

JOAQUÍN: Guadalajara, Guanajuato, San Miguel de Allende y ahora la capital. ¡Qué suerte[10] tiene David!

[1]*Welcome.*   [2]*Come*   [3]*Te... I envy you!*   [4]*food*   [5]*nos... we like*   [6]*to rent*   [7]*Listen*   [8]*me... tells me*   [9]*ya... has already seen*   [10]*luck*

PREPARATION: Ask students to work in pairs or small groups and make as many statements about the drawing as they can. Ask for volunteers to make statements about the picture, then ask questions of your own to draw attention to additional details.

De inmediato

1. ¿Para quién es la fiesta de cumpleaños?
2. ¿Qué les dice Jorge a los invitados cuando llegan?
3. ¿Cómo es la casa de Jorge, según Alfonsina?
4. ¿Cuántas personas viven en la casa?
5. ¿Por qué prefieren Joaquín y Jorge vivir en una casa?
6. ¿Dónde pueden hacer fiestas en la casa?
7. ¿Para qué ciudad sale hoy David?
8. ¿Qué ciudades ha visto David?

A ti te toca

Using the dialogue as a model and the following vocabulary, tell a classmate three things you and your friends can do where you live.

VARIATION: Ask students to tell some of the things they *cannot* do where they live.

abrir las ventanas
beber cerveza
cocinar
escribir en las
   paredes
escuchar la radio
hacer fiestas

lavar los platos / la ropa / las ventanas
practicar un instrumento musical
preparar la comida que nos gusta
trabajar en el jardín
ver televisión
¿ ?

EJEMPLO: En mi casa/apartamento/residencia podemos...

123

EN ACCIÓN

Antes de ver

In this chapter you will watch and listen as a series of people talk about where they live and their daily routines. Listen carefully for details. After viewing, share information with a classmate to create as detailed a description as possible of the living arrangements and routines of the people you have seen.

Una carta de David

Here is the first part of a letter that David has written to Tomás, an Argentine friend at the University of Wisconsin–Eau Claire.

Antes de leer

In this excerpt, David describes the typical Mexican colonial-style home. Before you read the letter, review the vocabulary for the parts of the house. Also, reread the **Faceta cultural** on **La vivienda** to prepare yourself for the content of the reading. What do you understand about the Mexican colonial period? What do you think a Mexican colonial-style home would look like? What might some of the differences be between that style and the typical brick or frame house found in most of the United States? What differences other than in construction materials might there be?

Next, read the questions that follow the letter to prepare yourself for the content. Then study the reading to find the information requested.

SUGGESTION: Bring photographs of typical colonial architecture and have students point out the features of the house that are mentioned in the reading.

NEW VOCABULARY: los balcones, el estilo; antiguas

La casa típica hispana

Querido Tomás:

No sé cómo son las casas en el lugar donde tú vives en la Argentina. Aquí en Guanajuato, muchas casas son de estilo colonial. Es decir, son muy parecidas[a] a las casas españolas antiguas del siglo XVIII. Estas casas tienen en común ciertas[b] características. Las paredes son gruesas[c] para mantener fresca[d] la casa. Algunas de las casas son blancas con tejas[e] rojas. Otras casas son de color rosado. No hay jardines al frente de las casas. Las ventanas tienen rejas[f] y están a la orilla[g] de la calle. Si la casa es de dos pisos, casi siempre tiene balcones en las ventanas del segundo piso. En el centro de la casa hay un patio. Desde[h] todos los cuartos de la casa se puede ver el patio, que sirve de jardín. Es un lugar bonito con árboles[i] y muchas flores[j].

[a] *similar*
[b] *certain*
[c] *thick*
[d] *cool*
[e] *roof tiles*
[f] *decorative iron bars*
[g] *edge*
[h] *From*
[i] *trees*
[j] *flowers*

Después de leer

1. ¿A qué se parecen las casas de estilo colonial en Guanajuato?
   a. a las casas de estilo colonial en la Argentina
   b. a las casas españolas del siglo XVIII
   c. a las casas de estilo colonial en el este de los EE. UU.
2. Según la lectura, ¿cómo se mantienen frescas las casas?
   a. con paredes gruesas
   b. con jardines al frente de las casas
   c. con tejas rojas
3. ¿De qué color son las casas?
   a. rojas o rosadas, con tejas blancas
   b. blancas o rojas, con tejas rosadas
   c. blancas o rosadas, con tejas rojas
4. ¿Qué tienen en las ventanas las casas de dos pisos?
   a. balcones
   b. cortinas
   c. tejas
5. ¿Qué hay en el centro de la casa?
   a. una cocina
   b. un cuarto
   c. un patio

Conjunto Los Tréboles

Su Auténtico Patrimonio...

Habitacional y comercial

VARIATION: (La casa típica en los EE.UU.) Have groups of students take responsibility for writing.
NEW VOCABULARY: al contrario, al frente, por eso, por otra parte, tampoco

La casa típica en los EE. UU.

Use the preceding reading passage as a model to describe a typical home in the United States or in your city. You may wish to write your paragraph from a contrastive point of view. For example, you may use the Mexican colonial home as a point of comparison. **Vocabulario útil: al contrario, mientras, o, pero, por eso, por otra parte, también, tampoco, y.**

SUGGESTION: Brainstorm features of the typical American house that are not mentioned in David's letter (average size of house, typical number of bedrooms, room arrangements, houses that have more than a single story, etc.) Help the students with unfamiliar structures and vocabulary. Encourage students to model their descriptions on David's letter.

EJEMPLO: La casa típica mexicana no tiene jardín al frente de la casa; tiene patio central. Al contrario, la casa típica estadounidense no tiene patio central, pero tiene jardín al frente.

El horario de Carmen y el de Celia

Carmen and her cousin Celia have very different schedules. Ask a classmate questions based on the chart. Your classmate will look at the chart and identify the person you are talking about.

EJEMPLO: ¿Quién se baña a las nueve y media? → Celia.

HORA	CARMEN	CELIA
7:00	se despierta y se levanta	duerme
7:30	se baña y se viste	
8:00	se va para la universidad	se despierta
8:30	estudia en la biblioteca	se levanta
9:00	tiene una clase de química	toma el desayuno
9:30		se baña
10:00		se viste
10:30	hace la tarea	se va para la universidad
11:00	toma café con los amigos	toma café con los amigos
11:30	estudia en la biblioteca	tiene una clase de inglés
12:00		
12:30	tiene una clase de física	trabaja en la librería
1:30		almuerza
2:30	almuerza	trabaja en la librería

FOLLOW-UP: Ask students to make a schedule of their own daily activities, including at least eight items. Then have them read the schedule to a classmate, who will write down the appropriate information. (**Me despierto a las ocho.** → **8:00 Se despierta.**)

SUGGESTION: Before arranging the students into pairs, have each one write down two sound and two silly excuses. When the students have finished the activity, ask for volunteers to give you some very good excuses and some very silly ones.

No puedo tomar el examen hoy porque...

Instructors hear a lot of excuses. Invent at least five excuses for not taking an exam, some of which are legitimate and some of which are ridiculous. Then read your sentences to your partner, who will act as the instructor. If your excuse sounds legitimate, your partner will say, "**Está bien. Ud. puede tomar el examen mañana.**" If your excuse is preposterous, your partner will reply, "**Lo siento, pero Ud. tiene que tomar el examen hoy.**" When you have finished reading your excuses, exchange roles with your partner.

EJEMPLO: —No puedo tomar el examen hoy porque me duelen la cabeza y el estómago.
—Está bien. Ud. puede tomar el examen mañana.

VOCABULARIO

Los verbos de cambio radical
Stem-changing verbs

almorzar (ue)	to eat lunch
devolver (ue)	to return (*something*)
dormir (ue)	to sleep
empezar (ie)	to start, begin
entender (ie)	to understand
jugar (ue)	to play (*a game, sport*)

mostrar (ue)	to show
pedir (i)	to ask for; to request
pensar (ie)	to think
• poder (ue)	to be able, can
preferir (ie)	to prefer
• querer (ie)	to want
recordar (ue)	to remember
repetir (i)	to repeat

servir (i)	to serve
soler (ue)	to be accustomed to, tend to
volver (ue)	to return (*from somewhere*)

Los verbos con algunas formas irregulares / *Verbs with some irregular forms*

dar (doy)	to give
decir (digo, dices, dice, decimos, dicen)	to say; to tell
hacer (hago)	to do; to make
oír (oigo, oyes, oye, oímos, oyen)	to hear
poner (pongo)	to put, place; to set
saber (sé)	to know
salir (salgo)	to leave
traer (traigo)	to bring
venir (vengo, vienes, viene, venimos, vienen)	to come
ver (veo)	to see

Los verbos con uso reflexivo / *Verbs used reflexively*

acostarse (ue)	to go to bed
afeitarse	to shave
bañarse	to bathe, take a bath
cepillarse	to brush (one's hair)
despertarse (ie)	to wake up, awaken
divertirse (ie)	to have fun, enjoy oneself
dormirse (ue)	to fall asleep
ducharse	to take a shower
irse	to go away
lavarse	to wash oneself
levantarse	to get up; to rise, stand up
llamarse → *Yo me llamo...*	to be called
maquillarse	to put on makeup
peinarse	to comb (one's hair)
ponerse (la ropa)	to put on (one's clothes)
quitarse	to take off (clothes)
reunirse (me reúno)	to meet, get together
secarse	to dry off
sentarse (ie)	to sit down
vestirse (i)	to get dressed

Otros verbos / *Other verbs*

celebrar	to celebrate
desayunar	to eat breakfast
lavar	to wash
pasar (por)	to go, pass (by)

En la urbanización / *In the neighborhood*

la casa (particular)	(private) home, house
el departamento, el piso	apartment, flat
el edificio	building
la residencia	dorm, residence hall
la urbanización, la colonia	neighborhood; housing development
el vecino / la vecina	neighbor
la vivienda	dwelling; housing

Palabras semejantes: el apartamento, el condominio.

En la ciudad y en el pueblo / *In the city and in the town*

las afueras	outskirts
el centro	downtown; center, middle
el coche	car
el gobierno	government
los pobres	the poor (*people*)
el pueblo	town; townspeople
el supermercado	supermarket
la zapatería	shoe store
la zona	zone, area
el norte	north
el sur	south
el oeste	west
el este	east

Palabra semejante: la capital.

En la casa / *In the house*

el armario	closet
el balcón	balcony
el baño	bathroom
la cocina	kitchen
el comedor	dining room
el cuarto	room; bedroom
el desván	attic
el dormitorio, la alcoba	bedroom
la escalera	stairs, stairway

el jardín	garden; yard; lawn
la pared	wall
el portal	porch
la sala	living room
el sótano	basement
el suelo	floor
el vestíbulo	foyer
la alfombra	rug; carpet
el aparato (eléctrico)	(electrical) appliance
la bañera	bathtub
la cama	bed
la cómoda	dresser
las cortinas	curtains
la ducha	shower
el espejo	mirror
la estufa	stove, range
el fregadero	kitchen sink
los gabinetes, las alacenas	cabinets
el horno (de microondas)	(microwave) oven
el inodoro	toilet
la lámpara	lamp
el lavabo	bathroom sink
la lavadora	washing machine
el lavaplatos	dishwasher
el librero	bookcase
la mesita	nightstand
los muebles	furniture, furnishings
la nevera	refrigerator
el reloj	clock; watch
la secadora	clothes dryer
el sillón	armchair, easy chair
el televisor	television set
el tocador	dresser, vanity

Palabras semejantes: el garaje, el patio, el refrigerador, el sofá.

El cuerpo / *The body*

la boca	mouth
el brazo	arm
la cabeza	head
la cara	face
el corazón	heart
el cuello	neck
el dedo	finger
el dedo del pie	toe
el diente	tooth
la espalda	back
el estómago	stomach
la garganta	throat
el hombro	shoulder
el labio	lip
la mano	hand
la nariz (*pl.* narices)	nose
el ojo (R)	eye
la oreja	ear
el pecho (R)	chest
el pelo	hair
el pie	foot
la pierna	leg
la rodilla	knee

Otros sustantivos / *Other nouns*

la barbacoa	barbecue
el café	coffee
el cambio	change
la cerveza	beer
el cumpleaños	birthday
la derecha	right (*direction*)
el dinero	money
el estilo	style, design
el fin	end
la firma	signature
la forma	shape, form
las gafas (de sol)	(sun)glasses
el grupo	group
la mentira	lie
el mundo	world
el *picnic*	picnic
el plato	plate; dish
el refresco	soft drink, soda pop
el regalo	gift, present
el siglo	century
el sitio	place
el socio / la socia	business partner, associate
el teléfono	telephone
la televisión	television (*image*)
la tele	T.V.
el tenis	tennis
el tipo	type, kind
el/la turista	tourist
la verdad	truth
la vez (*pl.* veces)	time, occurrence

Los adjetivos

algún, alguno/a	some, any
antiguo/a	old
cómodo/a	comfortable
distinto/a	different; distinct
económico/a	economical, affordable
enorme	enormous
ese/a	that
este/a	this
europeo/a	European
gran, grande (R)	large, big; great
hispano/a	Hispanic
importante	important
mayor	older, oldest; greater, greatest
pobre	poor
rápido/a	fast, rapid
rico/a	rich
rígido/a	rigid, inflexible
suficiente	enough
típico/a	typical
uniforme	uniform, consistent

Adjectives

Los adverbios

casi	almost, nearly
despacio	slowly
en este momento	right now, at this moment
generalmente	generally
muchas veces	many times, often
rápido	quickly, fast
tarde	late
temprano	early
todavía	still, yet

Adverbs

Las preposiciones

al frente (de)	in front (of)
antes (de)	before
conmigo	with me
contigo	with you (*fam.*)
después (de)	after
detrás (de)	behind
sin	without
enfrente (de)	in front (of)
sin	without

Prepositions

Palabras y expresiones útiles

acabar de (+ *inf.*)	to have just (*done something*)
al contrario	on the contrary
a tiempo	on time
de habla española	Spanish-speaking
de vacaciones	on vacation
hacer la cama	to make the bed
le duele(n)...	... hurt(s) you (*form.*)/ him/her
me gusta(n)...	I like . . .
mientras	while
poner la mesa	to set the table
por	for; through; along; by
por eso	that's why
por otra parte	on the other hand
por teléfono	by phone, on the telephone
tampoco	neither, (not . . .) either

Useful words and expressions

Otros Mundos

España

NOTE: The detailed suggestions for teaching the **Otros mundos** section cannot be accommodated in the margins of this *Instructor's Edition*. For this reason, notes for this section are in the *Instructor's Manual*.

NEW VOCABULARY: acaba de; europeo, mayores

Hola. ¿Qué tal? Me llamo Carmen Campos. Uds. me conocen;[1] soy amiga de David Nelson. Soy de España pero estudio en la Universidad de Wisconsin en Eau Claire.

Cuando estoy en España vivo con mi familia en Madrid, la capital del país. Aunque somos muchos (tengo seis hermanos), mi familia no vive en una casa particular. Tenemos un piso en un barrio antiguo y popular de la ciudad. El piso es grande; tiene cinco alcobas.

Mi padre es hombre de negocios. Tiene una zapatería cerca de la Plaza Mayor. Mi madre acaba de empezar un puesto de profesora de español y catalán para hombres de negocios europeos, japoneses y estadounidenses.

Mi mamá es de la provincia española de Cataluña. Mis abuelos todavía viven en Barcelona, la capital de Cataluña. Cuando yo era[2] niña, mi mamá, todos mis hermanos y yo pasábamos[3] el verano con mis abuelos en una casa de verano que tienen cerca de Sitges. Ahora somos mayores y tenemos trabajo y nuestros estudios. Trabajamos y estudiamos incluso[4] en el verano.

[1]*know* [2]*was* [3]*used to spend* [4]*even*

Plaza Mayor, Madrid. El concepto español de la plaza central se manifesta en el zócalo de las ciudades mexicanas.

¿Sabías que... ?[1]

- Madrid es la capital de España.
- Cuando pensamos en la España «típica», muchas veces pensamos en Andalucía.
- Barcelona fue[2] la sede[3] de los Juegos[4] Olímpicos en 1992.*
- El País Vasco es una de las comunidades autónomas de España.
- Ávila es una ciudad circundada[5] de murallas.[6]
- España e Inglaterra han luchado[7] por el Estrecho[8] de Gibraltar durante años.[9]
- Los moros[10] llegaron a España en 711* y se quedaron allí hasta 1492.*
- Granada fue la última ciudad que los españoles tomaron[11] para terminar la reconquista de España.

- Santiago de Compostela fue el destino[12] de muchas peregrinaciones[13] en la Edad Media.[14]

[12]destination [13]pilgrimages [14]Edad... Middle Ages

España en breve[1]

Capital: Madrid
Lenguas: el castellano (el español), el catalán, el gallego, el vascuence
Gobierno: monarquía constitucional
Moneda:[2] la peseta
Población: 40 millones de habitantes
Superficie: aproximadamente 200.000[†] millas cuadradas (el tamaño de los estados de Utah y Arizona juntos)

[1]brief [2]Currency

[1]¿Sabías... Did you know that . . . ? [2]was [3]seat [4]Games [5]surrounded
[6]walls [7]han... have fought [8]Strait [9]durante... for years [10]Moors [11]took

---

*1992: mil novecientos noventa y dos; 711: setecientos once; 1492: mil cuatrocientos noventa y dos
[†]200.000: doscientas mil

México y los mexicanos

NOTE: See the *Instructor's Manual* for suggestions on teaching **México y los mexicanos**.

NEW VOCABULARY: los habitantes, los hoteles, los restaurantes; millones; gigantesca; tanto

De viaje: México, Distrito Federal (D.F.)

La Ciudad de México, la ciudad más poblada[1] del mundo, tiene más de veinte millones de habitantes. Esta ciudad gigantesca, situada en el valle de Anáhuac, tiene sus aspectos positivos y sus aspectos negativos. La contaminación[2] es un problema enorme. Desde 1989 existen restricciones en la circulación[3] de coches. Sin embargo,[4] el valle que tanto admiró Cortés, muchas veces es apenas[5] visible.

A pesar de[6] esto, en México o el D.F. (nombres que le dan los habitantes a la capital), están los restaurantes más refinados, las mejores tiendas, los hoteles más lujosos[7] y los clubes nocturnos más animados de todo el país. En la Ciudad de México se concentra[8] la riqueza[9] de la nación. Es el centro del poder,[10] la sede[11] del gobierno. Es el lugar de las oportunidades.

[1]*populated* [2]*pollution* [3]*traffic* [4]*Sin... Nevertheless* [5]*hardly, barely* [6]*A... In spite of* [7]*luxurious* [8]*se... is concentrated* [9]*wealth* [10]*power* [11]*seat*

La contaminación es uno de los problemas más graves que sufre la sobrepoblada Ciudad de México, D.F.

Perspectivas de México: La ciudad y sus habitantes

Cuando una persona vive en una ciudad de más de veinte millones de habitantes, ¿qué efecto tiene en su perspectiva de la vida? ¿Es esta persona más realista? ¿más pesimista? ¿más optimista? En México, las ciudades (la población urbana) se asocian[1] con el desarrollo,[2] el alfabetismo,[3] mejor educación y altos ingresos.[4] El campo (la población rural) se asocia con la tradición (en este caso, con la pobreza[5] y el atraso[6] del país), el analfabetismo,[7] la baja escolaridad[8] y un nivel[9] de ingresos muy bajo.

En una encuesta realizada[10] en México, se hizo[11] una serie de preguntas a más de 3.500 personas de distintos grupos y se vio[12] que había[13] mucha diferencia de opinión. Una de las preguntas era:[14] «¿Cuáles son los factores necesarios para triunfar en la vida?» En general, los mexicanos estaban de acuerdo[15] en que los tres factores más importantes son:

una buena educación (24%)
la inteligencia (20%)
el trabajo duro[16] (14%).

Pero, si se comparan[17] los resultados de la encuesta entre la gente de la ciudad y la gente del campo, se ve[18] que tienen perspectivas diferentes.

POBLACIÓN URBANA	POBLACIÓN RURAL
buena educación	buena educación
inteligencia	inteligencia
trabajo duro	buena suerte[21]
relaciones personales	trabajo duro
salud[19]	posición
buena suerte	económica
posición económica	relaciones
intrepidez[20]	personales
posición social	salud
creatividad	posición social
falta de escrúpulos	intrepidez
	creatividad
	falta de escrúpulos

Las personas que visitan la capital mexicana pueden escoger entre todo tipo de hospedaje.

La gente del campo da más importancia a los factores que la persona no puede controlar (la buena suerte, la posición económica y la posición social) y un poco menos importancia a los factores como el trabajo duro y la intrepidez que la persona sí puede controlar. Quizás se puede decir que la población rural es más fatalista que la urbana en cuanto a su actitud[22] hacia lo que[23] se necesita para triunfar en la vida.

[1]se... are associated [2]development, progress [3]literacy [4]income [5]poverty [6]backwardness [7]illiteracy [8]level of education [9]level [10]carried out [11]was asked [12]se... it was seen [13]there was [14]was [15]estaban... agreed [16]hard [17]se... are compared [18]se... one sees [19]health [20]"guts" [21]luck [22]attitude [23]lo... what, that which

La vida urbana

NOTE: See the *Instructor's Manual* for suggestions for using the chapter-opening pages.

El monumento del Ángel de la independencia está en el bonito Paseo de la Reforma. Ésta pasa por el centro de la Ciudad de México.

En los elegantes centros comerciales de la capital, se puede encontrar todo lo que se necesita.

En las fruterías de la capital se puede encontrar una gran cantidad y variedad de frutas tropicales.

M E T A S

FUNCIONES

- to use numbers greater than 100 to talk about how much things cost and what year events happened

- to ask for and give directions and addresses

- to talk about stores and other places in town, shopping and sizes, and transportation

- to talk about events that took place in the past

GRAMÁTICA

- the use of infinitives with auxiliary verbs and verb phrases

- the preterite conjugations of regular verbs

- the forms and uses of demonstrative adjectives and pronouns

APPROPRIATE TESTING POINTS:
Diálogo (2), Lugares en la ciudad, Verbos y frases verbales + infinitivos, Diálogo (2), El transporte, **Quiz 1**
   Los números de 100 para arriba, Las direcciones, Diálogo (2), El pretérito, **Quiz 2**
   Diálogo (2), ¿De qué material es?, Adjetivos y pronombres demostrativos, **Quiz 3**
   Diálogo (1), En acción
   Chapter test

En una farmacia en Querétaro

NEW VOCABULARY: las aspirinas, la clínica, la excursión, la farmacia, el hospital, los museos, el supermercado; estoy segura de, quizá

David, Elena y Roger Austin y su familia hacen una excursión a Querétaro. Después de un día largo visitando las iglesias históricas y los museos, Roger pide que paren[1] en una farmacia.

DAVID: ¿Qué buscas?

ROGER: Mi mamá tiene jaqueca.[2] Necesito comprar aspirinas.

DAVID: Si no puedes encontrarlas,[3] podemos ir a otro lugar. ¿Hay algún supermercado cerca de aquí?

ELENA: Sí. Pero estoy segura de que tienen aspirinas en las farmacias.

DAVID: Oye, Roger, si es muy fuerte la jaqueca, quizá tu mamá necesite ir a una clínica o un hospital.

ROGER: Gracias, David, pero creo que el problema normalmente se resuelve[4] con la aspirina.

[1]*they stop* [2]*headache, migraine* [3]*find them* [4]*se... will resolve itself, will be all right*

PREPARATION: Focus students' attention on the drawing and ask them to describe the drawing.

De inmediato

Does the following information appear in the dialogue? Respond with **Es cierto** if the information is in the dialogue or **No dice** if it is not.

1. La mamá de Roger tiene jaqueca.
2. Roger busca aspirinas.
3. Elena está segura de que la farmacia tiene aspirinas.
4. La mamá de Roger necesita ir a una clínica.
5. Hay un hospital cerca.

A ti te toca

In groups of three, practice the preceding dialogue. Then tell each other six things you need to buy and six things you bought last week (**La semana pasada compré...**).

OPTIONAL: Have students use David's second line as a model to ask others whether the following establishments are nearby: **un aeropuerto, un centro comercial, una escuela secundaria, una pastelería, un videocentro.** (Write the places on the board or overhead.) Students can respond **Sí, está cerca. / No, está lejos. / No sé.**

LAS COSAS PARA LA CLASE	LAS COSAS PARA LA CASA O EL APARTAMENTO	LA ROPA
unos bolígrafos	unas alfombras	unas camisas
unos lápices	unos cassettes	unas gafas de sol
unos libros	una cómoda	unos pantalones
una mochila	unas sillas	unos zapatos
un diccionario	un teléfono	unos calcetines
¿ ?	¿ ?	¿ ?

En la universidad

NEW VOCABULARY: encuentras, mandar; el aeropuerto, el banco, la oficina de correos, la papelería, la pastelería, el postre, los sellos, los sobres, el videocentro, la zapatería; algo; excelente; miles; antes de

DIÁLOGO

En Eau Claire, los amigos de David se preparan[1] para ir a varios lugares.

ALFONSINA: Oye, Carmen, mañana es sábado. ¿Qué vas a hacer?

CARMEN: ¡Tengo miles de cosas que hacer! Mi prima Celia llega de Barcelona. Pero antes de ir al aeropuerto debo ir al banco, a la zapatería y a la biblioteca. Y necesito limpiar mi cuarto.

FELIPE: Oye, Tomás, necesito sellos y sobres especiales para mandar libros. ¿Dónde se compran[2]?

TOMÁS: Puedes buscarlos[3] en la librería estudiantil. Si no los encuentras[4] allí, puedes ir al centro, a la oficina de correos o a la papelería.

FELIPE: Gracias. Pues, voy a la oficina de correos ahora y si no los encuentro allí, los busco en la papelería. Hasta luego.

PREPARATION: Review the objects in the drawing. Then, make statements about the drawing and ask students to indicate whether each one is correct (**Es cierto**) or not (**No es cierto**).

MARISOL: ¡Joaquín! ¡Jorge! ¿Adónde van Uds.?

JORGE: Al videocentro. Mañana Carmen y su prima Celia vienen a nuestra casa para ver vídeos. ¿Quieres venir también?

MARISOL: Sí, cómo no[5]... y llevo algo de postre.

JOAQUÍN: ¿Vas a prepararlo tú?

MARISOL: Creo que no, Joaquín. Hay una pastelería excelente cerca de aquí.

[1]se... *get ready*   [2]se... *does one buy them*   [3]*look for them*   [4]Si... *If you don't find them*   [5]cómo... *of course*

De inmediato

Which of the characters from the preceding dialogues do you associate with the following statements?

1. Llega de Barcelona el sábado.
2. Tiene que ir al banco.
3. Debe limpiar su cuarto.
4. Va a mandar libros.
5. Van al videocentro.
6. Van mañana a casa de Jorge y Joaquín.
7. Va a llevar algo de postre.

A ti te toca

Ask four or five classmates whether they do the following activities frequently (**con frecuencia**) or rarely (**casi nunca**).

NEW VOCABULARY: los pasteles, los vídeos
OPTIONAL: Have students work in small groups to create sentences that tell something they want to, need to, have to, ought to, or can do. Point out lines from the dialogues to use as models.

EJEMPLO: comprar pasteles → —¿Con qué frecuencia compras pasteles?
—Casi nunca compro pasteles.
o —Compro pasteles con frecuencia.

1. ir al aeropuerto
2. ir al banco
3. ir a la zapatería
4. ir a la biblioteca
5. limpiar su cuarto
6. comprar sobres
7. mandar libros
8. ir al videocentro
9. ver vídeos

Lugares en la ciudad

Otros sitios

You can probably guess some place names without any difficulty, such as **el bar, el café, el hotel,** and **el hospital**. Others probably do not require too much thought to guess, such as **el banco, la clínica, el museo, el restaurante,** and **la universidad**. How many of the following can you guess?

el aeropuerto	la farmacia	el supermercado
la discoteca	la oficina	el teatro
la estación del tren	el parque	

Un puesto de regalos is *a souvenir* or *gift stand*. What are **un puesto de frutas** and **un puesto de discos**? Some place names are a bit more difficult; others may even be tricky.

la agencia de viajes	*travel agency*	la iglesia	*church*
la carnicería	*butcher shop, meat market*	la joyería	*jewelry store*
		el mercado	*market*
el centro comercial	*mall; business district*	la oficina de correos	*post office*
el cine	*movie theater*	la panadería	*bakery*
el colegio	*school*	la papelería	*stationery store*
el consultorio	*doctor's office*	la parada de autobuses	*bus stop*

la pastelería	*pastry shop*
la piscina	*swimming pool*
la tienda de juguetes	*toy store*
la tienda de ropa	*clothing store*
el videocentro	*video store*
la zapatería	*shoe store*

Actividades

A **¿Qué haces en este lugar?** Match the places in the left column with the appropriate activity.

¿Qué haces en... ?

1.	la carnicería	**a.**	Compro un libro.
2.	la universidad	**b.**	Compro aspirinas.
3.	la piscina	**c.**	Trabajo.
4.	el banco	**d.**	Visito a un amigo enfermo.
5.	la librería	**e.**	Bailo y escucho música.
6.	la joyería	**f.**	Estudio y aprendo.
7.	la discoteca	**g.**	Tomo el sol.
8.	el hospital	**h.**	Compro carne.
9.	la oficina	**i.**	Cambio un cheque de viajero.
10.	la farmacia	**j.**	Compro un brazalete.

NEW VOCABULARY: tomo el sol; el brazalete, la carne, el cheque de viajero, la oficina
EXPANSION: Ask students to create three items similar to those in this activity and write only the actions on the board. The class will try to guess where each action would take place. Accept all logical answers.

B **¿Dónde está... ?** Using the drawing of buildings that accompanies the vocabulary for this section and prepositional phrases from the list below, give the location of the following places relative to another place.

EJEMPLO: la parada de autobuses →
La parada de autobuses está enfrente del hotel.

a la derecha/ izquierda de	*to the right/left of*	encima de	*on top of*
al lado de	*next to*	enfrente de	*in front of*
alrededor de	*around, surrounding*	entre	*between*
cerca de	*near*	frente a	*facing*
debajo de	*under*	fuera de	*outside of*
dentro de	*inside of*	junto a	*next to*
detrás de	*behind*	lejos de	*far from*

1.	el cine	**5.**	la tienda de ropa
2.	la piscina	**6.**	el puesto de regalos
3.	la universidad	**7.**	el restaurante
4.	la oficina de correos	**8.**	el aeropuerto

NEW VOCABULARY: a la derecha/izquierda de, al lado de, alrededor de, debajo de, dentro de, detrás de, encima de, enfrente de, frente a, fuera de, lejos de
SUGGESTION: Ask students to work in small groups to generate as many statements as possible for each place listed.
VARIATION: Ask students to write five sentences that express, accurately or inaccurately, the relationship between two of the places shown in the drawing. They should read the sentences to the class, who will say whether each one is true (**Es cierto**) or false (**No es cierto**) and correct any inaccurate statements—El aeropuerto está dentro de la ciudad → —No es cierto. El aeropuerto está fuera de la ciudad.

OPTIONAL: Have students ask where their classmates go to purchase the following items: **alfombras, aretes, medicinas, panecillos, pantalones cortos, papel para cartas, un refresco frío, regalos para niños, sandalias.** —¿Adónde vas para comprar medicinas? —Voy a la **Farmacia la Ronda.**

Las tiendas

In the Hispanic world, shopping for food has traditionally meant going to a number of small specialty stores. To purchase food for a single meal, for example, one might go to a **carnicería** for meat, to a **panadería** for bread, to a **pastelería** for pastry, as well as to a **pescadería** (*fish market*), **verdulería** (*vegetable market*), **lechería** (*dairy*), **frutería** (*fruit market*), and perhaps even a **bodega** or **vinatería** (*wine shop*). Although supermarkets are increasingly common in larger cities, many people in the Hispanic world still prefer the social interaction involved in visiting a number of stores and talking with friends and neighbors while they make their purchases.

En México

The variety of shops is as diverse in Mexico as in other parts of the Hispanic world and the custom of shopping frequently is as true in Mexico as elsewhere. Markets are a convenient place to shop, as the many booths provide a variety of products and prices. In addition to food and clothing, one can find numerous crafts in every Mexican market. Even the **tianguis,** small local markets held in popular locations on certain days of the week, will carry hand-crafted objects from distant areas. The **tianguis** carry a variety of ceramics, jewelry, baskets, wooden objects, hand-woven and hand-embroidered articles, as well as the famous **amates**: paintings done in vibrant colors and with distinctive designs on thin sheets of wood bark. Larger markets, like El Mercado de San Juan de Dios in Guadalajara, sell the works of artisans from throughout Mexico.

Verbos y frases verbales + infinitivos

CONCEPTO

Sé hablar francés. **Debo estudiar** italiano. Pero **prefiero estudiar** ruso.

Ⓐ Los cursos de Carmen y los de otras personas. Look at the drawings that show what Carmen knows how to do (page 140), and what she should and prefers to do. Then answer the following questions.

1. ¿Qué lengua sabe hablar Carmen? ¿Y qué lengua(s) sabes hablar tú? ¿y Ⓟ?
2. ¿Qué debe estudiar Carmen? ¿y tú? ¿Debes estudiar biología o literatura? ¿Qué deben estudiar tus amigos?
3. ¿Qué prefiere estudiar Carmen? ¿y tú? ¿Prefieres estudiar ciencias naturales o ciencias sociales? ¿Prefieres estudiar lenguas o comercio?

Ⓑ El día de Jorge. Use the ideas illustrated in the following drawings to answer the questions about Jorge, then provide additional information, using the second structure provided. **NEW VOCABULARY:** tiene ganas de

EJEMPLO: ¿Qué necesita hacer Jorge? (No / tener / ganas de...) →
Jorge necesita dormir. No tiene ganas de trabajar más.

OPTIONAL: Ask students to work in small groups and use auxiliary verbs to create sentences that apply to all students in the group: **Debemos estudiar más.** Students should share three or four of their best sentences with the rest of the class.

1. ¿Qué sabe hacer Jorge? (También / querer...)

2. ¿Qué prefiere hacer Jorge? (Pero / deber...)

3. ¿Qué debe hacer Jorge? (Y en el próximo examen / ir / a...)

4. ¿Qué tiene ganas de hacer Jorge? (Pero, como no tiene dinero, / necesitar...)

Ⓒ Preguntas personales. Ask a classmate the following questions. Be prepared to report to the class on at least three of the items.

EJEMPLO: Mi compañero/a (no) prefiere (debe, puede, tiene ganas de, quiere, va a, sabe, necesita)...

1. ¿Qué prefieres estudiar, matemáticas o química? ¿sociología o música? ¿ ?
2. ¿Qué materia necesitas estudiar más? ¿y estudiar menos?
3. ¿Qué vas a hacer hoy después de la clase de español?
4. ¿Adónde debes ir esta noche? ¿a tu casa o apartamento? ¿a una fiesta? ¿a una discoteca? ¿ ?
5. ¿Qué puedes hacer este fin de semana?
6. ¿Adónde tienes ganas de ir para tus vacaciones? ¿a la playa? ¿a las montañas? ¿ ?
7. ¿Qué quieres hacer para tu cumpleaños?
8. ¿Sabes bailar el tango o la rumba?
9. ¿Prefieres comer comida china o mexicana? ¿francesa o japonesa?

VARIATION: Have students write their answers to the questions, leaving the margins clear. Then use the questions for a sign-here activity, where students with the same answer as the interviewer sign in the margin.

NEW VOCABULARY: bailar

El infinitivo con verbos y frases verbales auxiliares

$$\left.\begin{array}{ll} \text{deber} & \textit{should, ought [to]} \\ \text{ir a} & \textit{to be going [to]} \\ \text{necesitar} & \textit{to need} \\ \text{pensar (ie)} & \textit{to plan, intend} \\ \text{poder (ue)} & \textit{to be able} \end{array}\right\} \quad \left.\begin{array}{ll} \text{preferir (ie)} & \textit{to prefer} \\ \text{querer (ie)} & \textit{to want} \\ \text{saber} & \textit{to know how} \\ \text{tener ganas de} & \textit{to feel like} \\ \text{tener que} & \textit{to have [to]} \end{array}\right\} + \textit{infinitive}$$

Carmen habla francés. Carmen
$$\left\{\begin{array}{l} \text{sabe} \\ \text{puede} \\ \text{tiene ganas de} \\ \text{quiere} \\ \text{prefiere} \\ \text{piensa} \\ \text{va a} \\ \text{necesita} \\ \text{debe} \\ \text{tiene que} \end{array}\right\}$$ hablar francés.

SUGGESTION: Review the list of auxiliary verbs and verb phrases. Emphasize that **ir a, tener ganas de,** and **tener que** are set phrases. Ask students to write one phrase with each auxiliary. Ask several students to read their sentences for the entire class.

A number of verbs or verb phrases in Spanish can appear as auxiliaries to add aspects of meaning to other verbs. Many of these can also be paired with nouns, prepositional phrases, and other objects: **Mi amigo va a la tienda (necesita aspirinas, piensa en ti, prefiere café, quiere el suéter rojo, sabe la respuesta, tiene los libros).** Note: Some verbs change their meaning when used with an infinitive. **Deber** (*to owe*) → *should, ought to;* **pensar** (*to think*) → *to plan, intend;* **saber** (*to know*) → *to know how to.*

DIÁLOGO

El transporte

PREPARATION: Ask students the following questions as they look at the drawing. **¿Quiénes son las personas en este dibujo? ¿Qué miran? ¿Qué país ven en el mapa?**

NEW VOCABULARY: maneja, tienes razón; los camiones, las gasolineras, el sudeste, la supercarretera, el tránsito, el transporte; misma, recta

David y Elena piensan continuar su viaje al D.F. mañana. Conversan con Roger Austin en un parque en Querétaro sobre la ruta más directa a la capital.

DAVID: Esta supercarretera entre Querétaro y México va casi en línea recta[1] al sudeste.

ROGER: Tienes razón. Generalmente se maneja más rápido en esa carretera, y hay gasolineras al lado de la carretera. Pero también hay mucho tránsito —coches, camiones, autobuses...

[1] *straight*

DAVID: ¿Hay restaurantes al lado?

ELENA: Sí, hay muchos restaurantes.

DAVID: Roger, tengo otra pregunta. Dijiste **camiones** y **autobuses**. Para mí y para muchos mexicanos son la misma cosa. ¿Cuál es la diferencia entre **un camión** y **un autobús** para ti?

Summarize the content of the dialogue by combining items from the two columns.

1. Al lado de la supercarretera hay
2. La supercarretera va de
3. En la supercarretera hay
4. David pregunta cuál es la diferencia entre

a. un camión y un autobús
b. noroeste a sudeste
c. gasolineras y restaurantes
d. mucho tránsito

Using David's question from the last line of the dialogue as a model, form questions about differences between the following items. Working in pairs, take turns asking and answering the questions.

1. un hospital / una clínica
2. una blusa / una camisa
3. una carnicería / una panadería
4. un traje / un traje de baño

El transporte

Although David's question about the difference between an **autobús** and a **camión** may seem odd to you, it reflects the variety of Spanish words used in different regions to express the same concept. In most areas, an **autobús** is a *bus* and a **camión** is a *truck*. But in some parts of Latin America, such as Mexico, a *bus* can also be called a **camión**. In other areas of the Hispanic world, buses may have other names. In many parts of the Caribbean, for example, a *bus* is a **guagua**.

FOLLOW-UP: Ask students to talk to people from two different Spanish-speaking countries to find out what words they use for *bus* and *truck*.

En México

In Mexico the word for *bus* is **camión,** and the *bus station* is often called **la central camionera**. But terms used for city buses vary, which can be confusing. In Mexico City, for example, buses of specific types may be designated as **peseros** (minibuses that used to take you anywhere along a prescribed route for a peso, but now cost considerably more), **delfines** (express buses, hence the name *dolphins*), or **smurfs** (blue buses).

DIÁLOGO

En la universidad

NEW VOCABULARY: estacionar, hace buen tiempo, le gustan, vengo a pie; la bicicleta, el estacionamiento, el hielo, la nieve, la película, el sudoeste, el vuelo; éstos; antes de, según

Los miembros del Club Hispánico conversan antes de clase.

ALFONSINA: ¿Llegó tu prima, Carmen? ¿Qué tal el vuelo?
CARMEN: Bueno, a Celia no le gustan los vuelos transatlánticos, ¿sabes? Pero me dijo[1] que la película que vio fue[2] muy interesante.

LUISA: ¿Cómo vienes a clase normalmente?
FELIPE: Pues, las residencias no están lejos. Cuando hace buen tiempo, vengo en bicicleta. Si hay nieve o hielo, vengo a pie.

JOAQUÍN: Cuando Jorge y yo llegamos a la universidad después de las siete y media, frecuentemente no podemos encontrar dónde estacionar.
LEON: ¿Hay problemas con el estacionamiento en las universidades bolivianas?
JOAQUÍN: No tantos. Los alumnos que tienen carro son menos. Éstos usan el transporte público o vienen a pie o en bicicleta.

LUIS: Ahora David debe estar aquí, en el centro de México.
TOMÁS: Sí, y según sus planes, después va al sudoeste —a Acapulco— y luego al este —a Veracruz.

[1]me... *she told me*   [2]*was*

PREPARATION: Ask what means of transportation appear in the drawing, and provide the Spanish equivalents. Ask for other means of transportation, and provide the Spanish equivalents for the more common ones.

De inmediato

The following statements are incorrect. Use information from the preceding dialogues to change them to true statements.

1. Celia es la hermana de Carmen.
2. La película que vio Celia en el vuelo fue muy aburrida.
3. La residencia de Felipe no está cerca.
4. Si hace buen tiempo, Felipe viene a pie.
5. En Bolivia más alumnos tienen carro que en los EE. UU.
6. Ahora David está en el norte de México.
7. Después David va al este, a Veracruz, y luego al sudoeste, a Acapulco.

A ti te toca

NEW VOCABULARY: hace mal tiempo
OPTIONAL: Ask students to use Leon and Joaquín's dialogue as a model to discuss parking conditions on your campus.

In groups of four or five, indicate how you come to the university when the weather is good and when it's bad. **Vocabulario útil: a pie, en autobús, en bicicleta, en camioneta, en carro/coche/auto, en motocicleta, en taxi.**

EJEMPLOS: Cuando hace buen/mal tiempo...
Cuando hay nieve o hielo...

144

El transporte

VOCABULARIO

A **Definiciones.** Use the illustration to identify which means of transportation is being defined.

Actividades

1. Es un carro de alquiler[1] que se paga por la distancia que recorre.[2]
2. Va por el aire.
3. Es una bicicleta con motor.
4. Transporta a muchas personas y va sobre una carretera.
5. Sirve para transportar productos por tierra.[3]
6. Tiene sólo dos ruedas[4] y la fuerza[5] viene de la persona que la monta.[6]
7. Viaja sobre rieles.[7]
8. El impulso[8] viene del cuerpo.
9. Es un camión pequeño.

[1]de... *rented* [2]*it travels, runs* [3]*land* [4]*wheels* [5]*strength, power* [6]la... *rides it* [7]*rails* [8]*power, impulse*

B **El transporte aquí.** Complete the following paragraphs, choosing among the options in parentheses to reflect your own situation. Then read the paragraphs to a classmate. Finally, discuss with your classmate the similarities and differences between your descriptions. (Each choice is numbered.)

Aquí, mis amigos y yo preferimos venir a la universidad (en autobús, en coche, en bicicleta, a pie).[1] (Muchos, Pocos)[2] de mis amigos tienen su propio coche y (hay, no hay)[3] problemas con el estacionamiento. En esta universidad se usa el autobús (con frecuencia, con poca frecuencia).[4] (Las residencias, Los apartamentos)[5] están (cerca, lejos)[6] de los edificios donde tenemos las clases y hay (muchos, pocos)[7] estudiantes que vienen a clase (a pie, en bicicleta, en motocicleta).[8] Los profesores (viven, no viven)[9] cerca de la universidad. Vienen a la universidad (a pie, en coche).[10]   (*Continúa.*)

145

En esta ciudad (hay, no hay)[11] un buen sistema de transporte público. (Vemos, No vemos)[12] muchos taxis y autobuses en las calles y (hay, no hay)[13] estación de (autobús, tren).[14] Las carreteras que pasan cerca de la ciudad son (buenas, malas).[15] Hay (muchas, pocas)[16] supercarreteras en esta parte del estado.

VOCABULARIO

Los números de 100 para arriba

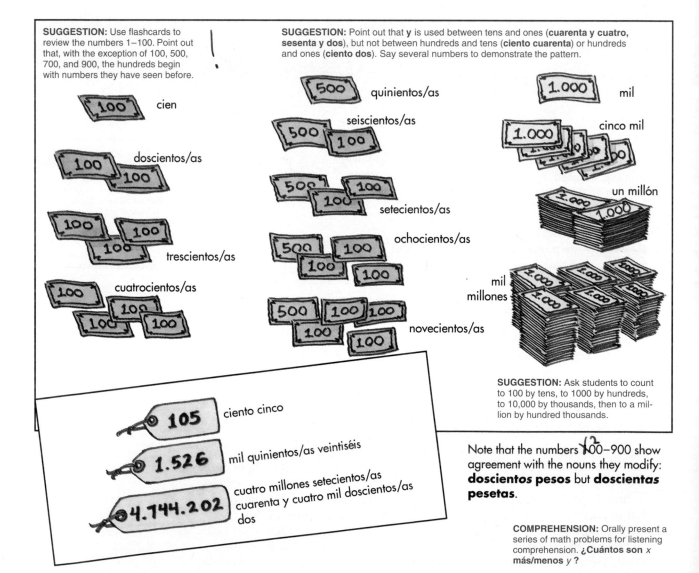

SUGGESTION: Use flashcards to review the numbers 1–100. Point out that, with the exception of 100, 500, 700, and 900, the hundreds begin with numbers they have seen before.

cien

doscientos/as

trescientos/as

cuatrocientos/as

SUGGESTION: Point out that **y** is used between tens and ones (**cuarenta y cuatro, sesenta y dos**), but not between hundreds and tens (**ciento cuarenta**) or hundreds and ones (**ciento dos**). Say several numbers to demonstrate the pattern.

quinientos/as

seiscientos/as

setecientos/as

ochocientos/as

novecientos/as

mil

cinco mil

un millón

mil millones

SUGGESTION: Ask students to count to 100 by tens, to 1000 by hundreds, to 10,000 by thousands, then to a million by hundred thousands.

ciento cinco

mil quinientos/as veintiséis

cuatro millones setecientos/as cuarenta y cuatro mil doscientos/as dos

Note that the numbers 100–900 show agreement with the nouns they modify: **doscientos pesos** but **doscientas pesetas**.

COMPREHENSION: Orally present a series of math problems for listening comprehension. **¿Cuántos son** *x* **más/menos** *y* **?**

Ⓐ El tránsito. The traffic director at a large university is preparing a report on the number of people and vehicles that pass through the various checkpoints on campus each day. Indicate how many of each she must report.

1. 8.539 coches
2. 272 camionetas
3. 539 personas en bicicleta
4. 128 personas en taxi
5. 214 autobuses
6. 17.816 estudiantes y profesores a pie
7. 367 personas en motocicleta

Ⓑ ¿Y el año? Pronounce the following important dates, then connect them to the event that occurred during that year. (If you are weak in world history, there are clues to help you. The numbers in parentheses indicate the sum of the digits in the date. For example, 1995 → 1 + 9 + 9 + 5 = 24.)

1. 711
2. 1492
3. 1519
4. 1776
5. 1810
6. 1848
7. 1898
8. 1904
9. 1936

SUGGESTION: Review the items to make sure that students understand the meanings of the phrases. Review pronunciation of the dates given. Encourage students to work through this activity by eliminating the easy items (e and h, for example) and then making educated guesses about the others.

El escudo de México

a. el comienzo de la conquista de México por Cortés (16)
b. el comienzo de la construcción del canal de Panamá (14)
c. el comienzo de la guerra civil española (19)
d. entran los moros en España (9)
e. el descubrimiento del Nuevo Mundo por Cristóbal Colón (16)
f. el Grito de Dolores: el comienzo de la guerra por la independencia mexicana de España (10)
g. la independencia cubana de España (26)
h. la independencia estadounidense de Inglaterra (21)
i. el Tratado de Guadalupe Hidalgo: los EE. UU. anexan a su territorio tierras del norte de México (21)

FOLLOW-UP" Write several "big-ticket" items on the board or overhead (e.g., **la Casa Blanca, una isla pequeña, un brazalete de oro y diamantes, un avión supersónico, el Palacio de Buckingham, la ciudad de ¿ ?**) Have students ask a classmate how much the items cost in **pelachas,** an imaginary currency that exchanges at 100 pelachas/dollar. —**¿Cuánto cuesta una estación de televisión? —¡Caramba! Cuesta doscientas mil millones de pelachas.**

Los números

Faceta cultural

The system of writing and expressing numbers in many Hispanic countries is somewhat different from that used in the United States. Commas are used where we would use a decimal point and vice versa. Thus the fraction *two and three-fourths* would be expressed as **2,75** and the number *one hundred thousand* would be **100.000.**

A *million* is **un millón** in the Hispanic world, but an English *billion* is **mil millones (1.000.000.000),** and a *trillion* is **un millón de millones (1.000.000.000.000),** or sometimes **un billón.**

Las direcciones

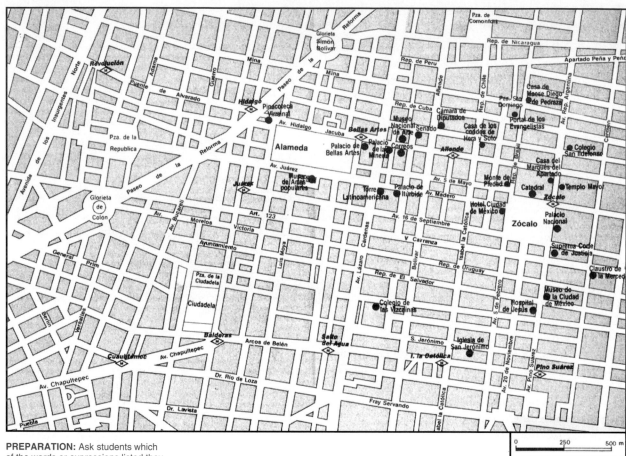

Otro vocabulario

la cuadra	*(city) block*
el kilómetro	*kilometer*
Está (Queda) a _____ de aquí.	*It's _____ from here.*
Está (Queda) a diez millas de aquí.	*It's ten miles from here.*
¿Cómo llego a _____?	*How do I get to _____?*
¿Cómo llego a la Calle Ocho?	*How do I get to 8th Street?*
¿Qué _____ debo tomar?	*What _____ should I take?*
¿Qué tren debo tomar?	*What train should I take?*
¿Dónde debo bajarme?	*Where should I get off?*
Siga derecho/recto.	*Go/Continue straight (ahead).*
Doble a la izquierda.	*Turn to the left.*
Doble a la derecha.	*Turn to the right.*

¿Cuál es tu dirección?	*What is your address?*
Vivo en la Avenida Zaragoza, número 493, apartamento B.	*I live at 493 Zaragoza Avenue, Apartment B.*
Vivo en la Calle Soledad, número 5520.	*I live at 5520 Soledad Street.*
Vivo en la Residencia Wilson, número 452.	*I live in Wilson Hall, number 452.*
los puntos cardinales	*cardinal points*
el norte	*north*
el sur	*south*
el este	*east*
el oeste	*west*
el nordeste	*northeast*
el sudeste	*southeast*
el noroeste	*northwest*
el sudoeste	*southwest*

Actividades

A **¿Dónde están?** Study the map of Mexico City's historical district and the list of prepositional phrases that follows. Write five or more statements that express, accurately or inaccurately, the relationship between two or more of the places shown on the map. Then, read your statements to the other students in the class, who will say whether each one is true (**Es cierto**) or false (**No es cierto**). Call on a classmate to correct the inaccurate statements.

a la derecha/ izquierda de	dentro de	frente a
al lado de	detrás de	fuera de
alrededor de	encima de	hacia
cerca de	enfrente de	junto a
debajo de	entre	lejos de

EJEMPLOS: La catedral está frente al Zócalo. → Es cierto.

La Avenida Chapultepec va alrededor de la Glorieta[1] de Colón. → No es cierto. El Paseo de la Reforma va alrededor de la Glorieta de Colón.

[1] *Traffic Circle*

NEW VOCABULARY: la catedral, el Zócalo, el paseo
SUGGESTION: Prepare students for this activity by reviewing the prepositions of location.

B **Mi dirección.** Work in groups of three or four students to practice asking for and giving your address. Remember that in Spanish the name of the street or residence hall comes first, followed by the number of the house, apartment building, or dormitory room.

C **Pueblo de origen y pueblo universitario.** Interview a classmate about where he or she is from and where he or she currently lives. Be prepared to report to the class what you discover.

SUGGESTION: You may wish to use questions 2, 5, 7, and 8 as the basis for a **miniencuesta**.

1. ¿Cómo se llama tu pueblo de origen?
2. ¿Cuántos habitantes tiene ese pueblo?
3. ¿Viven allí tus padres? ¿tus hermanos? ¿tus abuelos? ¿otros parientes?
4. ¿Cuáles son dos calles importantes del pueblo?

NEW VOCABULARY: la cartera; después; así que

FELIPE: ¿Dónde perdiste la cartera?

TOMÁS: No sé. Ayer trabajé en la librería y almorcé en el centro estudiantil. Por la noche salí con Alfonsina. Fuimos al cine.

FELIPE: ¿Tomaron café después?

TOMÁS: No, Alfonsina tenía que[4] estudiar, así que volvimos a las residencias después de la película.

FELIPE: ¿Y viste la cartera esta mañana?

TOMÁS: No, no la vi.[5]

FELIPE: Llama al cine. La cartera debe estar allí.

MARISOL: Jorge me dice que buscas trabajo.

JOAQUÍN: Sí, pero hay pocas oportunidades.

MARISOL: Ya sé. A mí me costó[6] mucho trabajo encontrar algo.

JOAQUÍN: Hoy fui[7] a los bancos, a la oficina de correos y al hospital. Hablé con el director del personal en cada sitio.

MARISOL: ¿Y?

JOAQUÍN: Nada. Llené[8] solicitudes de trabajo[9] y prometieron[10] llamarme.

[4]tenía... *had to* [5]no... *I didn't see it* [6]A... *For me it was* [7](*pret. of* ir) [8](*pret. of* llenar: *to fill out*) [9]solicitudes... *work applications* [10](*pret. of* prometer: *to promise*)

De inmediato

Complete the following sentences to form correct statements based on the dialogues.

1. ...fueron a la universidad y caminaron un rato.
2. En contraste con... , todo parece nuevo y moderno.
3. ...entre las universidades estadounidenses y las españolas son evidentes.
4. Ayer Tomás trabajó en... y almorzó en...
5. No tomaron café después porque Alfonsina...
6. Para buscar trabajo, Joaquín fue a... , a la oficina de correos y al...
7. Joaquín habló con... en cada sitio.

A ti te toca

OPTIONAL: Use Joaquín's second line as the basis of a Grandmother's Attic activity. E1. **Necesito trabajo. Hoy fui al banco para buscar un puesto.** E2. **Yo también necesito trabajo. Hoy fui al banco y al hospital para buscar un puesto.**

Using Felipe and Tomás's dialogue as a model, tell a classmate where you worked or studied yesterday and where you ate lunch. Mention also who you went out with last night. (You don't have to tell the truth!)

EJEMPLO: Ayer trabajé en una tienda de ropa y almorcé en un restaurante. No estudié y no salí con nadie.

El pretérito

NOTE: The activities in this section are designed to be easy enough that the student can work them inductively without the need for an extensive explanation.

Ayer **trabajé** en la biblioteca. Después **comí** en un restaurante. Y anoche **salí** con Carmen. Fuimos al cine.

Ⓐ ¿Cuándo lo hiciste[1]? Tell a classmate when you did each of the following activities. Vary your responses, using as many temporal adverbs as possible. Use **nunca** to say that you never did a particular action. **Vocabulario útil: anoche, ayer, anteayer, la semana pasada, el mes pasado, el semestre pasado, el año pasado.**

EJEMPLOS: estudiar → Estudié anoche.
beber café → Nunca bebí café.

1. estudiar el vocabulario
2. escribir cartas
3. hablar por teléfono
4. estacionar el carro en el centro
5. comer en un restaurante

[1] (*pret. of* hacer)

Actividades

NEW VOCABULARY: anteayer, la carta, la semana pasada, el mes pasado, el semestre pasado, el año pasado
SUGGESTION: Have students review the section on temporal adverbs in *Exploraciones* before proceeding with the activities.
SUGGESTION: Do all the activities in this section very quickly as whole-class activities, then redo them as pair/small-group activities after the complete paradigm for regular preterite tense verbs is introduced.

Ⓑ En el pasado. What did you do differently before today? Use the models to complete the following sentences. Read the sentences to a classmate, who will in turn report the information to the class.

EJEMPLOS: E1: Ahora estudio español pero el año pasado estudié inglés.
E2: Ahora (E1) estudia español pero el año pasado estudió inglés.
E1: Generalmente corro por la mañana pero ayer corrí por la tarde.
E2: Generalmente (E1) corre por la mañana pero ayer corrió por la tarde.

1. Comprendo la lección ahora pero anoche...
2. Generalmente compro en Sears pero el año pasado...
3. Hoy voy a comer en la cafetería pero ayer...
4. Esta noche no voy a mirar la tele pero anoche...
5. No me gusta tomar café pero el lunes...

Ⓒ Esta mañana. For a project in his sociology class, Jorge had to write down everything he did one morning before school. How did he describe his morning to his classmates? (His schedule is on page 154.)

VARIATION: Have students, working in pairs, take turns telling what time Jorge did things before school: **A las seis y media se despertó.**

EJEMPLO: 6:30 A.M.   despertarse → A las seis y media me desperté.

6:30 A.M.	despertarse
6:40 A.M.	levantarse
6:45 A.M.	bañarse
6:50 A.M.	lavarse los dientes
6:55 A.M.	vestirse
7:00 A.M.	comer huevos revueltos[1]
7:03 A.M.	tomar jugo de naranja[2]
7:05 A.M.	mirar el pronóstico del tiempo[3] en la tele
7:15 A.M.	salir de la casa
7:17 A.M.	tomar el autobús a la universidad
7:35 A.M.	entrar en mi primera clase

[1]huevos... *scrambled eggs*   [2]jugo... *orange juice*   [3]pronóstico... *weather forecast*

D **¿Qué hiciste[1] esta mañana?** What did you do this morning before you left for your first class?

Paso 1. Using Jorge's description of his morning from the previous activity as a model, tell a classmate at least six things you did this morning. Be prepared to share what you learn with the rest of the class.

EJEMPLO: Esta mañana me desperté a las seis y media y me levanté a las siete y cuarto. Luego, me bañé...

NEW VOCABULARY: luego

Paso 2. Of the things that you did this morning, which did your classmate do also? Tell the class what activities you had in common.

EJEMPLO: Esta mañana mi compañero/a de clase y yo nos despertamos temprano. Yo me desperté a las seis y mi compañero/a se despertó a las siete. Nos levantamos a las siete y cuarto. Yo me bañé y mi compañero/a se duchó. Luego, nos vestimos y tomamos el desayuno...

[1](*pret. of* hacer)   **PREPARATION:** Ask how the preterite forms compare to the present tense forms introduced previously. Point out the resemblances between all forms for the same subject and the similarity between preterite endings for **-er** and **-ir** verbs.

The preterite is one of two simple past tenses in Spanish; it is used to narrate or report what happened. You will study the other simple past tense, the imperfect, in **Capítulo 6.**

El pretérito

	trabajar		
yo	trabajé	nosotros/as	trabajamos
tú	trabajaste	vosotros/as	trabajasteis
Ud.	trabajó	Uds.	trabajaron
él/ella		ellos/ellas	

comer			
yo	comí	nosotros/as	comimos
tú	comiste	vosotros/as	comisteis
Ud. } él/ella }	comió	Uds. } ellos/ellas }	comieron

salir			
yo	salí	nosotros/as	salimos
tú	saliste	vosotros/as	salisteis
Ud. } él/ella }	salió	Uds. } ellos/ellas }	salieron

En el mercado

NEW VOCABULARY: cuestan; los aretes, el oro; aquéllos, estos; a ver

David y Elena van a un mercado en la capital donde se venden muchas joyas de plata.

ELENA: ¿Te gustan estos aretes?

DAVID: Sí, son muy elegantes.

ELENA: A ver... éstos son de plata y cuestan setenta y cinco mil pesos viejos, o sea,[1] setenta y cinco nuevos pesos. Los que vimos en la joyería costaban[2] más y eran[3] más pequeños.

DAVID: Sí, aquéllos costaban ciento veinte mil pesos viejos, o sea, ciento veinte nuevos pesos. Pero no eran de plata; eran de oro.

[1]o... *that is* [2]*cost* [3]*they were*

PREPARATION: Ask students about the people and objects depicted: **¿Quiénes son las personas en el dibujo? ¿Dónde están?**

Are the following statements true or false, based on the dialogue? Say **Es cierto** if the statement is true or **No es cierto** if it is false. Correct the false statements.

De inmediato

1. A David no le gustan los aretes.
2. David cree que los aretes son muy elegantes.
3. Los aretes en el mercado son de oro.
4. Los aretes en el mercado cuestan 60 nuevos pesos.

(*Continúa.*)

NEW VOCABULARY: caros

5. Los aretes en la joyería son más caros.
6. Los aretes en la joyería son más pequeños.

A ti te toca

Using the following chart for reference, work with a classmate to identify the cost of various items. One of you will say the current price of an article; the other will respond with the price of the article last year.

EJEMPLO: la aspirina $3 $2   →
—La aspirina cuesta tres dólares ahora.
—El año pasado costaba dos dólares.

		AHORA	EL AÑO PASADO
1.	una blusa	$40	$35
2.	una camisa	$30	$28
3.	una chaqueta	$75	$60
4.	un disco	$15	$13
5.	una silla	$100	$80

Faceta cultural

PREPARATION: You may wish to show students a listing of the current value, in dollars, of currencies in the Hispanic world. Ask students what they regard as a high rate of inflation. What is the highest rate of inflation they remember?

El valor del dinero

The different currencies of the Hispanic world have a variety of names. People spend **pesetas** in Spain, **quetzales** in Guatemala, **sucres** in Ecuador, **bolívares** in Venezuela, **colones** in Costa Rica and El Salvador, and **lempiras** in Honduras. Many countries use **peso** to designate the national currency, but the **pesos** from these countries do not have the same values.

Inflation has long plagued the economies of Latin American countries. In one year, at least three countries in this region—Ecuador, Peru, and Uruguay—had inflation rates that exceeded 50 percent. In this same period, only two Latin American countries, Mexico and Bolivia, managed to keep their inflation rate at 10% or less. The problem of inflation affects the economic growth of the region and may have an impact on the political stability of a country as well.

En México

David and Elena refer to **pesos viejos** and **nuevos pesos** as they shop in Mexico. The new peso was created in 1992 when the **peso viejo** had almost ceased to have any real value. At the time of the creation of the new peso, one U.S. dollar was worth approximately 3,000 Mexican pesos; with the creation of the new peso, a dollar was worth approximately three new pesos. (For additional information on the currency of the Hispanic world, see **Capítulo 8**.)

The currencies of Mexico and many Latin American countries vary so much that, between the time this book is printed and the time it reaches the hands of students, specific information on the value and the fluctuation of currencies will, no doubt, have changed.

FOLLOW-UP: Ask students to investigate one of the following topics and to report their findings to the class. 1. The names of the currencies of other Hispanic countries and the exchange rates. 2. The current inflation rates in several Hispanic countries.

¿Sabes de qué países son estos billetes?

En la universidad

DIÁLOGO

NEW VOCABULARY: la lana, el poliéster; en oferta, hace mucho frío

En la UW-EC, los amigos de David pasan la tarde en el centro comercial. Allí descansan y hablan de sus compras.

ALFONSINA: ¿Qué compraste, María?

MARÍA: Buscaba un abrigo de lana porque me dicen que aquí hace mucho frío en el invierno. Encontré un abrigo rojo de lana pero por fin decidí comprar el de poliéster porque costaba sólo ciento ochenta dólares.

ALFONSINA: El año pasado yo me compré uno de lana en oferta por ciento veinte dólares; pero es verdad que los abrigos de lana son caros.

CELIA: ¿Se puede comprar libros aquí también?

CARMEN: Sí, cuando vine[1] por primera vez a los EE. UU. en 1994, compraba[2] todos mis libros aquí. Y todavía lo hago, pero con menos frecuencia. A veces los libros aquí en esta librería cuestan más que en la librería de la universidad y a veces cuestan menos.

PREPARATION: Ask students questions about the art: **¿Qué compró Alfonsina/María/Jorge? ¿Cuánto costó/costaron?**

[1] (*pret. of* venir) [2] *used to buy, bought*

NEW VOCABULARY: las estatuas; éstas

JORGE: Encontré unas estatuas de madera preciosas para mi tía. Es coleccionista[3] de estatuas. Costaron trescientos dólares la pareja,[4] que parece mucho, pero sé que estatuas como éstas no se encuentran en mi país.

TOMÁS: Tienes razón. Esta tienda vende sólo artículos hechos a mano[5] en este estado.

[3]*collector* [4]*pair* [5]*hechos... handcrafted*

De inmediato

Which of the characters from the dialogue do you associate with the following statements?

1. Buscaba un abrigo de lana.
2. Compró un abrigo de lana.
3. Compró un abrigo de poliéster.
4. Compró dos estatuas de madera.
5. Sabe que la tienda vende sólo productos hechos a mano en Wisconsin.

A ti te toca

OPTIONAL: Ask students to use Jorge's line about his aunt to tell a partner what someone in your family collects (books, cassettes, coins [**monedas**], etc.). Use **nadie** if no one collects these items.

Using Carmen's line from the dialogue as a model, tell your partner two items that sometimes cost more in the university bookstore than in the supermarket and two that sometimes cost less. (Remember that the word for *nothing* in Spanish is **nada**.) **Vocabulario útil: la aspirina, los bolígrafos, los cuadernos, las gafas de sol, los lápices, los libros, el papel, las postales, ¿ ?**

NOTE: The structures presented in **A propósito** are for recognition only.
NEW VOCABULARY: ¿Cómo se dice... ?
SUGGESTION: Ask students to find other models of the impersonal **se** in the dialogues. Ask a series of questions using the impersonal **se** construction: **¿Cómo se dice** *thank you* (*shirt, winter,* etc.**) en español? ¿Cómo se dice** *río* (**bolígrafo, camiseta,** etc.**) en inglés? ¿Dónde se puede encontrar sellos (comida barata, joyas,** etc.**)?**

A propósito: El *se* impersonal

¿Se puede comprar libros aquí también? *Can you (a person) also buy books here?* Celia's words from the previous dialogue provide a good example of the impersonal construction with **se**. A verb in the third person singular can be used with **se** to refer to an action performed by an undefined or generic subject: *one, a person, people,* or *you.* Do not confuse this **se** with the third person reflexive pronoun, as in **Antonio se baña por la noche.** It might help you to remember that, in contrast with a reflexive construction, the impersonal with **se** cannot take an explicit subject, and will always use a singular verb form.

Practice using the impersonal with **se** when the subject of your verb is not specified or all-inclusive.

¿Cómo se dice _____ en español?	*How do you say _____ in Spanish?*
Se lee y se estudia en la biblioteca.	*One reads and studies in the library.*
¿Dónde se puede encontrar buenas camisas?	*Where can a person find good shirts?*

¿De qué material es?

PREPARATION: Review the items in the drawing, making sure that students understand what each one is and what it is made of. Ask students how many of them own the items indicated: **¿Cuántos de ustedes tienen ___?** Reinforce this vocabulary by touching items in the classroom or items you have brought to class while saying **¿De qué es? ¿Es de madera o es de ___?**

VOCABULARIO

| una estatua de cerámica | una estatua de madera | una camiseta de algodón | una blusa de poliéster | una mochila de nilón | ropa interior de seda |

| unos guantes y una gorra de lana | unos aretes de oro y plata | unas copas de cristal[a] | unos bolígrafos de plástico | una cartera y zapatos de cuero |

[a] *wine glasses*

Actividades

A **¿Es lógico?** Look at the following items and indicate whether or not the article described is common, using **(No) Es común** or **(No) Son comunes**.

1. unos aretes de algodón
2. una cartera de plástico
3. una copa de seda
4. un vestido de poliéster
5. unas frutas de cerámica
6. una camisa de seda
7. una mochila de madera
8. ropa interior de algodón

NEW VOCABULARY: la copa
EXPANSION: Ask students to make a list of five objects and what they are made of. With a classmate, students should take turns reading items from the list. The classmate will indicate whether the article described is common or not.—**un bolígrafo de madera** → —**No es común.**

B **¿De qué suele(n) ser?** Say what you believe the following items are generally made of. Then state the material you prefer for such items.

EJEMPLO: los calcetines → Los calcetines suelen ser de algodón, de nilón o de lana. Yo prefiero los calcetines de algodón.

1. los suéteres
2. una mesa
3. las joyas
4. las frutas decorativas
5. un vestido
6. los zapatos de tenis

EXTENSION: Ask students to propose additional items for this activity.

Se puede comprar amates como éste en los tianguis de México.

Adjetivos y pronombres demostrativos

NEW VOCABULARY: (demonstrative adjectives and pronouns)
PREPARATION: Before asking students to look at the drawing, use people and/or objects in the classroom to demonstrate the difference between the demonstrative adjectives. Have students look at the drawing and at the first series of captions. Point out the difference between **ese** and **aquel**. Point out that the distinction between **ese** (*that*—near you) and **aquel** (*that*—far away) does not exist in English.
NOTE: Although the **Real Academia de la Lengua Española** no longer requires accents on demonstrative pronouns unless there is the possibility of confusing them with demonstrative adjectives, *Para empezar* consistently uses accent marks on demonstrative pronouns.

Esta mujer es médica, **esa** mujer es profesora y **aquella** mujer es policía.

o **Esta** mujer es médica, **ésa** es profesora y **aquélla** es policía.

Esas mujeres son abogadas, **estas** mujeres son actrices y **aquellas** mujeres son peluqueras.

o **Esas** mujeres son abogadas, **éstas** son actrices y **aquéllas** son peluqueras.

Aquel hombre es mecánico, **ese** hombre es reportero y **este** hombre es enfermero.

o **Aquel** hombre es mecánico, **ése** es reportero y **éste** es enfermero.

Estos hombres son contadores, **aquellos** hombres son cocineros y **esos** hombres son granjeros.

o **Estos** hombres son contadores, **aquéllos** son cocineros y **ésos** son granjeros.

Actividades

Ⓐ ¿Quiénes son? Indicate the professions of the people in each drawing, following the model.

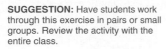

SUGGESTION: Have students work through this exercise in pairs or small groups. Review the activity with the entire class.

SUGGESTION: Ask students to compare people and things in the classroom. **Este libro es nuevo; esos libros son viejos. Esta mujer es rubia; esa mujer es morena.**

EJEMPLO: Estas mujeres son abogadas, esa mujer es mecánica y aquella mujer es enfermera.

1.

2.

3.

4.

5.

B **Me encanta(n), me gusta(n) o no me gusta(n).** Imagine that you are shopping for presents for friends, and you have just entered a boutique that carries items you love (**me encanta[n]**). Of the other places you visited, one store carries items that you like (**me gusta[n]**), and the market has items you don't care for at all (**no me gusta[n]**). Express how you feel about the items you've seen, following the model.

NEW VOCABULARY: me encanta(n)

EN EL MERCADO (−)	EN LA TIENDA (+)	EN LA BOUTIQUE (++)
el suéter rojo	el suéter negro	el suéter blanco
los calcetines rosados	los calcetines grises	los calcetines rojos
la blusa anaranjada	la blusa blanca	la blusa negra
los pantalones de nilón	los pantalones de seda	los pantalones de lana
los zapatos verdes	los zapatos de color café	los zapatos morados
los aretes de plástico	los aretes de plata	los aretes de oro

EJEMPLOS: No me gusta aquel suéter rojo del mercado. Me gusta ese suéter negro de la tienda. Pero me encanta este suéter blanco de la boutique.

No me gustan aquellos calcetines rosados del mercado. Me gustan esos calcetines grises de la tienda. Pero me encantan estos calcetines rojos de la boutique.

C **¿Quiénes son?** Using the drawings that accompany **Actividad A,** indicate the professions of the people depicted, following the model.

EJEMPLO: Estas mujeres son abogadas, ésa es mecánica y aquélla es enfermera.

SUGGESTION: (**¿Quiénes son?**) Before beginning Act. C, return to the drawings that accompany this **Concepto**. Read the captions that use demonstrative adjectives and then those using demonstrative pronouns for contrast. Ask students how demonstrative pronouns differ from demonstrative adjectives.
SUGGESTION: Have students compare **personas** for the mixed-sex groups in items 4 and 5: **Esta persona es dentista, ésa es cocinero, y aquélla es contadora.**
OPTIONAL: Ask students to compare objects they have with other, newer objects in a bookstore: **Tengo este libro, pero prefiero aquél en la librería porque es más nuevo.**

Demonstrative pronouns replace the noun in the sentence. There is no difference in pronunciation between the demonstrative adjectives and pronouns.

NEW VOCABULARY: el collar, la flor

Los adjetivos y pronombres demostrativos

DEMONSTRATIVE ADJECTIVES

this	este collar	*these*	estos collares
	esta flor		estas flores
that	ese collar	*those*	esos collares
	esa flor		esas flores
that (*over there*)	aquel collar	*those* (*over there*)	aquellos collares
	aquella flor		aquellas flores

DEMONSTRATIVE PRONOUNS

this one	éste, ésta	*these*	éstos, éstas
that one	ése, ésa	*those*	ésos, ésas
that one (*over there*)	aquél, aquélla	*those* (*over there*)	aquéllos, aquéllas

Prefiero este vestido. → Prefiero éste.
I prefer this dress. → *I prefer this one.*

Me gustan esos aretes. → Me gustan ésos.
I like those earrings. → *I like those.*

Me encanta aquel brazalete. → Me encanta aquél.
I love that bracelet (over there). → *I love that one (over there).*

DIÁLOGO

La capital

NEW VOCABULARY: a eso de, entonces

Los primos llegan al Zócalo. Ven el contraste entre lo europeo y lo indígena.[1]

DAVID: Esta ciudad es increíble, ¿no crees?

ELENA: ¡Sí! Dicen que es la ciudad más grande del mundo.

DAVID: No me gusta el tamaño[2] de la ciudad pero me fascinan[3] la variedad cultural, la historia y la importancia arqueológica de esta región.

ELENA: Bueno, entonces te van a encantar[4] las sorpresas[5] que tengo planeadas. Esta noche vas a vivir un poco la vida mexicana. Vamos con Roger a un partido de fútbol.[6] Y mañana vamos a hacer una excursión para ver una parte importante de la historia y arquitectura de México.

DAVID: ¿Adónde vamos a ir?

ELENA: A Teotihuacán. Ya sabes lo que es, ¿no?

DAVID: Claro que sé lo que es. ¡Qué bueno! Dicen que las ruinas son fabulosas. ¿Vamos solos?

ELENA: No, la familia de Roger va a ir también. Van a pasar por[7] nosotros a eso de las nueve.

SUGGESTION: You may wish to use pictures of Mexico City's Zócalo to introduce this dialogue.

[1]*lo... what is European and what is indigenous* [2]*size* [3]*me... fascinate me* [4]*te... you're going to love* [5]*surprises* [6]*partido... soccer game* [7]*pasar... to come by for*

1. ¿Cuál es la ciudad más grande del mundo?
2. ¿Qué le fascinan a David?
3. ¿Adónde van a hacer una excursión mañana?
4. ¿Cómo son las ruinas de Teotihuacán?
5. ¿Quiénes van a ir con David y Elena?
6. ¿A qué hora van a pasar por ellos?

In real life, things don't always happen right on the hour. Indicate approximately when you are going to do three of the following things today.

acostarme	estudiar	trabajar
bañarme	hacer la tarea	reunirme con amigos
comer	leer	¿ ?
correr	preparar la comida	
escribir una carta		

EJEMPLO: Voy a estudiar a eso de la una (las dos).

México, D.F.

PREPARATION: Ask whether any student has visited Boston, Philadelphia, or other historic cities in the country. How old were the oldest buildings there? Point out that the pre-Columbian and colonial sites in Mexico are older than most historical or archeological sites in the United States but are of more recent vintage than many sites in Europe and Asia.

Mexico City, a rapidly growing city of more than 20 million people, is expected to have 36 million inhabitants by the beginning of the twenty-first century. Not only is Mexico City the world's largest city, it is the oldest capital city in the western hemisphere; the current capital of Mexico is built on the site of the Aztec capital city of Tenochtitlán, founded in 1325.

Reminders of the conflict between European and Aztec civilizations can still be found even in the heart of the city. The Zócalo, the main square of the city and one of the largest squares in the world, occupies what was once an Aztec marketplace and the site of the fabled Halls of Montezuma. Near the Zócalo is the Aztec **Templo Mayor**. The temple, demolished and buried by the conquering Spaniards, was not discovered until 1978 during construction of the city's subway system. Facing the plaza is the **Catedral Metropolitana,** one of the world's largest churches. The cathedral was begun in 1573, but was not completed until nearly 250 years later. As a result, it reflects the most popular architectural styles of three centuries.

Mexico City lies in a large valley on what was, less than five centuries ago, a lake surrounded by mountains. The spongy subsoil, combined with the frequent earthquakes of the region, has had an enormous impact on the city's buildings. The **Catedral Metropolitana** is undergoing extensive repairs to save it from collapsing because of the instability of its foundation.

Mexico City, like many other large cities in the Hispanic world, is a city of contrasts and changes. There have been and will continue to be tremendous changes in Mexico's capital and throughout the rest of the country. But some values continue to transcend time and survive in the midst of change.

EN ACCIÓN

Antes de ver

In this chapter you will watch and listen to a series of people make purchases and ask for and get directions. Listen carefully for what they are purchasing and how much it costs, and try to remember as many of the details of the directions as you can.

Mi pueblo tiene de todo

On a separate sheet of paper, write about a town—your home town, the town in which your campus is located, or a fictitious town—that has everything. Mention five places in the town and what people do there. Next, in small groups, read your paragraph to your classmates, who will take notes on what you say. Then ask a few questions to check their comprehension.

NEW VOCABULARY: tiene de todo
SUGGESTION: Ask students to form groups to check compositions for errors before submitting them for a grade.

EJEMPLO: Mi pueblo tiene de todo. Tiene un hospital. Allí trabajan los médicos y enfermeros. También tiene un café adonde va para comer la gente de mi pueblo.

Miniencuesta

Paso 1. First, on a separate sheet of paper, write a list of five things you did last weekend. Next, ask your classmates if they did the same things that you did, and get a signature next to each activity from those who answer affirmatively.

EJEMPLOS: Trabajé todo el fin de semana. →   Escribí postales. →
E1: ¿Trabajaste este fin de semana?   E1: ¿Escribiste postales?
E2: Sí.   E2: No.
E1: Bien. Firma[1] aquí, por favor.   E1: Gracias.

Paso 2. Report to the class which of your classmates did the same things that you did.

EJEMPLO: Jorge y yo trabajamos este fin de semana.

[1] *Sign*

Las tiendas

Write a five- or six-sentence description in Spanish of a store or a place in your city. Share your description orally, one sentence at a time, with your classmates. Your classmates will try to guess the store or place you are describing before you read the last statement.

EJEMPLO: Es un edificio grande. La gente va allí para estudiar. Hay muchos libros en este edificio. Los profesores van allí con frecuencia. A veces los estudiantes duermen allí. Antes de los exámenes finales hay muchos alumnos allí.

Una carta de David

David has written the following letter to his friends in the **Club Hispánico** at UW-EC, in which he describes a market that he and Elena have just visited.

Antes de leer

Because the reading mentions what David did yesterday, first review the **Concepto** that deals with the conjugation of regular verbs in the preterite. Next, to prepare yourself for the content of the reading, re-read the **Faceta cultural** reading, **Las tiendas**. On a separate sheet of paper, list ten items you would expect to be able to buy in a large Mexican market. Then read the questions that follow the letter and study the reading to find the information requested.

De compras en el mercado

Queridos amigos: martes, el 17

Aquí estoy en México, D.F., la capital de México. No pueden imaginarse[1] qué grande es esta ciudad. Quiero contarles[2] una experiencia que tuve ayer con Elena y mis nuevos amigos, Roger y Jennifer Austin. Por ser[3] el cumpleaños de la Sra. Austin, fuimos[4] a un centro comercial para comprarle un regalo. No era un centro como el *Mall of the Americas* en Minneapolis. Al contrario, era un gran centro de tiendas y puestos bajo[5] techo.[6] El lugar se llama el Mercado San Juan. Allí se puede comprar de todo. Hay puestos en que uno puede comprar ropa, comestibles,[7] cosas para la casa, flores y muchas otras cosas.

Hay que regatear[8] con los dependientes[9] en cada tienda. ¡Imagínense![10] Intenté[11] comprar unas flores para la Sra. Austin. Estoy acostumbrado[12] a pagar unos veinte dólares por una docena[13] de rosas en los Estados Unidos e iba[14] a pagar lo mismo[15] aquí. Elena me dijo[16] que debía de[17] regatear el precio de las flores. Después de unos cinco minutos, salí del puesto con una bonita docena de rosas rosadas que sólo me costaron unos tres dólares y así aprendí el arte del regateo.

Hay un montón[18] de otras cosas interesantes en esta ciudad que voy a contarles cuando tenga tiempo de escribirles.

Su amigo,

David

---

[1]*imagine* [2]*to tell you* [3]*Por... Since it was* [4]*(pret. of* **ir**) [5]*under* [6]*roof* [7]*food items* [8]*to bargain* [9]*clerks* [10]*Imagine that!* [11]*I tried* [12]*accustomed* [13]*dozen* [14]*I was going* [15]*lo... the same* [16]*me... told me* [17]*debía... I should* [18]*vast quantity (lit., heap, pile)*

Después de leer

Choose the most logical response based on David's letter.

1. David fue al mercado porque...
   a. era el cumpleaños de la Sra. Austin
   b. era su cumpleaños
   c. era el cumpleaños de su prima Elena
2. El Mercado San Juan es...
   a. igual que el *Mall of the Americas*
   b. una tienda muy grande
   c. un grupo de tiendas y puestos bajo techo
3. ¿Qué se vende en el mercado?
   a. Hay de todo.
   b. Se vende sólo flores.
   c. Hay muy pocas cosas que comprar en el mercado.
4. Por las rosas, David...
   a. pagó veinte dólares
   b. usó su tarjeta de crédito
   c. aprendió a regatear
5. Las rosas que David compró eran
   a. blancas
   b. rosadas
   c. rojas
6. David va a escribirles a sus amigos
   a. cuando llegue a Acapulco
   b. cuando tenga tiempo
   c. el doce de febrero

VOCABULARIO

Los verbos	**Verbs**
andar, caminar	to walk
atraer (atraigo)	to attract
ayudar	to help
bailar	to dance
bajar(se)	to get off (*of a bus, train, . . .*)
costar (ue)	to cost
doblar	to turn
encontrar (ue)	to find
estacionar	to park
mandar	to send
manejar	to drive
pagar	to pay (for)

parecer (parezco)	to seem
quedar	to be (*location, distance*)
seguir (i, i)*	to continue
sigue/siga	continue (*fam./ form. command*)
le gusta(n)	you (*form.*)/he/she like(s)
me encanta(n)	I love
me/le gustó	I liked; you (*form.*)/he/ she liked

*__Seguir (i, i)__ has stem changes in the present and the preterite. See *Exploraciones* for more information on verbs with stem changes in the preterite.

Los lugares / *Places*

el aeropuerto	airport
la agencia de viajes	travel agency
el campo	country, rural area
la carnicería	butcher shop, meat market
el centro comercial	mall; business district
el cine	movie theater
el colegio	school
el consultorio	doctor's office
la cuadra	(city) block
la estación del tren	train station
la iglesia	church
la joyería	jewelry store
el mercado	market
la oficina	office
la oficina de correos	post office
la panadería	bakery
la papelería	stationery store
la parada de autobuses	bus stop
el parque	park
el paseo	boulevard, drive
la pastelería	pastry shop
la piscina	swimming pool
el pueblo universitario	campus
el puesto de discos	record stand, store
el puesto de frutas	fruit stand
el puesto de regalos	souvenir stand, gift stand
el supermercado	supermarket
la tienda de juguetes	toy store
la tienda de ropa	clothing store
el videocentro	video store
la zapatería	shoe store
el zócalo	public square

Palabras semejantes: el banco, la farmacia, el museo, el teatro.

El transporte / *Transportation*

el coche (R)	car
el autobús (R)	bus
el avión	airplane
el camión	truck; bus (*Mex.*)
la camioneta	pickup; van; station wagon
el estacionamiento	parking
la gasolinera	service station
la milla	mile
la motocicleta	motorcycle
la supercarretera	superhighway, expressway
el tránsito	traffic
el vuelo	flight

Palabras semejantes: el auto, la bicicleta, el carro, el tren, el kilómetro.

Los puntos cardenales / *Cardinal points*

el norte (R)	north
el sur (R)	south
el este (R)	east
el oeste (R)	west
el nordeste	northeast
el noroeste	northwest
el sudeste	southeast
el sudoeste	southwest

¿De qué es? / *What is it made of?*

el algodón	cotton
el cristal	crystal, glass
el cuero	leather
la lana	wool
la madera	wood
el oro	gold
la plata	silver
la seda	silk

Otros sustantivos / *Other nouns*

algo	something
el arete	earring
la ascendencia	heritage, ethnic background
la aspirina	aspirin
el brazalete	bracelet
la carne	meat
la carta	letter
la cartera	wallet
el collar	necklace
el/la comerciante	businessperson
la compra	purchase
el contraste	contrast
la copa	wine glass, goblet
el cheque de viajero	traveler's check
la dirección	direction; address
la estatua	statue
la excursión	tour; trip, excursion
la flor	flower

la gente (*sing.*)	people
el habitante	inhabitant
el hielo	ice
las joyas	jewelry
la nieve	snow
el pan	bread
el panecillo	roll (*of bread*)
el papel para cartas	stationery
el pastel	pastry; pie; cake
la película	film, movie
la población	population
el postre	dessert
el regateo	bargaining
el sello	stamp
el sobre	envelope
la tradición	tradition
la vida	life
el vídeo	video

Los números de cien para arriba
Numbers from 100 up

cien(to)	one hundred
doscientos/as	two hundred
trescientos/as	three hundred
cuatrocientos/as	four hundred
quinientos/as	five hundred
seiscientos/as	six hundred
setecientos/as	seven hundred
ochocientos/as	eight hundred
novecientos/as	nine hundred
mil	one thousand
millón	million
mil millones	one billion

Los adjetivos y pronombres demostrativos
Demonstrative adjectives and pronouns

este, esta (R)	this
estos, estas	these
ese, esa (R)	that (*nearby*)
esos, esas	those (*nearby*)
aquel, aquella	that (*remote*)
aquellos, aquellas	those (*remote*)

éste, ésta	this (one)
éstos, éstas	these (ones)
ése, ésa	that (one) (*nearby*)
ésos, ésas	those (ones) (*nearby*)
aquél, aquélla	that (one) (*remote*)
aquéllos, aquéllas	those (ones) (*remote*)

Los adjetivos
Adjectives

alto/a (R)	tall; high
avanzado/a	advanced
caro/a	expensive
evidente	evident
excelente	excellent
gigantesco/a	giant, gigantic
hispanohablante	Spanish-speaking
mismo/a	same
moderno/a	modern
orgulloso/a	proud
propio/a	own
recto/a	straight
seguro/a	sure

Los adverbios
Adverbs

a eso de	at about, at around, at approximately
anoche	last night
anteayer	day before yesterday
antes de	before
el año pasado	last year
ayer (R)	yesterday
(casi) nunca	(almost) never
después	after, afterward
entonces	then
luego	then, next
el mes pasado	last month
la semana pasada	last week
el semestre pasado	last semester
derecho	straight
inmediatamente	immediately
por fin	at last
tanto	so much

Las preposiciones
Prepositions

a la derecha de	to the right of
a la izquierda de	to the left of
al lado de	next to
alrededor de	around
bajo	under
cerca de (R)	near

debajo de	under
dentro de	inside of
detrás de	behind
encima de	on top of
enfrente de	in front of
entre (R)	between, among
frente a	facing, across from
fuera de	outside of
hacia	toward
junto a (R)	next to
lejos de	far from
acerca de	about
desde	from
según	according to

Palabras y expresiones útiles

Useful words and expressions

antes de + *inf.*	before (*doing something*)
así (que)	thus, so
A ver.	Let's see.

¿Cómo se dice... ?	How do you say . . . ?
dar la bienvenida	to welcome
de compras	shopping
en contraste con	in contrast with
en oferta	on sale
estar a	to be (*location, distance*)
estar de acuerdo	to agree, be in agreement
estar seguro/a	to be sure
hace buen/mal tiempo	the weather's nice/bad
hace (mucho) frío	it's (very) cold
ir/venir a pie	to walk, go/come on foot
nada	nothing; not at all
¿Qué te pareció... ?	What did you think about . . . ?
quizá(s)	maybe, perhaps
tener de todo	to have everything
tener razón	to be right
tomar el sol	to sunbathe
un poco	a little
un rato	a while

Otros Mundos

NOTE: The detailed suggestions for teaching the **Otros mundos** section cannot be accommodated in the margins of this *Instructor's Edition*. For this reason, notes for this section are in the *Instructor's Manual*.

Tres islas del Caribe

NEW VOCABULARY: atraen; la ascendencia, los comerciantes; avanzados, hispanohablantes, orgulloso; acerca de

¡Hola! ¿Cómo estás? Me llamo Felipe Castro Valenzuela. Soy de Puerto Rico y soy uno de los alumnos hispanohablantes de la Universidad de Wisconsin–Eau Claire. Quiero hablarles un poco acerca de mi familia y nuestra vida en Puerto Rico.

Nací[1] en San Juan, la capital de Puerto Rico. Mis abuelos y la mayoría de mis tíos y primos todavía viven allí. Pero cuando tenía once años[2] mi familia se trasladó[3] a un pueblo cerca de las selvas del Yunque donde mi padre trabaja de bioquímico.

Me siento orgulloso de mi familia y de mi país. Mi padre, Felipe Castro Wu, es de ascendencia puertorriqueña y china. Mi madre, Lola Valenzuela Sánchez, es puertorriqueña, de ascendencia borincana.[4] Mis abuelos son comerciantes. Uno de mis tíos vive en los Estados Unidos, en Nueva York.

Puerto Rico es una isla interesante. Tenemos una selva tropical muy famosa, el Yunque, y también tenemos ciudades coloniales que atraen a muchos turistas. Cuando termine mis estudios avanzados de biología en la Universidad de Wisconsin–Eau Claire, voy a volver a Puerto Rico para trabajar con mi padre.

[1]*I was born*   [2]*tenía... I was eleven*   [3]*se... moved*   [4]*indigenous Puerto Rican*

La Casa Blanca, en El Viejo San Juan, es la residencia del gobernador de la isla de Puerto Rico.

¿Sabías que... ?

- El nombre antiguo de Puerto Rico es Borinquén. Algunos puertorriqueños todavía usan el nombre **borincano** para afirmar sus orígenes indigenistas y su identidad independiente.
- Puerto Rico tiene los ingresos[1] más altos por persona de todos los países de la América Latina.

[1]*incomes*

La caña de azúcar es el producto principal de la isla de Cuba.

- La República Dominicana comparte[2] con Haití la isla de Santo Domingo. En Haití los habitantes hablan francés.
- Santo Domingo, la capital de la República Dominicana, es la ciudad europea más antigua del Nuevo Mundo.
- San Juan Bautista e Hispaniola son los nombres que Cristóbal Colón dio,[3] respectivamente, a las islas que hoy son Puerto Rico y la República Dominicana.
- San Juan y Santo Domingo son dos ciudades donde todavía se conservan[4] muestras[5] de la arquitectura colonial española de los siglos XVI y XVII.
- A pesar de los esfuerzos[6] para diversificar la economía de Cuba, el 85% de los ingresos por productos exportados todavía viene del azúcar.[7]
- Los Estados Unidos todavía tienen una base militar (establecida en 1903) en Guantánamo, en la isla de Cuba. Cuba es un país con el que[8] los EE. UU. no tienen relaciones diplomáticas.
- La Bahía de Cochinos fue el sitio de la invasión estadounidense a la isla de Cuba contra el régimen[9] comunista de Fidel Castro. En español la palabra **cochino** significa *pig*. Pero en Cuba **cochino** es también nombre de un pez.[10]
- José Martí fue un patriota cubano que murió[11] en la guerra por la independencia de Cuba de España. Sus *Versos sencillos*[12] son famosos incluso[13] en los EE. UU. La letra[14] de uno de los versos más famosos comienza: «Yo soy un hombre sincero de donde crece[15] la palma. Y, antes de morirme[16] quiero echar[17] mis versos del alma.[18]»

[2]*shares* [3]*(pret. of* dar*)* [4]*se... are preserved* [5]*evidence* [6]*efforts* [7]*sugar* [8]*el... which* [9]*regime* [10]*fish* [11]*died* [12]*simple* [13]*including, even* [14]*text* [15]*grows* [16]*I die* [17]*to give, present, bring forth* [18]*soul*

Tres islas del Caribe en breve

	PUERTO RICO	REPÚBLICA DOMINICANA	CUBA
Capital:	San Juan	Santo Domingo	La Habana
Lenguas:	español	español	español
Gobierno:	estado libre asociado	república	república
Moneda:	dólar	peso	peso
Población:	3.566.000	7.384.000	10.732.000
Superficie:	3.435 millas cuadradas (más grande que Delaware pero no tan grande como Connecticut)	18.704 millas cuadradas (tan grande como los estados de Vermont y New Hampshire juntos)	44.218 millas cuadradas (casi tan grande como Pensilvania)

SEIS

México y los mexicanos

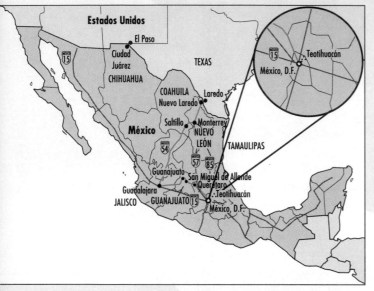

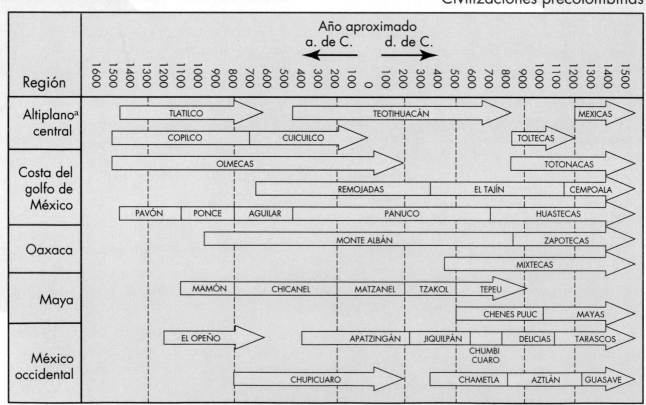

NOTE: See the *Instructor's Manual* for suggestions on teaching **México y los mexicanos**.

De viaje: México precolombino[1]

Uno de los aspectos más importantes de la cultura mexicana es la presencia de una variedad de grupos indígenas.[2] Esta presencia es una parte importante no sólo de la historia de México sino también del presente y del futuro del país.

Existieron culturas en México tres mil años antes de la llegada[3] de los españoles. Algunas de estas culturas eran mucho más avanzadas que los pueblos

[1]*pre-Columbian, before the arrival of Columbus to the New World* [2]*indigenous, Native American* [3]*arrival*

Civilizaciones precolombinas

Año aproximado
a. de C. ← → d. de C.

Región		
Altiplano[a] central	TLATILCO — TEOTIHUACÁN — MEXICAS; COPILCO — CUICUILCO — TOLTECAS	
Costa del golfo de México	OLMECAS — TOTONACAS; REMOJADAS — EL TAJÍN — CEMPOALA; PAVÓN — PONCE — AGUILAR — PANUCO — HUASTECAS	
Oaxaca	MONTE ALBÁN — ZAPOTECAS; MIXTECAS	
Maya	MAMÓN — CHICANEL — MATZANEL — TZAKOL — TEPEU; CHENES PUUC — MAYAS	
México occidental	EL OPEÑO — APATZINGÁN — JIQUILPÁN — DELICIAS — TARASCOS; CHUMBI CUARO; CHUPICUARO — CHAMETLA — AZTLÁN — GUASAVE	

[a]*Highland*

En esta cancha de pelota en Xochicalco hay dos ruedas de piedra por las que se pasaba la pelota de goma en los juegos.

europeos de la misma época. Muchas ya habían desaparecido[4] cuando llegó Cortés.

No se sabe[5] por qué desaparecieron civilizaciones como la olmeca y la maya. Pero pocas desaparecieron completamente. Muchos centros adoptaron aspectos de otras culturas para su propio uso. Un ejemplo es la ciudad de Xochicalco, que está cien millas al sudoeste de Teotihuacán. La arquitectura de Xochicalco es muy parecida[6] a la de Teotihuacán, y la cancha[7] de pelota es casi idéntica a las canchas que se encuentran[8] en las ciudades mayas de Uxmal y Chichén Itzá.

Todavía hay muchos misterios relacionados a las culturas indígenas precolombinas. Pero todos los días los arqueólogos descubren algo nuevo que nos ayuda a entender este aspecto fascinante de la cultura mexicana.

[4]habían... *had disappeared*   [5]No... *It is not known*   [6]*similar*   [7]*court*   [8]se... *are found*

Perspectivas de México: La presencia indígena actual[1]

La presencia indígena en México no es un fenómeno solamente del pasado. En al año 1990 más de seis millones de mexicanos, o casi el ocho por ciento de la población total, hablaban uno de 43 idiomas indígenas. De éstos, casi el veinte por ciento no hablaba español.

Algunos de los indios que viven en México hoy son descendientes de grandes civilizaciones como la azteca y la maya. El centro actual de los nahuas, descendientes de los aztecas, se encuentra[2] en el norte del estado de Puebla. Hay casi un millón de personas que todavía hablan nahua y que usan ropa que las identifica[3] como miembros de este grupo. Los descendientes de los mayas se encuentran en los estados mexicanos de Yucatán y Quintana Roo, y también en Guatemala.

La variedad de grupos indígenas en México es enorme. Es imposible hacer generalizaciones acerca de los grupos indígenas mexicanos que siguen sus costumbres distintivas. En su ropa, su lengua y sus características físicas, los grupos tienen poco en común. Aunque muchos no usan la ropa tradicional de su grupo todos los días, la ropa y la vida de estos mexicanos en los pueblos pequeños y aislados se contrastan en muchos aspectos con la ropa y la vida en los centros urbanos.

[1]*current, present-day*   [2]se... *is found*   [3]las... *identifies them*

Estas dos muchachas en el mercado en San Miguel de Allende llevan trajes regionales de colores brillantes.

173

6

Los pasatiempos

NOTE: See the *Instructor's Manual* for suggestions for using the chapter-opening pages.

NEW VOCABULARY: los pasatiempos

Los habitantes de Tzintzuntzán, en el estado de Michoacán, pasan la noche junto a las tumbas de sus antepasados el Día de los Muertos.

Hay que tener una piñata
navideña
para la posada.

Estos pescadores en el lago de Pátzcuaro, estado de Michoacán, pescan el famoso pez blanco.

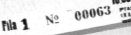

METAS

FUNCIONES

- to talk about your pastimes
- to talk about things that happened in the past
- to talk about weather and the seasons
- to express dates and to talk about holidays and celebrations
- to express your likes and dislikes

GRAMÁTICA

- the preterite conjugations of irregular verbs
- **gustar** and similar verbs
- the forms and uses of verbs in the imperfect

APPROPRIATE TESTING POINTS:
Diálogo (1), Los deportes y los pasatiempos, Verbos irregulares en el pretérito, **Quiz 1**
    Diálogo (2), El tiempo, los meses y las estaciones, Los días festivos, Gustar y verbos similares, **Quiz 2**
    Diálogo (2), El imperfecto, **Quiz 3**
    Diálogo (1), En acción
    Chapter test

Un partido especial

NEW VOCABULARY: me encanta, les gustó, le pareció, pasar (un programa); el fútbol (americano), la mitad, el partido; confundida

¡OJO! In this dialogue, the characters talk about a program they watched last night. In order to describe something in the past and to say what was going to happen, they use verbs conjugated in a past tense known as the *imperfect*. This tense is easy to recognize. The endings for regular **-ar** verbs use **-aba** and those for **-er** and **-ir** verbs use **-ía**. The imperfect of the irregular verb **ir** is **iba, ibas,…**

David, Elena y Roger van a un partido de fútbol. Allí hablan de otro partido que vieron en la televisión.

DAVID: ¿Vieron el partido de fútbol en la tele anoche?

ROGER: Yo sólo vi la mitad. No supe[1] hasta las diez que iban a pasar ese programa.

ELENA: Fue[2] un partido especial. No estaba programado.[3] Lo pusieron a última hora.[4]

DAVID: A mí me encanta el fútbol. ¿Qué le pareció el partido a tu familia, Roger?

ROGER: Pues, les gustó a todos. Pero, al principio[5] Jennifer estaba confundida porque creía que iba a ser un partido de fútbol americano.

[1](*pret. of* saber) *I found out*　　[2](*pret. of* ser)　　[3]*scheduled*　　[4]a… *at the last minute*　　[5]al… *at the beginning, at first*

De inmediato

Which of the characters do you associate with the following actions or feelings?

1. Vieron el partido de fútbol en la televisión anoche.
2. Sólo vio la mitad del partido.
3. No supo hasta las diez que iban a pasar ese programa.
4. Le encanta el fútbol.
5. Les gustó el partido de fútbol.
6. Estaba confundida.
7. Creía que iba a ser un partido de fútbol americano.

A ti te toca

Express to a classmate the sports or activities that you really enjoy.

EJEMPLO:　A mí me encanta el básquetbol. También me encanta bailar.

el básquetbol	bailar
el béisbol	cocinar
el boxeo	conversar con amigos/as
la clase de _____	correr
el fútbol	escribir cartas
el fútbol americano	escuchar música
el golf	hablar por teléfono
el ráquetbol	leer novelas/revistas
el tenis	levantarme tarde
el voleibol	¿ ?

·Los deportes y los pasatiempos

PREPARATION: Ask students to cover up the English translations of the items listed. For how many of the activities can they guess the meanings? After looking at the activities, ask them to guess the name of the categories under which the activities fall. Have them categorize the activities in the drawing.

VOCABULARIO

pescar

jugar (ue) al fútbol

jugar (ue) al boliche

jugar (ue) al golf

hacer alpinismo

esquiar

SUGGESTION: Point out that there is some variation in the terms for some activities: **el básquetbol = el baloncesto, las cartas = los naipes**.

jugar (ue) a las cartas

nadar

escuchar música

Otros deportes y pasatiempos

hacer / practicar / jugar al

DEPORTES INDIVIDUALES

hacer gimnasia	*to do gymnastics; to work out*
hacer los ejercicios aeróbicos	*to do aerobic exercises*
jugar (ue) al ráquetbol	*to play racquetball*
practicar el atletismo	*to participate in track and field*
practicar el boxeo	*to box*
practicar el ciclismo	*to go / participate in cycling*
practicar la lucha libre	*to wrestle*
practicar las artes marciales	*to do martial arts*

DEPORTES DE EQUIPO

jugar (ue) al básquetbol	*to play basketball*
jugar (ue) al béisbol	*to play baseball*
jugar (ue) al fútbol americano	*to play football*
jugar (ue) al voleibol	*to play volleyball*

COMPREHENSION: Ask students, working in small groups, to pantomime two or three sports/pastimes for their group to guess. Then ask students to present the best pantomimes for the entire class.

jugar al tenis

177

PASATIEMPOS AL AIRE LIBRE

acampar	*to camp*
cazar	*to hunt*
montar a caballo (en bicicleta, en motocicleta)	*to ride a horse (a bicycle, a motorcycle)*
pasear	*to take a walk, to stroll*
patinar	*to skate*
tomar el sol	*to sunbathe*
trotar	*to jog*

PASATIEMPOS DENTRO DE CASA

bailar	*to dance*
hablar por teléfono	*to talk on the telephone*
leer novelas/revistas	*to read novels/magazines*
sacar fotos	*to take pictures*
tejer	*to knit*
tocar el piano (el clarinete, la guitarra, la trompeta)	*to play piano (clarinet, guitar, trumpet)*
ver (veo) televisión	*to watch television*

Actividades

EXPANSION: When students have finished, read the name of a sport/pastime and ask students to tell you what sentence describes it.

A **¿De qué pasatiempo o deporte hablo?** Read the following descriptions and indicate which pastime or sport is being described.

1. Para este deporte se necesita una bicicleta.
2. Uno va con un rifle u otra arma en busca de un animal.
3. Se usa una pelota pesada,[1] de 12 a 16 libras.
4. Me siento en mi sillón favorito con un refresco y patatas fritas.[2]
5. Espero un día bonito y llevo la toalla[3] y la crema bronceadora.[4]
6. Se necesitan guantes y dos personas.
7. Es necesario tener una pelota y una cesta.[5]
8. Hay que tener un instrumento con 88 teclas.[6]
9. Hay dos personas, dos raquetas y una pelota. No hay red.[7]
10. Cuando hago este ejercicio para guardar la línea,[8] escucho música popular.

[1]*heavy* [2]*patatas... potato chips* [3]*towel* [4]*crema... suntan lotion* [5]*basket* [6]*keys* [7]*net* [8]*guardar... to keep (my) figure*

NEW VOCABULARY: raramente

EXPANSION: Have students ask a classmate how frequently he or she participates in five additional activities.

B **¿Con qué frecuencia?** Indicate how often you do the following, using **muchas veces, a veces, raramente,** or **nunca.**

EJEMPLO: ¿los ejercicios aeróbicos? →
Nunca hago los ejercicios aeróbicos.

1. ¿cazar?
2. ¿pescar?
3. ¿hacer gimnasia?
4. ¿jugar al boliche?
5. ¿jugar al tenis?
6. ¿bailar?
7. ¿jugar al fútbol americano?
8. ¿montar en bicicleta?
9. ¿jugar al golf?
10. ¿tomar el sol?
11. ¿hacer alpinismo?

SUGGESTION: Before putting students in pairs, ask them to make a list of six to eight sports/pastimes. Caution them about the activities that require **jugar a** and those that require **hacer** or **participar.**

C **¿Quién lo hace?** Ask a classmate whether he or she is involved in various sports and pastimes.

EJEMPLO: —¿Haces ejercicios aeróbicos?
　　　　　 —Sí, (No, no) hago ejercicios aeróbicos.

D **Mis amigos y mi familia.** What sports and leisure time activities are favored by your friends and family? For each of the following, identify one person you know who does that activity, then add one detail if you can. If you don't know anyone who does the activity, say **nadie**.

NEW VOCABULARY: nadie

EJEMPLO: jugar al fútbol americano →
　　　　　 Mi hermano Frank juega al fútbol americano. Juega los fines
　　　　　　　de semana en la universidad.
　　　　　 o Nadie juega al fútbol americano.

1. jugar al béisbol
2. jugar al tenis
3. pescar
4. cazar
5. practicar las artes marciales
6. bailar
7. pasear
8. ver televisión
9. leer novelas policíacas
10. tocar el piano (la guitarra, el clarinete)

EXPANSION: Ask students, using the list of activities, to express when their family and friends last participated in their favorite activities: **Mi hermano Frank jugó al fútbol el viernes pasado.**

Verbos irregulares en el pretérito

PREPARATION: Ask students to list verbs that are irregular in the present tense, and write the list on the board. Point out that many verbs with irregular forms in the present tense also have irregular preterite forms. Direct students' attention to the drawing. Read each caption and ask what the sentence means and what the infinitive of each verb is.

— pg #9 handout
— workbook pg #126, 127.

C O N C E P T O

SUGGESTION: Tell students that **quise** and **no pude** change meaning in the preterite. **Quise** = *I tried to,* **no pude** = *I didn't succeed.*

«**Traje** los libros a la residencia.»

«**Hice** mi tarea.»

«**Quise** leer una novela pero no **pude** concentrar más.»

«**Vi** televisión.»

«**Me puse** ropa nueva.»

«**Fui** a casa de mis amigos.»

«**Dije** muchas cosas cómicas.»

«**Tuve** que volver a casa a la una.»

Actividades

SUGGESTION: Do this very quickly as a whole-class activity. Then, ask which students did the same activities last night. Have students raise their hands in response.
EJEMPLO: ¿Cuántos de ustedes dijeron muchos chistes anoche?

✓ **A** **¿Quién lo hizo?** Who did the following activities, María or Luis?

1. dijo muchas cosas cómicas
2. fue a casa de unos amigos
3. trajo los libros a la residencia
4. hizo su tarea
5. quiso leer una novela
6. se puso ropa nueva
7. vio televisión con unas amigas
8. tuvo que volver a casa a la una

B **¿Qué hiciste tú?** During the last week, did you participate in any of the activities that Luis and María did? Make a list of these activities and then find someone in the room who has also done what you have listed.

EJEMPLO: E1: Luis y yo dijimos muchas cosas cómicas. Y tú, ¿dijiste muchas cosas cómicas también?

E2: No, no dije cosas cómicas, pero Luis y yo fuimos a casa de unos amigos. Y tú, ¿fuiste a casa de unos amigos?

E1: Sí, fui a casa de unos amigos.

SUGGESTION: Have students work in pairs or small groups to complete each of the sentences in as many ways as possible.

✓ **C** **En el pasado.** Complete the statements to tell what you did in the past.

1. Ayer me puse...
2. Una vez le dije una mentira[1] a...
3. El año pasado estuve en...
4. Anoche (no) hice la tarea de...
5. Una vez fui a...
6. Ayer (no) vi... en la tele.

[1] *lie*

Some of the most frequently used Spanish verbs are irregular in the preterite tense. These verbs are sometimes referred to as <u>unaccented preterites because</u> they do not have accents on the **yo** or the **Ud./él/ella** forms.

Los pretéritos irregulares

ir/ser	dar	ver
fui	di	vi
fuiste	diste	viste
fue	dio	vio
fuimos	dimos	vimos
fuisteis	disteis	visteis
fueron	dieron	vieron

decir	traer
dije	traje
dijiste	trajiste
dijo	trajo
dijimos	trajimos
dijisteis	trajisteis
dijeron	trajeron

OTROS PRETÉRITOS IRREGULARES

Verb	Stem	+	Endings
hacer	**hic-**		
querer	**quis-**		
venir	**vin-**		-e
			-iste
andar	anduv-		-o
estar	estuv-		-imos
poder	pud-		-isteis
poner	pus-		-ieron
saber	sup-		
tener	tuv-		

SUGGESTION: Ask students to note the groups into which these verbs can be divided. Can students find a logical division in the **Otros pretéritos irregulares** list? Ask how the endings for **decir/traer** differ from those of the **Otros pretéritos irregulares**.

Teotihuacán

NEW VOCABULARY: esperamos, hace mucho calor, subir, vámonos; la lluvia, la pirámide, el sol, los templos; estupendas; arriba

La familia Austin va con David y Elena a uno de los sitios arqueológicos más famosos de México, Teotihuacán.

ELENA: ¿Quiénes quieren subir la Pirámide del Sol?

ROGER: No sé, Elena. Hace mucho calor.

ELENA: Sí, pero desde arriba hay una vista magnífica. Sr. Austin, Ud. puede sacar unas fotos estupendas.

DAVID: Mira, Elena, ¿por qué no esperamos? Quizás después de pasear un rato...

ELENA: Bueno, la verdad es que no debemos esperar. En el verano muchas veces hay lluvia por la tarde.

DAVID: Bueno, entonces vámonos. Podemos ver los templos y las otras pirámides después.

SUGGESTION: Use photographs or a map of the site to show the location of the Pyramid of the Sun, the Pyramid of the Moon, and other major buildings at Teotihuacán.

De inmediato

Are the following statements true or false, based on the dialogue? Say **Es cierto** if the statement is true or **No es cierto** if it is false. Correct the false statements.

NEW VOCABULARY: hace mucho frío; el invierno; cierto
SUGGESTION: This works well as a pair activity.

1. Elena quiere subir la pirámide.
2. Roger no quiere subir la pirámide porque hace mucho frío.
3. Elena dice que el Sr. Austin puede sacar fotos desde arriba.
4. David no quiere esperar.
5. Roger quiere pasear un rato.
6. Elena dice que no deben esperar.
7. Elena dice que muchas veces en el invierno hay lluvia por la noche.
8. David dice que pueden ver los templos y las otras pirámides después.

A ti te toca

Use Elena's first line to ask your classmates which of them wants to do the following. Keep track of their responses and be prepared to report the results to the class.

EJEMPLO: practicar el vocabulario →
—¿Quiénes quieren practicar el vocabulario?
—Tres personas/estudiantes/alumnos quieren practicar el vocabulario.
o —Nadie quiere practicar el vocabulario.

OPTIONAL: Have students, working in pairs, use Elena and Roger's first lines to create new sentences. The first student will propose an activity. The second will say why it may not be a good idea. —**¿Quiénes quieren almorzar ahora?—No sé. No tengo mucha hambre.**

1. estudiar en la biblioteca
2. ver televisión esta noche
3. tener un examen mañana
4. ir de compras
5. visitar un museo histórico
6. conocer al presidente de los EE. UU.
7. manejar un Porsche
8. pasear un rato

181

The Hispanic countries in the Western Hemisphere offer a great diversity of geography and climates as well: the cold, dry deserts of Chile; the rain forests of the Amazon Basin; the Andean Mountains; and the Isthmus of Panama. Even within a single country, the contrasts may be dramatic.

It is important to remember that the seasons in areas south of the equator are reversed from those in the north. The coldest months in the United States are the warmest in Chile and Argentina. In addition, in many areas of the Hispanic world there are only two seasons—rainy (**la estación de las lluvias**) and dry (**la estación seca**).

En México

A wide variety of climates can be found in Mexico as well. In the northern desert states along the U.S. border, summer temperatures can exceed 100° F, whereas the winter months can be characterized by sub-freezing temperatures. Much of the state of Oaxaca consists of a semitropical highland, but a large part of its neighboring state to the southeast, Chiapas, is mountainous jungle. The central highlands, where Mexico City is located, enjoy rather moderate temperatures all year due to the high altitude and tropical latitude.

The northern central part of Mexico most closely approximates the typical four-season pattern of the midwestern part of the United States, although periods of cold will rarely bring snow, whereas the southern and coastal regions show seasonal changes in a less dramatic way.

VOCABULARIO

El tiempo, los meses y las estaciones

PREPARATION: Direct students' attention to the drawings. **¿Cómo se dice** *winter* (*spring,* etc.) **en español? Y, ¿cuáles son los nombres, en espanõl, de los tres meses, que**

¿Qué tiempo hace?

normalmente asociamos con el invierno (la primavera, etc.) Normalmente asociamos ciertas condiciones del clima con cada estación. Lean Uds. las frases en el dibujo.

¿Hace buen tiempo en el invierno (la primavera, etc.) o hace mal tiempo?

En el invierno hace mal tiempo. Hace frío y nieva.

En la primavera está nublado y llueve.

184

En el verano hace buen tiempo. Hace sol y hace mucho calor.

En el otoño hace fresco y también hace viento.

Otro vocabulario

¿Cómo es el clima?	*How is the climate?*
¿Qué tiempo hace?	*What's the weather like?*
Hay (mucha) neblina.	*There is (a lot of) fog. It's (very) foggy.*
Está (muy) húmedo.	*It's (very) humid.*
Está (muy) seco.	*It's (very) dry.*
Está templado.	*It's moderate. (The weather's moderate.)*

Ⓐ ¿Cuándo ocurre? Indicate what month or months you associate with each activity or fact.

Actividades

EJEMPLO: Se compra ropa nueva para el nuevo año escolar. → agosto

1. Se vuela[1] una cometa.[2]
2. Se vota[3] para elegir[4] al presidente de los EE. UU.
3. Salen las nuevas flores del año.
4. Generalmente este mes tiene veintiocho días, pero a veces tiene veintinueve.
5. Se comienzan las clases.
6. Se camina en la lluvia.
7. Por tradición es el mes de las bodas.[5]
8. Las hojas[6] de los árboles cambian de color.
9. Se celebra el Día de la Independencia de los EE. UU.
10. Es el mes más popular para ir de compras.

Y EN EL MUNDO HISPÁNICO

11. En México, se visitan los cementerios para recordar a los muertos.
12. En muchas ciudades del mundo hispano se celebra Carnaval.
13. En España se celebra el día del santo patrón del país.
14. Es el mes de las vacaciones de verano en los países al sur de la línea ecuatorial.

[1]*fly*   [2]*kite*   [3]*vote*   [4]*elect*   [5]*weddings*   [6]*leaves*

Ⓑ ¿Qué prefieres hacer cuando... ? Using the following activities or any others that occur to you, state what you prefer to do during each kind of weather.

me gusta / me encanta ... *(o no me....)*

EJEMPLO: Cuando hace frío, prefiero escuchar música.

1. Cuando hace buen tiempo...	cazar
2. Cuando hace sol...	esquiar
3. Cuando hace viento...	estudiar
4. Cuando llueve...	jugar a las cartas
5. Cuando hace fresco...	jugar al golf/tenis/voleibol
6. Cuando hay neblina...	leer novelas románticas
7. Cuando hace frío...	montar en bicicleta
8. Cuando nieva...	nadar
9. Cuando hace mal tiempo...	pasear
10. Cuando hace calor...	patinar
	pescar
	tocar un instrumento musical
	tomar el sol
	trotar
	ver televisión
	¿ ?

VOCABULARIO

Los días festivos

PREPARATION: Ask what celebrations are depicted in the drawings. Have students cover up the English translations of **Otras expresiones** and guess what the celebrations are.

SUGGESTION: Point out that **la Noche Vieja** is referred to by some as **la Víspera del Año Nuevo**. Ask students about **El Día de Acción de Gracias**. What is its origin? Is it apt to be celebrated in many Hispanic countries?

la Noche Vieja

el Día de los Enamorados

el Día de la Independencia

el Día de Gracias

la Navidad

un aniversario de bodas

un cumpleaños

28 de septiembre — 17 de marzo

Feliz cumpleaños Patricio

Feliz día de tu santo

un cumpleaños

el día del santo

Otro vocabulario

el Año Nuevo Chino	*Chinese New Year*	el Jánuca	*Hanukkah*
el barmitzvah	*Bar Mitzvah*	la Nochebuena	*Christmas Eve*
el Día de Año Nuevo	*New Year's Day*	la Pascua de los Hebreos	*Passover*
el día de la Raza	*Columbus Day*	la Pascua Florida	*Easter*
el Día de las Madres	*Mother's Day*	el Ramadán	*Ramadan*
el Día de los Muertos	*All Souls' Day*	el Rosh Hashana	*Rosh Hashana*
el Día de los Padres	*Father's Day*	la Semana Santa	*Holy Week*
el Día del Obrero/ trabajo/dor	*Labor Day*		

A **¿En qué fecha? ¿Qué tiempo hace?** *Paso 1*. Give the dates on which this country typically celebrates the holidays cited.

EJEMPLOS: la Navidad → Celebramos la Navidad el 25 de diciembre.
                  el Día de las Madres →
                          Depende del año, pero siempre es en el mes de mayo.

1. el Día de la Independencia de los EE. UU.
2. la Pascua Florida
3. la Noche Vieja
4. el Jánuca
5. el Día de los Padres
6. el Día de Gracias
7. el Día de los Enamorados
8. la Nochebuena
9. el Día de Año Nuevo

Paso 2. What weather do you associate with the preceding holidays? State at least two weather conditions for each one.

B **Preguntas.** Ask a classmate the following questions about celebrations and holidays.

1. ¿Cuántos años tienes? ¿Cuál es la fecha de tu cumpleaños?
2. ¿Cuál es tu día festivo favorito y por qué?
3. ¿Qué días festivos vas a la iglesia o al templo?
4. ¿Qué días festivos celebras con una fiesta?
5. ¿Qué días festivos haces una barbacoa?
6. ¿Quiénes celebraron un aniversario de bodas recientemente? ¿Cuántos años celebraron?

Actividades

NEW VOCABULARY: la fecha
OPTIONAL: Ask students to scan the drawings and the **Otro vocabulario** list to find other holidays whose dates are fairly predictable.
SUGGESTION: Review the seasons by asking students to state which season is associated with each holiday.

PREPARATION: Ask why we have holidays. (What purpose do they serve?) Do the students know of any cultures with no holidays? Ask whether any of our holiday traditions would seem strange to someone from another culture (e.g., candles on a birthday cake, decorating a tree at Christmas). Where did those traditions originate?

Las fiestas y los días festivos

Faceta cultural

The **fiesta,** according to Mexican author Octavio Paz, is an occasion for people to find an excuse to dress up, fix special food, gather with others and, in general, forget the cares of daily life. There is always something to celebrate. In addition to the holidays and celebrations that we may already be familiar with, families in most of the Hispanic world celebrate birthdays and saint's days (**el día del santo,** or simply **el santo**) with a party for family and friends. An individual's saint can be one of the saints that, on the religious calendar, corresponds to the day on which he or she was born. The **santo** can also be celebrated on the day of the religious calendar devoted to the saint after whom the person was named. Although this celebration has its origins in the Catholic church, not all Catholics throughout the world observe this custom.

A young woman's *fifteenth* birthday (not the sixteenth, as in the United States) traditionally calls for a special party, **la fiesta de quince años**. Although the ways in which this event is celebrated differ throughout the Hispanic world, there is almost always an elaborate party to mark an important step in the life of the **quinceañera,** or fifteen-year-old: the end of her childhood and the beginning of her adulthood.

Each community or parish may celebrate the festival of its patron saint with activities (fairs, parades, picnics, dances, and religious observances) that last from five to seven days. In the larger urban areas, which have many parishes, pleasant weather may bring a seemingly endless round of festivals as each parish celebrates its saint.

En México

NEW VOCABULARY: el Día de los Muertos, la quinceañera

SUGGESTION: Use pictures of **Día de los Muertos** commemorations to give students an idea of how the event is celebrated.

One traditional religious celebration held in Mexico on November 2 is *All Souls' Day,* or as it is known in Mexico, **El Día de los Muertos**. This is a day in which Mexicans remember and show respect for their friends and family members who have died. It is not a somber and sad occasion but rather a party and festival. Family members often attend a special mass and then go to the cemetery and eat a meal, including perhaps the favorite foods of the honored departed, and celebrate the time that they enjoyed with those they are remembering. One of the many traditional foods prepared that day is the **pan de muerto,** a sweet bread in the shape of bones, skeletons, or skulls. On this day also, children receive what some would call "ghoulish" toys, such as paper or sugar skulls, dancing skeleton marionettes, even miniature coffins with toy cadavers inside.

Another celebration unique to Mexico is the ceremony to commemorate Mexico's independence from Spain, referred to as **el Grito** (*the Shout* or *Cry*). Throughout Mexico, at 11:00 P.M. on September 15, the mayors of municipalities go to the most prominent balcony in the city to recite the words that Padre Miguel Hidalgo y Costilla used as a call to arms in 1810: "**Viva[1] la independencia,**" to declare Mexico's independence from Spain, "**Viva México,**" to embrace their new country, and "**Viva nuestra señora de Guadalupe,**" to celebrate the patron saint of the new country.

[1]*Long live*

Muchas personas compran calaveras de azúcar para conmemorar el Día de los Muertos.

FOLLOW-UP: Have students research one of the following and report their results to the class. (You may wish to have them use native informants other than library resources.)
1. **El santo:** Where and how is it celebrated? 2. **El Día de los Muertos:** What are the origins of this feast day and how is it celebrated in Mexico? How is it celebrated in other countries?

Gustar y verbos similares

PREPARATION: Ask students to focus on the drawings and the captions. Ask what is different about the verbs used and the present-tense verbs studied thus far.

NEW VOCABULARY: me molestan

«**Me gusta** el calor, pero no **me molestan** el frío y el viento. A João **le encanta** el calor pero no **le gustan** el frío y el viento. A nosotros **nos fascina** el verano, pero a João no **le gusta** nada el invierno.»

Actividades

* **Ⓐ Gustos personales.** Use the following scale to express your attitudes about the items or activities listed.

negativo   No me gusta(n) nada.
         Me molesta(n).
         No me gusta(n) (mucho).
         Me gusta(n) (un poco).
         Me interesa(n).
         Me gusta(n) mucho.
         Me fascina(n).
positivo   Me encanta(n).

parecer quedar faltar

EJEMPLO: bailar →   Me gusta mucho bailar.
                  o No me gusta bailar.

NEW VOCABULARY: me fascina(n), me interesa(n)

1. comprar regalos de Navidad
2. ver deportes en la tele
3. novelas de misterio
4. los exámenes
5. viajar
6. el verano
7. ir de compras
8. la nieve
9. tejer
10. trotar

PREPARATION: Before beginning the activities, write the following models on the board or overhead. Then have students, working in pairs, ask their classmate whether he or she likes various school subjects.—¿**Te gusta la contabilidad?** → —**Sí, (No, no) me gusta.** / —¿**Te gustan las matemáticas?** → —**Sí, (No, no) me gustan.**

Ⓑ ¿Qué te gusta(n) más? Ask a classmate which of the two items he or she likes more.

EJEMPLOS: esquiar / pasear →
              —¿Te gusta más esquiar o pasear?
              —Me gusta más esquiar.
              las novelas románticas / las novelas policíacas →
              —¿Te gustan más las novelas románticas o las novelas policíacas?
              —Me gustan más las novelas policíacas.

SUGGESTION: Have students practice third-person forms by reporting what they have learned about their partners. Then have them practice first-person plural forms by stating what they have in common with their classmates.

NEW VOCABULARY: las novelas policíacas/románticas

NEW VOCABULARY: el calor, el frío
EXPANSION: Have students work in small groups to devise three to five additional items and present them to the entire class.

1. ir de compras / ver televisión
2. jugar al boliche / jugar al golf
3. el frío / el calor
4. la primavera / el otoño
5. levantarte / acostarte
6. los coches americanos / los coches japoneses
7. ir a las montañas / ir a la playa

Preguntas personales. Ask a classmate the following questions about his or her likes, dislikes, and needs.

SUGGESTION: Remind students that ① (**individuo**) represents a person special to them, such as a boyfriend/girlfriend, husband/wife, best friend, roommate, or favorite relative.

1. ¿Te interesa la música *rock*? ¿Qué más te interesa?
2. ¿Le encanta a tu mamá tu ropa moderna? A tu mamá, ¿qué le encanta?
3. ¿Quién es tu persona especial? ¿Qué le gusta más a ①, dormir or comer? (A ① le...)
4. ¿Qué le molesta más a ①?
5. ¿Qué les fascina a los hombres? ¿a las mujeres? (Les...)
6. ¿Qué les falta para esta clase? (Nos falta[n]...)
7. ¿Cúantos minutos de clase nos quedan? (Nos...)

NEW VOCABULARY: les falta, nos quedan; el minuto

for quiz

Because the grammatical subject of Spanish verbs like **gustar** is not the person doing the liking but what is liked, only the third person singular and plural forms of the verb are typically used. A prepositional phrase (*a la profesora, a mis amigos*) may be/needs to be added to emphasize or clarify who is doing the liking.

gusta
gustan

SUGGESTION: Point out that in the sentence **A la profesora le molestan los errores,** the use of the object pronoun **le** is redundant but grammatically required.

Gustar y verbos similares

correr, bailar

(a mí)	**me**	
(a ti)	**te**	
(a Ud.)		
(a él/ella)	**le**	**gusta** + *infinitive or singular noun*
(a nosotros/as)	**nos**	**gustan** + *plural noun or series of nouns*
(a vosotros/as)	**os**	
(a Uds.)		
(a ellos/ellas)	**les**	

Me encanta la clase de español.
¿**Te gusta** escribir composiciones?
A la profesora **le molestan** los errores.
Nos quedan sólo dos semanas de clase antes de las vacaciones.
¿No **os interesa** ver películas extranjeras?
A mis amigos **les falta** tiempo para estudiar.

It sometimes helps to remember that **gustar** and similar verbs function like the English verb *to disgust*. (*This weather disgusts me.*) Try thinking of the actual and the literal meanings of these sentences.

Me encanta la clase de español.	*I love Spanish class.* (*Spanish class enchants me.*)
¿Te gusta escribir composiciones?	*Do you like to write compositions?* (*Is writing compositions pleasing to you?*)

La Universidad Nacional Autónoma de México

NEW VOCABULARY: teníamos mucha prisa

PREPARATION: Point out that the mosaic on the UNAM library is the largest in the world. It is the work of Juan O'Gorman, a Mexican muralist. On other parts of the campus there are murals by other artists. For example, the UNAM stadium is covered with a Diego Rivera mural.

David y Elena piensan ir con la familia Austin a la biblioteca de la Universidad Nacional Autónoma de México (UNAM) para ver los mosaicos[1] famosos.

ELENA: Uds. querían ver los famosos mosaicos, ¿no?

DAVID: Sí, claro. Cuando era niño, mi mamá me mostró fotos de los mosaicos en un libro que tenía de la UNAM.

ROGER: Cuando estuvimos aquí antes teníamos mucha prisa y no pudimos apreciar bien los colores.

ELENA: Ah, viniste con un grupo del Instituto Allende en San Miguel de Allende, ¿no?

ROGER: Sí. El instituto tiene una serie de excursiones para los alumnos. Pasamos tres días en el D.F. y en las afueras de la ciudad. Pero no vimos ni la mitad de lo que queríamos ver.

[1] *mosaics*

El mosaico más grande del mundo está en la biblioteca de la UNAM.

De inmediato

The following information is contained in the dialogue. Number the sentences to reflect the order in which the information was presented.

_____ Cuando David era niño su mamá le mostró fotos de los mosaicos.

_____ El Instituto Allende tiene una serie de excursiones.

_____ Roger y sus compañeros pasaron tres días en la capital.

_____ No pudieron apreciar bien los colores de los mosaicos.

_____ David y la familia de Roger quieren ver los famosos mosaicos.

_____ Roger estuvo antes en la UNAM.

_____ Roger vino antes con un grupo del Instituto Allende.

_____ Los compañeros de Roger tenían prisa.

OPTIONAL: 1. ¿Por qué querían ir David, Elena y Roger a la UNAM? 2. ¿Cuándo le mostró Ana fotos de los mosaicos a David? 3. ¿Por qué no pudieron apreciar los colores Roger y los otros estudiantes? 4. ¿Cuánto tiempo pasaron en la capital la última vez?

A ti te toca

With a classmate, share some memorable childhood experiences (real or imaginary) in which a relative bought, taught, or showed you something. Use clues from each of the following columns.

Cuando era niño/a	mi papá/mamá	me compró	su oficina
	mi tío/a	me enseñó	fotos de (un país)
Cuando tenía _____ años	mi abuelo/a	me mostró	un regalo
	mi bisabuelo/a[1]		una bicicleta
	¿ ?		a montar a caballo (cocinar, tocar un instrumento)
			¿ ?

[1] *great-grandfather/mother*

DIÁLOGO

En la universidad

NEW VOCABULARY: insistió en, se reúne; el baile, la importancia, el latino, las memorias, la misa, las reu- niones, las vacaciones; extranjeras; todos los veranos

El Club Hispánico se reúne en la biblioteca del departamento de lenguas extranjeras.

PREPARATION: La muchacha en el dibujo es una de los amigos de David cuando ella tenía quince años. ¿Quién es? ¿Qué lleva Marisol? ¿Qué está celebrando?

LA PROFESORA MARTÍNEZ: Pase, profesor Brewer. Estábamos hablando de nuestras memorias de la juventud.[1]

CELIA: ...y todos nos reuníamos los domingos en casa de mis abuelos.

LA PROFESORA MARTÍNEZ: ¿Teníais que viajar muy lejos para estas reuniones?

CELIA: No. Casi toda mi familia vivía en el mismo pueblo.

MARISOL: Mi familia se reunía con frecuencia también. Pero había ciertas fiestas más importantes que otras. Por ejemplo, yo tenía tres hermanas y no sé cuántas primas. Mi abuelo insistió en dar una estupenda fiesta de quinceañera para cada muchacha de la familia. Celebrábamos con una misa, una comida en un restaurante de primera categoría[2] y un baile en un hotel. Vinieron todos nuestros parientes y amigos.

EL PROFESOR BREWER: He oído decir[3] que la fiesta de quince años es muy importante para los latinos que viven en los EE. UU. ¿Es verdad, Luisa?

LUISA: Bueno, sí, la fiesta es muy importante pero creo que la misa tiene menos importancia para nosotros.

CELIA: En España, o por lo menos, entre mis amigas, hay muy pocas fiestas de este tipo.

JORGE: Las costumbres de la fiesta de quince años varían[4] un poco según el país pero las vacaciones de verano son importantes para todos. Luis, cuando eras niño, ¿salía tu familia para las vacaciones?

LUIS: Sí, todos los veranos, en agosto, mi madre nos llevaba a nuestra casa en las montañas. Mi padre tenía que seguir trabajando pero pasaba con nosotros los fines de semana.

[1]*youth* [2]*de... first class* [3]*He... I have heard (it said)* [4]*vary*

De inmediato

NEW VOCABULARY: si
VARIATION: Convert this into a true/false activity by inserting characters' names before the verbs.

Which of the characters do you associate with the following statements?

1. Le preguntó a Celia si ella y los otros miembros de la familia tenían que viajar muy lejos para las reuniones familiares.
2. Dijo que las vacaciones de verano eran importantes para todos.
3. Dijo que su familia se reunía los domingos en casa de sus abuelos.
4. Dijo que en las fiestas de quince años había menos énfasis en la misa.

192

5. Dijo que tenía tres hermanas.
6. Dijo que todos los veranos su madre llevaba a la familia a una casa en las montañas.
7. Dijo que casi toda su familia vivía en el mismo pueblo.
8. Le preguntó a Luis si su familia salía para las vacaciones.
9. Dijo que su abuelo insistió en dar una fiesta de quince años para cada muchacha de la familia.
10. Dijo que en su familia había ciertas fiestas más importantes que otras.

Describe your family when you were young, using Marisol's line about her sisters and the following example as models.

A ti te toca

EJEMPLO: Tenía un hermano, una hermana, dos padres, ocho tíos, cuatro abuelos y no sé cuántos primos.

A propósito: Los tiempos perfectos

In the dialogue on page 192, when Professor Brewer says **He oído decir que...** , he is using the present perfect tense to express what he has heard. The *present perfect* (equivalent to the English *have/has done*) and the *past perfect* (equivalent to the English *had done*) should be easy for you to recognize. They are formed with a conjugated form of the verb **haber** and the past participle. The verb **haber** is irregular in the present tense (**he, has, ha, hemos, habéis, han**), but is regular in the imperfect (**había, habías, habían, ...**). The form of **haber** is followed by a past participle, which will usually end with **-ado** (for **-ar** verbs) or **-ido** (for **-er** and **-ir** verbs), although there are many common irregular past participles. Study these examples of the present and past perfect tenses.

(conocer)	**Hemos conocido** a la profesora.	*We have met the instructor.*
(leer)	**He leído** este capítulo.	*I have read this chapter.*
(acostarse)	No **nos habíamos acostado** hasta la una y media y tuvimos que levantarnos a las cinco y media.	*We hadn't gone to bed until 1:30 and we had to get up at 5:30.*
(dormir)	La profesora tampoco **había dormido** bien la noche antes del examen.	*The instructor hadn't slept well the night before the exam either.*

El imperfecto

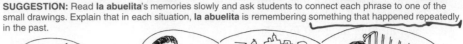

NEW VOCABULARY: las noticias

SUGGESTION: Read **la abuelita**'s memories slowly and ask students to connect each phrase to one of the small drawings. Explain that in each situation, **la abuelita** is remembering something that happened repeatedly in the past.

«Cuando yo era niña, tocaba el piano, bebía agua de un pozo,[1] leía las noticias de la revolución, iba a la capital una vez al año, dormía en la misma cama con mi hermana y me bañaba en el río.»

[1] *well*

Actividades

OPTIONAL: Ask a series of questions about students' habits when they were young. Do not require answers with a verb form, but be sure to model the correct response.

Ⓐ **En la secundaria.** Indicate whether or not you did the following things in high school.

EJEMPLO: bailar en las fiestas →
En la secundaria yo (no) bailaba en las fiestas.

1. tomar café
2. fumar[1]
3. practicar deportes
4. tocar la guitarra
5. ver telenovelas como «Hospital General»

[1] *to smoke*

SUGGESTION: Do this activity in small groups. Review for the entire class.

Ⓑ **El pasado y el presente.** Mention whether you did these things in the past, and compare them to what you do now.

EJEMPLO: asistir a la iglesia →
En el pasado yo asistía a la iglesia. Ahora todavía asisto. (Ahora ya no asisto.)
o En el pasado yo no asistía a la iglesia. Ahora sí asisto. (Ahora tampoco asisto.)

1. escribir poesía
2. correr
3. comer *pizza*
4. vivir en México
5. beber cerveza
6. vestirse como *punk*

OPTIONAL: Ask students, working in small groups, to tell how frequently they did the activities listed. Put a list of useful adverbs of time on the board or overhead: **a veces, de vez en cuando, frecuentemente, generalmente, los lunes/viernes/nunca, siempre, todos los días/meses/años**

Ⓒ **Lo que yo hacía...** Tell a classmate three things you used to do and three things you did not do when you were ten years old. If you need inspiration, you may use the following suggestions.

EJEMPLO: Cuando tenía diez años, (no) bailaba en las fiestas.

acostarse temprano
asistir a la escuela
bailar en las fiestas
escribir cartas a mis amigos
estudiar con mis amigos
jugar al fútbol americano

leer novelas para jóvenes
bañarse con mi hermano/a
recibir buenas notas
viajar con la familia
vivir en una ciudad grande
¿ ?

El imperfecto

VERBOS REGULARES	-ar (pescar)	-er (leer)	-ir (vestirse)
yo	pesc**aba**	le**ía**	me vest**ía**
tú	pesc**abas**	le**ías**	te vest**ías**
Ud., él/ella	pesc**aba**	le**ía**	se vest**ía**
nosotros/as	pesc**ábamos**	le**íamos**	nos vest**íamos**
vosotros/as	pesc**abais**	le**íais**	os vest**íais**
Uds., ellos/as	pesc**aban**	le**ían**	se vest**ían**

VERBOS IRREGULARES	ser	ir	ver
yo	era	iba	veía
tú	eras	ibas	veías
Ud., él/ella	era	iba	veía
nosotros/as	éramos	íbamos	veíamos
vosotros/as	erais	ibais	veíais
Uds., ellos/as	eran	iban	veían

You have already learned one of the past tenses for Spanish, **el pretérito**. Spanish has a second past tense called **el imperfecto**. It is used to describe repeated and habitual past actions and may be translated by *used to* or *was/were + -ing*.

There are only three irregular verbs in the imperfect: **ser**, **ir**, and **ver**.

SUGGESTION: Have students look at the imperfect endings for -ar, -er, and ir verbs. Which are identical? If you sense the need, provide a brief overview of the most common uses of the preterite and imperfect tenses.

Vamos a Acapulco

DIÁLOGO

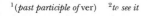

Después de varios días en la capital con la familia Austin, David y Elena van a la Central Camionera del Sur. Van a viajar en autobús a Acapulco.

DAVID: No quiero irme de aquí. Hay tantas cosas que no hemos visto[1] todavía.
ELENA: Sí, entiendo. Pero no es posible verlo[2] todo.
DAVID: Quizás la próxima vez. Bueno, ¿a qué hora sale el camión para Acapulco?
ELENA: A las diez. Es un viaje de seis horas. Llegamos a las cuatro de la tarde.

[1] (*past participle of* ver)   [2] *to see it*

PREPARATION: Direct students' attention to the drawing. Ask for volunteers to make sentences describing the drawing. Have students read the dialogue introduction.

NEW VOCABULARY: preferido

DAVID: ¿Habrá[3] mucha gente?

ELENA: Ahora no, porque estamos en verano, pero en el invierno Acapulco es el sitio preferido de miles de turistas que tratan de[4] escaparse[5] del frío.

[3]*Will there be* [4]tratan... *try to* [5]*escape, get away*

De inmediato

1. ¿Dónde están David y Elena?
2. ¿Por qué están allí?
3. ¿A qué hora salen para Acapulco?
4. ¿De cuántas horas es el viaje?
5. ¿Cree Elena que va a haber[1] muchas personas en Acapulco? ¿Por qué sí o por qué no?

[1]va... *there are going to be*

A ti te toca

Practice the preceding dialogue with a classmate, substituting another tourist area for Acapulco. You may need to change parts of the dialogue to work with the substitution.

EJEMPLO: (Ft. Lauderdale) ...Ahora sí, porque estamos en verano. Ft. Lauderdale es el sitio preferido de miles de turistas que tratan de escaparse de la ciudad.

EN ACCIÓN

Antes de ver

In this chapter you will watch and listen as a series of people talk about what they like (and don't like) to do, in general as well as at holiday time. Listen carefully and try to catch as many details as you can about their likes and dislikes.

Los horarios de Elena y David

David and Elena tend to follow different schedules. Using a chart like the one shown on page 198 as a guide, write their schedules on a separate sheet of paper as your instructor reads Elena's description of what she and David did yesterday.

El pronóstico de tiempo

NEW VOCABULARY: el pronóstico de tiempo

While David and Elena wait for the bus to Acapulco, Elena checks out the weather report for Mexico and the world.

Antes de leer

Before you read the weather report, review the vocabulary for weather and the seasons. Is Mexico north or south of the equator? Will it be summer or winter in late June? How about in Montevideo, Uruguay? And in Caracas, Venezuela? Now look at the format of the report and recall other weather reports you may have seen. What information do you expect it to contain?

Tiempo para hoy

Una depresión tropical continúa interaccionando con una onda tropical y aire húmedo del Pacífico, lo que ocasionará precipitaciones de 50 a 70 milímetros en Baja California Sur, Sonora, Sinaloa y Nayarit; de 20 a 50, en Chihuahua, Coahuila, Durango, Jalisco, Colima, Michoacán, Guerrero, Puebla, San Luis Potosí y Veracruz; de 10 a 20, Tlaxcala, Distrito Federal, estado de México, Morelos, Querétaro, Guanajuato, Hidalgo, Aguascalientes, Zacatecas, Tamaulipas y Veracruz, así como en la península de Yucatán. Por más de 70 milímetros se esperan en Chiapas.

Asimismo, la presencia de una onda cálida provocará temperaturas mayores de 40 grados centígrados en Sonora; de 35 a 40, en Baja California, Sinaloa, Chihuahua y Coahuila.

Reporte Imeca

El área metropolitana sigue teniendo una buena calidad de aire. En ninguna de las cinco zonas se ha rebasado la norma internacional, al mantenerse por debajo de los 100 puntos Imeca. La zona centro alcanzó de las 12 a las 13 horas el nivel más alto, con 85 puntos Imeca de ozono.

La Comisión Metropolitana para la Prevención y Control de la Contaminación pronostica para este día que la calidad del aire en el valle de México será "ocasionalmente no satisfactoria" de las 12 a las 14 horas.

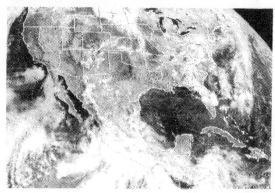

EL UNIVERSAL / AP

La imagen del satélite muestra un sistema anticiclónico sobre el golfo de México y mar Caribe

NEW VOCABULARY: principales

Temperaturas

En el país

MEXICO, D. F., 30 de junio.— Pronóstico para las principales ciudades, en las próximas 24 horas:

	Máxima	Mínima		Máxima	Mínima
Acapulco	34	25	Mexicali	45	25
Aguascalientes	26	16	Monterrey	32	23
Campeche	35	24	Morelia	27	15
Cancún	32	24	Nuevo Laredo	29	23
Ciudad Juárez	37	19	Oaxaca	30	16
Cuernavaca	29	15	Puebla	25	12
Chihuahua	34	21	Puerto Vallarta	32	21
Distrito Federal	25	13	Reynosa	30	23
Guadalajara	30	17	Tijuana	26	18
Guanajuato	26	16	Toluca	23	08
La Paz	38	19	Veracruz	31	23
Mazatlán	32	26	Villahermosa	35	24
Mérida	33	23	Zihuatanejo	32	21

En el mundo

NUEVA YORK, 30 de junio (AP).— Temperaturas registradas en las principales ciudades, en las últimas 24 horas:

	Mínima	Máxima		Mínima	Máxima
Amsterdam	10	23	Montevideo	06	15
Atenas	20	32	Montreal	09	20
Barcelona	14	24	Moscú	08	20
Berlín	10	18	Nueva Delhi	24	39
Buenos Aires	08	19	Nueva York	20	29
Caracas	16	26	Oslo	11	17
Chicago	16	31	París	13	26
El Cairo	22	36	Pekín	17	31
Ginebra	13	27	Roma	18	32
Londres	17	24	San Francisco	11	22
Los Angeles	18	26	Tokio	20	23
Madrid	20	31	Toronto	12	23
Miami	23	32	Viena	14	18

This report contains many cognates, the meanings of which should be fairly easy for you to guess. For example, what do you think **una depresión tropical** is? And **aire húmedo**? Scan the report to find other cognates so that you will have a clear idea of the content of the weather report before you read it. Now read the report and do the activity that follows.

Después de leer

Are the following statements true (**Es cierto**) or false (**No es cierto**)? If a statement is inaccurate, change it to make it accurate.

NEW VOCABULARY: nubes

1. Este pronóstico fue preparado para un día de invierno en México.
2. Según el pronóstico, va a llover en Nayarit.
3. Va a llover más en el Distrito Federal que en Michoacán.
4. El sistema anticiclónico ha producido nubes en Cuba.
5. La calidad del aire en el valle de México va a ser muy mala.
6. Una onda tropical causa la precipitación.
7. Hace más calor en Ciudad Juárez que en el resto de México.
8. Ayer, en Nueva York, la temperatura máxima fue la misma que la pronosticada para Nuevo Laredo y Cuernavaca hoy.
9. La temperatura máxima en la capital del Uruguay en las últimas 24 horas es igual que la temperatura mínima pronosticada para Morelia hoy.
10. Ayer, en Madrid, la temperatura máxima fue más alta que la máxima pronosticada para Oaxaca hoy.

Horarios

Carla and Frank, two of Professor Ramos's Spanish students, have somewhat different morning schedules. Write two short paragraphs describing what each of them did yesterday morning. Use expressions of time (**a las siete y media**) and connecting phrases (**y, después, entonces, luego**) as needed to make your narration as natural as possible.

HORA	CARLA	FRANK
6:30	despertarse	
7:00	levantarse	despertarse, levantarse
7:30	ponerse la ropa	tomar el desayuno
8:00	salir de la residencia	ponerse la ropa
8:30	ir a la biblioteca	salir de la casa
9:00	ir a la clase de español	ir a la clase de español
9:30		
10:00	ir al laboratorio de anatomía	ir a la oficina de la profesora de inglés
10:30		
11:00	ir a la clase de literatura norteamericana	ir a la cafetería
11:30		
12:00	volver a la residencia	ir a la clase de fotografía

Y en nuestra región...

Locate three cities mentioned in the article on page 197 that might be included in a weather report in your area. Using the high and low temperatures provided for the cities, create a logical forecast for those cities (rain, snow, heat, and so on) and present it to a partner, small group, or the entire class as if you were giving the early morning forecast on a local television channel.

EJEMPLO: La temperatura máxima para Monterrey hoy va a ser 32 grados centígrados con una mínima de 23. En Nuevo Laredo la máxima va a llegar a 29 y va a bajar a 23. Reynosa también va a tener una temperatura mínima de 23 grados y no va a hacer tanto calor allí como en Monterrey, pues la temperatura máxima va a llegar sólo a 30. No va a llover mucho en nuestra zona hoy.

Los verbos	Verbs
esperar	to wait (for)
ganar	to win; to earn
insistir (en)	to insist (on, upon)
pasar	to spend (*time*); to show (*a program on T.V.*)
perder (ie)	to lose; to miss (*an opportunity, a ride, a class*)
reunirse (me reúno)	to get together, meet
soportar	to stand, tolerate
subir	to go up; to climb; to get on (*a bus, train, etc.*)

Gustar y verbos parecidos	*Gustar and similar verbs*
encantar	to love (*something delights one*)
faltar	to lack
fascinar	to fascinate
gustar	to like (*something pleases one*)
interesar	to interest
molestar	to bother
parecer	to think (about); to seem
quedar	to remain

Los deportes	Sports
cazar	to hunt
el esquí	skiing
esquiar (esquio)	to ski
hacer (hago)	to do
los ejercicios aeróbicos	aerobics, aerobic exercises
gimnasia	gymnastics
hacer (hago) alpinismo	to go mountain climbing
jugar (ue)	to play
al fútbol	soccer
al fútbol americano	football
jugar (ue) al boliche	to bowl, go bowling
montar	to ride
a caballo	a horse, horseback
en bicicleta	a bicycle
en motocicleta	a motorcycle
nadar	to swim
pasear	to walk
patinar	to skate
pescar	to fish
practicar	to practice, do
las artes marciales	martial arts
el atletismo	track and field
el boxeo	boxing

el ciclismo	cycling
la lucha libre	wrestling
trotar	to jog

Palabras semejantes: el básquetbol, el béisbol, el golf, el ráquetbol, el tenis, el voleibol.

Los pasatiempos / *Pastimes*

acampar	to camp
bailar	to dance
hablar por teléfono	to talk on the telephone
jugar a las cartas	to play cards
leer	to read
sacar fotos	to take pictures
tejer	to knit
tocar (un instrumento musical)	to play (a musical instrument)
tomar una siesta	to take a nap

Palabras semejantes: el clarinete, la guitarra, el piano, la trompeta.

Las estaciones / *Seasons*

el invierno	winter
la primavera	spring
el verano (R)	summer
el otoño	autumn, fall

El tiempo y el clima / *Weather and the climate*

el calor	heat
la estación de las lluvias	rainy season
la estación seca	dry season
está (muy) húmedo	it is (very) humid
está (muy) nublado	it is (very) cloudy
está (muy) seco	it is (very) dry
está templado	it is moderate (the weather is moderate)
el frío	cold
hace (muy) buen tiempo	the weather is (very) nice
hace (mucho) calor	it is (very) hot
hace fresco	it is cool
hace (mucho) frío	it is (very) cold
hace (muy) mal tiempo	the weather is (very) bad
hace (mucho) sol	it is (very) sunny
hace (mucho) viento	it is (very) windy
hay (mucha) neblina	there is (a lot of) fog; it is (very) foggy

llover (llueve)	to rain (it rains; it is raining)
la lluvia	rain
nevar (nieva)	to snow (it snows; it is snowing)
la nieve	snow
la nube	cloud
el pronóstico (de tiempo)	(weather) forecast
el sol	sun
la temperatura	temperature
¿Cómo es el clima?	What is the climate like?
¿Qué tiempo hace?	What is the weather like?

Los meses (*Months*)

enero (R)**, febrero, marzo, abril, mayo, junio, julio, agosto, septiembre, octubre, noviembre, diciembre**

Los días festivos / *Holidays*

el aniversario de bodas	wedding anniversary
el Año Nuevo Chino	Chinese New Year
el Día de Año Nuevo	New Year's Day
el Día de los Enamorados	Valentine's Day
el Día de Gracias	Thanksgiving Day
el Día de la Independencia	Independence Day
el Día de las Madres	Mother's Day
el Día de las Muertos	All Souls' Day, Day of the Dead
el Día del Obrero	Labor Day
el Día de los Padres	Father's Day
el Día de la Raza	Columbus Day
el (día del) santo	saint's day
el Jánuca	Hanukkah
la Navidad	Christmas
la Nochebuena	Christmas Eve
la Noche Vieja	New Year's Eve
la Pascua de los Hebreos	Passover
la Pascua Florida	Easter
la Semana Santa	Holy Week

Palabras semejantes: el barmitzvah, el Ramadán, el Rosh Hashana.

Otros sustantivos

el árbol	tree
el baile	dance
el capítulo	chapter
la costumbre	custom
la época	cpoch, historical period
el equipo	team
la importancia	importance
el latino / la latina	Latin, Hispanic (*person*)
la memoria	memory
el minuto	minute
la misa	Mass
la mitad	half
las noticias	ncws
la novela policíaca/	detective/romance
romántica	novel
el partido	match, gamc
la pelota	ball
la pirámide	pyramid
la *pizza*	pizza
la quinceañera	*young woman turning 15 years old*
la residencia	dormitory, residence hall
la reunión	meeting, gathering
la revista	magazine
el templo	temple
las vacaciones (*pl.*)	vacation
la vista	vicw

Other nouns

Los adjetivos

acostumbrado/a a	accustomed to, used to
cierto/a	certain
confundido/a	confused
divorciado/a	divorced
estupendo/a	stupendous, fabulous
extranjero/a	foreign
muerto/a	dead
preferido/a	preferred, favorite
principal	main, principal
propio/a	own

Adjectives

Los adverbios

arriba	above, on top
casi	almost, nearly
todos los días/meses/ años	every day/month/year
ya	already; yet

Adverbs

Palabras y expresiones útiles

nadie	no one
no sólo... sino también...	not only . . . but also . . .
salir mal	to do poorly
si	if, whether
tener (mucha) prisa	to be in a (big) hurry
vámonos	let's go

Useful words and expressions

Otros Mundos

NOTE: The detailed suggestions for teaching the **Otros mundos** section cannot be accommodated in the margins of this *Instructor's Edition*. For this reason, notes for this section are in the *Instructor's Manual*.

La América Central

Las playas de Costa Rica atraen a muchos turistas.

Hola. Me llamo Jorge Dávila. Soy de la ciudad de Puntarenas, en Costa Rica. Puntarenas es el puerto más importante de mi país en el Océano Pacífico. Vine a los EE. UU. el año pasado porque algún día quiero trabajar en turismo y para esa carrera es muy importante saber bien el inglés. Me gusta leer novelas; una de mis novelas favoritas en inglés es *Jurassic Park* de Michael Crichton, porque tiene lugar en una isla ficticia cerca de Puntarenas.

Muchos de mis compañeros de clase creen que todos los países de la América Central son iguales. Pero, no es verdad. Tenemos semejanzas y diferencias. Costa Rica, así como los otros países centroamericanos, se independizó de España en 1821. Formamos parte del imperio mexicano desde 1822 hasta 1823. Después, los países de la América Central establecieron una federación que existió hasta 1838. Pero cada uno de los países centroamericanos tiene una identidad propia.

La mayoría de los habitantes de Costa Rica es de ascendencia europea. No tenemos ejército,[1] y tenemos la tasa de alfabetismo[2] más alta de todos los países de esta región. En la costa se cultivan la banana, el cacao y la caña de azúcar, pero en el altiplano, donde vive la mayoría de los habitantes, se cultiva el café. Aunque todavía importamos muchos productos de los países más industrializados, aquí se aumentan todos los días empresas industriales costarricenses.

[1] *army*   [2] tasa... *literacy rate*

El cincuenta por ciento de la tierra de Nicaragua consiste en bosques, montañas y volcanes.

¿Sabías que... ?

- Costa Rica recibió su nombre de Cristóbal Colón.
- En 1987, el presidente de Costa Rica, Óscar Arias Sánchez, recibió el Premio Nóbel de la Paz.
- El Salvador es el país más pequeño de la América Central.
- El Salvador es el tercer exportador de café del mundo, después de Brasil y Colombia (dos países mucho más grandes).
- El canal de Panamá tiene 51 millas de largo y costó $336.650.000.
- En Guatemala, el 60% de la población es de ascendencia maya.
- Tajumulco, un volcán apagado[1] en Guatemala, es el punto más alto de Centroamérica.

- Copán, en Honduras, y Tikal, en Guatemala, fueron los dos centros religiosos más importantes de la civilización maya clásica.
- Una mujer, Violeta Chamorro, fue elegida presidenta de Nicaragua en 1990.
- En Nicaragua, un país con muchos volcanes y lagos, sólo se cultiva el 10% de la tierra.

[1]*extinct*

La América Central en breve

	COSTA RICA	EL SALVADOR	PANAMÁ
Capital:	San José	San Salvador	Panamá
Lenguas:	español, dialectos criollos	español	español, inglés
Gobierno:	república	república	república
Moneda:	el colón	el colón	el balboa
Población:	3.111.000	5.418.000	2.426.000
Superficie:	19.575 millas cuadradas (más pequeño que la Virginia Occidental)	8.124 millas cuadradas (casi del tamaño de Massachusetts)	29.208 millas cuadradas (un poco más grande que Virginia Occidental)

	GUATEMALA	HONDURAS	NICARAGUA
Capital:	Guatemala	Tegucigalpa	Managua
Lenguas:	español, lenguas mayas	español	español
Gobierno:	república	república	república
Moneda:	el quetzal	el lempira	el córdoba
Población:	9.266.000	4.949.000	3.751.000
Superficie:	42.042 millas cuadradas (del tamaño de Tennessee)	43.277 millas cuadradas (un poco más grande que Tennessee)	50.193 millas cuadradas (más o menos del tamaño de Iowa)

NOTE: See the *Instructor's Manual* for suggestions on teaching **México y los mexicanos**.

México y los mexicanos

NEW VOCABULARY: los precios, los rayos; único

viando[18] hacia otros lugares turísticos en desarrollo.[19] Existían también otros problemas, como la congestión del tráfico, la proliferación de los barrios bajos[20] y la contaminación. De otras partes de México llegó gente en busca de trabajo y fue visible el contraste entre la vida opulenta de los ricos y la miseria de los pobres.

Pero gracias a un plan de reforma en Acapulco se han mejorado[21] los aseos[22] públicos, hay más recipientes para la basura[23] en las calles y las aceras[24] elevadas ayudan a descongestionar la circulación en

[1]*recreation* [2]*¡puede... it may be!* [3]*lodging, housing* [4]*a... behind* [5]*in front* [6]*resorts* [7]*se... stop* [8]*a... during* [9]*se... was made to be enjoyed* [10]*evenings, twilights* [11]*shows* [12]*After* [13]*se... gets lively* [14]*even* [15]*se... threw themselves into* [16]*charm* [17]*por... as a result* [18]*se... was going* [19]*en... under development* [20]*barrios... bad neighborhoods* [21]*se... have improved* [22]*lavatories* [23]*recipientes... garbage cans* [24]*sidewalks*

Las bonitas playas blancas de Acapulco no eran famosas hasta despues de la Segunda Guerra Mundial.

De viaje: Acapulco

Acapulco es único. Los mexicanos creen que es el lugar de recreo[1] más importante del mundo y ¡puede que lo sea![2] Acapulco tiene algo para todos: todo tipo de alojamiento,[3] todo tipo de precios... un lugar fabuloso con las montañas a sus espaldas[4] y el mar delante.[5]

En algunos balnearios[6] las actividades no se interrumpen[7] a lo largo[8] de las veinticuatro horas del día. Todo el mundo sabe que la noche se hizo para vivirla.[9] Los atardeceres[10] son perfectos para las grandes cenas y las diversiones: los espectáculos,[11] las discotecas.... Pasada[12] la medianoche todo se anima[13] aún[14] más.

Acapulco es una ciudad que ha tenido problemas. Se expandió demasiado rápidamente cuando una serie de constructores se lanzó a[15] levantar muchos hoteles. El lugar comenzó a perder su encanto;[16] por consiguiente[17] el turismo se fue des-

las calles de la ciudad. El programa de reforma también incluye la mejora[25] de los parques.

A pesar de las dificultades que tiene la ciudad (muy parecidas a las de otras ciudades), es fácil comprender por qué tres millones de visitantes acuden[26] anualmente a Acapulco. Es el dinamismo del lugar, la diversión, el clima. En Acapulco siempre hace sol. Incluso durante la estación de las lluvias, de junio a octubre, sigue brillando[27] el sol. En Acapulco, tomar el sol es un placer. Pero, es bueno recordar que en Acapulco los rayos de sol son más penetrantes que en el norte. ¡Cuidado con las quemaduras[28]!

[25]*improvement* [26]*come* [27]*shining* [28]*burns*

Se venden muchos chiles en los mercados mexicanos.

NEW VOCABULARY: cenar, tiene que ver con, el aceite, el aguacate, el aperitivo, el ave, las botanas, el cafecito, las calorías, la carne, la comida (fuerte), el chile, el chocolate, la dieta, el dulce, las especias, los frijoles, las frutas, las hierbas, el ingrediente, la leche, el limón, el maíz, el mango, la mezcla, el pan, el pavo, el pollo, el queso, la sopa seca, la taza, las tortillas, el trigo, el vaso, el vino; dulce, ligera, sabrosa; esencialmente

Perspectivas de México: La cocina[1] mexicana

Como muchas otras cosas en México, la comida mexicana es el resultado de una mezcla de culturas y pueblos durante siglos. Y es verdaderamente[2] rica, variada, original y única. Una influencia importante en la cocina mexicana tiene que ver con la llegada y colonización de los españoles, en el siglo XVI. Otra se debe a la presencia francesa y austríaca en el siglo XIX. La cocina mexicana actual es comida indígena enriquecida[3] con muchas cosas llegadas de Europa y África. Además de los dos ingredientes básicos de la comida mexicana, el maíz y los frijoles, los indígenas contribuyeron con exóticas frutas tropicales y hierbas, el chile, el cacao, el aguacate y un ave de carne muy sabrosa: el pavo. Los españoles aportaron[4] la carne, las aves de corral,[5] el queso, el trigo, el aceite y el vino. También introdujeron una manera de cocinar esencialmente mediterránea, muy característica. De Francia vienen, entre otras cosas, el pan y la pastelería.[6] Desde África llegaron el café, las especias y el mango. Esta mezcla, que es la actual cocina mexicana, es, para muchos, mejor que cualquiera[7] de sus antecesores.[8]

Aunque en México se hacen tres comidas al día, de cierta forma[9] son distintas de las de los EE. UU. Los mexicanos en el desayuno suelen tomar, al igual que[10] sus vecinos del norte o los europeos, jugo de naranja, huevos y café. Pero a diferencia de ellos[11] también pueden desayunar con **menudo** (callos[12] al estilo de Cuernavaca), **chilaquiles** (tortillas calientes en forma de tiras[13] cubiertas[14] con una crema espesa[15]) o **carne ranchera** (carne de res caliente, con frijoles), chocolate y pan dulce.

En la dieta mexicana, la comida fuerte es la de mediodía. Esta comida es fatal en cuanto a[16] calorías pero una delicia para el paladar:[17] para comenzar, un aperitivo con algunas botanas, sopa aguada,[18] sopa seca, carne o pollo (dos o tres platos distintos), frijoles, postre y un cafecito. La comida fuerte suele acompañarse con cerveza o **aguas frescas** (agua con jarabe[19] de fruta). Las más populares son las que tienen sabor[20] a limón o tamarindo.[21] Tanto las tortillas como[22] el pan al estilo francés acompañan cada plato, ya que[23] en las comidas informales a los mexicanos les gusta hacer tacos de todos los platos servidos en la mesa.

La cena se sirve entre las 6:30 de la tarde y medianoche. Consiste normalmente en algo más ligero que la comida: una taza de chocolate con pan o un vaso de leche con algún dulce o quizás un plato de frijoles o algo que haya quedado[24] de la comida. (En el pasado se comía también un tentempié[25] a media mañana y a media tarde[26] para mantener las fuerzas.[27]) Un proverbio que refleja[28] fielmente[29] esta costumbre de la cena ligera dice: «Desayunar como rey,[30] comer como príncipe y cenar como limosnero[31]».

[1]*cuisine* [2]*truly* [3]*enriched* [4]*contributed* [5]*de... domesticated* [6]*pastries* [7]*any* [8]*ancestors, predecessors* [9]*de... in some way* [10]*al... the same as* [11]*a... in contrast to them* [12]*tripe* [13]*strips* [14]*covered* [15]*thick, heavy* [16]*en... in terms of* [17]*palate* [18]*sopa... soup* [19]*syrup* [20]*flavor* [21]*tamarind (fruit)* [22]*Tanto... Tortillas as well as* [23]*ya... since* [24]*que... left over* [25]*pick-me-up* [26]*a... at mid-morning and at mid-afternoon* [27]*mantener... to keep up one's strength* [28]*reflects* [29]*faithfully* [30]*king* [31]*beggar*

NOTE: See the *Instructor's Manual* for suggestions on using the chapter-opening pages.

La comida

¿Has probado la comida mexicana? ¿Te gusta su sabor?

POR UN PESO

Hamburguesa

Una tortillera hace tortillas y las cocina en un comal grande.

Esta mujer tiene su puesto en el Mercado Hidalgo en Guanajuato.

METAS

FUNCIONES

- to discuss food and meals
- to read a menu and to order a meal

GRAMÁTICA

- use of the preterite in contrast with the imperfect
- comparisons of equality and inequality

APPROPRIATE TESTING POINTS:
Diálogo (2), Los comestibles, El pretérito y el imperfecto, **Quiz 1**
Diálogo (1), En la mesa, **Quiz 2**
Diálogo (2), Comparativos y superlativos, **Quiz 3**
Diálogo (1), En acción
Chapter test

207

DIÁLOGO

¿Cuándo comemos?

el almuerzo   la comida

PREPARATION: Direct students' attention to the drawings. Ask the following questions. **¿Se come el almuerzo por la mañana, por la tarde o por la noche? ¿Y cuándo se come la comida?** Ask students to focus on the title of the dialogue and on the dialogue introduction. **¿Dónde están los primos?** Have students skim the dialogue and ask **¿De qué hablan los jóvenes?**
SUGGESTION: Have students read the dialogue to each other in pairs.

NEW VOCABULARY: tienen hambre; el cereal, el desayuno, la ensalada, el helado, los huevos, el jamón, el pan (tostado), las papas, el pescado, el sándwich; caliente, raro; tal vez

David y Elena llegan a Acapulco. Después de tomar el sol, los primos tienen hambre y comienzan a hablar de la comida.

DAVID: ¿Sabes, Elena? El horario de las comidas en México todavía me parece un poco raro.
ELENA: Tal vez... pero ¡siempre comes con gusto[1]!
DAVID: Tienes razón. Me encanta la comida mexicana.
ELENA: ¿Verdad que el horario aquí es distinto? Pero, ¿cómo? A ver, ¿cuál es la comida más importante del día en los EE. UU.?
DAVID: Pues antes era el desayuno. La gente solía comer un desayuno enorme: fruta, huevos, jamón, pan tostado, papas, café y, a veces, cereal con leche. Pero, ahora muchos de mis compañeros en la universidad raramente desayunan, y nunca toman un desayuno caliente.
ELENA: ¿Y el almuerzo?
DAVID: Algo ligero... sopa, una ensalada o un sándwich con fruta o helado. Y comemos la comida fuerte por la noche.
ELENA: Pues, sí, los dos horarios son muy distintos. Ya sabes que nuestra comida fuerte es por la tarde y que por la noche comemos algo ligero. A veces la familia sale a cenar a un restaurante, sobre todo[2] ahora cuando muchas personas no pueden volver a casa para la comida principal. Las comidas tradicionales son un lujo[3] que reservamos para los días festivos. Recuerdo que cuando era niña, nuestra comida principal era a las dos y mi mamá preparaba sopa seca, carne... o pollo o pescado... ensalada, postre y fruta. Pero ahora generalmente no nos reunimos para la comida. ¡No tenemos tiempo!

[1] *gusto, appetite*   [2] sobre... *above all, especially*   [3] *luxury*

De inmediato

OPTIONAL: 1. ¿Por qué comenzaron David y Elena a hablar de la comida? 2. ¿Le gusta a David la comida mexicana o no le gusta? 3. ¿Qué solía comer la gente para el desayuno? 4. ¿Cuáles son algunas diferencias entre el horario de comidas mexicano y el estadounidense? 5. ¿Cómo era la comida principal en casa de Elena cuando (ella) era niña?

SUGGESTION: (A ti te toca) Remind students to use a plural form if they list two or more cuisines that they "love."

At which of the meals discussed in the dialogue (**el desayuno tradicional en los EE. UU., el almuerzo en los EE. UU., la comida principal tradicional en México**) would each of the following foods be eaten? (There may be more than one correct answer.)

la carne	los huevos	el pollo
el cereal	el jamón	el postre
la ensalada	el pan tostado	el sándwich
la fruta	las papas	la sopa seca
el helado	el pescado	

A ti te toca

David says, "**Me encanta la comida mexicana.**" Using the following suggestions, tell the class what kind(s) of food *you* love and why.

alemana	japonesa	cara	ligera	
china	mexicana	deliciosa	picante	
francesa	norteamericana	dulce	rápida	
italiana	¿ ?	frita	¿ ?	

NEW VOCABULARY: frita, picante

EJEMPLO: Me encanta la comida china porque no es cara y es rápida.

En la universidad

NEW VOCABULARY: estamos listos, estás loca; el aceite de oliva, la langosta, la paella, la pimienta, la sal, las servilletas, el vinagre

D I Á L O G O

SUGGESTION: Have students read the dialogues to each other in pairs.

Carmen y Celia llegan a la casa de Jorge y Joaquín, donde van a preparar la cena. Los dos hombres ya han puesto la mesa y esperan a las españolas.

CELIA: ¿Compraste langosta para la paella?

CARMEN: ¿Estás loca? En España, la abuela siempre le ponía langosta a la paella; pero en los EE. UU. la langosta cuesta mucho.

JORGE: Carmen dijo que iban a llegar a eso de las cinco, ¿no?

JOAQUÍN: Sí, pero primero tenían que pasar por el supermercado.

JORGE: ¿Ya pusiste las servilletas en la mesa?

JOAQUÍN: Sí, pero no pude encontrar la sal y la pimienta. ¿Dónde están?

JORGE: Pues ya las puse en la mesa, junto con el aceite de oliva y el vinagre para la ensalada.

JOAQUÍN: Entonces estamos listos.

PREPARATION: Direct students' attention to the drawing. **¿Quiénes son las personas en el dibujo?** Ask students to focus on the dialogue introduction. **¿Dónde están?** Have students skim the dialogues. **¿De qué hablan los estudiantes?**

De inmediato

¿Quién(es)... ?

1. puso servilletas en la mesa
2. no compró langosta
3. tenían que pasar por el supermercado
4. siempre le ponía langosta a la paella
5. dijo que iban a llegar sobre las cinco
6. no pudo encontrar la sal y la pimienta
7. puso el aceite de oliva y el vinagre en la mesa

OPTIONAL: 1. ¿De dónde son Carmen y Celia? 2. ¿Qué hicieron los hombres antes de llegar las españolas? 3. ¿Por qué no compró langosta Carmen? 4. ¿Qué van a preparar las señoritas para la cena?

A ti te toca

With a classmate, practice saying "Are you crazy?" Take turns asking the following questions, to which your partner will respond, "**¿Estás loco/a?**," followed by a logical comment. Try to invent at least two additional questions.

EJEMPLO: —¿El chófer te trajo a clase hoy?
            —¿Estás loco/a? No tengo chófer.

1. ¿Compraste flores para Ⓟ?
2. ¿Ya hiciste todas tus tareas para la semana entrante[1]?
3. ¿Te comparó un profesor de física con Albert Einstein?
4. ¿Dijiste que vas a tomar 50 unidades el semestre/trimestre que viene?
5. ¿Invitaste al rector (a la rectora) a nuestra fiesta el viernes?

[1] *upcoming*

Faceta cultural

Las tapas se comen con una copa de jerez u otro vino en los bares de España.

FOLLOW-UP: 1. What are **antojitos** and **tapas**? 2. What is a **merienda**? 3. What generalizations can be made about Hispanic meal patterns? 4. What time, generally speaking, is the midday meal in Mexico?

Las comidas

NEW VOCABULARY: la merienda

In the Hispanic world, breakfast often consists of coffee and rolls or bread, and a midmorning break with more coffee and rolls helps stave off hunger pangs until the main meal. Traditionally, all of the family members went home for the main meal, which was often followed by a **siesta** or a time for quiet activities. After school, children might also eat a light meal (**una merienda**) and their parents might have a glass of wine with **antojitos**[1] or **tapas**[1] in the early evening at a neighborhood café. Although the evening meal is typically very light, this pattern is changing. As more women work outside the home, the heavy midday meal has declined in popularity. In addition, in large cities, the time required for all family members to return home at midday is also a factor that discourages observation of traditional patterns.

The times at which one normally has meals in the Hispanic world may be very disconcerting to a visitor. The unwary traveler looking for lunch at noon or supper at 5:00 may find the restaurants closed. The midday meal is usually served around 2:00 and the evening meal rarely takes place before 8:00 or 9:00.* In some metropolitan areas, particularly in Spain, it is common to go out for an evening of entertainment and then have dinner at 11:00.

En México

Generalizations about Hispanic meal patterns do not necessarily apply to all countries, to all regions within a given country, or to every family within a particular region. In some homes in Cuernavaca, for instance, the midday meal, eaten around 2:00 P.M., is called **el almuerzo,** whereas the evening meal, generally served at 8:00, is **la comida**. In other homes, the midday meal, around 2:00, is referred to as **la comida** and the evening meal, also around 8:00, is **la cena**. In these homes, **el almuerzo** is often a light meal eaten in a restaurant two or three hours earlier than **la comida**. The use of **almuerzo** to refer to the midday meal may have much to do with the number of American students who routinely study at the language institutes in Cuernavaca. However, the use of **comida** to refer to the heavier midday meal and **cena** for the lighter evening repast is standard throughout Mexico.

[1] *snacks, hors d'œuvres*

---

*These hours for meals are observed in most restaurants; however, fast food restaurants—in the Hispanic world as well as in the United States—are open and serve at almost any time.

Los comestibles

Otras comidas y bebidas

LAS FRUTAS	FRUITS		
la banana	*banana*	el mango	*mango*
la cereza	*cherry*	la pera	*pear*
la fresa	*strawberry*	la toronja	*grapefruit*

211

LAS VERDURAS Y LEGUMBRES	VEGETABLES AND LEGUMES
el apio	celery
la calabaza	squash, pumpkin
la col	cabbage
los chícharos	peas
el chile	chili pepper
la ensalada	salad
las espinacas	spinach
los frijoles	beans
el pepino	cucumber
el tomate	tomato

LAS CARNES Y AVES	MEATS AND POULTRY
la carne de cordero	lamb
la carne de puerco	pork
la carne de res	beef
el huevo (duro/frito/ revuelto)	(boiled/fried/ scrambled) egg
el rosbif	roast beef
la ternera	veal
el tocino	bacon

EL PESCADO Y LOS MARISCOS	FISH AND SEAFOOD
el atún	tuna, tuna fish
los camarones	shrimp
el lenguado	sole, flounder
el pargo	red snapper

LOS POSTRES	DESSERTS
el dulce	candy, sweet
el flan	caramel custard
la galleta	cookie
la gelatina	gelatin
el helado	ice cream

el pan dulce	sweet bread
el pastel	pie
la torta	cake

LAS BEBIDAS	BEVERAGES
el agua	water
el café	coffee
el cafecito	coffee
la cerveza	beer
el champán	champagne
el chocolate	chocolate; hot chocolate
el jugo (de naranja/ manzana)	(orange/apple) juice
la leche	milk
la limonada	lemonade
el refresco	soft drink
el té (helado/caliente)	(iced/hot) tea
el vino	wine

OTRAS COMIDAS	OTHER FOODS
el arroz	rice
el cereal	cereal
los fideos	noodles
la mantequilla	butter
la mantequilla de cacahuetes/maní	peanut butter
la mayonesa	mayonnaise
el pan	bread
el pan tostado	toast
las papitas	potato chips
el queso	cheese
la sopa	soup
la sopa seca	pasta; rice

COMPREHENSION: Ask students to work with a classmate and state how they feel about various foods, using an expression that you've written on the board or overhead: **No me gusta(n) para nada. No me gusta(n) mucho. Me gusta(n) un poco. Me gusta(n). Me gusta(n) mucho. Me encanta(n).**

Actividades

SUGGESTION: Make sure there are no questions about the pronunciation and meaning of the items in Acts. A and B.
OPTIONAL: Ask students, working in small groups, to say the names of two food items. Their classmates will say whether the two items are a common combination: **El rosbif y las papas.** → **Es común. Los pepinos y el champán.** → **No es común.**

A Asociaciones. What do you associate with each of the following items?

EJEMPLO: el pan → la mantequilla, la mantequilla de maní, el sándwich, el pan dulce/tostado, agua...

1. el pollo
2. el rosbif
3. la ensalada
4. la manzana
5. la leche
6. el ajo
7. los sándwiches
8. el helado
9. los huevos

SUGGESTION: This activity works well when students are in pairs or small groups.

B ¿Qué comes tú? Describe what you eat or drink at the following times or for the following occasions. Begin your sentence with a phrase from the first column, continue with a phrase from the second column, then complete your thought with one or more foods or beverages.

A las siete de la mañana...
Para el Día de Gracias...
Después de las clases...
A mediodía...
Para la Pascua Florida...
Para mi cumpleaños...
Antes de acostarme...
En una fiesta...

me gusta comer/tomar...
normalmente como/tomo...
siempre como/tomo...

SUGGESTION: Encourage students to respond with phrases such as **¿Verdad? Yo también/tampoco**, and **Interesante. Yo sí/no.**

C **Preguntas personales.**

1. ¿Qué comes tú por la mañana? ¿a mediodía? ¿por la tarde?
2. ¿Tomas café? ¿vino? ¿cerveza? ¿mucha leche?
3. ¿Qué comes todos los días?
4. ¿Qué prefieres comer de postre?
5. ¿Qué comes entre comidas? ¿Qué bebes?
6. ¿Dónde y con quién comes tú?

SUGGESTION: This works well as a pair activity.
VARIATION: Have students interview you, being sure to change from familiar to formal address.

El pretérito y el imperfecto

El profesor Brewer **llegó** un poco tarde a la reunión del Club Hispánico. Cuando **entró** en la sala de clase...

PREPARATION: Read the captions and have students repeat them. Ask the following questions. **¿Qué le pasó al profesor Brewer ayer? ¿Qué pasaba en la clase cuando llegó? ¿Qué tiempo hacía? ¿Qué hacían Luisa y Marisol cuando entró el profesor?**

Marisol y Luisa **hablaban** de la hija de Luisa, Mercedes. Felipe **leía** una revista y Joaquín **dormía**. Afuera **llovía** y **hacía** viento.

A **¿Has prestado atención?** How well have you been paying attention to the places that David and Elena have visited, the people they have met, and the things they have done? Match the cities on the left with the events that occurred there to indicate where David and Elena were when these things happened.

Actividades

NEW VOCABULARY: prestar atención
SUGGESTION: If this proves too taxing for students' memories, have them find at least five that they remember or can figure out.

SUGGESTION: Make sure there are no questions about the pronunciation or meaning of the items.

EJEMPLO: Laredo → David y Elena estaban en Laredo cuando vieron a los padrinos de Elena.

1. Laredo	cenaron en la plaza de los Mariachis
2. Monterrey	compraron aspirinas en una farmacia
3. Saltillo	conocieron a Héctor y Matilde
4. Guadalajara	David conoció al Sr. Kolb
5. Guanajuato	fueron al partido de fútbol
6. San Miguel de Allende	la abuela le mostró fotos a David
7. Querétaro	llamaron a Ana, la madre de David
8. México, D.F.	David miró fotos con el padre de Elena
9. Teotihuacán	se encontraron con Roger Austin
	subieron una pirámide
	vieron a los padrinos de Elena
	visitaron a la Sra. Santos, la hermana del Sr. Kolb

NEW VOCABULARY: llamar a la puerta, perder, sonar; el ruido

PREPARATION: 1. Make sure students know the correct preterite forms of the infinitives in the right-hand column. 2. Have students identify who the symbols Ⓘ and Ⓟ represent: **¿Quién es tu persona especial? ¿Cuál es la relación entre Uds.?**

The uses of the preterite and the imperfect may seem confusing to you. Observe these two tenses carefully as they are used so that you can develop the ability to use them correctly.

Ⓑ **¿Qué hacías cuando... ?** Imagine that your day has been full of interruptions. Express what you were doing when the unexpected interruptions occurred, using the following phrases as clues.

SUGGESTION: This works well as a pair activity.

EJEMPLO: Escribía una carta...   oír / un ruido →
Escribía una carta cuando oí un ruido.

¿QUÉ HACÍAS?	INTERRUPCIÓN
1. Me bañaba...	entrar / Ⓘ
2. Tenía champú[1] en el pelo...	llamar / a la puerta
3. Leía el periódico...	llegar / mi(s) padre(s)
4. Estudiaba...	mi equipo favorito / perder
5. Estacionaba el coche...	mis amigos y yo / decidir / salir
6. Escribía una carta...	oír / un ruido
7. Escuchaba música...	sonar / el teléfono
8. Veía un partido de _____...	ver / a Ⓟ
9. Me acostaba...	ver / el accidente
10. ¿ ?	¿ ?

[1] *shampoo*

El pretérito y el imperfecto en contraste

PRETERITE

Used to

- talk about completed past events
- narrate a series of past actions

IMPERFECT

Used to

- talk about past actions in progress
- describe the background action or

IMPERFECT (*continued*)

conditions when something interrupted (*preterite*) or was occurring simultaneously (*imperfect*)

- describe habitual or continuous past actions
- express age and time in the past
- describe physical and mental states in the past

Eran las tres de la mañana cuando Luis **llegó**. TIME, ACTION

Hacía sol cuando Elena **se despertó**. DESCRIPTION, ACTION

Jorge y Joaquín **estudiaban** en casa cuando, de repente, Tomás **llamó** a la puerta. BACKGROUND ACTION, INTERRUPTION

Luisa **estaba** muy preocupada; pero cuando **vio** a Mercedes, **sabía** que su hija **estaba** bien. MENTAL STATE, ACTION, MENTAL STATE, PHYSICAL STATE

Esta mañana **me levanté, me bañé** y **me vestí** muy rápido. SERIES OF PAST ACTIONS

El profesor **explicaba** el problema mientras los alumnos buenos **escuchaban** y los malos **hablaban** o **dormían**. ACTIONS OCCURRING SIMULTANEOUSLY

NEW VOCABULARY: explicaba; el problema

En el mercado

DIÁLOGO

NEW VOCABULARY: anterior, fresco

SUGGESTION: Have students read the dialogue to each other in pairs.

Elena insiste en ir al mercado muy temprano para mostrarle a David la cantidad[1] de personas que se encuentran[2] allí a la madrugada.[3]

DAVID: Elena, ¿por qué teníamos que venir a las seis de la mañana?

ELENA: Porque todos vienen a esta hora para comprar la comida más fresca posible.

DAVID: Y ¿dónde estaba toda esa gente ayer? ¿Nadie vino de compras?

ELENA: Compraron ayer y anteayer y el día anterior.

DAVID: ¿Quieres decir que la gente viene al mercado todos los días? ... Ay, Elena, ¡mira qué fresco el pescado que trae este señor!

ELENA: Debe comprar para algún restaurante. En los restaurantes todo... pero todo[4]... tiene que ser fresco... la carne, las frutas, el pan... todo.

[1]*quantity, number* [2]*se... are found* [3]*dawn* [4]*pero... and I mean **everything***

PREPARATION: Direct students' attention to the drawing. Ask them to focus on the title of the dialogue and on the dialogue introduction. **¿Dónde están los primos?** Have students skim the dialogue. **¿De qué hablan los jóvenes?**

Match the phrases on the right with those on the left to explain why and when the characters in the dialogue acted as they did.

De inmediato

1. David y Elena van al supermercado a las seis porque
2. La gente va al mercado
3. El hombre del restaurante compra todos los días porque en el restaurante

todos los días

todo tiene que ser fresco

todos vienen a esta hora

OPTIONAL: 1. ¿Dónde están David y Elena? 2. ¿Por qué llegaron allí muy temprano? 3. ¿Cuántas veces por semana va la gente al mercado? 4. ¿Qué lleva el señor del restaurante?

A ti te toca

Imagine that you and a friend are thinking back to the things you had to do when you were younger, but you don't recall exactly *why* you had to do those activities. With a partner, take turns asking why you had to do certain activities, and answer the questions, using the cues given. Follow the model.

NEW VOCABULARY: salir bien, tanta

EJEMPLO: escribir todo el vocabulario antes del examen (salir bien en el examen) →
—¿Por qué tenía (yo) que escribir todo el vocabulario antes del examen?
—Tenías que escribir todo el vocabulario para salir bien en el examen.

1. practicar el clarinete todos los días (tocar bien en los conciertos)
2. practicar el atletismo cada mañana (correr más rápido en las competencias[1])
3. estudiar cada noche (saber las respuestas a las preguntas de Ⓟ)
4. acostarme temprano los días de clase (poder pensar mejor en clase)
5. ir al laboratorio de lenguas con tanta frecuencia (poder hablar con facilidad)
6. leer libros de historia todas las semanas (entender mejor el mundo actual)
7. lavarme los dientes (tener dientes sanos[2])

[1]*competitions* [2]*healthy*

VOCABULARIO

En la mesa

PREPARATION: As they look over the drawing and list, ask students to compare what they see with what they normally use.

COMPREHENSION: Using a child's tea set or a plastic table setting, give students commands such as **Pon el plato en la mesa.** Review prepositions with **Pon ___ a la derecha/izquierda de ___.**

el vinagre — el aceite — una copa — el azúcar — una taza — un plato hondo — un vaso — una botella — un plato chico — la sal — una servilleta — un plato — la crema — la pimienta — el tenedor — el cuchillo — la cuchara — la cucharita

Definiciones. Which items from the place setting best fit the description?

1. Le pongo estos dos ingredientes a una ensalada.
2. Uso este utensilio para comer la sopa.
3. Uso esto para tomar el vino.
4. Uso esto para limpiarme la boca después de comer.
5. Le pongo estos dos ingredientes al café.
6. Uso esto para tomar el café o el té.
7. Uso esto para cortar[1] la carne.
8. Uso estos para dar más sabor[2] a la carne o a las legumbres.

[1] *to cut* [2] *flavor, taste*

Un restaurante de primera[1]

NEW VOCABULARY: probar; la entrada, el plato fuerte, la salsa; sencillo

Elena y David deciden darse el lujo[2] de una comida especial en un restaurante elegante.

EL MESERO: Buenas noches, señores. ¿Qué desean comer esta noche? ¿Puedo traerles algo de aperitivo o de comer?

DAVID: Sí, por favor. Para empezar, yo voy a pedir los mariscos a la marinera.[3] Para la señorita, el aguacate relleno[4] con cebiche[5] de camarones. Y, para seguir, sopa de flor de calabaza para los dos. Pero, no podemos decidir lo que queremos de plato fuerte. ¿Qué nos recomienda Ud.?

EL MESERO: Bueno, la especialidad de la casa son los camarones acapulqueños.[6] Los camarones en este plato vienen con una salsa de mantequilla, ajo, tomate y perejil.[7]

ELENA: Como pedí camarones de entrada, prefiero algo más sencillo para el plato principal. ¿Qué tipo de pescado es el que preparan con cilantro[8]?

EL MESERO: Depende de lo que hay en el mercado cada día. Siempre compramos el pescado más fresco y con mejor aspecto.[9] Para este plato a veces usamos el lenguado o el pargo...

ELENA: Hmm. Hemos comido tanto pescado y tanto marisco en los últimos días que creo que voy a probar otra cosa esta noche. Veo que ustedes ofrecen[10] un plato muy viejo y muy tradicional que me gusta mucho. Voy a pedir ternera en salsa de ciruelas pasas.[11]

DAVID: Bueno, para mí, los camarones acapulqueños. Nunca me canso[12] de comer mariscos frescos. Y para tomar, una botella de vino blanco.

[1] *dc... first-class* [2] *luxury* [3] *a... sailor-style (usually in a spicy tomato sauce)* [4] *stuffed* [5] *marinated raw seafood*
[6] *Acapulco-style* [7] *parsley* [8] *coriander* [9] *appearance* [10] *offer* [11] *ciruelas... prunes* [12] *me... I tire*

De inmediato

The following statements are incorrect. Use information from the dialogue to change them to true statements.

1. Para empezar, David pide el aguacate relleno con cebiche de camarones.
2. Para seguir, Elena pide sopa de flor de calabaza y David pide ensalada.
3. La especialidad de la casa es el pescado con cilantro.
4. A veces usan el atún para el pescado con cilantro.
5. Como plato fuerte, David y Elena deciden pedir la especialidad de la casa.
6. Para tomar, David pide cerveza.
7. A Elena le encanto la ternera en salsa de mantequilla, ajo, tomate y perejil.

A ti te toca

List for your partner the ingredients in a simple dish (for example, a fruit or green salad, a sandwich) and see if he or she can guess what you are describing. You may use any of the following ingredients, and add others if necessary.

EJEMPLO —Este plato tiene pan, carne de res, lechuga, tomate, cebolla y salsa de tomate. A veces tiene tocino.
—Es una hamburguesa.

aceite	huevos	naranja	tomate
aguacate	jamón	pan	uvas
ajo	lechuga	papas	vinagre
banana	manzana	piña	zanahoria
cebolla	mayonesa	queso	¿ ?

DIÁLOGO

En la universidad

NEW VOCABULARY: deliciosa

El Club Internacional necesita dinero para algunos proyectos[1] y los miembros del club venden comida típica de sus países para reunir los fondos[2] necesarios para estos proyectos.

TOMÁS: Este año vinieron más estudiantes que el año pasado, ¿no?
ALFONSINA: Creo que sí. Los estudiantes hispanos del club tuvieron que buscar más ingredientes para preparar más gazpacho[3] y flan porque ya se les habían acabado.[4]
TOMÁS: Me parece que cada vez más los alumnos universitarios muestran interés en otras culturas... y están dispuestos[5] a probar comidas que no son típicas de los EE. UU.

[1] *projects* [2] *funds* [3] *cold tomato soup* [4] *se... had run out* [5] *ready*

CELIA: ¿Es buena la tortilla española[6]?
JOAQUÍN: Felipe, nuestro cocinero,[7] dice que sí.
CARMEN: Yo probé la tortilla y estaba deliciosa.

MARISOL: Los estudiantes de esta universidad comen más carne que en mi país.
EL PROFESOR BREWER: Es verdad. Es que en esta región no hay tanto pescado.
MARÍA: Pero incluso en la costa donde hay pescado, no hay nada tan popular como la hamburguesa entre los jóvenes de los EE. UU.

[6]tortilla... *potato-onion omelette* [7]*cook*

De inmediato

Are the following statements true or false, based on the dialogue? Respond **Es cierto** if the statement is true or **No es cierto** if it is false. Correct the false statements.

1. Alfonsina cree que este año vinieron más estudiantes que el año pasado.
2. Celia pregunta si la tortilla española es buena.
3. Carmen probó la tortilla mexicana.
4. Los estudiantes hispanos del Club Internacional venden gazpacho y tortillas.
5. Tomás dice que más y más estudiantes tienen interés en otras culturas.
6. Felipe dice que la tortilla española es horrible.
7. María cree que la comida típica preferida de los estudiantes en los EE. UU. es el pescado.
8. Marisol dice que comen menos carne en su país que en los EE. UU.

EXPANSION: Have students write additional true/false statements about the dialogue. They should read them to a partner or a small group.
OPTIONAL: 1. ¿Qué hacían los miembros del Club Internacional? ¿Por qué? 2. ¿Qué tuvieron que hacer los hispanos del club? ¿Por qué? 3. ¿Quién preparó la tortilla española? 4. Según Marisol, ¿cuál es la comida más popular entre los jóvenes de este país?

A ti te toca

Using the cues given, work with a classmate to construct questions and answers based on Celia and Joaquín's conversation.

EJEMPLOS: interesante / clase de _____ →
—¿Es interesante la clase de inglés?
—El profesor (La profesora) de inglés dice que sí.
o —Los estudiantes dicen que sí/no.

caros / libros →
—¿Son caros los libros?
—Todos dicen que sí.

buenos / exámenes
importantes / vacaciones
difíciles / composiciones
cara / comida en el centro estudiantil
importante / ir al laboratorio

difícil / encontrar dónde estacionar el coche
imposible / ganar dinero suficiente
fácil / esta actividad

Comparativos y superlativos

PREPARATION: Prepare an overhead transparency of the drawing with captions deleted for students to observe as you compare the characters. Work with the drawing by asking the following questions. **¿Quiénes son las personas del dibujo? ¿Cuál es la relación entre ellos? ¿Cuáles de ellos son altos? ¿Cuáles de ellos no son altos? ¿Cuáles de ellos son jóvenes? ¿Cuáles de ellos no son jóvenes? ¿Cuál de ellos es el más alto? ¿Cuál de ellos es la más baja? ¿Es Elena más alta que su tía? ¿Es Ana más alta que su sobrina?** Then begin Act. A.

NEW VOCABULARY: menor

Elena
21 años

Ana
44 años

Sandra
16 años

David
20 años

el Sr.
Nelson
49 años

la
abuelita
80 años

ELENA: Soy **tan alta como** mi tía pero soy **menor que** ella.
SANDRA: Soy **más alta que** mi mamá pero no soy **tan alta como** mi papá.
DAVID: Soy **más alto que** mi papá pero no tengo **tantos años como** él.
EL SR. NELSON: Soy **más bajo que** mi hijo pero él es **menor que** yo.
LA ABUELITA: Soy **la más baja** y **la mayor**.

Actividades

OPTIONAL: Have students, working in pairs, make as many sentences as possible comparing their height to members of their families or to famous people. Allow them to share their best efforts with the class. **Soy más alto/a que mi mamá. No soy más alto/a que Shaquille O'Neal.**
OPTIONAL: Have students, working in pairs, compare their ages with those of family members or famous people. **Soy mayor que mi prima Nancy. Soy mayor/menor que Ⓟ.**

Ⓐ ¿Quién es más alto/a y quién es mayor? *Paso 1.* Compare the height of the following characters, using the drawing as a reference.

EJEMPLOS: la abuelita / el Sr. Nelson →
La abuelita es más baja que el Sr. Nelson.

David / el Sr. Nelson →
David es más alto que el Sr. Nelson.

1. Ana / David
2. Ana / la abuelita
3. Sandra / Elena
4. David / Sandra
5. el Sr. Nelson / Ana
6. la abuelita / Elena

Paso 2. Now compare the ages of the same characters.

EJEMPLOS: la abuelita / el Sr. Nelson
La abuelita es mayor que el Sr. Nelson.
o La abuelita tiene más años que el Sr. Nelson.

Sandra / Ana →
Sandra es menor que Ana.
o Sandra tiene menos años que Ana.

E **¿Quién tiene más?** Look at the drawing and compare the purchases that
Marisol and María made for the International Club's food fair.

EJEMPLOS: maíz →
María compró más maíz que Marisol.

pollo →
Marisol compró menos pollo que María.

1. papas
2. uvas
3. salchichas
4. cebollas
5. biftec
6. huevos
7. pasteles
8. jugo de tomate

PREPARATION: Make sure students can name all the items in the drawing. Resolve any questions about the pronunciation or meaning of the items.
OPTIONAL: Ask students, working in small groups, to make statements comparing themselves to others in their group. Classmates may challenge their statements. E1: **Tengo más libros en mi mochila que Jason.** E2: **No lo creo. ¿Cuántos libros tienes?**/E1: **Tengo cinco.** E2: **Entonces, no es cierto. Tengo seis libros. Tengo más libros que tú.**

C **Compras idénticas.** By chance Tomás and Joaquín bought exactly the same
items for the International Club's food fair. Compare what they have
bought, following the models.

EJEMPLOS: jamón → Tomás compró tanto jamón como Joaquín

refrescos → Joaquín compró tantos refrescos como Tomás.

1. manzanas   4. pasteles   7. galletas
2. limones   5. gelatina   8. sopa
3. tocino   6. café   9. salchichas

PREPARATION: Make sure there are no questions about the pronunciation or meaning of the items.
OPTIONAL: Ask students, working in small groups, to make statements about their possessions or other aspects of their lives. They will then ask other students in the group to compare their lives. **Tengo cuatro clases hoy. ¿Tienes tantas clases como yo?** → **No, no tengo tantas clases como tú.** *o* **Sí, tengo tantas clases como tú.**

D **Yo soy más/menos _____ que ①.** Compare yourself to people you know,
using **más/menos** + *adjective* + **que** or **tan** + *adjective* + **como**.

EJEMPLO: bajo/a → Yo soy más bajo/a que mi padre.
o Yo no soy tan alto/a como mi padre.

1. inteligente   3. rico/a   5. simpático/a
2. guapo/a (bonita)   4. alto/a   6. delgado/a

PREPARATION: Have students identify who the symbol ① represents.
SUGGESTION: This activity works well when students are in pairs or small groups.
SUGGESTION: Encourage responses such as the following. **¿Verdad? Yo también. / Interesante. Yo no. / ¡Qué bien¡ / ¡Qué suerte tienes¡ / Sí, es verdad / Sí, tienes razón / Estoy de acuerdo.**

E **Preguntas personales**   NEW VOCABULARY: mejor, peor

1. ¿Quién es tu persona especial (①)? ¿Quién es más alto/a, ① o tú?
2. ¿Quién es mayor, ① o tú?
3. ¿Tienes tantas clases como ①?
4. ¿Quién estudia menos, ① o tú?
5. ¿Quién habla mejor el español, Ⓟ o tú?
6. ¿Quién es la persona más alta de esta clase?
7. ¿Cuál es la mejor clase de la universidad?
8. ¿Quién es el mejor actor de los EE. UU.? ¿la mejor actriz?
9. ¿Cuál es el peor equipo de fútbol americano?
10. ¿Quién es la persona más rica del mundo?

PREPARATION: Have students identify who the symbol ① represents.
¿Quién es tu persona especial? ¿Cuál es la relación entre Uds.?
SUGGESTION: This works well as a pair activity. The student receiving the questions should have his or her book closed.
VARIATION: Have students interview you, and be sure to change from familiar forms to formal forms.

The comparative forms of **viejo, joven, buen(o),** and **mal(o)** are irregular. Express *older* as **mayor,** *younger* as **menor,** *better* as **mejor,** and *worse* as **peor.**

Comparativos y superlativos

EQUALITY:	**tan**	+ *adjective/adverb*	+ **como**
	tanto/a/os/as	+ *noun*	+ **como**
INEQUALITY:	**más/menos**	+ *adjective/adverb/noun*	+ **que**
SUPERLATIVE:	**el/la/los/las**	+ *adjective/adverb/noun*	+ **de**

Statements of equality in the negative express *not as* (adjective/ adverb) or *not as many* (noun).

Elena es **tan** alta **como** su tía.
Jorge no es **tan** rico **como** su tío.

Los estudiantes no tienen **tantos** libros **como** el profesor.
Tomás compró **tanto** café **como** Joaquín.

Sandra es **más** alta **que** su mamá.
María tiene **más** manzanas **que** Marisol.

David es **menor** que Elena.
El Sr. Nelson es **mayor** que la Sra. Nelson.

David es **el más alto** de la familia.
La abuelita es **la mayor** de la familia.

DIÁLOGO

Un encuentro fortuito[1]

NEW VOCABULARY: el espacio; hermosa; de viaje

Al volver de hacer compras, Elena se encuentra con una mujer que conocía cuando estaba en el Politécnico.

ELENA: Alicia, ¿cómo estás? ¡Qué gusto de[2] verte!

ALICIA: ¿Qué tal, Elena? ¿Qué haces tú por aquí?

ELENA: Estoy de viaje con un primo de los EE. UU. ¿Y tú?

ALICIA: De vacaciones con mi hermana Concha. Esta noche volvemos a casa.

ELENA: Ah, ¿sí? Tu familia vive en Oaxaca, ¿no?

ALICIA: Sí, vivo con mis padres. Asisto a la universidad. Y Uds., ¿ya visitaron Oaxaca? Es una ciudad hermosa.

ELENA: Bueno, esta noche vamos a Oaxaca por autobús. Mi tío vive allí y nos invitó a visitarlo.

ALICIA: ¡Qué bueno! Si quieren, los llevo,[3] así no tienen que ir en autobús. Concha y yo tenemos la camioneta de mi padre y hay espacio de sobra.[4]

ELENA: Pues en cuanto[5] hagamos las maletas[6] las llamamos. Estoy segura de que vamos a divertirnos mucho en el viaje. Muchas gracias, Alicia, y ¡hasta pronto!

PREPARATION: Ask students to look at the drawing. Ask, who are these people and what are they doing? Ask students to focus on the title of the dialogue and on the dialogue introduction. Where are the characters? Have students skim the dialogue. **¿De qué hablan las jóvenes?**
SUGGESTION: Have students read the dialogue to each other in pairs.

[1] *chance, lucky*   [2] Qué... *How nice, What a pleasure*   [3] los... *I'll take you, I'll give you a ride*   [4] de... *extra, to spare*
[5] en... *as soon as*   [6] hagamos... *we pack*

Which of the characters in the preceding dialogue do you associate with these statements?

1. Asiste a la Universidad de Oaxaca.
2. Está de vacaciones con su hermana.
3. Está de viaje con su primo.
4. Está segura de que ella y David van a divertirse mucho en el viaje.
5. Su familia vive en Oaxaca.
6. Su tío vive en Oaxaca.
7. Tiene la camioneta de su padre.
8. Van a hacer las maletas.

De inmediato

SUGGESTION: Have one student read the first four items while the other has his or her book closed. Then they switch roles.
OPTIONAL: 1. ¿Con quién se encontró Elena? 2. ¿Por qué estaba Alicia en Acapulco? 3. ¿Qué ofreció hacer Alicia? 4. ¿Qué necesitaban hacer David y Elena antes de llamar a Alicia?

Tell a classmate five things you are sure of. Some suggestions are given, but try to be original in at least two of your sentences.

EJEMPLO: Estoy seguro/a de que la comida de la cafetería no es sabrosa.

voy a sacar una «A» en esta clase
Ⓘ me quiere
Ⓟ es inteligente
esta clase termina pronto
voy a aprender a hablar bien el español
esta actividad es muy fácil
¿ ?

A ti te toca

PREPARATION: Have students identify who the symbols Ⓘ and Ⓟ represent.

EN ACCIÓN

Antes de ver

In this chapter you will watch and listen as a series of people discuss what they like to eat. You will also see several people discuss what they like to eat and see several people order in a restaurant. Listen carefully and try to remember as many of the details as you can.

Yo, autor(a) esperanzado[1]

In order to write a story in Spanish that is set in the past, you will need to be able to use and differentiate the two past tenses for Spanish—the preterite and the imperfect. Review **El pretérito y el imperfecto en contraste** on page 214. Which tense would you use to set the scene by describing the weather and the setting? Which would you use to advance the action by telling what happened? And which would describe how someone felt at that time? Which would you use to express an action that was in progress at a given time? And

PREPARATION: Review the forms and uses of the preterite and imperfect. Make sure there are no questions about the pronunciation or meaning of the items.
OPTIONAL: Ask students to write original stories based on the model provided.

[1]hopeful

which would express an interrupting action? Look over the phrases listed in **Paso 1** to get a feel for the story you will be writing. When you write, some of the verbs will need to be in the preterite, others in the imperfect. Can you tell by glancing at the phrases which you will use in each case?

NEW VOCABULARY: gritar; oscura

Paso 1. Now it's time to write. Use one phrase from each of the following groups to create a very short story about a mysterious incident that occurred in the past. Although you do not need to add any words, remember that you will need to decide which past tense to use in each case.

1. (ser) un día hermoso.
   (ser) una tarde triste.
   (ser) una noche oscura.
2. (estar) nublado y no (haber) luna.
   (hacer) sol y fresco.
   (hacer) viento y (llover).
3. El policía (estar) nervioso porque...
   Ⓘ (estar) deprimido[2] porque...
   (Yo) (estar) contento/a porque...
4. (saber) que (haber) peligro.[3]
   (saber) que no (tener) problemas.
   (saber) que (tener) problemas.

5. (caminar) por la calle cuando...
   (preparar) para salir de casa cuando...
   (sentarse) en su oficina cuando...
6. Felipe (llamar) a la puerta.
   (sonar) el teléfono.
   (ver) a un hombre.
7. (contestar) inmediatamente.
   (gritar).
   (correr).

[2]*depressed* [3]*danger*

Paso 2. When you have finished writing the first draft of your story, exchange papers with a classmate. Mark any errors you see on your partner's paper. Then, playing the role of editor, improve this promising short work in two ways.

First, add details to the work that has already been done. Such details may include the story's setting (mountains, beach, city), the exact time when the incident took place, what the characters were wearing, and any additional actions that enhance the meaning of the story.

Second, write a few sentences to conclude the story.

Paso 3. Working in small groups, read your classmates' stories and decide which is a potential Pulitzer Prize winner. Each group may then decide how to present the story to the rest of the class; drama and mime are two possibilities if you do not want to read the story aloud. Remember, this is all for fun. If your creation is not chosen by the group, just remind yourself that they are probably ignorant churls who have been raised on television. Great art is rarely recognized by the masses.

OPTIONAL: Have students, in pairs, prepare, rehearse, and present the scenarios they have written.

Bajo en Calorías

Enchiladas de Queso Cottage
397.8 CAL.
11,000 NS 11.00

Ensalada de 8 Verduras
134.7 CAL.
12,000 NS 12.00

Pollo Asado con Manzana
618 CAL.
16,000 NS 16.00

Preparado de Manzana
138.1 CAL.
5,000 NS 5.00

Hamburguesa Asada
390.4 CAL.
12,000 NS 12.00

SUGGESTION: Indicate a targeted length for the students' skit, such as four or five lines per character.

PARA HABLAR

Por favor, señor/señora/señorita

With a classmate, act out the roles of a calorie-conscious diner and a waiter. The diner will specify what he or she wants; the waiter will recommend one or more dishes from the **Bajo en calorías** section of the menu (above left).

EJEMPLOS:
—Me gusta el pollo.
—Entonces le recomiendo el pollo asado con manzana.

—No me gusta comer carne.
—Entonces le recomiendo las enchiladas de queso *cottage*.

Una conversación oída por casualidad

While in a restaurant in Acapulco, Elena and David overheard the couple at the next table trying to convince their young son to order something from the child's menu.

Antes de escuchar

Because you know that the conversation you are about to hear takes place in a restaurant and will include the names of various food items, take this opportunity to review the food-related vocabulary for this chapter before proceeding. Next, read the exercises that pertain to the conversation to prepare yourself for the vocabulary and content of the program. Now you are ready to listen carefully to the dialogue for the first time.

Después de escuchar

Paso 1. As you listen to the dialogue, indicate with a check mark which of the following are mentioned.

_____ arroz	_____ gelatina	_____ pastel de queso
_____ biftec	_____ hamburguesa de	_____ pollo frito
_____ camarones	res	_____ rosbif
empanados[1]	_____ leche	_____ salchichas de pavo
_____ carne asada	_____ limonada	_____ sopa de fideos
_____ cerezas	_____ maíz	_____ tiras[2] de pescado
_____ cerveza	_____ nuggets de pollo	empanado
_____ ensalada	_____ papas fritas	
_____ frijoles	_____ pargo	

[1]*breaded*   [2]*strips, sticks*

Paso 2. Listen to the dialogue a second time and identify the speaker of the following lines. Use **A** for the mother, Alejandra; **C** for the father, Carlos; and **R** for their son, Roberto.

_____ **1.** Ay, Dios mío...
_____ **2.** En un restaurante debes hacer lo que te aconsejen[1] tus padres.
_____ **3.** Es un plato muy caro.
_____ **4.** Ésta es comida para niños pequeñitos.
_____ **5.** Esto es mucha comida para un niño de ocho años de edad.
_____ **6.** Mira lo que has hecho.
_____ **7.** Puedes comer todo lo que quieres en casa.
_____ **8.** Quiero carne asada con frijoles y arroz.

[1]*te... advise, tell you*

Una receta

Elena is trying to give David a recipe for a cereal-based treat that she read on the back of her cereal box that morning. David can't imagine what Elena is trying to tell him: he doesn't recognize the term **malvaviscos**, a main ingredient of the recipe, and Elena gives the instructions for making the dish out of sequence.

Antes de leer

Look at the photograph and the list of ingredients. What is the name of this popular treat in the United States? What do you think **malvaviscos** are? Now skim the instructions for making the treats. What English cognate do you see in the verb **revolviéndolos (revolver)**? In the context of a recipe, what might this verb mean? What cognate do you see in the verb **retire (retirar)**? **Fuego** means *heat* or *fire*. What should you do with the mixture at this point? What English cognate would be a logical translation of the verb **presione (presionar)**? What should you do with the mixture now? What common Spanish adjective can you find in the verb **enfriar**? What would be a logical translation of the verb? The noun **cera** means *wax* and **grasa** means *grease* or *fat*. What are logical meanings of the adjectives **encerado** and **engrasado** in the context of the recipe?

Now, read the jumbled list of steps Marisol took to prepare the Malva Krispis and put the steps in the most appropriate order.

MALVA KRISPIS

Ingredientes:
1/4 de taza de mantequilla o margarina
20 malvaviscos de tamaño regular ó
2 tazas de malvaviscos miniatura
5 tazas de RICE KRISPIS*

Forma de preparar:
Derrita la mantequilla en un recipiente grande a fuego lento. Agregue los malvaviscos revolviéndolos hasta que queden totalmente derretidos, cocine durante tres minutos más, revolviendo constantemente y retire del fuego. Añada los **RICE KRISPIS*** revolviéndolos hasta que queden totalmente cubiertos. Presione la mezcla con la ayuda de una espátula o papel encerado en un molde engrasado de 30 x 20 x 5 cm. Deje enfriar y córtese en cuadritos de 5 x 5 cm.

PARA HORNOS DE MICROONDAS:
Coloque la margarina y los malvaviscos en el horno en un recipiente grande y cocine a máxima potencia durante dos minutos. Revuelva la mezcla. Cocine durante otros dos minutos. Vuelva a mezclar hasta que quede suave. Añada los **RICE KRISPIS*** y mezcle nuevamente hasta que queden cubiertos, colóquelos en un molde y siga las instrucciones anteriores.

Después de leer: Marisol y los Malva Krispis

Marisol likes Malva Krispis and made them for her friends last night. Put her actions in the correct order.

_____ Agregó[1] los malvaviscos y los revolvió hasta que quedaran totalmente derretidos.[2]

_____ Derritió[3] la mantequilla en un recipiente[4] grande a fuego lento.[5]

_____ Dejó que los Malva Krispis se enfriaran y los cortó[6] en cuadritos.[7]

_____ Presionó la mezcla[8] en un molde[9] engrasado.

_____ Retiró la mezcla del fuego.

_____ Añadió los Rice Krispis revolviéndolos hasta que quedaran totalmente cubiertos.[10]

_____ Cocinó la mezcla durante tres minutos más.

[1]_She added_ [2]_melted_ [3]_She melted_ [4]_pan_ [5]_low_ [6]_she cut_ [7]_squares_ [8]_mixture_ [9]_pan_ [10]_covered_

VOCABULARIO

Los verbos	Verbs
cenar	to have dinner, supper
dejar	to let, allow
explicar	to explain
gritar	to yell, scream
probar (ue)	to try; to taste
sonar (ue)	to ring

Las frutas	Fruits
la cereza	cherry
el durazno	peach
la fresa	strawberry
el limón	lemon
la manzana	apple
la naranja	orange
la pera	pear
la piña	pineapple
la toronja	grapefruit
la uva	grape

Palabras semejantes: la banana, el mango.

Las verduras y legumbres	Vegetables and legumes
el aguacate	avocado
el ajo	garlic
el apio	celery
la calabaza	squash, pumpkin
la cebolla	onion
la col	cabbage
los chícharos	peas
el chile	chili pepper
la ensalada	salad
las espinacas	spinach
los frijoles	beans
la lechuga	lettuce
el maíz	corn
la papa	potato
las papas fritas	french fries
el pepino	cucumber
la zanahoria	carrot

Palabra semejante: el tomate.

Las carnes y aves	Meats and poultry
el biftec	(beef) steak
la carne de cordero	lamb
la carne de puerco	pork
la carne de res	beef
la chuleta	cutlet, chop
la hamburguesa	hamburger

el huevo (duro/frito/ revuelto)	(hard-boiled/fried/ scrambled) egg
el jamón	ham
el pavo	turkey
el pollo	chicken
el rosbif	roast beef
la salchicha	sausage
la ternera	veal
el tocino	bacon

El pescado y los mariscos / *Fish and seafood*

el atún	tuna, tuna fish
los camarones	shrimp
la langosta	lobster
el lenguado	sole, flounder
el pargo	red snapper

Los postres / *Desserts*

el dulce	candy, sweet
el flan	caramel custard
la galleta	cookie
el helado	ice cream
el pan dulce	sweet bread
el pastel	pie
la torta	cake

Palabra semejante: la gelatina.

Las bebidas / *Beverages*

el agua	water
el café (R)	coffee
el cafecito	coffee
la cerveza (R)	beer
el champán	champagne
el chocolate	chocolate; hot chocolate
el jugo (de naranja/ manzana)	(orange/apple) juice
la leche	milk
la limonada	lemonade
el refresco (R)	soft drink
el té (helado/caliente)	(iced/hot) tea
el vino	wine

Otras comidas / *Other foods*

el arroz	rice
la especia	spice
los fideos	noodles
la hierba	herb

la mantequilla	butter
la mantequilla de cacahuetes/maní	peanut butter
la paella	paella (*Spanish dish with rice, shellfish, fish, and often chicken and sausage, and flavored with saffron*)
las palomitas (de maíz)	popcorn
el pan	bread
el pan tostado	toast
las papitas	potato chips
el queso	cheese
la salsa	sauce
la sopa	soup
la sopa seca	pasta, rice
la tortilla	omlette (*Sp.*); tortilla (*round, flat bread made of corn or wheat flour*) (*Mex., Central Am.*)
el trigo	wheat

Palabras semejantes: el cereal, la mayonesa, el sándwich.

En la mesa / *On the table*

el aceite (de oliva)	(olive) oil
el azúcar	sugar
la botella	bottle
la copa (R)	wine glass, goblet
la crema	cream
la cuchara	soup spoon
la cucharita	teaspoon
el cuchillo	knife
la pimienta	pepper (*spice*)
el plato chico	saucer
el plato hondo	bowl
la sal	salt
la servilleta	napkin
la taza	cup
el tenedor	fork
el vaso	(drinking) glass

Palabras semejantes: el plato (R), el utensilio, el vinagre.

Otros sustantivos / *Other nouns*

el aperitivo	aperitif, cocktail
la botana	appetizer (*Mex.*)
la caloría	calorie
la comida	food; meal; lunch
la comida fuerte	main, heavy meal
el desayuno	breakfast
la dieta	diet
la entrada	entrée, main course
el espacio	space, room
el ingrediente	ingredient
la merienda	*light meal or snack eaten late afternoon*
la mezcla	mixture, mix, blend
el plato fuerte	main course
el precio	price
el premio	prize
el problema	problem
el rayo	ray
la receta	recipe
el ruido	noise

Los adjetivos / *Adjectives*

anterior	previous
asado/a	roasted; grilled
caliente	hot
delicioso/a	delicious
dulce	sweet
fresco/a	fresh; cool
frito/a	fried
hermoso/a	beautiful
ligero/a	light (*weight*)
menor	younger
oscuro/a	dark
peor	worse
picante	hot, spicy
raro/a	strange, odd
sabroso/a	delicious, tasty
sencillo/a	simple, easy
tanto/a	so much; *pl.* so many
único/a	unique

Los adverbios / *Adverbs*

demasiado	too much
esencialmente	essentially
tal vez	maybe, perhaps

Palabras y expresiones útiles / *Useful words and expressions*

de viaje	traveling
estar listo/a	to be ready
estar loco/a	to be crazy
llamar a la puerta	to knock (on the door)
prestar atención	to pay attention
salir bien/mal	to do well/poorly
tener hambre	to be hungry
tener que ver con	to have to do with

OTROS MUNDOS

Colombia y Venezuela

NOTE: The detailed suggestions for teaching the **Otros mundos** section cannot be accommodated in the margins of the *Instructor's Edition*. For this reason, notes for this section are in the *Instructor's Manual*.

Soy María Gómez y vivo en la ciudad de Cartagena, Colombia. Esta ciudad se encuentra en la costa del Caribe. Cartagena es una típica ciudad colonial española. La ciudad se fundó en 1533 y durante el siglo XVI sirvió como punto de embarque[1] a los barcos[2] españoles que llevaban a España los tesoros[3] que los conquistadores habían encontrado. Por eso, la ciudad sufrió constantes ataques de piratas y otros enemigos de España. Así que se construyeron grandes fortalezas,[4] que ahora son atracciones turísticas.

Dicen que Cartagena es una de las ciudades más pintorescas[5] de América Latina. Las plazas con sus árboles y las calles empedradas[6] nos hacen pensar en la historia gloriosa de esta ciudad que se estableció hace más de 450 años. Pero, como en casi todas las ciudades, lo nuevo existe al lado de lo antiguo. Por ejemplo, mi casa es de estilo colonial por fuera,[7] pero por dentro[8] tenemos todo lo moderno: televisor a colores, horno de microondas y hasta piscina pequeña.

[1]*embarkation* [2]*ships* [3]*treasures* [4]*fortresses* [5]*picturesque* [6]*cobblestone*
[7]*por... on the outside* [8]*por... on the inside*

(a la izquierda) La influencia colonial española es evidente en Cartagena, Colombia. (abajo) Aun en la casa del Libertador Simón Bolívar, en Caracas, se ve la influencia árabe en el patio y en la fuente.

¿Sabías que... ?

COLOMBIA

- Colombia es el único país sudamericano con costas en el Mar Caribe y el Océano Pacífico.
- La cuarta parte del territorio colombiano está destinado al cultivo del café.
- Bogotá, la capital de Colombia, es llamada «la Atenas Sudamericana» por su gran avance cultural y artístico.
- Gabriel García Márquez, el escritor colombiano (1928–) que escribió *Cien Años de Soledad*, ganó el premio Nóbel de Literatura en 1982.
- La primera línea aérea del Nuevo Mundo fue fundada en Colombia en 1919.

En Venezuela hay muchos yacimientos de petróleo como estos en el lago de Maracaibo.

VENEZUELA

- Venezuela ocupa el tercer lugar en el mundo como productor de petróleo crudo y sus derivados.
- Venezuela fue nombrada así porque parecía una pequeña Venecia.
- El lago de Maracaibo, el lago más grande de la América del Sur, es en realidad una extensión del golfo de Venezuela. El lago tiene más de 5.000 millas cuadradas. Un puente[1] en la salida del lado al golfo tiene más de cinco millas de largo y es uno de los puentes más largos del mundo.
- Simón Bolívar (1783–1830), uno de los líderes más importantes en la lucha de las colonias de independizarse de España, nació en Caracas, la capital de Venezuela.

[1] *bridge*

Colombia y Venezuela en breve

	COLOMBIA	VENEZUELA
Capital:	Bogotá	Caracas
Lengua:	español	español
Gobierno:	república	república federal
Moneda:	el peso	el bolívar
Población:	33.777.000 habitantes	20.189.000 habitantes
Superficie:	439.737 millas cuadradas (tres veces más grande que California)	352.000 millas cuadradas (casi tan grande como los estados de Arizona, Nuevo México y Nevada juntos)

OCHO

NOTE: See the *Instructor's Manual* for suggestions on teaching **México y los mexicanos**.

México y los mexicanos

De viaje: Oaxaca

El estado de Oaxaca es el territorio indígena[1] por excelencia en México. Los indígenas que predominan en el estado son los zapotecas y mixtecas, descendientes de los fundadores[2] de las antiguas civilizaciones de esta zona. También viven allí otros dieciséis grupos indígenas, todos con lenguas y culturas distintas. Los indígenas acuden[3] a la capital, la ciudad de Oaxaca, para vender sus mercancías,[4] especialmente sarapes,[5] ponchos y otras artesanías.[6]

Oaxaca es sitio también de más de 4.000 emplazamientos[7] arqueológicos, de los cuales sólo unos 800 han sido explorados. Ningún otro estado mexicano puede vanagloriarse[8] de tal[9] diversidad y riqueza[10] cultural. Cerca de la ciudad de Oaxaca se encuentran dos de los centros arqueológicos más importantes del país. Uno de ellos es Mitla, que se encuentra a 41 kilómetros de la ciudad. Los edificios de piedras labradas[11] y perfectamente ajustadas tienen un parecido[12] increíble con los frisos[13] de los

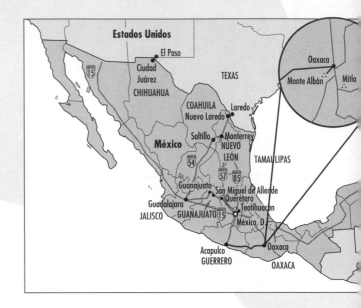

templos de los antiguos griegos. El otro de los centros arqueológicos notables es Monte Albán. Situada en una cordillera, Monte Albán domina desde las alturas[14] el amplio valle en que se encuentra el estado de Oaxaca. La ciudad sorprende[15] por su belleza[16] arquitectónica, pero más sorprende el hecho de[17] que pudiera ser erigida[18] en esas colinas por un pueblo que no tenía caballos[19] ni otras bestias de carga,[20] y que además no conocía la rueda.[21]

[1]*indigenous, native* [2]*founders* [3]*go* [4]*merchandise* [5]*colorful wool shawls* [6]*handicrafts* [7]*sites* [8]*boast* [9]*such* [10]*wealth* [11]*cut* [12]*resemblance* [13]*friezes* [14]*heights* [15]*surprises* [16]*beauty* [17]*hecho... fact* [18]*se... it could have been constructed* [19]*horses* [20]*burden* [21]*wheel*

Las ruinas de Monte Albán en el valle de Oaxaca indican que la civilización que aquí existió ocupaba más de 40 kilómetros cuadrados.

En el mercado de Oaxaca se puede ver a muchos indígenas.

Oaxaca es uno de los estados más pobres de México. Por el momento la vida en Oaxaca no tiene la grandeza[22] que tuvo en el pasado. Pero la gente mantiene su sencilla dignidad y buena voluntad,[23] y la capital es tranquila, limpia y acogedora,[24] con un aeropuerto moderno y restaurantes magníficos.

[22]grandeur   [23]will   [24]welcoming

Perspectivas de México: La historia y la actualidad[1] de México

¿Cuáles son las fuerzas[2] que determinan el carácter de un país? Para el México de hoy son importantes, entre otras, los logros[3] de las civilizaciones precolombinas, las hazañas[4] de la guerra de la independencia y la Revolución mexicana, y también los avances tecnológicos y económicos de México en los últimos años.

El mexicano es muy orgulloso[5] de su historia. ¿Qué se puede aprender de esta historia que nos ayuda a comprender el México de hoy? Los mexicanos son muy orgullosos de las culturas indígenas que existieron en su tierra antes de la llegada de Cortés. Hay una tendencia entre muchos mexicanos de considerar a los españoles como invasores.[6] Mientras más se va descubriendo[7] del estado avanzado de desarrollo de las culturas indígenas precolombinas, más se

entiende el orgullo que el mexicano siente por sus antepasados[8] indígenas.

Doña Josefa y el Padre Miguel Hidalgo son héroes mexicanos por su papel[9] en la guerra contra los españoles por la independencia. En esta etapa[10] de la historia mexicana los españoles son una fuerza negativa otra vez. Los españoles explotaron[11] las riquezas[12] de México, como las minas de Guanajuato, para su propio bien.[13] Al liberarse del dominio de los españoles, los mexicanos se declararon capaces[14] de decidir su propio destino.

La ejecución del emperador Maximiliano, en Querétaro, es otro episodio donde la historia mexicana muestra un rechazo[15] de lo extranjero.[16] Maximiliano y su mujer, Carlota, vinieron a México creyendo que el país había pedido[17] un emperador europeo. Pero, a pesar de[18] las buenas intenciones del emperador, el pueblo mexicano no lo aceptó y mostró su desagrado[19] de una manera violenta.

Porfirio Díaz, el presidente mexicano que volvió a abrir[20] las minas en Guanajuato, gobernó[21] en México durante más de tres décadas. Durante este período, conocido como «el Porfiriato», había muchas inversiones[22] e influencia extranjera en México. Estas inversiones, que beneficiaron a relativamente pocos mexicanos, fueron una de las causas de la revolución mexicana.

Cuando miramos el México de hoy, lo que vemos

es un país industrializado. Pero también es un país que todavía escucha las voces[23] de su pasado. Y hay que esperar[24] que estas voces desempeñen[25] un papel en el México de hoy y del futuro.

[1]current state   [2]forces   [3]achievements   [4]feats   [5]proud   [6]invaders   [7]se... is being discovered   [8]ancestors   [9]role   [10]period, phase   [11]exploited   [12]wealth   [13]propio... own good   [14]capable   [15]rejection   [16]lo... what is foreign   [17]había... had requested   [18]a... in spite of   [19]displeasure   [20]volvió... reopened   [21]governed   [22]investments   [23]voices   [24]hay... one must expect   [25]play

El emperador Maximiliano no fue aceptado por el pueblo mexicano. Fue ejecutado en 1867, por orden de Benito Juárez.

El mundo de los negocios

NOTE: See the *Instructor's Manual* for suggestions on using the chapter-opening pages.

OAXACA

recomendaciones
para el mejor uso
del servicio telefónico

- Para un mejor uso de su servicio de Larga Distancia, le recomendamos:

- • Hable claramente. Y así evitará repeticiones.

- • Organice sus llamadas. Tenga a la mano lápiz y papel, así como la documentación necesaria del asunto que va a tratar.

- • En cada llamada siempre anuncie que está llamando de otra población.

- • Anote el número completo al que va a hablar, incluyendo las claves de acceso por Lada.

ISTMO DE TEHUANTEPEC.

Conjunto zapoteco de terciopelo, bordado en hilo de algodón con grandes motivos florales. Resplandor y holán de encaje almidonado. En la cabeza lleva una jícara adornada para fiesta. Colección de Trajes Regionales: Museo de la Indumentaria Mexicana: "Luis Márquez Romay", del Claustro de Sor Juana A.C.

1993

SECCIÓN AMARILLA
Sí funciona...
y funciona muy bien.

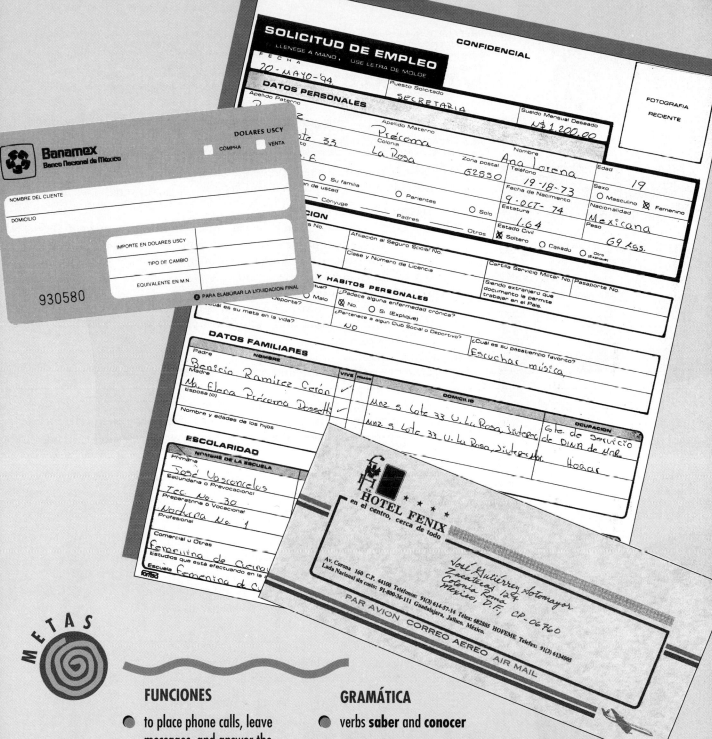

METAS

FUNCIONES

- to place phone calls, leave messages, and answer the telephone
- to make simple bank transactions
- to use and discuss postal services

GRAMÁTICA

- verbs **saber** and **conocer**
- additional uses of the preterite and the imperfect
- expressions with **tener**

APPROPRIATE TESTING POINTS:
Diálogo (2), Saber y conocer, El teléfono, **Quiz 1**

Diálogo (2), Los arreglos y las citas, Más sobre el pretérito y el imperfecto, **Quiz 2**

Diálogo (1), Expresiones con tener, **Quiz 3**

Diálogo (1), En accion
Chapter test

DIÁLOGO

Una llamada telefónica

NEW VOCABULARY: me equivoqué, marco, meto; la guía de teléfonos, la llamada (telefónica), el momento, la operadora, el recado, la tarjeta de crédito; ahora sí, bueno, ¿de parte de quién?

David y Elena hacen una llamada de Acapulco al tío de Elena, el Sr. Alfredo López Valderrama que vive y trabajo en Oaxaca.

SUGGESTION: Have students read the dialogue in groups of three.

DAVID: ¿Sabes el número?

ELENA: Sí, creo que sí. Déjame ver... para hacer la llamada con tarjeta de crédito, primero meto la tarjeta.... Luego marco: nueve... cinco... uno... seis... setenta y cuatro... noventa y ocho.... La línea está ocupada.

DAVID: La operadora te puede ayudar.

ELENA: No, primero voy a buscar en la guía de teléfonos para ver si... ah... me equivoqué... el número de teléfono es el 951-6-7489.* Ahora sí.

LA SECRETARIA: ¡Bueno!

ELENA: Con el Sr. Alfredo López Valderrama, por favor.

LA SECRETARIA: ¿De parte de quién?

ELENA: De Elena Muñoz López, su sobrina.

LA SECRETARIA: Un momento por favor, señorita.... No puede atenderla[1] en este momento, pero si Ud. quiere dejar un recado...

[1] *come to the phone (lit., attend to you)*

De inmediato

NEW VOCABULARY: la guía turística
OPTIONAL: 1. ¿Quién es el Sr. López Valderrama? 2. ¿Qué número marcó Elena primero? ¿Cuál era el número correcto? 3. ¿Quién contestó el teléfono? ¿Qué expresión usó para contestar? 4. Para saber quién llamaba, ¿qué preguntó la secretaria?

¿Es cierto o no es cierto?

OPTIONAL: Have students write additional true/false statements about the dialogue and read them to a partner or a small group.

1. El número de teléfono que Elena quiere llamar es el 951-6-7498.
2. Para usar el teléfono, Elena primero mete una tarjeta de crédito.
3. Para buscar un número de teléfono, Elena busca en la guía turística.
4. Cuando la secretaria contesta, dice «Bueno».
5. Alfredo López Valderrama no está en su oficina.

A ti te toca

With a classmate, use the preceding dialogue as a model to place a phone call to the office of a friend or family member.

EJEMPLO: E1: Déjame ver.... Marco (*phone number*).

E2: ¡Bueno!

E1: Con (*name*), por favor.

E2: ¿De parte de quién?

E1: De (*your name*), (*relationship*).

E2: Un momento, por favor, señor(a)/señorita.... No puede atenderlo/la en este momento, pero si Ud. quiere dejar un recado...

---

*Read as **9-5-1-6-74-89** or **951-6-74-89**.

En la universidad

NEW VOCABULARY: conozco, charlar, enviar; el/la agente de viajes, el cambio, la cuenta; absolutamente

Entre clases, los amigos se encuentran en el salón de descanso en el centro estudiantil. Pasan un rato charlando.

JORGE: Necesito llamar a mi agente de viajes. Conoces a Cheryl, ¿verdad?

JOAQUÍN: Creo que sí. ¿No es la que[1] trabaja para World Travel?

JORGE: Sí, exacto. ¿Sabes, por acaso,[2] cuál es su número?

JOAQUÍN: Pues, ¿qué sé yo? No la conozco bien. No sé su número de teléfono.

TOMÁS: ¿Qué tienes, Alfonsina? Pareces triste.

ALFONSINA: Sí, estoy deprimida. Mi cuenta de banco está vacía,[3] absolutamente vacía. No sé qué hacer. Tengo una beca[4] de un club cívico de mi ciudad, pero no me han enviado el dinero todavía. O puede ser que haya problemas con el cambio de nuevos pesos a dólares. No sé...

TOMÁS: No te pasa sólo a ti.[5] Conozco a otros estudiantes internacionales con el mismo problema. ¿Conoces al presidente del club? ¿Tal vez una llamada telefónica... ?

ALFONSINA: Sí, lo[6] conozco muy bien. Es amigo de mis padres. Buena idea.

MARISOL: En mi clase de literatura, leemos *El gringo viejo.* ¿Conocen las obras[7] de Carlos Fuentes?

CELIA: Sí, pero no las más recientes.

CARMEN: Dicen que es un novelista excelente. Celia, ¿sabes si en la biblioteca tienen todas sus novelas?

CELIA: Sé que tienen algunas, pero, ¿todas? ¿Quién sabe?

[1]La... *The one who* [2]por... *by chance* [3]*empty* [4]*scholarship* [5]No... *You're not alone (lit., It doesn't happen only to you.)* [6]*him* [7]*works*

Using the phrases on the right, complete the sentences on the left to explain who knows what or whom.

De inmediato

1. Joaquín conoce...
2. Joaquín no sabe...
3. Alfonsina tiene...
4. Tomás conoce...
5. Celia conoce...
6. Carmen pregunta si Celia sabe...

a. si en la biblioteca tienen todas las novelas de Fuentes.

b. a Cheryl, una agente de viajes que trabaja para World Travel.

c. a algunos estudiantes que tienen el mismo problema que Alfonsina.

d. el número de teléfono de Cheryl.

e. una cuenta de banco vacía.

f. las obras de Carlos Fuentes, pero no las más recientes.

A ti te toca

Ask a classmate if he or she is familiar with someone's artistic work. **Vocabulario útil: director(a), dramaturgo,[1] escritor(a), escultor(a), novelista, pintor(a), poeta.**

SUGGESTION: Encourage students to respond with phrases such as the following. **Sí, es verdad.** / **Sí, tienes razón.** / **¡Absolutamente!** / **Estoy de acuerdo.** / **Precisamente.**

EJEMPLOS: —¿Conoces las obras de Carlos Fuentes?
—Sí, conozco sus obras. Es un novelista excelente.

—¿Conoces las obras de Pedro Almodóvar?
—No, no conozco sus obras, pero sé que es un director de cine excelente.

[1] *playwright*

Faceta cultural

El teléfono

NEW VOCABULARY: las fichas

Although the phone system in Hispanic countries is similar to that in the United States, there are differences. *Tokens*, or **fichas**, may be required to use public phones in some countries, whereas phone cards are used in others. To make a long-distance call, one might have to go to a central location.

One feature that varies widely throughout the Hispanic world is how one answers the telephone. Appropriate ways of saying *hello* vary from **¡Bueno!** in Mexico, **¡Diga!** or **¡Dígame!** in Spain, to **¡Oigo!, ¿Qué hay?, ¡Hola!,** and **¡Aló!** in other countries.

FOLLOW-UP: 1. What are some differences between making calls in Hispanic countries and making calls in the U.S.? 2. What does one say when answering the telephone in Mexico? In Spain? In other countries? 3. What element in the phone number of the Stouffer hotel is the city code? The hotel's phone number? The country code?

En México

When calling Mexican phone numbers from outside Mexico, one must first dial 011 (the international access code), then 52 (the country code for Mexico), the city code (not unlike the area codes in the United States), and then the phone number. When calling long distance within Mexico, one must first dial 91, then the city code and phone number. Thus, to place a call from the United States to the Stouffer Presidente Oaxaca, a four-star hotel in a former convent built in Oaxaca in 1576, one would dial 011-52-951-6-06-11 (the city code for Oaxaca is 951). What series of numbers would you dial to call the hotel from, say, Acapulco? What series of numbers would you dial to call the hotel from another location in Oaxaca?

Los servicios de: **LOCATEL** 658-11-11

LOCATEL es un organismo desconcentrado del Departamento del Distrito Federal, creado con la finalidad de servir.
Un servicio para todos sin costo alguno, accesible a través de cualquier aparato telefónico.

Saber y conocer

«Yo **sé** todas las respuestas.»

«**Conozco** a David pero no **conozco** a su prima Elena.»

¿A quién conoces? ¿Qué sabes? Whom do you know and what do you know about your university?

Paso 1. Decide if you should begin the following questions with **¿Conoces...** or with **¿Sabes...** , according to the meaning.

EJEMPLOS: ...a todos los profesores de español? →
¿Conoces a todos los profesores de español?

...cuántos estudiantes asisten a esta universidad? →
¿Sabes cuántos estudiantes asisten a esta universidad?

1. ...dónde está el gimnasio?
2. ...a los miembros del equipo de básquetbol?
3. ...quién enseña las clases de francés?
4. ...a todos tus compañeros de clase?
5. ...si hay examen de español mañana?
6. ...cuándo terminan las clases este semestre?
7. ...al rector (a la rectora) de la universidad?

Paso 2. Now work with a classmate to ask and answer the questions from **Paso 1**.

EJEMPLOS: —¿Conoces a todos los profesores de español? →
—No, no conozco a todos los profesores de español.

—¿Sabes cuántos estudiantes asisten a esta universidad? →
—Sí, yo sé aproximadamente cuántos estudiantes asisten a esta universidad. Asisten unos doce mil quinientos estudiantes.

Saber y conocer

Spanish has two verbs that are translated as *to know*. **Saber** indicates knowing *facts, information,* or *how to do something*; **conocer** denotes *acquaintance* with a person, place, or thing.   (*Continúa.*)

Actividad

NEW VOCABULARY: el gimnasio, los miembros

NEW VOCABULARY: (*Paso 2*) aproximadamente
SUGGESTION: Have one student read an item while the other student has his or her book closed.
SUGGESTION: To practice using formal address, have students ask *you* the questions.
FOLLOW-UP: Ask students to make lists of people and places they know, facts they know, and things they know how to do. They will compare their lists with other students' to see whether they know the same things. **Conocemos a Ⓟ. Sabemos hablar español.**

PREPARATION: Have students repeat Mercedes's first line. Ask them whom/what she knows. Have students repeat her second line. Ask them whom/what she knows. Ask **¿Qué hace Mercedes? ¿Qué sabe ella? ¿Conoce Mercedes a David? ¿Conoce Mercedes a Elena?**

239

PRESENTE		PRETÉRITO		IMPERFECTO	
saber					
sé	sabemos	supe	supimos	sabía	sabíamos
sabes	sabéis	supiste	supisteis	sabías	sabíais
sabe	saben	supo	supieron	sabía	sabían
conocer					
conozco	conocemos	conocí	conocimos	conocía	conocíamos
conoces	conocéis	conociste	conocisteis	conocías	conocíais
conoce	conocen	conoció	conocieron	conocía	conocían

Note that **saber** is irregular in the present tense **yo** form and in the preterite, whereas the only irregular form of **conocer** is **conozco**.*

*Except for **hacer,** most infinitives in Spanish that end in **-cer** follow the conjugation pattern of **conocer**: **crecer** (*to grow*), **establecer** (*to establish*), **merecer** (*to deserve*), **ofrecer** (*to offer*), **parecer** (*to seem, look like*), **permanecer** (*to stay, remain*), **pertenecer** (*to belong*), **reconocer** (*to recognize*).

VOCABULARIO

El teléfono

PREPARATION: 1. Ask students to think about the telephone and how they use it every day. As they scan the illustrations and list, they can note the items that are particularly pertinent to them. 2. Work with the drawings by asking the following questions. **En el primer dibujo, ¿dónde está el Sr. Kolb? ¿Qué hace? ¿A quién llama? En el segundo dibujo, ¿cómo está el Sr. Kolb, contento o frustrado? ¿Por qué? En el tercer dibujo, ¿quién es la mujer? ¿Dónde está?**

marcar el número

colgar el auricular

la guía de teléfonos

«Hago una llamada de larga distancia a mi socio en Monterrey, Fernando Muñoz.»

«Llamé a Fernando, pero la línea estaba ocupada.»

«¿De parte de quién?»

Otro vocabulario

descolgar (ue) el auricular *Ibocuna* — to pick up the phone, receiver
equivocarse — to make a mistake; to get the wrong number
escuchar la señal de marcar — to listen to the dial tone
la ficha — token
¿Con quién hablo? — With whom am I speaking?

A **Cómo usar el teléfono.** Elena is trying to teach her young cousin how to use a pay phone, but the girl still has trouble sequencing the actions. Put her statements in a logical order. **Vocabulario útil: primero, después, entonces, luego, finalmente.**

__3__ Se escucha la señal de marcar.
__7__ Se cuelga el auricular.
__5__ Se marca el número.
__6__ Se habla con la persona con quien se quiere hablar.
__4__ Se depositan unas monedas o una ficha.
__2__ Se descuelga el auricular.
__1__ Se busca el número en la guía de teléfonos.

B **¿Es lógico o no es lógico?** Indicate whether or not the following statements are logical.

EJEMPLO: Antes de marcar el número es necesario descolgar el auricular.
→ Es lógico.

1. Es necesario escuchar la señal de marcar antes de marcar el número.
2. Descuelgo el auricular si la línea está ocupada.
3. Busco un número que no sé en la guía de teléfonos.
4. Digo, «¿De parte de quién?» cuando contesto el teléfono.
5. Suena el teléfono si la línea está ocupada.
6. Deposito monedas en un teléfono celular.

PREPARATION: Ask students to focus on the title of the dialogue and on the dialogue introduction. Where are the characters? What kinds of activities and objects would they anticipate finding in such a place?

SUGGESTION: Have students take turns reading the dialogue in groups of three.

Una transacción bancaria

NEW VOCABULARY: cambiar; la transacción bancaria

Los primos se divierten mucho en el viaje de Acapulco a Oaxaca. Llegan muy tarde a la ciudad y deciden quedarse en un hotel para no molestar al tío de Elena. Por la mañana David y Elena entran en un banco cerca de su hotel.

DAVID: Tengo que cambiar un cheque de viajero.
ELENA: Sí, es cierto. Ibas a hacerlo en Acapulco pero se te olvidó.[1]

[1]se... you forgot

NEW VOCABULARY: el dólar, la identificación, el pasaporte, la tarjeta de turismo, la tasa de cambio

EL CAJERO: ¿Quiere Ud. cambiar un cheque de viajero?

DAVID: Sí, señor. Un cheque de viajero de cien dólares.

EL CAJERO: Permítame ver su identificación, por favor... su pasaporte o su tarjeta de turismo.

DAVID: Aquí tiene mi pasaporte. ¿A cuánto está el cambio hoy?

EL CAJERO: Hoy la tasa de cambio está a 3,51 nuevos pesos el dólar, señor. Primero tiene que firmar este formulario,[2] por favor.

DAVID: ...Aquí tiene el formulario.

EL CAJERO: Bueno. Cien dólares a 3,51 nuevos pesos el dólar son trescientos cincuenta y un nuevos pesos. Aquí tiene su dinero.

DAVID: Gracias.

[2]*form*

De inmediato

The following is an abbreviated and confused version of David and Elena's visit to the bank. Identify who says each line—**C** for **el cajero, D** for David, or **E** for Elena—then put the lines in the correct order.

OPTIONAL: 1. ¿En qué ciudad se encuentran David y Elena? 2. ¿Dónde pasaron la noche? 3. ¿Qué tiene que hacer David? 4. ¿Qué necesita ver el cajero? 5. ¿A cuánto está la tasa de cambio?

1. C D E _____ Primero tiene que firmar este formulario.

2. C D E _____ Ibas a hacerlo en Acapulco pero se te olvidó.

3. C D E _____ Permítame ver su identificación.

4. C D E _____ ¿A cuánto está el cambio hoy?

5. C D E _____ Aquí tiene su dinero.

6. C D E _____ ¿Quiere Ud. cambiar un cheque de viajero?

7. C D E _____ Tengo que cambiar un cheque de viajero.

8. C D E _____ La tasa de cambio está a 3,51 nuevos pesos el dólar.

A ti te toca

Use the following model to carry out a brief conversation with a classmate regarding the items you both have brought to class today.

EJEMPLO: —Permítame ver tu cuaderno azul (bolígrafo rojo, libro de texto, etcétera).

o —Permítame ver tus zapatos nuevos (lápices de colores, aretes, etcétera).

—Aquí tienes. Permítame ver tu(s)...

En la universidad

PREPARATION: Ask students to describe the drawing. Have them focus on the title of the dialogue and on the dialogue introduction. Where are the characters? What kinds of activities and objects would they anticipate finding here? Have students skim the dialogue. **¿De qué hablan Tomás y Luis? ¿y Carmen y Celia?**

Tomás y Luis pasean en el centro comercial y hablan de lo que le pasó a Luis ayer con un proyecto para una de sus clases. Mientras tanto,[1] Celia y Carmen hablan de lo que hizo Celia ese día.

[1]Mientras... *Meanwhile*

NEW VOCABULARY: cerrar, se despidió de; los boletos de ida y vuelta, la cita, la fábrica, el método; pronto

TOMÁS: ¿Hiciste una cita con el gerente de la fábrica?

LUIS: Sí, le dije que necesitaba información para mi clase de economía. Pero, chico, el gerente es muy antipático.

TOMÁS: ¿Cómo que antipático?

LUIS: No me preguntó nada sobre la clase, ni quería saber nada de mí ni de por qué estudio economía en este país. Sólo me dio montones de[2] datos[3] y se despidió pronto porque esperaba una llamada de larga distancia.

TOMÁS: Chico, aquí es diferente. Les gusta ir al grano.[4] No quieren perder el tiempo.[5]

LUIS: Bueno, comprendo que es diferente, pero ¿es mejor este método? En este caso, creo que no.

———

CARMEN: ¿Qué hiciste ayer?

CELIA: Fui a una agencia de viajes. Llegué a las cinco e iban a cerrar pronto, pero todos estuvieron muy amables conmigo.

CARMEN: ¿Y qué buscabas allí?

CELIA: Nada de importancia: folletos[6] e información para una amiga sobre el precio de los boletos de ida y vuelta de aquí a Madrid.

[2]montones... *piles of, numerous*   [3]*facts*   [4]ir... *to get down to business*   [5]perder... *to waste time*   [6]*brochures*

De inmediato

Match the following characters with the actions or attitudes attributed to them in the dialogue: **Tomás, Luis, el gerente de la fábrica, los empleados de la agencia de viajes, Carmen, Celia.**

1. Es muy antipático.
2. Estuvieron muy amables.
3. Fue a la agencia de viajes.
4. No le preguntó nada a Luis sobre su clase de economía.
5. Le preguntó a Celia qué buscaba en la agencia de viajes.
6. Le preguntó a Luis si hizo una cita con el gerente de la fábrica.
7. Llegó a las cinco.
8. Pidió el precio de los boletos de ida y vuelta de Eau Claire a Madrid.
9. Hizo una cita con el gerente de la fábrica.
10. Se despidió de Luis porque esperaba una llamada.
11. Camina con Luis por el centro comercial.
12. Le dio información a Luis para su clase de economía.

OPTIONAL: 1. ¿Qué preguntó Tomás? 2. ¿Por qué fue Luis a ver al gerente de la fábrica? 3. ¿Qué le pareció el gerente a Luis? ¿Por qué? 4. ¿Adónde fue Celia ayer? ¿A qué hora llegó? 5. ¿Qué buscaba Celia allí?

A ti te toca

What did three of your classmates do yesterday? Be prepared to report to the class what you learned about them.

EJEMPLO: —¿Qué hiciste ayer?
   —Fui al supermercado (a la playa, a la casa de ①, al aeropuerto,...).
  o —Estudié en la biblioteca (en el laboratorio de lenguas, en casa, con ①,...)

Los arreglos y las citas

EN EL BANCO

el dinero en efectivo

los cajeros

LA CAJA

la tasa de cambio

cambiar/cobrar un cheque de viajero

las monedas

EN LA OFICINA DE CORREOS

ESTAMPILLAS

mandar un paquete

echar una carta al correo

las (tarjetas) postales

la carta

el buzón

PREPARATION: Ask students to look at the vocabulary while you read some of the words at random. Ask them if they associate items you suggest with **un banco, la oficina de correos,** or **los dos.**

Otro vocabulario

el boleto (de ida y vuelta)	(*roundtrip*) *ticket*	la tarjeta de turismo	*tourist card*
el cambio	*change*	la ventanilla	*ticket booth/ window*
la casa de cambio	*money exchange house*		
el correo (aéreo)	(*air*) *mail*	cambiar/cobrar un cheque	*to cash a check*
la cuenta	*account*	firmar	*to sign*
la entrevista	*interview*	hacer una cita	*to make an appointment*
el kilo(gramo)	*kilo*(*gram*)		
la libra	*pound*	llegar a tiempo	*to arrive on time*
la oficina de turismo	*tourist office*	pesar	*to weigh*
		recibir correspondencia	*to receive mail/ correspondence*
la onza	*ounce*	tardar	*to be late*
el pasaporte	*passport*		

SUGGESTION: For Acts. A and B, have students work in small groups and read each other's reordered paragraphs, discussing similarities and resolving discrepancies.

Actividades

A **Un cheque.** David is teaching a young cousin what needs to be done to cash a traveler's check, but his cousin has the order all wrong. Put her statements in a logical order. **Vocabulario útil: primero, después, entonces, luego, finalmente.**

_____ Se sale del banco.

_____ Se cuenta el dinero en efectivo, y monedas, que da el empleado.

_____ El empleado le da el dinero al cliente.

_____ Se firma el cheque de viajero que se quiere cobrar.

_____ Se va a la caja.

_____ Se cobra el cheque de viajero.

_____ Se entra en el banco.

OPTIONAL: Bring in slips of paper that can be filled out like traveler's checks. Ask one student to cash the traveler's check. He or she should call on classmates to indicate each action to be performed and the "traveler" should perform the actions mentioned. All students should be attentive to the order of actions described and should object if the sequence of actions is not logical.

B **Una carta.** Now David is teaching his young cousin how to mail a letter at the post office, but his cousin is still confused. Put her statements in a logical order. **Vocabulario útil: primero, después, entonces, luego, finalmente.**

_____ Se echa la carta al correo.

_____ Se escribe la dirección.

_____ Se escribe una carta.

_____ Se acerca[1] al buzón.

_____ Se va a la oficina de correos.

_____ Se pone la carta en un sobre.

_____ Se ponen las estampillas en el sobre.

[1]Se... _One goes up to_

Más sobre el pretérito y el imperfecto

PREPARATION: Work with the drawing by asking the following questions. **¿Quiénes son las personas del dibujo? ¿Cómo son las jóvenes físicamente? ¿Donde están? ¿Qué hacen?**
SUGGESTION: Work with the students to help them guess the meanings of the preterite verbs used in the dialogue.

LUISA: Cuando era niña **podía** hacer mis tareas fácilmente. Pero ahora, con todas mis actividades y responsabilidades, no tengo el tiempo necesario para terminar todas las tareas. Hablando de tareas, ¿cómo te fue en la de cálculo?

ALFONSINA: Pues, ¿sabes?, **quise** resolver el problema número ocho, pero **no pude**. A las cinco, **no quise** estudiar más y fui a la casa de Jorge. Allí **conocí** a una amiga de Jorge que se especializa en matemáticas. Ella **quería** ayudarme y **sabía** muy bien el concepto. Después de poco **pude** hacer el problema.

NEW VOCABULARY: se especializa; fácilmente; después de poco

Actividades

Ⓐ Las relaciones. State whether David already knew each person listed or if he met the person during his trip to Mexico.

EJEMPLOS: Roger (el estudiante de arte del Instituto Allende) →
David conoció a Roger en México.

Felipe (un estudiante en la UW-EC) →
David ya conocía a Felipe.

1. Amalia (la prima de Elena)
2. la profesora Martínez (una profesora en la UW-EC)
3. el Sr. Kolb (un amigo de la familia de Elena)
4. Raúl (el hermano de Amalia y el primo de Elena)
5. Jorge (un estudiante en la UW-EC)
6. Marisol (una estudiante en la UW-EC)

Ⓑ Decisiones. We all make decisions and some are more important than others. María recently decided that she wanted to do certain things and not others. Say what her decision was for each of the following choices.

EJEMPLOS: viajar a Chicago → María quería viajar a Chicago.
fumar marijuana → María no quiso fumar marijuana.

1. tomar un curso de francés
2. salir bien en el examen de matemáticas
3. copiar las respuestas de otro estudiante
4. tomar el sol y leer el libro de texto
5. mentir[1] a su amiga
6. beber mucho y manejar un coche después

[1] *to lie*

Ⓒ Niña típica. Mercedes is a typical child and often wants to avoid her mother's rules. Say whether Mercedes was allowed to do what she wanted or whether she was restrained by the rules.

EJEMPLOS: leer una novela →
Mercedes quería leer una novela y su mamá le dijo que podía.
salir a jugar sin permiso →
Mercedes quiso salir a jugar sin permiso pero no pudo.

1. beber Coca-Cola para el desayuno
2. tomar un vaso de leche con un sándwich para el almuerzo
3. comer torta de chocolate para el almuerzo
4. ir a la biblioteca después de la escuela
5. pasar la noche con una compañera de clase que su mamá no conocía
6. leer una revista *Teen* en la cama después de acostarse

Verbos de significado especial en el pretérito

INFINITIVO		IMPERFECTO	PRETÉRITO
conocer	*to know; to be acquainted with*	*knew, was acquainted with*	*met*
saber	*to know* (facts); *to know how*	*knew*	*found out, learned*
poder	*to be able, can; to have the ability*	*could*	*could and did, managed*
no poder	*to be unable, can't; not to have the ability*	*couldn't, didn't have the ability*	*couldn't and didn't, failed*
querer	*to want*	*wanted*	*tried*
no querer	*not to want*	*didn't want*	*refused*

These verbs undergo a change in meaning from the infinitive when used in the preterite tense. Note the differences between affirmative and negative expressions as well.

PREPARATION: (**Diálogo**) Ask students to focus on the title of the dialogue and on the dialogue introduction. Where are the characters? What kinds of activities and objects would they anticipate finding in such a place?

En la oficina de correos

DIÁLOGO

NEW VOCABULARY: tengo hambre, tengo prisa, tengo que... ; de acuerdo, ¡qué pena!

Por fin se comunican David y Elena con el tío Alfredo, quien los invita a pasar unos días en su casa. Antes de visitarlo, tienen que pasar por la oficina de correos porque David ha decidido mandar dos paquetes de recuerdos a su familia en Wisconsin.

ELENA: ¿Cuánto pesan esos paquetes?

DAVID: El grande pesa cinco kilos* aproximadamente. El pequeño debe pesar dos. Si tengo prisa, ¿puedo ponerles unas estampillas y echarlos al correo?

ELENA: Bueno, tienes que ir a la ventanilla allí porque tienen que pesar el paquete antes de mandarlo. Mientras tanto,[1] quiero comprar estampillas.

DAVID: Oye, cómprame unas para correo aéreo, por favor.

ELENA: De acuerdo. Ay, ¡qué pena! Escribí mal la dirección. Ahora tengo que comprar otro sobre.

DAVID: Espero que podamos hacer todo esto rápido. Tengo hambre, y me gustaría[2] almorzar antes de ir a la casa de tu tío.

[1]Mientras... *Meanwhile* [2]me... *I would like*

*A kilo (**kilogramo**) is equal to 2.2 pounds.

De inmediato

Correct the following sentences so that they accurately reflect the content of the dialogue.

1. David va a mandar tres paquetes.
2. El paquete más grande de David pesa 50 kilos.
3. David tiene que llevar los paquetes al buzón antes de mandarlos.
4. David le pide a Elena que le compre estampillas para tarjetas postales.
5. Elena escribió mal la dirección; ahora tiene que comprar otra estampilla.

A ti te toca

Ask a classmate how much something you brought to class today weighs.

EJEMPLO: —¿Cuánto pesa mi diccionario (libro, pluma,...)?
—No sé exactamente. Debe pesar un kilo (media libra, menos de tres onzas,...).

VOCABULARIO

Expresiones con *tener*

Actividades

Ⓐ **¿Qué tienes?** Using a **tener** expression, express how you are feeling based on the following information. There may be more than one acceptable response.

EJEMPLO: Estás en un maratón y la temperatura está a 100°F. →
           Tengo calor.   *o*   Tengo sed.

NEW VOCABULARY: cantar; las horas
SUGGESTION: This works well as a pair activity.
OPTIONAL: Ask students, working in groups of three, to choose three **tener** expressions to pantomime for the entire class. The class may vote for best actor, best overall group, and most original pantomime.
EXPANSION: Give students two minutes to write one or two additional "riddles" to share with the entire class.

1. Son las seis de la tarde. Después de cuatro horas de trabajo intenso, acabas de terminar la tarea.
2. Hace mucho calor y juegas al tenis por tres horas y media.
3. Son las ocho menos cinco de la mañana y tienes clase a las ocho. También tienes un examen en esa clase. Es tu materia más difícil.
4. Es la una y media de la mañana y todavía tienes más tarea que hacer.
5. Tienes que cantar enfrente de todos los estudiantes de la universidad.
6. Estás en un hotel. Es medianoche. Nieva mucho y hace frío afuera. Buscas una manta[1] extra pero no encuentras una.
7. Crees que la primera persona singular del verbo **saber** es **sabo**.
8. Crees que la primera persona singular del verbo **saber** es **sé**.

[1]*blanket*

B Ayer. Tell how you felt or did not feel yesterday at the times listed, using a **tener** expression. Then explain why you felt that way.

PREPARATION: Model this activity by having students ask how you felt at various times of the day.
SUGGESTION: Have students work in pairs. One student reads an item while the other has his or her book closed. Encourage students to respond with phrases such as the following. **¿Verdad? Yo también/tampoco. / Interesante. Yo sí/no. / Comprendo.**
SUGGESTION: Encourage students to use six different **tener** expressions and to be as creative as possible in their responses.

EJEMPLO: a las siete y media de la mañana →
           Tenía sueño porque me levanté temprano.
           o No tenía hambre porque tomé el desayuno a las siete.

1. a las diez de la mañana
2. a la una de la tarde
3. a las seis de la tarde
4. a las diez de la noche
5. a las ocho de la mañana
6. ¿ ?

Una característica hispana

DIÁLOGO

NEW VOCABULARY: la demora

Después de pasar unos días con el tío de Elena, David y Elena visitan el centro arqueológico de Monte Albán. Toman unos minutos para descansar y hablar de las famosas ruinas.

DAVID: ¡Qué lugar fantástico! No sabía nada de estas ruinas. Son de los mayas, ¿verdad?
ELENA: No, chico. Son de otros grupos indígenas,[1] los zapotecas y los mixtecas. No son tan bien conocidos[2] como los aztecas y los mayas, pero su civilización era muy avanzada, como puedes ver.
DAVID: Sí, las pirámides y los templos son maravillosos. Tu tío Alfredo nos dio tantas buenas ideas sobre cosas que deberíamos[3] ver y hacer en Oaxaca.
ELENA: Es un hombre encantador,[4] ¿no?
DAVID: Sí, muy simpático. ¿Sabes que me asombró[5] que él estuviera[6] listo para salir cuando llegamos? Creía que la demora era una característica de las personas hispánicas.

PREPARATION: Ask students to describe the drawing. Ask them to focus on the title of the dialogue and on the dialogue opener. Where are the characters? Have students skim the dialogue. **¿De qué hablan los jóvenes?**

[1]*indigenous, native*   [2]*known*   [3]*we should*   [4]*charming*   [5]*me... it amazed me*   [6]*was*

ELENA: Bueno.... No nos dejamos llevar por el reloj.[7] Si una persona necesita nuestra ayuda, la persona es más importante que la hora. Pero, esto está cambiando... sobre todo en el mundo de los negocios.

DAVID: Bueno pues, debemos regresar a Oaxaca dentro de poco para hacer las maletas. El autobús para Veracruz sale a las seis veintitrés de la tarde y no espera.

[7]No... *We don't let the clock control us.*

De inmediato

Do you associate Elena, David, or **el tío Alfredo** with the following statements?

OPTIONAL: 1. ¿Dónde están David y Elena? 2. ¿Quiénes construyeron lo que hoy son las ruinas de Monte Albán? 3. ¿Quién es Alfredo? 4. De qué característica hispana hablaron los primos?

1. Cree que en el mundo de los negocios la actitud tradicional hacia el tiempo está cambiando.
2. Creía que la demora era una característica de las personas hispánicas.
3. Dice que los hispanos no se dejan llevar por el reloj.
4. Les dio ideas sobre las cosas que deberían ver.
5. Sabe que el autobús para Veracruz no espera.
6. Le asombró que el tío estuviera listo cuando llegaron.

A ti te toca

Elena believes that "**La persona es más importante que la hora.**" Tell a classmate something similar that you believe.

la apariencia / la personalidad	la experiencia / el título
el dinero / la felicidad	el trabajo / la familia
	¿ ?

EJEMPLO: —La persona es más importante que la hora, ¿verdad?
—Sí, estoy de acuerdo.
o —No, no estoy de acuerdo. ¡Es al revés!

EN ACCIÓN

Antes de ver

In this chapter you will watch and listen as people perform a series of everyday functions, including using the telephone. After viewing, share information with a classmate, then try to role-play at least one of the situations you have seen.

El robo

Paso 1. Look closely at the drawing of a bank robbery for sixty seconds and try to remember as much detail as possible. Then close your book and tell a classmate what you saw, as if you were an eyewitness to the robbery. Your partner will take notes on what you describe, for use in the police report.

EJEMPLO: Alguien robó un banco con una pistola. En el banco había varias personas incluso...

SUGGESTION: Prepare students for this activity by reviewing the kinds of details they might want to mention in their report to the police: physical characteristics, clothes, colors, location of the people in the bank, and so forth.

Paso 2. Now work with your classmate, using the notes from the eyewitness account, to write a more complete description of the robbery. Your description should be from one-half page to one page in length. Be prepared to read your description to the class.

Una tarjeta postal

Paso 1. Imagine that you are spending a week in Guadalajara (or another location of your choice). On a separate sheet of paper, write a postcard-length note to a classmate about the trip you are taking. Start the note with **Querido/a** _____ (*Dear* _____) and use **Tu amigo/a** _____ as a closing. Remember that your space is limited to one-half of a postcard!

PREPARATION: Review the kinds of things tourists might include in a postcard (sites, weather, how they are feeling, . . .).

Saludos desde Guadalajara

PREPARATION: Ask students to review locations mentioned in this chapter or previous chapters to find information about the site they are visiting. Ask them to brainstorm about what one normally writes on a postcard. Be prepared to help with unfamiliar vocabulary, such as *Wish you were here.*
SUGGESTION: Have students read their postcards to a partner or a small group.

Paso 2. Imagine that a newly hired mail carrier (your instructor) accidentally distributes the postcards you have just written to the wrong addresses. With your classmates, play the role of snoopy neighbors who read the postcards and gossip with each other about their contents.

> EJEMPLO: ¿Sabes qué? Leí que el amigo de _____ está en Guadalajara y que...

Un recado

Steve, a student in a second-semester Spanish class, is in his Spanish instructor's office. The instructor is called away from the office for a short while and Steve is there alone. The phone rings and he decides to answer it.

Antes de escuchar

Have you ever tried to communicate with someone that did not speak your language well? What strategies could you use to get across an idea when the other person does not understand the key words? Would you prefer to be the one that was weak in the language or the one that had to help the other person understand? In either case, would communication be more or less difficult over the telephone?

Read the questions that pertain to each portion of the telephone call to alert yourself to the content of the conversation. Now, listen carefully to each part of the conversation. After listening, answer the questions that follow.

Después de escuchar

Paso 1. Primera parte

1. With whom does the caller wish to speak?
2. Why do Steve and the caller decide to speak Spanish instead of English?
3. Why can't the caller call back later?

Segunda parte

1. What is the caller's name?
2. What is the caller sending to Steve's instructor?
3. What does the caller mention about Steve's instructor giving a lecture?
4. At approximately what time did Steve and the caller finish the conversation?

Paso 2. Steve remembers that he has to leave before his Spanish instructor returns to the office, so he writes out the phone message for him. Imagine that you are Steve and write out the message for your instructor, including as many details as possible.

> EJEMPLO: Profesor Banderas:
>   Esta tarde, a las tres y media, llamó el profesor...

Paso 3. Imagine that you are in Steve's situation and have to communicate in Spanish over the telephone with someone you don't know. With a partner, act out a telephone conversation in which the caller needs to leave a long message for a friend.

El/La gerente ideal

Elena's uncle Alfredo has just received a recent issue of the San Francisco magazine *Avance hispano: La revista de las Américas,* in which the list below catches his attention.

Antes de leer

This reading presents a list of ten characteristics of an effective manager in to-day's business world. What qualities would you expect in a good manager? Would he or she need to be computer literate? Have a strong hold over the employees? Be a good friend to the employees? Be aware of the objectives of the company? Work with a classmate to produce a list of five qualities of a good company manager.

Next, quickly scan the article and the glosses to prepare yourself for the content. Circle the cognates that you find. Skim the article, looking for words with roots related to other words you know. For example, you know the verb **cono-cer**. What does the noun **conocimiento** mean? What part of speech is **geren-cial**? What familiar noun is it related to? What do you expect **una gerencia estratégica** to mean? What verb do you already know that is related to **segui-dores**? What do you think this noun means? Look for other words with familiar roots and try to guess their meanings.

Read each statement that follows the list and see which item in the list it refers to. Now, study the reading to decide if the statements that follow are true or false, based on the information presented in the reading.

Retos[a] del nuevo gerente

_Compromiso con el ambiente[b] externo para participar en el control de las tendencias futuras.

_Conocimiento de la informática.[c]

_Estar al día con los adelantos tecnológicos.

_Profundo conocimiento de la ciencia gerencial.

_Poseer una visión global del mundo y de las cosas...

_El ejecutivo-jefe tiene que ejercer una gerencia estratégica con claro conocimiento de su misión y objetivos.

_El ejecutivo-jefe dependerá del factor "humano" como clave[d] del éxito.[e]

_Hay que dar autonomía a los seguidores.

_Poder de adaptación. Sobrevivencia.[f]

_Ser un "líder"

[a] *challenges*
[b] *environment*
[c] *computer science*
[d] *key*
[e] *success*
[f] *survival*

Después de leer

¿Es cierto o no es cierto?

1. El nuevo (La nueva) gerente debe saber lo relacionado con computadoras.
2. El/La gerente tiene que dominar completamente a los trabajadores.
3. El/La gerente tiene que aprender a sobrevivir.
4. El/La gerente necesita tener objetivos y saber cuál es su misión.
5. Tener un conocimiento de la ciencia relativa a la gerencia no es importante.
6. El nuevo (La nueva) gerente no tiene que mantenerse al corriente de los avances tecnológicos.

VOCABULARIO

Los verbos	**Verbs**
cambiar	to cash; to change; to exchange
cantar	to sing
cerrar (ie)	to close
cobrar	to cash; to charge (*for a service*)
colgar (ue)	to hang up
conocer (conozco)	to know, be familiar with
charlar	to chat, talk
depositar	to deposit
descolgar (ue)	to pick up (*the phone, receiver*)
despedirse (i, i)	to say good-bye
echar al correo	to mail
enviar (envío)	to send
equivocarse	to make a mistake; to get the wrong number
especializarse	to major in
firmar	to sign
llegar a tiempo	to arrive on time
mandar (R)	to send, mail
marcar (el número)	to dial (the number)
pesar	to weigh
recibir	to receive
tardar	to be late

Expresiones con *tener*	**Expressions with tener**
tener (mucho) calor	to be (very) warm, hot
tener (mucho) frío	to be (very) cold
tener (mucha) hambre (R)	to be (very) hungry
tener (mucho) miedo	to be (very) afraid
tener (mucha) prisa (R)	to be in a (big) hurry
tener (mucha) razón (R)	to be (very) right
no tener razon (R)	to be wrong
tener (mucha) sed	to be (very) thirsty
tener (mucho) sueño	to be (very) sleepy
tener que + *inf.* (R)	to have to (*do something*)

Los arreglos y las citas	**Arrangements and appointments**
el boleto (de ida y vuelta)	(round-trip) ticket
la cita	appointment, date
la demora	delay
la entrevista	interview
la fábrica	factory
la oficina de turismo	tourist office
la tarjeta de turismo	tourist card
la ventanilla	ticket booth/window

Palabra semejante: el pasaporte.

En el banco / *At the bank*

la caja	teller's cage
el cajero / la cajera	teller, cashier
el cambio (R)	change; exchange
la casa de cambio	money exchange house
la cuenta	account
el cheque (de viajero)	(traveler's) check
el dinero (R)	money
el dinero en efectivo	cash
la moneda	coin
los negocios	business
la tasa (de cambio)	(exchange) rate
la transacción bancaria	bank transaction

Palabras semejantes: el dólar, la identificación.

En la oficina de correos / *At the post office*

el buzón	mailbox
el correo (aéreo)	(air)mail
la estampilla	stamp
la libra	pound
la onza	ounce
el paquete	package
la (tarjeta) postal (R)	postcard

Palabra semejantes: la correspondencia, el kilo(gramo).

Para usar el teléfono / *Using the telephone*

el auricular	receiver (*telephone*)
la ficha	token
la guía de teléfonos	telephone directory
la línea	line
la llamada (de larga distancia)	(long distance) call
el número de teléfono	telephone number

el recado	message
la señal de marcar	dial tone
la tarjeta de crédito	credit card

Palabra semejante: el operador / la operadora.

Otros sustantivos / *Other nouns*

el/la agente de viajes	travel agent
el gimnasio	gym, gymnasium
la guía turística	guidebook
la hora	hour; time
el método	method, way
el momento	moment

Un adjetivo / *An adjective*

deprimido/a	depressed

Los adverbios / *Adverbs*

absolutamente	absolutely
aproximadamente	approximately
fácilmente	easily
finalmente	finally, at last
pronto	soon

Palabras y expresiones útiles / *Useful words and expressions*

a tiempo	on time
¡Bueno!	Hello. (*Mex.*)
¿Con quién hablo?	With whom am I speaking?
De acuerdo.	Okay (by me).
¿De parte de quién?	May I ask who's calling?
después de poco	after a short while
La línea está ocupada.	The line is busy.
¡Qué pena!	What a shame!

NOTE: See the *Instructor's Manual* for suggestions on teaching **Otros mundos**.

Chile, el Perú y el Ecuador

Soy Alfonsina Gutiérrez y vengo del país más estrecho del mundo. Mi país, Chile, tiene unas 3.000 millas de costa. Mis padres son dueños de un balneario[1] en la famosa playa de Viña del Mar, primer centro turístico del país, al norte de la ciudad de Valparaíso. Cuando no estoy en los EE. UU., trabajo en el balneario donde doy lecciones de tenis a los turistas que vienen de todas partes del mundo. Claro, Uds. ya saben que aquí las estaciones son lo opuesto[2] de las suyas y la estación de turismo es desde noviembre hasta marzo.

De vez en cuando vamos a la capital, Santiago, para ir de compras y para ver a mis tíos. Mi tío es gerente de la mina de Chuquicamata, una de las minas de cobre más grandes del mundo. Pero, yo prefiero la vida tranquila junto al mar. Algún día me gustaría hacer un viaje al sur de mi país, a la Tierra del Fuego, una región que compartimos con la Argentina.

[1] *beach resort* [2] lo... *the opposite*

¿Sabías que... ?

CHILE
- Chile es uno de los países más cosmopolitas de Sudamérica.
  - Se dice que los vinos de Chile son unos de los mejores del mundo.
  - El desierto de Atacama es una de las zonas más áridas del mundo.
  - La famosa estatua El Cristo de los Andes es símbolo de paz y amistad entre Chile y la Argentina.
  - Gabriela Mistral fue maestra, diplomática y la primera mujer hispánica ganadora del Premio Nóbel de literatura.
- Pablo Neruda fue uno de los poetas más importantes de la lengua española.

(a la derecha) Estas iguanas marinas viven en las islas Galápagos. (abajo) El magnífico monumento del Cristo de los Andes se encuentra en la frontera entre Chile y la Argentina.

Nadie sabe ni cómo ni por qué fueron construidas las ruinas incas de Machu Picchu.

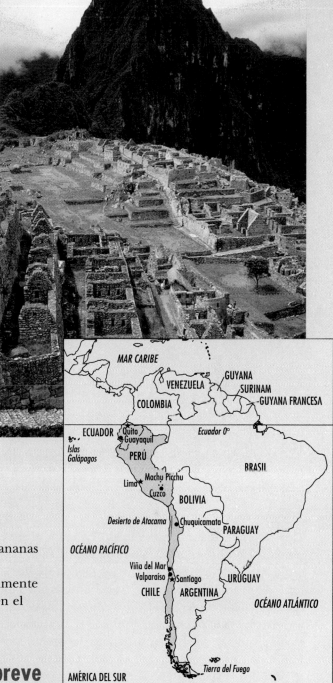

EL PERÚ

- El Perú es el principal país pesquero del mundo.
- La selva cubre más del 71% de la superficie del país.
- El quechua es, junto con el español, lengua oficial del Perú.
- Cuzco es la ciudad más antigua del hemisferio oeste.
- Machu Picchu, antigua ciudad-fortaleza, fue descubierta por el arqueólogo norteamericano Hiram Bingham.
- Hoy en día la comunidad chino-peruana se encuentra bien establecida.
- La papa es un alimento de origen peruano.

EL ECUADOR

- El puerto activo de Guayaquil es más importante económicamente que la ciudad de Quito, la capital.
- Las islas Galápagos, a unas 600 millas de la costa, pertenecen al Ecuador.
- El país debe su nombre al ecuador terrestre que atraviesa el país pocos kilómetros al norte de Quito.
- El Ecuador produce grandes cantidades de bananas pero el producto principal es el cacao.
- Los sombreros de Jipijapa (llamados comunmente *Panamá hats*) son, en realidad, fabricados en el Ecuador.

Chile, el Perú y el Ecuador en breve

	CHILE	EL PERÚ	EL ECUADOR
Capital:	Santiago	Lima	Quito
Lengua:	español	español y quechua	español
Gobierno:	república	república democrática	república
Moneda:	el peso	el inti	el sucre
Población:	13.786.000 habitantes	22.361.000 habitantes	10.751.000 habitantes
Superficie:	292.258 millas cuadradas (del tamaño del estado de Texas)	496.000 millas cuadradas (del tamaño de los estados de Texas, Colorado y Nuevo México juntos)	109.484 millas cuadradas (del tamaño del estado de Oregón)

257

México y los mexicanos

De viaje: Veracruz

NEW VOCABULARY: aunque

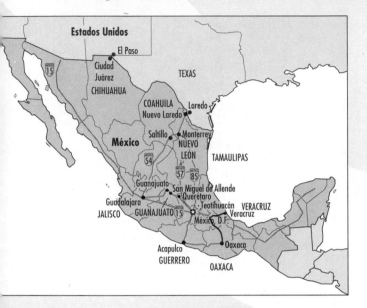

El estado de Veracruz está situado en una estrecha franja[1] de tierra entre el golfo de México y varias cadenas de montañas. La parte occidental de Veracruz es un terreno llano[2] de leves[3] ondulaciones y costa baja. Pero en el estado de Veracruz también se encuentra el Orizaba, el pico[4] más alto de México y el tercero de Norteamérica (después del Monte McKinley de Alaska y el Monte Logan de Canadá).

Veracruz es un estado industrializado y comercial: su puerto es el más activo del país. La industria se deriva esencialmente de la producción agropecuaria,[5] aunque se han desarrollado también otras industrias como la de productos químicos y la siderúrgica.[6] La economía del estado es básicamente agrícola y ganadera;[7] los productos más importantes son el café, el tabaco, los cereales y las frutas.

El estado de Veracruz ha gozado de[8] la influencia caribeña. Esto ha imprimido[9] en sus habitantes un carácter abierto y jovial. Los habitantes de la región, llamados **jarochos,** son muy aficionados a[10] la mú-

sica. Hay un estilo de música, **el huapango,** que es originario de este estado. El huapango tiene un ritmo muy vivo en la que los cantantes han de demostrar[11] una excelente capacidad de improvisación. Quizás el huapango más famoso en los EE. UU. es la canción «La Bamba».

La capital del estado de Veracruz es Jalapa (frecuentemente «Xalapa» en México), pero la ciudad más importante es el puerto de Veracruz. Es una ciudad alegre, y los veracruzanos tienen fama de ser los mexicanos más divertidos.

[1]estrecha... *narrow strip* [2]*flat* [3]*slight* [4]*peak* [5]*related to agriculture and cattle-raising* [6]*iron processing* [7]*cattle-raising* [8]*has enjoyed* [9]*imprinted, impressed* [10]aficionados... *fans of* [11]han... *have to show*

NEW VOCABULARY: casarse; la edad, el matrimonio; en cuanto a

Perspectivas de México: El matrimonio y los hijos

En México y en las culturas hispanas en general, se da un gran valor[1] a la familia y, en particular, a los hijos. Pero, ¿cuáles son los motivos que tienen los mexicanos para casarse? ¿Cuál es, según los mexicanos, la edad ideal para casarse? Y, ¿por qué, según los mexicanos, es importante tener hijos? Estas tres preguntas eran

[1]*value*

Veracruz es el puerto principal de México. Desde la fortaleza de San Juan de Ulúa se puede ver el puerto.

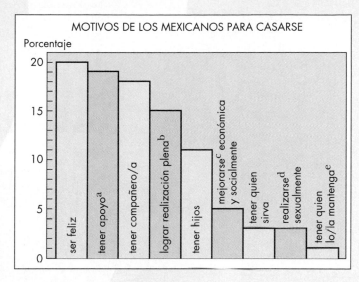

MOTIVOS DE LOS MEXICANOS PARA CASARSE

Porcentaje

- ser feliz
- tener apoyo[a]
- tener compañero/a
- lograr realización plena[b]
- tener hijos
- mejorarse[c] económica y socialmente
- tener quien sirva
- realizarse[d] sexualmente
- tener quien lo/la mantenga[e]

[a] support
[b] lograr... to be totally fulfilled
[c] to improve oneself
[d] to be fulfilled
[e] support

parte de una encuesta que se hizo a más de 3.500 mexicanos.

En México, son cinco los motivos para casarse que se destacan[2] y otros cuatro que se expresan con menor frecuencia. Los resultados de la encuesta están en la gráfica arriba y a la derecha.

En cuanto a la edad ideal para contraer matrimonio, casi todos los mexicanos entrevistados contestaron que el hombre debía tener cuatro años más que la mujer al casarse. Esta opinión parece basarse en parte en el papel tradicional del hombre de ser el que

El volcán Orizaba, siempre cubierto de nieve, domina el paisaje cerca de Puebla, México.

debe mantener[3] económicamente a la familia. Entre los entrevistados, los más pobres indicaron una edad ideal menor que la que respondieron los más adinerados.[4] Aquí están los resultados de la encuesta.

EDAD IDEAL PARA CASARSE

Entre quiénes	Para quién	Edad
los más pobres	la mujer	18
	el hombre	22
los más adinerados	la mujer	22 a 26
	el hombre	26 a 30

Hay marcadas[5] diferencias de opinión en cuanto a la razón para tener hijos. En general, en primer lugar resultó «por su cariño[6] y amor». Entre las personas alfabetas,[7] las razones de «trascender» y «perpetuarse» resultaron ser muy importantes. Entre las analfabetas,[8] fue mayor el número de los que respondieron «porque así lo quiere Dios», «porque contribuyen al ingreso[9] familiar» y «porque contribuyen con las cargas[10] de trabajo». Es evidente que las necesidades de la vida práctica influyen[11] mucho las opiniones de los mexicanos que tienen menos recursos[12] económicos.

[2] se... stand out [3] support [4] wealthy, monied [5] noticeable [6] affection [7] literate [8] illiterates [9] income [10] responsibilities [11] influence [12] resources

NEW VOCABULARY: los eventos, la vida

NOTE: See the *Instructor's Manual* for suggestions on using the chapter-opening pages.

Los eventos de la vida

Bautizo
Dafne Ríos Rivera

La pila bautismal de la Parroquia del Señor del Pueblo, recibió en días pasados a la pequeña **Dafne Ríos Rivera**, quien en brazos de sus padres, Héctor Ríos García y María de los Angeles Rivera de Ríos, recibió el primer sacramento que dicta la Iglesia Católica de manos del Reverendo Padre **Joaquín Orozco Gutiérrez.**

En tan importante celebración estuvieron presentes los padrinos de esta niña, los señores **Tobías Sánchez Hernández y Amalia Sánchez de Sánchez,** quienes obsequiaron a su ahijada el precioso vestido que llevó en esta especial ocasión y participaron devotamente del momento en que el sacerdote tocó la frente de **Dafne** con el agua bendita. Al término del acto religioso, familiares y amigos del matrimonio **Ríos Rivera** que ahí se congregaron felicitaron al mismo y le expresaron sus más sinceros parabienes por este importante acontecimiento en la vida de su pequeña, quien de esta manera se integró a la comunidad católica. Momentos después, en el domicilio de los anfitriones, los invitados disfrutaron de la convivio que los padres de

Dafne Ríos Rivera

AUTOPISTA DEL SOL, S.A. DE C.V.

Participa el sensible fallecimiento de nuestro contador general

 C.P. Enrique Angel Urbina Castillo

Acaecido el día 19 de junio de 1994 en la Ciudad de México, D.F.

Descanse en Paz.

En tu Graduación...

M E T A S

FUNCIONES

- to talk about important life events such as birth, death, marriage, and divorce

- to express opinions and values

- to ask another person to do something

- to speculate about the future

GRAMÁTICA

- the subjunctive and the concept of verbal mood

- the present subjunctive with some impersonal expressions, with some expressions of emotion, with the word **cuando,** and with some expressions of causation or influence

El nacimiento

¡OJO! In this dialogue, David and Elena make some value statements about their opinions of things that are going on (such as, "I'm so happy that . . . ," "It's a shame that . . . "). Such statements are followed in Spanish by special verb forms called the subjunctive. As you read this dialogue and others that follow, you will notice what seem to be unusual endings on these subjunctive forms. Present-tense subjunctive forms use the "opposite" endings.

INFINITIVES ENDING IN **-AR**	INFINITIVES ENDING IN **-ER** AND **-IR**
(yo) **-e**	(yo) **-a**
(tú) **-es**	(tú) **-as**
(Ud., él/ella) **-e**	(Ud., él/ella) **-a**
(nosotros/as) **-emos**	(nosotros/as) **-amos**
(vosotros/as) **-éis**	(vosotros/as) **-áis**
(Uds., ellos/ellas) **-en**	(Uds., ellos/ellas) **-an**

NEW VOCABULARY: me alegro de, dar a luz, era imposible, es lástima, nació; el bautizo, el mensaje, el nacimiento

PREPARATION: Ask students to describe the drawing. Ask them to focus on the title of the dialogue and on the dialogue introduction. **¿Dónde están los primos? ¿Qué necesita hacer Elena?** Have students skim the dialogue. **¿De qué hablan los jóvenes?**

La primera mañana en Veracruz, Elena recibe un mensaje explicando que necesita llamar a su madre. Elena hace la llamada y recibe buenas noticias.

ELENA: ¡Cuánto me alegro de que por fin Lucía haya dado a luz!
DAVID: Lucía es una de tus primas, ¿verdad?
ELENA: Sí, es la hermana de Amalia.
DAVID: ¿Y cuando tuvo el niño... o es niña?
ELENA: Es niña. Se llama María de la Concepción. Nació el día doce... el jueves pasado.
DAVID: ¿Ya celebraron el bautizo?
ELENA: Van a celebrarlo hoy porque era imposible que los padres de Miguel llegaran antes.[1]
DAVID: ¿Miguel?
ELENA: Sí, Miguel, el esposo de Lucía. Sus padres van a ser los padrinos.
DAVID: Es lástima que no podamos asistir al bautizo.

[1]que... *for Miguel's parents to arrive before that*

De inmediato

Indicate which of the following statements are true (**Es cierto**) and which are false (**No es cierto**) according to the dialogue.

1. Lucía, la hermana de Elena, acaba de dar a luz.
2. La niña de Lucía se llama María de la Concepción.
3. La niña nació el sábado pasado.
4. Celebraron el bautizo ayer.
5. Los padres de Miguel van a ser los padrinos.
6. David y Elena van a asistir al bautizo.

OPTIONAL: 1. ¿Quién es Lucía? 2. ¿Qué le pasó recientemente a Lucía? 3. ¿Cuándo nació la niña? 4. ¿Cuándo van a celebrar el bautizo? 5. ¿Quiénes van a ser los padrinos de la niña? 6. ¿Pueden asistir al bautizo David y Elena?

A ti te toca

Recount a recent birth in your family or among your friends. Mention whether the child is a boy or a girl, what his or her name is, the date and year of birth, and who the parents are as well as what their relationship is to you.

EJEMPLO: Es niño. Se llama Carlos Enrique Santos Fuentes. Nació el día dos de septiembre de 1995. Sus padres son Alejandro y Alicia Santos. Alejandro es mi primo, el hijo de mi tía Margarita.

En la universidad

NEW VOCABULARY: es increíble, es probable, es triste, espere, felicitarme, siento; el nombre

Los amigos y la Sra. de Nelson pasan el tiempo en la casa de Jorge y Joaquín.

CELIA: ¡No me digas!

CARMEN: Lo que tú oyes, mujer. Cristina espera otro niño en abril.

CELIA: Es increíble que Cristina tenga dos hijos ahora y que espere el tercero. Si estaba con nosotras en el colegio....

LA SRA. DE NELSON: Sí, mi hija. Tienes razón. Es triste que tu papá y tu abuelita no puedan venir para tu cumpleaños. Es que tu papá tiene que trabajar y tu abuelita es demasiado vieja para hacer viajes tan largos. Y ya sabes que David tampoco puede venir porque está en México.

SANDRA: Pero, vamos a hacer fiesta, ¿verdad? Y van a venir todos los otros parientes, ¿no?

LA SRA. DE NELSON: Sí, te haremos[1] una fiesta especial. Y todos los que puedan van a venir.

JORGE: Siento que hayas perdido[2] la llamada. Un hombre llamó de... larga distancia... pero de aquí... de los Estados Unidos.

JOAQUÍN: ¿No dio su nombre?

JORGE: No, pero... ahora recuerdo. Dijo que era tu padrino.

JOAQUÍN: Es probable que me haya llamado para felicitarme por ser el día de mi santo. Es importante que lo llame hoy.

[1]te... *we will throw you*   [2]hayas... *you missed*

PREPARATION: Ask students to describe the drawing. Ask students to focus on the dialogue introduction. **¿Dónde están los amigos?** Have students skim the dialogue. **¿De qué hablan los jóvenes?**

De inmediato

Which of the characters (Carmen, Celia, la Sra. Muñoz de Nelson, Sandra, Joaquín, or Jorge) communicates the following information?

1. Cristina espera otro niño en abril.
2. Una amiga que estaba con ellas en el colegio ya tiene dos hijos.

3. El papá de Sandra y su abuelita no pueden venir para su fiesta de cumpleaños.
4. Un hombre llamó a larga distancia.
5. El hombre que llamó dijo que era el padrino de Joaquín.

A ti te toca

Think of a friend or family member who has many children. Express your disbelief to a classmate over the number of children the person has.

EJEMPLO: E1: Es increíble que (*persona o personas*) tenga(n) (*número*) hijos.
E2: ¡No me digas!
E1: Lo que tú oyes, mujer/hombre.

Faceta cultural

Los padrinos

NEW VOCABULARY: la madrina, el padrino

People in Hispanic cultures may have different **padrinos** for their baptism, their first communion, their confirmation, and their wedding. The most important **padrinos**, however, are those chosen to take responsibility for children at the latter's baptism. The role of godparent is an important one and may have many ramifications. Godparents are expected to supervise their godchildren's spiritual education and to act as their guardians should their parents become unable to care for them. For this reason godparents are frequently chosen from among family members and friends of the parents.

The relationship between **padrino/madrina** and **ahijado/a** (*godchild*) is important, but equally important is the relationship formed between the **padrinos** and the child's parents. They become **compadres** and, as such, share the closeness and the mutual responsibilities of siblings. It is not uncommon for **compadres** and **padrinos** to be invited to family events as routinely as if they were family members.

FOLLOW-UP: 1. For which occasions might a Hispanic person choose **padrinos**? 2. Why are the **padrinos** at a child's baptism more important than those for other occasions? 3. In the past, whom did parents try to get for a child's **padrinos** if at all possible? Why? 4. What relationship besides godparent–godchild is formed when one agrees to be a godparent?

CONCEPTO

El subjuntivo

PREPARATION: Have students repeat Sandra's lines. Ask what sentiment **Me alegro de que** indicates. [happiness, emotion] Who is doing the wanting? [Sandra] Whom is she asking to come? [aunt and uncle] Have students repeat the second set of lines. What kind of sentiment does **Es importante que** indicate? [importance, value statement, attempt to influence] Ask if the arrival of Sandra's aunt and uncle in Eau Claire is in the present or in the future. Ask for the infinitives of the subjunctive verb forms. How do these forms compare to the present tense students have studied?

«Me alegro de que **planeen** un viaje a Eau Claire. Quiero que **vengan** para mi cumpleaños.»

«Es importante que **vayamos** a verte en este día especial. Vamos a llamarte cuando **lleguemos** a Eau Claire.»

(A) Ya sabemos. Using what you know about the following characters, combine elements from the columns to form logical sentences.

NEW VOCABULARY: les sorprende

1. Elena se alegra de que su prima Lucía
2. A David le molesta que él y Elena
3. A Carmen y Celia les sorprende que
4. A la Sra. Muñoz de Nelson le importa que su hija Sandra
5. Jorque siente que Joaquín
6. Es importante que Joaquín

a. no haya podido recibir la llamada de su padrino.
b. celebre su cumpleaños con la familia.
c. Cristina espere su tercer hijo.
d. haya dado a luz.
e. llame hoy a su padrino.
f. no puedan asistir al bautizo de la niña.

(B) En esta clase. Make statements that reflect your instructor's attitude about several aspects of Spanish class by combining elements from each column. Start each sentence with **Nuestro profesor** (**Nuestra profesora**) and use **no** as appropriate.

NEW VOCABULARY: recomienda
SUGGESTION: Students work in pairs to make the statements. Encourage responses such as ¿Verdad? / Interesante. / Comprendo. / Sí, es verdad. / Sí, tienes razón.
OPTIONAL: Have students intentionally say something that is not true about your attitudes about the class. Encourage responses to such incorrect statements with phrases such as the following. No, no es verdad/ cierto. / Creo que no.

EJEMPLOS: Nuestro profesor (Nuestra profesora) prefiere que no lleguemos tarde.

Nuestro profesor (Nuestra profesora) recomienda que vayamos al laboratorio de idiomas.

(no) prefiere	que (no)	lleguemos tarde
(no) pide		traigamos diccionarios a la clase
(no) recomienda		hablemos español en la clase
(no) insiste en		hagamos preguntas
		usemos computadoras
		repitamos las nuevas palabras
		durmamos en la clase
		salgamos temprano de la clase
		vayamos al laboratorio de lenguas
		practiquemos el español fuera de la clase

(C) La clase del profesor Brewer. Professor Brewer has scheduled conferences with some of his Spanish II students. Those in his first period class are quite serious students, whereas those in his second period class need to apply themselves a little more. What does he say about each one regarding these class expectations?

NEW VOCABULARY: en serio
EXPANSION: Give these infinitives with Sabe/Recomienda que and ask students to come up with the correct forms. 1. aprender el vocabulario: Heather? Michelle? 2. escribir las palabras nuevas: Charles? Scott? 3. tomar apuntes en clase: Dan? Bob? 4. participar en las actividades de la clase: Amy? Scott?

Primer período: Amy, Charles, Dan, Heather
Segundo período: Bob, Michelle, Natalie, Scott

EJEMPLO: hace/haga la tarea
Sabe que Heather...
Recomienda que Michelle... →
Sabe que Heather hace la tarea.
Recomienda que Michelle haga la tarea.

1. toma/tome el curso en serio
Sabe que Amy...
Recomienda que Bob...

2. sale/salga bien en los exámenes
Sabe que Dan...
Recomienda que Natalie...

3. estudia/estudie los nuevos
verbos
Sabe que Charles...
Recomienda que Scott...
4. lee/lea las lecciones dos veces
Sabe que Heather...
Recomienda que Natalie...

5. practica/practique el español
fuera de la clase
Sabe que Dan...
Recomienda que Bob...

Las formas del subjuntivo

VERBOS REGULARES

estudiar		querer		traducir	
estudie	estudiemos	quiera	queramos	traduzca	traduzcamos
estudies	estudiéis	quieras	queráis	traduzcas	traduzcáis
estudie	estudien	quiera	quieran	traduzca	traduzcan

VERBOS IRREGULARES

dar	**dé, des, dé, demos, deis, den**
estar	**esté, estés, esté, estemos, estéis, estén**
haber (hay)	**haya, hayas, haya, hayamos, hayáis, hayan**
ir	**vaya, vayas, vaya, vayamos, vayáis, vayan**
saber	**sepa, sepas, sepa, sepamos, sepáis, sepan**
ser	**sea, seas, sea, seamos, seáis, sean**

TO FORM THE PRESENT SUBJUNCTIVE

1. Use the **yo** form of the present
indicative.
2. Drop the final **-o**.
3. Add endings with **-e** to **-ar** verbs and
endings with **-a** to **-er**/**-ir** verbs.

hacer → hago

hag-

haga, hagas, haga, hagamos, hagáis, hagan

Me alegro de que (Uds.) **planeen** un viaje a Eau Claire.	*I'm pleased that you are planning a trip to Eau Claire.*
Quiero que (Uds.) **vengan** para mi cumpleaños.	*I want you to come for my birthday.*

Many sentences require the subjunctive in the second, or dependent, clause because the speakers express subjective attitudes toward the action. Four uses of the subjunctive will be practiced in separate sections of this chapter.

El subjuntivo con expresiones impersonales

CONCEPTO

«**Es posible que tengan** un examen la semana que viene. **Es importante que estudien** todo el capítulo. **Es triste que** no **podamos** pasar otro día en esta lección. Sin embargo, **es cierto que** van a salir bien.»

NEW VOCABULARY: es cierto, es claro, es verdad, es (im)probable, es malo, es necesario

PREPARATION: Model the sentences for the students. Ask what the infinitives of the verbs are. Ask what sentiment **Es posible** expresses. [possibility, doubt] What kind of sentiment does **Es importante que** indicate? [importance, value statement, attempt to influence] What sentiment does **Es triste que** indicate? [sadness, value statement, emotion] Ask them which verb forms in her statements are subjunctive? Which are indicative? What is the difference between **Es cierto** and **Es posible**?

+ *that . . .*

Otras expresiones impersonales

es claro		*it's clear*
es evidente	+ que + *indicative*	*it's evident*
es seguro		*it's certain*
es verdad		*it's true*
(no) es bueno		*it's (not) good*
(no) es (im)posible		*it's (not) (im)possible*
(no) es (im)probable		*it's (not) (im)probable*
(no) es increíble		*it's (not) incredible/unbelievable*
(no) es lástima		*it's (not) a shame, a pity, too bad*
(no) es malo		*it's (not) bad, unfortunate*
(no) es necesario	+ que + *subjunctive*	*it's (not) necessary*
no es cierto		*it's not certain*
no es claro		*it's not clear*
no es evidente		*it's not evident*
no es seguro		*it's not certain*
no es verdad		*it's not true*

Actividades

NEW VOCABULARY: el sueldo
PREPARATION: Make sure there are no questions about the pronunciation or meaning of the items.
OPTIONAL: After students have completed the easier activities, ask them to work in small groups to create original sentences similar to those in Act. A, that describe their reactions to current events.

A **Controversias.** Form logical sentences with elements from both columns.

1. Es bueno que
2. Es malo que
3. Es triste que
4. Es posible que
5. Es importante que
6. Es lástima que

la tecnología médica permita el nacimiento de algunos niños.

los jóvenes vayan a fiestas durante la semana.

algunos niños nazcan con problemas físicos y/o mentales.

mucha gente asista a la iglesia.

el nacimiento de algunos niños sea difícil.

yo gane $100.000 de sueldo en el año 2000.

una mujer sea gobernadora de este estado.

los republicanos ganen las elecciones del año 2000.

esta universidad (no) ponga mucho/más énfasis en los deportes.

SUGGESTION: Make sure there are no questions about the pronunciation or meaning of the items.
SUGGESTION: This works well as a pair activity. Students can tell each other the items they have chosen. Encourage responses such as **Estoy de acuerdo. / Comprendo. / Sí, es verdad. / Sí, tienes razón.**

B **El clima.** Make two statements about the climate of each of the four seasons in the place where you live. **Vocabulario útil: (no) es cierto que..., (no) es seguro que..., (no) es verdad que...**

EJEMPLO: En invierno donde vivo es verdad que hace frío. No es verdad que haya mucho viento...

hace/haga mucho calor
llueve/llueva frecuentemente
hay/haya mucho viento
nieva/nieve mucho

necesito/necesite un paraguas
está/esté húmedo
hace/haga frío

PREPARATION: Before beginning Act. C, ask students to give you the subjunctive form that corresponds to the indicative forms in the items.
SUGGESTION: This works well as a pair activity.
SUGGESTION: Give students a neutral response. **No me importa que...**
OPTIONAL: In small groups, students can record other students' opinions and report back to the class about what they think (i.e., **tres personas piensan que es bueno/malo que...**). The class can tally the results.

C **¿Qué piensas?** Do you think the following is good (**Es bueno que...**) or bad (**Es malo que...**)?

EJEMPLOS: Algunos estudiantes no vienen a clase. →
Es malo que algunos estudiantes no vengan a clase.

Los profesores son simpáticos. →
Es bueno que los profesores sean simpáticos.

1. Algunos profesores dan mucha tarea.
2. Los estudiantes van a la biblioteca para estudiar.
3. Algunos profesores hablan solamente español en la clase.
4. La biblioteca está abierta[1] los domingos por la noche.
5. Algunas universidades ponen mucho énfasis en los deportes.
6. Algunos jóvenes de secundaria beben cerveza.
7. Hay exámenes a nivel[2] universitario.
8. Algunos estudiantes copian de la tarea de otros.

[1]*open*   [2]*level*

OPTIONAL: Give students a neutral response. **No me importa que...**
EXTENSION: Have students write additional items and then, in pairs or in small groups, offer their statements (in the indicative). The others react.

D **Mis opiniones.** React to the following statements with an impersonal expression, using each expression only once. **Vocabulario útil: Es cierto/claro/evidente/seguro/verdad. (No) Es bueno/(im)posible/(im)probable/lástima/malo/necesario/triste. No es claro/evidente/seguro/verdad.**

EJEMPLO: El español es la mejor lengua del mundo. →
            Es cierto que el español es la mejor lengua del mundo.
            o Es posible que el español sea la mejor lengua del mundo.

1. La universidad es grande (pequeña).
2. Algunos estudiantes casi nunca hacen la tarea.
3. Este semestre/trimestre pasa rápidamente.
4. Ⓟ habla rápidamente en clase.
5. Mis padres pagan la matrícula para mis estudios universitarios.*
6. Hace mucho frío aquí en el invierno.
7. Hay muchos programas deportivos en la televisión los sábados.
8. Al Pacino es el mejor actor del cine.
9. Madrid está muy lejos de mi ciudad.

*¡OJO! There is a spelling change required for **-gar** verbs in the subjunctive:
g → gu.

Las expresiones impersonales y el modo del verbo

IMPERSONAL EXPRESSION	SECOND VERB
Generalization	→ Infinitive
Expression of certainty	→ Indicative
Expression of emotion, doubt, or attempt to influence	→ Subjunctive

IMPERSONAL EXPRESSION (MAIN CLAUSE)	SECOND VERB (DEPENDENT CLAUSE)
Any expression	No specified subject → use the infinitive

Es necesario	**estudiar** mucho.
It's necessary	*to study a lot.*
Es bueno	**estudiar** mucho.
It's good	*to study a lot.*

Any expression indicating certainty	Specified subject → use the indicative
Es cierto	que Jorge **estudia** mucho.
It's certain	*that Jorge studies a lot.*

Any expression *except* those indicating certainty	Specified subject → use the subjunctive
Es necesario	que Joaquín **estudie** mucho.
It's necessary	*for Joaquín to study a lot.*
No es verdad	que Joaquín **estudie** mucho.
It's not true	*that Joaquín studies a lot.*

Influencias religiosas

NEW VOCABULARY: el nombre de pila

Although many people in the Hispanic world have their children christened, serve as godparents to an infant, and attend a child's confirmation or a young adult's marriage, it is possible that none of the participants in the event may be particularly religious. In the Hispanic world, there are many religious customs that continue to be observed for cultural rather than religious reasons. Many non-practicing Catholics in the Hispanic world continue to observe the sacraments of baptism, a church marriage, and a religious burial.

The names given to children can be another indication of a presence of religion in the Hispanic world. Even the Spanish expression for *first name* reflects the importance of religion: a person's *first name* is his or her **nombre de pila**. The **pila** is the *baptismal font*. Thus, a person's **nombre de pila** is the name he or she received when baptized. The parents may choose a name for many reasons, including the fact that they simply liked the name, had a close friend or relative with the same name, or because it is the name of the saint for the day on which the child was born. Many names have religious significance. Popular names for women are María de la Concepción, Mercedes (*Mercies*), Luz (*Light*), Amada (*Beloved*), and Felicidad/Felisa (*Happiness*). Many men are named José María, Jesús, or Domingo.

FOLLOW-UP: Have students interview a native speaker to find out three more names with religious significance.

El subjuntivo con expresiones de emoción

PREPARATION: Model the sentences for the students. Point out that both sentences express emotion. Ask how Sandra feels. Ask how Inés (uncle Alfonso's wife) feels. Ask what the infinitives are of the subjunctive verb forms.

Estoy contenta de que estén aquí conmigo.

Me alegro de que tu tío Alfonso y yo podamos visitarte, niña.

Actividades

A **¡Tantas emociones!** Imagine that a new baby has been born into your family. Indicate with **sí** or **no** whether someone would express the following emotions.

1. ¡Me alegro de que el niño esté bien!
2. ¡Me gusta que el niño se parezca a mí!
3. ¡Siento que el niño se llame Onésimo!
4. ¡Temo que el niño sea muy feo!
5. ¡Espero que el niño tenga buena suerte en la vida!
6. ¡Me sorprende que el niño sea pelirrojo!
7. ¡Estoy muy contento de que la madre esté sufriendo!

B **Mis emociones.** Share with the class your feelings about various aspects of campus life by using the introductory phrases to complete the following sentences; add **no** where appropriate.

Espero que...
Estoy contento/a de que...
Me alegro de que...
Me fascina que...
Me gusta que...
Me interesa que...

Me molesta que...
Me sorprende que...
Siento que...
Temo que...
¿ ?

EJEMPLO: en esta universidad (dar) cursos de español/física/¿ ? →
Estoy contento/a de que en esta universidad den cursos de español.
o Me sorprende que en esta universidad no den cursos de arquitectura.

1. esta universidad (ser) demasiado grande/pequeña
2. mis amigos y yo (vivir) en una residencia estudiantil
3. los profesores (dar) buenas/malas notas
4. mis compañeros de clase y yo (ir) a España/México/¿ ?
5. los libros de texto para las clases (costar) mucho/poco
6. el equipo de fútbol norteamericano (ganar) con frecuencia
7. mi profesor(a) de _____ (recordar) mi nombre
8. (haber) muchos/pocos estudiantes en las clases
9. ¿ ?

NEW VOCABULARY: temo, tenga buena suerte
PREPARATION: Make sure there are no questions about the pronunciation or meaning of the items.
SUGGESTION: This works well as a pair activity. Have one student read the items while the other has his or her book closed.
EXTENSION: 7. Espero que el niño se haga abogado en el futuro. 8. Temo que el niño no aprenda a hablar español. 9. Me gusta que el niño tenga una nariz grande. 10. Me encanta que los padres del niño tengan mucho dinero ya.
EXPANSION: (Act. A.) Ask students, working in small groups, to create several sentences that one would or would not say about the new baby. Have each group read several of their sentences to the entire class, which will indicate if they are acceptable or not.

EXPANSION: Have students work in small groups to create original conclusions to at least five of the expressions of emotion in Act. B.

Las expresiones de emoción y el modo del verbo

ANY EMOTIONAL EXPRESSION (MAIN CLAUSE)	SECOND VERB (DEPENDENT CLAUSE)
	No change in subject → use the infinitive
Espero *I hope*	**salir** bien en el próximo examen. *to do well on the next exam.*
Me alegro de *I'm happy*	**poder** estudiar contigo hoy. *to be able to study with you today.*
Me sorprende *It surprises me*	**recibir** malas notas. *to receive bad grades.* (*Continúa.*)

Change in subject → use the subjunctive

Espero que tú **salgas** bien en el próximo examen.
I hope *that you will do well on the next exam.*

Me alegro de que Juan **pueda** estudiar contigo hoy.
I'm happy *that Juan is able to study with you today.*

Me sorprende que **recibas** malas notas.
It surprises me *that you receive bad grades.*

Nos molesta que Juan reciba malas notas.
It bothers us *that Juan receives bad grades.*

Les gusta que Juan estudie mucho.
They are glad *that Juan studies a lot.*

Emotional expressions are those in which someone expresses his or her feelings about a circumstance or event.

¡OJO! Many expressions of emotion, including **fascinar, gustar, interesar, molestar,** and **sorprender** use indirect object pronouns to indicate who is expressing emotion.

La boda

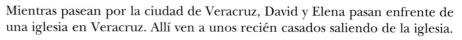

PREPARATION: Ask students to describe the drawing. Ask them to focus on the title of the dialogue and on the dialogue introduction. **¿Dónde están los primos? ¿Qué ven?** Have students skim the dialogue. **¿De qué hablan los jóvenes?**

NEW VOCABULARY: ahorre; la boda, los recién casados

Mientras pasean por la ciudad de Veracruz, David y Elena pasan enfrente de una iglesia en Veracruz. Allí ven a unos recién casados saliendo de la iglesia.

ELENA: Me encantan las bodas.

DAVID: ¿Verdad? Eres demasiado romántica. La boda es una tradición que cuesta más dinero cada año.

ELENA: Es que los novios siempre parecen tan contentos... ¿Y tú? ¿No esperas tener una ceremonia religiosa cuando te cases?

DAVID: Pues, sí. Pero sólo voy a casarme cuando tenga trabajo y ahorre el dinero suficiente. No quiero que ni mis padres ni los de ella[1] paguen la boda.

ELENA: ¿No es verdad que haya residencias para matrimonios en las universidades estadounidenses?

DAVID: Sí, es verdad que las hay. Y también hay muchos estudiantes que prefieren terminar sus estudios universitarios antes de casarse.

[1]ni... *either my parents or hers*

Here is Elena and David's conversation about weddings, but in an abbreviated and disorganized form. Identify the speaker as Elena (**E**) or David (**D**), then put their comments into logical order.

E   D   _____   Eres romántica; las bodas cuestan más dinero cada año.

E   D   _____   ¿No es verdad que en las universidades en los EE. UU. haya residencias para matrimonios?

E   D   _____   Los novios siempre parecen muy contentos.

E   D   _____   ¿No esperas tener una ceremonia religiosa cuando te cases?

E   D   _____   No quiero que ni mis padres ni mis suegros paguen la boda.

E   D   _____   Me encantan las bodas.

E   D   _____   Sólo voy a casarme cuando tenga trabajo y dinero.

E   D   _____   También hay muchos estudiantes que prefieren terminar sus estudios antes de casarse.

OPTIONAL: 1. ¿Qué acaban de ver David y Elena? 2. ¿Qué piensa David de la tradición de la boda? 3. ¿Cuándo va a casarse David? ¿Por qué va a esperar? 4. ¿Qué servicio para matrimonios ofrecen muchas universidades en los EE. UU.?
FOLLOW-UP: 1. ¿Ofrece servicios para matrimonios esta universidad? ¿Cuáles son? 2. ¿Hay recién casados en esta clase? ¿Cuándo se casaron?

Tell a classmate two things that you love, using the dialogue as a model.

EJEMPLOS: —Me encantan los bautizos y las fiestas de cumpleaños.
—¿Verdad? A mí también.

—Me encantan las hamburguesas y las papas fritas.
—¿Verdad? A mí no. A mí me encantan los camarones y las verduras.

En la universidad

PREPARATION: Ask students to describe the drawing. Then ask them to focus on the dialogue introduction. Have students skim the dialogues. **¿De qué hablan los jóvenes?**

DIÁLOGO

NEW VOCABULARY: la luna de miel; ¡Claro que sí!, hasta que, tan pronto como

Unos amigos de David van a un partido de béisbol, donde comen palomitas de maíz y charlan mucho.

MARÍA: ¿Adónde van Ángela y Jaime para la luna de miel?

MARISOL: No pueden hacer un viaje ahora. Tienen que esperar hasta que Ángela tenga dos semanas de vacaciones.

MARÍA: Pues, voy a comprarles un regalo de bodas tan pronto como tenga dinero. ¿Quieres ir conmigo al centro comercial?

MARISOL: ¡Claro que sí!

LUIS: Me dicen que el profesor Brewer está divorciado.

ALFONSINA: ¿Sí? Pues, creo que no, pero no estoy segura. ¿Quién te dijo eso?

LUIS: No recuerdo ahora. Es posible que no sea verdad.

JORGE: Es probable que el profesor no esté divorciado porque su esposa y él celebraron su aniversario de bodas recientemente. Invitaron a los otros profesores. ¿No recuerdas?

NEW VOCABULARY: la primera comunión

MERCEDES: ¿Cuándo vamos a ver a mi padre?

LUISA: Cuando terminen mis clases. Ya sabes eso.

MERCEDES: Es que pensaba en las fiestas que vamos a tener cuando lleguemos a la Florida.

LUISA: Sí, hija. Una fiesta para el cumpleaños de tu papá y la primera comunión de tu primo José.

De inmediato

Complete these statements by choosing the correct answer from among the choices provided.

OPTIONAL: 1. ¿Qué actividad planean Ángela y Jaime? 2. ¿Cuándo van a hacer el viaje? 3. ¿Qué va a hacer María? 4. ¿Por qué cree Jorge que el profesor Brewer no está divorciado? 5. ¿Cuándo van a ver Mercedes y Luisa al papá de Mercedes? 6. ¿Qué fiestas van a tener en la Florida?

FOLLOW-UP: 1. ¿A quién conoces que recientemente fue de luna de miel? ¿Adónde fue? ¿Por cuánto tiempo? 2. ¿A quiénes conoces que recientemente celebraron su aniversario de bodas? ¿Cuántos años de matrimonio celebraron? ¿Dónde lo celebraron? ¿Qué hicieron?

1. Jaime y Ángela van a esperar para hacer su viaje de luna de miel hasta que Ángela tenga _____.
   a. su luna de miel   **b.** suficiente tiempo   **c.** sus clases

2. María y Marisol van a comprarles un regalo de bodas a Ángela y Jaime en _____.
   a. dos semanas   **b.** el centro comercial   **c.** su luna de miel

3. A Luis le dicen que el profesor Brewer está _____.
   a. divorciado   **b.** de vacaciones   **c.** recién casado

4. El profesor Brewer _____ recientemente.
   a. vio a su padre   **b.** celebró su aniversario de bodas   **c.** se divorció

5. Luisa y Mercedes van a _____.
   a. la Florida   **b.** esperar dos semanas   **c.** casarse

---

A ti te toca

Tell your classmates what you can't do now or tomorrow, and what needs to happen before you can do it, using the dialogue as a model. You may want to use some of the following expressions.

NEW VOCABULARY: graduarme

ahorrar dinero
ayudar a _____
casarme
graduarme
hacer la tarea
jugar al béisbol
  (básquetbol, ¿ ?)

practicar el vocabulario
preparar la cena
ver televisión
viajar a _____
visitar a mi familia

EJEMPLOS: No puedo hacer la tarea ahora. Tengo que esperar hasta que tenga suficiente tiempo.

No puedo preparar la cena mañana. Tengo que esperar hasta que compre unas cebollas.

El subjuntivo con expresiones temporales

SUGGESTION: Ask students to look at the name of the **Concepto**. Ask them to give you some **expresiones temporales**. [ayer, hoy, mañana; cuando, hasta, antes, después].

PREPARATION: Ask students to describe the drawing. Model David's sentence for the students. Ask whether David's last year of school is in the present or the future. (Is it objective or subjective?) Ask them what infinitive the verb form **vuelva** comes from?

«Voy a estar en mi último año de universidad cuando **vuelva** a los Estados Unidos.»

Actividades

Ⓐ Lo voy a hacer cuando... Combine items from the columns with **cuando** to express when you will do the following activities. There may be more than one acceptable answer.

1.	Voy a estudiar	cuando
2.	Voy a comer	
3.	Voy a ponerme ropa formal	
4.	Voy a alquilar un vídeo	
5.	Voy a llamar a mi amigo	
6.	Voy a hablar francés	
7.	Voy a sacar fotos	
8.	Voy a saber hablar español	

compre un rollo de película.
desee divertirme.
encuentre mi libro de texto.
encuentre su número de teléfono.
haya una noche libre.
tenga hambre.
termine este libro.
vaya a México.
vaya a un baile elegante.
vengan mis padres a mi casa.
visite París.

NEW VOCABULARY: alquilar
SUGGESTION: Make sure there are no questions about the pronunciation or meaning of the items.
SUGGESTION: Acts. A and B work well with students in pairs. Students can share their statements with each other. Encourage responses such as the following. **¿Verdad? Yo también. / Interesante. Yo no. / ¡Qué bien! / ¡Qué suerte tienes! / Comprendo. / Sí, es verdad / Sí, tienes razón.**

Ⓑ Mis planes para el futuro. Complete the sentences to tell when you will do the following activities.

EJEMPLO: Voy a casarme cuando... →
Voy a casarme cuando encuentre a una persona muy especial.

1. Voy a ir de vacaciones cuando...
2. Voy a México cuando...
3. Voy a comprarme un coche caro cuando...
4. Cuando... , voy a celebrar mucho.
5. Cuando... , voy a dormir todo el día.
6. Voy a recibir muchos regalos cuando...
7. ¿ ?

EXTENSION: 8. Voy a tener mucho dinero cuando... 9. Voy a estar muy contento/a cuando... 10. Voy a estar triste cuando... 11. Conozco a una persona que va a ser rica cuando... 12. Vamos a tener un examen en esta clase cuando...

Las expresiones temporales y el modo del verbo

FIRST VERB + TIME EXPRESSION (MAIN CLAUSE)	SECOND VERB (DEPENDENT CLAUSE)
Habitual action	→ Indicative
Future or pending action or state of being	→ Subjunctive

FIRST VERB + TIME EXPRESSION		SECOND VERB (DEPENDENT CLAUSE)
		Habitual action → use the indicative
Generalmente estudio	cuando	**estoy** en mi habitación.
I usually study	*when*	*I'm in my room.*
		Future/uncertainty → use the subjunctive
Voy a estudiar esta noche	cuando	**esté** en mi habitación.
I'm going to study tonight	*when*	*I'm in my room.*

The subjunctive is required after various expressions of time when referring to future or pending events to indicate that they have not yet occurred or may not occur. There are several such expressions of time; but you will only practice using the indicative or the subjunctive after **cuando.**

Faceta cultural

El matrimonio y el divorcio

Hispanic couples tend not to marry until the groom is ready to take on the responsibilities of a family. Thus, young people who are still financially dependent on their families do not normally marry. Families often play an important role in the choice of marriage partners because the person marrying into the family will become an integral part of the family unit.

Although in some Hispanic countries a priest is authorized to conduct a civil and a religious ceremony at the same time, in countries that enforce the separation of church and state, these two ceremonies occur at different times because the church and state do not recognize each other's laws. If two ceremonies are required, it is the religious ceremony that is attended by family and friends. The civil ceremony is usually a relatively brief event held at the courthouse and normally precedes the religious ceremony.

Divorce in Hispanic countries has become increasingly possible in the twentieth century, but it is still generally less common than in the United States. In those areas where the Catholic Church is strong and influential, divorce is not easy to obtain and may carry a social stigma. Additionally, the grounds for divorce are not as broadly stated as in the United States. In the event that both a Catholic and a civil marriage have taken place, only the civil marriage can be dissolved; the religious marriage must be annulled by an ecclesiastical court.

En México

The two marriage ceremonies—by state and church—are required in Mexico, usually on different days. There is a distinct separation between church and state in Mexico: they do not recognize each other's laws.

FOLLOW-UP: 1. En el mundo hispano, ¿hasta cuándo esperan los prometidos para casarse? 2. ¿Cuáles son las dos ceremonias que muchos consideran necesarias para casarse en el mundo hispano? 3. ¿En cuál ceremonia suele participar toda la familia? 4. ¿Por qué son necesarias dos ceremonias en México?

Los eventos importantes de la vida

PREPARATION: Ask students to think about the important steps in a person's life. Have them cover up the English translations of the **Otro vocabulario** list. Which of the expressions do they know already or can they guess?

VOCABULARIO

el bautizo   la primera comunión   la boda

Otro vocabulario

dar a luz	*to give birth*	casarse (con)	*to get married*
nacer (nazco)	*to be born*	divorciarse	*to get a divorce*
el nacimiento	*birth*	el divorcio	*divorce*
la vida	*life*	la luna de miel	*honeymoon*
vivir	*to live*	el noviazgo	*engagement; courtship*
la graduación	*graduation*	el entierro	*burial, funeral*
graduarse (en) (me gradúo)	*to graduate (from)*	el velorio	*wake, vigil*
		morir (ue)	*to die*
el aniversario (de bodas)	*(wedding) anniversary*	la muerte	*death*

OPTIONAL: Read some of the life events in random order. Ask how students would respond to learning that a friend had experienced the event mentioned—with **Felicitaciones** or **Lo siento**?

OPTIONAL: Have students take three life events and put them in logical or illogical order. The class will respond to the sequence by saying **Es lógico** or **No es lógico: el divorcio, el matrimonio, el noviazgo → No es lógico. el nacimiento, el bautizo, el cumpleaños → Es lógico.**

277

Actividades

Ⓐ Los eventos de la vida. What life event is described? There may be more than one acceptable answer.

1. Los esposos celebran dieciocho años de estar juntos.
2. La persona ya no vive.
3. Los novios se casan.
4. Los novios viajan a las Cataratas de Niágara.
5. Los esposos se separan legalmente; ya no están casados.
6. El niño nace.
7. La persona termina sus estudios.
8. Es el estado de vivir.

Ⓑ Durante mi vida. Which five important life events have touched your life in some way? Explain how.

EJEMPLO: la muerte →
Mi abuelo murió recientemente a la edad de ochenta años.

DIÁLOGO

La muerte

NEW VOCABULARY: las esquelas de defunción, las notas necrológicas

El domingo por la mañana, David y Elena toman un café mientras leen el periódico en la terraza de un café cerca de su hotel. David comenta sobre una diferencia que ha notado entre los periódicos de su país y los de México.

DAVID: El periódico del domingo siempre trae muchas esquelas de defunción, ¿verdad?

ELENA: Sí. ¿Te sorprende? ¿No existe esta costumbre en los EE. UU.?

DAVID: Es cada vez más común en las ciudades con muchos habitantes hispanos. Pero nosotros solemos usar las notas necrológicas, que son distintas de las esquelas.

ELENA: Sí, las esquelas de defunción no refieren la vida y los méritos del difunto. Como ves, pueden ser un homenaje[1] de su familia, sus amigos, sus empleados, la compañía o la cofradía[2] a la que perteneció.

DAVID: Sí, mira ésta. Es de la familia en el aniversario de la muerte... otra diferencia entre una esquela de defunción y una nota necrológica.

[1] *homage, testimonial* [2] *religious or fraternal organization*

Match the questions with the appropriate short answer.

De inmediato

NEW VOCABULARY: en vez de
VARIATION: Ask these questions orally and have students find the answers in the dialogue.

1. ¿Cuándo se ven muchas esquelas de defunción en el periódico mexicano?
2. ¿Dónde existe la costumbre de publicar esquelas en los EE. UU.?
3. ¿Qué usan los estadounidenses en vez de las esquelas?
4. ¿Cuáles son dos de las diferencias entre una nota necrológica y una esquela de defunción?
5. ¿Quiénes publican las esquelas de defunción en los periódicos?

a. La familia, la compañía o a veces los empleados del difunto.
b. No refieren la vida y méritos del difunto y pueden aparecer en el aniversario de la muerte.
c. En el periódico del domingo.
d. Las notas necrológicas.
e. En las ciudades con muchos habitantes hispanos.

Describe to a classmate two things you tend to do in your daily routine. Follow the model.

A ti te toca

OPTIONAL: Have students make up three or four normal or bizarre "customs" for an imaginary country. Each student should tell a partner what the custom is and ask whether it exists in the partner's country. **—En mí país no nos alegramos al nacer un bebe, nos alegramos al morir un amigo. ¿No existe esta costumbre en tu país? —No, no es común.**

EJEMPLO: E1: Suelo acostarme a la una y levantarme a las once de la mañana. ¿Te sorprende?
E2: Sí, me sorprende. Yo suelo despertarme a las seis de la mañana y desayunar cereal, pan tostado y jugo de naranja. ¿Te sorprende?
E1: No, no me sorprende.

En la universidad

PREPARATION: Ask students to describe the photo. Have them focus on the dialogue introduction. **¿Dónde están los estudiantes? ¿Qué hacen?** Have students skim the dialogues. **¿De qué hablan los jóvenes?**

NEW VOCABULARY: se viste de luto

Después de las clases, los amigos de David toman un refresco en un bar cerca de la universidad. Hablan de unos aspectos de sus vidas actuales.

CARMEN: Celia, ¿la abuela todavía se viste de luto?
CELIA: Sí, mira estas fotos. En todas está vestida de luto e insiste en que los otros miembros de la familia también observen las costumbres tradicionales.

JORGE: La profesora Martínez no quiso planear la fiesta; prefería que los alumnos decidieran lo que iban a hacer.
JOAQUÍN: Bueno, eso significaba más trabajo para nosotros pero era mejor que tomáramos[1] las decisiones.

---

[1] *we make*

MARÍA: ¿Qué tienes que ir a buscar en el centro esta tarde, Alfonsina?

ALFONSINA: Voy a buscar una tarjeta. Tengo que escribirle a mi tía para darle el pésame[2] por la muerte de su cuñada.

[2]darle... *express condolences*

De inmediato

Who says or does the following: **la abuela,** Celia, **la profesora Martínez,** Joaquín, or Alfonsina?

1. Todavía se viste de luto.
2. Dice que la abuela insiste en que la familia observe las costumbres tradicionales.
3. No quiso planear la fiesta.
4. Prefería que los alumnos decidieran lo que iban a hacer.
5. Dijo que es mejor que los alumnos tomaran las decisiones.
6. Va a buscar una tarjeta.
7. Tiene que darle el pésame a su tía.

OPTIONAL: 1. ¿Cómo se viste la abuela de Carmen y Celia? 2. ¿Por qué no quiso planear la fiesta la profesora Martínez? 3. ¿Está de acuerdo Joaquín con la decisión de la profesora? 4. ¿Adónde va a ir Alfonsina? ¿Qué tiene que comprar? ¿Por qué?

A ti te toca

Practice the dialogue between María and Alfonsina with a classmate. Then exchange roles, substituting other places for **el centro** and responding appropriately. Some suggestions are provided.

la biblioteca	la papelería	la tienda (de
el centro	la pastelería	juguetes/
comercial	el puesto de	ropa)
la librería	discos/	el videocentro
la panadería	frutas/regalos	la zapatería
	el (super)mer-	¿ ?
	cado	

EJEMPLO: —¿Qué tienes que ir a buscar en la biblioteca esta tarde?
—Voy a buscar unos libros. Tengo que hacer un trabajo escrito para la clase de ciencias políticas.

NOTE: There are production activities for this concept in *Exploraciones*.
SUGGESTION: Have students find examples of the past subjunctive in the preceding dialogues of this chapter.

A propósito

When Jorge says, **"prefería que los alumnos decidieran... "** and Joaquín responds, **"era mejor que tomáramos las decisiones,"** they are using a verb form known as **el imperfecto del subjuntivo.** This past subjunctive form is used in the same situations that call for the present subjunctive, but to refer to past events. It is formed by taking the **ellos** form of the preterite, removing the **-on** ending, and adding the following endings: **-a, -as, -a, -´(r)amos, -ais, -an.** (Note that the **nosotros** forms take an accent on the vowel that immediately precedes the final **-r-: dediciéramos, esperáramos, nos graduáramos.**) Although you will not be expected to produce the past subjunctive, you need to be able to recognize the forms. Study these contrasts of the present and past subjunctive.

Me alegro de que **hagamos** los ejercicios en clase hoy.	*I'm happy that we're doing the exercises in class today.*
Ayer también me alegré de que los **hiciéramos** en clase.	*Yesterday I was also happy that we did them in class.*
Ahora la profesora insiste en que los estudiantes **vengan** a clase.	*Now the instructor insists that the students come to class.*
Pero en el pasado no insistía en que **vinieran** a clase.	*But in the past she did not insist that they come to class.*
Es necesario que los estudiantes **lean** el artículo con atención.	*It's necessary that the students read the article carefully.*
La última vez, fue necesario que **leyeran** el artículo de nuevo.	*Last time, it was necessary for them to read the article again.*

Costumbres funerarias

In the most traditional areas of the Hispanic world, full mourning is observed for as long as five years following the death of a spouse. Other Hispanics observe two years of mourning for a parent or a spouse, and one year for a sibling. Full mourning includes the wearing of only black clothing and a restriction on certain activities, including entertaining and amusement. In many areas, however, traditional customs such as **el luto** (*mourning*) and **el velorio** (*the wake*) are observed less rigorously than in the past. For example, some Hispanics observe **medio luto,** wearing only black and white or very dark colors, and others reduce the time of mourning to less than a year. Another custom associated with mourning and remembering loved ones who have died is **la novena,** in which acts of devotion, including prayers and masses, are observed over a nine-day period.

En México

The custom of wearing mourning clothes to show sorrow over the death of a friend or relative is only one way of remembering the dead. In Mexico, one of the customs of **el Día de los Muertos** is that of placing **ofrendas** on the graves. These offerings may include food, drink, incense, candles, and/or flowers. This custom may also be followed in the home with a family altar on which each departed family member is represented by a candle. Do you remember the date on which **el Día de los Muertos** is celebrated?

Faceta cultural

FOLLOW-UP: 1. What other restrictions are often associated with full mourning, traditionally? 2. What is a **novena**? 3. How are these customs changing in modern times? 4. What are **ofrendas** and with which celebration do we associate them?

El subjuntivo con expresiones causales o de influencia

PREPARATION: Model Jorge's line for the students. Ask what the subject of **quiero** is. [Jorge] Ask who Jorge hopes will come with him. [Joaquín] Model Joaquín's lines. Ask who wants to do the watching. What is the subject of **prefiero**? [Joaquín] What is the subject of **juegues**? [Jorge] Point out the change in subject. Ask what the infinitives of the subjunctive forms are.

JORGE: Voy a jugar al básquetbol, y **quiero** que **vengas** conmigo. ¿Puedes?
JOAQUÍN: Lo siento, amigo, pero no puedo. Quiero ver un programa especial en la tele. **Prefiero** que **juegues** con otra persona.

Actividades

PREPARATION: Have students identify who the symbol ① represents.
PREPARATION: Make sure there are no questions about the pronunciation or meaning of the items.
SUGGESTION: This works well as a pair activity.

Ⓐ Yo no quiero hacerlo. Living on your own means that there are always chores to be done. Imagine that you live in a house, but you want someone else to do your chores. Say that you want ① to do these things.

¡OJO! Recall that this text uses symbols to represent persons whom you will choose to include in your responses. For example, in this and subsequent activities, the icon ① (**individuo**) represents someone in your personal life (roommate, spouse, sister, and so on). When you see this symbol, state the name of the person to whom you wish to refer.

EJEMPLO: lavar los platos →
No quiero lavar los platos. Quiero que ① lave los platos.

1. limpiar el baño
2. preparar la comida
3. poner la mesa para la cena
4. arreglar la sala
5. hacer las camas
6. ir al supermercado
7. ¿ ?

PREPARATION: Review the vocabulary for members of the family.

Ⓑ ¿Quién en tu familia? Which of your relatives do you want or prefer to do the following? Explain why.

282

EJEMPLO: tomar un examen de matemáticas para mí →
Prefiero que mi cuñada tome un examen de matemáticas para mí porque es ingeniera y sabe mucho de matemáticas.
o No quiero que nadie en mi familia tome un examen de matemáticas para mí. Nadie en mi familia es fuerte en matemáticas.

SUGGESTION: This works well as a pair activity. Encourage responses such as the following. **¿Verdad? Yo también. / Interesante. Yo no. / Comprendo. / Sí, es verdad. / Sí, tienes razón.**

1. pasar una semana conmigo
2. viajar a México conmigo
3. decidir cuál ropa debo llevar a una cita importante
4. compartir una habitación conmigo
5. bailar conmigo
6. salir con mi mejor amigo/a
7. practicar las artes marciales conmigo
8. hacer mi tarea de _____
9. estacionar mi carro
10. ir de compras conmigo
11. subir las pirámides de Teotihuacán conmigo
12. acampar conmigo
13. arreglar mi cuarto
14. ¿ ?

Las expresiones causales o de influencia y el modo del verbo

EXPRESSION OF INFLUENCE (MAIN CLAUSE)		SECOND VERB (DEPENDENT CLAUSE)
No change of subject	→	Infinitive
Change of subject	→	Subjunctive

EXPRESSION OF INFLUENCE (MAIN CLAUSE)	SECOND VERB (DEPENDENT CLAUSE)
	No change of subject → use the infinitive
Insisto en *I insist on*	**pedir** una entrevista ahora mismo. *asking for an interview right now.*
Quiero *I want*	**estudiar** en esta universidad. *to study at this university.*
	Change of subject → use the subjunctive
Insisto en *I insist*	que **pidas** una entrevista ahora mismo. *that you ask for an interview right now.*
Prefiero *I prefer*	que tú **estudies** en esta universidad también. *that you also study at this university.*

The subjunctive is required when one party tries to influence the behavior of another; that is, when the subject in the main clause wants (prefers that, requests that, etc.) the subject in the dependent clause do something.

Faceta cultural

La quinceañera

An important event in the lives of young Hispanic women is **la fiesta de los quince años,** or fifteenth birthday celebration which acknowledges that the **quinceañera** is no longer a girl but is now making the transition to womanhood. The celebration often signals that she can dress more maturely, use makeup, and entertain potential suitors.

For Roman Catholics, the celebration for the **quinceañera** usually begins with a special mass in her honor attended by family and close friends. The party follows, also attended by family and friends, and features dancing, food, drink, and conversation. The traditional start of the celebration is the first dance, in which the **quinceañera** dances with her father or another significant man in her family. After this dance, the other guests may join in the dancing.

The party might consist of anything from a modest gathering in the family home to a gala social event in a rented banquet hall. At the upper levels of society, the celebrations can become extravagant, luxurious affairs in which the family presents the **quinceañera** to society. Not unlike high-society weddings in the United States, the young woman wears a special gown bought for the occasion and may be accompanied by several of her closest female friends, all of whom wear a gown of the same style. She may invite an equal number of young men (her **chambelanes,** or *attendants*) to participate in the ceremony. In many circles it is customary for the father to present a diamond ring to his daughter to mark the occasion. The **quinceañera**'s family hires a D.J. or a musical group to provide the music, and the decorations, food, beverages, and other arrangements are the finest available. The family may even rent limousines or horse-drawn carriages to transport the **quinceañera** and her entourage from the church to the banquet hall. The event is detailed in the society pages of the local newspaper as well.

FOLLOW-UP: Have students interview someone who has lived in a Hispanic country, and ask about the **fiesta de quince años** celebration in that country.

DIÁLOGO

PREPARATION: Ask students to describe the drawing. Ask them to focus on the title of the dialogue and on the dialogue introduction. **¿Dónde están David y Elena? ¿Qué hacen?** Have them skim the dialogue. **¿De qué hablan los jóvenes?**

¿Más película?

NEW VOCABULARY: el barco

David y Elena hacen el breve viaje por barco de Veracruz a la isla de los Sacrificios. Allí visitan el centro arqueológico de la isla.

ELENA: David, por favor. No quiero que saques más fotos aquí.
DAVID: ¿Por qué? Es uno de los sitios históricos más famosos de esta parte de México. Fue en esta isla donde Hernán Cortés vio que los aztecas hacían sacrificios humanos.
ELENA: Sí, es un lugar bastante interesante, pero pasado mañana vamos a Mérida, y después a Chichén Itzá. Vas a necesitar esos rollos de película. Sólo trajiste diez y en Chichén Itzá la película cuesta mucho.

284

DAVID: Ya lo sé. Pero he visto[1] tantas cosas que mis padres no han tenido la oportunidad de ver todavía. Quiero que vean las fotos del viaje para que ellos mismos decidan hacer el viaje.

ELENA: Comprendo. Pues, recomiendo que compres más película antes de salir para Chichén Itzá.

[1]he... *I have seen*

De inmediato

Complete the sentences using the phrases on the right to form correct statements based on the dialogue.

1. Elena no quiere que David saque...
2. La Isla de los Sacrificios es...
3. Pasado mañana, Elena y David van a...
4. En Chichén Itzá David va a necesitar...
5. David ha tenido la oportunidad de ver...
6. David quiere que...
7. Elena recomienda que...

a. cosas que sus padres nunca han visto.
b. David compre más película.
c. más fotos.
d. sus rollos de película.
e. sus padres decidan hacer un viaje a México.
f. un sitio turístico muy famoso.
g. Mérida.

EXPANSION: 1. ¿Qué es la Isla de los Sacrificios? ¿De dónde viene su nombre? 2. ¿Qué no quiere Elena que haga David? ¿Por qué? 3. ¿Adónde van pasado mañana? ¿Y después de eso? 4. ¿Por qué desea David sacar tantas fotos? 5. ¿Qué recomienda Elena que haga David antes de salir para Chichén Itzá?

A ti te toca

Practice the preceding dialogue with a classmate. Then tell your partner what you recommend buying before doing something else.

EJEMPLOS: Recomiendo que compres unas gafas de sol (un traje de baño) antes de ir a la playa (a la piscina).

Recomiendo que compres más ajos (cebollas) antes de preparar la sopa (la cena).

EN ACCIÓN

Antes de ver

In this chapter you will watch and listen as a series of people discuss important events that have happened in their lives. Listen carefully for details. After viewing, share information with a classmate to create as detailed a description as possible of those events.

La fiesta de los quince años

Elena reads the following article about a young girl's fifteenth birthday while she and David ride the bus to Chichén Itzá.

Antes de leer

Before you read the article, re-read the **Faceta cultural** about **La quinceañera**. Which of the following words or phrases do you expect to find in this reading?: **bailar, bautizo, boda, chambelanes, familia, felicitaciones, fiesta, flores, luna de miel, luto, música, noviazgo, padrinos, quince, sociedad, velorio**.

Look at the photo that accompanies the article (page 287). What role do the young men with Erika play in this celebration? Study the photo caption. Which young man might be Erika's cousin? Is he more likely to be related to Erika's father or to her mother? Next, skim the exercises that follow the article to prepare yourself for the content of the reading.

Now scan the article about Erika's **fiesta de los quince años** in order to complete the exercises that follow.

Festejaron[a] los 15 Años de Erika

1   **D**E un conjunto de cuerdas[b] fueron interpretadas las notas de la Marcha de Delgado, mismas que anunciaron la entrada al Sagrario Metropolitano de Erika Guerrero Martínez, quien enseguida participó de solemne ceremonia de acción de gracias.

2   El motivo, el haber llegado con toda dicha a su decimoquinto aniversario de existencia, por lo que por medio de la oración[c] agradeció al Todopoderoso los beneficios recibidos durante esos primeros quince años de su existencia.

3   El acto que se inició a las 19 horas se dignó oficiarlo el señor cura[d] de ese antiguo recinto, que para dicha celebración religiosa se vio sumamente concurrido por estimables familias de nuestra sociedad.

4   A ellas, previamente se les invitó por medio de lujosas cartulinas que suscribieron los esposos Vidal Guerrero Hernández y Rebeca Martínez de Guerrero.

5   Todo un ornato a base de gigantescos arreglos de albas[e] flores entrelazadas a verde follaje[f] e iluminación profusa, fue como se engalanó en tan especial ocasión la casa de Dios que sin duda conformó un marco de sin igual belleza.

6   Para ese día inolvidable, Erika lució un traje confeccionado en raso en seda en color durazno, con detalles delicados en rebordados en pedrería, encaje en la parte del talle y en las mangas[g] cortas, de escote amplio y de falda amplia. Tocado de flores en rosas al igual que su ramo[h] que llevó en sus manos, complementó su atavío.

7   A lo largo de la celebración litúrgica se escucharon obras de música sacra de un conjunto de violines.

8   Fueron padrinos de la homenajeada, Juan Ramón Guerrero Franco y María del Socorro Rivera de Guerrero.

9   Como chambelanes le acompañaron Ricardo Martínez Bárcenas, Gabriel Mariano Ortiz Malta, Oscar Valdivia Aguirre, Francisco Javier Melendias Amézquita y Juan Carlos González Hernández. Ellos con elegantes trajes de smokins en color blanco.

10   Bello fervorín dirigió en su momento el sacerdote[i] celebrante a la festejada durante el singular acto religioso.

11   Una vez finalizado el mismo, plena de dicha Erika en unión de su comitiva, abandonó el sacro recinto. Ya en el pórtico recibió parabienes y felicitaciones de sus invitados.

12   La fiesta que en su honor le ofrecieron luego sus padres, tuvo lugar[j] en un centro social, en donde al filo de la medianoche, la chica homenajeada[k] fue presentada en sociedad, luego de haber bailado con sus chambelanes su primer vals,[l] Cuento de los Bosques de Viena.

[a] *They celebrated with a party*
[b] conjunto... *string orchestra*
[c] *prayer*
[d] *priest*
[e] *white*
[f] *foliage*
[g] *sleeves*
[h] *bouquet*
[i] *priest*
[j] tuvo... *took place*
[k] *honored*
[l] *waltz*

Después de leer

Paso 1. Following are brief statements summarizing the general content of each paragraph in the article. Match each statement to the numbered paragraph to which it corresponds.

SUGGESTION: Ask for volunteers to give the number of the paragraph and the evidence in that paragraph that suggests what is being asked.

EJEMPLO: description of the church with the flowers → 5

_____ description of Erika's dress and flowers

_____ description of the music throughout the ceremony

_____ description of the reception

_____ Erika's guests congratulating her after Mass

_____ Erika's parents sending out the elegant invitations

_____ Erika's reason for a thanksgiving Mass: fifteen years of life

_____ list of escorts

_____ list of godparents

_____ music announcing the beginning of the thanksgiving Mass

_____ praise for the priest's role in the ceremony

_____ time of the Mass

Paso 2. Complete the following sentences based on information from the reading.

1. La ceremonia empezó a las...
   a. siete
   b. nueve
   c. cinco

2. La iglesia fue decorada con...
   a. cartulinas
   b. duraznos
   c. flores

3. Erika llevó un vestido de color...
   a. blanco
   b. durazno
   c. rosado

4. Sus padrinos fueron...
   a. Juan y María Guerrero
   b. Vidal y Rebeca Guerrero
   c. Juan y Rebeca Guerrero

5. Había _____ chambelanes que acompañaron a Erika.
   a. siete
   b. seis
   c. cinco

6. La fiesta en su honor tuvo lugar en...
   a. el Sagrario Metropolitano
   b. un centro social
   c. la casa de sus padres

ANSWERS: 1. a, 2. c, 3. b, 4. a, 5. c, 6. b

PREPARATION: Make sure there are no questions about the pronunciation or meaning of the items.

Erika Guerrero Martínez durante la misa de sus 15 años y con sus chambelanes Ricardo Martínez Bárcenas, Gabriel Mariano Ortiz Malta, Oscar Valdivia Aguirre, Francisco Javier Melendías Amézquita y Juan Carlos González Hernández.

La muerte de un señor distinguido

Imagine that you are in Mexico listening to the radio when the speaker announces the death of a prominent local citizen.

PARA ESCUCHAR

Antes de escuchar

Have you ever listened to an announcement of the death of a prominent person? What details are usually communicated by such an announcement? With a classmate, list in Spanish five pieces of information that are frequently given in a death announcement. What differences, if any, would you expect to find in an announcement in the Hispanic world?

Now listen carefully to the report. After listening, decide if the statements are true or false.

Después de escuchar

¿Es cierto o no es cierto?

1. El hombre que se murió se llamaba Alfredo Clemente Cepeda.
2. Murió ayer por la mañana.
3. El señor que se murió era periodista e intelectual.
4. Trabajó muchos años en un banco.
5. Ganó un premio de ciencias y artes.
6. El señor que se murió era soltero.

HANAYA
Floristería
y Jardinera, S.A. de C.V.
DISEÑOS ORIGINALES EN ARREGLOS FLORALES
AFILIADO A MEXIFLORA INTERNACIONAL
DISTRIBUIDOR AUTORIZADO **FLOR CALLI ARIC**
NUMERO UNO EN FLORES DE INVERNADERO
SERVICIO A DOMICILIO
ACEPTAMOS TARJETAS DE CREDITO
TELS.: **6-32-12 y 4-59-39**
(91-951)
ABASOLO 103 C.P. 68000 OAXACA, OAXACA.

PARA ESCRIBIR

Falleció el Sr. Clemente

Now imagine that someone comes into the room just after the announcement of Mr. Clemente's passing. Write a conversation in which you inform the other person of what has happened, including at least three details about Mr. Clemente's life. Each person should have at least four lines of dialogue. Then practice your dialogue with a classmate.

PARA HABLAR

Es evidente que puedes ver el futuro

Imagine that you are at a party pretending to be a palm reader. Tell several of your classmates what is in store for them in the future in terms of graduation, marriage, children, travel, employment, and so forth. Begin each of your statements with a form of **querer que... , es importante (probable, posible, triste, etc.) que... , alegrarse de que... , vas a casarte cuando... ,** and so on.

EJEMPLO: Es evidente que eres un(a) estudiante excelente. Es bueno que vayas a casarte pronto. Es importante que consigas una posición responsable en una empresa grande. Me alegro de que sepas qué quieres hacer con tu vida.

Los verbos / *Verbs*

ahorrar	to save
alegrarse de	to be glad
alquilar	to rent
casarse (con)	to be married (to)
divorciarse	to get a divorce
esperar (R)	to hope, expect; to wait (for)
felicitar	to congratulate
graduarse (en) (me gradúo)	to graduate (from)
morir (ue)	to die
nacer (nazco)	to be born
recomendar (ie)	to recommend
sentir (ie)	to regret; to feel
sorprender	to surprise
temer	to fear, be afraid of
vivir (R)	to live

Los eventos importantes de la vida / *Important steps/events in life*

el aniversario (de bodas)	(wedding) anniversary
el bautizo	baptism
la boda	wedding
el entierro	burial, funeral
la luna de miel	honeymoon
la muerte	death
el nacimiento	birth
el noviazgo	engagement; courtship
la primera comunión	first communion
el velorio	wake, vigil

Palabras semejantes: el aniversario, el divorcio, la graduación.

Otros sustantivos / *Other nouns*

el barco	boat, ship
la edad	age
la esquela de defunción	*newspaper ad to pay tribute to a dead person*
la madrina	godmother
el matrimonio	married couple; matrimony
el mensaje	message
el padrino	godfather
el nombre (de pila)	(first) name
la nota necrológica	obituary
el recién casado / la recién casada	newlywed
el sueldo	salary

Las expresiones impersonales / *Impersonal expressions*

Es... que (+ *indicative*)	It's . . . that
No es... que (+ *subjunctive*)	It's not . . . that
cierto (R)	(for) certain
claro	clear
evidente (R)	evident
seguro (R)	(for) certain
verdad	true
(No) Es... que (+ *subjunctive*)	It's (not) . . . that
bueno (R)	good
importante (R)	important
(im)posible	(im)possible
(im)probable	(im)probable
increíble	incredible
lástima	a shame, too bad
malo	bad, unfortunate
necesario	necessary
triste	sad

Palabras y expresiones útiles / *Useful words and expressions*

alguien	someone, somebody
aunque	although
casado/a	married
¡Claro que sí!	Of course!
dar a luz	to give birth
en cuanto a	regarding, with regard to
en serio	seriously
en vez de	instead of
hasta que	until
tan pronto como	as soon as
tener buena/mala suerte	to be lucky/unlucky
vestirse (i) de luto	to wear mourning clothes

NOTE: See the *Instructor's Manual* for suggestions on teaching **Otros mundos**.

Bolivia y el Paraguay

¡Saludos, amigos! Soy Joaquín Flores, de Bolivia. Vivo en una de las capitales del país, La Paz. Sí, es verdad. Mi país tiene dos capitales. La otra, que se llama Sucre, tiene menos de 100.000 habitantes y es constitucionalmente la capital de Bolivia. En ella reside la Corte Suprema de Justicia. Pero La Paz es la sede[1] del gobierno. También es la ciudad más grande e importante de mi país, con una población de más de un millón de habitantes. La Paz se encuentra en las altas montañas de los Andes.

Soy puro indio, como más del cincuenta por ciento de los habitantes de Bolivia. Mis abuelos maternos eran indios quechuas y mis abuelos paternos eran indios aymaraes. Estos pueblos indios son muy importantes en la historia precolombina de Bolivia y también durante la conquista. Los quechuas son los fundadores del imperio de los incas. Su idioma, el quechua, todavía se habla en muchas partes de la región andina. Los aymaraes eran otra tribu grande e importante que fue conquistada por los incas en el siglo XV. Su lengua se habla todavía en la región andina.

A veces, mi familia y yo vamos al pueblo peruano de Puno, a orillas[2] del lago Titicaca. El lago Titicaca es famoso por ser el lago navegable más elevado del mundo (a 12.506 pies de elevación). Se encuentran en el lago varias islas, unas de las cuales son célebres por sus tesoros arqueológicos.

Mis padres no son ricos, pero no somos pobres. Los dos trabajan bien duro para mantener a la familia, mi papá como minero en una mina de estaño[3] y mi madre como profesora de inglés y quechua en un colegio privado. Yo soy muy afortunado. Recibí una beca[4] de intercambio de un club cívico en La Paz, y sólo eso permite que yo esté aquí en los EE. UU.

[1] seat   [2] a... on the shores   [3] tin   [4] scholarship

¿Sabías que... ?

BOLIVIA

- El nombre oficial del país, la República de Bolivia, da homenaje a Simón Bolívar, el Libertador de Sudamérica.
- Bolivia es uno de los dos países del continente americano que no tiene costas marinas. ¿Sabes el nombre del otro?
- La Paz es la ciudad capital más alta del mundo.
- Bolivia tiene tres idiomas oficiales: el español, el quechua y el aymará.
- En 1660, Potosí era la ciudad más grande e importante del Nuevo Mundo por su riqueza mineral (plata, estaño, oro, plomo[1]).
- La llama, la vicuña y la alpaca abundan en Bolivia.

MAR CARIBE

VENEZUELA   GUYANA
COLOMBIA   SURINAM
   GUAYANA FRANCESA

ECUADOR

BRASIL

PERÚ   BOLIVIA
Puno   Lago Titicaca
   ★ La Paz
   ★ Sucre   PARAGUAY
      ★ Asunción
OCÉANO PACÍFICO   El Chaco

CHILE
   ARGENTINA   URUGUAY

OCÉANO ATLÁNTICO

AMÉRICA DEL SUR

[1] lead

EL PARAGUAY

- El Paraguay es el otro país del continente americano que no tiene costas marinas.
- Gran parte de los habitantes del Paraguay son bilingües: hablan español y guaraní.
- Casi el 95% de la población paraguaya es mestiza.
- El Gran Chaco es una llanura tropical dominada por la sequía[1] y las inundaciones. Fue objeto de una guerra entre el Paraguay y Bolivia durante los años 1932–1935, en parte por los depósitos de petróleo que se encuentran allí.
- El mate, un té amargo hecho de la planta yerba mate, es el té del Paraguay. Se toma por medio de una «bombilla».

[1] drought

(arriba) La lana de la alpaca, animal parecido a la llama y la vicuña, se usa para los suéteres tan deseados en los EE.UU. (a la izquierda) El Chaco, una inhospitaliaria región selvática, casi inexplorada, contiene grandes reservas de petróleo y ha sido motivo de conflictos entre Bolivia y el Paraguay.

Este estudiante argentino se refresca con un té de yerba mate.

Bolivia y el Paraguay en breve

	BOLIVIA	EL PARAGUAY
Capitales:	La Paz y Sucre	Asunción
Lenguas:	español, quechua y aymará	español y guaraní
Gobierno:	república	república
Moneda:	el peso boliviano	el guaraní
Población:	7.516.000 habitantes	4.798.000 habitantes
Superficie:	424.165 millas cuadradas (del tamaño de Texas y California juntos)	157.047 millas cuadradas (del tamaño de California)

NOTE: See the *Instructor's Manual* for suggestions on teaching **México y los mexicanos**.

México y los mexicanos

NEW VOCABULARY: el dios; sin embargo

De viaje: Mérida y Chichén Itzá

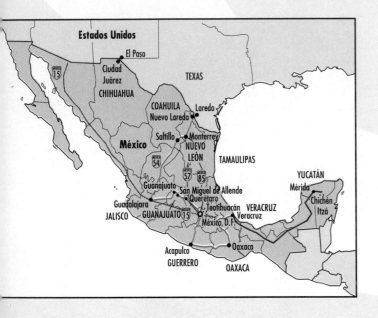

Existe una anécdota graciosa[1] sobre el origen del nombre de la península de Yucatán. En 1517, Francisco Hernández de Córdoba, explorador español, andaba a la caza de esclavos.[2] Equivocadamente[3] descubrió esta punta[4] de México. Al preguntarles a los indígenas el nombre de su tierra, respondieron: «tectetán», que quiere decir «no entendemos». Hernández de Córdoba malinterpretó la respuesta de los mayas y le dio a la tierra el nombre de Yucatán.

Mérida, la capital del estado de Yucatán, está construida sobre las ruinas de la antigua ciudad maya de T-hó (que se pronuncia «Te-O»). Los conquistadores, al ver las casas de la ciudad maya tan limpias y encaladas,[5] con sus molduras[6] de madera y sus adornos, la compararon inmediatamente con Mérida, la ciudad española. Por eso le pusieron ese nombre.

Pocos de los turistas que vienen a Mérida dejan el estado de Yucatán sin ver otras atracciones de la región. Cancún, con sus increíbles playas de arena fina, y la isla de Cozumel son dos atracciones turísticas que han gozado de[7] mucha popularidad recientemente. Sin embargo, estos centros turísticos del siglo XX no pueden competir con las verdaderas atracciones de la península de Yucatán: las ruinas de las civilizaciones precolombinas. Una de las más famosas es Chichén Itzá, a 120 kilómetros de Mérida. Chichén Itzá es el sitio de las ruinas más extensas y mejor conservadas de la cultura indígena mexicana.

En Chichén Itzá se encuentran el Castillo[8] (una impresionante pirámide que domina la zona), el templo de los Guerreros[9] y el patio de rituales toltecas con sus bajorrelieves[10] que muestran cómo eran decapitados los perdedores[11] de las competiciones. En Chichén Itzá está también el **chac-mool,** el dios de la lluvia en forma de un recipiente para los corazones de las víctimas de los sacrificios.

[1] *amusing*   [2] *andaba... was looking for slaves*   [3] *Mistakenly*   [4] *point*   [5] *whitewashed*   [6] *moldings*   [7] *han... have enjoyed*   [8] *Castle*   [9] *Warriors*   [10] *bas-reliefs*   [11] *losers*   **NEW VOCABULARY:** contaminen, luchar, proteger, reforestamos; la contaminación, la razón, el medio ambiente, la naturaleza, el plomo; en contra de, no sólo... sino (que)

Perspectivas de México: El medio ambiente

La preocupación[1] por el medio ambiente es un fenómeno reciente. En épocas anteriores había poca preocupación por los efectos que la industrialización y el desarrollo[2] económico tenían en la naturaleza. Ahora, México y otros países hispanos están tomando medidas[3] para luchar en contra de la contaminación y para proteger el medio ambiente.

En su tercer informe de gobierno en 1991, el presidente de México en esa época, Carlos Salinas de

[1] *concern*   [2] *development*   [3] *measures*

Gortari, habló de las medidas que México había tomado para combatir los problemas del medio ambiente. «Desde hace poco más de una década[4] iniciamos en México un proceso institucional, serio y consistente, para atacar los problemas del entorno...[5] particularmente en la zona metropolitana de la Ciudad de México...

«Gracias a un gran esfuerzo[6] tecnológico y de producción, el contenido[7] de plomo de las gasolinas se ha reducido en un 85%... Este año reforestamos 93 mil hectáreas,[8] cifra[9] que representa más del doble del promedio[10] anual de los últimos ocho años...

«México no sólo defiende recursos que pertenecen[11] a los mexicanos sino que contribuye a asegurar[12] la permanencia de cadenas[13] biológicas esenciales para la vida en el planeta. México no será receptor[14] de nuevas industrias que contaminen y que, por esta razón, no se aceptan en otros países.»

[4]desde... *a little more than a decade ago*   [5]*ambiente*   [6]*effort*
[7]*content*   [8]*hectares (1 hectare = 10,000 sq. meters)*   [9]*figure*
[10]*average*   [11]*belong*   [12]*sino... but also helps to ensure*
[13]*chains*   [14]*no... will not receive, accept*

En Quintana Roo, al sur de Cancún, el gobierno trata de recuperar los bosques.

10

El medio ambiente

NOTE: See the *Instructor's Manual* for suggestions on using the chapter-opening pages.

En un día claro el volcán Popocatépetl ofrece una vista magnífica.

Esta compañía que funde cobre fue construida en 1904 sin control de emisiones tóxicas.

En Chiapas, se puede ver la destrucción causada por la tala y quemadura de los bosques.

Estos científicos hacen sus investigaciones entre una colonia de pingüinos en la argentinos.

M E T A S

FUNCIONES

- to discuss nature and environmental issues
- to name common animals
- to order things from first to twelfth
- to discuss in greater detail topics from previous chapters

GRAMÁTICA

- review and expansion of grammar learned in previous chapters

APPROPRIATE TESTING POINTS:
Diálogo (2), El medio ambiente, En acción, **Quiz 1**
  Diálogo (2), Los animales, En acción, **Quiz 2**
  Los números ordinales, En acción, **Quiz 3**
  Episodios, Actividad comprensiva
  Chapter test

¿Y en tu país?

NEW VOCABULARY: tratamos de; las especies, la selva tropical; protegidos
PREPARATION: Ask students to describe the photo. Ask them to focus on the title of the dialogue and on the dialogue introduction. **¿Dónde están David y Elena?** Introduce/review terms related to archeology (**arqueología, civilización, indígenas, pirámide, templo**). Have students skim the dialogue. **¿De qué hablan los jóvenes?**

David y Elena llegan a su hotel en Mérida muy tarde. Allí pasan la noche, y el próximo día salen temprano para visitar las ruinas de Chichén Itzá. Ya en la zona arqueológica, ven la selva tropical, que cubre[1] la zona.

ELENA: ¿Hay muchos árboles en el estado donde tú vives?

DAVID: Sí, y hay bosques también, pero no son como las selvas mexicanas.

ELENA: ¿No? ¿Cuál es la diferencia? Me imagino que las especies de árboles son diferentes.

DAVID: Tienes razón. Otra diferencia es que los bosques de donde yo vivo no son tan grandes como las selvas de aquí. Pero los bosques más grandes están protegidos por el gobierno.

ELENA: En México también tratamos de proteger los bosques y las selvas.

[1] *covers*

En la sagrada ciudad maya de Chichén Itzá, en Yucatán, existen unos de los edificios precolombinos más elegantes del mundo.

De inmediato

EXTENSION: 4. ¿Hay muchos árboles en este estado? 5. ¿Hay bosques protegidos cerca de aquí? 6. ¿Quiénes de Uds. estuvieron alguna vez en una selva? ¿En dónde? 7. ¿Quiénes de Uds. visitaron alguna vez una zona arqueológica? ¿Cuál?

1. ¿Hay bosques en el estado donde vive David?
2. ¿Cuáles son dos diferencias entre los bosques de los EE. UU. y las selvas mexicanas?
3. En los EE. UU., ¿qué protección tienen los bosques más grandes?

A ti te toca

OPTIONAL: Have students use Elena's first line to ask a classmate about other geographical features: **¿Hay muchas montañas en el estado donde tu vives?**

Ask a classmate the difference between two things, two people, or two places.

EJEMPLO: —¿Cuál es la diferencia entre un bosque y una selva?
             —Un bosque es más pequeño que una selva.
          o —Un bosque tiene más pinos que una selva.

En la universidad

NEW VOCABULARY: causan; el aire, la destrucción, las inundaciones, los temblores, los terremotos; grave, puro

Unos estudiantes están visitando una exhibición sobre el medio ambiente.

JORGE: El problema de la destrucción de las selvas tropicales es muy grave. Vamos a perder miles de especies de plantas y animales.

JOAQUÍN: Es que no pensamos en el futuro. Sólo pensamos en tener hoy lo que queremos.

MARÍA: Los colombianos siempre decimos que el aire del campo de nuestro país es muy puro.

TOMÁS: En las pampas de la Argentina el aire es puro también. Por eso mucha gente que vive en las ciudades pasa allí los fines de semana.

CELIA: Me dicen que en México hay temblores con mucha frecuencia. ¿Es cierto?

MARISOL: Sí. En México y por toda la América Central son frecuentes los temblores. Y a veces hay terremotos que causan mucha destrucción. ¿No es así en España?

CELIA: No tenemos ni temblores ni terremotos pero tenemos muchas inundaciones.

PREPARATION: Ask students to describe the drawing. Ask them to focus on the dialogue introduction. **¿Dónde están los estudiantes?** Have students skim the dialogue. **¿De qué hablan los jóvenes?** Have students scan for words related to ecology and the environment.

De inmediato

Change the sentences so they agree with the content of the dialogues.

1. Jorge cree que el problema de la destrucción de las selvas tropicales no es grave.
2. Vamos a perder diez especies de plantas y animales.
3. En Colombia el aire del campo está completamente contaminado.
4. Muchos argentinos que viven en el campo pasan los fines de semana en la ciudad.
5. Hay temblores solamente en México.
6. En España hay temblores.

NEW VOCABULARY: contaminado
OPTIONAL: 1. ¿Hay temblores en esta región? ¿Hay inundaciones? 2. ¿Cuál es la probabilidad de que ocurra un temblor grande en esta región? ¿y una inundación?

A ti te toca

Tell a classmate in what countries the following conditions also occur.

EJEMPLO: En Colombia el aire del campo es muy puro. →
           En las pampas de la Argentina el aire es puro también.

1. En Brasil hay mucha destrucción de las selvas tropicales.
2. En los EE. UU. mucha gente que vive en las ciudades va al campo para escaparse del aire contaminado.
3. En México hay temblores con mucha frecuencia.
4. En el centro de los EE. UU. hay inundaciones con mucha frecuencia.

OPTIONAL: Ask students to use Celia's last line to tell what natural disasters tend to (or do not tend to) occur where they live: **No tenemos muchas inundaciones pero tenemos tornados.**

Las selvas tropicales

The destruction of one nation's rain forest can have an international impact. The global interdependence that makes people learn other languages must also make them learn to save their environment. As we learn more about the ecosystem of the rain forest, its richness and fragility amaze us. Within one forest there may exist plants and animals found nowhere else on earth. We cannot begin to imagine the present or future benefits these species may represent. Nor can we know what role a species plays within its own ecosystem . . . until it is gone and the entire ecosystem is thrown into chaos.

En México

The tropical rain forests of Mexico are found along its borders with Guatemala and Belize. In the Yucatan Peninsula, they are dotted with archaeological sites from the Mayans and other pre-Columbian indigenous cultures. Mexican authorities face a difficult situation: improving tourists' access to the sites—essential for the region's economic growth—while maintaining the fragile ecological balance and harmony necessary to preserve the environment. Improved roads invite visitors; care must be taken that the visitors and their vehicles do not damage the ruins or the rain forests.

FOLLOW-UP: Have students research the location and situation of one or two rainforests in North or South America.

PREPARATION: Ask students to think about the topics related to the environment they hear and read about. Have them scan the new vocabulary—with the translations covered—to find cognates and guessable words.

El medio ambiente

SUGGESTION: Ask students to describe each of the drawings.

la contaminación

la lluvia ácida

el agua subterránea

una inundación

un incendio

un tornado

Otro vocabulario

el arbusto	*bush*
la calidad (del agua/aire / de la tierra)	*quality (of the water/air/earth [soil])*
la capa de ozono	*ozone layer*
la ecología	*ecology*
la especie (en peligro)	*(endangered) species*
el huracán	*hurricane*
el planeta	*planet*
la planta	*plant*
la selva tropical	*(tropical) rain forest*
el temblor	*tremor, small earthquake*
el terremoto	*earthquake*
la tierra	*land; earth*
la tormenta	*storm*

COMPREHENSION: Read the new vocabulary in a random order. Ask whether students associate the words with earth (**la tierra**), wind (**el viento**), or fire (**el fuego**).

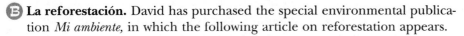

Actividades

A **Nuestro medio ambiente.** Match each word with its definition.

1. el aire
2. la contaminación del aire
3. un temblor
4. la inundación
5. un tornado
6. un incendio
7. la lluvia ácida
8. la ecología
9. una especie en peligro

a. lo que quema[1] el bosque
b. animal o planta al borde[2] de extinción
c. movimientos de la tierra
d. estudio de la interacción de plantas, animales y el medio ambiente
e. líquido peligroso[3] que cae de la atmósfera
f. lo que respiramos
g. revoluciones rápidas del aire
h. algo sucio y gris que cubre[4] una ciudad como una nube
i. lo que cubre un lugar con agua

[1] *burns* [2] *al... on the verge* [3] *dangerous* [4] *covers*

NEW VOCABULARY: respiramos; sucio
VARIATION: Reverse the activity. Give students the definition orally and have them give the vocabulary word.
EXPANSION: Give students two minutes to write one or two additional definitions, which they then share with a partner, a small group, or the entire class.

B **La reforestación.** David has purchased the special environmental publication *Mi ambiente,* in which the following article on reforestation appears.

Paso 1. What do you know about reforestation projects in your country or in others? Who typically initiates them: the government, private enterprise, non-profit groups, or groups of citizens? What is involved in a reforestation project? To get an idea of the task involved in reforesting, how many trees do you think could be planted on a hectare*? About how many trees would it take to replant 100,000 hectares?

Because of the topic and source, this article uses somewhat more difficult language than most of the articles you have read. However, reading the article is not an impossible task due to the many cognates, the meanings of which should be fairly easy for you to guess. Scan the article looking for cognates and look at the English glosses so you can get a feel for the general idea of the story. Now read the title of the article and skim the article

PREPARATION: Familiarize students with the glossed vocabulary by giving them the English equivalents and having them find the Spanish words and phrases in the text. Encourage students to read the text in Spanish rather than translating the text into English.

---

*A *hectare* is a metric measurement equal to 10,000 square meters, roughly equivalent to 2.5 acres.

quickly, without looking up any of the words. Which of the following sentences best summarizes the content?

a. The current annual level of reforestation in the Mexican state of Morelos is alarmingly low due to a lack of human and material resources.

b. The government of Mexico is making a concerted effort to save the forests by replanting the forests and educating the Mexican citizens.

c. 100,000 hectares of forest will be clear-cut in Mexico this year, up from 90,000 hectares last year—3 million trees were felled in the state of Morelos alone.

d. The North American Free Trade Agreement mandates the replanting of the Mexican forests, which will ultimately save them.

Now read the report and do the activity that follows.

Cien mil hectáreas se reforestan en este año

NEW VOCABULARY: sembrar; los recursos

A diferencia de[1] años anteriores en los que el nivel[2] de reforestación en el estado de Morelos fue muy bajo, en el presente se hará[3] la mayor reforestación que se ha visto[4] en muchos años, pues se cuenta con los recursos materiales y humanos para una óptima labor.

Durante 1990 se reforestaron un total de 90 mil hectáreas en todo el país, mientras que en este año, por medio de la Secretaría de Agricultura y Recursos Hidráulicos (S.A.R.H.), se superarán[5] las 100 mil. En el estado de Morelos se dio inicio al programa sembrando más de tres millones de árboles. Para poder llevar a cabo[6] una labor tan compleja, es necesaria la participación de diversos sectores, por lo que se estima que el diciembre próximo se formarán más de dos mil comités municipales forestales, el doble de los que existían hasta hace un año.[7]

Nuestros bosques, además de tener gran importancia para la vida misma, pueden constituir una gran fuerza para la economía de los países. En el caso de México, el bosque habrá de adquirir una importancia económica fundamental en el intercambio[8] que se iniciará por el Tratado de Libre Comercio de la América del Norte. Para prepararnos para este intercambio, debemos implementar programas que rescaten[9] las áreas que han sido taladas.[10] Sobre todo, necesitamos programas de educación forestal para salvar[11] nuestro entorno ambiental y aprovechar[12] el recurso.

[1]A... *In contrast with* [2]*level* [3]se... *will be carried out* [4]se... *has been seen* [5]se... *it will surpass* [6]llevar... *carry out* [7]hasta... *until one year ago* [8]*exchange* [9]*rescue* [10]*clear-cut* [11]*save* [12]*employ usefully*

Mi Ambiente — Al Servicio del Automovilista y la Ecología

México D.F. Junio de 1993   Año I   Tomo I   Número 10   Director General: Adolfo Montiel Talonia

Paso 2. Complete the statements in the first column with phrases from the second column.

OPTIONAL: 1. ¿Qué recursos tienen en Morelos en mayor cantidad este año que en años anteriores? 2. ¿Cuántas hectáreas se reforestaron en 1990? 3. ¿Qué significa S.A.R.H.? 4. ¿Cuántos árboles van a sembrar en el estado de Morelos este año? 5. ¿Qué se van a formar el diciembre próximo? 6. ¿Cómo son importantes para México los bosques?

1. _____ Además de ser importantes para la vida misma, los bosques pueden constituir...
2. _____ Para una labor tan compleja como lo es la reforestación, es necesaria...
3. _____ S.A.R.H. significa...
4. _____ En el intercambio que se iniciará por el Tratado de Libre Comercio de la América del Norte...
5. _____ Se estima que el diciembre próximo se formarán...
6. _____ En 1990 se reforestaron...
7. _____ Este año el número de hectáreas reforestadas va a superar
8. _____ Este año se hará la mayor reforestación que se ha visto en muchos años...

a. porque hay muchos recursos humanos y materiales.
b. el bosque va a adquirir una importancia económica fundamental.
c. la participación de diversos sectores.
d. Secretaría de Árboles y Ríos Hermosos.
e. más de dos mil comités municipales forestales.
f. una gran fuerza para la economía.
g. Secretaría de Agricultura y Recursos Hidráulicos.
h. un total de 90 mil hectáreas en todo México.
i. las 100 mil hectáreas.

Paso 3. Now place the sentences from the previous activity in logical order to form a synopsis of Mexican reforestation efforts.

EN ACCIÓN

Sanciones a industriales

While David and Elena are taking a break from seeing the ruins at Chichén Itzá, they hear on the radio a story about how the government of Mexico is levying fines on industries that fail to comply with environmental laws.

Antes de escuchar

Before you listen to the report, skim the incomplete transcript of the passage and look at the English glosses in order to have a better idea of the content of the report you will hear. What do you think an ecological audit (**una auditoría**

PREPARATION: Familiarize students with the glossed vocabulary by giving them the English equivalents and having them find the Spanish words and phrases in the text. Discuss any other unfamiliar vocabulary.

ecológica) is? Who do you think conducts them? Who do you think undergoes them? In the first paragraph, what is the subject of **han asumido**? In the second paragraph, where did the money come from? Why was a penalty imposed on some group? (What was not installed?) In the third paragraph, what area of research was most likely to undergo an environmental audit?

Next, look at the context of the words that are missing. What part of speech do you predict each one will be? Are the nouns masculine or feminine? On a separate sheet of paper, write the numbers 1–12, allowing yourself room to fill in the missing words.

Now listen to the passage as you read the transcript. As you listen, write the words that are missing from the transcript. Listen to the passage a second time to check your answers and fill in what you have missed. Then answer the questions that follow.

Los industriales, como sector de la sociedad que aporta[a] ____[1] a la ____[2] nacional, han asumido el papel[b] que les corresponde en la ____[3] de los recursos naturales de todo el ____.[4]

De esta ____[5] los datos[c] de la Procuraduría[d] Federal de Protección al ____[6] señalan[e] que desde ____[7] del año pasado a la fecha[f] se ha logrado recaudar[g] 3,5 ____[8] de dólares, producto de las «auditorías ecológicas»[h] practicadas mediante[i] once mil inspecciones. En ello los ____[9] han asumido las consecuencias por no haber instalado a ____[10] los equipos[j] reductores de sustancias contaminantes.

En el caso del ____[11] de México, ____[12] se realizaron siete de las once mil inspecciones efectuadas[k] en todo el país, la dependencia[l] citó en sus informaciones que el sector más visitado para la realización de[m] «auditorías ecológicas» fue el sector químico.

[a]*contributes* [b]*role* [c]*data* [d]*Office* [e]*point out* [f]*la... the present (day)* [g]*collect (especially taxes)* [h]auditorías... *ecological audits, investigations* [i]*by means of* [j]*equipment* [k]*conducted* [l]*branch office* [m]para... *to conduct*

Después de escuchar

EXPANSION: Ask questions regarding pollution control in this country. **¿Quién tiene la responsabilidad de controlar la contaminación en este país? ¿Quién tiene que asegurar que las leyes se cumplen?** etc.

1. ¿Quiénes han asumido un papel en la preservación de los recursos naturales?
2. ¿Cómo se llama la organización federal responsable de las «auditorías ecológicas»?
3. ¿Cuántos dólares se ha logrado recaudar?
4. ¿Qué no instalaron a tiempo los industriales?
5. En México, ¿cuál es el sector más visitado para la realización de «auditorías ecológicas»?

El ser humano y la naturaleza

Literature often reflects the prevailing philosophy of a particular historical period. However, the relationship between human beings and the world around them is a recurring theme in Hispanic literature.

Antes de leer

Think about the literature of your own country as well as that of other countries you have studied. Other than language, what are some differences between them? What themes do you recall? What differences might you expect to find between the literatures of specific groups within the international Hispanic community? What might influence one writer but not another? What might influence all of them but in different ways?

Now read the two poems that follow. Pay attention to the tone of each and the messages the poets attempt to convey.

Rima XVII

GUSTAVO ADOLFO BÉCQUER (ESPAÑA, 1836–1870)

Hoy la tierra y los cielos me sonríen;
hoy llega al fondo[1] de mi alma[2] el sol:
hoy la he visto[3]... la he visto y me ha mirado...
    ¡Hoy creo en Dios!

Obras completas (1870)

[1] *bottom, depths* [2] *soul* [3] la... *I have seen her*

NEW VOCABULARY: me sonríen; los cielos
SUGGESTION: Read the poems outloud, pantomiming and hamming shamelessly to help students understand both meaning and tone.

Lo fatal

RUBÉN DARÍO (NICARAGUA, 1867–1916)

Dichoso[1] el árbol, que es apenas[2] sensitivo,
y más la piedra dura, porque ésa ya no siente,
pues no hay dolor más grande que el dolor de ser vivo,
ni mayor pesadumbre[3] que la vida consciente.

  Ser, y no saber nada, y ser sin rumbo cierto,[4]
y el temor de haber sido,[5] y un futuro terror...
Y el espanto[6] seguro de estar mañana muerto,
y sufrir por la vida, y por la sombra,[7] y por
lo que no conocemos y apenas sospechamos.[8]
Y la carne que tienta[9] con sus frescos racimos,[10]
y la tumba[11] que aguarda[12] con sus fúnebres ramos,[13]
¡y no saber a dónde vamos,
ni de dónde venimos... !

Cantos de vida y esperanza (1905)

[1] *Lucky* [2] *scarcely* [3] *heaviness* [4] rumbo... *sure course* [5] temor... *fear of having been*
[6] *terror* [7] *darkness* [8] *we suspect* [9] *tempts* [10] *clusters* [11] *tomb* [12] *awaits* [13] fúnebres... *funeral wreaths*

NEW VOCABULARY: el dolor, la piedra; dura, vivo

Después de leer

1. ¿Cuál es el tono del poema de Bécquer? ¿y del poema de Darío?
   a. alegre **b.** triste **c.** enojado **d.** deprimido
2. ¿Qué palabras y expresiones en los poemas indican este tono?
3. ¿Cuál es la actitud de Bécquer a la naturaleza?
   a. La naturaleza es viva pero es indiferente al ser humano.
   b. La naturaleza es viva y se preocupa por el ser humano.
   c. La naturaleza no es viva.

SUGGESTION: Have students memorize one or both of the poems and recite or write them for extra credit.

4. ¿Cuál es la actitud de Darío a la naturaleza?
   a. La naturaleza es más dichosa que el ser humano porque no puede sentir.
   b. La naturaleza es menos dichosa que el ser humano porque no puede sentir.
   c. Ni la naturaleza ni el ser humano puede sentir.
5. ¿Según Darío, ¿de qué tiene miedo el ser humano?
6. Bécquer era español mientras Darío era nicaragüense. ¿Qué efectos puede tener esta diferencia?
7. ¿Qué poema te gusta más y por qué?

Mi parque favorito

Describe in detail your favorite state or national park. Include the following details.

1. dónde está
2. cómo es el paisaje[1]
3. qué actividades se puede hacer allí
4. por qué motivo el gobierno decidió conservar el lugar

Finally, state what you think of the park and make any recommendations or observations about the site for others who might consider going there.

[1]*landscape*

Animales mitológicos

NEW VOCABULARY: el buho, el jaguar, el mono, el murciélago, la serpiente

David y Elena admiran las ruinas de Chichén Itzá y hablan de los artefactos que ven allí.

DAVID: ¡Qué interesante! Hay figuras de animales en casi todas las ruinas que hemos visto.

ELENA: Es cierto. Hay muchas semejanzas[1] entre las culturas de los toltecas, los mayas y los aztecas. Por ejemplo, las divinidades de una cultura lo son también de otra. Uno de los dioses más importantes de los aztecas fue Quetzalcóatl. Pero, ¿Sabías que la imagen de Quetzalcóatl fue adorado primitivamente por los toltecas. Ah... y también por los mayas quienes lo llamaban[2] Kukulcán.

DAVID: **Quetzalcóatl** significa **serpiente emplumada**,[3] ¿verdad?

ELENA: Sí. Hay muchos animales en la mitología indígena, especialmente el jaguar, el mono, el buho y el murciélago. Todos representan algo importante.

[1]*similarities*   [2]lo... *called him*   [3]*plumed*

DAVID: También admiramos animales en nuestra cultura. A ver... el jaguar porque es fuerte y rápido y el buho porque es sabio.[4] Pero... ¿el murciélago?

ELENA: Para los zapotecas, el murciélago representa la oscuridad[5] y la muerte.

DAVID: Pues, cuando regresamos al D.F., me gustaría[6] ir de nuevo[7] al Museo Nacional de Antropología para aprender más de las culturas precolombinas de México.

[4]*wise*   [5]*darkness*   [6]*I would like*   [7]*de... again*

Complete the sentences in the left column with phrases from the right column.

1. _____ Algunos de los animales de la mitología indígena son...

2. _____ Quetzalcóatl fue también adorado por...

3. _____ En las ruinas de las grandes civilizaciones indígenas aparecen...

4. _____ Hay muchas semejanzas entre...

5. _____ Para los zapotecas el murciélago representa...

6. _____ **Quetzalcóatl** significa...

7. _____ Uno de los dioses más importantes de los aztecas fue...

a. figuras de animales.

b. el jaguar, el mono, el buho y el murciélago.

c. la oscuridad y la muerte.

d. Kukulcán.

e. las culturas de los toltecas, los mayas y los aztecas.

f. Quetzalcóatl.

g. los mayas, que lo llamaban Kukulcán.

h. serpiente emplumada.

i. Chichén Itzá.

OPTIONAL: Read the following list of words and ask students whether they refer to **un sitio arqueológico, un dios mitológico** or **un animal**. The list: **un jaguar, Quetzalcóatl, un murciélago, Chichén Itzá, una serpiente emplumada, Kukulcán, un mono, un buho.**

David and Elena tell why we admire certain animals. Referring to the following suggestions, describe for the class what or whom we (don't) admire in our culture, and why.

PERSONAS
los atletas profesionales
los actores
las madres
los médicos
los músicos profesionales
los políticos
¿ ?

COSAS, ANIMALES, CONCEPTOS
la belleza[1]
la corrida de toros
el dinero
las flores
la muerte
los tigres
¿ ?

NEW VOCABULARY: la corrida de toros, los políticos, los tigres

EJEMPLOS: En nuestra cultura admiramos a los actores porque son ricos y muy guapos.

En nuestra cultura admiramos los tigres porque son muy fuertes.

[1]*beauty*

En la universidad

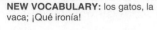

NEW VOCABULARY: los gatos, la vaca; ¡Qué ironía!

Unos estudiantes visitan la feria[1] estatal de Wisconsin donde ven muchas exhibiciones de animales.

CELIA: ¿Por qué no les gusta a los norteamericanos la corrida de toros?
CARMEN: Dicen que es cruel.
CELIA: ¡Qué ironía! Cuando ellos comen animales y también los usan en sus experimentos científicos.... ¿Cómo pueden criticar la corrida de toros?

ALFONSINA: A la esposa del profesor Brewer le encantan los gatos. ¿A ti te gustan, Marisol?
MARISOL: Sí, me gustan... pero los animales domésticos no tienen en México la aceptación que tienen aquí.

FELIPE: Tomás, ¿cuál es tu animal favorito?
TOMÁS: Pues... creo que es la vaca.
FELIPE: Chico, ¿hablas en serio?
TOMÁS: Claro. En la Argentina, el ganado[2] es una de las industrias más importantes del país.

[1] *fair* [2] *livestock*

PREPARATION: Ask students to describe the drawing. Ask them to focus on the title of the dialogue and on the dialogue introduction. **¿Dónde están los estudiantes?** Have students skim the dialogues. **¿De qué hablan los estudiantes?**

De inmediato

SUGGESTION: Have one student read an item while the other refers to the dialogue for the answer.

To whom do the following statements refer: Celia, **los norteamericanos, la Sra. Brewer,** Marisol, Felipe, or Tomás?

1. Dice que los norteamericanos comen animales y los usan en experimentos científicos.
2. Creen que la corrida de toros es cruel.
3. Le encantan los gatos.
4. Le gustan los gatos.
5. Dice que en México los animales domésticos no tienen la aceptación que tienen en los EE. UU.
6. Le preguntó a Tomás cuál era su animal favorito.
7. La vaca es su animal favorito.

OPTIONAL: (A ti te toca) Have students express what they, their families, or their friends love, using Alfonsina's line as a model.

A ti te toca

SUGGESTION: Encourage responses such as **¿Verdad? / Interesante. / ¡Qué bien! / Comprendo. / Sí, es verdad. / Sí, tienes razón.**

Tell the class about an important industry in your city, region, country, or in another country. Remember what you have read about other Hispanic countries in **Otros Mundos**.

EJEMPLO: En Venezuela, el petróleo es una de las industrias más importantes.

La corrida de toros

Although many people in the United States regard bullfighting as a cruel sport, within the Hispanic world it is generally seen as a highly stylized and ritualized art. Each aspect of the bullfight is dictated by tradition, from the clothes worn by the matador (**el traje de luces**) and the decision of which matador fights the first bull, to the function of the various members of the entourage (**la cuadrilla**).

Bullfighting may be known as the national pastime (**la fiesta nacional**) of Spain, but many feel that soccer (**el fútbol**) currently has a greater following. Bullfighting is still popular in Mexico, but in other Hispanic countries, it may not exist or may be severely restricted.

En México

Although virtually every major city in Mexico has a bullring and many smaller cities and towns promote bullfights during local fiestas, the major arenas are located in Mexico City and Guadalajara. In the capital, the Plaza de Toros Monumental México seats 64,000 people and most Sunday afternoons during the primary season (usually December through April), it is full. The corridas start promptly at 4:00 P.M., and the impressive opening ceremonies are quite colorful. There arc almost always six fights featuring three matadors. Ticket prices are determined by location of the seats: **sol** tickets, for seating in the full sun, are the least expensive; **sombra** seats, for seating in shaded areas which are considered more comfortable, are more expensive.

FOLLOW-UP: 1. ¿Cómo se dice *bullfight* en español? 2. ¿Cómo se llama el traje de los matadores? 3. ¿Qué día asiste más público a las corridas? 4. ¿Cuáles son los meses de la temporada de corridas en México?

Los animales

PREPARATION: Ask students to scan the drawings and the list—with the translations covered—to find cognates and guessable words.

el cerdo
la cabra
la vaca
la oveja
el caballo
el toro
el gallo

el mono
el tigre
la cebra
el elefante
el león
la jirafa
la culebra
el hipopótamo
el rinoceronte

Otro vocabulario

el águila (*f.*)	*eagle*	la mariposa	*butterfly*
la ardilla	*squirrel*	la mosca	*fly*
el canguro	*kangaroo*	el oso	*bear*
el coyote	*coyote*	el pájaro	*bird*
la foca	*seal*	el perro	*dog*
la gallina	*chicken*	el pez (tropical)	(*tropical*) *fish*
el gato	*cat*	la rata	*rat*
el insecto	*insect*	el ratón	*mouse*
el lobo	*wolf*	la zorra	*fox*

Actividades

Ⓐ ¿Qué animal es? Identify each animal.

1. Este animal es el mejor amigo del hombre.
2. Este animal da leche.
3. Este animal puede volar.
4. Este animal es muy listo.[1]
5. Este animal tiene un cuello muy largo.
6. Este animal es el mejor amigo de los vaqueros.[2]
7. Este animal canta en la madrugada.[3]
8. Este animal no tiene patas[4] pero se mueve rápidamente sobre la tierra.
9. Este animal nos da lana.
10. Este animal se cuelga[5] de los árboles en las selvas.

[1]*smart, sharp*　[2]*cowboys*　[3]*dawn*　[4]*feet*　[5]*se... hangs*

Ⓑ Preguntas personales.

1. ¿Tienes animales domésticos en tu casa? ¿Qué son? ¿Cuántos tienes?
2. En tu opinión, ¿son los gatos más limpios o más sucios que los perros? ¿Por qué?
3. ¿Crees que los gatos son más inteligentes que los perros?
4. ¿Tienes un animal que no sea doméstico? ¿Qué es?
5. ¿Cuál es el animal que más te gusta ver en el zoológico?
6. En tu opinión, ¿qué animal es el más rapido? ¿el más fuerte? ¿el más inteligente? ¿el más feo? ¿el más gordo? ¿el más alto?

EN ACCIÓN

Monos en Veracruz

Elena reads the following article in a welcome magazine she picked up in the hotel in Veracruz. In it, she discovers that not all immigrants to Veracruz are human.

Antes de leer

When Charles Darwin visited the Galapagos Islands, he found many animals there that had traveled from far away lands. Many of these animals had adapted physically and behaviorally to their new environment and had made it their own. The horse is one animal that is not native to the United States but is not usually thought of as an immigrant. What others can you name? What conditions are necessary for a species to survive in a new environment?

Scan the article to find the following information: What animal is discussed? What part of the state of Veracruz has it adopted? Has the species fit in well in the new environment?

Now read the article and do the activity that follows.

Unos inmigrantes ideales

Llegaron al estado de Veracruz desde Puerto Rico y establecieron su hogar[1] en la isla de Totogadillo. Aunque algunos murieron, se reprodujeron moderadamente y formaron una notable familia. Resultaron prolíficos, vienen de buena cepa[2] y como si hubieran asistido al mejor colegio, demuestran buenos modales.[3] Ahora hasta son practicantes del buceo[4] y de manera espontánea y con cierta alegría reciben al visitante. En cuanto el turista se acerca,[5] ellos demuestran felicidad.[6] Sólo hay que llevarles un buen regalo, de preferencia comida.

Por si Ud. no adivina[7] de quiénes se trata,[8] le diremos que es un grupo de macacos, simpáticos monos que son la atracción de los visitantes. Esos monos se consideran parte del equilibrio ecológico de esta región. Desde su llegada a México, fueron bien aceptados.

[1]*home* [2]*stock* [3]*manners* [4]*skin diving* [5]*se... comes near* [6]*happiness* [7]*guess* [8]*se... we are talking*

Después de leer

¿Es cierto o no es cierto?

1. Vinieron de Costa Rica.
2. Establecieron su hogar en la isla de Totogadillo.

OPTIONAL: 1. ¿De qué isla son los monos originalmente? 2. ¿Cómo se llama la isla donde viven ahora? 3. ¿Cómo reaccionan los monos al ver a turistas? 4. ¿Cuál es su regalo preferido? 5. ¿Son bien aceptados o no en México?

3. Reciben al visitante de manera espontánea y con alegría.
4. A los monos no les gusta la comida que traen los turistas.
5. El nombre de este grupo de monos es macaco.
6. Estos monos no forman parte del equilibrio ecológico de la región.

PREPARATION: Read the following list of words and ask students whether the words relate to **la geografía, el tiempo, los meses,** or **las estaciones**. The list: **la meseta, la primavera, la tormenta, el valle, enero, el viento.**

OPTIONAL: 1. ¿En cuántos continentes hay países hispánicos? 2. ¿Dónde quedan los centros turísticos más visitados en España? 3. ¿Por qué se dice que el río Amazonas es único? 4. ¿Cuáles son las dos estaciones del año en los lugares donde no hay cuatro?

EXPANSION: When students have listened to the selection twice, have them work in small groups (with maps if desired) to add more details to their graphs. Have them share their results with the rest of the class, proceeding by country or by geographical feature.

Clima y topografía

Before you listen to a passage about the climate and topography of the Hispanic world, review the vocabulary from **La geografía** in **Capítulo 1** and that from **El tiempo, los meses y las estaciones** in **Capítulo 6**. Next, copy the following grid onto another sheet of paper, leaving room to write ten to fifteen words in each box.

Now listen to the passage once to get a general idea of the content. After listening, fill in from memory as much of your grid as you can. (**¡OJO!** Information is not provided for some of the boxes.) Listen a second time to check your answers and fill in what you have missed.

	España	México	El Caribe, América Central y América del Sur
montañas	en el norte y...	la Sierra Madre Occidental y...	
playas			
tiempo			
ríos			
selva			

Los números ordinales

EL HIPÓDROMO: LA QUINTA CARRERA DE CABALLOS

noveno · octavo · quinto · primero · séptimo · cuarto · segundo · décimo · sexto · tercero

Otro vocabulario

undécimo/a (11º, 11ª)	*eleventh (11th)*
duodécimo/a (12º, 12ª)	*twelfth (12th)*
último/a	*last*

A **No es verdad.** The following statements about the ranking of places are inaccurate. In each item, the correct answer is always one number higher than what is stated. Correct the statements, using the cues provided.

Actividades

EJEMPLO: En cuanto al número de habitantes, el estado de Michoacán es el quinto estado más grande de México.
(Guanajuato—quinto; Michoacán—¿ ?) →
No, Guanajuato es el quinto; Michoacán es el sexto.

1. En cuanto al número de habitantes, Nueva York es la tercera ciudad más grande del mundo. (Seoul en la Corea del Sur—tercera; Nueva York—¿ ?)
2. En cuanto al número de habitantes, Buenos Aires es la octava ciudad más grande del mundo. (Río de Janeiro—octava; Buenos Aires—¿ ?)
3. En cuanto al tamaño, la América del Sur es el tercer continente más grande del mundo. (la América del Norte—tercero; la América del Sur—¿ ?)

(Continúa.)

4. En cuanto al tamaño, África es el primer continente del mundo.
   (Asia—primero; África—¿ ?)

B **¿Qué lugar ocupan?** Rank these people and things.

1. Enero es el _____ mes del año.
2. La cena es la _____ comida del día.
3. El domingo es el _____ día de la semana. **¡OJO!**
4. Jorge es «sophomore» en la universidad; está en su _____ año.
5. El número diez es el _____ número.
6. El «fa» es la _____ nota en una octava del piano.
7. La esposa del presidente de los EE. UU. es la _____ Dama.[1]
8. La «e» es la _____ letra del alfabeto español.
9. Tomás Jefferson fue el _____ presidente de los EE. UU., después de
   Washington y Adams.
10. La última entrada[2] en el juego[3] de béisbol es la _____.

[1]*Lady*   [2]*inning*   [3]*game*

PREPARATION: For number 3, remind students that Sunday is the first day of the week on the Hispanic calendar.
EXPANSION: Ask students to make up three or four additional items following the models provided in the activity.

EN ACCIÓN

PREPARATION: Familiarize students with the glossed vocabulary by providing the English equivalents and having them find the Spanish words and phrases in the poem.
SUGGESTION: You may wish to ask a native speaker of Spanish to record the poem for you to play back in class.
FOLLOW-UP: 1. ¿Quién escribió este poema? ¿En qué año? 2. ¿Cuáles son algunas palabras de origen africano o caribe-africano? 3. ¿Qué palabras sugieren los movimientos de la culebra? 4. ¿Qué palabras y frases del poema se refieren al cuerpo o a la apariencia de la culebra?

Un canto mágico

Many writers have used literature to express the various ethnic influences in their country. The poems of Cuban Nicolás Guillén often convey the African influence in the Caribbean.

Antes de escuchar

In the following poem, some of the repeated words are not Spanish but of African or African-Caribbean origin and are used to give the poem the feeling of an African chant. The word **sensemayá,** for example, is a magical incantation to protect a man who is about to kill a poisonous snake.

Throughout history, humans have worshipped or admired many animals. For example, for the Zapotecs, the bat represented darkness and death. For what reasons might a culture worship the snake? What might a snake represent to that culture? What are some actions or movements that you associate with snakes? Scan the poem and list the verbs used to convey the snake's actions. What do they mean?

Now, listen to this famous work as you read along with the poem.

Sensemayá

Canto para matar una culebra

NICOLÁS GUILLÉN (CUBA, 1902–1989)

¡Mayombe—bombe—mayombé!
¡Mayombe—bombe—mayombé!
¡Mayombe—bombe—mayombé!

La culebra tiene los ojos de vidrio;
la culebra viene y se enreda en un palo;[1]
con sus ojos de vidrio, en un palo,
con sus ojos de vidrio.

La culebra camina sin patas;[2]
la culebra se esconde en la yerba;[3]
caminando se esconde en la yerba,
caminando sin patas.

¡Mayombe—bombe—mayombé!
¡Mayombe—bombe—mayombé!
¡Mayombe—bombe—mayombé!

Tú le das con el hacha[4] y se muere:
¡dale ya!
¡No le des con el pie, que te muerde,
no le des con el pie, que se va!

NEW VOCABULARY: muerde

Sensemayá, la culebra,
sensemayá.
Sensemayá, con sus ojos,
sensemayá.
Sensemayá, con su lengua,
sensemayá.
Sensemayá, con su boca,
sensemayá.

¡La culebra muerta no puede comer;
la culebra muerta no puede silbar;[5]
no puede caminar,
no puede correr!
¡La culebra muerta no puede mirar;
la culebra muerta no puede beber;
no puede respirar,
no puede morder!

¡Mayombe—bombe—mayombé!
Sensemayá, la culebra...

[1] *se... wraps itself around a rod*   [2] *legs*   [3] *se... hides in the grass*   [4] *Tú... You hit him with the hatchet*   [5] *hiss*

> ¡Mayombe—bombe—mayombé!
> *Sensemayá, no se mueve...*
> ¡Mayombe—bombe—mayombé!
> *Sensemayá, la culebra...*
> ¡Mayombe—bombe—mayombé!
> *¡Sensemayá, se murió!*
>
> West Indies Ltd. (1934)

Animales y legumbres en las noticias

The following selections discuss nature and the interactions between humans and nature.

Antes de leer

What does the title of this activity suggest these articles will be about?

The first article deals with the smuggling of items out of Russia. According to the title of the article, what do you think the contraband is? Why do you think a government might make it illegal to remove any member of a particular species from the country?

The second and third articles deal with the beneficial nature of certain living things. According to the title of each article, what plant or animal is discussed in each article, and what advantage does its presence provide?

Now, read the articles and do the activities that follow.

Saquean[1] águilas de Rusia

Como cualquier país tercermundista,[2] la Comunidad de Estados Independientes (Rusia) está siendo saqueada de sus aves de rapiña.[3] Recientemente un cargamento[4] de águilas imperiales fue confiscado en una aduana alemana. Este país se ha negado a devolver los animales con el pretexto de que morirán por falta de protección.

Según el periódico ruso *Commersant,* el comercio de aves raras hacia el extranjero[5] es el segundo negocio ilegal del país, después del tráfico de drogas. El contrabando de la fauna rusa pasa tranquilamente por Moscú y San Petersburgo, con destino a Alemania, Finlandia y a las repúblicas checa y eslovaca. Otros pasos están en Vladivostok y Rhabarovsk, cuando las aves son enviadas al sudeste de Asia.

[1] *They are plundering*   [2] *Third World*   [3] *aves... birds of prey*   [4] *shipment*   [5] *hacia... abroad*

Las coles absorben venenos[1] de la tierra

El doctor Alan Baker de la universidad británica de Sheffield ha descubierto que las coles tienen la facultad de absorber venenos de la tierra y hacerlos desaparecer.

[1] *toxins*

Baker y su pareja en tareas de investigación han sembrado coles en terrenos del norte del Reino[2] Unido —saturados de cadmio, zinc y níquel— y como resultado encontraron que las coles «limpian» el suelo más eficazmente que muchos productos químicos y según ellos «sin ningún riesgo de posibles efectos colaterales». Los dos científicos creen que las coles pueden salvar[3] terrenos arruinados por la contaminación industrial, pero no han aclarado si esas coles «limpiadoras» siguen siendo comestibles[4] o ya no.

[2]*Kingdom*   [3]*save*   [4]*edible*

FOLLOW-UP: 1. ¿Qué descubrieron el Dr. Baker y su pareja? 2. ¿Qué minerales saturaban los terrenos investigados por el Dr. Baker y su pareja? 3. ¿Podemos comer las coles que usaron para limpiar el suelo?

No mate las arañas patonas,[1] son útiles contra mosquitos

Como buenos amos de casa, debemos estar enterados[2] de que los fertilizantes y ciertas sustancias son unos de los principales contaminantes de ríos y lagos, por el abuso de muchos productos que usamos en casa y que arrojamos[3] después. Pero hay medidas[4] que podemos tomar para evitar[5] este problema.

Por ejemplo, evitemos al máximo utilizar aerosoles para eliminar a los insectos. Algo muy importante: ¡Por favor!, no mate a las «arañas patonas»; tal vez desagradables, estas arañas nos ayudan a acabar con los mosquitos. ¿Y las telarañas[6]? Pues, podemos limpiarlas con una jerga[7] húmeda.

[1]*arañas... daddy-longlegs (harvestmen)*   [2]*informed*   [3]*we throw out*   [4]*measures*   [5]*avoid*   [6]*spider webs*   [7]*cloth*

FOLLOW-UP: 1. ¿Cuál es el tema de este artículo? 2. ¿Por qué mencionan las arañas patonas? 3. ¿Cuál es un método de matar insectos que puede ser destructivo para el medio ambiente?

Después de leer

Paso 1. Match the items in the first column with the most closely related item in the second column.

1. águilas
2. animales
3. arañas patonas
4. coles
5. minerales
6. negocio ilegal
7. Rusia
8. Sheffield

a. absorber venenos
b. aves de rapiña
c. cadmio, níquel
d. comer mosquitos
e. Comunidad de Estados Independientes
f. fauna
g. tráfico de drogas
h. universidad británica

Paso 2. Choose one of the articles and write a brief synopsis of its contents. Be prepared to share your synopsis with a partner or a small group.

Con este huevo no empolló/concluyó otra especie más. Ayúdenos a suspender la secuencia mortal, uniéndose a Pronatura.

Cuanto desée saber, obténgalo por teléfono, fax o correo.

PRONATURA
Nuevo León 144 Col. Hipódromo Condesa
06100 México, D.F.
Tel: 286-9642 Fax: 286-9480

EPISODIOS

Paso 1 PARA ESCUCHAR

PREPARATION: For each scene, have students point out key vocabulary in Spanish that would help them identify it.

For each statement your instructor reads, give the number of the corresponding drawing.

Paso 2 PARA ESCRIBIR

EXAMPLES: 1. La señora tomó un taxi para ir al centro. (No, no es cierto.) 2. La señora compró estampillas en el correo. (Es cierto.)

Write six statements about the **episodios** scenes, three of which are true, three of which are false. Then read your statements to a classmate, who will respond with either **Sí, es cierto** or **No, no es cierto.** Then switch roles and listen to your classmate's sentences, responding appropriately.

EXPANSION: Have students correct any false statements.

Paso 3 PARA ESCRIBIR

Rewrite the following paragraph so that it accurately reflects the situations in the drawings.

SUGGESTION: Have students work in pairs to read each other's corrected paragraphs, discuss similarities, and resolve discrepancies.

Una tarde, una señorita joven sale de su casa para ir de compras. Lleva pantalones cortos y una camiseta porque hace un poco de calor. Toma el metro a la plaza comercial en las afueras de la ciudad. Primero baja en la farmacia para comprar aspirinas. Después, va a una tienda de ropa, al lado de la far-

316

macia, donde compra una blusa y un suéter. Luego, entra en la lechería para comprar queso. Finalmente, compra unas frutas frescas antes de tomar el metro para regresar a casa. Ya en casa, toma una siesta en su habitación.

Paso 4

VARIATION: Have students describe what the **señora** did (preterite), was doing (imperfect), or was going to do (**ir a** + inf.) in each of the scenes.

In small groups, describe what the **señora** is doing in each of the scenes. Each student should make at least two statements about each scene without repeating information given by the other students.

Paso 5

PREPARATION: Ask students which form of address (**tú** or **Ud.**) would be appropriate in this situation.

Imagine that you overheard the conversation between the **señora** and the clerk at the stationery store. Write out the conversation, in which each character has at least five lines. Include appropriate greetings, expressions of courtesy, and farewells, and be sure to use the formal forms of address.

SUGGESTION: Have students prepare, rehearse, and present their dialogues to the class.

Paso 6

Write five sentences that describe the scenes. Then write five sentences that describe what is *not* happening. **Vocabulario útil: (No) Es cierto/claro/evidente/seguro/verdad que... (No) Es bueno/importante/(im)posible/(im)probable/lástima/malo/necesario/triste que...**

EJEMPLOS: Es evidente que hace un poco fresco.
No es verdad que la señora compre ropa.

PREPARATION: Ask whether subjunctive or indicative will be required after sentences that begin with **es cierto, es posible, es claro; es lástima, es evidente, es necesario.** Review the formation of the present subjunctive.

Paso 7

PREPARATION: Review question words and word order in question formation. You may wish to write the question words on the board.

First write five questions that can be answered by looking at the scenes. Each question must begin with a different interrogative word (**¿cómo?, ¿dónde?, ¿quién?,** and so on). Then ask a classmate to answer your questions.

EJEMPLOS: —¿Qué compró la señora en la papelería?
—La señora compró papel para cartas y sobres en la papelería.

—¿Quién entra en la cocina?
—La hija de la señora entra en la cocina.

PARTICIPA EN LA PRESERVACION DEL AMBIENTE
PEMEX
VANGUARDIA DEL CAMBIO

ACTIVIDAD COMPRENSIVA

SUGGESTION: Have students make lists of words that fit several categories present in the drawing (i.e., physical descriptions, geographical features, animals, nationalities, professions, furniture, body parts, and descriptive adjectives).

Working with a classmate, describe the following drawing in detail.

NOTE: The purpose of the drawing is to review vocabulary from previous chapters.

VOCABULARIO

Los verbos	*Verbs*	El medio ambiente	*The environment*
cantar	to sing; to crow	el agua subterránea	ground water
causar	to cause	el arbusto	bush
contaminar	to pollute; to contaminate	la calidad	quality
criticar	to criticize	la capa de ozono	ozone layer
luchar	to fight; to struggle	el cielo	sky; heaven
morder (ue)	to bite	la contaminación	pollution
proteger (protejo)	to protect	la especie (en peligro)	(endangered) species
reforestar	to reforest, replant a forest	el huracán	hurricane
		el incendio	fire
respirar	to breathe	la inundación	flood
sembrar (ie)	to plant	la lluvia ácida	acid rain
sonreír (sonrío)	to smile	la naturaleza	nature
volar (ue)	to fly	la piedra	stone, rock

318

el plomo	lead (*metal*)
el recurso	resource
la selva tropical	(tropical) rain forest
el temblor	tremor, small earthquake
el terremoto	earthquake
la tierra	earth; land; soil
la tormenta	storm

Palabras semejantes: el aire, la destrucción, la ecología, el planeta, la planta, el tornado.

Los animales — *Animals*

el águila (*f.*)	eagle
la ardilla	squirrel
el buho	owl
el caballo	horse
la cabra	goat
el canguro	kangaroo
la cebra	zebra
el cerdo	pig
la culebra	snake
la foca	seal
la gallina	chicken, hen
el gallo	rooster
el gato	cat
la jirafa	giraffe
el león	lion
el lobo	wolf
la mariposa	butterfly
el mono	monkey
la mosca	fly
el murciélago	bat
el oso	bear
la oveja	sheep
el pájaro	bird
el perro	dog
el pez (*pl.* **los peces**) **tropical**	tropical fish
el ratón	mouse
el rinoceronte	rhinoceros
el toro	bull
la vaca	cow
la zorra	fox

Palabras semejantes: el coyote, el elefante, el hipopótamo, el insecto, el jaguar, la rata, la serpiente, el tigre.

Otros sustantivos — *Other nouns*

la corrida de toros	bullfight
el dios	god
el dolor	pain
el periódico	newspaper
el político / la politica	politician
la razón	reason

Los números ordinales — *Ordinal numbers*

primer(o)/primera (**1ʳ, 1º, 1ª**) (R)	first (1st)
segundo/a (**2º, 2ª**) (R)	second (2nd)
tercer(o)/tercera (**3ʳ, 3º, 3ª**) (R)	third (3rd)
cuarto/a (**4º, 4ª**)	fourth (4th)
quinto/a (**5º, 5ª**)	fifth (5th)
sexto/a (**6º, 6ª**)	sixth (6th)
séptimo/a (**7º, 7ª**)	seventh (7th)
octavo/a (**8º, 8ª**)	eighth (8th)
noveno/a (**9º, 9ª**)	ninth (9th)
décimo/a (**10º, 10ª**)	tenth (10th)
undécimo/a (**11º, 11ª**)	eleventh (11th)
duodécimo/a (**12º, 12ª**)	twelfth (12th)
último/a (R)	last

Los adjetivos — *Adjectives*

contaminado/a	contaminated, polluted
duro	hard
grave	serious (*problem or condition*)
limpio/a	clean
protegido/a	protected
puro/a	pure
sorprendido/a	surprised
sucio/a	dirty
vivo/a	alive, living

Palabras y expresiones útiles — *Useful words and expressions*

en contra de	in opposition to, against
no... sino (que)	not . . . but rather
¡Qué ironía!	How ironic!
sin embargo	however, nevertheless
tratar de + *inf.*	to try (*to do something*)
tratar de + *noun*	to deal with, speak about (*an issue*)

La Argentina y el Uruguay

Saludos desde la Argentina. Me llamo Tomás Garibaldi. Es posible que Uds. estén sorprendidos al oír mi apellido, Garibaldi. Soy puro argentino pero mi abuelo paterno vino a la Argentina de Italia. En la Argentina hay muchas personas de apellido italiano, alemán o inglés. Sus antepasados emigraron a la Argentina hace años por razones políticas y económicas.

Vivo en la ciudad de Córdoba, un centro ganadero[1] que se dedica a la producción de leche, carne, cuero y piel.[2] Mi padre y mi tío son dueños de muchas tierras agrícolas y su compañía, Hermanos Garibaldi, emplea a muchos gauchos, o sea a los vaqueros[3] argentinos. Ellos trabajan con el ganado y cultivan trigo, maíz, alfalfa y frutas en nuestros campos en la Pampa.

Mi familia no vive en el campo sino en la ciudad. Desde allí, mi padre y su hermano manejan la compañía. Mi madre es profesora de inglés en la Universidad de Córdoba. Es por su parte que recibí una beca para estudiar inglés en Wisconsin.

[1]*cattle*   [2]*hides*   [3]*cowboys*

NEW VOCABULARY: sorprendidos

¿Sabías que... ?

LA ARGENTINA
- La Argentina es el país más cosmopolita de la América Latina.
- Más del 90% de los argentinos son de origen europeo.
- Los habitantes de Buenos Aires, la capital, se llaman **porteños.**

- Parte de las famosas cataratas[1] del Iguazú está en la Argentina.
- El gaucho reina en la Pampa, una inmensa llanura tan extensa como los estados de Illinois, Missouri e Iowa juntos.
- San Carlos de Bariloche ofrece oportunidades excelentes para el esquí en el invierno —de julio a septiembre— y para la pesca en el verano —de diciembre a marzo.
- El escritor argentino Jorge Luis Borges (1899–1986) ganó muchos premios internacionales por sus obras literarias.
- El tango, un famoso baile, tiene su origen en la Argentina.
- Las vidas de Juan y Eva Perón, famosos políticos argentinos, están inmortalizadas en la obra teatral estadounidense *Evita*.

MAR CARIBE
VENEZUELA
GUYANA
SURINAM
GUAYANA FRANCESA
COLOMBIA
ECUADOR
BRASIL
PERÚ
BOLIVIA
OCÉANO PACÍFICO
PARAGUAY
Cataratás del Iguazú
Córdoba
URUGUAY
Montevideo
CHILE
Buenos Aires
Punta del Este
Pampa
Río de la Plata
San Carlos de Bariloche
ARGENTINA
OCÉANO ATLÁNTICO
AMÉRICA DEL SUR

EL URUGUAY
- La mayor parte de los habitantes del Uruguay son de origen europeo.
- El Uruguay posee unas de las playas más hermosas del mundo. Punta del Este, a 80 kilómetros al este de la capital, se considera la Riviera de Sudamérica.
- La ganadería es la industria más importante del Uruguay. Se dice que el Uruguay produce la mejor carne del mundo.
- Hay un promedio de 8,4 ovejas por habitante uruguayo.

[1]*waterfalls*

La Argentina y el Uruguay en breve

	LA ARGENTINA	EL URUGUAY
Capital:	Buenos Aires	Montevideo
Lengua:	el español	el español
Gobierno:	república	república
Moneda:	el peso	el nuevo peso
Población:	32.663.000 de habitantes	3.121.000 de habitantes
Superficie:	1.065.189 millas cuadradas (cuatro veces más grande que Texas)	68.037 millas cuadradas (aproximadamente del tamaño del estado de Washington)

Este gaucho argentino compite en un rodeo.

NOTE: See the *Instructor's Manual* for suggestions on teaching **México y los mexicanos**.

México y los mexicanos

De viaje: A una hora de la capital

NEW VOCABULARY: extraño

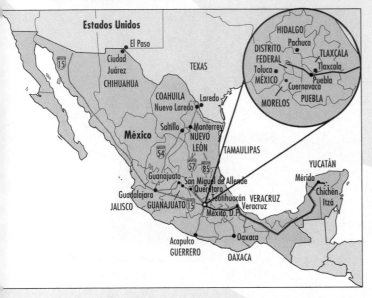

México, D.F., no es la única ciudad de importancia en la parte central del país. Partiendo[1] en varias direcciones de este centro metropolitano, y a aproximadamente una hora de viaje en automóvil, hay varios estados que valen la pena conocer.

Morelos

Al sur de México, D.F., se encuentra el estado de Morelos, que aprovisiona de azúcar al resto del país. La capital del estado, Cuernavaca, es donde los aztecas solían veranear[2] en la época prehispánica. Hernán Cortés inició en esta ciudad la construcción de su palacio con la intención de pasar en él los veranos. En el siglo XIX, el emperador Maximiliano y su esposa, Carlota, la valoraron[3] como centro residencial. Hoy Cuernavaca es lugar de residencia de estadounidenses, algunos europeos y, sobre todo, artistas, escritores y celebridades. También es el sitio elegido[4] por muchos mexicanos capitalinos[5] para pasar los fines de semana.

México

A sólo 65 kilómetros al oeste de México, D.F. se encuentra Toluca, capital del estado de México. Toluca es una ciudad moderna, de medio millón de habitantes y de gran actividad industrial. Es una ciudad provincial típica, con algunos edificios de estilo victoriano, iglesias coloniales, una gran plaza central y calles estrechas.[6] Se dice que, saliendo de la capital y entrando en el valle de Toluca, se encuentra el verdadero México: seco, de campos dorados, cactos y casas de adobe.

Hidalgo

El estado de Hidalgo, al norte de la capital del país, tiene una economía eminentemente agrícola. Aquí se cultivan alfalfa, trigo, tomate, maíz, caña de azúcar, cebada,[7] chile verde, papa, habas,[8] ajo, manzana, perón,[9] aguacate, café, naranja y mango. Pero hoy Hidalgo es también un estado intensamente industrializado gracias al petróleo, las fundiciones[10] y la proximidad a la Ciudad de México. Pachuca, la capital del estado, es una ciudad colonial de calles empedradas.[11]

Puebla

El estado de Puebla es montañoso, con numerosos valles. No es extraño oír lenguas nativas en ciertas partes del territorio de Puebla, ya que en él habitan muchos indígenas totonacas, mixtecas y otomíes.

El gran suceso[12] histórico que tuvo lugar en Puebla fue la batalla del 5 de mayo de 1862. Fue entonces cuando el ejército[13] mexicano con el apoyo[14] de algunos batallones indios derrotó[15] al ejército francés. El aniversario de este enfrentamiento[16] se celebra anualmente en todo México y entre los de ascendencia[17] mexicana en los EE. UU.

---

[1]*Departing* [2]*to spend the summer* [3]*la... valued it* [4]*chosen* [5]*residents of the capital city* [6]*narrow* [7]*barley* [8]*large beans similar to lima beans* [9]*variety of apple* [10]*foundries* [11]*cobblestone* [12]*event* [13]*army* [14]*support* [15]*defeated* [16]*confrontation* [17]*heritage*

Perspectivas de México:
El progreso y sus consecuencias

Durante el siglo XX México ha cambiado mucho. Ha pasado de ser un país esencialmente agrícola a uno moderno y en vías de desarrollo,[1] que depende de la industria y la tecnología para sobrevivir.[2] ¿Cuáles son las variables que definen los índices de modernización y desarrollo[3]? En el aspecto del desarrollo de México en el siglo XX se destacan[4] la duración de vida, el Producto Nacional Bruto[5] (PNB) y la urbanización.

En México, la duración de vida al nacer casi se ha doblado en los últimos cincuenta años, de 37 años en promedio[6] a 64, un incremento de casi el 75%. Desde principios[7] del siglo hasta el año 1993, la tasa[8] de mortalidad descendió por más del 85%, de 33,6 a sólo 4,8 muertes por año por cada mil habitantes. La principal consecuencia de esto es un crecimiento[9] exponencial de la población, que se ha incrementado[10] por más de cinco veces desde el año 1900.

El indicador que se emplea con más frecuencia

CAMBIOS DEMOGRÁFICOS		
aspecto	*cambio*	*años*
duración de vida	↑ el 74%	1940–1990
tasa de mortalidad	↓ el 78%	1900–1980
población	↑ el 500%	1900–1990

para evaluar el bienestar[11] de una población es el PNB por persona. El PNB por persona es el total del valor[12] de servicios y productos proveídos[13] en el país durante un año, dividido por el número de personas en el país. En México, entre 1895 y 1980, la población creció[14] por más de cinco veces mientras que el PNB per cápita avanzó más de 36 veces. El creci-

miento rápido del PNB per cápita durante este período indica una vitalidad económica.

Sin embargo, el progreso en México ha traído dificultades. Por ejemplo, México está cambiando de una economía agrícola a una economía industrial, basada principalmente en la manufactura y la industria petrolera. Este cambio produce un traslado[15] de la población de los campos a los centros urbanos. Esta urbanización trae consigo[16] toda clase de problemas, incluso, por ejemplo, una falta de viviendas adecuadas, contaminación, tráfico sofocante y crimen de menor cuantía.[17]

Algunas creencias,[18] tradiciones y valores del pasado también se ven amenazados[19] por los cambios. Con la transferencia de tecnología y del estilo de vida de las naciones avanzadas hay también la adopción del sistema de valores de estas naciones. En el cambio, las sociedades sufren la pérdida[20] gradual de la identidad nacional, que es mayor en proporción a la rapidez con que avanzan hacia su desarrollo. Esta situación provoca en la sociedad una crisis de valores y una búsqueda[21] de mecanismos de reafirmación de su identidad, aunque la esencia de esta identidad consta[22] ahora de un nuevo sistema de valores.

No es decir que ya no existe la vida tradicional del campesino,[23]. Al contrario, en todas las regiones del país hay familias que están bien contentas con su vida en el campo, cultivando la tierra y cuidando su ganado[24] en su propio terreno. Sin embargo, en México, como en todos los países, los cambios que acompañan la tecnología tendrán que ser enfrentados[25] a medida que se presentan.[26]

[1] en... *developing* [2] *survive* [3] *development* [4] se... *stand out* [5] *Gross* [6] en... *on the average* [7] *the beginning* [8] *rate* [9] *growth* [10] se... *has increased* [11] *well-being* [12] *value* [13] *provided* [14] *grew* [15] *movement* [16] *with it* [17] de... *petty* [18] *beliefs* [19] se... *are being threatened* [20] *loss* [21] *search* [22] *is made up* [23] *peasant* [24] *cattle* [25] tendrán... *will have to be faced* [26] a... *as they arise*

Las
comunicaciones

NEW VOCABULARY: Las comunicaciones

NOTE: See the *Instructor's Manual* for suggestions on using the chapter-opening pages.

(arriba) El disco satélite, como éste en Caracas, Venezuela, ha cambiado la transmissión de noticias en todo el mundo.
(a la derecha) En los quioscos de la Ciudad de México se pueden comprar revistas y periódicos de toda clase.

Para dar mejor servicio telefónico a la república, en Telefónicas Mexicanas se usan ahora computadoras.

Las computadoras son necesarias en los negocios y en la vida diaria. Estos jóvenes miran las computadoras en un centro comercial en el D.F.

METAS

FUNCIONES

- to discuss several means of communication
- to discuss the role of computers and other technology
- to discuss in greater detail topics from previous chapters

GRAMÁTICA

- review and expansion of grammar learned in previous chapters

APPROPRIATE TESTING POINTS:
Diálogo (2), La tecnología, En acción, **Quiz 1**
Diálogo (2), La informática, En acción, **Quiz 2**
Episodios, Actividad comprensiva
Chapter test

De nuevo en la capital

NEW VOCABULARY: darse cuenta (de), la antropología, las culturas, la llegada; indígena, precolombinas; actualmente; de nuevo

PREPARATION: Ask students to describe the drawing. Ask them to focus on the title of the dialogue and on the dialogue introduction. **¿Dónde están los primos? ¿Qué hacen?** Have students skim the dialogue. **¿De qué hablan los jóvenes?**
OPTIONAL: Have students ask a classmate what they have recently realized: **¿De qué te has dado cuenta recientemente?** The partner should answer with **Me he dado cuenta de** + *noun phrase* or **Me he dado cuenta de** + *verb phrase.*

El viaje de Chichén Itzá a México, D.F. es largo pero fascinante. Desde el autobús, David y Elena ven cafetales,[1] bananales[2] y varios pueblos pintorescos.[3] Por fin llegan a la capital, donde descansan un día antes de ir de nuevo al Museo Nacional de Antropología. Ahora los primos charlan enfrente del museo.

DAVID: ¿Sabes, Elena? Cuando estuvimos aquí por primera vez, no pude comprender la importancia de algunas de las cosas que vimos.
ELENA: Por eso querías regresar, ¿no?
DAVID: Sí. Por nuestro viaje, me he dado cuenta de la importancia de las culturas precolombinas en México.
ELENA: Para entender el México de hoy, tienes que comprender también el efecto que tuvo la llegada de los españoles en el siglo XVI. Su presencia lo cambió todo.
DAVID: Claro que sí, pero yo creía que muchos mexicanos actualmente rechazaban[4] la herencia[5] que recibieron de los españoles.
ELENA: Es que nos identificamos más con la cultura indígena. Pero todo el mundo sabe que la influencia española en México es poderosa.[6]

[1]*coffee plantations* [2]*banana plantations* [3]*picturesque* [4]*rejected* [5]*heritage* [6]*powerful*

De inmediato

EXTENSION: 7. ¿Qué hicieron David y Elena en la capital antes de ir al museo? 8. ¿Por qué quería David regresar al museo? 9. ¿Fue grande o pequeño el efecto que tuvo la llegada de los españoles a México en el siglo XVI?

1. ¿Cómo fue el viaje de Chichén Itzá a México, D.F.?
2. ¿Qué no pudo comprender David cuando estuvo por primera vez en el Museo Nacional de Antropología?
3. ¿Qué aprendió David por su viaje?
4. Según Elena, para entender el México de hoy, ¿qué hay que comprender? ¿Por qué?
5. ¿Creía David que muchos mexicanos rechazaban su herencia española o que se identificaban con ella?
6. Según Elena, ¿con qué cultura se identifican más muchos mexicanos, la europea o la indígena?

A ti te toca

OPTIONAL: Ask students to describe a road trip they have made, using the first two lines of the dialogue as a model: **El viaje de Nueva Orleans a Louisville es largo pero fascinante. Desde el carro se pueden ver ríos, bosques, montañas y varias ciudades interesantes.**

Discuss with classmates which ethnic heritage you and your family most identify with. If necessary, refer to the list of adjectives of nationality in **Capítulo 2**. **Vocabulario adicional: africano/a, árabe, europeo/a central (occidental/oriental[1]/septentrional),[2] judío/a,[3] mediterráneo/a, polaco/a, vietnamita.**

EJEMPLO: —Creo que nos identificamos más con la cultura europea occidental. ¿Y Uds.?
—Nosotros nos identificamos más con la cultura judía.

[1]*Eastern* [2]*Northern* [3]*Jewish*

En la universidad

NEW VOCABULARY: apaga; los artículos, los números, la radio, el volumen

Mercedes y unos compañeros del Club Hispánico ven la influencia de los medios de comunicación en su vida.

LUISA: Mercedes, por favor, apaga la radio. Tengo mucho que hacer y, con esta música, no puedo pensar.

MERCEDES: Bueno, mamá, pero todos mis amigos escuchan la radio. Y esta canción de Gloria Estefan es muy popular. Además, tiene un ritmo muy interesante. ¿No puedes esperer hasta que termine la canción?

LUISA: Pues, si no bajas el volumen por lo menos, me vas a dar dolor de cabeza.

PREPARATION: Ask students to describe the drawing. Have students skim the dialogues. **¿De qué hablan los jóvenes?**

JORGE: ¿Adónde vas?

JOAQUÍN: A la biblioteca.

JORGE: ¿Por qué?

JOAQUÍN: Quiero leer el *Miami Herald*. Esta mañana oí una noticia en la televisión sobre unas manifestaciones estudiantiles[1] en España. Quiero ver si el periódico trae más detalles.[2]

JORGE: ¡Qué interesante! Espera hasta que termine de lavar los platos y voy contigo.

CELIA: ¿Tienes algunos números de *Cambio 16*? En España leía todos los artículos en cada número de la revista, sin falla.[4]

CARMEN: Yo también, pero ahora leo *El Carillón.*

CELIA: ¿Qué es eso?

CARMEN: Es un periódico para hispanohablantes que viven en los Estados Unidos. Es muy interesante.

SUGGESTION: Tell students something you do every day without fail, using **sin falla.** **¿Qué haces tú todos los días / cada semana sin falla?**

[1]manifestaciones... *student protests, demonstrations*   [2]*details*   [3]sin... *without fail*

De inmediato

Match the following characters with the source of information or entertainment to which they refer in the dialogues.

1. Carmen
2. Celia
3. Joaquín
4. Mercedes

a. un periódico en español publicado en los Estados Unidos

b. una canción popular en la radio que todos los amigos escuchan cuando estudian

c. una noticia en la televisión sobre manifestaciones estudiantiles

d. una revista española

e. un periódico internacional publicado en la Florida

OPTIONAL: ¿Es cierto o no?
1. Mercedes tiene mucho que hacer. 2. Todos los amigos de Mercedes escuchan la radio. 3. Mercedes quiere apagar la radio. 4. Joaquín va a la librería para leer el periódico. 5. Jorge está lavando los platos. 6. A Celia le encanta leer *Cambio 16*. 7. Carmen tiene algunos números de *Cambio 16*.

A ti te toca

Discuss with a classmate a newspaper or magazine that you enjoy reading, using the following exchange as a guide.

EJEMPLO: E1: ¿Tienes algunos números de _____?
E2: No leo ese periódico / esa revista.
E1: ¿Qué sueles leer?
E2: Leo _____.
E1: ¿Qué es eso?
E2: Es un periódico / una revista que trata de (es para)...

VOCABULARIO

La tecnología

el disco

la videocasetera

los auriculares

el radio

la grabadora

la televisión por satélite

el estéreo

el altavoz

el tocador de discos compactos

la calculadora

el radiocassette portátil

Otro vocabulario

la cámera de vídeo	*video camera*
la computadora portátil	*portable computer*
la máquina de escribir	*typewriter*
el micrófono	*microphone*
la radio	*radio (medium)*
el teléfono celular	*cellular telephone*
la televisión por cable	*cable television*
el tocador de discos láser	*laser disc player*

A **Aparatos indispensables.** Identify the objects described.

1. Esta tecnología permite recibir por un disco las transmisiones de imágenes.
2. Este aparato recibe del aire las transmisiones de sonidos.
3. Se usan para escuchar en privado los sonidos de un estéreo o una grabadora.
4. Este aparato nos permite ver vídeos.
5. Se usa este aparato para sumar.[1]
6. Esto permite escuchar música y caminar o correr al mismo tiempo.

VARIATION: Reverse this activity. Give the name of the object and ask students to choose the most logical definition.

[1]*add*

B **Comparaciones.** Indicate whether you had the following items years ago and whether you have them now.

OPTIONAL: Ask students to work in small groups, conducting a **miniencuesta** to find out who in the group owns what and/or how many of each. Have students share the results with the entire class.

EJEMPLO: una computadora personal →
       Hace diez años no tenía computadora en mi casa. Tampoco/
       Pero tengo computadora ahora.
      o Hace diez años tenía computadora en mi casa. También/No
       tengo computadora ahora.

1. un estéreo
2. discos compactos
3. un radiocassette portátil
4. televisión por cable
5. televisión por satélite
6. una videocasetera
7. un tocador de discos láser
8. un micrófono

C **La tecnología.** Write brief descriptions in Spanish of three electrical or electronic items that you have. You can describe what the item is used for or how it works, but do not identify the item itself. The descriptions will be collected and read aloud; then the class will try to identify each item.

OPTIONAL: Ask students to indicate which electrical or electronic items they want (or don't want) and why: **Quiero un estéreo porque me encanta escuchar música.**

EJEMPLO: Cuando voy a la playa, llevo este aparato conmigo para escuchar música. → Es un radiocassette portátil.

EN ACCIÓN

Alfonsina hace una llamada

Alfonsina decides to make a phone call using the Spanish-language service. Before listening to the conversation, read the following sentences, which are paraphrased from the conversation. As you listen to Alfonsina's conversation with the operator, indicate the order in which the sentences appear in the conversation.

_____ Deseo hablar con la Sra. González.
_____ La conecto ahora mismo.
_____ ¿En qué puedo servirle?
_____ Soy Alfonsina Castro Cota.
_____ ¿Puede Ud. cargarlo a mi tarjeta de crédito?

_____ Marco el número de la casa.
_____ ¿Puede Ud. darme el número de la tarjeta?
_____ Marco el número 0.

En la _Tele·Guía_

Their first evening back in the capital city, David and Elena decide to stay at their hotel and rest from the long trip. They look at the following page from the _Tele·Guía,_ a guide listing the week's television programming.

Antes de leer

Before you begin the reading, think about the information usually contained in similar television guides in English. In addition to the date and time of the show, what information needs to be provided for the guide to be useful to the reader? What information is helpful, though not essential? Do such guides typically list the actors in the films listed? How about those in weekly series? And in soap operas? In news programs? Do the guides list film directors and producers? How about for news programs? For game shows? For cartoons? For which of the following kinds of shows do you typically see a synopsis of the story in a guide: films, weekly series, sports, game shows, soap operas, cartoons?

Study the information contained in the 8:00–9:00 time slots. What do you think the following words mean: **noticiario, tortugas, dibujos animados, conductores, producter**?

Now scan the reading for the information necessary to do the activities that follow.

Viernes ¡CARNE PROPIA
NOCHE   FEB 15

GONZALO VEGA
OCTAVIO
EDITH GONZALEZ
NATALIA

MARIANA LEVY
DULCE OLIVIA
EDUARDO YANEZ
LEONARDO

⑬ JUEGOS Y JUGADORES. Comentarios, entrevistas y Trivia deportiva con la asistencia del público. Conductor: Raúl Orvañanos. Productor: Luis Manuei Jaramillo. Coordinador de producción: Juan Manuel Mendoza. Asistentes: Jaqueline Chavarin, Gerardo Martinez.

8:00 ❷ LA TELARAÑA. Teleteatro. Producción: Rafael Baledón, hijo. Dirección: Rafael Baledón, padre.
❹ MUCHAS NOTICIAS. Noticiario. Loliya Ayala.
❺ LAS TORTUGAS NINJA. Dibujos animados.
❾ ABIGAIL. Telenovela venezolana. Original de Inés Rodena y María Luján. Adaptación: Ana Mercedes Escamez. Ca-

herine Fullop (Abigail Guzmán); Fernando Carrillo (Carlos Alfredo Ruiz); Hilda Abrahams (Maria Clara Martinez). **Capitulo 65.**
⑪ ENLACE. Noticiario. Mayté Noriega, Maria Elena Meneses.
⑬ MIKE Y ANGELO. Melodrama.
8:30 ❺ DIMENSION DESCONOCIDA.
⑪ HOY EN LA CULTURA. Noticiario Cultural. Conductores: Rubén González Luengas, Lourdes Christlieb. Productor: Victor Manuel González Morales. Realizacion: Fabian Hernández.
⑬ CASOS Y COSAS DEL DEPORTE. Escenas cnuscas en diversos escenarios.
9:00 ❷ AMOR DE NADIE. Telenovela. Original de Eric Vonn. Producción: Carla

Estrada. Dirección de escena: Miguel Córcega. Dirección de cámaras: Alejandro Frutos.

1.—LUCIA MENDEZ ....**Sofía**
2.—FERNANDO SAENZ.......**Edmundo**
3.—GERMAN ROBLES ....**Belarmino**
4.—MONICA MIGUEL ....**Socorro**
5.—BARBARA CORCEGA ....**Emma**
6.—ROSARIO ZUÑIGA.........**Marcelina**
7.—MIGUEL PIZARRO................**Pablo**
8.—ISMAEL LARUMBE.............**Román**
9.—IRMA LOZANO ....**Bety**
10.—PATRICIA MARTINEZ.......**Zenaida**

Capítulo 114.—Amelia acepta ver a Rafael en una cafetería y él le dice que en esos treinta años no ha podido olvidar la pasión que una vez sintiera por ella. Sofía se resiste a dejar España sin haber encontrado a su hijo. Emma cuenta todo lo que le pasó en su pueblo a Perla y a Elena. Luis sugiere a Sofía que contraten un investigador. Ella alega que no tiene suficiente dinero. Maggi sugiere pedir ayuda económica a Raúl pero Sofía se niega. Ofelia ante la idea de deshacerse de Vera acepta respaldarla ante Renato. Nancy llega con el niño con Raúl y éste sonríe satisfecho. Nancy le pregunta cuándo van a casarse y al ver que él la elude le advierte que no se va a burlar de ella. Venciendo su rechazo, Sofía telefonea a Raúl pidiendo su ayuda pero él le dice que no le importa lo que le pase a ella o al niño, que no lo moleste.

4 PELICULA.
La Gran Veta. (Aventuras). ★★★ Charlton Heston, Kim Basinger. Un par de gemelos, uno malo y uno bueno, se dan el quien vive en busca del precioso metal y descubren una gran veta que los pone muy nerviosos.

5 PELICULA.
La Mosca. (Horror). ★★★ Jeff Goldblum, Genna Davies. Sin quererlo, un científico se teletransporta en una extraña máquina con una mosca polizón, y luego se convierte genéticamente en el insecto.

9 PELICULA.
Ojos de Juventud. (Melodrama). ★★★ Joaquín Pardavel, Elsa Aguirre. Un anciano trata de proteger a una mujer, demasiado bella para ser buena, y se queda con un hijito de ella en sus brazos.

11 ESPECIALES DEL ONCE. Ediciones especiales de la producción diaria de Canal 11.

13 IMEVISION INFORMA. Noticiario. Raúl Rodríquez, Elizabeth Ojeda.

9:30 **2 EN CARNE PROPIA. Telenovela.**
Producción y dirección de escena: Carlos Téllez. Original y adaptación: Carlos Olmos. Dirección de cámaras: Carlos Sánchez Zúñiga.

1—GONZALO VEGA................**Octavio**
2—EDITH GONZALEZ ....**Natalia**
3—RAUL MERAZ..............**Don Alfonso**
4—ANGELICA ARAGON ....**Magdalena**
5—JUAN PELAEZ ....**Jerónimo**
6—NORMA LAZARENO ....**Gertrudis**

¡TELE-GUIAS! —TAQUILLA.—Una historia de fantasmas "Ghost"; otra de amor con una mujer bonita "Pretty Woman", y una tercera con tortugas de tamaño humano como protagonistas resultaron las cintas más taquilleras de Hollywood en 1990.—EFE.

PAGINA 74

Paso 1

1. ¿Cuántas películas hay en esta hoja? ¿Cuáles son de los EE. UU.?
2. ¿Cuántos programas de noticias hay? ¿A qué hora ponen estos programas?
3. ¿Cuántas telenovelas hay? Si ponen cinco episodios, o capítulos, cada semana, ¿por aproximadamente cuántas semanas han pasado «Amor de nadie» en la tele mexicana?
4. ¿Qué programas reconoces? ¿Cómo se llaman en inglés?

Paso 2. Which program(s) fit the following descriptions?

1. Es una producción venezolana.
2. Un hombre se convierte en insecto.
3. Presenta escenas de diversos deportes.
4. Un hombre viejo ayuda a una mujer hermosa.
5. Este programa incluye entrevistas.
6. Incluye la participación del público.

Paso 3. With all her traveling, Elena had not kept up with her favorite soap opera, "Amor de nadie." Use the *Tele·Guía* to bring her up to date.

1. Amelia...
2. Rafael...
3. Sofía...
4. Emma...
5. Luis...
6. Maggi...
7. Ofelia...
8. Nancy...

a. acepta respaldar a Vera
b. se encuentra con Rafael en una cafetería
c. cuenta todo lo que le pasó en su pueblo
d. le dice a Amelia que no puede olvidarla
e. le pregunta a Raúl cuándo van a casarse
f. no quiere dejar España sin encontrar a su hijo
g. le recomienda a Sofía que contraten un investigador
h. le sugiere a Sofía que le pida ayuda económica a Raúl
i. sonríe satisfecho

Diferencias en la programación

NEW VOCABULARY: la falta, la programación, la variedad

Write a short paragraph in which you compare the programming for this time period with that you would find in your own country. Then express your opinion about the schedule given.

EJEMPLO: Hay más... durante este período en México que en los EE. UU. En los EE. UU., los viernes por la noche, normalmente hay... ; en México no. Me gusta la variedad. No me gusta la falta de...

En el quiosco

NEW VOCABULARY: conseguir; el noticiero, el quiosco; unas cuantas

David y Elena se encuentran enfrente de un quiosco, donde tratan de decidir qué comprar para su viaje mañana a los EE. UU.

DAVID: ¿Quieres comprar algunas revistas para leer en el avión?
ELENA: No, ayer compré los números más recientes de *Vanidades* y de *Buenhogar*. Tu mamá recibe *Buenhogar* en casa, ¿no?
DAVID: Sí. Dice que lo que más le gusta son las recetas de cocina. Y ahora es mucho más fácil conseguir los ingredientes para preparar platos hispanos en los EE. UU.
ELENA: Mira, David. En *El Universal* anuncian en primera plana[1] otro acuerdo económico entre México y los EE. UU.
DAVID: Sí, ya lo sé. Comentaron ese acuerdo anoche en el noticiero... ¿Sabes?, voy a comprarme unos periódicos para llevárselos a la profesora Martínez y también para ver si me documento[2] mejor sobre lo que está pasando en el mundo.
ELENA: Buena idea. Y yo me compro unas cuantas revistas para jóvenes para llevárselas a Sandra.

[1]primera... *first page* [2]me... *bring myself up to date*

Match the phrases on the right with the statements on the left.

1. David pregunta si Elena quiere comprar...
2. Ayer Elena compró...
3. A la mamá de David le gustan más...
4. Ahora en los EE. UU. es más fácil conseguir...
5. En *El Universal* anuncian en primer plano...
6. Elena decide comprar...

a. unas cuantas revistas para jóvenes
b. unos periódicos para llevárselos a la profesora Martínez
c. otro acuerdo económico entre México y los EE. UU.
d. los números más recientes de *Vanidades* y de *Buenhogar*
e. las recetas de cocina en *Buenhogar*
f. revistas para leer en el avión
g. los ingredientes para preparar algunos platos hispanos

OPTIONAL: Ask students which of the characters mentioned in the dialogue would most likely read each of the following publications: *Buenhogar,* **el periódico, la revista para jóvenes,** *El Universal, Vanidades.*

Using the model, discuss with a classmate two things it is easier to get nowadays.

EJEMPLO: E1: Es mucho más fácil ahora conseguir programas para la computadora.
E2: Sí, estoy de acuerdo. También es más fácil obtener películas extranjeras.
E1: Sí, tienes razón.

OPTIONAL: Ask students to give the name of a magazine or newspaper that they read and to tell what they like most about it. They should use David's second line as a model: **Lo que más me gusta de** *Newsweek* **son las noticias internacionales.**

En la universidad

PREPARATION: Ask students to describe the drawing. Ask them to focus on the dialogue introduction. **¿Dónde están los jóvenes? ¿Qué hacen? ¿De qué hablan?** Have students pick out the words in the conversation that suggest some kind of disaster or calamity.

NEW VOCABULARY: calcular; el canal, el desastre, los informes

Los amigos están mirando con interés las noticias que presentan en el canal de lengua española.

JOAQUÍN: ¿Qué están haciendo, amigos?

JORGE: Sabías que hubo un terremoto fuerte esta mañana, ¿no? Pues, en el canal en español que hay en el sistema de tele por cable, están pasando cada quince minutos informes especiales sobre el terremoto. ¡Es terrible! Hay tanta destrucción que todavía no han podido mandar reporteros y cámaras al sitio del desastre.

JOAQUÍN: ¡Qué horror!

MARISOL: Dijeron que se calculaba el número de muertos en más de doscientas personas pero que no se podía saber el número de heridos.[1]

---
[1] *injured*

NEW VOCABULARY: me pregunto, suceder; la fuerza

JOAQUÍN: ¿Han oído si el área afectada llega hasta la costa... o si se centra en las montañas como suele suceder?

ALFONSINA: No sé, pero temen que vaya a haber otros temblores casi tan fuertes como el primero.

JOAQUÍN: Yo recuerdo haber visto[2] fotos en el periódico de los efectos de algunos de los terremotos que sufrieron en esa zona antes... Es increíble la fuerza destructiva de la naturaleza. Me pregunto cómo la gente puede seguir viviendo allí cuando los terremotos son tan frecuentes.

JORGE: Escuchen. Interrumpen el programa con otro informe especial...

LA VOZ DEL LOCUTOR: ...y esta tragedia ha atraído la atención del mundo entero. Hace sólo quince minutos el senado[3] aprobó,[4] a pedido del Presidente, la institución[5] de un fondo especial de tres millones de dólares para ayudar a los damnificados[6] por el terremoto. La Cruz[7] Roja está solicitando contribuciones especiales. Al final de este programa les daremos la dirección que la Cruz Roja ha indicado para enviar estas contribuciones. Y, ahora... acaban de informarnos que nuestro reportero ha llegado a San Cristóbal y que está listo para darnos la primera versión de lo que ha sucedido. Todavía no podemos enviarles una transmisión visual; sólo nos llega la voz de Juan Felipe Aranda...

JORGE: Joaquín, tengo que ir a clase. Mira qué es lo que pasa. Hablamos después.

JOAQUÍN: Está bien. Hasta luego.

[2]haber... *having seen*   [3]*Senate*   [4]*approved*   [5]*establishment*   [6]los... *those affected, injured*   [7]*Cross*

De inmediato

OPTIONAL: 1. ¿Qué miran los amigos? 2. ¿Con qué frecuencia pasan informes especiales sobre el desastre? 3. ¿Por qué no se puede mandar reporteros y cámaras al sitio del terremoto? 4. ¿Qué número de muertos se calcula? 5. ¿Son frecuentes o infrecuentes los terremotos en esa zona? 6. ¿Qué solicita la Cruz Roja? 7. ¿Cómo se llama la ciudad donde ocurrió el terremoto?

Are the following statements true or false according to the dialogue? Respond **Es cierto** if the statement is true or **No es cierto** if it is false. Correct the false statements.

1. Los amigos están escuchando las noticias del terremoto.
2. Están pasando informes especiales cada media hora.
3. En el periódico dijeron que había más de doscientos muertos.
4. Temen que vaya a haber otros temblores fuertes.
5. Joaquín se pregunta cómo la gente puede vivir en una zona donde no hay terremotos.
6. La Cruz Roja aprobó la institución de un fondo especial de tres millones de dólares para ayudar a los damnificados.
7. El nombre del pueblo donde sucedió el terremoto es San Juan.
8. Cuando pasan el primer informe desde el sitio del terremoto, no pueden poner transmisión visual.

PREPARATION: (A ti te toca) Review regular and irregular preterites. Ask which words in the dialogue express people's emotions about disasters.

A ti te toca

Tell a classmate about two disasters you remember having seen photos of in the newspapers or on television in the last few years.

accidente de aviación	inundación
choque de coche(s)/tren(es)	terremoto
erupción de un volcán	tormenta
huracán	tornado
incendio	

EJEMPLO: Yo recuerdo haber visto fotos en la televisión (el periódico) de una inundación terrible que ocurrió en Iowa, Illinois y Missouri. Muchas personas perdieron su casa por las aguas. También recuerdo haber visto los incendios en el parque nacional Yellowstone. ¡Qué cosa!

PREPARATION: Ask students to describe the photo.

La leyenda de los volcanes de Puebla

Many indigenous peoples have legends to explain aspects of nature. Such is the case with Mexico's snow-capped volcanoes in the state of Puebla: Popocatépetl (elevation 5,450 meters or 17,887 feet) and Ixtaccíhuatl (elevation 5,287 meters or 17,343 feet). In the indigenous language **náhuatl,** the names **Popocatépetl** and **Ixtaccíhuatl** mean, respectively, *Smoking Mountain* and *Sleeping Woman*. According to legend, Popo (as his friends called him) was a warrior in love with Ixtaccíhuatl, daughter of the emperor. Popo marched off to war, and during his absence, Ixtaccíhuatl mistakenly heard that Popo had died. The princess died of heartbreak and grief. When Popo learned of the death of his beloved, he built the two mountains. He placed her body in the northern mountain, while he remained in the mountain to the south, keeping vigil beside her with a torch. Some **poblanos,** or *residents of the state of Puebla*, insist even today that the pale corpse of Ixtaccíhuatl can still be seen stretched out on the snow-covered crest of the volcanic mountain.

Faceta cultural

El Popocatépetl es la segunda montaña más alta de México. Los habitantes de Puebla tienen esta magnífica vista.

La informática

la computadora

la pantalla

la impresora

el disco

el disco duro

el ratón, el *mouse*

las teclas

el teclado

Otro vocabulario

autocopiar	*to make a copy*
guardar ficheros	*to save files*
imprimir	*to print*
introducir datos	*to input data*
perder ficheros	*to lose files, crash*
la aplicación	*application (software)*
el fichero	*file*
el lector de discos	*disk drive*
la programación	*programming*

PREPARATION: Make sure students know the English names of all the components shown. **¿Cuántos de Uds. tienen computadora? ¿Quiénes usan las computadoras de la universidad pero no tienen su propia computadora?**
COMPREHENSION: Use a series of sequential statements about the operation of computers to check students' comprehension. Ask them to respond **Es lógico** or **No es lógico**. Example: **Primero pierdo los ficheros y después introduzco datos. → No es lógico.**

Actividades

VARIATION: Reverse this activity. Give the name of the object and ask students to choose the most logical definition.

Ⓐ **Definiciones.** Provide the computer-related term for the following definitions. There may be more than one possible answer for each.

1. Usamos esto para introducir datos.
2. Usamos esto para guardar ficheros.
3. Usamos esto para imprimir un documento electrónico.
4. Vemos el documento electrónico aquí.
5. Es la ciencia de trabajar con computadoras.
6. Hacemos esta acción en caso de que haya una pérdida de ficheros.
7. Este componente de un sistema personal de computadoras tiene una capacidad de memoria muy grande.

PREPARATION: Review vocabulary related to courses and fields of study available to students at your institution.

Ⓑ **Necesidades.** Students with different academic specialties need different kinds of technical support to help them in their studies. With a classmate, choose six of the following academic areas to discuss.

Paso 1. Tell your partner what two pieces of equipment a student would need to succeed in each area in school (one item can be for relaxation). Your partner will take notes on what you say.

EJEMPLO: música → Una persona que estudia música necesita un estéreo y una grabadora.

1. biología
2. teatro
3. ciencias sociales
4. matemáticas
5. inglés
6. ingeniería
7. farmacia
8. química
9. lenguas extranjeras
10. psicología

Paso 2. Now ask your classmate the following questions about the equipment he or she has mentioned.

1. ¿Para qué necesita un estudiante de (**especialización**) un(a) (**aparato**)?
2. ¿Cuál de las dos cosas que mencionaste para un estudiante de (**especialización**) es más importante?

Preguntas

1. ¿Usas una computadora para hacer tu tarea de español? ¿Por qué sí o por qué no?
2. ¿Es posible introducir letras y signos[1] del español con esa computadora o tienes que escribirlos a mano?
3. ¿De qué marca es la computadora personal ideal?
4. En tu opinión, qué componentes tiene un sistema ideal de computadora personal? ¿Conoces a alguien que tenga tal sistema?
5. ¿Te interesa la programación de computadoras? ¿Por qué sí o por qué no?
6. ¿Cuál es una de las ventajas de usar computadoras? ¿Cuál es una de las desventajas?

[1] *symbols*

NEW VOCABULARY: los anuncios

Los anuncios para los hispanos en los EE. UU.

Faceta cultural

As the Hispanic presence in the United States continues to grow, more and more advertising agencies are attempting to appeal to this particular segment of the buying public, which is being recognized as an important cultural force. There is some controversy, however, regarding which language to use in appealing to the Hispanic market.

Many who advocate the use of English believe that the use of Spanish would be demeaning and would imply that Americans of Hispanic heritage are not fully integrated into the mainstream culture. Those who believe that Spanish should be used to appeal to the Hispanic market disagree. They point to the fact that Hispanics in the U.S. are extremely proud of their heritage. Even fully assimilated bilingual-bicultural individuals of Hispanic background retain many traditional customs and often speak Spanish at home or with friends. The advocates of Spanish as the language of choice in advertisements for the Hispanic public regard this usage as a recognition of the pride that Hispanics have in their identity.

EN ACCIÓN

PARA HABLAR

Lujos[1]

Paso 1. Imagine that you know a student who owns the most up-to-date technology available. What items does he or she use on a typical day? Using this student's daily schedule, suggest ways in which he or she might use electrical or electronic equipment during these activities.

EJEMPLO: A las seis y media de la mañana corre y usa su grabadora de cassette *Walkman.*

6:00	Corre.
7:00	Prepara el desayuno.
9:00	Busca un libro en la biblioteca.
11:00	Prepara la tarea de cálculo.
3:00	Se relaja en su apartamento.
5:00	Llama a su novia.
8:00	Escribe una composición.
10:00	Se divierte.

[1] *Luxuries*

338

Paso 2. Now tell a classmate what modern equipment you use during five of your own daily activities. Your partner will take notes and report to the class.

EJEMPLO: A las ocho de la mañana me despierto. Uso los auriculares y el estéreo.

Un pedido del profesor Ramos

Professor Ramos has asked Tomás to do a favor for him. Tomás knows he will have some trouble completing the task, so he turns to his friends for some assistance.

Antes de escuchar

Are you familiar with the literature of your country? What authors or poets from your country have you read extensively? What literary genre are you most familiar with: novels, essays, short stories, or poetry? If you were asked to record a work of literature from your country, what piece would you choose?

In the conversation you will hear, the speakers discuss their favorite works of literature. Before you listen, review various ways to express likes and dislikes: auxiliary verbs + infinitives (**Capítulo 5**), **gustar** and similar verbs (**Capítulo 6**), and verbs that express emotion (**Capítulo 9**). Next, scan the statements that follow to get an idea of what to listen for. Now listen to the conversation and do the following activity.

Después de escuchar

Match the phrases on the right with those on the left to make complete and correct statements.

1. Tomás necesita la ayuda de Celia y Jorge porque el profesor Ramos le pidió...
2. El problema de Tomás es que no sabe...
3. A Celia le encanta...
4. Celia dice que los novelistas españoles son...
5. Uno de los poetas favoritos de Celia es...
6. Tomás dice que Celia no parece ser...
7. Jorge dice que sería difícil grabar una novela porque es...
8. Los poemas que Jorge va a grabar fueron escritos...
9. Celia dice que los cuentos argentinos son...
10. Tomás va a grabar...

a. un microcuento de Enrique Anderson Imbert.
b. muy extensa.
c. Gustavo Adolfo Bécquer.
d. la literatura.
e. una mujer romántica.
f. nada de literatura.
g. grabar selecciones para su clase.
h. por Jesús Maldonado.
i. excelentes.
j. famosos.

PREPARATION: Familiarize students with the glossed vocabulary by providing the English equivalents and having them find the Spanish words and phrases in the text. Encourage students to read the text in Spanish rather than translating the text into English.

Un microcuento argentino

Tomás plans to record the following short story for Professor Ramos. Read the story and do the activity that follows.

Sala de espera

ENRIQUE ANDERSON IMBERT (ARGENTINA, 1910–)

Costa y Wright roban una casa. Costa asesina a Wright y se queda con[1] la valija[2] llena de joyas y dinero. Va a la estación para escaparse en el primer tren. En la sala de espera, una señora se sienta a su izquierda y le da conversación. Fastidiado,[3] Costa finge con un bostezo[4] que tiene sueño y que va a dormir, pero oye que la señora continúa conversando. Abre entonces los ojos y ve, sentado a la derecha, el fantasma[5] de Wright. La señora atraviesa[6] a Costa de lado a lado con la mirada[7] y charla con el fantasma, quien contesta con simpatía.[8] Cuando llega el tren, Costa trata de levantarse, pero no puede. Está paralizado, mudo y observa atónito[9] cómo el fantasma toma tranquilamente la valija y camina con la señora hacia el andén,[10] ahora hablando y riéndose.[11] Suben, y el tren parte. Costa los sigue con los ojos. Viene un hombre y comienza a limpiar la sala de espera, que ahora está completamente desierta. Pasa la aspiradora por el asiento donde está Costa, invisible.

El gato de Chesire (1965)

[1]*se... keeps* [2]*valise* [3]*annoyed* [4]*yawn* [5]*ghost* [6]*looks straight through with her look* [7]*de... from one side to the other* [8]*friendliness* [9]*astonished* [10]*platform* [11]*laughing*

NEW VOCABULARY: deja de + *inf.,* mata, reconoce
SUGGESTION: This works well as a pair activity. The student receiving the clues should have his or her book closed.
OPTIONAL: Have students write additional true/false statements to read to the class.

Después de leer

¿Es cierto o no es cierto?

1. Costa roba a Wright.
2. Costa mata a Wright.
3. Costa piensa escaparse por tren.
4. En la estación una señora se sienta a la derecha de Costa.
5. La señora deja de hablar cuando Costa finge dormir.
6. El fantasma de Wright habla con la señora.
7. Cuando llega el tren, Costa toma la valija y sube.
8. El hombre que limpia la sala de espera reconoce a Costa.

SUGGESTION: Ask students to analyze the meaning of the story. How could Wright come to the train station if he is dead? What is the function of the woman in the story? Could the story be interpreted in more than one way?

Dos poemas románticos

Celia is going to record three very brief poems by nineteenth-century Spanish poet Gustavo Adolfo Bécquer for Professor Ramos's students. Before you listen, study the words in the following vocabulary list to better understand the poems.

PREPARATION: (Para escuchar) Have students quiz each other on the **Vocabulario útil.** Have them read the statements that follow so that they will know the kinds of things to listen for. Make sure they know how to say the key vocabulary words in each item.

NEW VOCABULARY: grabar; los cuentos; chistoso

clavar	*to nail; to affix*	diera	*I would give*
la mirada	*look, glance*	los suspiros	*sighs*
la sonrisa	*smile*	las lágrimas	*tears*
el cielo	*sky; heaven*		

Now listen to the poems and do the activity that follows.

Después de escuchar

To which poem does the statement refer? Indicate whether the information is expressed in the first poem (**Rima A**), the second (**Rima B**), or the third (**Rima C**).

1. The poet says that he doesn't know what he would give for a kiss from his beloved.
2. The poet's loved one has blue eyes.
3. The poet asks his beloved where love goes when it is forgotten.
4. The poet's loved one asks him to define poetry.
5. The poet says that he would give the heavens for a smile from his beloved.
6. The poet says that sighs are air.
7. The poet tells his loved one that she is poetry.
8. The poet says that tears are water and end up in the sea.
9. The poet says that he would give a world for a glance from his beloved.

Nueve Treinta
Noticiero Cultural
En Canal 22 la cultura siempre es noticia

nueve:
30

canal 22

Con Myriam Moscona y José Gordon

Dirección de noticias: Guadalupe Alonso
Jefe de información: Bruce Swansey

De lunes a viernes a las 21:30 hrs.

Un viaje a México

Imagine that you were lucky enough to accompany David and Elena on their trip through Mexico. During your last week there, you decide to write a letter to your Spanish class telling them all about your trip. In your letter of ten to twelve sentences, indicate where you went, what you saw, whom you met, and what you liked or didn't like about the trip.

PARA ESCRIBIR

EPISODIOS

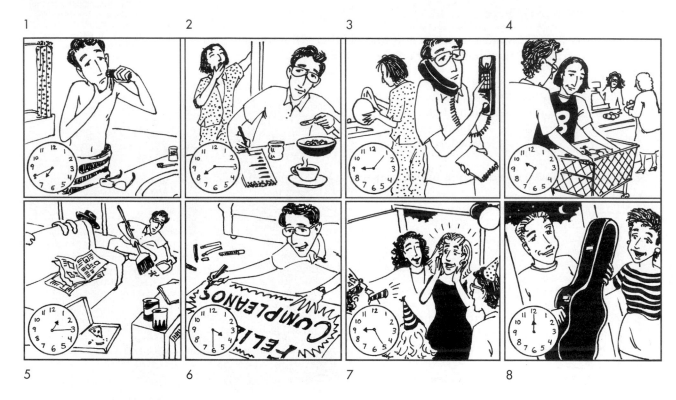

5 6 7 8

Paso 1

PREPARATION: For each scene, have students suggest key vocabulary in Spanish that would help them identify it.

Write the number of the scene that illustrates each statement you hear.

Paso 2

EXAMPLES: 1. Jorge toma huevos con tocino para el desayuno. (No, no es cierto.) 2. Jorge se levantó antes de Joaquín. (Es cierto.)

Write six statements about the **Episodios** scenes, three of which are true, and three of which are false. Then read your statements to a classmate, who will respond with either **Sí, es cierto** or **No, no es cierto**. Then switch roles and listen to your partner's sentences, responding appropriately.

EXPANSION: Have students correct any false statements.

Paso 3

SUGGESTION: Have students work in pairs to read each other's corrected paragraphs, discuss similarities, and resolve discrepancies.

Rewrite the following paragraph so that it accurately reflects what you see in the scenes.

Joaquín se levantó temprano, se duchó y se afeitó mientras Jorge dormía hasta tarde. Se preparó huevos con tocino y pan tostado con mermelada para el desayuno, y escribió una lista de cosas que comprar. Los amigos fueron al supermercado antes de llamar a los invitados. Jorge y Joaquín no necesitaban limpiar la casa porque todo estaba ordenado. Jorge hizo una tarjeta pequeña que anunciaba el aniversario del profesor. No se divirtió haciendo la carta. Jorge y Joaquín dieron una fiesta en honor del Profesor Brewer, que celebraba su aniversario de bodas. El profesor llegó a la fiesta a las diez menos veinticinco. Sabía de la fiesta así que no fue una sorpresa. Ninguno de los miembros del Club Hispánico vino a la fiesta. Alfonsina trajo su guitarra. Todos se aburrieron y se fueron temprano.

Paso 4

VARIATION: Have students describe what Jorge and Joaquín *did* (preterite), *were doing* (imperfect), or *were going to do* (**ir a** + *inf.*) in each of the scenes.

In small groups, describe what Jorge or Joaquín is doing in each of the scenes. Each student should formulate at least two statements about each scene without repeating information given by other students.

Paso 5

PREPARATION: Ask students which form of address (**tú** or **Ud.**) would be appropriate in this situation.

Imagine that you overheard Jorge and Joaquín in the kitchen outlining the day's activities. Write out the conversation, in which each character has at least five lines.

SUGGESTION: Have students prepare, rehearse, and present their dialogues to the class.

Paso 6

Write five sentences that describe the scenes. Then write five sentences that describe what is *not* happening. Begin each sentence with a phrase from the following list.

> (No) Es cierto/claro/evidente/seguro/verdad que...
> (No) Es bueno/importante/(im)posible/(im)probable/lástima/ malo/necesario/triste que...

EJEMPLOS: Es evidente que Marisol no sabe que la fiesta es en su honor.
No es verdad que Jorge mire el fútbol.

PREPARATION: Ask whether subjunctive or indicative will be required after sentences that begin with **es cierto, es posible, es claro; es lástima, es evidente, es necesario.** Review the formation of the present subjunctive.

Paso 7

First, write five questions that can be answered by looking at the scenes. Each question must begin with a different interrogative word (**¿cómo?, ¿dónde?, ¿quién?,** and so on). Then ask a classmate to answer your questions.

PREPARATION: Review question words and word order in question formation. You may wish to write them on the board.

EJEMPLOS: —¿A qué hora se levantó Joaquín?
—Se levantó a las ocho y cuarto de la mañana.

—¿Quién entró en la cocina mientras desayunaba Jorge?
—Joaquín entró en la cocina.

ACTIVIDAD COMPRENSIVA

SUGGESTION: Have students make lists of words that fit several categories present in the drawing (i.e., stores / shops / public places in town; means of transportation; foods and table settings; professions; family relationships).

Working with a classmate, describe the following drawing in detail.

NOTE: The purpose of the drawing is to review vocabulary from previous chapters.

VOCABULARIO

Los verbos	Verbs		
		grabar	to record
apagar	to turn off	imprimir	to print
autocopiar	to make a copy	matar	to kill
	(*of a program, a*	preguntarse	to wonder
	software application)	reconocer (reconozco)	to recognize
calcular	to estimate, calculate	suceder	to happen, occur
conseguir (i) (consigo)	to get, obtain	sugerir (ie)	to suggest

344

La tecnología / *Technology*

el altavoz (*pl.* altavoces)	loudspeaker
los auriculares	headphones
la cámara de vídeo	video camera
la computadora	computer
la computadora portátil	portable computer
el disco	satellite dish
la grabadora	tape recorder
la maquina de escribir	typewriter
el radio	radio (set)
la radio	radio (*the medium*)
el radiocassette portátil	portable radio-cassette player, boom box
el teléfono celular	cellular phone
la televisión por cable	cable TV
la televisión por satélite	satellite TV
el tocador de discos compactos	compact disc (CD) player
el tocador de discos láser	laser disc player
la videocasetera	video cassette recorder, VCR

Palabras semejantes: la calculadora, el estéreo, el micrófono.

La informática / *Computer science*

la aplicación	application (*software*)
el disco	disk
el disco duro	hard drive
el fichero	file
la impresora	printer
el lector de discos	disk drive
la pantalla (R)	screen
la programación	programming
el ratón, *mouse*	mouse
la tecla	key (*on keyboard*)
el teclado	keyboard

Otros sustantivos / *Other nouns*

el amor	love
la antropología	anthropology
el anuncio	announcement; advertisement; advertising

el artículo	article
el canal	channel
las comunicaciones	(mass) communication(s)
el cuento	story; short story
la cultura	culture
el desastre	disaster
la especialización	(academic) major; specialization
la falta	lack
la fuerza	force, strength
el informe	report, paper
el noticiero	newscast
el número	issue (*of a magazine*); number
el programa	program
el quiosco	kiosk, stand
la telenovela	soap opera
la variedad	variety
el volumen	volume

Los adjetivos / *Adjectives*

chistoso/a	funny, comical; witty
extraño/a	strange, odd
indígena	indigenous, native
precolombino/a	pre-Columbian

Palabras y expresiones útiles / *Useful words and expressions*

actualmente	currently, nowadays
darse cuenta (de)	to realize
dejar de + *inf.*	to stop (*doing something*)
de nuevo	again
guardar ficheros	to save files
introducir (introduzco) datos	to input data
perder (ie) ficheros	to lose files, crash
seguir (i) (sigo) + *present progressive*	to continue (*doing something*)
unos cuantos / unas cuantas	a few
valer la pena	to be worth (it)

Otros Mundos

NOTE: See the *Instructor's Manual* for suggestions on teaching **Otros mundos.**

El Brasil

Bom día. (Así se dice **buenos días** en portugués.) Soy João Alvares Cabral y voy a hablar en español y no en portugués, la lengua de mi país, Brasil. El español no es mi idioma natal. Tuve que aprenderlo en la universidad, como Uds.

No vivo ni en Río de Janeiro ni en São Paulo, las ciudades más grandes y famosas de mi país. Vivo en la capital, Brasilia, con mi mamá, que ocupa un puesto en el gobierno.

Hay muchas partes de mi país que nunca he visitado porque es tan grande. Después de graduarme en la universidad, voy a hacer un viaje a la cuenca del Amazonas. Hay allí densas selvas con toda clase de animales, pájaros y plantas silvestres. También voy a visitar las playas de Río de Janeiro, especialmente la de Copacabana, una de las más hermosas del mundo.

¿Por qué hablamos portugués en el Brasil? Pues, porque en 1493, el Papa Alejandro VI dividió el Nuevo Mundo entre España y Portugal para evitar disputas entre las dos naciones. Esto permitió que Portugal tuviera el derecho de establecer colonias en el Nuevo Mundo. Entonces aquí estamos nosotros los brasileños, los únicos que hablamos portugués, entre todos los países latinoamericanos.

¿Sabías que... ?

- El Brasil es el país más grande de la América del Sur en extensión y población.
- En 1960 inauguraron la nueva capital Brasilia en un lugar en donde antes sólo había selva.
- São Paulo es la ciudad más populosa y la más importante del país industrial y económicamente. También es una de las ciudades más populosas de todo el mundo.
- El río Amazonas es el río más voluminoso del mundo—extiende unas 4.000 millas y en

El famoso Carnaval brasileño se celebra antes de empezar la Cuaresma.

lugares tiene más de 6 millas de ancho. Con sus tributarios forma una red de ríos navegables de más de 15.800 millas.

- La costa del Brasil extiende unas 4.603 millas.
- El Brasil produce más de la mitad de todo el café producido en el mundo y también es segundo en el mundo en la cantidad del cacao producido.
- El Brasil tiene las minas de hierro más grandes del mundo.
- El Brasil tiene una reputación internacional por la excelencia de su fútbol, baloncesto y voleibol.
- La celebración del Carnaval en Río de Janeiro es una de las más famosas del mundo. Tiene lugar los tres días y las cuatro noches antes del Miércoles de Ceniza.

El Brasil en breve

Capital:	Brasilia
Lenguas:	portugués (oficial) y tupí-guaraní (idiomas indígenas)
Gobierno:	república federativa
Moneda:	cruzeiro
Población:	158.000.000 habitantes
Tamaño:	3.286.470 millas cuadradas (el tamaño de los 48 estados contiguos de los EE. UU.)

Brasilia, la capital brasileña en el interior del país, fue inaugurada en 1960.

DOCE

México y los mexicanos

De viaje: De vuelta a los Estados Unidos

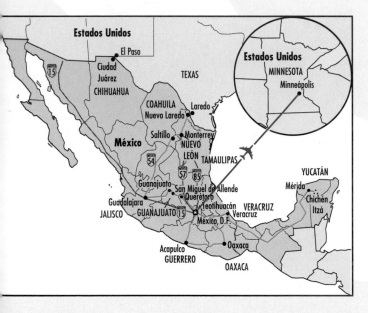

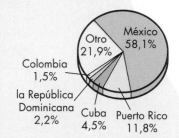

Hasta cierto punto ésta es la historia de todos los inmigrantes a los EE. UU. En tres generaciones, los miembros de una familia pasan de ser inmigrantes que no tienen conocimiento ni del idioma ni de las costumbres de su nuevo país, a ser ciudadanos que saben de sus raíces[1] sólo a través de los cuentos de sus abuelos. Quizás la asimilación sea un problema más significativo para el pueblo hispano porque, en contraste con otros pueblos inmigrantes, muchos hispanos se han mudado[2] a los EE. UU. con el propósito de eventualmente volver a su patria.[3] El pueblo hispano

[1]*roots*   [2]*se... have moved*   [3]*homeland*

Hay más de 22 millones de hispanos en los EE. UU. Más de la mitad viene de México y vive en Texas, Nuevo México y California. La mayor concentración de cubanos se encuentra en la Florida. Los puertorriqueños, los dominicanos y los colombianos que viven en los EE. UU. residen principalmente en los estados industrializados del nordeste.

Un problema de muchos hispanos en los EE. UU. puede ser la falta de asimilación y de interés en formar parte de la cultura mayoritaria. Hay muchas ciudades de los EE. UU. donde la población hispana es tan grande como para vivir y trabajar sin hablar ni una palabra de inglés. Pero la asimilación trae otro problema. Muchos hispanos en los EE. UU. han notado que sus hijos ya no hablan español y que no se identifican con el país de origen de sus padres.

¿QUIÉN SOY YO?

Cerca de la mitad de todos los que respondieron a la encuesta escogieron clasificaciones singulares de identidad propia.

De origen mexicano

Mexican-American	205
mexicano	186
Hispanic	116
Mexican	76
American	59
Spanish-American	46
Spanish	34
hispano	26
latino	24
chicano	14

De origen cubano

cubano	181
americano	43
hispano	14
Spanish-American	13
Hispanic	12
latino	8

De origen puertorriqueño

puertorriqueño	255
americano	33
Spanish-American	29
hispano	15
Hispanic	12
Neorican*	11

- Ninguno de los respondientes de origen cubano eligió llamarse **cubano-americano**.
- Muchos respondientes seleccionaron dos o más etiquetas de identificación propia como aceptables.
- Uno de cada cinco usa un término general, tal como **hispano**, **latino** o **estadounidense**.

*Neorican es el término que se usa para los puertorriqueños neoyorquinos.

en los EE. UU. también se distingue de los otros grupos de inmigrantes porque su llegada ha sido predominantemente un fenómeno del siglo XX, una época en la que mucha gente ha llegado a creer que la asimilación no es tan importante como el mantenimiento de la identidad cultural.

Los hispanos en los EE. UU. están entre dos culturas, la mayoritaria del país y la hispana. No importa cuál sea su decisión de asimilarse o no, sin duda serán objeto de la crítica de los miembros de una o ambas culturas.

Perspectivas de México: César Chávez (1927–1993)

César Chávez se dedicó a hacer reconocer[1] y defender la dignidad del trabajador agrícola y a luchar por los derechos[2] humanos, la justicia social y la no violencia. Tomó como símbolo de su lucha[3] al héroe de la Revolución mexicana, Emiliano Zapata, que también luchó[4] por los derechos de los que se ganaban la vida trabajando en el campo. Fue uno de los fundadores y dirigente de la *United Farm Workers of America.* En los años sesenta[5] logró[6] algo que se consideraba imposible hasta aquel momento: logró que los jornaleros,[7] muchos de ellos mexicanos y filipinos, que trabajaban en las fincas[8] de California, se declararan en huelga[9] para protestar las condiciones de su trabajo. Varias veces, para de-

mostrar la importancia vital de «La Causa», él mismo se declaró en huelga de hambre.

Como Presidente de la *United Farm Workers of America,* César Chávez firmó un acuerdo[10] junto con el Director del Instituto Mexicano del Seguro Social en una ceremonia presidida por el Presidente Salinas de Gortari. Con este acuerdo, el gobierno mexicano se comprometió[11] a proporcionar[12] servicios médicos completos a las familias que viven en México de los trabajadores mexicanos en los EE. UU. César Chávez también recibió el Águila Azteca, que es, según el periodico *La Paloma,* «la distinción más alta que otorga[13] México a los ciudadanos[14] de otras naciones que se han distinguido por sus destacadas[15] contribuciones al mejoramiento y difusión de los valores esenciales que, en todos los ámbitos,[16] promueve[17] el país de México».

[1]*known* [2]*rights* [3]*fight* [4]*fought* [5]*los... the sixties* [6]*he accomplished* [7]*day laborers* [8]*farms* [9]*strike* [10]*agreement* [11]*se... promised* [12]*provide* [13]*awards* [14]*citizens* [15]*outstanding* [16]*arenas, spheres* [17]*promotes*

César Chávez, líder sindicalista, luchó por los derechos de los trabajadores agrícolas.

Los hispanos en los EE. UU.

NOTE: See the *Instructor's Manual* for suggestions on using the chapter-opening pages.

(arriba) A lo largo de la costa de California se puede apreciar la influencia hispánica en la arquitectura de las iglesias. (a la derecha) La película norteamericana *Stand and Deliver* se basa en los logros de este maestro, Jaime Escalante. El papel principal fue interpretado por Edward James Olmos.

(arriba) Entre Santa Fe, Nuevo México, y el sur del estado de Colorado es evidente la mezcla de lo español y lo indígena, como en este edificio de Taos, Nuevo México. (a la derecha) El tejano Henry Cisneros es Secretario de Vivienda y Desarrollo Urbano en el gabinete del presidente Bill Clinton. (abajo, a la derecha) Muchos deportistas norteamericanos famosos, como la jugadora de tenis Mary Joe Fernández, son de ascendencia hispánica.

METAS

FUNCIONES

- to discuss themes related to the growing numbers of Hispanic residents in the United States

- to read about and discuss the three principal Hispanic groups in the United States—people of Mexican, Cuban, and Puerto Rican origin

- to examine and discuss issues related to the "English Only" movement in the United States

- to discuss in greater detail topics from previous chapters

GRAMÁTICA

- review and expansion of grammar learned in previous chapters

APPROPRIATE TESTING POINTS:
Diálogo (2), En acción, **Quiz 1**
Diálogo (1), En acción, **Quiz 2**
Episodios, Actividad comprensiva
Chapter test

En los EE. UU.

David y Elena llegan al aeropuerto de Mineápolis donde se encuentran con la familia de David.

DAVID: ...y saqué muchas fotos. Quiero que Uds. vean...

LA SRA. NELSON: Ya, David, ya.... Quiero que nos cuentes todo, pero primero, quiero saludar a mi sobrina. Elena m'ija,[1] ¿cómo estás? ¿Qué tal la familia en México?

ELENA: Bien, todos están muy bien. Me alegro mucho de verla, tía, a Ud. y a toda la familia. Estoy un poco cansada, claro, pero... ¡qué gusto[2] estar con Uds.!

LA SRA. NELSON: Gracias, Elena. Tu mamá y yo hemos hablado mucho de la posibilidad de esta visita... y ¡por fin!,[3] aquí estás.

ELENA: Sí, por fin llegó ese día. Y ahora soy yo la que va a sacar muchas fotos. Pero... ¿no debo hablar inglés? Sé que el tío Harvey y que mi prima Sandra hablan español, pero, ¿no sería[4] mejor que habláramos inglés?

EL SR. NELSON: Bueno, mi español no es perfecto, así que prefiero que hablemos español en casa para practicarlo. ¿Está bien? Tú vas a tener muchas oportunidades de practicar el inglés durante tu visita.

[1]*endearing term used with someone much younger (lit.* mi hija, *my child)*   [2]*qué... what a pleasure*   [3]*¡por... finally!*
[4]*no... wouldn't it be*

De inmediato

David and Elena's reunion with David's family is presented here in an abbreviated and random manner. Identify who says each line, and then put the lines in order.

_____ Bien, todos están muy bien.

_____ Elena, ¿cómo estás? ¿Qué tal la familia en México?

_____ Saqué muchas fotos.

_____ ¿No sería mejor que habláramos inglés?

_____ Quiero que nos cuentes todo.

_____ Mi español no es perfecto.

_____ Sí, por fin llegó ese día.

_____ Tu mamá y yo hemos hablado mucho de la posibilidad de esta visita... y ¡por fin!, aquí estás.

A ti te toca

What principal language is spoken in each of the following countries? Your partner will start by saying what country you are in. Then you will respond by mentioning what language it would be best to speak there.

EJEMPLO: —Estamos en España.
    —¿No sería mejor que habláramos español?

1. Alemania
2. el Brasil
3. China
4. Francia
5. Inglaterra
6. Italia
7. el Japón
8. Rusia
9. Holanda

En la universidad

Los miembros del Club Hispánico se reúnen en el jardín de la casa del profesor Brewer.

EL PROFESOR BREWER: Ayer vi a Sandra, la hermana de David. Me dijo que David y su prima llegaron el lunes. Necesitamos darles una fiesta de bienvenida.[1]

MARISOL: ¡Muy buena idea! ¿Y qué dice David? ¿Qué tal el viaje? ¿Fueron a Morelia, mi ciudad? ¿Visitaron a mis padres?

EL PROFESOR BREWER: No, creo que no. Es que en un viaje tan corto uno no tiene tiempo de ver todo lo que quisiera.[2]

TOMÁS: ¿La fiesta es el sábado?

LA PROFESORA MARTÍNEZ: Sí, es para darle la bienvenida a la prima de David.

LUIS: Va a estar aquí muy poco tiempo, ¿no?

EL PROFESOR RAMOS: Sí, unas pocas semanas. Pero quiere conocer a los amigos de David... sobre todo[3] a los del Club Hispánico.

CELIA: Podemos preparar una paella especial.

CARMEN: Elena es mexicana; quizás no le guste la paella.

JORGE: ¡Qué va![4] Los mexicanos son muy cosmopolitas. Seguro que le gusta a Elena probar la comida de otros países.

CELIA: Probablemente ya la ha probado.

JOAQUÍN: Tengo una idea. ¿Por qué no preparamos platos típicos de todos nuestros países?

MERCEDES: ¿Puedo ir yo a la fiesta de bienvenida también?

LUISA: Sí, m'ija. David me presentó a Elena ayer en el supermercado, y ella me dijo que le interesaba saber algo de las experiencias de los hispanohablantes aquí en los EE. UU.

MARÍA: Entonces, le va a interesar conocer a Mercedes. Sus abuelos son cubanos y, aunque ella nació aquí, habla español y conserva[5] muchas costumbres de sus antepasados.[6]

[1]*welcome* [2]*would like* [3]*sobre... above all, especially* [4]*¡Qué... No way!* [5]*she retains, keeps* [6]*ancestors*

De inmediato

Are the following statements true or false based on the dialogues? Respond **Es cierto** if the statement is true or **No es cierto** if it is false. Correct the false statements.

1. El profesor Brewer vio a la hermana de David recientemente.
2. Sandra dijo que David y Elena llegaron el domingo.

3. David fue a Morelia y vio a la familia de Marisol.
4. La fiesta para darle la bienvenida a Elena es el viernes.
5. Elena va a estar en los EE. UU. durante varios meses.
6. Celia piensa preparar arroz con pollo.
7. Según Jorge, los mexicanos no son cosmopolitas.
8. Joaquín sugiere que todos preparen platos típicos de México.
9. A Elena le interesan las experiencias de los hispanohablantes en los EE. UU.
10. Los abuelos de Mercedes son mexicanos.

A ti te toca

Practice the following exchanges with a partner. Be ready to report to the class what you discover.

1. E1: ¿Qué te interesa saber que ya no sabes?
   E2: Me interesa saber (algo de) _____.
2. E1: ¿Con quién hablaste ayer?   E1: ¿Qué te dijo?
   E2: Ayer hablé con _____.   E2: Me dijo que _____.

REPORTAJE
1. _____ me dijo que le interesaba saber más sobre _____.
2. _____ me dijo que _____ le dijo ayer que _____.

EN ACCIÓN

En Oaxaca

David finally gets the chance to talk about the trip when Elena, David, and David's family arrive at the Nelson home. Listen to him as he gives details about the visit to Oaxaca.

Antes de escuchar

Now that you know David will be talking about the trip to Oaxaca, you may wish to refresh your memory of what David and Elena did by re-reading the last dialogue in **Capítulo 7** and the dialogues set in Mexico in **Capítulo 8**. Because David will be discussing events that happened in the past, review the forms and uses of the preterite and the imperfect in **Capítulos 5, 6,** and **7**. Next, skim the statements in **Después de escuchar** to get the gist of what you will be listening to.

Now, listen to David talk about the visit to Oaxaca and do the activity that follows.

Después de escuchar

Reorder the following statements so that they accurately summarize what David told his family.

_____ Alfredo invitó a Elena y David a almorzar.

_____ Alfredo les habló de Oaxaca y sus alrededores.

_____ Elena y David fueron con Concha y Alicia de Acapulco a Oaxaca.

_____ Todos comieron enchiladas de pollo y la ensalada especial de la casa.

_____ Elena y David se dieron cuenta de que tenían poco dinero en efectivo.

_____ Elena y David pasaron unos días en la casa de Alfredo y él les mostró varios lugares de interés en la ciudad.

_____ Elena y David llegaron a Oaxaca muy tarde y se hospedaron en un hotel que conocían Concha y Alicia.

_____ En el restaurante se sentaron en un patio muy lindo.

OPTIONAL: 1. ¿Quiénes son Concha y Alicia? 2. ¿Dónde se situaba el hotel que recomendaron Concha y Alicia? 3. Al llegar al hotel, ¿qué hicieron David y Elena? 4. ¿Qué hicieron los primos la mañana siguiente antes de llamar a Alfredo? ¿Por qué? 5. ¿Dónde encontraron David y Elena a Alfredo? 6. ¿Qué almorzaron? 7. ¿Qué hicieron los tres durante la visita a Oaxaca?

¡Buen provecho![1]

In the following poems, the poet celebrates the goodness of these simple, but tasty and healthful, staples of Mexican cuisine while pointing out their role in the daily struggle of the poor against hunger.

Antes de leer

Before reading these poems, what foods other than rice do you think are staples in the diet of the Mexican poor? What nutritional advantages do the foods have? What other advantages can you think of (for example, price and taste)? A quality that a poor person might look for in a food is that **la comida mata hambre**. What do you think this means?

You have learned that **abuelita** is an endearing, or affectionate, way of saying **abuela**. In Spanish, the diminutive of a word is used to express affection. The diminutive is often formed by adding **-ito/a** or **-cito/a** to the end of a word. Scan the first poem. What diminutives do you find? (**¡OJO!** Some words that end in **-ito** are not diminutives.) What do the diminutive forms mean?

Before you read the poems, read their titles and the glosses that accompany the poems to prepare yourself for the content.

Now read the poems and do the activities that follow.

[1]¡Buen... *Enjoy your meal!*

PREPARATION: Familiarize students with glossed vocabulary. Have them look over the follow-up questions in **Paso 1** to prepare them for the content of the poems. Encourage them to read the text in Spanish rather than translating the text into English.

Loa[1] al frijol

JESÚS MALDONADO (EE. UU.)

Frijolito pinto,
Frijolito lindo,
Rico[2] caldudito[3]
Traes el apetito.

Frijolito chico,
Frijolito rico,
Reinas[4] cuando frito
Matas[5] hambrecito.

[1]*Praise*   [2]*Delicious*   [3]*diminutive of* caldo, *broth*   [4]*You reign*   [5]*You kill*

El trío mexicano

JESÚS MALDONADO (EE. UU.)

Tortillas con mantequilla
Parientes de Pancho Villa,
Bistec de los mexicanos
De placeres soberanos.[1]

El rico café saluda,
A matar hambres ayuda.
Sabroso humilde[2] trío
Me contentas cuando frío.

[1]placeres... *sovereign pleasures*   [2]*humble*

Después de leer

Paso 1

> **SUGGESTION: Pasos 1** and **2** work well with students in small groups. Have groups compare their answers or poems with other groups when they have finished.

1. If the diminutive implies affection in "Loa al frijol," what is the poet's attitude toward beans?
2. The poet mentions two ways to prepare beans in the first poem. What are they, and what different effects do they have on the person eating?
3. In "El trío mexicano," what are the three elements that constitute the trio?
4. In the second poem the poet uses two images to describe tortillas with butter: **parientes de Pancho Villa** and **bistec de los mexicanos**. What qualities is the poet attempting to portray with these images?

> **SUGGESTION:** Provide an example—either this one, one you create, or one that you and the class write together. **Jamón rojo, / Jamón salado, / Un rico sándwich de jamón. / Como mi sándwich. / Jamón fresco, Jamón frío, / Preparo mi sándwich con lechuga, queso y mayonesa. / ¡Quisiera compartirlo contigo!**

Paso 2. Using the style of the first poem, write a new poem. You may use the following formula.

Lines 1 and 2: the name of the food
Lines 1, 2, and 3: three adjectives used to describe the food
Line 3: the name of something made with the food
Line 4: an action phrase
Lines 5 and 6: repeat the name of the food with two adjectives to describe the food
Line 7: another action phrase
Line 8: another action phrase

English Only y la lengua oficial

Professor Brewer asked his advanced Spanish students to find articles on the controversial English Only movement. One of the articles is presented here.

> **PREPARATION:** Familiarize students with the glossed vocabulary. Have them look over the follow-up activities to prepare for the content of the reading. Encourage them to read the text in Spanish rather than translating the text into English.

Antes de leer

Few issues related to the Hispanic population of the United States have been as sensitive as those of bilingual education and the English Only movement. What reasons would someone have for wanting English as the only official language in the United States? Do you think that having English as the official language would give immigrants an incentive to learn the language more quickly? In your opinion, if a U.S. school educates a child for twelve years without ever requiring that the child learn English, is the school doing the child a service or a disservice in the long run? Do you think a country's official language should be the only language allowed in public buildings and at public events? This might exclude individuals who do not speak English from being informed voters, from serving as jurors, and even from understanding their own court proceedings. Do you think such a change would be beneficial in the long run to the United States? Would it be beneficial to the immigrants?

Now read the article and do the activities that follow.

English Only

Los partidarios[1] del movimiento llamado *English Only* (**Sólo Inglés**) alegan que este movimiento está creciendo.[2] Tiene una filosofía simple: El inglés es, y debe permanecer[3] para siempre, la única lengua oficial del pueblo de los Estados Unidos. El movimiento tiene objetivos muy claros. Primero, sus partidarios quieren imponer[4] la asimilación a los millones de inmigrantes que han entrado a los EE. UU. en los últimos veinte años. Segundo, quieren que los documentos del gobierno sean publicados solamente en inglés. Tercero, desean que los discursos[5] públicos y los debates políticos que tienen la autorización del gobierno sean limitados al inglés.

[1]*supporters* [2]*growing* [3]*remain* [4]*to impose* [5]*speeches*

Después de leer

Paso 1. Complete the statements in the first column with phrases from the second column.

1. El movimiento Sólo Inglés está...
2. La filosofía del movimiento es que...
3. Los partidarios de Sólo Inglés quieren imponer la asimilación a...
4. Quieren que...
5. Quieren limitar...

   a. los discursos públicos oficiales al inglés.
   b. el inglés debe ser la única lengua oficial de los EE. UU.
   c. millones de inmigrantes recientes.
   d. los documentos públicos sean publicados sólo en inglés.
   e. creciendo en popularidad.

Paso 2. Ask a classmate what he or she thinks about the movement to declare English as the official language. (Note that the questions here are to stimulate thought and discussion and are not necessarily representative of any particular movement.) Be prepared to report to the class what you discover.

1. ¿Crees que es bueno tener leyes que regulen los idiomas que se puede usar en un país? ¿Por qué sí o por qué no?
2. ¿Crees que el inglés debe ser el único idioma oficial de los EE. UU.?

3. ¿Crees que es necesario imponer la asimilación a los inmigrantes recién llegados? ¿Por qué sí o por qué no?

4. ¿Cuáles son algunos aspectos negativos de tener comunidades en un país que no tienen un idioma en común? ¿Y algunos aspectos positivos?

5. ¿Crees que las personas que no saben inglés tienen derecho[1] a votar o a entender los procesos jurídicos[2]? ¿Por qué sí o por qué no?

6. ¿Crees que los alumnos deben ser castigados[3] o físicamente o por recibir malas notas si no hablan inglés en las clases? ¿Por qué sí o por qué no?

[1] *the right* [2] *judicial, legal* [3] *punished*

DIÁLOGO

La fiesta de bienvenida

PREPARATION: Ask students to describe the drawing. Ask them to focus on the title of the dialogue and on the dialogue introduction. **¿Dónde están los amigos? ¿Qué hacen? ¿Qué cosas asocian Uds. con una fiesta de bienvenida?** Have students skim the dialogue. **¿De qué hablan las personas?**

El sábado por la noche, los miembros del Club Hispánico celebran una fiesta en la casa del Profesor Brewer para darle la bienvenida a Elena.

DAVID: Profesor Brewer, quiero presentarle a mi prima, Elena Muñoz López.
EL PROFESOR BREWER: Mucho gusto, Elena.
ELENA: Encantada, Profesor Brewer. Es un placer estar aquí con Uds. Y ésta debe ser Mercedes, la hija de Luisa, ¿no? ... ¿Te gusta la escuela de aquí, Mercedes? ¿Es mejor que la escuela a que asistías en Florida?
MERCEDES: Sí, me gusta; es muy parecida a mi antigua[1] escuela. Pero las clases comienzan muy temprano; tengo que levantarme a las seis para vestirme y tomar el desayuno.

LUIS: La mujer que está con David es la prima de Uds., ¿verdad?
SANDRA: Sí, la mamá de Elena es la hermana de nuestra mamá. Elena es de México, de Monterrey.
LUIS: Sabe manejar, ¿no?
SANDRA: Sí, tiene licencia mexicana pero no la va a necesitar pues mis padres piensan llevarla a algunos sitios de interés aquí en los EE. UU.

TOMÁS: Carmen y tú prepararon... digo, preparasteis la paella, ¿no? Estaba muy rica.
CELIA: ¿Te gustó? Tuvimos que buscar los ingredientes en varias tiendas, pero valió la pena. Creo que a todos les gustó. El padre de David se sirvió dos porciones.
TOMÁS: ¿Ya hablasteis con David?
CELIA: Sí. Le gustó el viaje a México pero está contento de estar de regreso.

[1] *former*

TOMÁS: ¿Qué va a hacer el año que viene? ¿Va a seguir[2] sus estudios aquí o va a volver a México?

CELIA: David me dijo que va a seguir sus estudios aquí pero es posible que cambie de especialización. Después de su viaje le interesan mucho la antropología y la historia.

[2] *continue*

Which of the characters do you associate with the following statements?

De inmediato

1. Es un placer estar aquí con Uds.
2. Las clases comienzan muy temprano.
3. Mis padres piensan llevarla a algunos sitios de interés aquí en los EE. UU.
4. El padre de David se sirvió dos porciones.
5. David me dijo que va a seguir sus estudios aquí.

OPTIONAL: 1. ¿Cuándo fue la fiesta? 2. ¿Cuáles eran las dos cosas que quería saber Luis? 3. ¿Qué especializaciones le interesan a David? 4. ¿Qué piensa Mercedes de su escuela en Eau Claire? 5. ¿Qué le pareció la paella a Tomás?

Practice the following exchanges with a classmate.

A ti te toca

E1: ¿Te gusta esta universidad?
E2: ...
E1: ¿Qué vas a hacer el año que viene? ¿Vas a seguir tus estudios aquí?
E2: ...
E1: ¿Es posible que cambies de especialización?
E2: ...

La inmigración y la influencia hispana

Faceta cultural

The United States ranks fifth in the world in terms of the number of residents of Hispanic origin, after Mexico, Spain, Colombia, and Argentina. Well over 22 million people in the United States, or one-tenth of the country's population, identify themselves as being of Hispanic descent. This group is not homogeneous, however. The U.S. Hispanic population is diverse, varying in many ways, including country of origin and socioeconomic factors.

The term *Hispanic* is not accepted by many who speak (or whose ancestors spoke) Spanish. Some prefer the term *Latino*, whereas others opt for designations that specify their ethnic heritage: *Mexican, Cuban, Puerto Rican,* or whatever the case may be. Because definitions of *Hispanic* typically refer to origin in Spain or Latin America, some "Hispanics" argue that these definitions exclude Caribbean cultures. This text uses *Hispanic* to refer to all individuals of Spanish-speaking background, regardless of their native language or country of birth.

Contrary to popular belief, most Hispanics in the United States are not recent arrivals to the country. Many trace their presence in what is now the United States back to the nineteenth century and even earlier, when the lands their ancestors occupied belonged to Mexico, not to the United States. Others are fourth- or fifth-generation descendants of people who came to the United States to work early in the twentieth century.

Many of those whose roots in this country go the deepest do not regard themselves as Hispanic. They may recognize that they bear a Hispanic surname, but they no longer speak Spanish, nor do they and their children hold traditional Hispanic values or practice Hispanic customs. Others may have lost touch with their Hispanic roots, but on certain special occasions they observe family customs that can be traced to Hispanic ancestors.

Although there is virtually no Spanish-speaking culture in the world that does not have a presence in the United States, there are three main groups of Hispanics represented. The largest group is composed of those who originally came from Mexico; this group is located primarily in California and the southwest part of the United States. The second largest group is that of Puerto Rican ancestry; these people are found largely in New York and other urban centers of the Northeast. The most recent group consists of Cuban-Americans, predominantly found in south Florida. Although some of its members have resided in this country for generations, many others came to the United States in the late 1950s, early 1960s, in 1980, and again in 1994 to escape the government of Fidel Castro.

The Hispanic influence in the United States varies to some degree from one region of the country to another, but it is undeniable. One of the most tangible pieces of evidence of the importance of Spanish in this country is the number of Spanish place names found in the United States. Spanish explorers and early Mexican settlers left their linguistic marks all over the continent. From Boca Ratón to San Francisco, there are many American cities whose names are derived from Spanish. Names of many rivers (**el Río Grande**), mountains (**Sangre de Cristo** in southern Colorado and northern New Mexico), and states (**Nevada**) are also of Hispanic origin.

Spanish is also a part of our everyday language. There are a number of Spanish words that appear verbatim in an English dictionary: **patio, mosquito,** and **plaza,** to name a few. Still other English words (*vanilla, lariat, desperado, lasso*) come from Spanish but are not identical to their counterparts: **vainilla, reata, desesperado,** and **lazo**.

The **tacos** and **enchiladas** we order at our favorite Tex-Mex restaurant may bear only a passing resemblance to the original dish, but they attest nonetheless to the Hispanic presence in our country. Furthermore, Mexican dishes share the limelight with Caribbean and Spanish dishes. Spanish **tapas** have recently been featured in several popular U.S. magazines, including *Time* and *Newsweek.*

From the popularity of Gloria Estefan and the Miami Sound Machine to that of ''La Bamba,'' the Hispanic presence in the entertainment industry is increasingly felt. There are few Americans who don't know the names Raúl Julia or Ricardo Montalbán. **Salsa** is hot as a musical genre. Many popular athletes, such as Juan González and José Canseco, are well known by Hispanics and non-Hispanics alike.

Although most people recognize the names of Henry Cisneros and Antonia Novello, there are fewer well-known Hispanics in politics than in the film, music, and sports industries, and many enjoy name recognition solely on a local basis. Nevertheless, it is clear that the group that will constitute the largest minority in the United States by the year 2050 is having a cultural impact. The Hispanic community is only now beginning to realize its power.

En México

FOLLOW-UP: As a homework assignment, have students come up with five additional items in one of the following categories: Spanish place names, English words of Spanish origin, Hispanic dishes that are not Tex-Mex, famous Hispanics in the United States.

Mexico itself has been the country of choice for many immigrants from other nations around the world. For example, in the nineteenth century, many Germans settled in Mexico, notably in the north, where they became active in such areas as ranching, manufacturing, and beer brewing. So strong is their influence on Mexican ways of life that a Mexican variety of the polka is often included in the folklore ballets popular all over Mexico. In the 1930s, many Spaniards fleeing the Franco regime settled in Mexico. More recently, refugees from political unrest in nearby Central American countries have crossed the southern Mexican border.

EN ACCIÓN

La educación bilingüe y el bilingüismo

While she waits for David to run errands at the university, Elena hears an editorial on the Spanish-language television channel.

Antes de escuchar

PREPARATION: Have students look over the follow-up activities to prepare for the content of the passage.

What are the advantages and disadvantages of offering bilingual education in schools? Do you feel that immigrant children tend to use it as a way to avoid learning English? Have you ever lived in an area where bilingual education was offered? What public reaction have you heard about it?

This editorial contains many words you may not understand. Before listening, review this list to prepare yourself for the content of the editorial.

el creole haitiano	*Haitian Creole*	los carteles	*billboards; posters*
		los discursos	*lectures*
el urdu	*Urdu (language used in India and Pakistan)*	los partidarios	*supporters*
		la enseñanza	*teaching*
el blanco	*target*	recaudar fondos	*to raise money*
se enfurecen	*(they) get angry*	alcanzar	*to reach*

Now listen to the editorial and do the activities that follow.

Después de escuchar

Paso 1. ¿Es cierto o no es cierto?

1. Los inmigrantes recientes a los EE. UU. vinieron sólo de países hispanos.
2. En Nueva York ofrecen educación bilingüe en chino, creole haitiano, coreano, italiano, griego, vietnamita, árabe, hindú, urdu y ruso.
3. A algunos que no saben español no les gusta ver carteles en este idioma.
4. El bilingüismo y la educación bilingüe son la misma cosa.
5. Según este editorial, el movimiento Sólo Inglés no se opone a la educación bilingüe sino al bilingüismo.

Paso 2. Ask a classmate what he or she thinks about the conflict between the English Only movement and bilingual education. Be prepared to report to the class what you discover.

SUGGESTION: The student receiving the questions should have his or her book closed.
VARIATION: Have students interview you, being sure to change from familiar to formal address.
VARIATION: Students can work in small groups. They can record the group's answers and report back to the class about what they do and do not have in common as a group (using **nosotros** forms).

1. ¿Crees que los inmigrantes tienen derecho a la educación bilingüe?
2. ¿Piensas que la educación bilingüe en las escuelas ayuda de alguna forma a los EE. UU.?
3. ¿Crees que el movimiento Sólo Inglés se refiere a todos los inmigrantes que residen en los EE. UU. o sólo a los hispanos?
4. En tu opinión, ¿es el bilingüismo una cosa negativa o positiva?

Recuerdos en inglés... y en español

Hispanic writers often record memories of their childhood in English. Note how Ponce uses both English and Spanish to recall an incident of her World War II childhood in Los Angeles. Read the story and answer the questions that follow.

PREPARATION: Have students, in small groups, brainstorm what they imagine life to have been like as a Hispanic in Los Angeles during WWII.

Recuerdo: How I changed the war and won the game

MARY HELEN PONCE (EE. UU., 1938–)

During World War II I used to translate the English newspaper's war news for our adopted grandmother Doña Luisa and her friends. All of them were *señoras de edad,* elderly ladies who could not read English, only their native Spanish.

Every afternoon they would gather on Doña Luisa's front porch to await Doña Trinidad's son who delivered the paper to her promptly at 5 P.M. There, among the *geranios* and pots of *yerba buena,*[1] I would bring them the news of the war.

At first I enjoyed doing this, for the *señoras* would welcome me as a grown-up. They would push their chairs around in a semicircle, the better to hear me. I would sit in the middle, on a *banquito*[2] that was a milk crate. I don't remember how I began to be their translator but because I was an obedient child and at eight a good reader, I was somehow coerced or selected.

I would sit down, adjust my dress, then slowly unwrap the paper, reading the headlines to myself in English, trying to decide which news items were the most important, which to tell first. Once I had decided, I would translate them into my best Spanish for Doña Luisa and her friends.

The news of a battle would bring sighs of *Jesús, María y José, Ay Dios mío,* from the ladies. They would roll their eyes toward heaven, imploring our Lord to protect their loved ones from danger. In return they vowed to light candles or to make a *manda,* a pilgrimage to *la Virgen de San Juan* in the nearby town of Sunland. Once I read them the highlights of the war I was allowed to play ball with my friends.

One day we had an important ball game going, our team was losing, and it was my turn at bat. Just then Doña called me. It was time for *las noticias.* Furious at this interruption yet not daring to disobey, I dropped the bat, ran to the porch, ripped open the paper, pointed to the headlines and in a loud voice proclaimed: "*Ya están los japoneses en San Francisco... los esperan en Los Ángeles muy pronto,*" or "The Japanese have landed in San Francisco; they should be in Los Angeles soon."

"*Jesús, María y José, Sangre de Cristo, Ave María purísima*" chanted *las*

SUGGESTION: Point out that **doña** is a title of respect often used for an elderly woman. It is used with the woman's first name.

[1]yerba... *mint*   [2]*small bench*

señoras as I dashed off to resume my game. "*Dios mío ya vámonos, ya vámonos*" they said as chairs were pushed aside, "*vamos a la iglesia... a rezarle[3] al Señor.*"

After that I was able to translate according to whim—and depending on whether or not I was up to bat when the paper arrived.

[3]*pray*

Después de leer

1. What Spanish phrases does the author define in the story?
2. What Spanish phrases would not be understood by readers who do not know Spanish? What impact does the loss of that information have on such readers?
3. Why do you think the author chose to use Spanish words when she did? What patterns do you see in the kinds of words and phrases she chose to use in Spanish? For example, is she more likely to use Spanish for direct or indirect quotes? For noun or verb phrases?
4. Explain the significance of the title of the story.

El lugar donde dormí

Imagine that a friend is writing and directing a film about the nights of an average college student and wants to use you as the typical student. The director needs to know, in detail, what a recent evening was like for you after you got home. On a separate sheet of paper, write a ten- to fifteen-sentence composition in which you describe the night for your friend. Include the following details.

1. what you looked like as you walked in
   - how you felt
   - what you were wearing
2. what your room looked like as you walked in
   - the furniture, accessories, and electronic devices (include relative age, size, and color)
   - the location of the objects in the room relative to each other, such that the director can accurately set up the stage from your description
3. what you did before going to bed (Did you listen to music, take a shower, brush your teeth?)

First, decide what you want to mention. Jot down Spanish words and expressions that you might need, then write a draft of your composition. (Do not try to write the composition in English and translate it to Spanish!) Look over what you've written. Have you included the information requested? Are your descriptions complete and interesting? Check your grammar. Do the verbs agree with their subjects? Do the adjectives agree with the nouns they modify? Have you used past tenses appropriately—the preterite for completed actions in the past and the imperfect for descriptions? Finally, check spelling, accent marks, and punctuation, then prepare a clean copy of your composition to turn in.

EPISODIOS

1   2   3   4

5   6   7   8

Paso 1

PREPARATION: For each scene, have students suggest key vocabulary in Spanish that would help them identify it.

Write the number of the drawing that corresponds to each statement you hear.

Paso 2

EXAMPLES: 1. Luisa se arregló a las ocho menos quince. (No, no es cierto.) 2. Luisa tuvo una clase de matemáticas ese día. (Es cierto.)

Write six statements about the **Episodios** scenes, three of which are true, three of which are false. Then read your statements to a classmate who will respond with either **Sí, es cierto** or **No, no es cierto**. Then switch roles and listen to your classmate's sentences, responding appropriately.

EXPANSION: Have students correct any false statements.

Paso 3

SUGGESTION: Have students work in pairs to read each other's corrected paragraphs, discuss similarities, and resolve discrepancies.

Rewrite the following paragraph so that it accurately reflects what you see in the scenes.

Luisa se maquilló antes de ducharse. Decidió ponerse jeans y una blusa verde porque tenía que trabajar en la librería ese día. Llevó a Mercedes a la escuela de verano y después fue a la universidad en su coche. En la clase de sociología, la profesora explicó una teoría complicada y todos los estudiantes le pusieron atención. En la cafetería habló con una amiga que la invitó a ir al cine. Luisa aceptó la invitación porque tenía mucho tiempo libre. En el centro estudiantil no pasaba nada extraordinario ese día. En casa, por la tarde, Luisa y su compañera de cuarto, Mercedes, prepararon hamburguesas en la cocina. Después, Luisa se divirtió con un videojuego mientras Marisol limpiaba la casa. Más tarde, antes de acostarse, Luisa recibió un telegrama. Esa noche se durmió temprano.

Paso 4

VARIATION: Have students describe what Luisa *did* (preterite), *was doing* (imperfect), or *was going to do* (**ir a** + *inf.*) in each of the scenes.

In small groups, describe what Luisa is doing in each of the scenes. Each student should make at least two statements about each scene without repeating information given by the other students.

Paso 5

PREPARATION: Ask students which form of address (**tú** or **Ud.**) would be appropriate in this situation.

SUGGESTION: Have students prepare, rehearse, and present their dialogues to the class.

Imagine that you overheard the conversation between Luisa and the man at the circulation desk in the library. Write out the conversation. Make sure each character has at least five lines. Include appropriate greetings, expressions of courtesy, and farewells.

Paso 6

PREPARATION: Ask whether subjunctive or indicative is required after sentences that begin with **es cierto, es posible, es claro; es lástima, es evidente, es necesario.** Review the formation of the present subjunctive.

Use the following phrases to write five sentences that describe the scenes. Then write five sentences that describe what is *not* happening.

(No) Es cierto/claro/evidente/seguro/verdad que...
(No) Es bueno/importante/(im)posible/(im)probable/lástima/ malo/necesario/triste que...

EJEMPLOS:　Es verdad que Luisa estudia matemáticas.
　　　　　No es verdad que Luisa salga con el joven.

Paso 7

PREPARATION: Review question words and word order in question formation. You may wish to write them on the board.

First write five questions that can be answered by looking at the scenes. Each question must begin with a different interrogative word (**¿cómo?, ¿dónde?, ¿quién?,** and so on). Then ask a classmate to answer your questions.

EJEMPLOS:　—¿Qué ropa se puso Luisa para ir a sus clases?
　　　　　—Luisa se puso una falda, una camiseta y sandalias (para ir a sus clases).

　　　　　—¿Qué hizo Mercedes antes de acostarse?
　　　　　—Mercedes jugó un vídeojuego (antes de acostarse).

ACTIVIDAD COMPRENSIVA

Working with a classmate, describe the following drawing in detail.

NOTE: The purpose of the drawing is to review vocabulary from previous chapters.

SUGGESTION: Have students make lists of words that fit several categories present in the drawing (i.e., physical descriptions of the characters, their personality characteristics, their feelings at the moment, food items).

OTROS MUNDOS

NOTE: See the *Instructor's Manual* for suggestions for teaching **Otros mundos.**

Los EE. UU.

Bienvenidos a Miami, una ciudad verdaderamente hispánica. Uds. ya me conocen; soy Luisa de la Vega López de Vargas. Quiero hablarles de un país importante en el mundo de habla hispana: los EE. UU. Sí, es verdad. Hay unos 22 millones de personas de origen hispánico, como yo, en los EE. UU., o sea, el 9% de toda la población. Hay tres grupos principales de hispanos—los mexicanos, puertorriqueños y cubanos. También hay más de 5 millones de habitantes procedentes de otros países hispánicos.

En mi opinión, mi ciudad es una de las más cosmopolitas del mundo. Aquí hay un poco de todo. Es el puerto principal de entrada para los miles de imigrantes que llegan cada año de Latinoamérica y de España. Entre los hispanos aquí en Miami los cubanos somos el grupo más grande, pero es incorrecto pensar que somos el único porque hay tantos habitantes de otros grupos hispánicos como cubanos. También llegan millones de turistas de todas partes del mundo que quieren visitar mi ciudad y mi estado. Ellos forman parte vital del ambiente cosmopolita de Miami.

Un barrio de Miami que celebra sus orígenes cubanos es la Calle Ocho. Llamado «la pequeña Habana», este sector de Miami tiene una concentración de restaurantes, clubes y tiendas que son por la mayor parte como una extensión de la capital de Cuba antes de Castro. Cada año, celebramos en marzo Carnaval Miami, una semana de festivales que atrae a más de un millón de personas, todas bailando, cantando, divirtiéndose en la Calle Ocho las 24 horas del día. La realidad es que Miami y sus afueras forman una de las regiones más vibrantes, más excitantes, más progresivas del país y del mundo. Ojalá que Uds. vengan a visitarnos pronto.

¿Sabías que... ?

- Por el número de hablantes, el español es el idioma que ocupa el segundo lugar en los EE. UU. después del inglés.
- Según el censo de 1990, Nueva York tiene el mayor número de hispanos, seguida por Los Ángeles, Chicago y San Antonio.
- El 40% de los hispanos en los EE. UU. tienen menos de dieciocho años.
- Puerto Rico es un estado libre asociado[1] de los EE. UU. Los puertorriqueños son ciudadanos de los EE. UU. con todos los derechos que

[1]estado... *commonwealth*

tienen todos los otros ciudadanos de los EE. UU., incluso el derecho de votar en las elecciones nacionales. El 60% de todos los puertorriqueños reside en el continente[2] de los EE. UU.

- La abogada Sonia Sotomayor fue la primera mujer puertorriqueña electa para un cargo en una corte federal en el territorio continental y en 1992 era la única juez federal latina en Nueva York.
- Antonia Novello mantuvo posiciones altas en varios Institutos Nacionales de Salud antes de ser nombrada Inspectora General de Sanidad de los EE. UU. por el entonces presidente Reagan. Fue la primera mujer, la primera hispana, y la primera puertorriqueña en ocupar esa posición.
- Henry González, congresista de San Antonio, Texas, fue elegido en 1960 con el amplio apoyo de anglos, hispanos y africano-americanos. Es el primer representante mexicano-americano de Texas. En 1994 continuaba sirviendo su cargo.
- Ellen Ochoa formó parte de la tripulación[3] de la nave espacial Discovery en abril de 1993, siendo la primera hispana en una misión al espacio.

[2]mainland [3]crew

(en la pàgina 368) En el sector la Pequeña Habana, en Miami, Florida, uno puede gozar de la comida cubana. (a la izquierda) Miami Beach es un lugar cosmopolita. Estas personas se sientan al aire libre en Ocean Drive.

LOS HISPANOS EN LOS EE. UU. EN BREVE

	De origen mexicano	De origen puertorriqueño	De origen cubano	Otros grupos
población (en millones)	13,5	2,7	1,1	5,1
% de la población hispana	60,3	12,0	4,9	22,8
% de la población total	5,4	1,1	0,4	2,1
concentración geográfica	el suroeste	Nueva York	Florida	todas partes

Appendix 1

Verbs

Some of the verb forms in these tables are not intended for active use in the text, but are occasionally found in the readings and **Diálogos.** Note that additional verb forms not listed in these tables also exist in Spanish, for example, the perfect tense forms: preterite perfect indicative (**hube hablado**), future perfect indicative (**habré hablado**), conditional perfect indicative (**habría hablado**), present perfect subjunctive (**haya hablado**), and past perfect subjunctive (**hubiera hablado**).

A. Regular verbs: Simple tenses

INFINITIVE PRESENT PARTICIPLE PAST PARTICIPLE	INDICATIVE					SUBJUNCTIVE		COMMANDS
	PRESENT	IMPERFECT	PRETERITE	FUTURE	CONDITIONAL	PRESENT	PAST	
hablar	hablo	hablaba	hablé	hablaré	hablaría	hable	hablara	habla tú, no
hablando	hablas	hablabas	hablaste	hablarás	hablarías	hables	hablaras	hables
hablado	habla	hablaba	habló	hablará	hablaría	hable	hablara	hable Ud.
	hablamos	hablábamos	hablamos	hablaremos	hablaríamos	hablemos	habláramos	hablemos
	habláis	hablabais	hablasteis	hablaréis	hablaríais	habléis	hablarais	hablen
	hablan	hablaban	hablaron	hablarán	hablarían	hablen	hablaran	
comer	como	comía	comí	comeré	comería	coma	comiera	come tú, no
comiendo	comes	comías	comiste	comerás	comerías	comas	comieras	comas
comido	come	comía	comió	comerá	comería	coma	comiera	coma Ud.
	comemos	comíamos	comimos	comeremos	comeríamos	comamos	comiéramos	comamos
	coméis	comíais	comisteis	comeréis	comeríais	comáis	comierais	coman
	comen	comían	comieron	comerán	comerían	coman	comieran	
vivir	vivo	vivía	viví	viviré	viviría	viva	viviera	vive tú, no
viviendo	vives	vivías	viviste	vivirás	vivirías	vivas	vivieras	vivas
vivido	vive	vivía	vivió	vivirá	viviría	viva	viviera	viva Ud.
	vivimos	vivíamos	vivimos	viviremos	viviríamos	vivamos	viviéramos	vivamos
	vivís	vivíais	vivisteis	viviréis	viviríais	viváis	vivierais	vivan
	viven	vivían	vivieron	vivirán	vivirían	vivan	vivieran	

B. Regular verbs: Perfect tenses

INDICATIVE

PRESENT PERFECT		PAST PERFECT	
he	hablado	había	hablado
has	comido	habías	comido
ha	vivido	había	vivido
hemos		habíamos	
habéis		habíais	
han		habían	

C. Irregular verbs

INFINITIVE PRESENT PARTICIPLE PAST PARTICIPLE	INDICATIVE					SUBJUNCTIVE		COMMANDS
	PRESENT	IMPERFECT	PRETERITE	FUTURE	CONDITIONAL	PRESENT	PAST	
andar	ando	andaba	anduve	andaré	andaría	ande	anduviera	anda tú, no
andando	andas	andabas	anduviste	andarás	andarías	andes	anduvieras	andes
andado	anda	andaba	anduvo	andará	andaría	ande	anduviera	ande Ud.
	andamos	andábamos	anduvimos	andaremos	andaríamos	andemos	anduviéramos	andemos
	andáis	andabais	anduvisteis	andaréis	andaríais	andéis	anduvierais	anden
	andan	andaban	anduvieron	andarán	andarían	anden	anduvieran	
caer	caigo	caía	caí	caeré	caería	caiga	cayera	cae tú, no
cayendo	caes	caías	caíste	caerás	caerías	caigas	cayeras	caigas
caído	cae	caía	cayó	caerá	caería	caiga	cayera	caiga Ud.
	caemos	caíamos	caímos	caeremos	caeríamos	caigamos	cayéramos	caigamos
	caéis	caíais	caísteis	caeréis	caeríais	caigáis	cayerais	caigan
	caen	caían	cayeron	caerán	caerían	caigan	cayeran	
dar	doy	daba	di	daré	daría	dé	diera	da tú, no des
dando	das	dabas	diste	darás	darías	des	dieras	dé Ud.
dado	da	daba	dio	dará	daría	dé	diera	demos
	damos	dábamos	dimos	daremos	daríamos	demos	diéramos	den
	dais	dabais	disteis	daréis	daríais	deis	dierais	
	dan	daban	dieron	darán	darían	den	dieran	
decir	digo	decía	dije	diré	diría	diga	dijera	di tú, no
diciendo	dices	decías	dijiste	dirás	dirías	digas	dijeras	digas
dicho	dice	decía	dijo	dirá	diría	diga	dijera	diga Ud.
	decimos	decíamos	dijimos	diremos	diríamos	digamos	dijéramos	digamos
	decís	decíais	dijisteis	diréis	diríais	digáis	dijerais	digan
	dicen	decían	dijeron	dirán	dirían	digan	dijeran	
estar	estoy	estaba	estuve	estaré	estaría	esté	estuviera	está tú, no
estando	estás	estabas	estuviste	estarás	estarías	estés	estuvieras	estés
estado	está	estaba	estuvo	estará	estaría	esté	estuviera	esté Ud.
	estamos	estábamos	estuvimos	estaremos	estaríamos	estemos	estuviéramos	estemos
	estáis	estabais	estuvisteis	estaréis	estaríais	estéis	estuvierais	estén
	están	estaban	estuvieron	estarán	estarían	estén	estuvieran	

A-1

C. Irregular verbs (continued)

INFINITIVE / PRESENT PARTICIPLE / PAST PARTICIPLE	INDICATIVE PRESENT	IMPERFECT	PRETERITE	FUTURE	CONDITIONAL	SUBJUNCTIVE PRESENT	PAST	COMMANDS
haber habiendo habido	he has ha hemos habéis han	había habías había habíamos habíais habían	hube hubiste hubo hubimos hubisteis hubieron	habré habrás habrá habremos habréis habrán	habría habrías habría habríamos habríais habrían	haya hayas haya hayamos hayáis hayan	hubiera hubieras hubiera hubiéramos hubierais hubieran	
hacer haciendo hecho	hago haces hace hacemos hacéis hacen	hacía hacías hacía hacíamos hacíais hacían	hice hiciste hizo hicimos hicisteis hicieron	haré harás hará haremos haréis harán	haría harías haría haríamos haríais harían	haga hagas haga hagamos hagáis hagan	hiciera hicieras hiciera hiciéramos hicierais hicieran	haz tú, no hagas haga Ud. hagamos hagan
ir yendo ido	voy vas va vamos vais van	iba ibas iba íbamos ibais iban	fui fuiste fue fuimos fuisteis fueron	iré irás irá iremos iréis irán	iría irías iría iríamos iríais irían	vaya vayas vaya vayamos vayáis vayan	fuera fueras fuera fuéramos fuerais fueran	ve tú, no vayas vaya Ud. vayamos vayan
oír oyendo oído	oigo oyes oye oímos oís oyen	oía oías oía oíamos oíais oían	oí oíste oyó oímos oísteis oyeron	oiré oirás oirá oiremos oiréis oirán	oiría oirías oiría oiríamos oiríais oirían	oiga oigas oiga oigamos oigáis oigan	oyera oyeras oyera oyéramos oyerais oyeran	oye tú, no oigas oiga Ud. oigamos oigan
poder pudiendo podido	puedo puedes puede podemos podéis pueden	podía podías podía podíamos podíais podían	pude pudiste pudo pudimos pudisteis pudieron	podré podrás podrá podremos podréis podrán	podría podrías podría podríamos podríais podrían	pueda puedas pueda podamos podáis puedan	pudiera pudieras pudiera pudiéramos pudierais pudieran	
poner poniendo puesto	pongo pones pone ponemos ponéis ponen	ponía ponías ponía poníamos poníais ponían	puse pusiste puso pusimos pusisteis pusieron	pondré pondrás pondrá pondremos pondréis pondrán	pondría pondrías pondría pondríamos pondríais pondrían	ponga pongas ponga pongamos pongáis pongan	pusiera pusieras pusiera pusiéramos pusierais pusieran	pon tú, no pongas ponga Ud. pongamos pongan
querer queriendo querido	quiero quieres quiere queremos queréis quieren	quería querías quería queríamos queríais querían	quise quisiste quiso quisimos quisisteis quisieron	querré querrás querrá querremos querréis querrán	querría querrías querría querríamos querríais querrían	quiera quieras quiera queramos queráis quieran	quisiera quisieras quisiera quisiéramos quisierais quisieran	quiere tú, no quieras quiera Ud. queramos quieran

C. Irregular verbs (continued)

INFINITIVE / PRESENT PARTICIPLE / PAST PARTICIPLE	INDICATIVE PRESENT	IMPERFECT	PRETERITE	FUTURE	CONDITIONAL	SUBJUNCTIVE PRESENT	PAST	COMMANDS
saber / sabiendo / sabido	sé	sabía	supe	sabré	sabría	sepa	supiera	sabe tú, no
	sabes	sabías	supiste	sabrás	sabrías	sepas	supieras	sepas
	sabe	sabía	supo	sabrá	sabría	sepa	supiera	sepa Ud.
	sabemos	sabíamos	supimos	sabremos	sabríamos	sepamos	supiéramos	sepamos
	sabéis	sabíais	supisteis	sabréis	sabríais	sepáis	supierais	sepan
	saben	sabían	supieron	sabrán	sabrían	sepan	supieran	
salir / saliendo / salido	salgo	salía	salí	saldré	saldría	salga	saliera	sal tú, no
	sales	salías	saliste	saldrás	saldrías	salgas	salieras	salgas
	sale	salía	salió	saldrá	saldría	salga	saliera	salga Ud.
	salimos	salíamos	salimos	saldremos	saldríamos	salgamos	saliéramos	salgamos
	salís	salíais	salisteis	saldréis	saldríais	salgáis	salierais	salgan
	salen	salían	salieron	saldrán	saldrían	salgan	salieran	
ser / siendo / sido	soy	era	fui	seré	sería	sea	fuera	sé tú, no seas
	eres	eras	fuiste	serás	serías	seas	fueras	sea Ud.
	es	era	fue	será	sería	sea	fuera	seamos
	somos	éramos	fuimos	seremos	seríamos	seamos	fuéramos	sean
	sois	erais	fuisteis	seréis	seríais	seáis	fuerais	
	son	eran	fueron	serán	serían	sean	fueran	
tener / teniendo / tenido	tengo	tenía	tuve	tendré	tendría	tenga	tuviera	ten tú, no
	tienes	tenías	tuviste	tendrás	tendrías	tengas	tuvieras	tengas
	tiene	tenía	tuvo	tendrá	tendría	tenga	tuviera	tenga Ud.
	tenemos	teníamos	tuvimos	tendremos	tendríamos	tengamos	tuviéramos	tengamos
	tenéis	teníais	tuvisteis	tendréis	tendríais	tengáis	tuvierais	tengan
	tienen	tenían	tuvieron	tendrán	tendrían	tengan	tuvieran	
traer / trayendo / traído	traigo	traía	traje	traeré	traería	traiga	trajera	trae tú, no
	traes	traías	trajiste	traerás	traerías	traigas	trajeras	traigas
	trae	traía	trajo	traerá	traería	traiga	trajera	traiga Ud.
	traemos	traíamos	trajimos	traeremos	traeríamos	traigamos	trajéramos	traigamos
	traéis	traíais	trajisteis	traeréis	traeríais	traigáis	trajerais	traigan
	traen	traían	trajeron	traerán	traerían	traigan	trajeran	
venir / viniendo / venido	vengo	venía	vine	vendré	vendría	venga	viniera	ven tú, no
	vienes	venías	viniste	vendrás	vendrías	vengas	vinieras	vengas
	viene	venía	vino	vendrá	vendría	venga	viniera	venga Ud.
	venimos	veníamos	vinimos	vendremos	vendríamos	vengamos	viniéramos	vengamos
	venís	veníais	vinisteis	vendréis	vendríais	vengáis	vinierais	vengan
	vienen	venían	vinieron	vendrán	vendrían	vengan	vinieran	
ver / viendo / visto	veo	veía	vi	veré	vería	vea	viera	ve tú, no veas
	ves	veías	viste	verás	verías	veas	vieras	vea Ud.
	ve	veía	vio	verá	vería	vea	viera	veamos
	vemos	veíamos	vimos	veremos	veríamos	veamos	viéramos	vean
	veis	veíais	visteis	veréis	veríais	veáis	vierais	
	ven	veían	vieron	verán	verían	vean	vieran	

D. Stem-changing and spelling change verbs

INFINITIVE PRESENT PARTICIPLE PAST PARTICIPLE	INDICATIVE					SUBJUNCTIVE		COMMANDS
	PRESENT	IMPERFECT	PRETERITE	FUTURE	CONDITIONAL	PRESENT	PAST	
pensar (ie) pensando pensado	pienso	pensaba	pensé	pensaré	pensaría	piense	pensara	
	piensas	pensabas	pensaste	pensarás	pensarías	pienses	pensaras	piensa tú, no pienses
	piensa	pensaba	pensó	pensará	pensaría	piense	pensara	piense Ud.
	pensamos	pensábamos	pensamos	pensaremos	pensaríamos	pensemos	pensáramos	pensemos
	pensáis	pensabais	pensasteis	pensaréis	pensaríais	penséis	pensarais	
	piensan	pensaban	pensaron	pensarán	pensarían	piensen	pensaran	piensen
volver (ue) volviendo vuelto	vuelvo	volvía	volví	volveré	volvería	vuelva	volviera	
	vuelves	volvías	volviste	volverás	volverías	vuelvas	volvieras	vuelve tú, no vuelvas
	vuelve	volvía	volvió	volverá	volvería	vuelva	volviera	vuelva Ud.
	volvemos	volvíamos	volvimos	volveremos	volveríamos	volvamos	volviéramos	volvamos
	volvéis	volvíais	volvisteis	volveréis	volveríais	volváis	volvierais	
	vuelven	volvían	volvieron	volverán	volverían	vuelvan	volvieran	vuelvan
dormir (ue, u) durmiendo dormido	duermo	dormía	dormí	dormiré	dormiría	duerma	durmiera	
	duermes	dormías	dormiste	dormirás	dormirías	duermas	durmieras	duerme tú, no duermas
	duerme	dormía	durmió	dormirá	dormiría	duerma	durmiera	duerma Ud.
	dormimos	dormíamos	dormimos	dormiremos	dormiríamos	durmamos	durmiéramos	durmamos
	dormís	dormíais	dormisteis	dormiréis	dormiríais	durmáis	durmierais	duerman
	duermen	dormían	durmieron	dormirán	dormirían	duerman	durmieran	
sentir (ie, i) sintiendo sentido	siento	sentía	sentí	sentiré	sentiría	sienta	sintiera	
	sientes	sentías	sentiste	sentirás	sentirías	sientas	sintieras	siente tú, no sientas
	siente	sentía	sintió	sentirá	sentiría	sienta	sintiera	sienta Ud.
	sentimos	sentíamos	sentimos	sentiremos	sentiríamos	sintamos	sintiéramos	sintamos
	sentís	sentíais	sentisteis	sentiréis	sentiríais	sintáis	sintierais	sientan
	sienten	sentían	sintieron	sentirán	sentirían	sientan	sintieran	
pedir (i, i) pidiendo pedido	pido	pedía	pedí	pediré	pediría	pida	pidiera	
	pides	pedías	pediste	pedirás	pedirías	pidas	pidieras	pide tú, no pidas
	pide	pedía	pidió	pedirá	pediría	pida	pidiera	pida Ud.
	pedimos	pedíamos	pedimos	pediremos	pediríamos	pidamos	pidiéramos	pidamos
	pedís	pedíais	pedisteis	pediréis	pediríais	pidáis	pidierais	pidan
	piden	pedían	pidieron	pedirán	pedirían	pidan	pidieran	
reír (i, i) riendo reído	río	reía	reí	reiré	reiría	ría	riera	
	ríes	reías	reíste	reirás	reirías	rías	rieras	ríe tú, no rías
	ríe	reía	rió	reirá	reiría	ría	riera	ría Ud.
	reímos	reíamos	reímos	reiremos	reiríamos	riamos	riéramos	riamos
	reís	reíais	reísteis	reiréis	reiríais	riáis	rierais	rían
	ríen	reían	rieron	reirán	reirían	rían	rieran	
seguir (i, i) (ga) siguiendo seguido	sigo	seguía	seguí	seguiré	seguiría	siga	siguiera	
	sigues	seguías	seguiste	seguirás	seguirías	sigas	siguieras	sigue tú, no sigas
	sigue	seguía	siguió	seguirá	seguiría	siga	siguiera	siga Ud.
	seguimos	seguíamos	seguimos	seguiremos	seguiríamos	sigamos	siguiéramos	sigamos
	seguís	seguíais	seguisteis	seguiréis	seguiríais	sigáis	siguierais	sigan
	siguen	seguían	siguieron	seguirán	seguirían	sigan	siguieran	

D. Stem-changing and spelling change verbs (continued)

| INFINITIVE PRESENT PARTICIPLE PAST PARTICIPLE | INDICATIVE | | | | | SUBJUNCTIVE | | COMMANDS |
	PRESENT	IMPERFECT	PRETERITE	FUTURE	CONDITIONAL	PRESENT	PAST	
construir (y)	construyo	construía	construí	construiré	construiría	construya	construyera	construye tú,
construyendo	construyes	construías	construiste	construirás	construirías	construyas	construyeras	no construyas
construido	construye	construía	construyó	construirá	construiría	construya	construyera	construya Ud.
	construimos	construíamos	construimos	construiremos	construiríamos	construyamos	construyéramos	construyamos
	construís	construíais	construisteis	construiréis	construiríais	construyáis	construyerais	construyan
	construyen	construían	construyeron	construirán	construirían	construyan	construyeran	
producir (zc)	produzco	producía	produje	produciré	produciría	produzca	produjera	produce tú, no
produciendo	produces	producías	produjiste	producirás	producirías	produzcas	produjeras	produzcas
producido	produce	producía	produjo	producirá	produciría	produzca	produjera	produzca Ud.
	producimos	producíamos	produjimos	produciremos	produciríamos	produzcamos	produjéramos	produzcamos
	producís	producíais	produjisteis	produciréis	produciríais	produzcáis	produjerais	produzcan
	producen	producían	produjeron	producirán	producirían	produzcan	produjeran	

Appendix 2

Grammar Summary Tables

A. Personal pronouns

	SUBJECT	OBJECT OF PREPOSITION	REFLEXIVE	INDIRECT OBJECT	DIRECT OBJECT
I	yo	mí	me	me	me
you (fam. sing.)	tú	ti	te	te	te
you (form. sing.)	usted (Ud.)	usted (Ud.)	se	le	lo/la
he	él	él	se	le	lo
she	ella	ella			la
we	nosotros/as	nosotros/as	nos	nos	nos
you (fam. pl.)	vosotros/as	vosotros/as	os	os	os
you (pl.)	ustedes (Uds.)	ustedes (Uds.)	se	les	los/las
they	ellos	ellos	se	les	los
they (f.)	ellas	ellas			las

B. Possessive adjectives

my	mi, mis	*our*	nuestro/a, nuestros/as
your (fam. sing.)	tu, tus	*your (fam. pl.)*	vuestro/a, vuestros/as
your (sing.)	su, sus	*your (form. pl.)*	su, sus
his		*their*	
her			

C. Demonstrative adjectives and pronouns

	ADJECTIVES	PRONOUNS	NEUTER PRONOUNS
this, these	este/esta, estos/estas	éste/ésta, éstos/éstas	esto
that, those (*not close to speaker*)	ese/esa, esos/esas	ése/ésa, ésos/ésas	eso
that, those (*farther from speaker*)	aquel/aquella, aquellos/aquellas	aquél/aquélla, aquéllos/aquéllas	aquello

D. *Por* and *para*

POR		PARA	
through, by	por el parque, por teléfono	*destination*	para México
length of time	por una hora	*time*	cinco minutos para la una
during	por la noche	*deadline*	para el lunes
in place of	Hoy trabajo por Carlos.	*recipient*	Trabajo para mis hijos.
quantity	por mil pesos		Es un regalo para Cecilia.
means	por avión		
per	por ciento		

E. Preterite and imperfect

PRETERITE		IMPERFECT	
completed event	comí	*event in progress*	comía
completed state	estuve	*ongoing state*	estaba
completed series of actions	bailé, canté	*("used to," was/were + -ing)*	bailaba, cantaba
interrupting action	toqué	*simultaneous action*	leía, miraba

F. Indicative and subjunctive

INDICATIVE		SUBJUNCTIVE	
assertion	es verdad que	*possibility*	es posible que
belief	creer que	*doubt*	dudar que
knowledge	saber que	*emotional reaction*	estar contento/a de que
		attempt to influence	querer que
cuando + *habitual action*	cuando trabajo, siempre...	*cuando + future action*	mañana, cuando trabaje...

Spanish-English Vocabulary

The Spanish-English Vocabulary contains all the words that appear in the text, with the following exceptions: (1) many close or identical cognates that do not appear in the chapter vocabulary lists; (2) most conjugated verb forms; (3) diminutives ending in **-ito/a**; (4) absolute superlatives ending in **-ísimo/a**; (5) most adverbs ending in **-mente**; (6) much vocabulary that is glossed in the text; and (7) much vocabulary from realia and authentic readings. Active vocabulary is indicated by the number of the chapter in which a word or given meaning first appears; vocabulary that is glossed in the text is not considered to be active vocabulary and is not numbered. Only meanings that are used in the text are given.

The gender of nouns is indicated, except for masculine nouns ending in **-o** and feminine nouns ending in **-a**. Stem and spelling changes are indicated for verbs as follows: **dormir (ue, u); llegar (gu).**

Words beginning with **ch, ll,** and **ñ** are found under separate headings, following the letters **c, l,** and **n,** respectively.* Similarly, **ch, ll,** and **ñ** within words follow **c, l,** and **n,** respectively. For example, **coche** follows **cocinero, calle** follows **calor,** and **añadir** follows **anuncio.**

The following abbreviations are used:

adj.	adjective	*inv.*	invariable form	*poss.*	possessive
adv.	adverb	*i.o.*	indirect object	*p.p.*	past participle
conj.	conjunction	*irreg.*	irregular	*prep.*	preposition
d.o.	direct object	*L.A.*	Latin America	*pron.*	pronoun
f.	feminine	*lit.*	literally	*R*	Repaso (review vocabulary)
fam.	familiar	*m.*	masculine	*refl. pron.*	reflexive pronoun
form.	formal	*Mex.*	Mexico	*s.*	singular
gram.	grammatical term	*n.*	noun	*Sp.*	Spain
inf.	infinitive	*obj. (of prep.)*	object (of a preposition)	*sub. pron.*	subject pronoun
interj.	interjection	*pl.*	plural		

A

a at, to (1); **a base de** based on; **a caballo** (on) a horse, horseback (6); **a causa de(l)** because of, on account of; **a consecuencia** as a result; **a diferencia de** unlike; **a domicilio** in-home, to your home; **a eso de** at about, at around, at approximately (5); **a fuego lento** by slow fire, low flame, or heat (*cooking*); **a la derecha (de)** to the right (of) (5); **a la disposición de** at the disposal of; **a la izquierda (de)** to the left (of) (5); **a la larga** in the long run, in the end; **a la marinera** sailor-fashion; **a la plancha** broiled, grilled; **a la veracruzana** in the style of Veracruz; **a lo largo de** throughout; **a media mañana** in the/at midmorning; **a media tarde** in the/at midafternoon; **a menudo** frequently; **a partir de** from (*specific time, amount, etc.*) onward; **a pesar de** in spite of; **a pie** on/by foot (5); **a propósito** by the way; **a punto de** (+ *inf.*) about to (*do something*); **¿a qué hora?** (at) what time?; **a tiempo** on time (4); **a través de** through, by

---

*Several language academies have recently decided that **ch** and **ll** should no longer be considered separate letters of the Spanish alphabet. Because it is difficult to predict what effect the decision of the academies may have on Spanish usage throughout the world, this vocabulary list treats **ch** and **ll** as separate letters.

means of; **a última hora** at the last moment; **a veces** sometimes, at times (3); **a ver** let's see (5)

abandonar to leave

abierto/a *p.p.* open; sincere, frank

abnegación *f.* self-denial

abogado/a lawyer (3)

abrazo hug, embrace (1)

abrigo overcoat (2)

abril *m.* April (6)

abrir (*p.p.* **abierto/a**) to open (3)

absolutamente absolutely (8)

absorber to absorb

abuelito/a grandpa/grandma (1, 2R)

abuelo/a grandfather/grandmother (2); **abuelos** grandparents (2); grandfathers

abundar to be plentiful

aburrido/a bored (1); boring (2); **estar** (*irreg.*) **aburrido/a** to be bored (1); **ser** (*irreg.*) **aburrido/a** to be boring (2)

aburrirse to become bored, be bored

abusar to abuse

abuso *n.* abuse

acabar to finish; to run out of; to use up completely; **acabar con** to destroy, wipe out; **acabar de** (+ *inf.*) to have just (*done something*) (4)

acampar to camp (6)

acapulqueño/a Acapulcan, from Acapulco

acaso *adv.* by chance, perchance; **por acaso** by chance

accidente *m.* accident

acción *f.* attitude; action (*of an actor or speaker*); **Día** (*m.*) **de Acción de Gracias** Thanksgiving Day; **en acción** in action, at work

aceite *m.* oil (7); **aceite de oliva** olive oil (7)

aceptación *f.* acceptance

aceptar to accept

acera sidewalk

acerca de *prep.* about, concerning (5)

acercarse (**qu**) (**a**) to approach, draw near (to)

ácido/a: lluvia ácida acid rain (10)

aclarar to clarify

acogedor(a) *adj.* welcoming, inviting

acompañar to accompany

aconsejar to advise, counsel

acontecimiento event

acostar (**ue**) to put to bed; **acostarse** to go to bed (4)

acostumbrado/a (**a**) *adj.* accustomed (to), used (to) (6)

acrílico acrylic

actitud *f.* attitude; **cambio de actitud** change in attitude

actividad *f.* activity

acto ceremony; **acto de velación** *ceremony of veiling the bride and bridegroom at the nuptial mass*

actor *m.* actor (3)

actriz *f.* (*pl.* **actrices**) actress (3)

actual *adj.* current, present-day

actualidad *f.* present time; **en la actualidad** at the present time, nowadays

actualmente *adv.* currently, nowadays (11)

actuar (**actúo**) to act

acuático/a *adj.* aquatic

acudir (**a**) to go or come (to); to come or go to the aid or assistance (of)

acuerdo agreement; **de acuerdo** agreed; OK (by me) (8); **de acuerdo con** in agreement with; **estar** (*irreg.*) **de acuerdo** to agree, be in agreement (5)

achiote *m.* annatto (*dyestuff*)

adaptación *f.* adaptation

adecuado/a adequate

adelanto advance; improvement

además (**de**) besides, in addition (to)

adherir (**ie, i**) to adhere, stick (to)

adinerado/a *adj.* wealthy, affluent, well-to-do

adiós good-bye (1)

adivinar to guess

adjetivo *gram.* adjective (1); **adjetivo demostrativo** *gram.* demonstrative adjective (5)

administrador(a) de empresas administrator, businessperson (3)

admirar to admire

admitir to admit; to accept

adonde *adv.* where

¿adónde? (to) where? (2)

adopción *f.* adoption

adoptar to adopt

adoptivo/a adoptive; **hijo/a adoptivo/a** adopted child

adorar to adore; to worship

adorno ornament, decoration; trimming

adquirir (**ie**) to acquire; to purchase

aduana customs office (1)

adverbial *gram.* adverbial (3)

adverbio *gram.* adverb (1)

advertir (**ie, i**) to warn

aéreo/a: correo aéreo airmail (8); **línea aérea** airline

aeróbico/a: danza aeróbica aerobic dancing; **hacer** (*irreg.*) **(los) ejercicios aeróbicos** to do aerobics, aerobic exercises (6)

aerolínea airline

aeromozo/a flight attendant

aeropuerto airport (5)

afectar to affect

afeitarse to shave (4)

afición *f.* fondness, liking

aficionado/a (**a**) fan, enthusiast (of)

afirmar to affirm, assert

afortunado/a *adj.* lucky, fortunate

africano/a *n., adj.* African

afuera *adv.* outside

afueras *n. f. pl.* outskirts (*of a town*) (4)

agencia de viajes travel agency (5)

agente *m., f.* agent; salesperson (3); **agente de viajes** travel agent (8)

ágil agile

agosto August (6)

agradable pleasant (2)

agradecer (**zc**) to thank for; to be grateful for

agregar (**gu**) to add

agrícola *adj.* agricultural

agricultura agriculture; **Secretaría de Agricultura y Recursos Hidráulicos** Department of Agriculture and Water Resources

agrícola of or pertaining to farms

agrimensor land surveyor

agropecuario/a *adj.* pertaining to agriculture and cattle raising

agua *f.* (*but* **el agua**) water (7); **agua mineral (con gas)** (carbonated) mineral water; **agua subterránea** ground water (10); **aguas frescas** *Mex.* water with fruit juice

aguacate *m.* avocado (7)

aguado/a *adj.* watery; clear (*soup*)

aguafiestas *m., f. s.* kill-joy

aguardar to wait (for)

águila *f.* (*but* **el águila**) eagle (10)

aguileño/a *adj.* hawk-nosed

ahí there

ahora now (1); **ahora mismo** right now

ahorrar to save (9)

ahuecar (**qu**) to hollow; to loosen

aire *m.* air (10); **al aire libre** outdoors, in the open air; **contaminación** (*f.*) **del aire** air pollution

aislado/a isolated

ajeno/a another's

ajiaco *L.A. dish of boiled meat and vegetables, seasoned with chili*

ajo garlic (7)

ajustado/a tight, close-fitting

al (*contraction of* **a** + **el**) to the; **al** + *inf.* upon, while, when (*doing something*); **al aire libre** outdoors, in the open air; **al (año, mes, etcétera)** per (year, month, etc.); **al borde de** on the verge of; **al contrario** on the contrary (4); **al corriente** up to date; **al día** per day; **al fin** finally, at last; **al frente (de)** in front (of) (4); **al igual** equally; **al lado (de)** next (to) (5); by the side (of); **al**

margen de outside of; **al principio** at first, in the beginning; **al revés** backwards

alabar to praise; to celebrate

alacena cabinet (4)

albo/a white

alcanzar (c) to reach; to attain; to obtain

alcoba bedroom (4)

alegar (gu) to allege, profess; to argue, dispute

alegrarse (de) to be glad/happy (about) (9)

alegre *adj.* joyful, happy

alegría happiness, joy, pleasure

alemán *n. m.* German (language)

alemán, alemana *n., adj.* German

Alemania Germany (2)

alfabetismo literacy; **tasa de alfabetismo** literacy rate

alfabeto alphabet

alfabeto/a *adj.* literate

alfombra rug (4); carpet (4)

alfombrado/a carpeted

álgebra *f.* (*but* **el álgebra**) algebra (3)

algo *pron.* something (5); anything; *adv.* somewhat, a little

algodón *m.* cotton (5)

alguien someone, anyone

algún, alguno/a some, any (4); **algún día** some day; **alguna vez** once, ever; **algunas veces** sometimes, at times

alianza alliance (*by marriage*)

aliarse (yo me alío) to ally, unite in a league

alimento food (*item*)

aliviar to alleviate, relieve

alma *f.* (*but* **el alma**) soul

almacén *m.* department store

almohadón *m.* large cushion

almorzar (ue) (c) to eat lunch (4)

almuerzo lunch (3)

aló hello (*telephone*)

alojamiento *n.* lodging

alpinismo mountain climbing; **hacer** (*irreg.*) **alpinismo** to go mountain climbing (6)

alquilar to rent (9)

alrededor de *prep.* around (5)

alrededores *n. m. pl.* space around; surroundings, outskirts

altar *m.* altar

altavoz *m* (*pl.* **altavoces**) loudspeaker

altiplano high plateau

alto/a tall (2, 5R); high (5); **alta calidad** *f.* high quality

altura height; elevation

alubia bean

alumno/a student, pupil (1)

allá there, over there (3)

allí there (1)

ama [*f.* (*but* **el ama**)] **de casa** housewife; homemaker (*female*) (3)

amable kind, nice

amanecer (zc) to dawn

amargo/a bitter

amarillo/a yellow (2); **fiebre** (*f.*) **amarilla** yellow fever

amate *m.* Mexican bark painting; Mexican fig tree

Amazonas *m. s.* Amazon (river)

amazónico/a Amazonian; **selva amazónica** Amazon jungle

ambición *f.* ambition

ambiental *adj.* pertaining to the atmosphere or setting

ambiente *m.* environment, atmosphere; **medio ambiente** environment

ámbito sphere; field, area

ambos/as both

amenazado/a threatened

América: América Central Central America; **América del Norte** North America; **América del Sur** South America; **América Latina** Latin America

americano/a *n., adj.* American; **fútbol** (*m.*) **(norte)americano** football (6); **liga americana** American (baseball) League

amigo/a friend (1)

amistad *f.* friendship

amo de casa homemaker (3)

amor *m.* love (11)

amplio/a large; wide; comprehensive

amurallar to wall, defend with walls

analfabetismo illiteracy

analfabeto/a illiterate person

analizar (c) to analyze

anaranjado/a *adj.* orange (2)

anatomía anatomy

anciano/a elderly person

andar (*irreg.*) to walk (5); **andar a la caza** (**de**) to be on the hunt (for)

andén *m.* railway platform

anécdota anecdote

anexar to annex

ángel *m.* angel

angustia anguish, distress

anhelar to long or yearn for, covet

anillo ring

animado/a lively; full of life; **dibujo animado** cartoon

animal *m.* animal; **animal doméstico** pet

animar to enliven, brighten

ánimo: estado de ánimo state of mind

aniversario anniversary (9); **aniversario de bodas** wedding anniversary (6)

anoche last night (5)

Antárdita Antarctica

ante before; in the presence of

anteayer day before yesterday (5)

antecedente *m., f.* predecessor, ancestor

antecesor(a) ancestor, forebear

antepasado/a ancestor, forebear

anterior previous (7), preceding; **día** (*m.*) **anterior** yesterday; **noche** (*f.*) **anterior** the night before

antes *adv.* sooner, before; **antes (de)** *prep.* before (4); **antes de** + *inf.* before (*doing something*) (5); **antes de Cristo** before Christ (B.C.)

anticiclónico/a *adj.* anticyclonic, of/with high atmospheric pressure

antiguo/a old (4); ancient; former

Antillas *f. pl.* Antilles, West Indies

antipático/a not likable, obnoxious (2)

antojito appetizer

antropología anthropology (11)

anual annual

anunciar to announce

anuncio announcement (11); advertisement (11); **anuncio de matrimonio** wedding announcement; **anuncios** advertising (11)

añadir to add

año year; **año escolar** school year; **Año Nuevo Chino** Chinese New Year (6); **año pasado** last year (5); **año que viene** next year; **años de casados** years of marriage; **¿cuántos años tienes?** how old are you (*s. fam.*)? (1); **cumplir** _____ **años** to turn _____ years old; **dentro de** _____ **años** within _____ years; **Día** (*m.*) **de Año Nuevo** New Year's Day (6); **durante** (_____) **años** for (_____) years; **hace** _____ **años** _____ years ago; **tener** (*irreg.*) _____ **años (de edad)** to be _____ years old (2); **tengo** _____ **años** I'm _____ years old (1); **todos los años** every year (6)

apadrinar to act as godparent to

apagado/a dead, extinct (*volcano*)

apagar (gu) to turn off (*lights, appliance*)

aparato appliance (4); device; **aparato eléctrico** electrical appliance (4)

aparecer (zc) to appear

apartamento apartment, flat (4)

aparte *m.* aside (*theater*)

apasionado/a ardent, impassioned

apellido family name, surname, last name (1)

apenas scarcely, hardly

aperitivo aperitif, cocktail (7)

apetito appetite

apio celery (7)

aplicación *f.* application (*software*) (11); appliqué

apoderarse de to seize, take hold of

aportar to contribute; to bring, furnish

apoyo support

apreciar to like, have a regard for; to evaluate, appraise; to value

aprender (a) to learn (how to) (3)

aprobar (ue) to approve; to pass, adopt (*bill, law, etc.*)

apropiado/a appropriate

aprovechar to make good use (of)

aprovisionar to supply, furnish

aproximadamente approximately (8)

aproximado/a approximate

apurarse to hurry

aquel, aquella *adj.* that (*remote*) (5); **aquél, aquélla** *prom.* that one (*remote*) (5); **en aquel entonces** back then, in those days

aquellos/as *adj.* those (*remote*) (5); **aquéllos/as** *pron.* those (ones) (*remote*) (5)

aquí here (1); **aquí (muy) cerca** (very) near here

árabe *n. m.* Arabic (language); *adj.* Arab

araña spider; **araña patona** daddy-longlegs spider

árbol *m.* tree (6)

arbusto bush (10)

arcilla clay

archipiélago archipelago

ardilla squirrel (10)

área *f.* (*but* **el área**) area

arena sand

arete *m.* earring (5)

Argentina Argentina (2)

argentino/a *n., adj.* Argentine (2)

árido/a arid

aritmética arithmetic

arma *f.* (*but* **el arma**) arm, weapon

armario wardrobe, closet

armonía harmony

arpón *m.* harpoon

arqueológico/a archaeological

arqueólogo/a archaeologist

arquitecto/a architect

arquitectónico/a architectural

arquitectura architecture (3)

arras *f. pl. thirteen coins given by the bridegroom to the bride at a wedding*

arreglar to fix (3); to arrange, straighten up (*room*) (3)

arreglo arrangement (8); agreement, compromise; **arreglo personal** personal grooming

arriba above, on top (6); up, upwards; **desde arriba** from the top; **para arriba** and up (*with numbers*) (5)

arrojar to put forth; to shed; to throw out

arroz *m.* (*pl.* **arroces**) rice (7)

arruinado/a ruined, destroyed

arte *f.* (*but* **el arte**) art (3); **artes marciales** martial arts (6); **bellas artes** fine arts (3); **practicar (qu) las artes marciales** to do martial arts (6)

artesanía *s.* crafts

artículo article (11); **artículo definido** *gram.* definite article

artista *m., f.* artist (3)

artístico/a artistic

asado/a roasted (7); grilled (7); **carne** (*f.*) **asada** roasted meat; **cochinillo asado** roast suckling pig

ascendencia ancestry

asegurar to guarantee, make safe; **asegurarse** to make sure

aseo público public bathroom

asesinar to assassinate, murder

asesinato assassination, murder

así thus, so (5); **así como** as well as; **así que** therefore, consequently

asiento seat

asimilación *f.* assimilation

asimilarse to assimilate, be assimilated

asistencia assistance; attendance, presence

asistente *m., f.* assistant, helper; **asistente graduado** graduate assistant; **asistente residencial** resident assistant

asistir (a) to attend (3)

asociación *f.* association

asociado/a: estado libre asociado free associated state

asociar to associate; **asociarse (con)** to be associated (with)

asombrar to amaze, astonish (6)

aspecto aspect; appearance

aspiración *f.* aspiration

aspiradora vacuum cleaner; **pasar la aspiradora** to vacuum

aspirar a to aspire after

aspirina aspirin (5)

astronauta *m., f.* astronaut

asturiano/a Asturian

asumir to assume (*role, reponsibilities, etc.*)

asunto matter, subject; affair, business

atacar (qu) to attack

ataque *m.* attack

atardecer *m.* evening, twilight

ataviado/a dressed, adorned

atavío dress, adornment

Atenas Athens

atención *f.* attention; **poner** (*irreg.*) **atención** to pay attention; **prestar atención** to pay attention (7)

atender (ie) to attend to; to serve

atentado murder or attempted murder, attempt upon the life (*of a person*)

Atlántico: Océano Atlántico Atlantic Ocean

atleta *m., f.* athlete (2)

atlético/a athletic; **entrenador** (*m.*) **atlético** athletic trainer

atletismo track and field (6); **practicar (qu) el atletismo** to practice, do track and field (6)

atmósfera atmosphere

atónito/a astonished, aghast

atracción *f.* attraction

atractivo/a attractive (2); engaging, charming

atraer (*like* **traer**) to attract (5)

atraso backwardness

atravesar (ie) to cross, span, bridge; to go through

atún *m.* tuna, tuna fish (7)

audífonos *m. pl.* earphones

auditoría ecológica ecological audit

aumentar to increase

aun *adv.* even

aún *adv.* still, yet

aunque although (9)

auricular *m.* receiver (*telephone*) (8); earpiece; headphone; **descolgar (gu) el auricular** to pick up the phone

austríaco/a *n., adj.* Austrian

auto car (5), automobile

autobús *m.* bus (1, 5R); **chófer** (*m.*) **del autobús** bus driver (1); **estación** (*f.*) **de autobuses** bus station (1); **parada de autobús** bus stop

autocopiar to make a copy of (*program, software application*) (11)

automóvil *m.* automobile

autonomía autonomy

autónomo/a autonomous

autopista motorway; freeway

autor(a) author (3)

auxiliar *adj.* auxiliary

auxilio help, aid, relief

avance *n. m.* advance

avanzado/a advanced (5)

avanzar (c) to advance

avanzo balance sheet

ave *f.* (*but* **el ave**) bird; *pl.* poultry (7); **ave de rapina** bird of prey; **ave de corral** domestic fowl

avenida avenue (1)

aventura adventure

avión *m.* airplane (5)

¡ay! *interj.* oh! (1), alas!; **ay, lo siento** oh, I'm sorry (1)

ayer *adv., n., m.* yesterday (3)

aymará *n. m., f., adj.* Aymara; *member of or related to indigenous group from the area around Lake Titicaca in Peru and Bolivia*

ayuda help, assistance

ayudar to help (5)

azteca *n. m., f.* Aztec

azúcar *m.* sugar (7); **caña de azúcar** sugar cane

azul blue (2)

B

bachillerato *course of studies equivalent to high school, junior college*

bahía bay (1); **Bahía de Cochinos** Bay of Pigs (*Cuba*)

bailar to dance (5)

bailarín, bailarina dancer

baile *m.* dance (6)

bajar to descend, go down; to lower; to drop; **bajarse** to get off (*bus, train, etc.*) (5)

bajo *prep.* under (5); **bajo techo** under a roof

bajo/a *adj.* short (*in height*) (2); low; **bajo en calorías** low in calories; **barrio bajo** slum; **de baja estatura** short

bajorrelieve *m.* bas-relief

balboa *m. Panamanian monetary unit*

balcón *m.* balcony (4)

Baleares: Islas (*f. pl.*) **Baleares** Balearic Islands

balneario resort, spa

ballet *m.* ballet

banana banana (7)

bananal *m.* banana plantation

bancario/a *adj.* banking, bank; **transacción** (f.) **bancaria** bank transaction (8)

banco bank (5); bench

bandera flag

banquete *m.* banquet

bañarse to bathe, take a bath (4); to swim

bañera bathtub (4)

baño bathroom (4); bath; **traje** (*m.*) **de baño** swimsuit (2)

bar *m.* bar (5)

barato/a inexpensive, cheap

barba beard (2)

barbacoa barbecue (4)

barbarie *f.* barbarism; barbarity

barco boat, ship (9)

barmitzvah *m.* Bar Mitzvah (6)

barranca canyon; abyss

barrio neighborhood; quarter, district; **barrio bajo** slum

basar to base, found; **basarse en** to be based on

base *f.* base, basis; **a base de** based on

básico/a basic

basílica basilica

básquetbol *m.* basketball (6); **jugar (ue) (gu) al básquetbol** to play basketball (6)

bastante rather, quite, fairly; sufficiently; a lot

basura garbage

basurero trash can

batalla battle

batallón *m.* battalion

bateador(a) (baseball) batter

bautista *n. m.* baptizer; *adj.* Baptist

bautizar (c) to baptize, name

bautizo baptism (9)

bebé *m.* baby

beber to drink (3)

bebida beverage (7), drink

beca scholarship

béisbol *m.* baseball (6); **jugar (ue) (gu) al béisbol** to play baseball (6)

beisbolista *m., f.* baseball player

belleza beauty

bello/a beautiful; **bellas artes** *f. pl.* fine arts (3)

bendición *f.* benediction, blessing

beneficiar to benefit

beneficio benefit, profit

beso kiss (1)

bestia de carga beast of burden

biblioteca library (1)

bibliotecario/a librarian

bicicleta bicycle (5); **montar en bicicleta** to ride a bicycle (6)

bien *n. m.* good; *adv.* well, fine (1); **muy bien** very well, fine (1); **pasarlo bien** to have a good time; **que le vaya bien** hope all goes well (for you [*form. s.*]) (1); **que te vaya bien** hope all goes well (for you [*fam. s.*]) (1); **salir** (*irreg.*) **bien** to do well (7)

bienestar *m.* well-being; happiness

bienvenida: dar (*irreg.*) **la bienvenida** to welcome (5); **fiesta de bienvenida** welcoming party

bienvenido/a *adj.* welcome

biftec *m.* (beef)steak (7)

bigote *m.* moustache (2)

bilingüe bilingual; **educación** (*f.*) **bilingüe** bilingual education

bilingüismo bilingualism

billón *m.* billion

biología biology (3); **cadena biológica** food chain

bioquímico/a biochemist

bistec *m.* steak

blanco *n.* target; **televisor** (*m.*) **en blanco y negro** black and white television

blanco/a white; **la Casa Blanca** the White House; **pelo blanco** gray/ white hair (2); **vino blanco** white wine

blandir to brandish, swing

blando/a soft; mild, bland

blusa blouse (2)

boca mouth (4); **limpiarse la boca** to brush one's teeth

bocadillo sandwich

bocina (telephone) receiver

boda wedding (ceremony) (9); **aniversario de bodas** wedding anniversary (6)

bodega wine shop

bola: queso de bola cottage cheese

boleto ticket (8); **boleto de ida y vuelta** round-trip ticket (8)

boliche *m.* bowling; **jugar (ue) (gu) al boliche** to bowl, go bowling (6)

bolígrafo ballpoint pen (3)

bolívar *m. Venezuelan monetary unit*

boliviano/a *n., adj.* Bolivian

bombilla light bulb

bondad *f.* goodness; kindness

bonito/a pretty (2)

bordado/a embroidered

borde: al borde de on the verge of

borincano/a *n., adj.* indigenous Puerto Rican

Borinquén *ancient name of Puerto Rico*

borrador *m.* blackboard eraser (3)

bosque *m.* woods, forest (1)

bostezo yawn

botana *Mex.* appetizer (7)

botella bottle (7)

boutique *f.* boutique

boxear to box (*sport*)

boxeo *n.* boxing (*sport*) (6); **practicar (qu) el boxeo** to practice, do boxing (6)

Brasil *m.* Brazil (2)

brasileño/a *n., adj.* Brazilian (2)

bravo: Río Bravo Rio Grande

brazalete *m.* bracelet (5)

brazo arm (4); **tomados/as del brazo** arm-in-arm

breve short, brief; **en breve** shortly; at a glance

brillante brilliant

brillar to shine

brindar to offer

británico/a *n., adj.* British

broche *m.* brooch

bronceador(a): crema bronceadora suntan lotion

bruto: producto nacional bruto gross national product

buceo scuba diving

buen, bueno/a *adj.* good (1); **buena suerte** good luck; **buenas costumbres** good manners; **buenas noches** good evening, good night (1); **buenas noticias** good news; **buenas tardes** good afternoon (1); **buenos días** good morning (1); **buen provecho** enjoy your meal (*lit.*, good appetite); **de**

buena cepa of acknowledged good quality; **hace (muy) buen tiempo** the weather's (very) nice (5, 6R); **hierba buena** mint; **(no) es bueno que ...** it's (not) good that . . . (9); **tener** (*irreg.*) **buena suerte** to be lucky (9); **yerba buena** mint

bueno *adv.* well; OK; *Mex.* hello (*telephone*) (8); **¡qué bueno!** *interj.* how nice! (1)

bufete *m.* lawyer's office

buho owl (10)

bulevar *m.* boulevard

burlarse de to make fun of

busca: en busca de in quest of

buscar (qu) to look for (3)

búsqueda search, quest

buzo diver

buzón *m.* mailbox (8)

C

caballo horse (10); **carrera de caballos** horse race; **montar a caballo** to ride a horse, ride horseback (6)

caber: no cabe duda there is no doubt

cabeza head (4); **dolor** (*m.*) **de cabeza** headache; **me duele la cabeza** I have a headache

cable: televisión (*f.*) **por cable** cable television (11)

cabo: llevar a cabo to carry out, accomplish

cabra goat (10)

cacahuete *m.* peanut; **mantequilla de cacahuetes** peanut butter (7)

cacao cocoa

cacto cactus

cada *inv.* each, every; **cada vez más** more and more

cadena chain; **cadena biológica** food chain; **cadena de montañas** mountain range

cadmio cadmium

caer (*irreg.*) to fall

café *m.* coffee (4, 7R); café (5); brown (*color*) (2); **de color** (*m.*) **café** brown (2)

cafecito coffee

cafetal *m.* coffee plantation

cafetería cafeteria

caja teller's cage (8); cashier's desk

cajero/a cashier (3, 8R); bank teller (8)

calabaza squash (7); pumpkin (7)

calamar *m.* squid, calamary

calavera skull

calcetín *m.* sock (2)

calculadora calculator (11)

calcular to estimate, calculate (11)

cálculo calculus (3)

caldo de gallina chicken broth, bouillon, soup

calendario calendar (3)

caléndula pot marigold

calidad *f.* quality (10); **alta calidad** high quality; **calidad de vida** quality of life

cálido/a warm

caliente hot (7); **té** (*m.*) **caliente** hot tea (7)

calificación *f.* grade

calor *m.* heat (6); **hace (mucho) calor** it is (very) hot (6); **tener** (*irreg.*) **(mucho) calor** to be (feel) (very) warm, hot

caloría calorie (7); **bajo/a en calorías** low in calories

caluroso/a hot

callado/a quiet (2), silent

calle *f.* street (1)

callos *m. pl.* tripe

cama bed (4); **hacer** (*irreg.*) **la cama** to make the bed (4)

cámara chamber, house (*legislative body; board, council*); camera; **cámara de vídeo** video camera (11); **dirección** (*f.*) **de cámaras** director of photography

camarón *m.* marine shrimp or prawn; *pl.* shrimp (7)

cambiar to change (8); to cash (8); to exchange (*currency*) (8); **cambiar de** to change; **cambiar de colores** to change colors; **cambiar un cheque (de viajero)** to cash a (traveler's) check

cambio change (4); exchange (8); **¿a cuánto está el cambio?** how much is the exchange rate?; **cambio de actitud** change in attitude; **casa de cambio** currency exchange house (8); **tasa de cambio** exchange rate (*currency*) (8); **verbo de cambio radical** *gram.* stem-changing verb (4)

caminar to walk (5)

camino path, road, way

camión *m.* truck (5); *Mex.* bus

camionero/a: central (*f.*) **camionera** *Mex.* main bus station

camioneta pickup (5); van (5); station wagon (5)

camisa shirt (2)

camiseta T-shirt (2)

campana bell

campesino/a farm worker, peasant

campo country, rural area (5); field, ground; **casa de campo** country house; **día** (*m.*) **de campo** day in the country

campus *m.* (university) campus

Canadá *m.* Canada (2)

canadiense *n., adj.* Canadian (2)

canal *m.* channel (11); canal; **Canal de Panamá** Panama Canal

Canarias: Islas (*f. pl.*) **Canarias** Canary Islands

canción *f.* song

candelabro candelabrum

cancha court; **cancha de pelota** ball court

canela cinnamon

canguro kangaroo (10)

canoa canoe

cansado/a tired (1)

cansar(se) to tire, grow weary

cantante *m., f.* singer

cantar to sing (8, 10R); to crow (10)

cantidad *f.* quantity

canto *n.* singing; chant, song

caña de azúcar sugar cane

capa de ozono ozone layer (10)

capacidad *f.* capacity, capability, ability

capaz (*pl.* **capaces**) capable

capital *f.* capital (city) (4)

capitalino/a inhabitant of a capital city

capitolio capitol

capítulo chapter (6)

captar to win, secure

cara face

carácter *m.* character; **caracteres** *pl.* personality

característica *n.* characteristic (2)

característico/a *adj.* characteristic

caramelo caramel

cardinal: dirección (*f.*) **cardinal** cardinal direction (*north, south, east, west*) (5)

carga load, burden; **bestia de carga** beast of burden

cargamento cargo, shipment

cargar (gu) to charge; to debit

cargo: tener (*irreg.*) **a su cargo** to be in charge of

Caribe *n. m.* Caribbean; **Mar** (*m.*) **Caribe** Caribbean Sea

caribeño/a *adj.* Caribbean

caridad *f.* charity

cariñoso/a loving, affectionate

carnaval *m.* carnival (*season of merrymaking before Lent, especially the three days before Ash Wednesday*)

carne *f.* meat (5); flesh; **carne asada** roasted meat; **carne de cordero** lamb (7); **carne de puerco** pork (7); **carne de res** beef (7); **carne ranchera** *dish of beef and beans*; **en carne propia** in the flesh

carnicería butcher shop, meat market (5)

caro/a expensive (5)

carrera race; career, profession; course of studies; **carrera de caballos** horse race

carretera highway (1) road; **Carretera Panamericana** Pan-American Highway (1)

carro car (5), automobile

carta letter (5); playing card; **echar una carta al correo** to mail a letter (8); **echar una carta en el buzón** to mail a letter; **jugar (ue) a las cartas** to play cards (6); **papel** (*m.*) **para cartas** stationery (5)

cartel *m.* billboard; poster

cartera wallet (5)

cartulina fine cardboard or construction paper Bristol board; card, invitation

casa house (2); **amo/ama** (*f.* [*but* **el ama**]) **de casa** homemaker (3); **casa de cambio** currency exchange house (8); **casa de campo** country house; **casa de verano** summer (vacation) house; **casa particular** private home, house (4); **en casa (de)** at (the) home (of) (3); **especialidad** (*f.*) **de la casa** specialty of the house; **la Casa Blanca** the White House

casadero/a marriageable

casado/a married; **años** (*m. pl.*) **de casados** years of marriage; **recién casado/a** *n.* newlywed (9)

casarse (con) to get married (to)

cascabel: serpiente (*f.*) **de cascabel** rattlesnake

cascada waterfall

casero/a: labores (*f. pl.*) **caseras** household tasks, chores

casi almost, nearly (4)

caso case, event; affair

cassette *m.* cassette (2)

castaño/a brown; chestnut, hazel; **ojos castaños** brown eyes (2); **pelo castaño** brown hair (2)

castellano Castilian or Spanish language

castellano/a *n., adj.* Castilian

castigar (gu) to punish

castigo punishment

castillo castle

casualidad: por casualidad by chance

catalán *m.* Catalan (language)

Cataluña Catalonia

catarata waterfall; **Cataratas de Niágara** Niagara Falls; **Cataratas del Iguazú** Iguazú Falls

catedral *f.* cathedral

categoría: de primera categoría first-class

católico/a *n., adj.* Catholic

catorce fourteen (1)

caucho rubber, gum elastic

causa cause; **a causa de(l)** because of, on account of (the)

causación *f.* causation

causar to cause (10)

cazar (c) to hunt (6); **andar** (*irreg.*) **a la caza (de)** to be on the hunt (for)

cazuela earthen cooking pan

cebada barley

cebiche *m. spiced dish of raw fish marinated in lemon juice*

cebolla onion (7)

cebra zebra (10)

ceder to surrender

celebración *f.* celebration

celebrar to celebrate (4)

celebridad *m., f.* celebrity (*well-known person*)

celular: teléfono celular cellular telephone (11)

cementerio cemetery

cena dinner (3)

cenar to have dinner, supper (7)

centavo cent

centígrado/a centigrade

central *n. f.* head or main office; *adj.* central; **América Central** Central America; **central camionera** *Mex.* main bus station; **plaza central** central, main square/plaza

centrarse to be centered

centro downtown (4); center, middle (4); **centro comercial** mall (5), shopping center; business district (5); **centro estudiantil** (university) student union

Centroamérica Central America

centroamericano/a Central American

cepa: de buena cepa of acknowledged good quality

cepillarse to brush (one's hair or teeth) (4)

cera wax

cerámica ceramic (5); ceramics, tile, pottery

cerca *adv.* nearby, near (1, 5R), close; **aquí (muy) cerca** (very) near here; **cerca de** *prep.* near to (1, 5R), close to

cercano/a *adj.* close by

cerdo pig (10)

cereal *m.* cereal (7)

ceremonia ceremony

cereza cherry (7)

cero zero (1)

cerrar (ie) to close (8)

certamen *m. competition for a literary, artistic, or scientific prize*

cerveza beer (4, 7R)

cesta basket

ciclismo cycling (6), bicycling; **practicar (qu) el ciclismo** to practice, do cycling (6)

ciclista *m., f.* cyclist

ciclo cycle

cielo sky (10); heaven (10)

cien, ciento one hundred (5); **por ciento** percent (2)

ciencia science; *pl.* sciences; **ciencia gerencial** managerial science; **ciencias naturales** natural sciences; **ciencias políticas** *pl.* political science (3); **ciencias sociales** social sciences (3); **ciencias veterinarias** *pl.* veterinary science (3)

científico/a *n.* scientist; *adj.* scientific

cierto certain, sure (6); true (6); **es cierto** that's true, it's true (2); **hasta cierto punto** to a certain point; **(no) es cierto que...** it's (not) certain that . . . (9)

cifra figure, number

cilantro coriander

cinco five (1); **faltan cinco para la una** it's five 'til one (1)

cincuenta fifty (1)

cine *m.* movie theater (5); movies; **estrella del cine** movie star; **ir** (*irreg.*) **al cine** to go to the movies

cinta ribbon; film

circulación *f.* traffic, movement (*of vehicles, etc.*); **circulación de coches** traffic

círculo circle

circundar to surround

ciruela pasa prune

cita appointment (8); date (8); **hacer** (*irreg.*) **una cita** to make an appointment (8)

citar to cite, quote

ciudad *f.* city (1); **ciudad universitaria** (college, university) campus

ciudadanía citizenship

ciudadano/a citizen

ciudadela citadel

civil: guerra civil civil war

civilización *f.* civilization

civilizado/a civilized

clarinete *m.* clarinet (6)

claro/a clear, obvious; **¡claro que sí!** *interj.* of course! (9); **(no) es claro que...** it's (not) clear that . . . (9)

clase *f.* class (1); **clase de español** Spanish class (1); **clase media** middle class; **compañero/a de clase** classmate (1); **dar** (*irreg.*) **clases** to teach; **sala de clase** classroom (1)

clásico/a classical

clasificación *f.* classification

clasificarse (qu) to classify oneself

clavar to nail; to affix

clave *n. f.* key; *adj. inv.* key

cliente *m., f.* client, customer

clima *m.* climate (6); **¿cómo es el clima?** what is the climate like? (6)

clínica clinic (5)

cloro chlorine
club *m.* club (1); **club nocturno** nightclub
cobrar to cash (8); to charge (*for a service*) (8); **cobrar un cheque (de viajero)** to cash a (traveler's) check; **llamada por cobrar** collect call
cobre *m.* copper
cocido *Sp. dish of boiled meat and vegetables*
cocina kitchen (4); cuisine
cocinar to cook (3); **cocinar a máxima potencia** to cook on high heat
cocinero/a *n.* cook (3)
coche *m.* car, automobile (4); **circulación** (*f.*) **de coches** traffic
cochinillo asado roast suckling pig
cochino pig, hog; type of fish (*Cuba*); **Bahía de Cochinos** Bay of Pigs (*Cuba*)
código postal postal code, zip code
cofradía brotherhood, society
cohesión *f.* cohesion
coincidencia coincidence; **por coincidencia** by coincidence
cojín *m.* cushion; **forro de cojín** cushion cover
col *f.* cabbage (6)
coleccionista *m., f.* collector
colectivo/a *adj.* collective
colegio secondary/high school (3)
colgar (ue) (gu) to hang up (8); **colgarse** to hang, suspend oneself
colina hill (1)
colocar (qu) to place
Colombia Colombia (2)
colombiano/a *n., adj.,* Colombian (2)
colón *m.* monetary unit of Costa Rica and El Salvador
Colón: Cristóbal Colón Christopher Columbus
colonia neighborhood; housing development (4); colony
colonial colonial
colono/a *m. f.* colonist, settler
color *m.* color (2); **cambiar de colores** to change colors; **de color café** brown (2); **televisor** (*m.*) **en colores** color television
collar *m.* necklace
comal *m.* flat earthenware cooking pan
comando command
combatir to combat, fight
combinar to combine
comedor *m.* dining room (4)
comentar to comment
comentario commentary; talk, gossip
comenzar (ie) (c) to begin
comer to eat (3); to eat the noonday meal; **comer fuera** to eat out, in a restaurant

comercial *adj.* commercial, mercantile; **centro comercial** mall (5), shopping center; business district (5); **plaza comercial** mall; shopping center; business district
comerciante *m., f.* merchant, trader
comercio business, commerce; trade; **libre comercio** free trade
comestibles *m. pl.* food
cometa kite
comida food (7); meal (7); lunch (7); **comida fuerte** main, heavy meal (7); **comida principal** main meal of the day; **entre comidas** between meals
comienzo beginning, start
comité *m.* committee
comitiva procession, retinue
como as a; like; since; **así como** as well as; **tan... como** as . . . as; **tan pronto como** as soon as (9); **tanto/a ... como** as much . . . as; **tantos/as ... como** as many . . . as
¿cómo? how? (2); what?; **¿cómo eres?** what are you (*fam. s.*) like? (2); **¿cómo es el clima?** what is the climate like? (6); **¿cómo están ustedes?** how are you (*pl.*)? (1); **¿cómo estás?** how are you (*fam. s.*)? (1); **¿cómo está usted?** how are you (*form. s.*)? (1)
cómoda dresser (4)
cómodo/a comfortable (4)
compacto: disco compacto compact disc (CD) (2, 11); **tocador** (*m.*) **de discos compactos** compact disc (CD) player (11)
compañero/a companion (1); friend; **compañero/a de clase** classmate (1); **compañero/a de cuarto** roommate
compañía company; society
comparación *f.* comparison
comparar to compare
comparativo *gram.* comparative term
compartir to share
competencia competition
competente competent, qualified
competición *f.* competition
competir (i, i) to compete
complejo/a *adj.* complex
complementario/a complementary
complemento *gram.* object
completar to complete
completo/a complete; entire; perfect
complicado/a complicated
componente *m.* component
composición *f.* composition
compra *n.* purchase (5); **de compras** shopping (5); **hacer** (*irreg.*) **las compras** to go shopping, do one's shopping; **ir** (*irreg.*) **de compras** to go shopping

comprar to buy (3)
comprender to understand (3)
comprensión *f.* understanding
comprensivo/a comprehensive; understanding
comprometerse to commit oneself
compromiso commitment, pledge, obligation; undertaking
computación *f.* computer science (3)
computadora computer; **computadora personal** personal computer; **computadora portátil** portable computer
común common; **en común** in common
comunicación *f.* communication; *pl.* mass communication (11)
comunicar (qu) to communicate; **comunicarse** to correspond
comunidad *f.* community; commonwealth
comunión: primera comunión first communion (9)
comunista *adj.* communist
con with (2); **acabar con** to destroy, wipe out; **con cuidado** carefully; **con destino a** bound for, going to; **con facilidad** easily; **con ganas** willingly, happily; **con gas** carbonated; **con gusto** with pleasure; **con menor (mucha/poca) frecuencia** less (very/ not very) frequently; **con permiso** excuse me (1); **¿con quién hablo?** with whom am I speaking? (8)
concentración *f.* concentration
concentrarse to concentrate
concepción *f.* conception
concepto concept (3)
concierto concert
concurrido/a *p.p.* attended
conde *m.* earl, count
condición *f.* condition
condominio condo, condominium (4)
conducir (*irreg.*) to drive (*vehicle*)
conducta conduct, behavior
conductor(a) director
conectar to connect
confeccionar to make, prepare (*especially by hand*)
conferencia conference; public lecture
confiar (yo confío) (en) to confide (in); to trust (in)
confirmar to confirm (3)
confiscar (qu) to confiscate
conflictivo/a *adj.* conflicting
conflicto conflict
conformar to adapt, bring into harmony
confrontación *f.* confrontation
confundido/a confused (6)
confundirse to get or become confused
congregar (gu) to congregate, assemble

conjunción *f. gram.* conjunction (1)
conjunto ensemble; complex; **conjunto de cuerdas** string (*instrument*) ensemble
conmemorar to commemorate
conmigo with me (4)
conocer (zc) to know, be familiar with (8); to meet (*someone*) (8)
conocimiento knowledge
conquista conquest
conquistador(a) conqueror
consciente conscious, aware
consecuencia consequence; **a consecuencia** as a result
conseguir (i, i) (ga) to get, obtain (11)
consejero/a counselor, adviser (3)
consenso consensus, consent
conservar to maintain, preserve
consideración *f.* consideration
considerar to consider
consiguiente: por consiguiente consequently, therefore
consistente consistent
constante constant; continual
constar to consist of, be composed of
constitución *f.* constitution
constitucional: monarquía constitucional *type of monarchy in which the powers of the monarch are limited by the constitution*
constituir (y) to constitute; to be
construcción *f.* construction
consultorio doctor's office (5); **consultorio del/de la dentista** dentist's office
contabilidad *f.* accounting
contador(a) accountant (3)
contaminación *f.* pollution (10); **contaminación del aire** air pollution
contaminado/a *adj.* contaminated, polluted
contaminador(a) *adj.* contaminating, polluting
contaminante *n. m.* contaminant; *adj.* contaminating
contaminar to pollute, contaminate (10)
contar (ue) to tell
contemplar to contemplate
contener (*like* **tener**) to contain
contenido *s.* contents
contento/a happy (1); **estar** (*irreg.*) **contento/a** to be happy (1)
contestar to answer
contigo with you (*fam. s.*) (4); **¿y contigo?** and with you (*fam. s.*)? (1)
contiguo/a contiguous, adjoining
continente *m.* continent
continuación: a continuación immediately after, below
continuar (yo continúo) to continue, go on

continuo/a continuous
contra against; **en contra de** in opposition to, against (10)
contrabando smuggling; contraband, smuggled goods
contraer (*like* **traer**) to contract, get; **contraer matrimonio** to get married
contrario: al contrario on the contrary (4); **por el contrario** on the contrary
contrastar to contrast
contraste *m.* contrast (5); **en contraste con** in contrast with (5)
contratar to hire
contrayente *m., f.* contracting party (*to a marriage*)
contribución *f.* contribution
contribuir (y) to contribute
control *m.* control
controlar to control
controversia controversy
convención *f.* agreement
conversación *f.* conversation
conversar to converse, talk (3)
convertirse (ie, i) (en) to become
convivencia *n.* living together with others
conyugal matrimonial
cónyuge *m., f.* spouse
cooperación *f.* cooperation
coordinador(a) coordinator
copa wineglass, goblet (5, 7R); cup
copia copy; **copia fotostática** photostat; photocopy
corazón *m.* heart (4)
corbata tie (*clothing*) (2)
cordero: carne (*f.*) **de cordero** lamb (7)
cordial cordial, warm, sincere
cordillera mountain range
Corea Korea; **Corea del Sur** South Korea
coreano Korean (language)
corral: ave (*f.* [*but* **el ave**]) **de corral** domestic fowl
correcto/a correct
correo mail; post office; **correo aéreo** airmail (8); **echar (una carta) al correo** to mail (a letter) (8); **oficina de correos** post office (5)
correr to run (3); to jog
corresponder to correspond; to pertain, belong (to)
correspondencia mail, correspondence (8); **recibir correspondencia** to receive mail/correspondence
corrida de toros bullfight (10)
corriente: al corriente up to date
corsario corsair, privateer
cortar to cut
corte *m.* cut (*of clothes*); *f.* court (*judicial*); **corte** (*f.*) **de honor** wedding

party; **corte** (*f.*) **suprema** Supreme Court
cortesía courtesy (1), politeness; **expresión** (*f.*) **de cortesía** courtesy expresssion (1)
cortina curtain (4)
corto/a short (*length*) (2); **onda corta** shortwave; **pantalones cortos** shorts (2)
cosa thing (1)
cosechar to harvest
cosmopolita *n.* cosmopolite; *adj.* cosmopolitan
costa coast (1); **Costa Rica** Costa Rica (2)
costar (ue) to cost (5)
costarricense *n. m., f.; adj.* Costa Rican (2)
costo cost, price, expense
costumbre *f.* custom (6); habit; **buenas costumbres** good manners
cotidiano/a daily
cottage: **queso** *cottage* cottage cheese
coyote *m.* coyote
creación *f.* creation
crear to create
creatividad *f.* creativity
crecer (zc) to grow
crecimiento growth
crédito credit; **tarjeta de crédito** credit card (8)
creencia belief
creer (y) (en) to believe (in), think (3)
crema cream (7); **crema bronceadora** suntan lotion
criada maid
crianza rearing, bringing up
crimen *m.* crime
criollo/a *n., adj.* Creole
crisis *f.* crisis
cristal *m.* crystal (5)
Cristo Christ; **antes de Cristo** before Christ (B.C.)
Cristóbal Colón Christopher Columbus
criterio criterion
crítica criticism
criticar (qu) to criticize (10)
crudo: petróleo crudo crude oil
cruz *f.* (*pl.* **cruces**) cross; **Cruz Roja** Red Cross
cruzar (c) to cross
cruzeiro *Brazilian monetary unit*
cuaderno notebook (3)
cuadra block (*of houses*)
cuadrado/a *adj.* square; **milla cuadrada** square mile
cuadrilla quadrille (*bullfighter's squad*)
cuadro square
cual which; **por lo cual** for which reason, because of which

¿cuál(es)? what?, which? (2); *pron.* which
  one(s)?
cualidad *f.* quality
cualquier(a) any
cuando when; **de vez en cuando** from
  time to time
¿cuándo? when? (2)
cuantía: de menor cuantía of little
  importance
cuanto: en cuanto as soon as; **en cuanto
  a** regarding, with regard to (9); **unos
  cuantos/as** a few (11)
¡cuánto! *interj.* how (much)!
¿cuánto/a? how much? (2); **¿a cuánto
  está el cambio?** how much is the
  exchange rate?; **¿cuánto tiempo?** how
  long? (2)
¿cuántos/as? how many? (1, 2R);
  ¿cuántos años tienes? how old are you
  (*s. fam.*)? (1)
cuarenta forty (1)
Cuaresma Lent (*forty-day period of
  penitence and fasting beginning on Ash
  Wednesday and ending on Easter*)
cuarto *n.* room (4); bedroom (4);
  quarter (1); **compañero/a de cuarto**
  roommate; **menos cuarto** quarter to
  (*with time*) (1); **y cuarto** quarter past
  (*with time*) (1)
cuarto/a *adj.* fourth (10); **cuarta parte**
  one fourth
cuatro four (1)
cuatrocientos/as four hundred (5)
Cuba Cuba (2)
cubano/a *n., adj.* Cuban (2)
cubanoamericano/a *n., adj.* Cuban
  American
cubrir (*p.p.* **cubierto/a**) to cover;
  cubrirse to cover oneself
cuchara soup spoon (7); spoon
cucharita teaspoon (7)
cuchillo knife (7)
cuello neck (4)
cuenca del Amazonas Amazon river
  basin
cuenta check, bill (8); **darse** (*irreg.*)
  cuenta (de) to realize (11)
cuento story (11); short story (11);
  cuento infantil children's story
cuerda string; **conjunto de cuerdas**
  string (*instrument*) ensemble
cuero leather (5)
cuerpo body (4)
cuestión *f.* question, matter in discussion
cuidado care, keeping; **con cuidado**
  carefully; **¡cuidado!** *interj.* take care,
  be careful!
cuidar to take care of
culebra snake (10)
cultivar to cultivate, farm; to raise, grow

cultivo cultivation, farming; raising,
  growing
culto worship
cultura culture (11)
cultural cultural
cumpleaños *m. s.* birthday (4); **feliz
  cumpleaños** happy birthday; **fiesta de
  cumpleaños** birthday party; **tarjeta de
  cumpleaños** birthday card
cumplir: cumplir _____ años to turn
  _____ years old; **cumplir con** to fulfill
  (an obligation)
cuna cradle; place of birth
cuñado/a brother-in-law; sister-in-law;
  cuñados brothers- and sisters-in-law;
  brothers-in-law
cuota membership fee
cura *m.* Roman Catholic priest
cursar to study (*a subject*) (3)
curso course (3); school year
cuyo/a whose

CH

Chac Mool *m. Maya-Toltec rain god*
Chaco *South American plain region*
chambelán *m. male attendant participating
  in a girl's fifteenth birthday celebration*
champán *m.* champagne (7)
champiñón *m.* mushroom
champú *m.* shampoo
chao 'bye (1)
chaqueta jacket (2)
charlar to chat, talk (8)
charreada *Mex.* rodeo
charro *Mex.* cowboy
chayote *m. edible fruit of a West Indian
  vine*
checo/a *n., adj.* Czech
cheque *m.* check (8); **cambiar un cheque**
  to cash a check; **cheque de viajero**
  traveler's check (5, 8R); **cobrar un
  cheque** to cash a check
chicano/a Chicano, Mexican-
  American
chico/a *n.* child; boy, girl; *adj.* small;
  plato chico saucer (7)
chícharo pea (7)
chicharrón *m.* pork rind (*fried crisp*)
Chichimecas *ancient indigenous group of
  northern Mexico*
chilaquiles *m. Mexican dish of strips of corn
  tortilla covered with a thick sauce*
chile *m.* chili pepper (7)
chimenea chimney
China China (2)
chino *n.* Chinese (language)
chino/a *n., adj.* Chinese (2); **Año Nuevo
  Chino** Chinese New Year (6)
chiste *m.* joke (6)

chistoso/a funny, comical (11); witty
  (11)
choclo *L.A. green ear of maize*
chocolate *m.* chocolate (7); hot
  chocolate (7)
chófer *m.* chauffeur, driver; **chófer del
  autobús** bus driver (1)
choque *m.* collision
chuleta cutlet, chop (7)
churrasco *L.A. dish of broiled or barbecued
  meat*
chusco/a droll, funny

D

dama lady, woman
damnificado/a injured party
danza dance; dancing; **danza aeróbica**
  aerobic dancing
dar (*irreg.*) to give (4); to strike; **dar a
  luz** to give birth (9); **dar clases** to
  teach; **dar el pésame** to present one's
  condolences; **dar inicio a** to start (up);
  dar la bienvenida to welcome (5); **dar
  una fiesta** to give/throw a party; **darse
  cuenta (de)** to realize (11); **darse la
  mano** to shake hands
datar de to date from
dato fact; datum; **introducir (zc) datos**
  to input data (11)
de *prep.* of, from (1); **de acuerdo**
  agreed; OK (by me) (8); **de color** (*m.*)
  café brown (2); **de compras** shopping
  (5); **de día** during the day; daytime;
  ¿de dónde? (from) where? (2); **de
  edad** old, elderly; **de espaldas** to one's
  back; **de estatura mediana** (of)
  average height (2); **de habla española**
  Spanish-speaking (4); **de inmediato**
  immediately; **de lado a lado** from one
  side to the other; **de la mañana** A.M.,
  in the morning (1); **de (la) noche**
  P.M., at night (1); **de larga distancia**
  long distance (8); **de largo** in length;
  de la tarde P.M., in the afternoon (1);
  de menor cuantía of little importance;
  de nada you're welcome (1); **de nuevo**
  again (11); **de parte de** on behalf of;
  ¿de parte de quién? may I ask who's
  calling? (8); **de peso mediano** (of)
  average weight(2); **de punto** *adj.*
  knitted; **¿de qué es?** what is it made
  of? (5); **¿de quién?** whose? (2); **de
  repente** suddenly; **de sobra** more
  than enough, ample; **de turno** on
  duty; **de vacaciones** on vacation (4);
  de veras truly, really; real, genuine;
  ¿de veras? really? (2); **de vestir**
  adj. dress; **de vez en cuando** from
  time to time, sometimes; **de viaje**

traveling (7); **de vuelta a** returning to

debajo de *prep.* under (5); below, beneath; **por debajo de** under, below

debate *m.* debate

deber ought to, should (3); to owe; **deber (de)** + *inf.* must, have to; ought to, should (*do something*)

debidamente duly, properly

debido a owing to, on account of

débil weak (2)

debilitar to weaken, debilitate

década decade

decapitar to decapitate, behead

decidir to decide (3)

décimo/a tenth (10)

decimocuarto/a fourteenth

decimoquinto/a fifteenth

decimosexto/a sixteenth

decir (*irreg.*) to say (4), tell (4); **decir mentiras** to tell lies; **diga, dígame** *Sp.* hello (*telephone*); **es decir** that is to say; **¡no me digas!** *interj.* you're kidding! (2); **oír** (*irreg.*) **decir** to hear tell; **querer** (*irreg.*) **decir** to mean

decisión *f.* decision; **tomar la decisión** to make the decision (9)

declaración *f.* declaration; statement

declarar to declare; **declararse** to declare oneself

declinar to decline

decoración *f.* decoration

decorar to decorate

decorativo/a decorative

dedicarse (qu) a to devote oneself to; to make a specialty of

dedo finger (4); **dedo del pie** toe (4)

defecto defect, fault

defender (ie) to defend

definición *f.* definition

definido/a: **artículo definido** *gram.* definite article

definir to define

defunción: **esquela de defunción** *newspaper announcement to pay tribute to a dead person* (9)

dejar to let, allow (7); to leave (behind); to relinquish, let go; **dejar de** + *inf.* to stop (*doing something*); **dejarse** + *inf.* to abandon oneself (*to doing something*)

del (*contraction of* **de** + **el**) of/from the (1)

delante ahead

delegar (gu) to delegate

delfín *m.* dolphin

delgado/a slender (2), thin

delicado/a delicate

delicia delight

delicioso/a delicious (7)

demás the other, the rest of the

demasiado *adv.* too much (7); too

democrático/a democratic

demográfico/a demographic

demora delay (8)

demostrar (ue) to demonstrate, show; to prove

demostrativo/a: **adjetivo demostrativo** *gram.* demonstrative adjective (5); **pronombre** (*m.*) **demostrativo** *gram.* demonstrative pronoun (5)

denso/a dense

dentista *m., f.* dentist (1); **consultorio del/de la dentista** dentist's office

dentro: **dentro de** inside of (5); **dentro de poco** soon; **por dentro** on the inside

departamento apartment, flat (4); department

dependencia dependence, dependency; staff; branch office

depender (de) to depend (on)

dependiente *m., f.* clerk (3)

deporte *m.* sport (6)

deportista *n. m., f.* sportsman/ sportswoman, athlete; *adj.* sports-minded

deportivo/a *adj.* sports

depositar to deposit (8)

depósito deposit

depredación *f.* depredation, plundering

depresión *f.* depression

deprimido/a depressed

derecha *n.* right; right-hand side; **a la derecha (de)** to the right (of)

derecho *n.* right; *adv.* straight (5); **derechos humanos** human rights; **seguir (i, i) (ga) derecho** to keep going straight ahead; **tener** (*irreg.*) **derecho a** to be entitled to

derivado derivate, derivative

derivarse de to derive, be derived from

derretir (i, i) to melt, thaw

derrotar to defeat

desagradable unpleasant (2)

desagrado displeasure

desaparecer (zc) to disappear

desarrollado/a developed

desarrollo development; **desarrollo económico** economic development, growth; **en vías de desarrollo** developing

desastre *m.* disaster

desayunar to eat breakfast (4)

desayuno breakfast (7)

descansar to rest

descanso rest; alleviation; peace

descender (ie) to descend, go down

descendiente *m., f.* descendent

descolgar (ue) (gu) el teléfono to pick up the phone (8)

descongestionar to lessen or relieve the congestion of

desconocido/a unknown

describir (*p.p.* **descrito/a**) to describe

descripción *f.* description (2); **descripción física** physical description (2)

descubierto/a discovered

descubrimiento discovery

descubrir (*p.p.* **descubierto/a**) to discover

desde *prep.* from (5); since

desear to wish, desire

desembarcar (qu) to disembark, land, put ashore

desembarque *m.* landing

desempeñar to play (*a part*)

desempleo: **tasa de desempleo** unemployment rate

desértico/a desert-like

desesperado/a desperate; hopeless

desfilar to parade; to march past

desgraciadamente unfortunately

deshacerse (*irreg.*) **de** to get rid of

desierto desert (1)

desierto/a deserted

desinterés *m.* disinterest; lack of self-interest

desmoldar to remove from a mold

despacio slowly (4)

despedida farewell (1), good-bye; **fiesta de despedida** farewell party (1)

despedir(se) (i, i) (de) to say good-bye to (8)

despertarse (ie) to wake up, awaken (4)

desposado/a *n.* newlywed

déspota *m.* despot

después *adv.* later, afterwards; after; **después de** *prep.* after (4); **después de poco** after a little while/bit (8)

destacado/a outstanding, distinguished; marked

destacar (qu) to stand out, be conspicuous

desteñir (i, i) to discolor, fade

destinado/a (a) destined (for)

destino destiny, fate; **con destino a** bound for, going to

destrucción *f.* destruction

destructivo/a destructive

destructor(a) destructive

desubicación *f.* displacement; homelessness

desván *m.* attic (4)

desventaja disadvantage

desviado/a deviated

detalle *m.* detail

detective *m.* detective

deterioro deterioration
determinar to determine; to distinguish; to cause, bring about
detrás de *prep.* behind (5)
devastar to devastate
devoción *f.* devotion
devolver (ue) (*p.p.* **devuelto/a**) to return (*something*) (4)
día *m.* day; **al día** per day; **algún día** someday; **buenos días** good morning (1); **de día** during the day; daytime; **de hoy en quince días** in two weeks; **día anterior** yesterday; **Día de Acción de Gracias** Thanksgiving Day; **Día de Año Nuevo** New Year's Day (6); **día de campo** day in the country; **Día de Gracias** Thanksgiving Day (6); **Día de la Independencia** Independence Day (6); **Día de la Raza** Columbus Day (6); **día de la semana** day of the week (3), weekday; **Día de las Américas** Day of the Americas (6); **Día de las Madres** Mother's Day (6); **Día del Obrero** Labor Day (6); **Día de los Enamorados** Valentine's Day (6); **Día de los Muertos** Day of the Dead (*November ?*) (6); **Día de los Padres** Father's Day (6); **día del santo** saint's day (of the saint for whom one is named) (6); **Día de Viernes Santo** Good Friday; **día feriado** holiday; **día festivo** holiday (6); **estar** (*irreg.*) **al día** to be up to date, current; **feliz día de tu santo** happy saint's day; **hoy (en) día** today, nowadays; **hoy es el día doce (trece...)** today is the twelfth (thirteenth . . .) (1); **ocho días** a week; **¿qué día es hoy?** what day is today? (1); **todo el día** all day; **todos los días** every day (6)
diablo: pobre diablo poor devil
dialéctica *s.* dialectics, arguments
dialecto dialect
diálogo dialogue
diario/a daily
dibujo drawing; **dibujo animado** cartoon
diccionario dictionary (2)
diciembre December (6)
dicha happiness
dicho/a said, mentioned
dichoso/a happy; fortunate
diecinueve nineteen (1)
dieciocho eighteen (1)
dieciséis sixteen (1)
diecisiete seventeen (1)
diente *m.* tooth (4); **lavarse los dientes** to brush one's teeth
dieta diet (7)
diez ten (1)

diferencia difference; **a diferencia de** unlike
diferente different
difícil difficult, hard (3)
dificultad *f.* difficulty
difunto/a deceased (*person*)
difusión *f.* diffusion; spreading
diga, dígame *Sp.* hello (*telephone*)
dignarse to deign, condescend
dignidad *f.* dignity
dimensión *f.* dimension
dinamismo dynamism
dinero money (3); **dinero en efectivo** cash (8)
Dios *m. s.* God (10)
dios(a) god
diplomático/a *n.* diplomat; *adj.* diplomatic
dirección *f.* direction (5); address (5); **dirección cardinal** cardinal direction (*north, south, east, west*) (5); **dirección de cámaras** director of photography; **dirección de escena** (stage) director
directo/a direct
director(a) director, manager
dirigente *m., f.* leader, director
dirigir (j) to direct; to lead
disco record (2); satellite dish (11); (computer) disk (11); **disco compacto** compact disc (2, 11); **disco duro** hard drive (11); **lector de discos** (computer) disk drive (11); **mercado de discos** record store; **puesto de discos** record stand/store (5); **tocador de discos compactos** compact disc (CD) player (11); **tocador de discos láser** laser disk player (11)
discoteca disco, discotheque (5)
discurso lecture; speech
discutir to discuss, argue about, dispute
diseñar to design
diseño *n.* design
disfrutar (de) to enjoy
disket: porta disket (*m.*) disk carrying case
disminuir (y) to diminish, decrease
disposición: poner (*irreg.*) **a la disposición de** to put at (*someone's*) disposal
dispuesto/a inclined; ready; prepared
disputa dispute
distancia distance; **llamada de larga distancia** long distance (telephone) call (8)
distante distant
distinción *f.* distinction
distinguir (ga) to distinguish; **distinguirse** to distinguish oneself; to make oneself different or noticeable

distintivo/a distinctive
distinto/a different (4); distinct (4)
distribución *f.* distribution
Distrito Federal Federal District (*of Mex.*); Mexico City
diversidad *f.* diversity
diversificar (qu) to diversify
diversión *f.* amusement, entertainment
diverso/a diverse, different
divertido/a fun, funny (2)
divertirse (ie, i) to have fun, enjoy oneself (4)
dividido/a divided
divinidad *f.* divinity
división *f.* division
divorciado/a divorced (6)
divorciarse to get a divorce (9)
divorcio divorce (9)
doblar to turn (5); to double; to fold
doble double, twofold
doce twelve (1)
docena dozen
doctor(a) doctor
documento document
dólar *m.* dollar (8)
dolor *m.* pain (10); **dolor de cabeza** headache
doméstico/a domestic; **animal** (*m.*) **doméstico** pet
domicilio domicile, residence; **a domicilio** in-home, to your home
dominación *f.* domination
dominar to dominate
domingo Sunday (3)
dominicano/a *n., adj.* Dominican (2)
don *title of respect used with a man's first name*
donde where
¿dónde? where? (1, 2R); **¿adónde?** (to) where? (2); **¿de dónde?** (from) where? (2)
doña *title or respect used with a woman's first name*
dorado/a golden
dormir (ue, u) to sleep (4); **dormirse** to fall asleep (4)
dormitorio bedroom (4)
dos two (1)
doscientos/as two hundred (5)
drogas: tráfico de drogas drug trafficking
ducha *n.* shower (4)
ducharse to take a shower (4)
duda doubt; **no cabe duda** there is no doubt; **no hay duda** there's no doubt; **sin duda** doubtless, no doubt, without a doubt
duele(n): le duele(n)... . . . hurt(s) you (*form. s.*)/him/her (4)
dueño/a owner; landlord

dulce *n. m.* candy (7); sweet (7); *adj.* sweet (7); **pan** (*m.*) **dulce** sweet bread (7); **dulzura** sweetness
duodécimo/a twelfth (10)
duque *m.* duke
duración *f.* duration
durante during (2)
durar to last, continue
durazno peach (7)
duro/a hard (10); **disco duro** hard drive (11); **huevo duro** hard-boiled egg (7)

E

e *used instead of* **y** *before words beginning with* **i** *or* **hi**
eclesial *adj.* ecclesiastic(al)
ecología ecology (10)
ecológico/a ecological; **auditoría ecológica** ecological audit
economía *s.* economics; economy
económico/a economical, affordable (4); economic; **desarrollo económico** economic development, growth
ecuador *m.* equator
ecuatorial: línea ecuatorial equator
ecuestre *adj.* equestrian
echar to cast; to emit, send forth; **echar (una carta) al correo** to mail (a letter) (8); **echar (una carta) en el buzón** to mail (a letter)
edad *f.* age (9); **de edad** old, elderly; **edad media** Middle Ages; **tener** (*irreg.*) _____ **años de edad** to be _____ years old (2)
edición *f.* edition
edificio building (1)
educación *f.* education; breeding, manners; **educación bilingüe** bilingual education
EE. UU. *abbrev. of Estados Unidos* United States, U.S.A., U.S.
efectivo: dinero en efectivo cash (8)
efectivo/a effective
efecto effect; **en efecto** in fact, indeed
efectuar (yo efectúo) to effect, carry out
¿eh? right? (2)
ejecución *f.* execution
ejecutivo/a executive; **ejecutivo/a jefe** chief executive
ejemplo example; **por ejemplo** for example
ejercer (z) to exercise, perform; to exert
ejercicio exercise; **hacer** (*irreg.*) **(los) ejercicios aeróbicos** to do aerobics, aerobic exercises (6)
ejército army
ejote *m.* string bean
el the *m. definite article*
él *sub. pron.* he; *obj.* (*of prep.*) him

elaborar to elaborate
elección *f.* choice; *pl.* election
eléctrico/a: aparato eléctrico electrical appliance (4)
electrónico/a electronic
elefante *m.* elephant
elegancia elegance
elegante elegant
elegir (i, i) (j) to select, choose
elevado/a raised; high
elevar to raise
eliminar to eliminate
elote *m. Mex. ear of green Indian corn*
eludir to avoid, evade
ella *sub. pron.* she; *obj.* (*of prep.*) her
ello it, that
ellos/as *sub. pron.* they; *obj.* (*of prep.*) them
embargo: sin embargo however, nevertheless (10)
embarque: punto de embarque point of departure (*of a ship*)
emborracharse to get drunk
emergencia: sala de emergencia emergency room (*of a hospital*)
emigración *f.* emigration
emigrar to emigrate
eminentemente notably, highly
emisión *f.* emission
emoción *f.* emotion
emocionado/a (emotionally) moved, touched
emocional: estado emocional emotional state
emotividad *f.* emotionality
empanada turnover
empanado/a breaded
empanizado/a breaded
empedrado/a paved with stones
emperador emperor
emperatriz empress
empezar (ie) (c) to start, begin (4)
emplazamiento location
empleado/a employee (3)
emplear to employ; to use
emplumado/a feathered; covered, adorned with feathers
empresa firm, company; **administrador(a) de empresas** administrator, businessperson (3)
en in, on (1); at; **en acción** in action, at work; **en aquel entonces** back then, in those days; **en breve** shortly; at a glance; **en busca de** in quest of; **en carne propia** in the flesh; **en casa (de)** at (the) home (of) (3); **en común** in common; **en contra de** in opposition to, against (10); **en contraste con** in contrast with (5); **en cuanto** as soon as; **en cuanto a** regarding, with regard to (9); **en efecto** in fact, indeed; **en**

este momento right now, at this moment (4); **en fin** in short; **en general** in general; **en oferta** on sale (5); **en parte** partly; **en peligro** endangered (10); **en primer lugar** in the first place; **en privado** in private; **en punto** sharp, on the dot (1); **en realidad** really; **en seguida** right away, immediately; **en serio** seriously (9); **en todas partes** everywhere; **en torno a** about, regarding; **en total** total (2), in all; **en vez de** instead of (9); **en vías de desarrollo** *adj.* developing; **televisor** (*m.*) **en blanco y negro / en colores** black and white / color television
enamorado/a sweetheart; person in love; **Día** (*m.*) **de los Enamorados** Valentine's Day (6)
enamorarse (de) to fall in love (with)
encaje *m.* lace
encalado/a whitewashed
encantado/a delighted (1); pleased to meet you (1)
encantador(a) charming, delightful
encantar to love (6), enchant, delight (*something delights one*); **me encanta(n)...** I love . . . (5)
encanto enchantment
encargarse (gu) de to take charge of; to attend to
encendido/a lit, ignited
encerado/a waxed
encima (de) on top (of) (5)
encontrar (ue) to find (5); **encontrarse** to be found, situated; **encontrarse con** to meet with, run into
encuentro meeting; encounter
encuesta survey, poll (2)
endémico/a endemic (*peculiar to particular people or locality*)
enemigo/a enemy
enero January (3, 6R)
énfasis *m. s.* emphasis
enfermedad *f.* sickness
enfermería nursing (*profession*) (3)
enfermero/a nurse (3); **enfermero/a público/a** public health nurse
enfermo/a sick (1); **estar** (*irreg.*) **enfermo/a** to be sick (1)
enfrentamiento confrontation
enfrentar to confront, cause to face
enfrente (de) in front (of) (5); opposite
enfriar (yo enfrío) to cool, make cool
enfurecerse (zc) to become infuriated
engalanar to adorn, bedeck
engrasado/a greased
enigmático/a enigmatic
enlace *m.* wedding; link; connection
enlazar (c) to link, join; to lasso

enojado/a angry (1); **estar** (*irreg.*) **enojado/a** to be angry (1)
enorme enormous (4)
enredarse to get entangled
enriquecido/a enriched
ensalada salad (7); **ensalada de frutas** fruit salad
ensayo essay
enseñanza *n.* teaching
enseñar to teach (3); to show (3)
entender (ie) to understand (4)
enterarse de to learn, be informed of; to find out about
entero/a entire, whole
entierro burial, funeral (9)
entonación *f.* intonation
entonces then (5), in that case; **en aquel entonces** back then, in those days
entorno environment, surroundings
entrada entrée, main course (7); admission ticket; entrance
entrante coming, next; **semana entrante** next week
entrar to enter
entre *prep.* between, among (3, 5R); **entre comidas** between meals
entregar (gu) to hand in, over
entrelazado/a entwined
entremés *m. s.* appetizer
entremetido/a meddlesome
entrenador(a) atlético/a athletic trainer
entrevista interview (8)
entrevistado/a interviewed
entusiasmado/a enthused, excited (1)
enviar (yo envío) to send (8)
envidiar to envy
episodio episode
época epoch, historical period (6)
equilibrado/a balanced
equilibrio equilibrium, balance
equipo team (6); equipment
equivalente *adj.* equivalent
equivocado/a mistaken, wrong; **número equivocado** wrong (telephone) number
equivocarse (qu) to make a mistake (8), be mistaken; to get the wrong number (8)
erigido/a erected, built
erosión *f.* erosion
error *m.* error
erupción *f.* eruption (*volcanic*)
es he/she/it is (1); **es cierto** that's true, it's true (2); **es la una** it's one o'clock (1); **es medianoche** it's midnight (1); **es mediodía** it's noon (1); **es preciso** it's necessary
esbelto/a slender, graceful
escabeche *m. preserving sauce made with vinegar, laurel, etc.*

escalera stairs, stairway (4)
escapar(se) to escape
escena scene; **dirección** (*f.*) **de escena** (stage) director
escenario stage; setting
esclavitud *f.* slavery
esclavo/a slave
escoger (j) to choose, select
escolar *adj.* of or pertaining to school; **año escolar** school year
escolaridad *f.* level of education
esconder(se) to hide
escote *m.* neckline
escribir (*p.p.* **escrito/a**) to write (3); **máquina de escribir** typewriter; **trabajo escrito** written work, paper
escritor(a) writer (3)
escritorio desk
escrúpulo scruple
escuchar to listen (to) (3); to mind, heed; **escuchar música** to listen to music (6)
escuela school; **escuela de verano** summer school; **escuela secundaria** secondary/high school (3)
escueto/a plain, unadorned
ese, esa *adj.* that (*nearby*) (4, 5R); **ése, ésa** *pron.* that one (*nearby*) (5)
esencia essence
esencial essential
esencialmente essentially (7)
esfuerzo effort
eslovaco/a *n.* Slovak; *adj.* Slovakian
esmeralda emerald
eso that, that thing, that fact; **a eso de** at about, at around, at approximately (5); **por eso** that's why (4); therefore
esos/as *adj.* those (*nearby*) (5); **ésos/as** *pron.* those (ones) (*nearby*) (5)
espacio space, room (7)
espada sword
espalda back (4); **de espaldas** to one's back
espanto terror, fright
España Spain (1, 2R)
español *m.* Spanish (language) (1); **clase** (*f.*) **de español** Spanish class (1)
español(a) *n.* Spaniard; *adj.* Spanish (2); **de habla española** Spanish-speaking (4)
espátula spatula
especia spice (7)
especial *adj.* special
especialidad (*f.*) **de la casa** specialty of the house
especialización *f.* (*academic*) major (11); specialization (11)
especializarse (c) to major (8); to specialize (8)

especie *f.* species (10); **especie en peligro** endangered species (10)
espectacular spectacular
espectáculo show
espejo *n.* mirror (4)
espera: sala de espera waiting room
esperanza hope, hopefulness
esperanzado/a hopeful
esperar to wait (for) (6); to hope (9); to expect (9)
espeso/a thick, heavy
espía *m., f.* spy
espinacas *f. pl.* spinach (7)
esponsales *m. pl.* betrothal
espontáneo/a spontaneous
esposo/a husband/wife (2); **esposos** married couple, spouses(2); husbands
esquela de defunción newspaper announcement to pay tribute to a dead person (9)
esqueleto skeleton
esquema *m.* outline, chart; scheme, plan
esquí *m.* skiing (6)
esquiar (yo esquío) to ski (6)
esquina corner
establecer (zc) to establish; **establecerse** to establish oneself
estación *f.* station (1); season; **estación de autobuses** bus station (1); **estación de las lluvias** rainy season (6); **estación del tren** train station (5); **estación seca** dry season (6)
estacionamiento *n.* parking (5)
estacionar to park (*vehicle*) (5)
estadio stadium
estadista *m.* statesman
estadística *s.* statistics (*science*) (3)
estado state (1); condition; **estado de ánimo** state of mind; **estado emocional** emotional state; **estado físico** physical state; **estado libre asociado** free associated state
Estados Unidos *pl.* United States (1, 2R)
estadounidense *n. m., f.* person from the United States; *adj.* U.S., from the United States, American (1, 2R)
estampilla stamp (8)
estaño tin
estar (*irreg.*) to be (1); **¿cómo están ustedes?** how are you (*pl.*)? (1); **¿cómo estás?** how are you (*fam. s.*)? (1); **¿cómo está usted?** how are you (*form. s.*)? (1); **está (muy) húmedo** it is (very) humid (6); **está (muy) nublado** it is (very) cloudy (6); **está (muy) seco** it is (very) dry (6); **está templado** it is moderate (the weather is moderate) (6); **estar a** to be (*location, distance*) (5); **estar aburrido/a** to be bored (1); **estar al día** to be up to date, current;

estar de acuerdo to agree, be in agreement (5); **estar de regreso** to be back (*from another place*); **estar de vacaciones** to be on vacation; **estar de viaje** to be on a trip; **estar listo/a** to be ready (7); **estar loco/a** to be crazy (7); **estar seguro/a** to be sure (5)

estatal *adj.* (pertaining to) state; **feria estatal** state fair

estatua statue (5)

estatura: de baja estatura short; **de estatura mediana** (of) average height (2)

este *n. m.* east (4, 5R)

este/a *adj.* this (4, 5R); **esta noche** tonight (2); **esta tarde** this afternoon (2); **en este momento** right now, at this moment (4); **éste/a** *pron.* this one (5)

estéreo stereo (11)

estilo style (4); design (4)

estimar to judge, think; to esteem, hold in regard

esto this, this thing, this matter; **por esto** for this reason

estómago stomach (4)

estos/as *adj.* these (5); **éstos/as** *pron.* these (ones) (5)

estrategia stategy

estrecho/a narrow; **Estrecho de Gibraltar** Strait of Gibraltar

estrella star; **estrella del cine** movie star

estudiante *m., f.* student (1)

estudiantil *adj.* student; **centro estudiantil** (university) student union; **residencia estudiantil** dormitory

estudiar to study (3); **estudiar para** (*professional title*) to study to be (*professional title*)

estudio study; *pl.* studies, schooling (3)

estudioso/a studious (2)

estufa stove, range (4)

estupendo/a stupendous, fabulous (6)

etapa stage

etcétera et cetera

eterno/a eternal

etiqueta etiquette, ceremony, formality; label; **etiqueta de identificación** identification label; luggage tag

Europa Europe

europeo/a *n., adj.* European (4)

evaluar (yo evalúo) to evaluate

evento event

evidente evident (5); **(no) es evidente que...** it's (not) evident that . . . (9)

evitar to avoid

evolución *f.* evolution

¡exacto! *interj.* exactly!

examen *m.* exam, test (1)

excelencia excellence

excelente excellent (5)

excepción *f.* exception

excepcional exceptional

exceso excess

excitante exciting

excursión *f.* tour (5); trip, excursion (5)

exhibición *f.* exhibition

exhibir to exhibit, show, display

existencia existence

existir to exist

éxito success

exitoso/a successful

exótico/a exotic

expandir to extend, expand, spread

experiencia experience

experimentador(a) experimentor

experimento experiment

explicar (qu) to explain (7)

explorador(a) explorer

explorar to explore

explotar to exploit

exponencial exponential

exportado/a exported

exportador(a) exporter

expresar to express

expresión *f.* expression (1); **expresión de cortesía** courtesy expression (1)

exquisito/a exquisite; delicious

extender(se) to spread, extend

extensión *f.* extension, expanse; spreading

extenso/a vast; long, lengthy

exterior *m.* exterior, outside

externo/a external

extinción *f.* extinction

extinguirse (ga) to die

extranjero *n.* foreign country

extranjero/a *adj.* foreign (6); **lengua extranjera** foreign language

extrañar to miss (*feel the absence of*)

extraño/a strange, odd (11)

extraordinario/a extraordinary

extremo/a extreme

extrovertido/a extroverted, outgoing (2)

F

fabada Asturian (*Sp.*) *stew made of pork and beans*

fábrica factory (8)

fabricado/a manufactured

fábula fable

fabuloso/a fabulous

facciones *f. pl.* features (*of the face*)

faceta facet

fácil easy (3)

facilidad: con facilidad easily

fácilmente easily (8)

factor *m.* factor

facultad *f.* ability, skill; school/college (*of a university*) (3); **Facultad de Filosofía y Letras** School of Liberal Arts (3); **Facultad de Ingeniería** School of Engineering (3)

falda skirt (2)

falso/a false

falta *n.* lack (11)

faltar to lack (6); **faltan cinco para la una** it's five 'til one (1)

falla: sin falla without fail

fallecer (zc) to die

familia family (1); **familia nuclear** nuclear family

familiar *n. m.* relative; *adj.* household; (*pertaining to the*) family; familiar

familiarizar (c) to familiarize

famoso/a famous

fanático/a fanatic; fanatical

fantasma *m.* ghost

fantástico/a fantastic

fáquir *m.* fakir (*Muslim or Hindu religious ascetic or mendicant monk commonly considered a wonder worker*)

farmacia pharmacy (5)

fascinación *f.* fascination

fascinante fascinating

fascinar to fascinate (6); to enchant

fastidiado/a annoyed

fatal bad; deadly, fatal; unavoidable

fatalista fatalistic

favor: por favor please (1)

favorito/a favorite (2)

fe *f.* faith

febrero February (6)

fecha date (*calendar*) (6)

federación *f.* federation

federal federal; **Distrito Federal** Federal District (*Mex.*); Mexico City; **procuraduría federal** attorney general's office

federativo/a federative

felicidad *f.* happiness

felicitaciones *f.* congratulations

felicitar to congratulate (9)

feliz (*pl.* **felices**) happy; **feliz cumpleaños** happy birthday; **feliz día de tu santo** happy saint's day

femenino/a *adj.* feminine; female

fenómeno phenomenon

feo/a ugly (2)

feria estatal state fair

feriado/a: día (*m.*) **feriado** holiday

fertilizante *m.* fertilizer

fervorín *m.* short prayer

festejada festivity, celebration

festejar to celebrate

festival *m.* festival

festivo/a: día (*m.*) **festivo** holiday (6)
fibra fiber
ficticio/a fictitious
ficha token (8)
fichero (computer) file (11); **guardar ficheros** to save (computer) files (11); **perder (ie) ficheros** to lose (computer) files, crash (11)
fideo noodle (7)
fiebre (*f.*) **amarilla** yellow fever
fiel faithful, true
fiesta party (1); holiday; **dar** (*irreg.*) **una fiesta** to give/throw a party; **fiesta de bienvenida** welcoming party; **fiesta de cumpleaños** birthday party; **fiesta de despedida** farewell party (1); **fiesta de los quince años, la quinceañera** *party given to celebrate a young woman's fifteenth birthday;* **fiesta de primavera** spring festival; **fiestas patrias** *holidays celebrating a nation's history;* **hacer** (*irreg.*) **una fiesta** to have/throw a party
figura figure
fijo/a fixed, set; **precio fijo** fixed, set price
filipino/a *n., adj.* Filipino; *adj.* Philippine, from the Philippines
filo edge
filosofía philosophy; **Facultad** (*f.*) **de Filosofía y Letras** School of Liberal Arts (3); **filosofía y letras** humanities, liberal arts
filósofo/a philosopher
fin *m.* end (4); purpose; **al fin** finally, at last; **en fin** in short; **fin de semana** weekend (3); **por fin** at last (5)
final *n. m.* end; *adj.* final
finalizar (c) to conclude
finalmente finally (8)
finca farm
fingir (j) to feign, pretend
Finlandia Finland
fino/a fine
finura fineness
firma signature (4)
firmar to sign (8)
física *s.* physics (3); **laboratorio de física** physics laboratory (3)
físico/a physical (2); **descripción** (*f.*) **física** physical description (2); **estado físico** physical state
flan *m.* caramel custard (7)
flor *f.* flower (5)
Florida: Pascua Florida Easter (6)
foca seal (10)
foco focus, focal point
folklórico/a folkloric
follaje *m.* foliage
folleto pamphlet, brochure

fondo bottom; fund; **recaudar fondos** to raise money
forestal *adj.* forest
forma shape, form (4); manner, method; **forma de preparar** method of preparation; **mantenerse** (*irreg.*) **en forma** to keep in shape
formación *f.* education
formal *adj.* formal
formar to form; to make; to constitute
formulario form
forro de cojín cushion cover
fortaleza fortress
fortificación *f.* fortification
fortuito/a fortuitous
foto *f.* photograph, photo (2); **sacar (qu) fotos** to take pictures (6), photos
fotografía photograph (2); photography
fotógrafo/a photographer
fotostática: copia fotostática *n.* photostat; photocopy
frac *m.* full-dress coat
francés *n. m.* French (language)
francés, francesa *adj.* French (2)
Francia France (2)
franja strip (*of land*)
frase phrase, sentence
frecuencia frequency; **con menor (mucha/poca) frecuencia** less (very/not very) frequently
frecuente frequent
fregadero kitchen sink (4)
frente: frente a facing, across from (5); **al frente (de)** in front (of) (4)
fresa strawberry (7)
fresco/a fresh (7); cool (7); **aguas** (*f.* [*but* **el agua**]) **frescas** *Mex.* water with fruit juice; **hace fresco** it is cool (weather) (6)
frijol *m.* (kidney) bean (7)
frío cold (6); **hace (mucho) frío** it's (very) cold (weather) (5, 6R); **tener** (*irreg.*) **(mucho) frío** to be (very) cold (8)
friso frieze
frito/a fried (7); **huevo frito** fried egg (7); **papa frita** *L.A.* french fry (potato) (7); **patata frita** *Sp.* french fry (potato)
frontera border (*political*) (1)
fronterizo/a *adj.* border
fruta fruit (7); **ensalada de frutas** fruit salad; **jarabe** (*m.*) **de fruta** fruit juice; **puesto de frutas** fruit stand (5)
frutería fruit market
fuego fire; **a fuego lento** by slow fire, low flame, or heat (*cooking*)
fuente *f.* fountain; source, origin

fuera *adv.* out, outside; **comer fuera** to eat out, in a restaurant; **fuera de** *prep.* outside of (5); out of; **por fuera** from or on the outside
fuerte strong (2); **comida fuerte** main, heavy meal (7); **plato fuerte** main course (7)
fuerza force, strength (11)
fumar to smoke
función *f.* function
funcionar to function, work, run
fundación *f.* foundation
fundador(a) founder
fundamento foundation
fundar to found, establish
fundir to found, melt (*metals*)
fúnebre *adj.* funeral; funereal, sad
funerario/a funerary
furioso/a furious (1)
fútbol *m.* soccer (6); **fútbol (norte)americano** football (6); **jugar (ue) (gu) al fútbol/fútbol (norte)americano** to play soccer/football (6)
futbolista *m.* football or soccer player
futuro *n.* future (3)
futuro/a *adj.* future

G

gabinete *m.* cabinet (4)
gachupín, gachupina *L.A. Spaniard who settles in Latin America*
gafas *f. pl.* (eye)glasses (4); **gafas de sol** sunglasses (4)
galgo greyhound
gallego Galician (language)
galleta cookie (7)
gallina chicken, hen (10); **caldo de gallina** chicken broth, bouillon, soup
gallo rooster (10)
ganadería cattle raising
ganadero/a pertaining to cattle or cattle raising
ganado cattle, livestock
ganador(a) winner
ganancia gain, profit
ganar to gain; to earn; to win; **ganarse la vida** to earn one's livelihood
ganas: tener (*irreg.*) **ganas de** + *inf.* to feel like (*doing something*) (5); **con ganas** willingly, happily
garaje *m.* garage (4)
garantizar (c) to guarantee
garganta throat (4)
garra claw; talon; clutch
gas *m.* gas; **agua** (*f.* [*but* **el agua**]) **mineral con gas** carbonated mineral water
gasolina gasoline

gasolinera service station (5)
gastar to spend
gasto expense
gato cat (10)
gaucho horseman (*cowboy of Southern Latin America*)
gazpacho *cold soup made with tomatoes, bread, garlic, olive oil, and other vegetables*
gelatina gelatin (7)
gemelo/a twin; **hermano/a gemelo/a** twin brother/sister
generación *f.* generation
general *adj.* general; **en general** in general
generalización *f.* generalization
generalmente generally
generar to generate
gente *f. s.* people (5)
geografía geography (1, 3R)
geográfico/a geographic; **término geográfico** geographic term (1)
geología geology (3)
geranio geranium
gerencia management; managership
gerencial pertaining to management; **ciencia gerencial** managerial science
gerente *m., f.* manager (3)
gigantesco/a giant, gigantic (5)
gimnasia *s.* gymnastics; **hacer** (*irreg.*) **gimnasia** to do gymnastics (6)
gimnasio gymnasium (8)
glorieta *circle or square with streets converging on it*
glorioso/a glorious
gobernación: secretaría de la gobernación Department of the Interior
gobernador(a) governor
gobernar (ie) to govern
gobierno government (4)
golf *m.* golf (6); **jugar (ue) (gu) al golf** to play golf (6)
golfo gulf (1)
golondrina swallow
goma: pelota de goma rubber ball
gordo/a fat (2)
gorra cap (2)
gozar (c) to enjoy
grabadora tape recorder
grabar to record (11)
gracias thank you; **Día** (*m.*) **de Acción de Gracias** Thanksgiving Day; **Día** (*m.*) **de Gracias** Thanksgiving Day (6); **gracias a** thanks to; **muchas gracias** thanks a lot, thank you very much (1)
gracioso/a cute
grado degree (*temperature*)
graduación *f.* graduation (9)
graduado/a: asistente (*m.*) **graduado** graduate assistant

gradual gradual
graduarse (yo me gradúo) (en) to graduate (from) (9)
gráfica *n.* graph; diagram
gráfico/a graphic; illustrated
gramática grammar
gran, grande large, big (2, 4R); great (4)
granja farm
granjero/a farmer (3)
grasa grease, fat
grave serious
griego/a *n., adj.* Greek
gringo/a *n., adj. L.A.* foreigner, especially American
gris gray (2); **ojos grises** hazel/gray eyes (2)
gritar to yell, scream (7)
grito shout, cry
grueso/a thick; big, heavy
grupo group (4); **grupo minoritario** minority group
guacamole *m.* avocado dip
guagua bus (*Caribbean islands*)
guante *m.* glove (2)
guapo/a good-looking, handsome (2)
guaraní *m. Paraguayan indigenous group*
guardar to save, keep safe; **guardar ficheros** to save (computer) files (11); **guardar la línea** to watch one's figure
guatemalteco/a *n., adj.* Guatemalan
guayabera *loose-fitting man's shirt worn in tropical climates* (2)
guerra war; **guerra civil** civil war; **Guerra Hispanoamericana** Spanish-American War; **Guerra Mundial** World War
guerrero warrior, soldier
guía *m., f.* guide; *f.* guide(book); **guía** (*f.*) **de teléfonos** telephone directory (8); **guía** (*f.*) **de turismo** tourist guidebook; **guía** (*f.*) **turística** tourist guidebook (8)
guisado/a cooked, stewed
guitarra guitar (6)
gustar to be pleasing; to like (something pleases one) (6); **me gusta(n)...** I like . . . (4); **me gustó...** I liked . . . (5)
gusto *n.* taste; like, preference; **con gusto** with pleasure; **el gusto es mío** the pleasure is mine (1); **mucho gusto** pleased to meet you (1); **tanto gusto en conocerte/lo/la** so pleased to meet you (*fam./form. s.*) (1)
gustoso/a gladly, willingly

H

haber *irreg. infinitive form of* hay; to have (*auxiliary*); to be; to take place
habilidad *f.* ability, skill; talent

habitación *f.* room
habitante *m., f.* inhabitant (5)
habitar to live, reside in; to inhabit
habitual habitual
habla: de habla española Spanish-speaking (4)
hablador(a) talkative, gossipy (1, 2R)
hablante *m., f.* speaker
hablar to talk (3); to speak (3); **¿con quién hablo?** with whom am I speaking? (8); **hablar por teléfono** to talk on the telephone (6)
hacer (*irreg.*) (*p.p.* **hecho/a**) to make (3, 4R); to do (3, 4R); **hace ___ años ___** years ago; **hace fresco** it is cool (weather) (6); **hace (mucho) calor** it is (very) hot (6); **hace (mucho) frío** it is (very) cold (weather) (5, 6R); **hace (mucho) sol** it is (very) sunny (6); **hace (mucho) viento** it is (very) windy (6); **hace (muy) buen tiempo** the weather's (very) nice (5, 6R); **hace (muy) mal tiempo** the weather's (very) bad (5, 6R); **hacen** you (*pl.*)/they do, are doing (3); **hacer alpinismo** to go mountain climbing (6); **hacer gimnasia** to do gymnastics (6); **hacer juego** to match (*articles of clothing*); **hacer la cama** to make the bed (4); **hacer la tarea** to do one's homework; **hacer las compras** to go shopping, do one's shopping; **hacer las maletas** to pack one's suitcases; **hacer (los) ejercicios aeróbicos** to do aerobics, aerobic exercises (6); **hacer negocios** to do business; **hacer preguntas** to ask questions; **hacer un viaje** to take a trip; **hacer una cita** to make an appointment (8); **hacer una fiesta** to have/throw a party; **hacer una llamada** to make a call; **hacerse** to become; **haces** you (*fam. s.*) do, are doing (3); **¿qué tiempo hace?** what is the weather like? (6)
hacia toward (5)
hacha *f.* (*but* **el hacha**) ax
haitiano/a *n., adj.* Haitian
hambre *f.* (*but* **el hambre**) hunger; **huelga de hambre** hunger strike; **tener** (*irreg.*) (**mucha**) **hambre** to be (very) hungry (7)
hamburguesa hamburger (7)
hasta *prep.* until (3); *adv.* even; **hasta cierto punto** to a certain point; **hasta luego** see you later (1); **hasta mañana** see you tomorrow (1); **hasta pronto** see you soon; **hasta que** *conj.* until (9)
hay there is, there are (1); **hay (mucha) neblina** there is (a lot of) fog; it is (very) foggy (6); **hay que + *inf.*** it's

necessary to (*do something*); **no hay de qué** you're welcome (1); **no hay duda** there's no doubt; **¿qué hay?** what's going on? (1); **¿qué hay de nuevo?** what's new? (1)

hazaña deed, feat, exploit

hebreo/a Hebrew; **Pascua de los Hebreos** Passover (6)

hectárea hectare

hecho *n.* fact, event

hecho/a *adj.* made, done; **hecho/a a mano** handmade

helado ice cream (7)

helado/a frozen; iced; **té** (*m.*) **helado** iced tea (7)

hemisferio hemisphere

heredar to inherit

herencia heritage, inheritance; heredity

herido/a wounded person

hermano/a brother/sister (2); **hermano/a gemelo/a** twin brother/sister; **hermanos** brothers and sisters; brothers (2)

hermoso/a beautiful (7); handsome, good-looking

héroe *m.* hero

hidráulico/a hydraulic; **recursos** (*m. pl.*) **hidráulicos** water resources; **Secretaría de Agricultura y Recursos Hidráulicos** Department of Agriculture and Water Resources

hielo ice (5)

hierba herb (7); **hierba buena** mint; **hierba mate** *plant from which tea* (**mate**) *is made in southern Latin America*

hierro iron

hígado liver

hijo/a son/daughter (2); **hijo/a adoptivo/a** adopted child; **hijo/a ilegítimo/a** illegitimate child; **hijo/a político/a** son-in-law/daughter-in-law; **hijos** children (2); sons

himno nacional national anthem

hindú *n. m., f.; adj.* Hindu

hipódromo hippodrome, race track

hipopótamo hippopotamus

hispánico/a *n., adj.* Hispanic

hispano/a *n., adj.* Hispanic (4)

Hispanoamérica Latin America

hispanoamericano/a *n., adj.* Hispanic-American; **Guerra Hispanoamericana** Spanish-American War

hispanohablante Spanish-speaking (5)

historia history (3); story, tale

histórico/a historical, historic

hogar *m.* home

hoja leaf; sheet (*of paper*); printed or written sheet; **hoja de papel** sheet of paper

hola hello, hi (1)

Holanda Holland

holandés, holandesa *n., adj.* Dutch

hombre *m.* man (2); **¡hombre!** *interj.* well!, man!; **hombre de negocios** businessman (3)

hombro shoulder (4)

homenaje *m.* homage; tribute; **rendir (i, i) homenaje a** to pay or do homage to

homenajeado/a *person to whom respect, admiration, etc., is shown through a public ceremony*

hondo/a deep; **plato hondo** bowl (7)

honor *m.* honor; **corte** (*f.*) **de honor** wedding party

hora time (1); hour (8); time of day (8); **¿a qué hora?** (at) what time?; **a última hora** at the last moment; **¿qué hora es?** what time is it? (1)

horario schedule (3)

hornear to bake (*specifically bread*)

horno oven (4); **horno de microondas** microwave oven (4)

horror *m.* horror; **¡qué horror!** *interj.* what an atrocity!

hospedaje *m.* lodging

hospedarse to lodge, have lodgings (in), stay

hospital *m.* hospital (5)

hotel *m.* hotel (5)

hoy today (1); **de hoy en quince días** in two weeks; **hoy (en) día** today, nowadays; **hoy es el día doce (trece...)** today is the twelfth (thirteenth . . .) (1); **¿qué día es hoy?** what day is today? (1)

huachinango *Mex.* red snapper

huapango *musical rhythm and dance that originated in Veracruz, Mexico*

hubo (*preterite of* **haber**) there was

huelga de hambre hunger strike

huevo egg (7); **huevo duro** hard-boiled egg (7); **huevo frito** fried egg (7); **huevo revuelto** scrambled egg (7)

humanidad *f.* humanity

humano/a *adj.* human; **derechos** (*m. pl.*) **humanos** human rights; **recursos** (*m. pl.*) **humanos** human resources; **ser** (*n. m.*) **humano** human being

húmedo/a humid, damp, wet; **está (muy) húmedo** it is (very) humid (6)

humilde humble; meek

humor: sentido del humor sense of humor

humorístico/a humorous, funny

huracán *m.* hurricane (10)

I

ida: boleto de ida y vuelta round-trip ticket (8)

idea idea

ideal ideal

idealista *m., f.* idealist

idéntico/a identical

identidad *f.* identity

identificación *f.* identification (8); **etiqueta de identificación** identification label; luggage tag

identificar (qu) to identify; **identificarse con** to identify oneself with

ideología ideology

idioma *m.* language; **idioma natal** native language; **idioma oficial** official language

ido/a *adj.* past, bygone

iglesia church (5)

igual *adj.* equal, same; **al igual** *adv.* equally; **igual a/que** the same as; **sin igual** unrivaled, matchless

igualdad *f.* equality

igualmente likewise, same to you, same here (1)

ilegal illegal

ilegítimo/a illegitimate; **hijo/a ilegítimo/a** illegitimate child

iluminación *f.* illumination

iluminado/a illuminated

imagen *f.* image

imaginarse to imagine

imitar to imitate

impacto impact

imperfecto *gram.* imperfect tense; **imperfecto del subjuntivo** *gram.* past subjunctive tense

imperio empire; **imperio romano** Roman Empire

implementar to implement

imponer (*like* **poner**) to impose

importancia importance (6)

importante important (4); **(no) es importante que...** it's (not) important that . . . (9)

importar to be important, matter; to import

importe *m.* amount, value, cost

importunar to annoy, disturb

imposible impossible (2); **(no) es imposible que...** it's (not) impossible that . . . (9)

impresionante impressive

impresora printer (11)

imprimir to print (11)

improbable improbable (9); **(no) es improbable que...** it's (not) improbable that . . . (9)

improvisación *f.* improvisation

impulso impulse
inaugurar to inaugurate
inca *n. m.* Inca
incaico/a *adj.* Inca, Incan
incendio fire (10)
incienso incense
incierto/a uncertain, problematical
incluido/a included
incluir (y) to include
incluso *adv.* including, even
inconcebible inconceivable
incorrecto/a incorrect, inacccurate
increíble incredible, unbelievable; **(no)
    es increíble que...** it's (not) incredible
    that . . . (9)
incrementar to increase
incremento *n.* increase
indefinido/a: artículo indefinido
    indefinite article
independencia independence; **Día** (*m.*)
    de la Independencia Independence
    Day (6)
independiente independent
independizarse (c) to make oneself
    independent; to win freedom
indicador *m.* index, indicator
indicar (qu) to indicate, point
    out
indicativo *gram.* indicative tense;
    presente (*m.*) **del indicativo** *gram.*
    present indicative tense
índice *m.* index
indígena *n. m., f.* native person; *adj.*
    indigenous, native (11)
indigenista *adj. pertaining to the
    indigenismo movement, a Latin American
    sociopolitical movement in favor of
    indigenous peoples*
indio/a *n., adj.* Indian
individuo individual, person
**indocumentado/a: trabajador(a)
    indocumentado/a** undocumented,
    illegal worker
industria industry
industrial *n. m.* manufacturer; *adj.*
    industrial
industrialización *f.* industrialization
industrializado/a industrialized
inexplorado/a unexplored
infantil: cuento infantil children's
    story
infinitivo *gram.* infinitive
influencia *n.* influence
influir (y) to influence
información *f.* information; journalistic
    report, news
informar to inform
informática computer science
informe *m.* report (11)
infortunio misfortune

ingeniería *n.* engineering (3); **Facultad**
    (*f.*) **de Ingeniería** School of
    Engineering (3)
ingeniero/a engineer (3)
Inglaterra England (2)
inglés *m.* English (language)
inglés, inglesa *n.* English person; *adj.*
    English (2)
ingrediente *m.* ingredient (7)
ingreso coming in (*of money*); *pl.*
    earnings
inhospitalario/a inhospitable
iniciar(se) to begin, start
inicio initiation; beginning; **dar** (*irreg.*)
    inicio a to start (up)
inmediatamente immediately (5)
inmediato/a *adj.* immediate; **de
    inmediato** *adv.* immediately
inmenso/a immense
inmigrante *n. m., f.; adj.* immigrant
inocencia innocence
inodoro toilet (4)
inolvidable unforgettable
inscripción *f.* registration
insecto insect
insistir (en) to insist (on, upon) (6)
inspección *f.* inspection
inspirar to inspire; **inspirarse en** to take
    as a model or subject
instalación *f.* installation, plant
instalar to install
institucional institutional
instituto institute
instrucciones *f. pl.* instructions,
    directions
instrumento instrument; **tocar (qu) un
    instrumento musical** to play a musical
    instrument (6)
integrar to integrate
intelectual *n. m., f.* intellectual (person)
inteligencia intelligence
inteligente intelligent (2)
intención *f.* intention
intenso/a intense
intentar to try, attempt
interacción *f.* interaction
interaccionar to interact
intercambio *n.* exchange
interés *m.* interest
interesado/a person or party concerned
interesante interesting (2)
interesar to interest (6); to be
    interesting
interior *n. m., adj.* interior; **ropa interior**
    underwear, undergarments (2)
internacional international
interpretado/a interpreted
interrogativo/a: palabra interrogativa
    gram. interrogative word (2)
interrupción *f.* interruption

interrumpir to interrupt, suspend
intervención *f.* intervention
inti *m. Peruvian monetary unit*
íntimo/a intimate; private, personal;
    close
intrepidez *f.* (*pl.* **intrepideces**)
    intrepidity, courage
introducción *f.* introduction
introducir (*like* **producir**) to introduce;
    insert; **introducir datos** to input
    data (11)
introvertido/a introverted
inundación *f.* flood (10)
invadir to invade
invasión *f.* invasion
invasor(a) invader
invención *f.* invention
inventario inventory
inversión *f.* inversion; investment
investigación *f.* investigation; research
investigador(a) investigator
invierno winter (6)
invitación *f.* invitation
invitado/a person invited, guest
invitar to invite (3)
ir (*irreg.*) to go (1); to ride, be
    transported; **ir a** + *inf.* to be going to
    (*do something*) (1); **ir a pie** to walk, go
    on foot (5); **ir al cine** to go to the
    movies; **ir de compras** to go shopping;
    ir de vacaciones to go on vacation;
    irse to go away (4), leave; **que te/le
    vaya bien** hope all goes well (for you
    [*fam./form. s.*]) (1); **va** he/she/it goes
    (1); you (*form. s.*) go (1); **vamos** we
    are going (6); **vámonos** let's go (6)
ironía irony; **¡qué ironía!** *interj.* how
    ironic! (10)
irónico/a ironic
irregular irregular (4)
irremediable hopeless
isla island (1); **Islas Baleares** Balearic
    Islands; **Islas Canarias** Canary
    Islands
istmo isthmus (1)
Italia Italy
italiano Italian (language) (3)
italiano/a *n., adj.* Italian
intención *f.* intention
itinerario itinerary
izquierda *n.* left (*direction*); **a la izquierda
    de** to the left of

J

jabón *m.* soap
jaguar *m.* jaguar (10)
jamón *m.* ham (7)
Jánuca *m.* Hanukkah (6)
Japón *m.* Japan (2)

japonés *m.* Japanese (language) (3)
japonés, japonesa *n.* Japanese person; *adj.* Japanese (2)
jaqueca migraine; headache
jarabe *m.* syrup; **jarabe** (*m.*) **de fruta** fruit juice
jardín *m.* garden (4); yard (4); lawn (4)
jaripeo rodeo, bronco busting (*Mex.*)
jarocho/a *n., adj.* person from Veracruz, Mexico
jeans *m. pl.* jeans (2)
jefe/a boss
jengibre *m.* ginger
jerez sherry
jerga rag
Jipijapa *village in Ecuador famous for the straw hats the inhabitants weave*
jirafa giraffe (10)
jonrón *m.* home run
jornalero/a day laborer
joven *n. m., f.* young person; *adj.* young (1, 2R)
joya jewel (5); *pl.* jewels; jewelry (5)
joyería jewelry store (5)
joyero/a jeweler
judía green bean
judío/a *n., adj.* Jewish
juego game; **hacer** (*irreg.*) **juego** to match (*articles of clothing*); **Juegos Olímpicos** Olympic games
jueves *m. s.* Thursday (3)
jugador(a) player
jugar (ue) (gu) (al) to play (a game, sport) (4, 6R); **jugar a las cartas** to play cards (6); **jugar al básquetbol** to play basketball (6); **jugar al béisbol** to play baseball (6); **jugar al boliche** to bowl, go bowling (6); **jugar al fútbol** to play soccer (6); **jugar al fútbol (norte)americano** to play football (6); **jugar al golf** to play golf (6); **jugar a los naipes** to play cards; **jugar al ráquetbol** to play racquetball (6); **jugar al tenis** to play tennis (6); **jugar al voleibol** to play volleyball (6)
jugo juice (7); **jugo de naranja/manzana** orange/apple juice (7)
juguete *m.* toy; **tienda de juguetes** toy store
julio July (6)
junio June (6)
junto: junto a next to (1, 5R), alongside of; **junto con** along with
juntos/as together
jurídico/a legal
justicia justice
justo *adv.* exactly
juventud *f.* youth

K

kilo(gramo) *m.* kilogram (*approximately 2.2 pounds*) (8)
kilómetro kilometer (5)

L

la the (*f.s. definite article*); *d.o.* you (*form. s.*), her, it (*f.*)
labio lip (4)
labor *f.* labor, work, task; **labores caseras** household tasks, chores
laboratorio laboratory; **laboratorio de lenguas/física/química** language/physics/chemistry laboratory (3)
labrado/a cut, carved
lacio: pelo lacio straight hair (2)
lado side; **al lado (de)** by the side of; next to; **de lado a lado** from one side to the other
lago lake (1)
lágrima tear
lamentar to be sorry, regret
lámpara lamp (4)
lana wool (5)
langosta lobster (7)
lanza lance, spear
lanzarse (c) to launch
lápiz (*pl.* **lápices**) pencil (3)
largo/a long (2); **a la larga** in the long run, in the end; **a lo largo de** throughout; **de largo** in length; **llamada de larga distancia** long distance (telephone) call (8)
las the (*f. pl. definite article*); *d.o.* you (*form. pl.*), them (*f.*)
láser: tocador (*m.*) **de discos láser** laser disk player (11)
lástima: (no) es lástima que... it's (not) a shame/a pity/too bad that . . . (9); **¡qué lástima!** *interj.* what a shame!
latín *m.* Latin (language) (3)
latino/a *n.* Latin, Hispanic (person) (6); *adj.* Latin, Hispanic; **América Latina** Latin America
Latinoamérica Latin America
latinoamericano/a *adj.* Latin American
lavabo bathroom sink (4)
lavadora washing machine (4)
lavandería laundry
lavaplatos *m. s.* dishwasher (4)
lavar to wash (4); **lavarse** to wash oneself (4); **lavarse las manos** to wash one's hands; **lavarse los dientes** to brush one's teeth
lazo bow, knot; tie, bond; lasso, lariat
le *i.o.* to/for you (*form. s.*), him, her, it; **le duele(n)... . . .** hurt(s) you (*form. s.*)/him/her (4)

lección *f.* lesson
lector (*m.*) **de discos** (computer) disk drive (11)
lectura reading
leche *f.* milk (7)
lechería milk shop
lechuga lettuce (7); head of lettuce
leer (y) to read (3, 6R)
legal: tutor(a) legal legal guardian
legumbre *f.* legume (7)
lejía bleach
lejos *adv.* far away; **lejos (de)** *prep.* far (from) (5)
lempira *m. Honduran monetary unit*
lengua language; tongue; **laboratorio de lenguas** language laboratory (3); **lengua extranjera** foreign language; **lengua oficial** official language
lenguado sole, flounder (7)
lento: a fuego lento by slow fire, low flame, or heat (*cooking*)
león *m.* lion (10)
les *i.o.* to/for you (*form. pl.*), them
letra letter (*of the alphabet*); words (*of a song*); **Facultad** (*f.*) **de Filosofía y Letras** School of Liberal Arts (3); **filosofía y letras** humanities, liberal arts
levantar to build, erect; **levantar pesas** to lift weights; **levantarse** to get up (4); to rise, stand up (4)
leve slight
leyenda legend
liberación *f.* liberation, release
liberarse to free oneself
libertad *f.* liberty
libertador(a) liberator
libra pound (8)
libre free; **al aire libre** outdoors, in the open air; **estado libre asociado** free associated state; **libre comercio** free trade; **lucha libre** wrestling (6); **tiempo libre** free, spare time
librería bookstore (1)
librero bookcase (4)
libro book (1); **libro de texto** textbook
licencia licence
licenciado/a lawyer
líder *m.* leader
liga: liga americana American (baseball) League; **liga mayor** major league (baseball); **liga nacional** National (baseball) League
ligero/a light(weight) (7)
limitar to limit; **limitar con** to border on or upon
limón *m.* lemon (7)
limonada lemonade (7)
limosnero/a beggar

limpiador(a) *adj.* cleaning
limpiar to clean (3); **limpiarse la boca** to brush one's teeth
limpio/a clean (10)
lindo/a pretty, lovely; nice
línea line (8); **guardar la línea** to watch one's figure; **la línea está ocupada** the line is busy (8); **línea aérea** airline; **línea equatorial** equator
liquidación *f.* bargain sale
líquido liquid
lista list
listo/a ready; clever; **estar** (*irreg.*) **listo/a** to be ready (7)
literario/a literary
literatura literature (3)
litúrgico/a liturgic(al)
lo *d.o.* you (*form. s.*), him, it (*m.*); **lo mismo** the same thing; **lo que** what, that which; **lo siento** I'm sorry (1)
loar to praise, eulogize
lobo wolf (10)
localidad *f.* locality; area; place
loco/a: estar (*irreg.*) **loco/a** to be crazy (7)
locutor(a) radio announcer
lógico/a logical (2)
lograr to achieve; to gain, obtain, attain
logro achievement
loro parrot
los the (*m. pl. definite article*) *d.o.* you (*form. pl.*), them (*m.*)
lúcido/a bright, shining
lucir (zc) to show, display
lucha fight; **lucha libre** wrestling (6); **practicar (qu) la lucha libre** to practice, do wrestling (6); to wrestle
luchar to fight (10); to struggle (10)
luego then, next (5); later; **hasta luego** see you later (1)
lugar *m.* place (1); **en primer lugar** in the first place; **tener** (*irreg.*) **lugar** to take place
lujo luxury
lujoso/a luxurious
luna moon; **luna de miel** honeymoon (9)
lunes *m. s.* Monday (3)
luto mourning; **medio luto** mourning for which the mourners wear black and white or very dark colors; **vestirse (i, i) de luto** to wear mourning clothes (9)
luz (*f. pl.* **luces**) light; **dar** (*irreg.*) **a luz** to give birth (9); **traje** (*m.*) **de luces** *suit of clothes worn by bullfighters*

LL

llama flame
llamada call; **hacer** (*irreg.*) **una llamada** to make a call; **llamada de larga distancia** long distance (telephone) call (8); **llamada de persona a persona** person-to-person call; **llamada por cobrar** collect call; **llamada telefónica** telephone call
llamar to call (3); **llamar (a la puerta)** to knock (on the door) (7); **llamarse** to be called (4)
llano/a flat, level
llanura plain (1)
llegada arrival
llegar (gu) (a) to arrive (in, at) (3); **llega (a)** he/she/it arrives (in, at) (1); **llegar a** + *inf.* to come to (*do something*); **llegar a tiempo** to arrive on time (8); **llegar tarde** to arrive late
llenar to fill out
lleno/a full
llevar to wear (3); to carry (3); to take (3); to have been (*in a certain place for a period of time*); **lleva** he/she/it wears, is wearing (2); **llevo** I wear, am wearing (2); **llevar a cabo** to carry out, accomplish
llorar to cry
llover (ue) to rain (6)
lluvia rain (6); **estación** (*f.*) **de las lluvias** rainy season (6); **lluvia ácida** acid rain (10)

M

macaco macaque monkey
madera wood (5)
madrastra stepmother
madre *f.* mother (2); **Día** (*m.*) **de las Madres** Mother's Day (6)
madrugada dawn, early morning
maestro/a teacher (3)
mágico/a magic(al)
magnífico/a magnificent
maíz *m.* (*pl.* **maíces**) corn (7)
majestuoso/a majestic
mal *adv.* badly; incorrectly; ill, poorly (1); **muy mal** very ill, poorly (1); **salir** (*irreg.*) **mal** to do poorly (7)
mal, malo/a *adj.* bad; unfortunate; **hace (muy) mal tiempo** the weather's (very) bad (5, 6R); **(no) es malo que...** it's (not) bad/unfortunate that . . . (9); **tener** (*irreg.*) **mala suerte** to be unlucky (9)
maletas: hacer (*irreg.*) **las maletas** to pack one's suitcases
malgastar to waste
malinterpretar to misinterpret
malsano/a unhealthy
malvavisco marshmallow
mamá mom, mother (1)
mancha stain
mandar to send (5); to mail

mandarín *m.* Mandarin (language)
mando command
manejar to drive (5)
manera manner, way
manga sleeve
mango mango (7)
maní *m.* peanut; **mantequilla de maní** peanut butter (7)
manifestación *f.* demonstration
mano *f.* hand (4); **darse** (*irreg.*) **la mano** to shake hands; **hecho/a a mano** handmade; **lavarse las manos** to wash one's hands
manta blanket
mantel *m.* tablecloth
mantener (*irreg.*) to maintain; to hold; **mantenerse en forma** to keep in shape
mantenimiento maintenance
mantequilla butter (7); **mantequilla de cacahuetes/maní** peanut butter (7)
manufactura manufacture
manzana apple (7); **jugo de manzana** apple juice (7)
mañana *n.* morning; *adv.* tomorrow; **a media mañana** in the/at midmorning; **de la mañana** A.M., in the morning (1); **hasta mañana** see you tomorrow (1); **pasado mañana** the day after tomorrow (3); **por la mañana** in the morning
mapa *m.* map
maquillarse to put on makeup (4)
máquina machine; **máquina de escribir** typewriter
mar *m.* sea (1); **Mar Caribe** Caribbean Sea; **Mar Mediterráneo** Mediterranean Sea
maratón *m.* marathon
maravilloso/a marvelous, wonderful
marcar (qu) to dial (8); to mark (*as noteworthy*); **marcar el número** to dial a telephone number (8); **señal** (*f.*) **de marcar** dial tone (8)
marcial: artes (*f.* [*but* **el arte**]) **marciales** martial arts (6)
marco picture frame
marcha march; **poner** (*irreg.*) **en marcha** to start, put in motion
margarina margarine
margen: al margen de outside of
mariachi *n. m. Mex.* member of a Mariachi band; *adj.* Mariachi
marido husband; *pl.* married couple; husbands
marinero/a: a la marinera sailor-fashion (*culinary style*)
marino/a *adj.* marine, sea
mariposa butterfly (10)
mariscos *m. pl.* seafood (7); shellfish
martes *m. s.* Tuesday (3)
marzo March (6)

más more (1); most; **cada vez más** more and more; **más o menos** more or less; **más** (+ *adj.*) **que** more (+ *adj.*) than, (*adj.*)-er than (2); **más que nada** more than anything; **más tarde** later; **¿quién más?** who else? (1)

masa dough

matador *m.* matador (*bullfighting*)

matar to kill (11)

mate: yerba (hierba) mate *plant from which tea* (**mate**) *is made in southern Latin America*

matemáticas *f. pl.* mathematics (3)

materia school subject (3)

material *n. m.* material; equipment; *adj.* material

materno/a maternal

matrícula registration fee

matrimonio married couple (9); matrimony (9); **anuncio de matrimonio** marriage announcement; **contraer** (*like* **traer**) **matrimonio** to get married

máximo *n.* maximum

máximo/a *adj.* maximum

maya *n. m., f.; adj.* Mayan

mayo May (6)

mayonesa mayonnaise (7)

mayor older, oldest (4); greater, greatest (4); biggest; main, major; **liga mayor** Major League (baseball); **plaza mayor** central, main square/plaza; **por la mayor parte** in the majority, on the whole

mayoreo large quantities, wholesale

mayoría majority

mayoritario/a pertaining to the majority

me *d.o.* me; *i.o.* to, for me; *refl. pron.* myself; **me encanta(n)...** I love . . . (5); **me gusta(n)...** I like . . . (4); **me gustó...** I liked . . . (5)

mecánico/a mechanic (3)

mecanismo mechanism

media: y media half past (*with time*) (1)

mediano/a: de estatura mediana (of) average height (2); **de peso mediano** (of) average weight (2)

medianoche *f.* midnight; **es medianoche** it's midnight (1)

mediante *adv.* by means of, with the help of, through

medias *f. pl.* stockings, pantyhose (2)

medicina medicine (3)

médico/a *n.* doctor, physician (3); *adj.* medical

medida: tomar medidas to take measures, steps

medio *n.* means; **medio ambiente** environment; **medio luto** *mourning for which the mourners wear black and white*

or very dark colors; **por medio de** by means of

medio/a *adj.* half; middle; **a media mañana** in the/at midmorning; **a media tarde** in the/at midafternoon; **clase** (*f.*) **media** middle class; **edad** (*f.*) **media** Middle Ages

mediodía *m.* noon, midday; **es mediodía** it's noon (1)

mediterráneo/a Mediterranean; **Mar** (*m.*) **Mediterráneo** Mediterranean Sea

mejilla cheek

mejor better (1); best (1)

mejora improvement

mejoramiento improvement

mejorar to improve

melocotón *m.* peach

melodrama *m.* melodrama

memoria memory (6)

mencionar to mention

menor younger (7); least; lesser; **de menor cuantía** of little importance

menoreo small quantities; retail

menos less; least; fewer; except; **más o menos** more or less; **menos cuarto** quarter to (*with time*) (1); **por lo menos** at least

mensaje *m.* message (9)

mentira lie (4); **decir** (*irreg.*) **mentiras** to tell lies

menú *m.* menu

menudo: a menudo frequently

mercado market (5); **mercado de discos** record store

mercancía merchandise

merecer (zc) to deserve

merideño/a *person from Mérida, Mexico*

merienda light meal or snack eaten late afternoon (7)

mérito merit; worth

merluza hake (*fish*)

mes *m.* month (3); **mes pasado** last month (5); **todos los meses** every month (6)

mesa table (1); **mesa para el profesor / la profesora** table for the professor (1); **poner** (*irreg.*) **la mesa** to set the table (4)

mesero/a waiter/waitress

meseta plateau (1)

mesita nightstand (4)

mestizo/a *n., adj.* mestizo

meta goal

metal *m.* metal

metate *m. Mex.* stone on which maize, etc., is ground

meter to put in/into (8)

metodista *n. m., f.; adj.* Methodist

método method, way (8)

metro subway

metrópoli *f.* metropolis

metropolitano/a metropolitan

mexicano/a *n.* Mexican; *adj.* Mexican (1, 2R); **ser** (*irreg.*) **mexicano/a** to be Mexican (1)

mexicanoamericano/a *n., adj.* Mexican American

México Mexico (1, 2R)

mezcla mixture, mix, blend (7)

mezclar to mix, blend

mí *obj.* (*of prep.*) me

mi(s) *poss.* my (1)

microcuento short short story

micrófono microphone (11)

microondas: horno de microondas microwave oven (4)

miedo: tener (*irreg.*) **(mucho) miedo** to be (very) afraid (8)

miel: luna de miel honeymoon (9)

miembro/a member (8)

mientras while (4); **mientras que** while; whereas; **mientras tanto** meanwhile

miércoles *m. s.* Wednesday (3)

mil *m.* (one) thousand (5); **mil millones** (one) billion (5)

milímetro millimeter

militar *m.* soldier

milla mile; **milla cuadrada** square mile

millón *m.* million (5); **mil millones** (one) billion (5)

mina mine

mineral *adj.* mineral; **agua** (*f.* [*but* **el agua**]) **mineral (con gas)** (carbonated) mineral water

minero/a miner

miniatura miniature

miniencuesta brief survey, question- naire

minifalda miniskirt

mínimo *n.* minimum

mínimo/a *adj.* minimum

ministro: primer ministro Prime Minister

minoritario/a: grupo minoritario minority group

minúsculo/a small, trifling

minuto minute (6)

mío/a(s) *poss.* my, (of) mine; **el gusto es mío** the pleasure is mine (1)

mira: punto de mira lookout point

mirada look, glance

mirar to look at (3); **¡mira!** *interj.* look! (1); **mirar la televisión** to watch television

misa Mass (6)

miseria misery

misión *f.* mission

Misisipí: río Misisipí Mississippi River

mismo/a same (5); self; selfsame; myself, yourself, herself, itself, etc. (*for emphasis*); **ahora mismo** right now; **lo mismo** the same thing; **sí mismo/a(s)**

himself, herself, itself, oneself, themselves (*for emphasis*)

misterio mystery; **novela de misterio** mystery novel

mitad *f.* half (6)

mito myth

mitología mythology

mitológico/a mythological

mixteca *m., f. member of indigenous group of southern Mexico*

mixto/a mixed

mochila backpack; bookbag (1)

moda fashion

modelar to model

modelo model

modernización *f.* modernization

moderno/a modern (5)

modista *m. f.* designer

modo manner, way; *gram.* mood

molcajete *m.* large stone or earthenware mortar

molde *m.* mold

moldura molding

molestar to bother (6)

molinillo hand mill; coffee grinder

molino de viento windmill

momento moment (8); **en este momento** right now, at this moment (4); **por el momento** for the present

monarquía constitucional *type of monarchy in which the powers of the monarch are limited by the constitution*

moneda coin (8); money

monja nun

mono monkey (10)

monotonía monotony

monstruo monster

montaña mountain (1); **cadena de montañas** mountain range; **montañas Rocosas** Rocky Mountains

montañoso/a mountainous

montar to ride (6); **montar a caballo** to ride a horse; ride horseback (6); **montar en bicicleta** to ride a bicycle (6); **montar en motocicleta** to ride a motorcycle (6)

montón *m.* heap, pile

monumento monument

morado/a purple (2)

moral *f.* morale

morder (ue) to bite (10)

moreno/a dark-haired, dark-skinned (2)

morir(se) (ue,u) (*p.p.* **muerto/a**) to die (9)

moro/a *n.* Moor; *adj.* Moorish

mortalidad: tasa de mortalidad death rate

mosaico mosaic

mosca fly (10)

Moscú Moscow

mostrar (ue) to show (4); to exhibit

motel *m.* motel

motivo motive

motocicleta motorcycle (5); **montar en motocicleta** to ride a motorcycle (6)

motor *m.* motor

mouse *m.* (computer) mouse (11)

moverse (ue) to move

movimiento movement

muchacho/a young man/woman (2); boy/girl (2)

mucho *adv.* a lot (2), much

mucho/a *adj.* much (1); (*pl.*) many, a lot (of) (1); **muchas gracias** thanks a lot, thank you very much (1); **muchas veces** many times, often (4); **mucho gusto** pleased to meet you (1)

mudarse to move (*change one's residence*)

mudo/a mute, silent

muebles *m. pl.* furniture, furnishings (4)

muerte *f.* death (9)

muerto/a *n. m.* dead person; *adj.* dead; killed; **Día** (*m.*) **de los Muertos** Day of the Dead (*November 2*) (6)

mujer *f.* woman (2); wife; **mujer de negocios** businesswoman (3); **mujer policía** (female) police officer (1)

multicínemas *m. s.* movie theater with various screens

multietnicidad *f.* multiethnicity (*having various ethnic backgrounds*)

multitud *f.* multitude

mundial *adj.* world; **Guerra Mundial** World War

mundo world (4); **mundo de los negocios** business world; **Nuevo Mundo** New World

municipio municipality, city

mural *m.* mural

muralista *m., f.* muralist

muralla wall, rampart

murciélago bat (10)

museo museum (5)

música music (3); **escuchar música** to listen to music (6)

musical: instrumento musical musical instrument (6); **tocar (qu) un instrumento musical** to play a musical instrument (6)

músico/a musician (3)

muy very (1); **muy bien** very well, fine (1); **muy mal** very ill, poorly (1)

N

nacer (zc) to be born (9)

nacimiento birth (9)

nación *f.* nation

nacional national; domestic; **himno nacional** national anthem; **liga nacional** National League (baseball); **producto nacional bruto** gross national product

nacionalidad *f.* nationality (2)

nada nothing (1, 5R), not anything; not at all (5); **de nada** you're welcome (1); **más que nada** more than anything; **nada de particular** nothing much (1), nothing in particular; **para nada** at all

nadar to swim (6)

nadie no one (6), nobody, not anybody

nahua *m., f. member of indigenous group of Mexico that preceded the Aztecs; m.* **Nahua** *language*

naipes: jugar (ue) (gu) a los naipes to play cards

naranja orange (7); **jugo de naranja** orange juice (7)

nariz (*pl.* **narices**) *m.* nose (4)

narración *f.* narration

natación *f.* swimming

natal *adj.* native; **idioma** (*m.*) **natal** native language

natural natural; **ciencias naturales** natural sciences; **recursos naturales** natural resources

naturaleza nature (10)

Navidad *f.* Christmas (6); **vacaciones** (*f. pl.*) **de Navidad** Christmas vacation

navideño/a Christmas

neblina fog, mist; **hay (mucha) neblina** there is (a lot of) fog, it is (very) foggy (6)

necesario/a necessary (9); **(no) es necesario que...** it's (not) necessary that . . . (9)

necesidad *f.* necessary

necesitar to need (3); **necesita** he/she/it needs (2); **necesito** I need (2)

necrológico/a: nota necrológica obituary (9)

negarse (ie) (gu) to refuse

negativo/a *adj.* negative

negocio business (8); *pl.* business; **hacer** (*irreg.*) **negocios** to do business; **hombre** (*m.*) **de negocios** businessman (3); **mujer** (*f.*) **de negocios** businesswoman (3); **mundo de los negocios** business world

negro: televisor (*m.*) **en blanco y negro** black and white television

negro/a *adj.* black (2); **ojos negros** black/dark eyes (2)

neovolcánico/a neovolcanic

neoyorquino/a *adj.* of New York City

nervioso/a nervous (1); **estar** (*irreg.*) **nervioso/a** to be nervous (1)
nevar (ie) to snow (6)
nevera refrigerator (4)
ni neither, nor
Niágara: Cataratas de Niágara Niagara Falls
nieto/a grandson/granddaughter (2); **nietos** grandchildren; grandsons
nieve *f.* snow (5, 6R)
nilón *m.* nylon (5)
ningún, ninguno/a no, none, not any
niño/a boy/girl (2); child (2); **niños** children; boys
níquel *m.* nickel (*chemical*)
nivel *m.* level
no no (1); not (1); **¿no?** right? (1); isn't he/she/it?, aren't you/we/they? (2); **no hay de qué** you're welcome (1); **¡no me digas!** *interj.* you're kidding! (2); **no... sino que** not . . . but rather (10); **no sólo... sino también...** not only . . . but also . . . (6); **ya no** no longer
nobel: premio Nóbel Nobel Prize
nocturno: club (*m.*) **nocturno** nightclub
noche *f.* night; **buenas noches** good evening, good night (1); **de (la) noche** P.M., at night (1); **esta noche** tonight (2); **la noche anterior** the night before; **Noche Vieja** New Year's Eve (6); **por la noche** at night (3); in the night; **toda la noche** all night
Nochebuena Christmas Eve (6)
nombrar to name, nominate
nombre *n.* name (9); **nombre de pila** first name (9); **nombre de soltera** maiden name
nominalización *f. gram.* nominalization (*converting another part of speech into a noun*)
nopal *m.* prickly pear cactus
nordeste *m.* northeast (5)
noroeste *m.* northwest (5)
norte *m.* north (4, 5R); **América del Norte** North America; **Polo Norte** North Pole
Norteamérica North America
norteamericano/a *n., adj.* North American (1, 2R); **fútbol** (*m.*) **norteamericano** football (6)
nos *d.o.* us; *i.o.* to, for us; *refl. pron.* ourselves; **nos vemos** see ya (1)
nosotros/as *sub. pron.* we; *obj.* (*of prep.*) us
nota note (*musical*); grade; **nota necrológica** obituary (9)
notar to note, observe, remark

noticia news *pl.* news (6); **buenas noticias** good news
noticiario newscast
novecientos/as nine hundred (5)
novela novel (6); **novela de misterio** mystery novel; **novela romántica/policíaca** romance/detective novel (6)
novelista *m., f.* novelist
novena *nine-day period of mourning*
noveno/a ninth (10)
noventa ninety (1)
noviazgo engagement (9); courtship (9)
noviembre *m.* November (6)
novio/a boyfriend/girlfriend (1)
nube *f.* cloud (6)
nublado/a: está (muy) nublado it is (very) cloudy (6)
nuclear: familia nuclear nuclear family
nuera daughter-in-law (2)
nuestro/a(s) *poss.* our (3); (of) ours; **Nuestra Señora** our Lady (*Virgin Mary*)
nueve nine (1)
nuevo/a new (2); **Año Nuevo Chino** Chinese New Year (6); **de nuevo** again (11); **Día** (*m.*) **de Año Nuevo** New Year's Day (6); **Nuevo Mundo** New World; **¿qué hay de nuevo?** what's new? (1)
número number (1); issue (*of a magazine*) (11); **marcar (qu) el número** to dial a telephone number (8); **número de teléfono** telephone number (1); **número equivocado** wrong (telephone) number; **número ordinal** ordinal number (10)
numeroso/a numerous
nunca never (3)

O

o or (1); **o sea** in other words
objetivo *n.* objective
objeto object
obligación *f.* obligation
obligar (gu) to oblige, compel
obligatorio/a obligatory, compulsory
obra piece of work
obrero/a worker, laborer (3); **Día** (*m.*) **del Obrero** Labor Day (6)
obscuro/a dark
observar to observe
obsoleto/a obsolete
obtener (*like* **tener**) to obtain
ocasión *f.* occasion
ocasionar to cause; to stir up
occidental *adj.* western
océano ocean (1); **Océano Atlántico** Atlantic Ocean; **Océano Pacífico** Pacific Ocean

octavo/a eighth (10)
octubre *m.* October (6)
ocupación *f.* occupation (3)
ocupado/a busy (1); **estar** (*irreg.*) **ocupado/a** to be busy (1); **la línea está ocupada** the line is busy (8)
ocupar to occupy; to take up (*time*); **ocuparse de** to be in charge of; to attend to
ocurrir to happen, occur
ochenta eighty (1)
ocho eight (1); **ocho días** a week
ochocientos/as eight hundred (5)
oda ode
odiar to hate
oeste *m.* west (4, 5R)
oferta offer; **en oferta** on sale (5)
oficial *adj.* official; **idioma** (*m.*)/**lengua oficial** official language
oficiar to officiate
oficina office (5); **oficina de correos** post office (5); **oficina de turismo** tourist office (8)
oficio occupation, trade (3)
ofrecer (zc) to offer
ofrenda religious offering; offering, present
oír (*irreg.*) to hear (4); **oír decir** to hear tell; **¡oye!** *interj.* hey!; listen! (1)
ojalá (que) I hope, wish that
ojo eye (2, 4R); **ojos grises** hazel/gray eyes (2); **ojos negros** black/dark eyes (2)
Olimpiadas *f. pl.* Olympic games
Olímpicos: Juegos (*m. pl.*) **Olímpicos** Olympic games
oliva: aceite (*m.*) **de oliva** olive oil (7)
olmeca *indigenous group of southern Mexico* (*near Veracruz*)
olor *m.* odor, smell
olvidar to forget
olla pot, stewpot
once eleven (1)
onda wave; **onda corta** shortwave
ondulación *f.* undulation
onza ounce (8)
opción *f.* option
operación *f.* (mathematical) operation
operador(a) (telephone) operator (8)
operar to operate
opinar to form, express, or hold an opinion
opinión *f.* opinion
oponerse (*like* **poner**) **(a)** to be opposed (to)
oportunidad *f.* opportunity
oposición *f.* opposition
optimista *n. m., f* optimist; *adj.* optimistic (1, 2R)

óptimo/a optimal, best
opuesto/a *adj.* opposite
opulento/a opulent
oración *f.* prayer
orden *m.* order, command; order (*sequence*)
ordenado/a orderly, tidy
ordinal: número ordinal ordinal number (10)
oreja (outer) ear (4)
organismo organism
organización *f.* organization
organizador(a) organizer
orgullo pride
orgulloso/a proud (5)
oriental eastern
orientarse to orient oneself, find one's way about
origen *m.* origin; **país** (*m.*) **de origen** native country; **pueblo de origen** hometown
original *adj.* original
originario/a native
originarse to originate, arise
orilla shore; border, edge
ornato adornment; show
oro gold (5)
oscuridad *f.* darkness
oscuro/a (*adj.*) dark (7)
oso bear (10)
ostra oyster
otomí *m., f.* member of indigenous group of central Mexico
otoño autumn, fall (3, 6R)
otorgar (gu) to award; to grant
otro/a other (1); another (1); **otra vez** again; **por otra parte** on the other hand (4)
oveja *s.* sheep (10)
¡oye! *interj.* hey!; listen! (1)
ozono ozone; **capa de ozono** ozone layer (10)

P

paciencia patience
paciente *m., f.* patient
pacífico/a: Océano Pacífico Pacific Ocean
padre *m.* father (2); priest; *pl.* parents (2); fathers; priests; **Día** (*m.*) **de los Padres** Father's Day (6)
padrino godfather; *pl.* godparents (*of a baptism, first communion, confirmation, or wedding*); godfathers
paella paella (*dish made with rice, shellfish, and often chicken or rabbit, flavored with saffron*)
pagar (gu) to pay (for) (5)
país *m.* country (1); **país de origen**

native country; **País Vasco** Basque region (*Sp.*)
paisaje *m.* landscape
pájaro bird (10)
palabra word (1, 3R); **palabra interrogativa** *gram.* interrogative word (2); **palabra semejante** cognate (1)
palacio palace
paladar *m.* palate
paleta popsicle
palma palm tree
palmar *m.* palm plantation
palo stick
paloma dove, pigeon
palomitas *f. pl.* popcorn (7)
pampa pampa, grassland
pan *m.* bread (7); **pan dulce** sweet bread (7); **pan tostado** toast (7)
panadería bakery (5)
panameño/a *n., adj.* Panamanian (2)
panamericano/a: Carretera Panamericana Pan-American Highway (1)
panecillo roll (*of bread*) (5)
pantalones *m. pl.* pants (2); **pantalones cortos** shorts (2)
pantalla screen (3, 11R)
pantano swamp, marsh
pañuelo handkerchief
papa *L.A.* potato (7); **papa frita** french fry (potato) (7); **papita** potato chip (7)
papá *m.* dad, father (1)
papel *m.* paper (3); role, part; **hoja de papel** sheet of paper; **papel para cartas** stationery (5)
papelería stationery store (5)
papi *m.* daddy
papita potato chip (7)
paquete *m.* package (8)
par *m.* pair; equal; **sin par** unequaled, incomparable
para *prep.* (intended) for; for, in order to (*be/do something*) (1); for, by (*specified future time*); for a; 'til (*with time*); to; toward (*a place*); **estudiar para** (*professional title*) to study to be (*professional title*); **para arriba** and up (*with numbers*) (5); **para nada** at all; **para que** *conj.* in order that, so that
parabién *m.* congratulation
parada de autobuses bus stop (5)
paraguas *m. s.* umbrella (2)
paralelo *n.* parallel
paralizado/a paralyzed
parar to stop
pardo/a brown
parecer (zc) to seem (5), appear; to think (about) (6); **parecerse** to look

like; **¿qué te pareció... ?** what did you think about . . . ? (5)
parecido resemblance
parecido/a *adj.* similar (to), like
pared *f.* wall (4)
pareja pair; partner
parentesco relationship
pargo red snapper (7)
pariente *m., f.* relative (2)
parque *m.* park (5)
párrafo paragraph
parrilla grill; **a la parrilla** grilled
parrillada *dish consisting of grilled meats*
parte *f.* part: **cuarta parte** one fourth; **de parte de** on behalf of; **¿de parte de quién?** may I ask who's calling? (8); **en parte** partly; **en/por todas partes** everywhere; **por la mayor parte** in the majority, on the whole; **por otra parte** on the other hand (4); **por su parte** as far as he/she is concerned
participación *f.* participation
participante *m., f.* participant
participar to participate
particular *adj.* private; extraordinary; **casa particular** private home, house (4); **nada de particular** nothing much (1), nothing in particular
partidario/a *m., f.* supporter
partido match, game (*sports*) (6)
partir to divide; to depart; **a partir de** from (*specific time, amount, etc.*) onward
pasado *n.* past
pasado/a *adj.* past, former (*with time*), gone by; **año pasado** last year (5); **mes** (*m.*) **pasado** last month (5); **pasado mañana** the day after tomorrow (3); **semana pasada** last week (5); **semestre** (*m.*) **pasado** last semester (5); **verano pasado** last summer
pasaporte *m.* passport (8)
pasar to happen; to pass (4); to spend (*time*) (5); to show (*program on T.V.*) (5); **pasar de ser** to go beyond being; **pasar la aspiradora** to vacuum; **pasarlo bien** to have a good time; **pasar por** to go, pass by (4); to pass, slip through; to pick up; **¿qué pasa?** what's happening? (1)
pasatiempo pastime
Pascua: Pascua de los Hebreos Passover (6); **Pascua Florida** Easter (6)
pasear to walk (6)
paseo boulevard, drive (5)
pasión *f.* passion
paso step
paso/a dried (*fruit*); **ciruela pasa** prune
pastel *m.* pie (7), cake, pastry; **pastel de queso** cheesecake

pastelería pastry shop (5), bakery
pata foot (*of an animal*), hoof, paw
patata *Sp.* potato; **patata frita** french fry (potato)
paterno/a paternal
patinar to skate (6)
patineta skateboard
patio patio (4)
pato duck
patona: araña patona daddy-longlegs spider
patria one's country, native country; **fiestas patrias** *holidays celebrating a nation's history*
patrimonio estate, heritage, endowment
patriota *m., f.* patriot
patrocinador(a) sponsor
patrón, patrona: santo patrón patron saint
pavo turkey (7)
paz *f.* (*pl.* **paces**) peace
peculiaridad *f.* peculiarity
pecho chest (4)
pedir (i, i) to ask for (4); to request (4); to order
pedrería jewelry, precious stones
peinarse to comb (*one's hair*) (4)
pelar to peel
película film, movie (5); film (*photography*); **rollo de película** roll of film
peligro danger; **en peligro** endangered (10); **especie** (*f.*) **en peligro** endangered species (10)
peligroso/a dangerous
pelirrojo/a redheaded (2)
pelo hair (2, 4R); **pelo blanco** gray/white hair (2); **pelo lacio** straight hair (2)
pelota ball (6); **cancha de pelota** ball court; **pelota de goma** rubber ball
peluquero/a hair stylist, barber (3)
pena: valer (*irreg.*) **la pena** to be worth (it) (11); **¡qué pena!** *interj.* what a shame! (8)
penetrante *adj.* penetrating; piercing
península peninsula (1)
pensar (ie) to think (4); to intend
pensión *f.* boarding house (3)
peor worse (7); worst
pepino cucumber (7)
pequeño/a small, little (2)
pera pear (7)
percebe *m.* barnacle
perdedor(a) loser
perder (ie) to lose (7); to miss (*opportunity, ride, class*) (7); **perder el tiempo** to waste time; **perder ficheros** to lose (computer) files, crash (11)

pérdida loss
perdón forgive me; (1); excuse me; pardon
peregrinación *f.* pilgrimage
perejil *m.* parsley
perezoso/a lazy (2)
perfecto/a perfect
periódico newspaper
periodista *m., f.* journalist (3)
período period
permanecer (zc) to stay, remain
permanencia permanence
permanente permanent
permiso permission; **con permiso** excuse me (1)
permitir to permit, allow
pero *conj.* but (1)
perpetuarse (me perpetúo) to be perpetuated
perro dog (10)
persecución *f.* persecution
persona person; **llamada de persona a persona** person to person call
personaje *m.* character
personal *n. m.* personnel; *adj.* personal; **arreglo personal** personal grooming; **computadora personal** personal computer; **pronombre** (*m.*) **personal** *gram.* personal pronoun
personalidad *f.* personality
perspectiva perspective
pertenecer (zc) to belong
peruano/a *n., adj.* Peruvian
pesa weight; **levantar pesas** to lift weights
pesado/a heavy; boring, dull, tiresome
pesadumbre *f.* sorrow, grief
pésame: dar (*irreg.*) **el pésame** to present one's condolences
pesar to weigh (8); **a pesar de** in spite of
pesca *n.* fishing
pescadería fish shop
pescado fish (7)
pescador(a) fisherman/woman
pescar (qu) to fish (6)
peseta *Spanish monetary unit*
pesimista pessimistic (1, 2R)
peso weight; *monetary unit of Argentina, Bolivia, Chile, Colombia, Cuba, Dominican Republic, Puerto Rico, Uruguay;* **de peso mediano** of average weight (2); **nuevo peso** *Mexican monetary unit since 1992;* **peso viejo** *Mexican monetary unit prior to 1992*
pesquero/a (pertaining to) fishing
petróleo petroleum; **petróleo crudo** crude oil
petrolero/a (pertaining to) petroleum

petrolífero/a *adj.* (pertaining to) petroleum
pez *m.* (*pl.* **peces**) fish (10); **pez tropical** tropical fish (10)
piano piano (6)
picante hot (*spicy*) (7)
picar (qu) to be hot (*spicy*)
picnic *m.* picnic (4)
pico (mountain) peak
pie *m.* foot (4); **dedo del pie** toe (4); **ir** (*irreg.*) **a pie** to walk, go on foot (5); **venir** (*irreg.*) **a pie** to walk, come on foot (5)
piedra stone, rock (10)
piel *m.* leather; fur
pierna leg (4)
pijama *m. s.* pajamas (2)
pila: nombre (*m.*) **de pila** first name (9)
pimienta pepper (*spice*) (7)
pingüino penguin
pino pine tree
pintar to paint
pinto/a spotted, speckled
pintor(a) painter
pintoresco/a picturesque
piña pineapple (7)
piñata *suspended decorated figure filled with candy and small prizes, broken by a blindfolded person with a stick*
pirámide *f.* pyramid (6)
pirata *m.* pirate
piscina swimming pool (5)
piso apartment, flat (4); floor, story
pistola pistol
pizarra chalkboard (3)
pizza pizza
placer *m.* pleasure
plan *m.* plan (3); arrangement
plancha: a la plancha grilled
planeamiento *n.* planning
planear to plan
planeta *m.* planet (10)
plano: en primer plano on the first page
planta plant (10); plant (*equipment and buildings necessary to carry on any industrial business*); **planta silvestre** wild plant
plantar to plant
plástico plastic (5)
plata silver (5)
plato plate (4, 7R); dish (4); **plato chico** saucer (7); **plato fuerte** main course (7); **plato hondo** bowl (7); **plato principal** main course; **primer plato** first course; **segundo plato** second course (*of a meal*)
Platón Plato
playa beach (1)
plaza plaza, square (5); **plaza central**

central, main square/plaza; **plaza comercial** mall; shopping center; business district; **plaza mayor** central, main square/plaza

pleno/a full, complete

plomo lead (10)

pluma pen

pluriempleo moonlighting

población *f.* population (5)

poblado/a populated

poblador(a) inhabitant

poblano/a *person from Puebla, Mexico*

pobre *n. m., f.* poor person; *adj.* poor; **los pobres** the poor (*people*) (4); **pobre diablo** poor devil

pobreza poverty

poco *adv.* little (5); a little bit; **dentro de poco** soon; **después de poco** after a little while/bit (8)

poco/a *adj.* few, little (1)

poder (*irreg.*) *v.* to be able, can (4)

poder *n. m.* power

poderoso/a powerful

poema *m.* poem

poesía poetry

poeta *m.* poet

policía *m.* (male) police officer (1); **mujer** (*f.*) **policía** (female) police officer (1)

policíaco/a (pertaining to the) police; **novela policíaca** detective novel (6)

poliéster *m.* polyester (5)

politécnico/a polytechnic

política *s.* politics; policy

político/a *n.* politician (10); *adj.* political; **ciencias** (*f. pl.*) **políticas** political science (3); **hijo/a político/a** son-in-law/daughter-in-law

polizón *m.* stowaway

Polo Norte North Pole

pollo chicken (7)

poner (*irreg.*) (*p.p.* **puesto/a**) to turn on; to put, place (4); to set (4); to make, cause to become; to show (*on television*); to put on; to add; **poner a la disposición de** to put at (*someone's*) disposal; **poner atención** to pay attention; **poner en marcha** to start, put in motion; **poner la mesa** to set the table (4); **ponerse (la ropa)** to put on (one's clothes) (4)

popularidad *f.* popularity

populoso/a populous

por for (4); through (4); along (4); by (4); in; because of; due to; around; in exchange for; per; on account of; for the sake of; **pasar por** to go, pass by (4); **por acaso** by chance; **por casualidad** by chance; **por ciento** percent (2); **por coincidencia** by

coincidence; **por consiguiente** consequently, therefore; **por debajo de** under, below; **por dentro** on the inside; **por ejemplo** for example; **por el contrario** on the contrary; **por el momento** for the present; **por eso** that's why (4); therefore; **por esto** for this reason; **por favor** please (1); **por fin** at last (5); **por fuera** from or on the outside; **por la mañana** in the morning; **por la mayor parte** in the majority, on the whole; **por la noche** at night (3); in the night; **por la tarde** in the afternoon; **por lo cual** for which reason, because of which; **por lo menos** at least; **por medio de** by means of; **por otra parte** on the other hand (4); **por primera vez** for the first time; **por su parte** as far as he/she is concerned; **por supuesto** of course; **por teléfono** by phone, on the telephone (4); **por todas partes** everywhere; **por última vez** for the last time; **televisión** (*f.*) **por cable** cable television (11); **televisión** (*f.*) **por satélite** satellite television (11)

porcentaje *m.* percentage

porción *f.* portion

porfiriato *period of time during which Porfirio Díaz was president of Mexico (1876, 1877–1880, and 1884–1911)*

¿por qué? why? (2)

porque *conj.* because (2); for; in order that

porqué *n. m.* reason, motive

porta disket (*m.*) disk carrying case

portal *m.* porch (4)

portátil *adj.* portable; **computadora portátil** portable computer (11); **radiocassette** (*m.*) **portátil** portable radio-cassette player, boom box (11)

porteño/a *resident of Buenos Aires, Argentina*

Portugal *m.* Portugal (2)

portugués *m.* Portuguese (language) (3)

portugués, portuguesa *n.* Portuguese person; *adj.* Portuguese (2)

posada *Mexican Christmas festivity lasting nine days*

posarse to alight; to perch, sit

poseer (y) to possess

posesión *f.* possession

posibilidad *f.* possibility

posible possible (9); **(no) es posible que...** it's (not) possible that . . . (9)

posición *f.* position

positivo/a positive

postal *n. f.* postcard (1, 8R); *adj.* postal;

código postal postal code; **tarjeta postal** postcard (8)

posteriormente afterwards, subsequently

postrarse to prostrate oneself; to kneel down

postre *m.* dessert (5)

potencia: cocinar a máxima potencia to cook on high heat

pozo *n.* well

pozole *m. Mex. dish or soup of green Indian corn, meat, and chili*

practicante *m., f.* one who practices (*something*)

practicar (qu) to practice (3, 6R); to do, participate in (*sports*) (6)

práctico/a practical

precio price; **precio fijo** fixed, set price

precioso/a precious; beautiful

precipitación *f.* precipitation

precisamente precisely, exactly

preciso: es preciso it is necessary

precolombino/a pre-Columbian (11)

predominante predominant, prevailing

predominar to predominate; to prevail

preferencia preference

preferido/a preferred, favorite (6)

preferir (ie, i) to prefer (4)

pregunta *n.* question (2); **hacer** (*irreg.*) **preguntas** to ask questions

preguntar to ask (3); **preguntarse** to wonder (11)

prehispánico/a *n., adj.* pre-Hispanic

premio prize (7); **premio Nóbel** Nobel Prize

prenda article of clothing

prensa press, newspapers

preocupación *f.* preoccupation; worry, anxiety

preocupado/a (por) worried (about) (1); **estar** (*irreg.*) **preocupado/a (por)** to be worried (about) (1)

preocupar to preoccupy; to worry

preparación *f.* preparation

preparado *n.* preparation

preparar to prepare, (3); to make ready; **forma de preparar** method of preparation; **prepararse** to prepare oneself, get ready

preposición *f. gram.* preposition (1)

presencia presence

presentar to present; to introduce; to show, display; to show (*on television*); **presentar en sociedad** to debut; **quiero presentarle a...** I'd like you (*form. s.*) to meet . . . (1); **quiero presentarte a...** I'd like you (*fam. s.*) to meet . . . (1)

presente *n. m.* present; *gram.* present tense; **presente del indicativo** *gram.* present indicative tense; **presente del**

subjuntivo *gram.* present subjunctive tense

preservación *f.* preservation

presidente/a president

presidido/a presided over

presionar to press

prestar to lend, loan; to give; **prestar atención** to pay attention (7)

pretérito *gram.* preterite tense

pretexto *n.* pretext, excuse

previamente previously

primavera spring (6); **fiesta de primavera** spring festival

primer, primero/a first (3, 10R); **en primer lugar** in the first place; **en primer plano** on the first page; **por primera vez** for the first time; **primera comunión** first communion (9); **primer ministro** prime minister; **primer plato** first course

primitivamente primitively

primo/a cousin (1)

primordial primordial, fundamental

principal *adj.* main, principal (6); **comida principal** main meal of the day; **plato principal** main course

príncipe *m.* prince

principio beginning, start; **al principio** at first, in the beginning

prisa: tener (*irreg.*) **(mucha) prisa** to be in a (big) hurry (6, 8R)

privado: en privado in private

privado/a private

probable probable (9); **(no) es probable que...** it's (not) probable that . . . (9)

probar (ue) to try (7); to taste (7)

problema *m.* problem (7)

procedente coming, originating

proceder to proceed

proceso process

procuraduría federal attorney general's office

producción *f.* production

producir (*irreg.*) to produce

producto product; **producto nacional bruto** gross national product

productor(a) producer

profesión *f.* profession (3)

profesional *n. m., f.* professional person, white-collar worker (3); *adj.* professional

profesionista *n. m., f.* professional person, white-collar worker (*Mex.*)

profesor(a) professor (1); **mesa para el profesor/la profesora** table for the professor (1)

profundo/a profound; deep

profuso/a profuse, abundant

programa *m.* program (11)

programación *f.* programming (11)

programar to program

progresivo/a progressive

progreso progress

proliferación *f.* proliferation

prolífico/a prolific

promedio *n.* average

promesa *n.* promise

prometer to promise

prometido/a fiancé/fiancée

promover (ue) to promote

promulgar (gu) to proclaim

pronombre *m. gram.* pronoun; **pronombre demostrativo** *gram.* demonstrative pronoun (5); **pronombre personal** *gram.* personal pronoun

pronosticar (qu) to forecast

pronóstico (de tiempo) (weather) forecast (6)

pronto soon (8); **hasta pronto** see you soon; **tan pronto como** as soon as (9)

pronunciar to pronounce (3)

propio/a *adj.* own (6); one's own; proper; **en carne propia** in the flesh

proponente *m., f.* proponent

proponer (*like* **poner**) to propose

proporción *f.* proportion

proporcionar to provide, supply

propósito purpose, intention; **a propósito** by the way

próspero/a prosperous

protagonista *m., f.* protagonist; hero, heroine

protección *f.* protection

proteger (j) to protect (10)

protegido/a (por) protected (by) (10)

protesta *n.* protest

protestar to protest

provecho: buen provecho enjoy your meal, (*lit.*, good appetite)

proveer (y) to provide

proverbio proverb

provincia province

provincial provincial

provocar (qu) to provoke; to cause

proximidad *f.* proximity

próximo/a next, following

proyecto project

prueba proof

psicología psychology (3)

publicar (qu) to publish

público *n.* public

público/a *adj.* public; **aseo público** public bathroom; **enfermero/a público/a** public health nurse; **relaciones** (*f. pl.*) **públicas** public relations

pueblo town (4); townspeople (4);

people (*body of persons*); **pueblo de origen** hometown

puente *m.* bridge

puerco: carne (*f.*) **de puerco** pork (7)

puerta door (1); **llamar a la puerta** to knock on the door (7); **tocar (qu) a la puerta** to knock (on the door)

puerto port, harbor; **Puerto Rico** Puerto Rico (2)

puertorriqueño/a *n., adj.* Puerto Rican (2)

pues *adv.* well (2); then (2)

puesto stall, stand; post, employment; **puesto de discos** record stand/store (5); **puesto de frutas** fruit stand (5); **puesto de regalos** souvenir stand, gift stand (5)

pulpo octopus

punta point, sharp end

punto point, dot; **a punto de** + *inf.* about to (*do something*); **de punto** *adj.* knitted; **en punto** sharp, on the dot (1); **hasta cierto punto** to a certain point; **punto de embarque** point of departure (*of a ship*); **punto de mira** lookout point; **punto de vista** point of view

pupila pupil (*of the eye*)

pupitre *m.* student desk (1)

puro/a pure (10)

Q

que that, who; than; **así que** therefore, consequently; **hasta que** until (9); **lo que** what, that which; **mientras que** while; whereas; **que** + *subjunctive* I hope + (*verb form*); **que te/le vaya bien** hope all goes well (for you [*fam./ form. s.*]) (1); **que viene** *adj.* next, coming; **tener que** + *inf.* to have to, (*do something*) (5, 8R); **tener que ver (con)** to have to do (with) (7); **ya que** since, inasmuch as

qué: no hay de qué you're welcome

¿qué? what?, (1, 2R); which?; **¿a qué hora?** (at) what time?; **¿de qué es?** what is it made of? (5); **¿por qué?** why? (2); **¿qué día es hoy?** what day is today? (1); **¿qué hay?** what's going on? (1); **¿qué hay de nuevo?** what's new? (1); **¿qué hora es?** what time is it? (1); **¿qué pasa?** what's happening? (1); **¿qué tal?** what's up? (1); **¿qué te pareció...?** what did you think about . . . ? (5); **¿qué tiempo hace?** what is the weather like? (6)

¡qué...! *interj.* what . . . !; **¡qué** + *adj./ adv.!* how + *adj./adv.!* (2); **¡qué** + *noun!* what a . . . !; **¡qué bueno!** how

satisfecho/a satisfied
se (*impersonal*) one; *refl. pron.* yourself
 (*form.*), himself, herself, yourselves
 (*form.*), themselves
sea: o sea in other words
secadora clothes dryer (4)
secar (qu) to dry; **secarse** to dry off (4)
seco/a dry; dried; **está (muy) seco** it is
 (very) dry (6); **estación** (*f.*) **seca** dry
 season (6); **sopa seca** pasta, rice
secretaría secretary's office; **Secretaría**
 de Agricultura y Recursos Hidráulicos
 Department of Agriculture and Water
 Resources; **Secretaría de la**
 Gobernación Department of the
 Interior; **Secretaría de Turismo**
 Department of Tourism
secretario/a secretary (3)
secreto/a *adj.* secret
sector *m.* sector
secundaria high school; **escuela**
 secundaria high school
sed: tener (*irreg.*) **(mucha) sed** to be
 (very) thirsty (8)
seda silk (5)
sede *f.* headquarters
sedentario/a sedentary
seguida: en seguida right away,
 immediately
seguidor(a) follower
seguir (i, i) (ga) to continue (5); to
 follow; **seguir** + *present progressive* to
 continue (*doing something*) (11); **seguir**
 derecho/recto to keep going straight
 ahead; **siga** continue (*form. command*)
 (5); **sigue** continue (*fam. command*) (5)
según according to (5)
segundo *n.* second (*of time*)
segundo/a *adj.* second (3, 10R); **segundo**
 plato second course (*of a meal*)
seguro/a sure (5); certain; **estar** (*irreg.*)
 seguro/a to be sure (5); **(no) es**
 seguro que... it's (not) sure that . . .
 (9); **seguro social** Social Security
seis six (1)
seiscientos/as six hundred (5)
selección *f.* selection
seleccionar to choose
selecto/a select, choice
selva jungle (1); **selva amazónica**
 Amazon jungle; **selva tropical**
 (tropical) rain forest (10)
selvática *adj.* wild; jungle
sello stamp (5)
semana week (2); **día** (*m.*) **de la semana**
 day of the week (3), weekday; **fin** (*m.*)
 de semana weekend (3); **semana**
 entrante next week; **semana pasada**
 last week (5); **semana que viene** next
 week; **Semana Santa** Holy Week (6);
 todas las semanas every week

sembrar (ie) to plant (10)
semejanza similarity
semestre *m.* semester (2); **semestre**
 pasado last semester (5)
semilla seed
senado Senate
sencillo/a simple, easy (7)
senda path, pathway
sensibilidad *f.* sensibility; sensitivity
sensitivo/a sensitive (*of the senses*)
sensualidad *f.* sensuality
sentado/a seated
sentarse (ie) to sit down (4)
sentido del humor sense of humor
sentimiento feeling
sentir (ie, i) to regret (9); to feel (9); to
 feel sorry; **lo siento** I'm sorry (1);
 sentirse to feel
señal (*f.*) **de marcar** dial tone (8)
señalar to show, indicate
señor (Sr.) *m.* Mr. (2); sir (2);
 gentleman (2); **Señor** Lord, God
señora (Sra.) Mrs. (2); ma'am (2); lady
 (2), woman; **Nuestra Señora** our Lady
 (*Virgin Mary*)
señores (Sres.) *m. pl.* Mr. and Mrs.;
 gentlemen
señorita (Srta.) Miss (2); young lady (2)
separar(se) to separate
septiembre *m.* September (6)
séptimo/a *adj.* seventh (10)
sequía drought
ser (*irreg.*) *v.* to be (2); **¿cómo eres?**
 what are you (*fam. s.*) like? (2); **¿cómo**
 es el clima? what is the climate like?
 (6); **es la una** it's one o'clock (1); **es**
 medianoche it's midnight (1); **es**
 mediodía it's noon (1); **es preciso** it is
 necessary; **pasar de ser** to go beyond
 being; **ser aburrido/a** to be boring
 (2); **son** they are (1); you (*pl.*) are
ser (*n. m.*): **ser humano** human being;
 ser querido loved one
serie *f. s.* series
serio: en serio seriously (9)
serio/a serious (2)
serpiente *f.* serpent, snake (10);
 serpiente de cascabel rattlesnake
servicio service; **servicio a domicilio** in-
 home service
servidor(a) servant
servilleta napkin (7)
servir (i, i) to serve (4); **servir de** to be
 used as, serve as or for
sesenta sixty (1)
setecientos/as seven hundred (5)
setenta seventy (1)
severamente severely
sexismo sexism
sexo sex
sexto/a sixth (10)

si if, whether (6)
sí yes (1); *inv. refl. pron. used as obj.* (*of*
 prep.) himself, herself, itself, oneself,
 themselves; **¡claro que sí!** *interj.* of
 course! (9); **sí mismo/a(s)** himself,
 herself, itself, oneself, themselves (*for*
 emphasis)
sicología psychology
siderúrgico/a siderurgical (*pertaining to*
 the metallurgy of iron and steel)
siempre always (1)
sierra mountain range (1)
siesta nap, siesta
siete seven (1)
siglo century (4)
significar (qu) to mean
significativo/a significant
signo sign
siguiente *adj.* following
silbar to whistle
silencio silence
silencioso/a silent
silueta silhouette
silvestre wild; **planta silvestre** wild
 plant
silla chair
sillón *m.* armchair, easy chair (4)
simbólico/a symbolic
simbolizar (c) symbolize
símbolo symbol
simpatía congeniality
simpático/a nice, friendly (2)
sin *prep.* without; **sin duda** doubtless, no
 doubt, without a doubt; **sin embargo**
 however, nevertheless (10); **sin falla**
 without fail; **sin igual** unrivaled,
 matchless; **sin par** unequaled,
 incomparable; **sin que** *conj.* without;
 sin querer(lo) unintentionally
singular unique; extraordinary; *gram.*
 singular
sino but (rather); **no... sino que** not . . .
 but rather (10); **no sólo... sino**
 también... not only . . . but also . . . (6)
sistema *m.* system
sitio place (4); site
situación *f.* situation
situado/a located
smokins: traje (*m.*) **de smokins** tuxedo
soberano/a supreme
sobra: de sobra more than enough,
 ample
sobre *n. m.* envelope (5); *prep.* about
 (3), above, on, around; **sobre todo**
 above all, especially
sobrecama bedspread
sobresaliente outstanding
sobrevivencia survival
sobrevivir to survive
sobrino/a nephew/niece (2); **sobrinos**
 nephews and nieces

sobrio/a sober, temperate
social: seguro social Social Security;
  ciencias (*f. pl.*) **sociales** social sciences
  (3)
socialización *f.* socialization
sociedad *f.* society; **presentar en
  sociedad** to debut
socio/a partner (4)
sociología sociology (3)
sociológico/a sociological
socorro help, aid
sofá *m.* sofa, couch (4)
sofocante *adj.* suffocating, stifling
sol *m.* sun (6); **gafas de sol** sunglasses
  (4); **hace (mucho) sol** it is (very)
  sunny (6); **tomar el sol** to sunbathe
  (5)
solamente only
soleado/a sunny
soledad *f.* solitude
solemne solemn
soler (ue) to be accustomed to, tend
  to (4)
solicitar to ask for
solicitud *f.* application
sólido/a *adj.* solid
sólo *adv.* only (1); **no sólo... sino
  también...** not only . . . but also . . .
  (6)
solo/a *adj.* alone
soltar (ue) to untie, unfasten; to
  release
soltero/a unmarried man/woman;
  nombre (*m.*) **de soltera** maiden name
solución *f.* solution
sombra shade; shadow
sombrero hat
son they are (1); you (*pl.*) are
sonar (ue) to ring (7)
sonido sound
sonreír (i, i) (yo sonrío) to smile (10)
sonrisa *n.* smile
soñar (ue) to dream
sopa soup (7); **sopa aguada** soup; **sopa
  seca** pasta, rice (7)
soportar to stand, tolerate (6)
sordidez *f.* (*pl.* **sordideces**) sordidness
sorprendente *adj.* surprising
sorprender to surprise (9), be surprising
sorprendido/a surprised (10)
sorpresa surprise
sospechar to suspect
sótano basement (4)
su(s) *poss.* his (1), her (1), its, your
  (*form. s., pl.*), their
suave soft
subir (a) to go up (6); to climb (6); to
  get on (*bus, train, etc.*) (6)
subjuntivo *gram.* subjunctive mood;
  imperfecto del subjuntivo *gram.* past
  subjunctive tense; **presente** (*m.*) **del**

subjuntivo *gram.* present subjunctive
  tense
sublime sublime
substancia substance; **substancia química**
  n. chemical
substituir (y) to substitute
subterráneo/a: agua (*f.* [*but* **el agua**])
  subterránea ground water (10)
subvencionar to subsidize
suceder to happen, occur (11)
suceso event
sucio/a dirty
sucre *m. Ecuadorean monetary unit*
Sudamérica South America
sudamericano/a *n., adj.* South
  American
sudeste *m.* southeast (5)
suegro/a father-in-law/mother-in-law
  (2); **suegros** in-laws (2); fathers-in-law
sueldo salary (9)
suelo floor
sueño dream; **tener** (*irreg.*) **(mucho)
  sueño** to be (very) sleepy (8)
suerte *f.* luck; **buena suerte** good luck;
  tener (*irreg.*) **buena/mala suerte** to be
  lucky/unlucky (9)
suéter *m.* sweater (2)
suficiente enough (4)
sufrir to suffer, endure; to undergo
sugerir (ie, i) to suggest (11)
sujeto *gram.* subject
sumamente exceedingly, extremely
sumar to add
superar to exceed
supercarretera superhighway,
  expressway (5)
superficie *f.* surface; area
superlativo *n. gram.* superlative
supermercado supermarket (5)
supervivencia survival
suplicar (qu) to implore, pray
suponer (*like* **poner**) to suppose, assume
supremo/a: Corte (*f.*) **Suprema**
  Supreme Court
supuesto: por supuesto of course
sur *m.* south (4, 5R); **América del Sur**
  South America; **Corea del Sur** South
  Korea
suramericano/a *n., adj.* South
  American
surgir (j) to appear, arise
suroeste *m.* southwest (5)
surtido selection, assortment
suscribir (*p.p.* **suscrito/a**) to subscribe
suspiro *n.* sigh
sustancia substance
sustantivo *gram.* noun (1)
sustituir (y) to substitute
suyo/a(s) *poss. s., pl.* your, (of) yours
  (*form.*); his, (of) his; her, (of) hers;
  its; their, (of) theirs

T

tabaco tobacco
tabla table, chart
taco taco (*tortilla filled with meat, beans,
  vegetables*)
taíno/a *member of indigenous group that
  occupied the Antilles*
tal such, such a; **¿qué tal?** what's up?
  (1); **tal vez** maybe, perhaps (7)
tala *n.* felling of trees; **tala y quemadura**
  slash and burn
talar to fell (*trees*)
talento talent
talle *m.* waist
tamaño size
tamarindo tamarind (*fruit*)
también also, too (2); **no sólo... sino
  también...** not only . . . but also . . . (6)
tampoco not either; neither (4)
tan as, so; **tan... como** as . . . as; **tan
  pronto como** as soon as (9)
tanto *adv.* so much (5); **mientras tanto**
  meanwhile
tanto/a so much; *pl.* so many; **tanto/a...
  como** as much . . . as; **tanto gusto en
  conocerte/lo/la** so pleased to meet
  you (*fam./form. s.*) (1); **tantos/as...
  como** as many . . . as
tapa snack
taquilla (box office) receipts
taquillero/a *adj.* that sells a lot of
  tickets
tarasco/a *member of indigenous group of
  central Mexico*
tardar to be late (8)
tarde *n. f.* afternoon, evening; *adv.* late
  (4); **a media tarde** in the/at
  midafternoon; **buenas tardes** good
  afternoon (1); **de la tarde** P.M., in the
  afternoon (1); **esta tarde** this
  afternoon (2); **llegar (gu) tarde** to
  arrive late; **más tarde** later; **por la
  tarde** in the afternoon; **todas las
  tardes** every afternoon
tarea homework (3); **hacer** (*irreg.*) **la
  tarea** to do one's homework
tarjeta card; **tarjeta de crédito** credit
  card (8); **tarjeta de cumpleaños**
  birthday card; **tarjeta de turismo**
  tourist card (8); **tarjeta postal**
  postcard (8)
tasa: tasa de alfabetismo literacy rate;
  tasa de cambio exchange rate
  (*currency*) (8); **tasa de desempleo**
  unemployment rate; **tasa de
  mortalidad** death rate
taxi *m.* taxi (5)
taza cup (7)
te *d.o.* you (*fam. s.*); *i.o.* to, for you (*fam.
  s.*); *refl. pron.* yourself (*fam. s.*); **¿qué te**

pareció...? what did you think about . . . ? (5)

té *m.* tea (7); **té helado/caliente** iced/hot tea (7)

teatro theater (5)

tecla key (*of a keyboard*) (11)

teclado keyboard (11)

tecnología technology (11)

tecnológico/a technological

techo roof; **bajo techo** under a roof

teja roof tile

tejer to knit (6)

tejido fabric, textile

tejolote *m. Mex.* stone pestle

tela cloth, fabric

telaraña spider web

telefonear to telephone

telefónico/a *adj.* telephone; **llamada telefónica** telephone call

teléfono telephone (4); **descolgar (ue) (gu) el teléfono** to pick up the phone (8); **guía de teléfonos** telephone directory (8); **hablar por teléfono** to talk on the telephone (6); **número de teléfono** telephone number; **por teléfono** by phone, on the telephone (4); **teléfono celular** cellular phone (11)

telegrama *m.* telegram

teleguía television programming guide

telenovela soap opera (11)

teleteatro *stage production shown on television*

teletransportar to teleport, teletransport

tele(visión) *f.* television (*image*) (4); **mirar la televisión** to watch television; **televisión por cable** cable television (11); **televisión por satélite** satellite television (11); **ver (*irreg.*) televisión** to watch television (6)

televisor *m.* television set (4); **televisor en blanco y negro/en colores** black and white/color television

tema *m.* topic, theme

temblor *m.* tremor, small earthquake (10)

temer to fear, be afraid of (9)

temor *m.* fear

temperatura temperature (6)

templado/a: está templado it is moderate (the weather is moderate) (6)

templo temple (6)

temporada season

temporal *gram.* temporal (*pertaining to time*)

temprano early (4)

tendencia tendency

tender (ie) to tend, have a tendency

tenedor *m.* fork (7)

tener (*irreg.*) to have (1, 2R); to be the matter with, ail; **¿cuántos años tienes?** how old are you (*fam. s.*)? (1); **tener _____ años (de edad)** to be _____ years old (2); **tener buena/mala suerte** to be lucky/unlucky (9); **tener derecho a** to be entitled to; **tener de todo** to have everything (5); **tener ganas de** + *inf.* to feel like (*doing something*) (5); **tener lugar** to take place; **tener (mucha) hambre** to be (very) hungry (7, 8R); **tener (mucha) prisa** to be in a (big) hurry (6, 8R); **tener (mucha) razón** to be (very) right (5, 8R); **tener (mucha) sed** to be (very) thirsty (8); **tener (mucho) calor** to be (feel) (very) warm, hot (8); **tener (mucho) frío** to be (very) cold (8); **tener (mucho) miedo** to be (very) afraid (8); **tener (mucho) sueño** to be (very) sleepy (8); **tener que** + *inf.* to have to (*do something*) (5, 8R); **tener que ver (con)** to have to do (with) (7); **tener verificativo** to take place, come true; **tengo _____ años** I'm _____ years old (1)

tenis *m.* tennis (4); **jugar (ue) (gu) al tenis** to play tennis (6); **zapatos** (*m. pl.*) **de tenis** tennis shoes (2)

tentempié *m.* light meal, snack

teoría theory

tercer, tercero/a third (3, 10R)

tercermundista *adj.* third-world

terminación *n. f. gram.* ending

terminar to finish (3)

término term; **término geográfico** geographic term (1)

ternera veal (7)

terraza sidewalk café

terremoto earthquake (10)

terreno terrain, ground

terrestre terrestrial, pertaining to the Earth

territorio territory

terror *m.* terror

tesoro treasure

texto text; textbook; **libro de texto** textbook

textura texture

ti *obj.* (*of prep.*) you (*fam. s.*)

tianguis *m. s. Mex.* small market

tiempo time (2); weather (6); **a tiempo** on time (4); **¿cuánto tiempo?** how long? (2); **hace (muy) buen/mal tiempo** the weather's (very) nice/bad (5, 6R); **llegar (gu) a tiempo** to arrive on time (8); **perder (ie) el tiempo** to waste time; **pronóstico de tiempo** weather forecast (6); **¿qué tiempo hace?** what is the weather like? (6);

tiempo libre free, spare time

tienda store (1); **tienda de juguetes** toy store (5); **tienda de ropa** clothing store (5)

tierra earth (10); land (10); soil (10)

tigre *m.* tiger

tímido/a shy, timid (2)

tinta ink

tío/a uncle/aunt (2); **tíos** uncles and aunts (2); uncles

típico/a typical (4)

tipo type, kind (4)

tira narrow strip

título title

tiza chalk (3)

tlaxcalteco/a *person from Tlaxcala, Mexico*

toalla towel

tocador *m.* dresser, vanity (4); player; **tocador de discos compactos** compact disc (CD) player (11); **tocador de discos láser** laser disk player (11)

tocar (qu) to touch; to play (*musical instrument, song, etc.*); **tocar (a la puerta)** to knock (on the door); **tocarle a uno** to be one's turn; **tocar un instrumento musical** to play a musical instrument (6)

tocino bacon (7)

todavía still, yet (4)

todo *n. m.* all, everything; **sobre todo** above all, especially; **tener (*irreg.*) de todo** to have everything (5)

todo/a *adj.* every, all (3); **en/por todas partes** everywhere; **toda la noche** all night; **todas las semanas** every week; **todas las tardes** every afternoon; **todo el día** all day; **todos los días/meses/años** every day/month/year (6)

Todopoderoso Almighty (God)

tolteca *n. m., f.; adj.* Toltec (*indigenous group of central Mexico*)

tomados/as del brazo arm-in-arm;

tomar to take (3); to eat (3); to drink (3); **tomar el sol** to sunbathe (5); **tomar la decisión** to make the decision (9); **tomar medidas** to take measures, steps

tomate *m.* tomato (7)

tonto/a *n.* silly, dummy; *adj.* foolish, silly (1, 2R)

torero bullfighter

tormenta storm (10)

tornado tornado (10)

torno: en torno a about, regarding

toro bull (10); **corrida de toros** bullfight (10)

toronja grapefruit (7)

torre *f.* tower

torta cake (7)

tortilla (*Sp.*) omelette; (*Mex., Central*

America) **tortilla** (*round, flat bread made of corn or wheat flour*)

tortillero/a tortilla maker

tortuga tortoise, turtle

tostado: pan (*m.*) **tostado** toast (7)

total *n. m.* total; *adj.* total; **en total** total (2), in all

totonaca *n. m., f. member of ancient indigenous group that inhabited the Veracruz region of Mexico*

tóxico/a toxic, poisonous

trabajador(a) *n.* worker; *adj.* hardworking (2); **trabajador(a) indocumentado/a** undocumented, illegal worker

trabajar to work (3)

trabajo work (3); job; **trabajo escrito** written work, paper

tradición *f.* tradition (5)

tradicional traditional

traducir (*like* **producir**) to translate

traer (*irreg.*) to bring (4)

tráfico traffic; **tráfico de drogas** drug trafficking

tragedia tragedy

trágico/a tragic

traje *m.* suit (2); **traje de baño** swimsuit (2); **traje de luces** *suit of clothes worn by bullfighters*; **traje de smokins** tuxedo

tranquilo/a calm, tranquil

transacción *f.* transaction (8)

transatlántico/a transatlantic

transcurrir to pass, elapse

transferencia transfer

transformar to transform

transición *f.* transition

tránsito traffic (5)

transmisión *f.* transmission

transmitir to transmit; to broadcast

transportar to transport

transporte *m.* transportation (5)

tras (de) *prep.* after, behind

trascendencia transcendence

trascender (ie) to transcend

trasladarse to move

traslado *n.* moving, transfer

tratado treaty

tratar to treat, deal with (*a subject*); **tratar (de)** to deal with, speak about (*a subject*) (10); **tratar (de)** + *inf.* to try to (*do something*) (10); **tratarse de** to be the matter or subject discussed

través: a través de through, by means of

trébol *m.* three-leaf clover

trece thirteen (1)

treinta thirty (1)

tremendo/a tremendous

tren *m.* train (5); **estación** (*f.*) **del tren** train station (5)

tres three (1)

trescientos/as three hundred (5)

tribu *f.* tribe

tribulación *f.* tribulation, affliction

trigo wheat (7)

trimestre *m.* trimester (3)

triste sad (1); **(no) es triste que...** it's (not) sad that . . . (9)

triunfar to triumph

trompeta trumpet (6)

tropical tropical; **pez** (*m.*) **tropical** tropical fish; **selva tropical** (tropical) rain forest (10)

trotar to jog (6)

tu(s) *poss.* your (*fam. s.*) (1)

tú *sub. pron.* you (*fam. s.*)

tucán *m.* toucan

tumba tomb, grave

tuna prickly pear, *fruit of the prickly pear*

turismo tourism; **guía de turismo** tourist guide book; **oficina de turismo** tourist office (8); **secretaría de turismo** Department of Tourism; **tarjeta de turismo** tourist card (8)

turista *m., f.* tourist (4)

turístico/a *adj.* tourist; **guía turística** tourist guidebook (8)

turnarse to take turns

turno: de turno on duty

tutor(a) legal legal guardian

tuyo/a(s) *poss.* your, (of) yours (*fam. s.*)

U

u or (*used instead of* **o** *before words beginning with* **o** *or* **ho**)

ubicación *f.* location, position

último/a last (3, 10R); **a última hora** at the last moment; **por última vez** for the last time

umbral *m.* threshold

un, uno/a one (1); a, an (*indefinite article*); *pron.* one (*person, someone*); **es la una** it's one o'clock (1); **faltan cinco para la una** it's five 'til one (1); **una vez** once; **una vez al/a la** + *time period* once every (*time period*)

undécimo/a eleventh (10)

único/a unique (7); only

unidad *f.* unit

unido/a: Reino Unido United Kingdom; **Estados** (*m. pl.*) **Unidos** United States

uniforme *n. m.* uniform; *adj.* uniform, consistent (4)

unión *f.* union, marriage; association

unirse to get married

universidad *f.* university (1)

universitario/a *adj.* university (3); **ciudad** (*f.*) **universitaria** (college, university) campus

unos/as some, several; a few

urbanización *f.* neighborhood (4); housing development (4)

urbano/a urban

urdu *m.* Urdu (*language used in India and Pakistan*)

uruguayo/a *n., adj.* Uruguayan

usar to use (8); to wear

uso use (4); usage

usted (Ud., Vd.) *sub. pron.* you (*form. s.*); *obj.* (*of prep.*) you (*form. s.*)

ustedes (Uds., Vds.) *sub. pron.* you (*form. pl.*); *obj.* (*of prep.*) you (*form. pl.*)

utensilio utensil (7)

útil useful (2), helpful

utilizar (c) to use, make use of

uva grape (7)

V

va he/she/it goes (1); you (*form. s.*) go (1)

vaca cow (10)

vacaciones *f. pl.* vacation (6); **de vacaciones** on vacation (4); **estar** (*irreg.*) **de vacaciones** to be on vacation; **ir** (*irreg.*) **de vacaciones** to go on vacation; **vacaciones de Navidad** Christmas vacation; **vacaciones de verano** summer vacation

vainilla vanilla

valer (*irreg.*) **la pena** to be worth (it) (11)

valija suitcase

valor *m.* value

valorar to value

vals *m.* waltz

valle *m.* valley (1)

vámonos let's go (6)

vamos we are going (1)

vanagloriarse to boast (of)

vanidad *f.* vanity

vaquero cowboy

variable *n. f.* variable

variado/a varied, diverse

variar (yo varío) to vary, change; to diversify

variedad *f.* variety (11)

varios/as *pl.* various, several

Vasco/a: País (*m. s.*) **Vasco** Basque region (*Sp.*)

vascuense *m.* Basque (language)

vaso (drinking) glass (7)

vaya: que te/le vaya bien hope all goes well (for you *fam./form. s.*) (1)

vecindario neighborhood

vecino/a *n.* neighbor (4); *adj.* neighboring

vegetación *f.* vegetation

vegetal *m.* vegetable

vehículo vehicle; **vehículo de recreación** recreation vehicle, RV

veinte twenty (1)

veinticinco twenty-five (1)

veinticuatro twenty-four (1)

veintidós twenty-two (1)

veintinueve twenty-nine (1)

veintiocho twenty-eight (1)

veintiséis twenty-six (1)

veintisiete twenty-seven (1)

veintitrés twenty-three (1)

veintiuno twenty-one (1)

vela candle

velación: acto de velación *ceremony of veiling the bride and bridegroom at the nuptial mass*

velorio wake (9)

vencer (z) to overcome; to conquer

vendedor(a) salesperson

vender to sell (3)

veneno poison, venom

venezolano/a *n., adj.* Venezuelan (2)

Venezuela Venezuela (2)

venir (*irreg.*) to come (4); **que viene** *adj.* next, coming; **venir a pie** to walk, come on foot (5)

venta sale, selling

ventaja advantage

ventana window (1)

ventanilla ticket booth/window (8)

ver (*irreg.*) to see (4); **a ver** let's see (5); **nos vemos** see ya (1); **tener** (*irreg.*) **que ver (con)** to have to do (with) (7); **ver televisión** to watch television (6)

veracruzano/a *adj.* from Veracruz (*Mex.*) **a la veracruzana** in the style of Veracruz

veranear to summer, spend the summer

verano summer (2, 6R); **casa de verano** summer (vacation) house; **escuela de verano** summer school; **vacaciones** (*f. pl.*) **de verano** summer vacation; **verano pasado** last summer

veras: de veras truly, really; real, genuine; **¿de veras?** really? (2)

verbal *gram.* verbal

verbo *gram.* verb (1); **verbo de cambio radical** *gram.* stem-changing verb (4); **verbo con uso reflexivo** *gram.* verb used reflexively; **verbo regular** *gram.* regular verb (3)

verdad *f.* truth (4); **¿verdad?** right? (1); isn't he/she/it?, aren't you/we/they? (2); **(no) es verdad que...** it's (not) true that . . . (9)

verdadero/a true, real

verde green (2)

verdulería greengrocer's shop

verdura vegetable (7)

vergonzoso/a shameful, disgraceful, scandalous

verificativo: tener (*irreg.*) **verificativo** to take place; to come true

versión *f.* version

verso verse; poem; line

verter (ie, i) to pour

vestíbulo foyer (4)

vestido dress (2); clothing

vestir (i, i) to dress; **de vestir** *adj.* dress; **vestirse** to get dressed (4); **vestirse de luto** to wear mourning clothes (9)

veta vein, lode (*of mineral or precious metal*)

veterinario/a veterinarian (3); **ciencias** (*f. pl.*) **veterinarias** veterinary science (3)

vez *f.* (*pl.* **veces**) time, occurrence (4); **a veces** sometimes, at times (3); **alguna vez** once, ever; **algunas veces** sometimes, at times; **cada vez más** more and more; **de vez en cuando** from time to time, sometimes; **en vez de** instead of (9); **muchas veces** many times, often (4); **otra vez** again; **por primera/última vez** for the first/last time; **tal vez** maybe, perhaps (7); **una vez** once; **una vez al/a la** + *time period* once every (*time period*)

viajar to travel (3)

viaje *m.* trip (1), voyage; **agencia de viajes** travel agency (5); **agente** (*m., f.*) **de viajes** travel agent (8); **de viaje** traveling (7); **estar** (*irreg.*) **de viaje** to be on a trip; **hacer** (*irreg.*) **un viaje** to take a trip

viajero/a traveler; **cheque** (*m.*) **de viajero** traveler's check (5)

vías: en vías de desarrollo *adj.* developing

vibrante vibrant

víctima *m., f.* victim

victoria victory

victoriano/a Victorian

vida life (9); **calidad** (*f.*) **de vida** quality of life; **ganarse la vida** to earn one's livelihood

vídeo video (5); **cámara de vídeo** video camera (11)

videocasetera videocassette recorder, VCR (11)

videocentro video store (5)

videojuego video game

vidrio glass

viejo/a old (2); **Noche** (*f.*) **Vieja** New Year's Eve (6)

viento wind; **hace (mucho) viento** it is (very) windy (6); **molino de viento** windmill

viernes *m. s.* Friday (3); **los viernes** on

Fridays; **(Día** [*m.*] **de) Viernes Santo** Good Friday

vietnamita *n. m., f.; adj.* Vietnamese

vigilancia: puesto de vigilancia observation post

vigilar to watch (over); to hold a vigil (at)

villa town

vinagre *m.* vinegar (7)

vinatería wine shop

vino wine (7); **vino blanco** white wine

violencia violence

violento/a violent

violín *m.* violin

virgen *m., f.* virgin

visión *f.* vision

visita *n.* visit (3)

visitante *m., f.* visitor

visitar to visit (3)

vista view; **punto de vista** point of view

visual *adj.* visual

vitalidad *f.* vitality

¡viva! *interj.* long live!

vivienda dwelling (4); housing (4)

vivir to live (3)

vivo/a alive, living (10)

vocabulario vocabulary

volar (ue) to fly (10)

volcán *m.* volcano (1)

volcánico/a volcanic

voleibol *m.* volleyball (6); **jugar (ue) (gu) al voleibol** to play volleyball (6)

volumen *m.* volume (11)

voluntad *f.* goodwill

volver (ue) (*p.p.* **vuelto/a**) to return (*from somewhere*) (4); **volver a** + *inf.* to (*do something*) again

vos *sub. pron. L.A.* you (*fam. s., pl.*); *obj.* (*of prep.*) *L.A.* you (*fam. s., pl.*)

vosotros/as *sub. pron. Sp.* you (*fam. pl.*); *obj.* (*of prep.*) *Sp.* you (*fam. pl.*)

votar to vote

voto vote

voz *f.* (*pl.* **voces**) voice

vuelo flight (5)

vuelta turn; **boleto de ida y vuelta** round-trip ticket (8); **de vuelta a** returning to

vuestro/a(s) *poss. Sp.* your (*fam. pl.*); of yours (*fam. pl.*)

Y

y and (1); **¿y contigo?** and with you (*fam. s.*)? (1); **y cuarto** quarter past (*with time*) (1); **y media** half past (*with time*) (1); **¿y tú?** and you (*fam. s.*)? (1); **¿y usted?** and you (*form. s.*)? (1); **¿y ustedes?** and you (*pl.*)? (1)

ya *adv.* already (6); yet (6); now; at

once; **¡ya!** *interj.* oh yes!, I see; of course; **ya no** no longer; **ya que** since, inasmuch as

yanqui *m., f.* Yankee, American (of U.S.)

yerba (hierba) grass; herb; **yerba buena** mint; **yerba mate** *plant from which tea (**mate**) is made in southern Latin America*

yerno son-in-law (2)

yo *sub. pron.* I

Z

zanahoria carrot (7)

zapatería shoe store (5)

zapato shoe (2); **zapatos de tenis** tennis shoes (2)

zapoteca *n. m., f., adj.* Zapotec; *member of or related to indigenous group of southern Mexico*

zócalo *Mex.* public square, central plaza

zona zone, area (4)

zoológico zoo

zorra fox (10)

Index

This index is divided into three parts, Culture, Grammar, and Vocabulary. Topics in the **Facetas culturales, México y los mexicanos,** and **Otros mundos** sections are listed under Culture only.

CULTURE

bullfighting, 307
busses, 143
calendars, 94
celebrating birthdays and saints' days, 187–188
Chávez, César, 349
countries. *See* **Otros mundos**
currency, 156–157
educational system, 77–78, 87–88
family life, 37, 43, 258–259, 275
food
   meal patterns, 210
   Mexican cuisine, 205
   shopping, 140
greeting customs, 16–17
Hispanics in the U.S., 348–349, 359
holidays and festivals, 187–188
housing, 107–108, 124
indigenous populations, 173
Laredo (Texas) and Nuevo Laredo (Mexico), 2
marriage and divorce, 275
meals and mealtimes, 210
Mexico
   and the U.S., 103
   Baja California Norte, 31
   el Bajío (Guanajuato, Hidalgo, Querétaro), 102
   Chihuahua, 31
   Coahuila (Saltillo), 36
   cuisine of, 205
   demographic changes, 323

environmental concerns, 292–293
family life, 205
Guerrero (Acapulco), 204–205
Hildago (Pachuca), 322–323
history, 232–233
Jalisco (Guadalajara), 72
Mexico (Toluca), 322
Mexico City, 132–133, 163
Morelos (Cuernavaca), 322
Nuevo Leon (Monterrey), 36
Oaxaca (Mitla), 232–233
Puebla, 322–323
Tamaulipas (Nuevo Laredo), 2, 31
Teotihuacan, 182
Tlaxcala, 322–323
traditional clothing, 51
Veracruz, 258–259
Yucatan (Chichen Itza, Merida), 292–293
mourning customs, 281
names of professions, 83
numbers, expressing, 147
Otros mundos (*country descriptions*)
   Argentina, 320–321
   Bolivia, 290–291
   Brazil, 346–347
   Chile, 256–257
   Colombia, 230–231
   Costa Rica, 202–203
   Cuba, 171
   Dominican Republic, 171
   Ecuador, 256–257

   El Salvador, 203
   Guatemala, 203
   Haiti, 171
   Honduras, 203
   Nicaragua, 203
   Panama, 203
   Paraguay, 290–291
   Peru, 256–257
   Puerto Rico, 170–171
   Spain, 130–131
   Uruguay, 320–321
   United States, Hispanic influence in, 368–369
   United States, Puerto Rico, 369
   Venezuela, 230–231
open markets (**los tianguis**), 140
phone calls, 238
physical types, 119
pre-Columbian history, 172–173
professional
   goals, 73
   names and titles, 83
rain forests, 298
religious influences, 270
shopping for food, 140
telling time, 24–25, 35
transportation, 143
twenty-four hour clock, 24
university education, 77–78, 87–88
U.S. ads in Spanish, 337
volcanos, legends, 335
weather and seasons, 183–184

GRAMMAR

a
   + **el**, 95
   + infinitive, 85
   personal, 94–95
A propósito... (grammar for recognition)
   imperfect (past) subjunctive, 280–281.
     See also Appendix 1

impersonal **se**, 158
past (imperfect) subjunctive, 280–281.
   See also Appendix 1
perfect tenses, 193. *See also* Appendix 1
progressive forms, 113
abbreviations, 59n
adjective(s)
   agreement of, 23–24, 45, 62

adjective(s) (*continued*)
   comparative forms of, 220–222
   demonstrative, 160–162, 168. *See also* Appendix 2
   listed (*vocabulary*), 22, 34, 54–55, 61–62, 71
   meaning after **ser** and **estar**, 14–15, 80–81

A-45

VOCABULARY

38: Stephanie Maze/Woodfin Camp and Associates; **50:** Steve Allen/Gamma Liaison; **51:** Kolvoord/The Image Works; **72:** Bob Daemmrich/The Image Works; **73:** (top) Byron Augustin/D. Donne Bryant Stock Photography; (bottom) Frerck/Odyssey/Chicago; **74:** Jeff Greenberg/The Image Works; **75:** (top left) Nancy D'Antonio; (top right) Jeff Greenberg/Photo Researchers Inc.; (bottom left) Frerck/Odyssey/Chicago; (bottom right) Cameramann/The Image Works; **103:** M. Rangell/The Image Works; **104:** (left) Frerck/Odyssey/Chicago; (right) Nancy D'Antonio; **105:** (left) Bob Daemmrich/The Image Works; (top right) D. Donne Bryant; (bottom right) D. Donne Bryant; **130:** Frerck/Odyssey/Chicago; **132:** Macduff Everton/The Image Works; **133:** Tim Rautert/Visum/Woodfin Camp and Associates; **134:** Frerck/Odyssey/Chicago; **135:** (left) Byron Augustin/D. Donne Bryant Stock Photography; (right) Peter Menzel/Stock, Boston; **140:** Bob Daemmrich/The Image Works; **147:** Bettmann Archives; **163:** D. Donne Bryant; **170:** Chip and Rosa Maria de la Cueva Peterson; **171:** Barry Parker/Odyssey/Chicago; **173:** (top) D. Donne Bryant; (bottom) Frerck/Odyssey/Chicago; **174:** (left) Frerck/Odyssey/Chicago; (right) Frerck/Odyssey/Chicago; **175:** Frerck/Odyssey/Chicago; **188:** Peter Menzel/Stock, Boston; **191:** D. Donne Bryant; **202:** (top) Max and Bea Hunn/D. Donne Bryant Stock Photography; (bottom) Byron Augustin/D. Donne Bryant Stock Photography; **204:** Eric Carle/Stock, Boston; **205:** Macduff Everton/The Image Works; **206:** Dave Bartruff/Stock, Boston; **207:** (left) Randall Hyman/Stock, Boston; (right) Cary Wolinsky/Stock, Boston; **210:** Macduff Everton/The Image Works; **230:** (left) Frerck/Odyssey/Chicago; (right) Frerck/Odyssey/Chicago; **231:** Randall/The Image Works; **232:** Frerck/Odyssey/Chicago; **233:** (top) Frerck/Odyssey/Chicago; (bottom) Bettman Archives; **236:** Peter Menzel/Stock, Boston; **256:** Chip and Rosa Maria de la Cueva Peterson; **256–257:** Inga Spence/D. Donne Bryant Stock Photography; **257:** Cary Wolinsky/Stock, Boston; **258–259:** Frerck/Odyssey/Chicago; **259:** Frerck/Odyssey/Chicago; **279:** Robert Frerck/Woodfin Camp and Associates; **291:** (left) Chip and Rosa Maria de la Cueva Peterson; (top right) Patti Murray/Animals Animals; (bottom right) Carlos Goldin/D. Donne Bryant Stock Photography; **292:** Frerck/Odyssey/Chicago; **294:** George F. Riley/Stock, Boston; **295:** (left) James D. Nations/D. Donne Bryant Stock Photography; (top right) Peter Chartrand/D. Donne Bryant Stock Photography; (bottom right) Jan Haleska/Photo Researchers Inc.; **296:** Robert Fried/Stock, Boston; **321:** Frerck/Odyssey/Chicago; **324:** (satellite dish) Crandall/The Image Works; (inset) D. Donne Bryant; **325:** (left) Peter Menzel/Stock, Boston (right) Frerck/Odyssey/Chicago; **335:** Frerck/Odyssey/Chicago; **346–347:** Juca Martins /D. Donne Bryant Stock Photography; **347:** Rick Browne/Stock, Boston; **349:** Rod Lamkey Jr./Gamma Liaison; **350:** (left) Frerck/Odyssey/Chicago; (right) George Rose/Gamma Liaison; **351:** (top) Donald Dietz/Stock, Boston; (middle) Reuters/Bettmann Newsphotos; **368–369:** (bottom) Reuters/Bettmann Newsphotos; Okonewski/The Image Works; **369:** Piero Guerrini/Woodfin Camp and Associates.

REALIA **Pages 66, 67:** Adapted from *Los valores de los mexicanos* by Enrique Alduncín Abitia (Mexico, D.F.: Banamex, 1989); **148:** *México*, Carmet Miret and Eduardo Suárez, eds., (Barcelona: Laertes, S.A. de Ediciones), **172:** (Civ. precolombinas) Adapted from *Three Thousand Years of Art and Life in Mexico* by Ignacio Bernal (New York: Harry N. Abrams); **175:** (Novela) Fondo de Cultura Económica; **197:** From *El Informador*, Guadalajara, Mexico. Weather graphics courtesy of Accu-Weather, Inc., 619 West College Avenue, State College, PA 16801. (814) 237-0309. © 1994; **226:** Kellogg Company; **246:** Banco Santander 1994, Banco Santander and Flame Design. Reproduced with permission of Banco Santander, the trademark and copyright owner; **251:** Tarjetas Permacolor; **253:** *Avance hispano*; **260:** Altecard S.A. de C.V.; **261:** (En tu graduación) Hallmark Corporation; **286, 287:** *El Occidental*; **300:** *Mi Ambiente*; **330–331:** *Tele-Guía*; **338:** © 1994 Visa International. All rights reserved. VISA, Bands Design and Dove Design are registered trademarks of Visa International; **348:** (¿Quién soy yo?) *El tiempo latino*; **360:** Epic Records.

READINGS **Page 3:** From *Literatura Chicana: Texto y Contexto*, edited by Antonia Casteñada Schuler (Englewood Cliffs, N.J.: Prentice-Hall, 1972); **37:** Adapted from *Los valores de los mexicanos* by Enrique Alduncín Abitia (Mexico, D.F.: Banamex, 1989); **73:** Adapted from *Los valores de los mexicanos*; **133:** From *Los valores de los mexicanos*; **156:** From *El Carillón*, May 1993; **204–205:** From *Los libros del viajero: Mexico* (Madrid: Aguilar, S.A. de Ediciones, 1989); **258:** (El matrimonio) From *Los valores de los mexicanos*; **300:** From *Mi ambiente: Al servicio del automovilista y la ecología*, Editorial Nuestra; **302, 309:** From *Mi ambiente*; **313:** "Sensemayá" by Nicolás Guillén. Reprinted with permission; **314:** (Saquean águilas): From *Mi ambiente*; **323:** From *Los valores de los mexicanos*; **348:** Reprinted by permission from *The Christian Science Monitor* © 1993 The Christian Science Publishing Society. All rights reserved; **349:** Adapted from *La paloma*; **355, 356:** (Maldonado poems) From *Literatura Chicana: Texto y Contexto*, edited by Antonia Casteñada Schuler (Englewood Cliffs, N.J.: Prentice-Hall, 1972); **363:** "How I Changed the War and Won the Game" by Mary Helen Ponce was first published in *Corazón de Aztlán*, Los Angeles, February 1982. Reprinted with permission.

About the Authors

Dave McAlpine is Professor of Spanish and Director of the Division of International and Second Language Studies at the University of Arkansas at Little Rock, where he also directs the masters program in second language education. He received his B.A.E. from Wayne State College, his M.A. from the Universidad Internacional, and his doctorate from the University of South Dakota. McAlpine is vice-chair of the Central States Conference on the Teaching of Foreign Languages.

Leon Book is Associate Professor of Foreign Languages at Southeast Missouri State University in Cape Girardeau, where he teaches all levels of Spanish as well as methodology and other education courses. He is an active member of the Foreign Language Association of Missouri and has served on the Board of Directors of the Central States Conference on the Teaching of Foreign Languages. He received his B.S.Ed. and M.A.Ed. from Southeast Missouri State and his Ph.D. from Florida State University.

Karen Hardy Cárdenas is Professor of Spanish and Head of the Department of Foreign Languages at South Dakota State University. She received her B.A. from Grinnell College and her M.A. and Ph.D. from the University of Kansas. She has taught a wide variety of courses in Spanish language, literature, and culture. She is active in the profession, having held offices in her state organization as well as having served as Recording Secretary for the Central States Conference on the Teaching of Foreign Languages.

Listening Passages*

*These passages are included in the *Audiocassette Program*.

CAPÍTULO 1

Para escuchar
Una llamada telefónica (page 29)

Paso 1

—Bueno, habla David Nelson.

—...

—¡Alfonsina! ¡Imposible! ¿Cómo estás? ¿Qué pasa?

—...

—Todos estamos muy bien, gracias.

—...

—Sí, estoy en la casa de mi abuelita. Hmm... un momentito, Alfonsina, perdón. [*aparte*] No, Elena, todo está bien. Es una amiga de Wisconsin. Lo siento, Alfonsina. Mi prima Elena estaba un poco preocupada, pero todo está bien ahora.

—...

—No, no, son las tres y media aquí también. No hay problema. En Monterrey es la misma hora que en Wisconsin. ¿Por qué llamas?

—...

—Hmm... ah, sí. Comprendo. Bueno, el número de teléfono de Sandra en Chicago es el 635-2259.

Paso 2

—...

—De nada. Y, ¿cómo están todos mis amigos en Eau Claire?

—...

—Oh, sí, Alfonsina, ¡todo está bien, absolutamente perfecto! Estoy muy entusiasmado.

—...

—No, Monterrey y Saltillo no están en la costa. Están en el centro del país en un valle. Hay montañas muy altas aquí cerca, también. Y, hay un río en la ciudad de Monterrey. ¡Es fantástico!

—...

—Okay, comprendo. ¡Qué bueno oír noticias de los Estados Unidos! Saludos a todos.

—...

—Adiós, Alfonsina.

CAPÍTULO 2

Para escuchar
Un reportaje sobre el béisbol　(page 65)

Paso 1

—No hay duda que el béisbol es un deporte muy popular. Pues, hoy es, en efecto, un deporte internacional.

—Sí, hombre. Para los japoneses, es uno de sus pasatiempos favoritos. Por ejemplo, ¿viste la película con Tom Selleck, «El Sr. Béisbol»?

—Pues, no todavía, pero indica la popularidad del béisbol en Japón. En Japón, sabes, el beisbolista Sidharita Oh es considerado el Babe Ruth japonés.

—¡Qué jugador! Un bateador sin par. Su récord japonés de jonrones es igual al récord de jonrones de los beisbolistas estadounidenses Babe Ruth y Hank Aaron.

Paso 2

—Bueno, te digo que en Latinoamérica, muchas personas tienen mucho interés en las ligas profesionales que están en muchos países latinoamericanos.

—Sí. La gente va frecuentemente a los estadios locales.

—Y también, en las Ligas Mayores en los Estados Unidos...

—Son la Liga Nacional y la Liga Americana respectivamente.

—Exacto. Digo que los venezolanos, los panameños, los cubanos, los puertorriqueños, los dominicanos (entre otros) y nosotros mexicanos todos tenemos «hijos nativos» en las Ligas Mayores de los Estados Unidos.

—Por ejemplo, entre nosotros mexicanos, Fernando Valenzuela es un héroe nacional. Muy popular.

—Tú sabes que los antepasados de José Canseco y Danny Tartabull son cubanos.

—Sí, claro que lo sé. ¿Sabes tú que David Concepción y Andrés Galarraga son beisbolistas venezolanos?

—¡Qué temporada tuvo Galarraga en 1993 para los Rockies de Colorado!

—Excepcional, de veras. ¿Y qué tal Juan González, Iván Rodríguez y Rubén Sierra? Son jugadores jóvenes de Puerto Rico que tienen mucho talento.

—Ese González es fantástico.

CAPÍTULO 3

Para escuchar
El horario de Luisa (page 96)

Mi amiga Luisa quiere ser abogada. Este semestre tiene cinco materias. Los lunes, miércoles y viernes tiene una clase de inglés a las nueve de la mañana. Los lunes, miércoles y viernes también va a su clase de cálculo a las diez. Después, a las once, los lunes, martes, miércoles y viernes Luisa tiene una clase de francés. Los jueves va al laboratorio para practicar la lengua. Los martes y los jueves a las nueve toma una clase de política. También los martes y los jueves, a las dos, tiene una clase de biología. El laboratorio de biología es a las tres los miércoles. Tiene dieciocho unidades en total. ¡Es una mujer muy trabajadora!

CAPÍTULO 6

Para escuchar
Los horarios de Elena y David (page 196)

Ayer me desperté a las seis menos cuarto. Me levanté a las seis. Me vestí rápidamente y salí del cuarto del hotel a las seis y media. David es muy perezoso y no se levantó hasta las siete, pero se vistió inmediatamente y a las siete y cuarto entró en el restaurante del hotel donde yo lo esperaba. Después del desayuno, a las ocho, David volvió a su cuarto pero yo fui a un quiosco cerca del hotel y compré dos revistas. A las nueve David bajó otra vez y a las nueve y cuarto tomamos un taxi al otro hotel donde los Austin nos esperaban.

CAPÍTULO 7

Para escuchar
Una conversación oída por casualidad (page 225)

ALEJANDRA: Mira, Roberto, la lista de platos especiales para niños tiene muchas cosas que te gustan.

CARLOS: Sí. Ofrecen hamburguesas de res y salchichas de pavo. Y con cualquiera de los dos platos puedes pedir papas fritas.

ROBERTO: No quiero nada de la lista para niños. Quiero carne asada con frijoles y arroz.

ALEJANDRA: No, Roberto. Es mucha comida para un niño de ocho años.

CARLOS: Tu mamá tiene razón, Roberto. Es mucha comida... y es un plato muy caro.

ALEJANDRA: Y, ¿qué te parecen las tiras de pescado empanado o los nuggets de pollo?

ROBERTO: Ésta es comida para niños pequeñitos. Yo ya estoy grande, mamá. Sabes que quiero ser jugador de fútbol... y los jugadores de fútbol tienen que comer mucho.

CARLOS: Puedes comer todo lo que quieras en casa, pero en un restaurante debes hacer lo que te aconsejen tus padres.

ROBERTO: Bueno, papi, si no quieren que coma la carne asada, voy a pedir... camarones empanados.

CARLOS: Ay, Dios mío, Alejandra, este niño es imposible. No, Roberto, los camarones son muy caros. Son más caros que la carne asada.

ALEJANDRA: Paciencia, Carlos, paciencia. Mira lo que has hecho. El niño está llorando. No llores, mi vida. Mira, si pides algo de la lista para niños, después puedes pedir algo de postre. ¿Qué te parece?

ROBERTO: ¿De veras, mami? Bueno, entonces voy a pedir las tiras de pescado y después pastel de queso con cerezas. Y para beber, un vaso enorme de limonada.

ALEJANDRA: Está bien. Y para mí, Carlos, el pollo frito. Y ¿qué vas a pedir tú, Carlos?

CARLOS: Rosbif, maíz, una ensalada... y una cerveza grande, bien fría.

CAPÍTULO 8

Para escuchar
Un recado (page 252)

Paso 1, primera parte

STEVE: Hello?

EL PROFESOR MENA: Hola, Tom. Soy yo, Alejandro. ¿Cómo estás?

STEVE: Excuse me. Do you speak English?

EL PROFESOR MENA: Perdón. ¿Cómo? Quiero hablar con Tom Banderas. ¿Quién es Ud.?

STEVE: Uh, . . . uh . . . Soy uno de sus estudiantes. ¿Habla Ud. inglés?

EL PROFESOR MENA: Ah, comprendo. No, lo siento. Hablo muy poco inglés.

STEVE: ¡Oh, no! Es un problema, señor, porque yo hablo muy poco español.

EL PROFESOR MENA: Yo creo que tú hablas español mejor de lo que yo hablo inglés. Necesito dejar un recado. ¿Comprendes?

STEVE: No, no comprendo. ¿Dejar un qué?

EL PROFESOR MENA: Un recado. Yo digo algo y tú escribes en un papel lo que digo para dárselo a Tom. ¿Comprendes ahora?

STEVE: Ah sí, comprendo. Pero, señor, es mi segundo semestre de español. Yo no puedo escribir un... un...

EL PROFESOR MENA: Un recado.

STEVE: Sí, un recado.

EL PROFESOR MENA: Sí puedes. Yo no voy a hablar muy rápido, y si necesitas, puedo repetir. ¿Está bien? ¿No hay problema?

STEVE: ¿No puede Ud. llamar a mi profesor más tarde?

EL PROFESOR MENA: Lo siento, pero no puedo. Tengo que salir de viaje inmediatamente, y no voy a poder llamar ni mañana ni el día siguiente. La información es importante para Tom. ¿Quieres tratar?

STEVE: Sí, ¿por qué no?

Paso 1, segunda parte

EL PROFESOR MENA: Bueno. Yo soy Alejandro Mena. Soy profesor de comercio en el Instituto Tecnológico de Monterrey, México.

STEVE: El profesor Mena. Instituto Tecnológico de Monterrey.

EL PROFESOR MENA: Precisamente. ¿Cómo te llamas tú?

STEVE: Uh, ¿perdón? Oh, ¿cómo te llamas? Sí. Me llamo Steve.

EL PROFESOR MENA: Mucho gusto, Steve.

STEVE: El gusto es mío, profesor.

EL PROFESOR MENA: Tu profesor quería la fotocopia de un artículo de nuestro periódico sobre nuestra economía. Encontré el artículo esta tarde. Mi secretaria va a mandarle el artículo por fax esta tarde. ¿Comprendes?

STEVE: Sí, señor. Un artículo sobre la economía hoy por fax. ¿Es todo?

EL PROFESOR MENA: No, hay más. Queremos invitar a Tom a venir a Monterrey en octubre para dar una conferencia sobre la educación universitaria de idiomas en los EE. UU. Nuestro instituto va a pagar todos los gastos.

STEVE: ¿Todos los qué?

EL PROFESOR MENA: Los gastos. Lo que cuesta. Tom no tiene que pagar nada. Nosotros pagamos.

STEVE: Ah, sí. Comprendo. Conferencia en Monterrey en octubre. Su instituto paga todo.

EL PROFESOR MENA: Muy bien. Eres buen estudiante, Steve, y un secretario excelente.

STEVE: Muchas gracias. Ud. es muy amable. Okay, necesito escribir que hoy es jueves, es el 15, y son las tres y media aquí. ¿Son las tres y media allí?

EL PROFESOR MENA: Sí, exacto. Bueno, yo tengo que irme ahora. Mis saludos a Tom, y repito: muchas gracias.

STEVE: De nada.

EL PROFESOR MENA: Adiós, Steve.

STEVE: Adiós, profesor Mena.

CAPÍTULO 9

Para escuchar
La muerte de un señor distinguido (page 287)

Ayer falleció a las 2:20 de la tarde el Sr. Alfredo Clemente Cepeda, destacado servidor público, periodista e intelectual de esta ciudad. Por muchos años, él sirvió de gerente del Banco Nacional de Depósito. Recordamos que en 1992 ganó el Premio Nacional de Ciencias y Artes porque supo captar con sobresaliente sensibilidad el corazón de nuestro país. Su esposa, hijos, hijos políticos, nietos y demás familiares lo participan a Ud. con profundo dolor, suplicándole ruegue a Dios Nuestro Señor por el eterno descanso de su alma.

CAPÍTULO 10

Para escuchar
Sanciones a industriales (page 301)

Los industriales, como sector de la sociedad que aporta recursos a la economía nacional, han asumido el papel que les corresponde en la preservación de los recursos naturales de todo el país.

De esta manera los datos de la Procuraduría Federal de Protección al Ambiente señalan que desde agosto del año pasado a la fecha se ha logrado recaudar 3,5 millones de dólares, producto de las «auditorías ecológicas» practicadas mediante once mil inspecciones. En ello los industriales han asumido las consecuencias por no haber instalado a tiempo los equipos reductores de sustancias contaminantes.

En el caso del Valle de México, donde se realizaron siete de las once mil inspecciones efectuadas en todo el país, la dependencia citó en sus informaciones que el sector más visitado para la realización de «auditorías ecológicas» fue el químico.

Para escuchar
Clima y topografía (page 310)

El mundo hispánico es muy amplio. Hay veintiún países donde se habla español. Hay países hispánicos en cuatro continentes y en una serie de islas. No es una sorpresa, entonces, que la geografía y el clima del mundo hispánico sean muy variados.

En España hay montañas en el norte y en la parte central. En el sur hay playas y allí están algunos de los centros turísticos más visitados del país. En el invierno hay nieve en las montañas; en el verano hace sol y calor en muchas partes del país.

La variedad de clima y geografía es aun más evidente en Hispanoamérica. Allí hay islas del Caribe que reciben la visita de muchos turistas y, de vez en cuando, de un huracán. Hay cordilleras de montañas en la América del Norte y en la América del Sur. Las cordilleras más famosas de México son la Sierra Madre Occidental y la Sierra Madre Oriental. En la América del Sur, cuando pensamos en montañas, es imposible no pensar en los Andes.

Una descripción del mundo natural de la América del Sur no es completa sin mencionar el río Amazonas y la selva que está en la cuenca del Amazonas. Hay muchos otros ríos y lagos en el mundo hispano pero el Amazonas es único; es el río más grande del mundo.

En gran parte del mundo hispánico hay cuatro estaciones al año: la primavera, el verano, el otoño y el invierno. Pero en algunos lugares hay sólo dos estaciones: una estación de lluvia y una estación seca.

Para escuchar
Un canto mágico (page 312)

SENSEMAYÁ

Canto para matar una culebra

¡Mayombe—bombe—mayombé!
¡Mayombe—bombe—mayombé!
¡Mayombe—bombe—mayombé!

La culebra tiene los ojos de vidrio;
la culebra viene y se enreda en un palo;
con sus ojos de vidrio, en un palo,
con sus ojos de vidrio.

La culebra camina sin patas;
la culebra se esconde en la yerba;
caminando se esconde en la yerba,
caminando sin patas.

¡Mayombe—bombe—mayombé!
¡Mayombe—bombe—mayombé!
¡Mayombe—bombe—mayombé!

Tú le das con el hacha y se muere:
¡dale ya!
¡No le des con el pie, que te muerde,
no le des con el pie, que se va!

Sensemayá, la culebra,
sensemayá.
Sensemayá, con sus ojos,
sensemayá.
Sensemayá, con su lengua,
sensemayá.
Sensemayá, con su boca,
sensemayá.

¡La culebra muerta no puede comer;
la culebra muerta no puede silbar;
no puede caminar,
no puede correr!

¡La culebra muerta no puede mirar;
la culebra muerta no puede beber;
no puede respirar,
no puede morder!

¡Mayombe—bombe—mayombé!
Sensemayá, la culebra...
¡Mayombe—bombe—mayombé!
Sensemayá, no se mueve...
¡Mayombe—bombe—mayombé!
Sensemayá, la culebra...
¡Mayombe—bombe—mayombé!
¡Sensemayá, se murió!

Para escuchar
Paso 1 (page 316)

You will hear six statements about the scenes on page 316 of your book. The statements will be read twice. On a separate sheet of paper, write the number of the scene that illustrates each statement you hear.

1. Después de comprar el periódico de la ciudad en el quiosco, la señora subió al autobús.
2. La señora tuvo que esperar porque un hombre de pelo rizado que llevaba sombrero compraba estampillas también.
3. Después de una tarde larga en la ciudad, la señora se sentó en la cocina de su casa para escribirle una carta a una amiga.
4. Cuando salió de la tienda con sus compras bajo el brazo, el autobús ya había pasado y tuvo que esperar otro.
5. La señora charlaba con el dependiente mientras escogía unas chuletas de puerco deliciosas para la cena.
6. La señora, que llevaba un suéter porque hacía fresco de la mañana, salió de su casa para ir al centro, donde iba a hacer sus compras del día.

CAPÍTULO 11

Para escuchar
Alfonsina hace una llamada (page 329)

ALFONSINA: A ver, marco el número 0, luego el número de la casa...
el 0–11–52–4–51–4–31–11. (*ring, ring, ring*)

OPERATOR: Thank you for using AT&T. How may I help you?

ALFONSINA: AT&T Español, por favor.

OPERATOR: One moment, please, and I'll connect you.

LA OPERADORA: Bueno, AT&T Español. ¿En qué puedo servirle?

ALFONSINA: Bueno, quisiera hablar de persona a persona con la Sra. Dora
González. Quiero que Ud. lo cargue a mi tarjeta.

LA OPERADORA: Sí, señorita. Favor de darme su número de la tarjeta de crédito.

ALFONSINA: Es el 5–0–1–5–69–23–45–75–91.

LA OPERADORA: Gracias. ¿De parte de quién?

ALFONSINA: De Alfonsina Castro Cota.

LA OPERADORA: Gracias, señorita. La voy a conectar.

Para escuchar
Un pedido del profesor Ramos (page 339)

TOMÁS: Oigan... Celia, Jorge. Necesito su ayuda.

CELIA: ¿Qué hay, Tomás? Pareces preocupado.

TOMÁS: Es que el profesor Ramos me pidió que yo grabara algunas selecciones
para su clase de literatura.

JORGE: ¿Y? Esto no debe ser un problema.

TOMÁS: Es que no sé nada de literatura... pues, casi nada. ¿Qué recomiendan
que yo grabara?

CELIA: Pues, a mí me encanta la literatura. ¿Sabes?, hay muchos novelistas españoles que son excelentes... Pero también me gustan algunos poetas del
siglo XIX, como el poeta romántico, Gustavo Adolfo Bécquer.

TOMÁS: ¿Un poeta romántico? Eso me sorprende. No pareces ser una mujer
muy romántica...

CELIA: Bueno, realmente no lo soy. Pero las rimas de Bécquer son tan lindas.
Puedo grabarte algunas si lo deseas.

TOMÁS: Está bien. Gracias. ¿Y tú, Jorge?

JORGE: Bueno, como Celia, prefiero la literatura moderna... especialmente la novela y el ensayo... pero sería difícil grabar una selección tan extensa. Espera. Tengo otra idea. Hay un cuentito, casi una fábula, escrito por Rubén Darío. Es muy chistoso. A todos les gusta mucho. ¿Quieres que te lo grabe?

TOMÁS: Sí, claro, cómo no. Y ahora, ¿qué puedo grabar yo?

CELIA: ¿No estudiaste la literatura de tu país? Son muy famosos los cuentos argentinos.

TOMÁS: ¡Caramba! Gracias, Celia, claro. Ya sé lo que voy a grabar. Uno de los microcuentos de Enrique Anderson Imbert.

Para escuchar
Dos poemas románticos (page 340)

XXI

«¿Qué es poesía?», dices mientras clavas
en mi pupila tu pupila azul.
«¿Qué es poesía?» ¿Y tú me lo preguntas?
Poesía... eres tú.

XXIII

Por una mirada, un mundo;
por una sonrisa, un cielo;
por un beso... , ¡yo no sé
qué te diera por un beso!

XXXVIII

Los suspiros son aire y van al aire.
Las lágrimas son agua y van al mar.
Dime, mujer: cuando el amor se olvida,
¿sabes tú adónde va?

Para escuchar
Paso 1 (page 342)

You will hear six statements about the scenes on page 342 of your book. The statements will be read twice. On a separate sheet of paper, write the number of the scene that illustrates each statement you hear.

1. Cuando Marisol entró en la sala, le sorprendió que todos sus amigos de la universidad le hubieran preparado una fiesta sorpresa por ser el día de su cumpleaños.

2. A María le gustó que Tomás llegara a la fiesta —aunque fuera medianoche— porque ella no sabía que Tomás sabía tocar un instrumento musical.

3. Mientras Jorge tomaba su cereal con leche y escribía una lista de cosas que hacer, uno de sus compañeros de casa se levantó y entró en la cocina todavía en su pijama.

4. Aunque era bastante temprano para un sábado, Jorge se levantó. Después de ducharse y secarse, se afeitó y se lavó los dientes y luego se arregló.

5. Mientras Joaquín, desanimado, cansado y todavía en pijama, limpiaba la cocina, Jorge hizo unas llamadas para invitar a sus amigos a su casa.

6. Para arreglar la sala, Jorge tuvo que barrer el suelo y quitar de los muebles la ropa y los restos de la comida de la noche anterior.

CAPÍTULO 12

Para escuchar
En Oaxaca (page 354)

Nos encontramos en Acapulco con Concha y Alicia, dos amigas de Elena, y ellas nos llevaron en su carro hasta Oaxaca. Las muchachas conocían un pequeño hotel cerca de la plaza y Elena y yo decidimos pasar la noche allí para no molestar al tío de Elena a esa hora. Llegamos muy tarde y nos acostamos casi en seguida. Por la mañana Elena y yo nos dimos cuenta de que teníamos muy poco dinero en efectivo y fuimos al banco. Después, llamamos al tío de Elena, Alfredo López Valderrama, y pasamos por su oficina. Él nos invitó a almorzar en un restaurante muy elegante.

En el restaurante nos sentamos en un patio muy lindo con muchos árboles y flores. Comimos enchiladas de pollo con guacamole, la ensalada especial de la casa y tomamos cerveza. El tío Alfredo nos habló mucho de Oaxaca y sus alrededores. Después, nos invitó a pasar unos días en su casa porque no quería que la hija de su hermana se quedara en un hotel. Durante la visita, Alfredo nos mostró varios lugares de interés en Oaxaca y nos ayudó con los planes para ver otros sitios históricos de la ciudad.

Para escuchar
La educación bilingüe y el bilingüismo (page 362)

Es útil hacer una distinción entre la educación bilingüe y el bilingüismo. La educación bilingüe tiene entre sus objetivos la enseñanza del inglés. Los proponentes de la educación bilingüe mantienen que las protestas contra la educación bilingüe son en realidad contra el bilingüismo: la habilidad de hablar, leer, pensar y soñar en dos lenguas.

Esta distinción no la hacen con frecuencia los partidarios de Sólo Inglés. A los partidarios del movimiento Sólo Inglés no les preocupa la dificultad de los recién llegados de aprender inglés. Nunca han tratado de recaudar fondos para programas que sirvan para alcanzar ese objetivo. El movimiento se define por su oposición al español.

Para escuchar
Paso 1 (page 365)

You will hear six statements about the scenes on page 365 of your book. The statements will be read twice. On a separate sheet of paper, write the number of the scene that illustrates each statement you hear.

1. Luisa, quien suele ser una estudiante muy seria, casi se durmió en la clase de cálculo aunque la lección era importante y la profesora era una de sus favoritas.
2. Después de acostarse, Luisa recibió una llamada de su esposo, algo que le encantó aunque era muy tarde.
3. Luisa y Mercedes se compraron pollo frito ya preparado para la cena; luego Luisa preparó una ensalada mientras su hija ponía la mesa.
4. Un joven le habló a Luisa con mucho interés en ella, pero Luisa no quería tener nada que ver con él.
5. Mientras Luisa leía la lección para la clase de ciencias políticas, notó que su hija, ya lista para ir a la cama, tenía sueño. Con una sonrisa, Luisa le dijo a Mercedes que se acostara.
6. Antes de que se levantara su hija, muy temprano todavía, Luisa se bañó y se lavó el pelo, se maquilló y luego se vistió. Le esperaba un día muy largo.